NATURAL BORN SEER

"A seer shall the Lord my God raise up,
who shall be a choice seer …"

The Book of Mormon, 2 Nephi 3:6

NATURAL BORN SEER

JOSEPH SMITH | AMERICAN PROPHET

1805-1830

Richard S. Van Wagoner

SMITH-PETTIT FOUNDATION
SALT LAKE CITY

To Brandon, Travis, Jordan, Austin, Shayni, Dylan,
Carter, Kelly Anne, Ashlee, Hayden, Hailie, Sophie,
and all other grandchildren yet unborn

For my part, I shall ever claim the right
of thinking and judging for myself,
and of fully and freely expressing my views,
whether these correspond with those of others
or differ from them.
This I conceive to be a high and holy privilege,
and its exercise a sacred duty.

—Robert Richardson (1806-76),
qtd. in John M. Bland, "Men Who Would Be 'Kings'"

The opinions expressed in this book are not necessarily those of the Smith-Pettit Foundation.

 Printed on acid-free paper. Composed, printed, and bound in the United States of America. Distributed by Signature Books Publishing LLC. www.signaturebooks.com

Designed by Jason Francis.
Index compiled by Jani Fleet.

Frontispiece: Lithograph of Joseph Smith, ca 1847, published by Moses Martin and derived from a painting by Sutcliffe Maudsley. All illustrations, unless otherwise noted, are courtesy of the Smith-Pettit Foundation.

2020 2019 2018 2017 2016 5 4 3 2 1

LIBRARY OF CONGRESS CATALOGING-IN-PUBLICATION DATA

Names: Van Wagoner, Richard S., author.

Title: Natural born seer : Joseph Smith, American prophet, 1805-1830 / Richard S. Van Wagoner.

Description: Salt Lake city: Smith-Pettit Foundation, 2016. | Includes bibliographical references and index.

Identifiers: LCCN 2015038867 | ISBN 9781560852636 (alk. paper)

Subjects: LCSH: Smith, Joseph, Jr., 1805-1844. | Church of Jesus Christ of Latter-day Saints–History–19th century. | LCGFT: Biographies.

Classification: LCC BX8695.S6 V36 2016 | DDC 289.3092–dc23 LC record available at http://lccn.loc.gov/2015038867

CONTENTS

INTRODUCTION

The more original religious life is always lyric ... and its essence is ... to feel an invisible order ... [wherein] the common sense values really vanish. [There is a] genuine antagonism between common-sense religion ... and that of the more extravagant prophets of whatever kind. Each is foolish to the other, for each lives in the light of a different world.

—William James, No. 64 (#4476), *Manuscript Essays and Notes,* 311-12

History abounds with figures whom time and tradition have sculpted into icons. Virtues are magnified, vices ignored or forgotten. "All cultures have their heroes," writes psychologist Len Oakes, "and no hero is more mysterious, or more extraordinary, than God's messenger—the prophet."[1] The Mormon prophet Joseph Smith Jr. (1805-44), a contemporary of Thomas Jefferson, Abraham Lincoln, Andrew Jackson, Davy Crockett, Lewis and Clark, Ralph Waldo Emerson, Mark Twain, and Horace Greeley, among other notables, is as much an enduring charismatic American icon as the rest. As founder of the Church of Jesus Christ of Latter-day Saints (Mormon or LDS), Joseph occupies my earliest memories in the crayon-marked chapel hallways of Mormon "Junior" Sunday School. My patriarchal blessing, which most LDS Church members receive as an adolescent, urged me to "be ever mindful of Joseph Smith's life and mission," a charge I have never taken lightly.

To be immortalized, it seems best that one die young. An untimely death at age thirty-eight helped to make Joseph a cultural obsession especially among his followers. The martyred hero continues to inspire faith nearly two centuries later and is beloved by millions worldwide. Despite dozens of biographies intent on portraying the real original, however, I believe much is left to be revealed of the complex, controversial Mormon prophet.

1. Len Oakes, *Prophetic Charisma,* 1.

A creative religious genius and singular soul with an ability to foster and nurture faith and devotion in fellow seekers, Smith's index of accomplishments is lengthy and in many ways unique: "author and proprietor" of the Book of Mormon, Bible revisionist, founder of a millenarian church, oracle of messages from God, architect of robust communities, would-be banker, newspaper editor, city mayor, husband to dozens of wives, spiritual father of the State of Utah, and omnipotent prophet, priest, and king whom millions of adherents testify restored in its fullness the lost primitive gospel of Jesus Christ.

Joseph was an eclectic, syncretic innovator, not a systematic theologian. Many of his religious inspirations were largely gleaned from his nineteenth-century environment, ruminated over, confirmed by what he said was God's spirit, then refined and enhanced through an incremental process of trial-and-error development that in many ways is still on-going among his successors. Believers refer to this process as continuous revelation; non-believers as the natural expression of human intellect and reason. But much of the homespun image of the young farm boy's metamorphosis from village scryer or glass looker to God's mouthpiece has been embellished to the point of distortion by a heavy overcoat of hyperbole, mythologizing, and wishful thinking.

Late in his career, two months before his murder, the young prophet, who at various times referred to himself as *Gazelam, Enoch,* and *Baurak Ale,* made a rather baffling statement. "You don't know me," he told 20,000 friends, family members, and followers who had gathered for a funeral. "You never knew my heart. No man knows my history. I cannot tell it; I shall never undertake it. I don't blame anyone for not believing my history. If I had not experienced what I have, I could not have believed it myself."[2] This paradox of the well-known unknown may be seen through the diverse eyes of a few of his intimates:

> Joseph Smith, the Prophet and Seer of the Lord, has done more, save Jesus only, for the salvation of men in this world, than any other man that ever lived in it. —John Taylor[3]

> [Joseph Smith] ... was a high handed transgresser [sic] of a character so

2. *History of the Church,* 6:317.

3. Doctrine and Covenants 135:3 (1844); hereafter cited parenthetically in the text as D&C. Unless otherwise noted, all quotations from this canonized book of Mormon scripture are from the current (1981) LDS edition. John Taylor served as third president of the Church of Jesus Christ of Latter-day Saints from 1880 to 1887.

heaven daring that he transfe[r]red his allegiance from the Lord to the devil so as to be one of Satan's servants instead of the Lord[']s. —Sidney Rigdon[4]

No man or woman in this generation will get a resurrection and be crowned without Joseph Smith saying so. —Brigham Young[5]

That Smith admired and lusted after many men's wives and daughters, is a fact, but they could not help that. They or most of them considered his admiration an insult, and treated him with scorn. In return for this scorn, he generally managed to blacken their reputations. —William Law[6]

John D. Lee, executed for his crimes at the infamous 1857 Mountain Meadows Massacre, called Joseph "a perplexing mystic with singular power to command the loyalty and devotion of his disciples."[7] John C. Bennett, once a member of the First Presidency who became one of Joseph's bitterest enemies, admitted that Smith had a "mysterious power which even now I fail to fathom."[8] "The ideal prophet differs widely from the real person," asserted nineteenth-century spiritualist Joel Tiffany. "To one, ignorant of his character, he may be idealized and be made the impersonation of every virtue. He may be associated in the mind with all that is pure, true, lovely and divine. Art may make him, indeed, an object of religious veneration. But remember, the Joseph Smith thus venerated, is not the real, actual Joseph Smith ... but one that art has created."[9] Martyrdom helped to make Joseph an obsession; with time, desire, and memory, he became an idea, an image, a myth.

Carl L. Becker, in his 1931 presidential address to the American Historical Association, observed: "In order to understand the essential nature of anything, it is well to strip it of all superficial and irrelevant accretions—in short, to reduce it to its lowest terms."[10] For most of my adult life, I have researched, in various ways, the life of the Mormon prophet, trying conscientiously to peel back the layers of veneer that have obscured Joseph's essential self. Early, I came to the conclusion that much of the lacquer was applied,

---

4. Sidney Rigdon to Jesse Crosby (Oct. 1872), Revelation, Section 70 in Copying Book A. Rigdon served as first counselor to Joseph Smith in the First Presidency from 1833 to 1844.

5. Brigham Young, unpublished discourse, Oct. 8, 1854.

6. William Law to Wilhelm Wyl, Jan. 20, 1887, qtd. in Lyndon W. Cook, *William Law,* 106. Law served in the First Presidency from 1841 to 1844.

7. Robert Glass Cleland and Juanita Brooks, *A Mormon Chronicle,* vii.

8. John Cook Bennett, *The History of the Saints, or, An Exposé of Joe Smith and Mormonism,* 10.

9. Joel Tiffany, "Mormonism–No. II," 170.

10. Carl L. Becker, "Everyman His Own Historian," 20.

not only by well-meaning enthusiasts and vociferous enemies, but by Joseph himself, to shield aspects of his paradoxical nature from fuller disclosure. "What we have in Mormon historiography," writes perceptive non-Mormon observer Jan Shipps, "is two Josephs."[11]

The dichotomy of certain controversial aspects of the prophet's life is camouflaged in misdirection and secrecy. After he disengaged himself from the ultimately unprofitable treasure digging and divination activities of his youth, he refocused his energies into what Shipps insightfully terms "propheteering." In this venture he was more successful, both in giving his life purpose and enhancing—for the remainder of his lifetime—the financial and social security of his extended family. His crusade to reshape aspects of his life retrospectively, to refashion especially his early years, has been the focus of my inquiry as a sympathetic, though not uncritical, Mormon for more than three decades. The following synopsis, expanded in the biography, is what I have come to believe is the essence of Joseph Smith's youth. (While some of the examples date from later in Joseph's life, I believe they nonetheless speak to the character of the man who was once the boy.)

Born in rural Vermont in 1805, Joseph spent his earliest years there and in neighboring New Hampshire. His youth centered on subsistence farming with his family. Despite hard work and the generally shrewd, speculative Yankee ingenuity of his parents, stability and economic security eluded the family throughout his boyhood. Poverty was early his fate, and necessity served as midwife for much of his creative expression. Parents Joseph Smith Sr. and Lucy Mack Smith were God-fearing people who, like others of the day, also practiced folk magic. Joseph Jr. was reportedly born with an amnion facial veil or caul. Some people believed this birth omen to be a sign of good fortune, a harbinger of future greatness.

In young Smith's case, the superstition was well founded. His inventiveness, his appetite for adventure and novelty, and his prowess as a "glass looker," as many termed his divining technique, helped to nurture a budding reputation for himself in upstate New York and Pennsylvania. Joseph, like thousands in the world, was a "natural born seer,"[12] with a reputation for locating lost animals and household objects, underground water, even hidden and buried treasure. The young clairvoyant soon began to see visions in seer stones, first to supplement his family's income. This supernatural

11. Jan Shipps, "The Prophet Puzzle," in Waterman, *The Prophet Puzzle,* 44.
12. T. B. H. Stenhouse, *Rocky Mountain Saints,* 209.

enlightenment, which Joseph later referred to as "the Gift and Power of God," enabled the budding seer to envision—or to "translate," he termed it—the text of a gold bible from the depths of his "peep" stone. Joseph could not translate any ancient languages, but the Book of Mormon, as he subsequently related, "was communicated to him, *direct from heaven.*"[13] The presence of a physical text, or golden plates, was not needed—nor do eyewitness accounts indicate that they were used in any way—during the production of the Book of Mormon.

After most first- and second-generation Mormon leaders died, their successors showed little or no interest in Joseph's folk magical practices. Increasingly, manifestations of the so-called occult arts were embarrassing. For the most part, these elements of the prophet's early career were suppressed or rewritten as Mormonism moved closer culturally to mainstream Christianity. Instead of the events surrounding the coming forth of the Book of Mormon, Church leaders began to emphasize what today is known in the faith as the "First Vision." Smith asserted, years after the fact, that God and his son Jesus appeared to him in 1820 when he was a mere fourteen years old. The factual historicity of Joseph's account is complicated by the lack of contemporary evidence for such an occurrence. Neither family members, neighbors, newspapers, clergymen, early Mormon converts, nor even anti-Mormon detractors mentioned such an event at that time—at least, not in any known contemporary written account. Furthermore, the teenage boy, at that point in his theological development, manifested unsettled, irresolute views of the Godhead. His understanding of God's existence, even his name, was a process of prolonged development rather than the result of a single resplendent manifestation.

The "First Vision" story, so important to modern Mormonism, was not shared with the faithful generally until about 1842. (There were some minor exceptions, but Joseph's vision was not widely published until the early 1840s.) In the late 1820s and early 1830s, as the Church of Christ (the name first given to Joseph's movement) began to evolve, its hallmark was the proclaimed marvelous events surrounding the coming forth of the Book of Mormon; Joseph's proclaimed vision of God was more of a personal conversion experience. Yet even that portrayal by Smith is clouded

13. Matthew Livingston Davis (1773-1850), writing to "My Dear Mary," qtd. in Andrew F. Ehat and Lyndon W. Cook, *The Words of Joseph Smith,* 34. Davis was a Washington correspondent for the *New York Enquirer* when he heard Joseph Smith deliver this information in a public lecture.

by inconsistencies. Evidence from friends and enemies alike conveys the impression that, from age fourteen until age twenty, and possibly beyond, Joseph was more involved in folk magic treasure seeking ventures than in what believers today may understand as explicitly religious activities.

Most of us, including Joseph Smith, do not possess a strongly developed sense of motivational self-awareness. We have little understanding of the seemingly mysterious but natural workings of the mind and the effects it produces. The boy Joseph's visions were effected through the faculty of *scrying,* a form of divination used for centuries to energize the subconscious and to seek communication with the otherworldly. Friends and foes alike describe Joseph's use of seer stones in his gazing activities which included money digging, envisioning the Book of Mormon, and receiving revelations he said were God-sent. Once Joseph reached maturity and left the folk magical world with its unsavory elements essentially behind, his intentions became clear. Convinced both intellectually and spiritually that all other religions were corrupt, the young man concluded that he had been divinely commissioned to renew faith in the primitive gospel of the New Testament and to direct the world in building God's kingdom on earth in preparation for the advent of the Lord Jesus and the long promised Millennium which he claimed was "nigh at hand" (D&C 1:12, 35:15, 49:6, 104:4, 133:17). This all-encompassing vision and ultimate focus became the central mission of Joseph's life. His message announcing the dawning of a new millennial age of unbounded prosperity for believers—what he called the fullness of times—convinced some people of the region. Following the charismatic prophet and his teachings, they were drawn into the fold.

"We need genius," contends American literary critic Harold Bloom, "in the particular sense of turning to the genius of others in order to redress a lack in oneself, or finding in genius a stimulus to one's own powers, whatever these may emerge as being."[14] Joseph Smith could not have been born in a more relevant epoch. His overtly secular-spiritual crusade, favored by the restlessness of his time, was graced by his innate genius and charisma. No one can create a following without discontent. Dissatisfaction with the existing order was the fertile soil from which sprang the Mormon revolution. Smith's dynamism drew the displeased and disappointed to him with vivid, compelling new revelations of a better life.

Modern society seems almost to expect eventual deceit from its public

14. Harold Bloom, *Genius,* 5.

figures. "Our ships in the Tonkin Gulf were attacked last night by forces of the North Vietnamese Navy," lied U.S. President Lyndon B. Johnson in a statement made to justify increased American participation in Vietnam.[15] And in a 1970 meeting, President Richard M. Nixon told the group to continue doing what was necessary in Cambodia but to tell the public that the United States was merely providing support to South Vietnamese forces when necessary to protect U.S. troops.[16] Aggrieved by criticism surrounding his plans to lay a wreath at the Bittburg Cemetery in West Germany, President Ronald Reagan described his emotional reaction to "what he had personally witnessed as an American army officer assisting in the liberation of a German concentration camp," despite the fact that Reagan, a special "liaison officer" serving in Hollywood, never left the United States during World War II.[17] And millions of Americans watched their president, Bill Clinton, stare into television cameras and lie: "I did not have sex with that woman." Later, elaborating on his "lifelong effort to lead parallel lives," Clinton wrote: "I was trying to protect my family and myself. … I believed that the contorted definition of 'sexual relations' enabled me to do so."[18] In the shadows and contours of Joseph Smith's wonder-filled life lie similar contradictions.

Janus is the Roman god of gates and doors, beginnings and endings, and hence is often represented with two faces looking in opposite directions. Being Janus-faced means to present oneself to the world, and perhaps to oneself, in more than one way, to be many-sided, and hence to have a divided self. Joseph Smith crafted a magnificently confident adult facade which concealed a character capable of being both forthright and duplicitous. "The full genius of language is inseparable from the impulse to concealment and fiction," states one scholar.[19] The historical record clearly demonstrates that on occasion Joseph used evasive, euphemistic, confusing, and self-contradictory language to conceal aspects of his inner self. He also developed a penchant for redefining the truth, particularly regarding the women in his life. In what follows, I am not suggesting that Joseph's life was dominated by deception. But I do believe it is an important trait—one of many that define

15. Lyndon Johnson, qtd. in Charles V. Ford, *Lies! Lies! Lies!,* 31.
16. Cal Woodward, "Documents Show Nixon Misled Public on Cambodian Actions," A5.
17. M. Shaller, *Reckoning with Reagan,* qtd. in Ford, *Lies! Lies! Lies!,* 2-3.
18. William Jefferson Clinton, *My Life,* 811, 774.
19. Ford, *Lies! Lies! Lies!,* 23.

his character and personality. Ignoring the prophet's duplicitous self will result in a failure to understand the man.

"What a thing it is for a man to be accused of committing adultery, and having seven wives," Joseph mused to a crowd of thousands a month before his assassination, "when I can only find one."[20] Yet historians have thoroughly documented that the Mormon prophet was secretly involved with more than thirty women at this time, a fact that caused substantial conflict with his legal wife, Emma Hale.[21] The Smiths' marital discord was known only to a few in Joseph's intimate circle. One of his loyal secretaries recorded the essential truth of the prophet's deception in his relationship with the wife of his youth. To appease Emma's anger over his hidden liaisons, a besieged prophet, fearful Emma would "obtain a divorce & leave him," told his aide that "he had to tell [Emma] he would relinquish all for her sake." Joseph, however, quickly added that "he should not relinquish any thing."[22] This double life led directly to his death a year later. "It was secret things which had cost Joseph and Hyrum their lives," Emma observed two months after the Smith brothers' murders.[23] A chain reaction occurred when the *Nauvoo Expositor* began to publish unsavory details of the prophet's private life. As city mayor, Smith called for the destruction of the printing press and was then arrested for his actions and their repercussions. A vengeful mob stormed the jail where he was being held and murdered him and Hyrum.

Secrets often are attended and protected by lies. There were reasons for Joseph's secretiveness. His covert polygamy was only one side of a multi-sided lifestyle. A few other examples show his ability to make his way through a web of calculated subterfuge. In an 1843 memorial "To the Honorable Senate and House of Representatives of the United States, in Congress Assembled," Smith wrote: "My father, who stood several times in the battles of the American Revolution, till his companions in arms had been shot dead at his feet, was forced from his home in Far West, Missouri."[24] Yet Father Smith, born in 1771, was only four years old when the first shots of the Revolution were fired, just twelve when the Treaty of Paris ended the war.

20. *History of the Church,* 6:409.

21. For treatments of Joseph Smith's polygamy, see Linda King Newell and Valeen Tippets Avery, *Mormon Enigma,* chaps. 7-10; Richard S. Van Wagoner, *Mormon Polygamy,* chaps. 2-5; B. Carmon Hardy, *Solemn Covenant,* chaps. 1-3; Todd Compton, *In Sacred Loneliness;* and George D. Smith, *Nauvoo Polygamy: "But We Called It Celestial Marriage ..."* See also Brian C. Hales, *Joseph Smith's Polygamy,* 3 vols. (Salt Lake City: Greg Kofford Books, 2013).

22. William Clayton, in George D. Smith, *Intimate Chronicle,* 117.

23. Ibid., 144.

24. *History of the Church,* 6:92.

There are parts of human beings that remain unquantifiable or are qualities of a special stamp. But denial was perhaps the most common reaction when Joseph Smith was cornered, particularly by women who knew him in his private moments. "She lied about me," Joseph allegedly said of Sarah Pratt, a married woman who had rebuffed his advances. "I never made the offer [of sex] which she said I did." The prophet had previously threatened Sarah: "If you should tell, I will ruin your reputation, *remember that.*"[25] Unintimidated, she told her husband, Orson, anyway. When later confronted, the prophet replied: "I will not advise you to break up your family—unless it were asked of me. Then I would coun[se]l you to get a bill from your wife and marry virtuous women—and a new family but if you do not do it [I] shall never throw it in your teeth."[26]

Another example which unfolded in Nauvoo, Illinois, contributed to the deaths of a number of new converts. In an August 15, 1841, letter to an Illinois land agent from whom he had purchased large tracts of Mississippi River bottomland, the prophet complained: "I presume you are no stranger to the part of the city plat we bought of you being a deathly sickly hole, and that we have not been able in consequence to realize any valuable consideration from it, although we have been keeping up appearances, and holding out inducements to encourage immigration, that we scarcely think justifiable in consequence of the mortality that almost invariably awaits those who come from far distant parts."[27]

Despite the admission that the mosquito-infested river bottoms he owned were a "deathly sickly hole," Joseph was in such a desperate financial dilemma that he "kept up appearances" and continued to promote real estate sales in that unhealthy locale. As late as April 13, 1843, while greeting a company of newly disembarked English Saints, Joseph announced grandiloquently: "Some persons may perhaps inquire which is the most healthful location. I will tell you. The lower part of the town is most healthful. In the upper part of the town are the merchants, who will say that I am partial ... but the lower part of the town is much the most healthful; and I tell it [to] you in the name of the Lord."[28] This untruthful claim influenced many unsuspecting Saints to purchase the malarial and yellow-fever

25. Bennett, *The History of the Saints,* 231; emphasis his.

26. "Minutes of the Quorum of the Twelve," Jan. 20, 1843. See also Richard S. Van Wagoner, "Sarah M. Pratt," 72.

27. *History of the Church,* 4:407.

28. Ibid., 5:357.

plagued bottomlands. For some, death was their reward for heeding the prophet's advice.

A charming high achiever in articulating his vision and persuading other people to embrace it, Joseph admitted, "Although I do wrong, I do not the wrongs that I am charged with doing; the wrong that I do is through the frailty of human nature, like other men. No man lives without fault."[29] Yet even this confession reshapes and minimizes his faults. Prominent early twentieth-century Mormon Church historian and leader B. H. Roberts attested that Joseph

> claimed for himself no special sanctity, no faultless life, no perfection of character, no inerrancy for every word spoken by him. And as he did not claim these things for himself, so can they not be claimed for him by others; for to claim perfection for him, or even unusual sanctity, would be to repudiate the revelations themselves which supply the evidence of his imperfections, whereof, in them, he is frequently reproved.
>
> Joseph Smith was a man of like passions with other men; struggling with the same weaknesses; subjected to the same temptations; under the same moral law, and humiliated at times, like others, by occasionally, in word and conduct, falling below the high ideals presented in the perfect life and faultless character of the Man of Nazareth.[30]

No doubt in the minds of most Christians, Jesus was never deceitful. Joseph Smith, on the other hand, sometimes was. Although this modern prophet is the ultimate expert on his own biography, how far should we go in accepting without question his and others' retrospective accounts of his life as entirely factual? How historically accurate are the prophet's narratives of the coming forth of the Book of Mormon, the First Vision, and restoration of ancient priesthood authority? In what ways, if any, are such accounts akin, for example, to Joseph's public and false denials of polygamy? How are we to evaluate character when it comes to God's spokesmen? Some scholars view lying as "characteristic of all life and a significant part of human interactions."[31] David Nyberg argues that deception is "rather an essential component of our ability to organize and shape the world … to cope with uncertainty and pain, to be civil and to achieve privacy as needed, to survive as a species and to flourish as persons."[32] I do not deny the prevalence or

29. Joseph Fielding Smith, *Teachings of the Prophet Joseph Smith,* 258.
30. B. H. Roberts, *Comprehensive History of the Church,* 2:360.
31. Ford, *Lies! Lies! Lies!,* 280.
32. D. Nyberg, *The Varnished Truth,* 219.

roles of deception and dishonesty in society. I merely ask about their place and function in the lives of people revered as God's messengers.

Some may point out that many ancient prophets, who spoke as they were inspired, were weak and sinful men, yet acted as approved agents of the Most High. And as Joseph said, in a paraphrase of 1 Corinthians 1:27, God chooses "the weak things of this world to confound the wise." My own perspective is of a creator whose principal attributes are truth and love—and who still expects, despite our repeated failures, honesty and integrity from each of us. Historian Alice Felt Tyler commented:

> For many he [Joseph Smith] was to be the prophet and favored confidant of God, the founder of the only true church, and the father and messiah of his people. To countless thousands of others he has seemed a liar and a deliberate charlatan. ... Conscious or unconscious charlatan, self-deceived or flamboyantly triumphant in his ability to take advantage of the gullibility of others, true or false prophet, the crude, uneducated, neurotic farmer and treasure hunter became a man of unusual powers of leadership and of remarkable success as an organizer. Valid or invalid in its fundamental tenets, the Mormon church became a fact, and Joseph Smith was its Prophet.[33]

As non-Mormon historian Nathan O. Hatch observes: "Historians of Mormonism who themselves are Latter-day Saints have also constructed their history in ways that are theologically faithful. In Mormon discourse about their own history, the most powerful magnet arranging the iron filings of the historical evidence is the conviction that Joseph Smith was a divine prophet."[34] For many Mormon believers, it is easy to assume that Joseph's theology is divine, given, and secure, his pronouncements absolute, immutable, guaranteed. But history continually teaches us the heavy price such certitude may exact. I am a descendant of some who were with Joseph Smith in the beginning, and have no doubt been influenced by, drawn upon, and benefitted from the heritage of my believing ancestors. It is, in part, to honor their commitment to the truth, as they believed it, that I have not presumed to write a biography in the tradition of apologetic history. First and foremost, I am an investigative biographer, interested in both truth and falsehood and their ramifications, disinclined to move along a velvet rope with the crowd while keeping a respectful distance from Joseph Smith.

33. Alice Felt Tyler, *Freedom's Ferment,* 89.
34. Nathan O. Hatch, "Mormon and Methodist," 36.

The prophet was blessed with consummate creative genius and vision, with near boundless personal charisma, yet also was burdened with character flaws suitable to a Sophoclean tragedy. Religious leaders, like all leaders, demand up-close-and-personal scrutiny. There is nothing disrespectful or demeaning about subjecting such men and women to the same common-sense analysis by which we measure philosophers, politicians, professors, and all other human beings. One should not ignore Joseph Smith's darker nooks and crannies; one should study his persona *in toto.* "We need not follow our researches in any spirit of fear and trembling," admonished B. H. Roberts. "We desire only to ascertain the truth; nothing but the truth will endure; and the ascertainment of the truth and the proclamation of the truth in any given case, or upon any subject, will do no harm to the work of the Lord which is itself truth."[35]

I believe there is virtually nothing on which all people agree entirely, no matter how absolute and seemingly obvious. We see and experience reality through our own perceptions and according to our own predispositions. I include myself and my readers here. We see what we want to see, what we need to see. We often identify and define ourselves by myths and stories. The accumulation of two centuries of charged, romanticized imagery has helped to create an iconic Joseph Smith. That fact and its accompanying mind set tend to shield many believers from information that might up-end the shared complacency, even ignorance, regarding their church's founder. I believe that a hardy voice of critical scrutiny, asking probing questions and exploring and sharing new ideas, nourishes both individuals and organizations. With Roberts, I believe that truth can only be strengthened by serious-minded investigation. The practical value of good critical history is that it helps us to acquire a healthier identity and approach to living.

I treat the early years of the Mormon prophet as I would approach an archaeological dig. The deepest levels, those deposited first and least contaminated by subsequent accumulates, are of primary interest in my pursuit of the historical Joseph. Mindful of the prophet's controversial reputation, I try to remain sensitive to the impact that some of the more problematic elements of his behavior may have on believers. But truth is often best evidenced in the detail. "Fix Reason firmly in her seat," advised Thomas Jefferson, "and call to her tribunal every fact, every opinion. Question with boldness even

35. B. H. Roberts, *New Witnesses for God,* 1:503.

the existence of a God; because, if there be one, he must more approve the homage of reason than of blindfolded fear."[36]

"We are naturally prone to believe that the light of culture shines brightest in our own circle," writes historian Lester D. Stephens. "Our ideas, our beliefs, and our customs seem to us to be sanctified; those of others seem to suffer the defects of inferiority, or at the least they are viewed as unenlightened."[37] Human nature being what it is, I believe we should thoroughly scrutinize the assertions of religious individuals and communities which promote what, to common sense, may seem strange, mysterious, or marvelous. Most adherents to any religious belief system, whether Catholicism, Buddhism, Hinduism, Islam, Judaism, Mormonism, or Protestantism, are confident that their history and dogmas are true. Frequently they assert that they have the witness of the Spirit (or its equivalent) in their souls, a fire in their bones (Jer. 20:9). But one's personal belief should never be based solely on unchallenged, emotive impressions, common though they may be to religious experience. Nor should one routinely discount the fantastical merely because he has not experienced it in his own life. "Prove all things," the Apostle Paul admonished (1 Thess. 5:21). Before assuming that someone else speaks—or does not speak—for God, a believer—or a non-believer—should carefully examine her own spiritual quest. You must "study it out in your mind," Joseph's compilation of revelations counsels, and "*then* you must ask me if it be right." Then and only then, said Joseph, will God "cause that your bosom shall burn within you; therefore you shall feel that it is right" (D&C 9:8; emphasis mine). My focus throughout this work is informed and tempered by such advice and by my own intellectual curiosity.

Acknowledgments

This book could not have been completed without the assistance of archives, special collections, and library staffs at the Church History Library of the Church of Jesus Christ of latter-day Saints (Salt Lake City, Utah); the J. Willard Marriott Library, University of Utah (Salt Lake City); the Harold B. Lee Library, Brigham Young University (Provo, Utah); and the Utah State Historical Society (Salt Lake City). Special assistance was provided by Bob Clark, Wesleyan Methodist Archivist (Indianapolis, Indiana); Beth Hoad, Palmyra Historian (Palmyra, New York); J. Taylor Hollist (Oneonta, New York); and Stan Larson (Marriott Library).

36. Thomas Jefferson, qtd. in John E. Remsburg, "Six Historic Americans," 1.
37. Lester D. Stephens, "The Uses of History," 100.

In addition, I wish to thank artist Kurt Gray for the illustrations and cartographer Ken Rust for the maps. Special acknowledgment to the Smith-Pettit Foundation for its support. I also appreciate the contributions of colleagues Scott G. Kenney and Martha Bradley-Evans, editor Lavina Fielding Anderson, historians H. Michael Marquardt and Dan Vogel, and longtime friend George D. Smith. Last, I could not—and would not—have attempted this undertaking without the advice, guidance, and editing of Mary C. Van Wagoner.

1 | GOODLY PARENTS

I raised them in the fear of God. When they were two or three years old I told them I wanted them to love god with all their hearts. I told them to do good ... I presume there never was a family more obedient than mine—I did not have to speak to them only once[.]

—Lucy Mack Smith, qtd. in William Clayton, Conference Minutes, Nauvoo, Illinois, Oct. 8, 1845, in Dan Vogel, *Early Mormon Documents*, 1:223

Though not generally recognized as a pivotal year in world history, 1805 boasts some memorable events. Thomas Jefferson, triumphantly reelected as U.S. President a year earlier, was presiding over a nation of nearly 6 million. Prosperity was returning to the country in the wake of renewed European wars. On January 11, Michigan became the country's newest territory. Three months later, on April 7, Meriwether Lewis and William Clark left Fort Mandan for points west, beginning the process of filling in the American canvas. Later that month, U.S. Marines and Berber allies attacked Barbary pirates on the shores of Tripoli, capturing the city of Derna, and putting an imperishable line in the future "Marines' Hymn." A month later in Milan's cathedral, Napoleon was crowned King of Italy. On August 9, Zebulon Pike was commissioned to explore the territory of the Louisiana Purchase. In October, during the Napoleonic Wars, a British fleet under the command of Admiral Lord Nelson at the Battle of Trafalgar, off the coast of Spain, defeated a combined French and Spanish armada. Nelson was killed, but Napoleon's effort to invade England was stopped. On November 7, after ascending the Missouri River and struggling overland to the mouth of the Columbia, Lewis and Clark's Corps of Discovery first glimpsed the Pacific Ocean.

As 1805 neared its close, deep in the backwoods of New England's Vermont, an American cultural and religious prodigy was born. There on December 23, the future seer and prophet of Mormonism, fourth son and fifth child of Joseph Smith Sr. and Lucy Mack Smith, entered the world atop the high ridge of land between Royalton and Sharon, Windsor County. He would later speak of himself in a prophecy voiced in the words of the Hebrew Bible patriarch Joseph in which the future seer "shall be called after me; and it shall be after the name of his father. And he shall be like unto me" (Book of Mormon, 2 Ne. 3:14-15). This new Vermonter, like his father, was named Joseph Smith.

The Smith surname, perhaps the most common in Great Britain, belonged to "artificers in wood as well as metal—in fact to all mechanical workers, hence its great frequency."[1] Noted Western American historian Dale Morgan wrote of Joseph and Lucy Smith:

> The senior Smith brought much to the making of a prophet, his stalwart body, his hatred of the farm, his skeptical views on denominational religion, his love for the strange and the marvelous, his inventive fancy, his will to rise above the circumstances of his life. His wife Lucy, too, had a contribution that was not less vital. Shrewd, strong-willed, warm-hearted, garrulous, passionately devoted to her family, credulous and even superstitious, on the homeliest of terms with God, who manifested his mind and will to her in dreams and "providences," Lucy was to see all these characteristics abundantly reflected in her third son—and ultimately in the church he founded.[2]

Like Nephi, whose voice introduces the Book of Mormon, Joseph Jr. later declared that he too had been "born ... of goodly Parents who spared no pains to instructing me in christian religion."[3] His mother later said that she and her husband raised their children "in the fear of God," and from the time "they were 2 or 3 year[s] old [we taught them] that they may love God with all their hearts."[4] All his life, Joseph Jr. remembered the "kind ... parental words" that had been "written on the tablet of my heart."[5] And younger brother William said that both parents "pourd out their souls to God, the donner [donor] of all Blessings, to ... guard their children and keep them

1. Mary Audentia Anderson, *Ancestry and Posterity of Joseph Smith and Emma Hale,* 51. Recent research suggests that "the Smiths were Irish" (Michael De Groote, "DNA Shows Joseph Was Irish").

2. John Phillip Walker, *Dale Morgan on Early Mormonism,* 221. Joseph was actually the fourth-born son, but the eldest had been stillborn.

3. Dean C. Jessee, *The Personal Writings of Joseph Smith,* 4.

4. William Clayton, Conference Minutes, Nauvoo, Illinois, Oct. 8, 1845, in Vogel, *Early Mormon Documents,* 1:223.

5. *History of the Church,* 5:126.

from sin and from all evil works."[6] Like many of their peers, Joseph and Lucy Smith, though God-fearing Christians, were also superstitious country folk. They believed in, and fostered in their children, not only the principles of the Christian gospel, but also a magical world view suffused with enchantment, numerology, astrology, hidden treasure, dowsing, seer stones, divining rods, talismans, apparitions, fortune telling, omens, magic squares, magic circles, magic parchments, and other occult powers of nature.[7]

For example, Joseph Sr. told Vermont neighbors that when baby Joseph first made his appearance in the family's rustic log cabin on that cold Vermont day, he was "born with a veil over [his] face."[8] This birth veil or *caul*, an intricate, filmy membrane that occasionally covers the head and face of a newborn, was believed by ingenuous persons like the Smiths to be an omen of good fortune, a sign that the child was destined for greatness, gifted with a sixth sense, and immune to drowning.[9]

One account asserts that caulbearers are especially adroit in "finding underground water supplies," presumably through dowsing, and in "knowing when weather patterns will change, predicting when fish and other food supplies will become plentiful." Many born in the caul are "natural healers which may be manifested by the laying on of their hands, or remotely from a distance." Furthermore, caulbearers reportedly enjoy other mystical gifts, including "great ability in matters of judgment and ruling nations."[10]

In addition to Joseph Sr.'s arcane reference about the baby Joseph's

---

6. William B. Smith, "Notes on Chamber's Life of Joseph Smith," 29.

7. The most comprehensive treatment of these elements of Smith family lore is D. Michael Quinn, *Early Mormonism and the Magic World View*.

8. Qtd. in "Green Mountain Boys to Thomas C. Sharp," Feb. 15, 1844.

9. *Caul*, from the Gaelic *call*, meaning a veil or hood (Virginia S. Thatcher, *The New Webster Encyclopedic Dictionary)*. In ancient Rome, Aelius Lampridius, writing of Antonine Diadumenius, said he was so called from "being born into the world with a band of membrane round his forehead in the shape of a diadem, and he enjoyed a perpetual state of felicity from this circumstance" ("Caul," www.fact-index). According to some, the following were born in caul: Moses, Buddha, Marduk (ruler and king of Mesopotamia), Alexander the Great, Lord George Gordon Byron, and Sigmund Freud (Andrea Deno, "Sigmund Freud, 1856:1939"; "Caul," www.healthlink; "Caul, or Face Veil, Occasionally Present at Birth"; "Cauls," www.theshadowlands). Over the course of European history, the folk belief developed that possessing a baby's caul ensured its owner against drowning. Women often sold such cauls to sailors on the open market (Thomas Rogers Forbes, *The Midwife and the Witch,* 94-111; "Caul," www.fact-index; "Old Wives Tales"). In the Brothers Grimm fairy tale "The Devil with the Three Golden Hairs," the story's hero "came into the world with a caul on" (Jacob and Wilhelm Grimm, *Household Tales,* 1:119-25).

Amniomancy is a form of divination practiced using a caul. "Wise women" would inspect the membrane and foretell the baby's future based on their findings. A red caul suggested happy days or good fortune; a gray or dark one foretold misfortune ("Amniomancy").

10. "What Is So Special about the Caul?"

spiritual veil, perhaps anticipating his son's future as a soothsayer, a seer with second sight, he added that "he intended to procure a stone for [the boy] to see all over the world with."[11] Lucy Smith, who sometimes used seer stones herself, years later acknowledged the family's participation in "trying to win the faculty of Abrac[,][12] drawing Magic circles[,] or sooth saying." She stressed that they did not neglect other family business while engaged in mystical or occult pursuits.[13]

Joseph and Lucy Smith's Vermont, a state of New England tucked into the northeast corner of the country, is rich in American lore. When Europeans arrived on the eastern seaboard, the land that would become Vermont was populated by the Algonquin, Iroquois, and Abenaki, who hunted, gathered, and fished in its heavily wooded hillocks. The first European to see this craggy land was Jacques Cartier, a French explorer, in 1535. In 1609, Samuel de Champlain sailed the lake that now bears his name. The French no doubt made their explorations during warmer months, for when they gazed upon the elevations that form the spine of the state, they named them *les verts monts* ("the green mountains"), a name anglicized as Vermont.

English settlers first came to the area in 1724 to build Fort Dummer on the site of present-day Brattleboro, downstate from Joseph Smith's birthplace. The French settled in the Chimney Point area in 1731. Struggles for supremacy between the two European powers continued for four decades. In 1763, at the end of the French and Indian Wars, England was granted the territory that includes present-day Vermont in the Treaty of Paris. In the ensuing confusion, both New Hampshire and New York claimed the region.

---

11. "Green Mountain Boys to Thomas C. Sharp."

12. In early America, "The Faculty of Abrac" was a well-known phrase linking magic and divinity. *Abracadabra,* a word analogous to *Abraxas,* was reportedly coined by Basilides, an Egyptian Gnostic to invoke the aid of beneficent spirits against disease and misfortune. D. Michael Quinn has noted that "this word was often used as a talismanic spell in the form of a triangle, Abrac occupying the holy seventh line, with the single letter A as the bottom end point. From 1798 to 1829 American encyclopedias published this charm" *(Magic World View,* 69). The Gnostic physician Serenus Sammonicus gave precise instructions about the mystical use of Abraxas in averting or curing agues and fevers. "The paper on which the word was written had to be folded in the form of a cross, suspended from the neck by a strip of linen so as to rest on the pit of the stomach, worn in this way for nine days, and then, before sunrise, cast behind the wearer into a stream running to the east" ("Abracadabra, A Magical Formula Used by the Gnostics"). Another source has noted that the abracadabra triangle has been found on written charms in old buildings throughout England and Wales. "The written charms are the result of a farmer or householder's need to have their property or livestock protected by a supernatural spell. The person in need would contact the local cunning-person and ask him/her for a charm to protect the desired creatures or buildings" ("Written Charms").

13. Lavina Fielding Anderson, *Lucy's Book,* 323.

Originally organized to drive New Yorkers from Vermont, the Green Mountain Boys, led by Ethan Allen, won fame by capturing Fort Ticonderoga from the British on May 10, 1775, in the early days of the Revolutionary War.

In 1777, immediately after the United States gained its independence, Vermont declared its own emancipation—a move intended to resolve the complicated boundary disputes among New York, New Hampshire, and Vermont. For fourteen years, the Republic of Vermont was governed by home rule. The sovereignty maintained its own postal system, coined money, naturalized citizens from other countries, affirmed an independent system of laws and legislation, and conducted trade and maintained diplomacy with foreign governments (including the United States). On May 4, 1791, Vermont, with a population of 85,341, became the first state to join the original thirteen in an expansion of American union.[14]

Vermont's rugged, rocky terrain and unpredictable weather initially discouraged extensive agriculture. The region's first settlers were primarily subsistence farmers, cultivating only what they and their immediate community needed. A son of Massachusetts, Joseph Smith Sr., with his older brother Jesse, ascended the Connecticut and White River Valleys, before arriving during the summer of 1791 at Tunbridge, Orange County, in the heart of the new state of Vermont. The hardy Smith brothers, both in their early twenties, began felling trees to create a homestead on the 83-acre farm that their parents, Asael Smith and Mary Duty Smith, had just purchased. This property lay in the southern portion of the township in what was termed the Tunbridge Gore.[15] By November, the entire Smith clan—parents and eleven children—had crowded into the fourteen-by-ten-foot log cabin that the Smith boys had built and covered with elm bark.

Tunbridge was a small village with slightly fewer than 500 people in 1791. No more than a hundred families were scattered about the town's thirty-six square miles of knobby land when Asael and Mary Smith moved to the area. Smith family members were pioneers in this part of Tunbridge which abutted the North Royalton boundary, and the area was known as the Smith settlement, set off as School District Thirteen.

---

14. See "Vermont Timeline."

15. "Gore," in surveying terminology, refers to a triangular piece of property lying outside a survey line and therefore not included in a township's original survey. Tunbridge Gore was eventually added to Tunbridge township by legislative act, year not specified. Larry C. Porter, "A Study of the Origins of the Church of Jesus Christ of Latter-day Saints in the States of New York and Pennsylvania, 1816-1831," 11.

Jesse Smith was appointed a school trustee; Joseph later became a school teacher in the precinct.[16]

Joseph Smith Sr. had been born in Topsfield, Massachusetts, on July 12, 1771, as King George III was attempting to restore the declining power of the British monarchy. On March 8, 1772, Joseph's parents had him baptized a Congregationalist, an affiliation he shrugged off in his youth. A great-great grandson described him as "a clean appearing young man, with a face substantial in cut as the granite of the New England hills he was raised among, with good shoulders, and with arms and hands like a man ought to have—a man's man."[17] Like George Washington, Joseph Sr. stood six feet two, towering over most men of his day. Reportedly ramrod straight, and "remarkably well proportioned," as young Joseph later noted, Joseph Sr.'s adult weight was near 200 pounds. Like his father Asael, "a powerfully built man capable of handling two men of average size with very little difficulty,"[18] Joseph Sr. was strong and active. As a youth, "he was famed as a wrestler, and Jacob like, he never wrestled with but one man whom he could not throw."[19] One of his grandsons recollected that "in stature he had no superior in the family. Not one of his sons excelled him in physical appearance—not one to my memory."[20] Another stated that he "was very tall; his nose was very prominent ... [and his son] Joseph looked very much like him."[21] William Hyde, a close friend in Palmyra, remarked: "I don't believe [Joseph Sr., during 1828-29] missed a night without stopping with me for at least three hours." He described Joseph Sr. as a "solemn looking duck ... always seemed to be in deep study."[22]

Edward Stevenson remembered that "Father Smith was not a man of many words, but, sober-minded, firm, mild and impressive."[23] William Smith, later reminiscing about his father, noted that "his occupation in early life was that of a School teacher." He added that "he was a man well letter[e]d in [the] Common branches of our english Studies[.] He also was a

16. Evelyn M. Wood Lovejoy, *History of Royalton, Vermont, with Family Genealogies, 1769-1911,* 645.

17. Warren L. Van Dine, "Some Descriptive Material about [a] List of Nine Prominent People of Salisbury Descent (from the Wilkins J. Salisbury-Catherine Smith marriage of 1831)," 14. Van Dine, who was born after Joseph Sr.'s death, likely heard these traits from his grandmother, Katharine Smith Salisbury, who lived until 1900.

18. Ibid., 10.

19. *History of the Church,* 4:191.

20. Joseph F. Smith, "Remarks Made ... following the Reading of the Preceding Paper," *Journal of History,* 1:41.

21. Ephraim Hatch, *Joseph Smith Portraits,* 11.

22. William Hyde, "Interview."

23. Richard L. Anderson, *Investigating the Book of Mormon Witnesses,* 142.

teacher of music [by] note to a concidera[b]l[e] extent."[24] "My opinion of him was high," said William Hyde, adding that he did not know of a subject Joseph Smith could not "discuss intelligently." The school teacher's "memory was something extraordinary," Hyde noted; "he could repeat several chapters of a book verbatim after it had been read rapidly."[25] A third-hand source, reporting accounts he had heard while visiting Palmyra, New York, in 1831, noted that Joseph Sr. "was a great story teller, full of anecdotes picked up in his peregrinations—and possessed a tongue as smooth as oil and as quick as lightning."[26] Orsamus Turner, a Palmyra neighbor, attested, less enthusiastically, that Father Smith displayed a "good deal of ... Scriptural knowledge," and was "a great babbler, credulous ... prone to the marvelous."[27]

Lucy, Joseph's wife of forty-four years by the time of his death in 1840, was born to Solomon Mack and Lydia Gates Mack on July 8, 1775, in Gilsom, New Hampshire, three months after the first shots of the American War for Independence were fired at Lexington, Massachusetts.[28] Age twenty-one in 1753, Solomon enlisted in the British-supervised colonial militia for the French and Indian Wars and saw action at Half-way Brook, New York, in 1755. Later, he served as a baggage-master for the commander of Fort Edwards. After his reenlistment in 1758, he narrowly escaped with his life on several occasions. In his forties during the Revolutionary War, he served in an artillery unit, then, with sons Jason and Stephen, found employment as a seaman on East Coast privateers. While she was growing up, Lucy delighted in hearing her father tell of his adventures. But Solomon Mack, a restless wandering soul who also labored as a tradesman and farmer, was frequently away from home on lengthy ventures. From ages nine through seventeen, Lucy did not see her eccentric father. When he did finally return, the adventurer was impoverished. Even though the family was poor and living in wilderness-like conditions, Lucy's mother, Lydia Gates Mack, managed to create for her eight children a home rich in spiritual and cultural experiences. Her husband later described her as "<a> most worthy <and invaluable> companion ... for I soon discovered that she was not only pleasant and agreable by reason of the polish of Education but she also possessed that

24. William Smith, "Notes," 33.

25. Hyde, Interview.

26. James G. Bennett, "Mormonism."

27. Orsamus Turner, *History of the Pioneer Settlement,* 48.

28. Unless otherwise noted, my narrative of this portion of Lucy's life is based on her own account in Anderson, *Lucy's Book,* 235-58.

inestimable jewel which in a wife and Mother of a family is truly a pearl of great price namily <a> truly pious and devotional Charecter."[29]

Lydia had grown up in a well-to-do home and, prior to marriage, had been a cultured schoolteacher. Her education proved to be a blessing during her husband's absence, when full responsibility for the children's education and temporal welfare fell upon her shoulders. Although Lucy does not specify how Lydia supported the family, she took pains to recount that Lydia schooled her children in secular matters and also enhanced their piety through Bible study, prayer, and morning and evening devotionals. Lucy traced her own "principles of early piety" to being "taught me when My Mother called me with my brothers and sisters around her knee and instructed [us] to feel our constant dependance upon God[,] our liability to transgression and the necessity of prayer and also discoursed to [us] of our accountability to our father in Heaven—of death and a judgement to come."[30] Lucy's brother Solomon recalled that "their mother's percepts and example ... had a more lasting influence upon their future char[a]cter" than any other single factor.[31]

Lucy inherited her mother's strength, decorum, and exceptional gift of language—a largess she passed along to her own children. From her father came an innate power of command, an ability to speak directly and plainly, which destined her to be a woman of determined—or stubborn—action. The youngest of eight children, Lucy was evidently loved, and sometimes favored, above the rest, although not overly doted on by her family. A compassionate lay nurse, and burden-bearer, she became the mainstay in caring for her sister Lovina, whose young life was slowly extinguished by virulent tuberculosis, then called consumption. A married sister, Lovisa Mack Tuttle, died of the same malady in 1794. The loss of her beloved sisters and the lack of comfort given by the severe religious creeds of that day left Lucy lonely and despondent. The grief, Lucy would later describe in her memoir, "was preying upon my health, and threatened my constitution with serious injury." Her brother Stephen, visiting from Tunbridge, Vermont, witnessed her depression and persuaded their parents to let him take Lucy to his home. "I was pensive and melancholy," she reported, and "and often in my reflections I thought that life was not worth possessing."[32] The trip to Vermont, probably the first time she had left her native New Hampshire, proved to be a lifesaver.

---

29. Anderson, *Lucy's Book,* 227.
30. Ibid., 55.
31. Ibid., 228.
32. Psychiatrist Robert D. Anderson observes in his study of Joseph Smith, *Inside the Mind*

Lucy's parents were divided on religion. For much of his life, Solomon believed in the doctrine of the universal salvation of all humanity as taught by Universalists. Lydia, on the other hand, was a staunch Congregationalist who conveyed Puritan beliefs and demands to her family. This confusion within her home must have been unsettling to Lucy. The deaths of Lovisa and Lovina were both scenes of Christian faith and fortitude; and although not baptized at the time of these deaths, Lucy was a believing Christian. Yet the young woman could find neither comfort nor peace of mind in the despairing darkness that enveloped her soul. "In the midst of this anxiety of mind," she would later say, "I determined to obtain that which I had heard spoken of so much from the pulpit—a change of heart." Although she focused her energies into reading the Bible and praying "incessantly," she despaired over finding an acceptable denomination. "If I remain a member of no church," she thought, "all religious people will say I am of the world." But if she joined a denomination, she reasoned, "the rest will say I am in error." In language and thought inspired by her Seeker heritage, the Christian primitivist pattern that decades later inspired her son Joseph, Lucy reflected, "how can I decide in such a case as this, seeing they are all unlike the Church of Christ, as it existed in former days!"[33]

While Lucy found no comfort in organized religion at the time, she did find solace in true love. Stephen Mack, her brother, operated a Tunbridge mercantile, tinning business, and tavern in partnership with John Mudget. At Mack and Mudget's store where she worked, the diminutive Lucy (one inch shy of five feet)[34] met the powerfully built, gentle-voiced young farmer Joseph Smith, an acquaintance of her brother. She later characterized the entire Asael Smith family as "worthy[,] respectable[,] amiable[,] and intelligent." After a year's courtship, the blue-eyed lovers were wed on January 24, 1796, by Tunbridge Justice of the Peace Seth Austin.[35]

The couple began life in relatively prosperous circumstances. Asael, Joseph's father, gave his son and his bride part ownership of his "old farm" on the Tunbridge property. They lived on the original cleared section of the

of Joseph Smith, 17: "This language suggests a depression that had approached suicidal proportions. Depression is a recurring illness, sometimes with symptoms of exhaustion, physical complaints, and religious preoccupation."

33. For an excellent treatment of Seekerism, see Dan Vogel, *Religious Seekers and the Advent of Mormonism.*

34. Vivian McConkie Adams, "All Prophets Knew." Adams is the great-great-great-granddaughter of Lucy Mack Smith.

35. "Record of Births, Deaths, Marriages." For evidence that both Smiths had blue eyes, see Vida E. Smith, "Character Sketch of Lucy Mack Smith," 406-7.

farm, "working it on shares," while Asael and his four youngest sons developed the rest.[36] Lucy also received a dowry. While she and Joseph were preparing to travel to New Hampshire to visit her parents, brother Stephen and his partner were discussing an appropriate wedding gift for her. "Lucy ought to have something worth naming," Mudget said, "and I will give her just as much as you will." "Done," replied Stephen. "I will give her five hundred dollars in cash." "Good," added Mudget, "and I will give her five hundred dollars more!" The prospect of a thousand-dollar bequest made Lucy a virtual heiress, and she wisely set aside the money for the future.[37] The money ultimately saved the family from financial ruin.

Sometime between mid-1796 and the spring of 1797, Lucy became pregnant. Many years later, reflecting on the loss of this first child, a stillborn son, Joseph Sr. said: "The Lord in his just providence has taken from me, at an untimely birth, a son."[38] However common it may have been to lose children in childbirth during this period, the death was no less difficult for the young couple since their unbaptized son was thereby doomed to hell, according to Calvinistic theology. Joseph Sr. sought spiritual comfort through Universalism, the faith of both his father, Asael, and his father-in-law, Solomon. In Universalist theology, everyone is ultimately saved; no one is damned. Proponents emphasize God's love and mercy over a desire to punish.

The Universalist movement—with universal salvation as its central theme—developed in America during the 1700s within the Congregational churches in New England. In 1803, the New Hampshire Convention summarized Universalist beliefs as: "We believe there is one God, whose nature is love, revealed in one Lord Jesus Christ, by one Holy Spirit of Grace, who will finally restore the whole family of mankind to holiness and happiness."[39] Universalism thus jettisoned the excess baggage of historical theology, including the concept that authority is derived from creeds. Emphasis was on a few simple, rational principles, which included a largely positive view of human nature, a rejection of the Trinity, the assertion of universal salvation, and the belief that religious wisdom is ever changing. Consequently, Universalists promoted the idea that human understanding of life and death, the world and its mysteries, is never final or complete. Asserting that revelation

36. "Records of Junius F. Wells."

37. By comparison, in 1825 when the Smith family was struggling to keep the Manchester farm, Lemuel Durfee Sr. purchased the entire property, including cleared land and frame house, for a little over $1,000 (Porter, "A Study of the Origins of the Church," 37).

38. Joseph Smith Sr., "Blessing on Hyrum Smith," Joseph Smith Sr., Introductory Comments.

39. Russell E. Miller, *The Larger Hope,* 45-46.

is continuous, Universalism celebrates unfolding truths to teachers, prophets, and sages throughout the ages.[40]

In December 1797, Joseph Smith, with father Asael, brother Jesse, and other Tunbridge men, signed declarations of membership in the Universalist Society. The signers, in compliance with Vermont law, also declared their exemption from "any tax towards the support of any teacher of any different denomination whatever," a reference to the usual town tax assessed for support of the established Congregational Church.[41]

William Smith later wrote that "[m]y father[']s ... faith in the Universal restoration doctrin[e] ... often brought him in Contact with the advocates of the doctrin[e] of endless misrey" as opposed to his "belief [in] the ultimate and final redemption of all mankind to heaven and happiness." Joseph Sr. may also have joined the Anabaptist Society in 1799.[42] This group rejected the doctrine of infant baptism and other Calvinistic tenets which taught that unbaptized infants would go to hell.[43]

The Smiths eked out an existence on their Tunbridge farm for nearly six years. During this period, Lucy gave birth to two more sons, Alvin in 1798 and Hyrum in 1800. In 1802, the Smiths rented out their farm and moved to Randolph, seven miles away. There they opened a mercantile—probably at the urging of Stephen Mack, whose Tunbridge emporium was successful. Randolph, a bit larger than Tunbridge, was named to honor Edmund Randolph, an aide to General George Washington. Six months after the family settled into this small community, Lucy, then twenty-seven, caught a cold, which after weeks of upper respiratory distress evolved into what she called a "hectic fever."[44] The local physician diagnosed her as consumptive, the condition that had killed both her sisters, and held out little hope of recovery. As her health spiraled downward, she and other family members foresaw she would soon join Lovisa and Lovina in death. Lucy feared dying. "I do not know the ways of Christ," she lamented. In her dismay, there appeared before her a "dark and lonesome chasm, between myself and the Savior, which I dared not attempt to pass."

A grief-stricken Joseph, kneeling at his wife's bedside, took Lucy's hand

40. Jon Butler, *Awash in a Sea of Faith,* 220.

41. "An Act for Supporting Ministers of the Gospel," 3.

42. "Tunbridge Anabaptist Society Petition." Because there were two Joseph Smiths in the area, it is not clear if this Anabaptist member was Father Smith.

43. Vogel, *Early Mormon Documents,* 1:633-36.

44. My narrative of Lucy's illness and recovery is based on her account in Anderson, *Lucy's Book,* 276-81.

and exclaimed amid sobs, "Oh, Lucy! My wife! My wife! You must die! The doctors have given you up; and all say you cannot live." That night, Lucy, unable to sleep, began praying with all the fervor of her soul. She "begged and pleaded" with the Lord, as she later told the story, to "spare my life, in order that I might bring up my children, and be a comfort to my husband." She made a covenant with God that, if he would let her live, she would serve him. A voice then spoke: "Seek and ye shall find; knock, and it shall be opened unto you. Let your heart be comforted; ye believe in God, believe also in me."[45]

Lucy's mother, Lydia, who was nursing her daughter and caring for her two small grandsons, noticed the improvement the next morning and exclaimed: "Lucy, you are better!" Her daughter replied, "Yes, mother, the Lord will let me live, if I am faithful to the promise which I made to him, to be a comfort to my mother, my husband, and my children."

Lucy's physical strength slowly returned, but her mind remained "considerably disquieted" on spiritual matters. As soon as she was able to leave her home, she sought out Deacon Davies, a local clergyman whom she "regarded as exceedingly pious." The cleric and his family were greatly concerned about Lucy's physical comfort in their home. "[H]elp her in—run, build a fire, make the room warm—fill the tea-kettle—get the great armchair," were confirmations of the family's tenderness. But Lucy, afire with the "miraculous manner of my recovery," expected her host to validate her experience, to marvel at the Lord's work and praise his name. When the parson's conversation was not "seasoned with one word in relation to Christ or godliness," the young mother felt "sickened and disgusted ... and returned home very sorrowful and much disappointed."

Mindful of her covenant with God, Lucy visited the churches in the community in search of "some congenial spirit who could enter into my feelings, and thus be able to strengthen and assist me in carrying out my resolutions." Hearing that a devout Presbyterian was to preach, Lucy attended, expecting to hear the "Word of Life." However, the sermon left her disheartened, convinced that the preacher "neither understood nor appreciated the subject upon which he spoke." She concluded that "there was not then upon earth the religion which I sought." Unable to find a denomination that coincided with her religious convictions, she resorted to reading the Bible and taking "Jesus and his d[is]ciples for an ensample." Convinced from her

45. This reference combines portions of both Luke 11:9 and John 14:1.

scripture reading that baptism was necessary for salvation, she found a minister who agreed to baptize her without insisting she join his sect.

Many years later, while reflecting on the impact of this early period of her spiritual life, Lucy said:

> Then I ~~first~~ began to feel most sensibly the want of a living instructor in matters of salvation[,] but how ~~much~~ intensely I felt this deficiency when a few years afterwards I found myself on the very verge of the [e]ternal world and although I had an intense desire for salvation yet I was totally devoid of any satisfactory Knowledge or understanding of the Laws or requirements of that being ~~to~~ before whom I expected shortly to appear but I labored faithfully in prayer to God struggling to be freed from the power of death.—when I recovered I sought unceasingly for some one ~~to~~ who could impart to … [me] some deffinite Idea of the requirements of Heaven with regard to mankind[,] but like Esaw seeking his blessing I found them not[,] though I saught the same with tears—~~In this for years~~ for days and months and years I continued asking God continually to reveal to me the hidden treasures of his will—~~but~~ although I was always [s]trenghtened from time [to time] still I did not receive a direct [answer] to my prayers for the space 20 years[.] I had always believed confidently that God would ~~a some time~~ raise up some one who would be able to effect a reconciliation among those who desired to do his will at the expense of all things else.[46]

While Lucy made religious seeking a continuous activity, her husband remained aloof from a similar quest. Many years later, bowed with age and poor health, Joseph Sr. lamented, "It is a source of grief to me that I have not been more fruitful to the Lord in days which are past than I have: I have not always set that example before my family that I ought; I have not been diligent in teaching them the commandments of the Lord, but have rather manifested a light and trifling mind: But in all this I have never denied the Lord. Notwithstanding all this my folly, which has been a cause of grief to my family."[47] As if religious turmoil were not enough to weigh down the Smiths in Randolph, Joseph's mercantile business, like most of his economic efforts, ended in failure after less then a year.

Prospects for the store had initially seemed promising. The proprietor was enthusiastic as the village needed a trading store. In addition, the

46. Anderson, *Lucy's Book,* 464-65.
47. Joseph Smith Sr., Introductory Comments.

establishment was amply stocked with $1,800 worth of new merchandise obtained on credit from Boston. Small village mercantiles, like Smith's and his brother-in-law Stephen Mack's, were general stores displaying an eclectic stock ranging from coal oil to calico to canned oysters. Dry goods (fabric), crockery, cutlery, edged tools, ropes and twine, tobacco, tea, and coffee presumably were included in the inventory. Cash was not plentiful, and most customers traded commodities for store-bought goods or credit, settling annually when crops were sold. A charitable proprietor, if he were not careful, could easily become overextended. Within his first season of operation, it became apparent to Smith that his store was not thriving. To recoup his potential losses, he became an exchange intermediary or broker in ginseng, a perennial aromatic herb found in the New England woods. The root, highly valued in the Orient as a tonic (or stimulant) and aphrodisiac, was nearly worth its weight in gold.

The use of ginseng, meaning "man root" because it sometimes resembles a human body, was documented in China as early as the first century B.C.E. In the early 1700s, the discovery of ginseng near Montreal set off a "wild ginseng rush" in America. By 1773, two years after Joseph Smith's birth, a sloop sailing from Boston for China carried 110,000 pounds of the white root.[48] A plague raged in China while the Smiths lived in Randolph, and crystalized ginseng was being sought as a remedy. The demand was high, and so were profits for successful middlemen. Smith invested everything he owned to broker the crystallization and export of the root to Oriental markets.[49] The fall ginseng harvest was phenomenal, which was fortunate because the failure of the village store forced the family to move back to the Tunbridge farm that Asael had given them. A merchant named Stevens from nearby Royalton offered Smith $3,000 for his yield. But Joseph, hoping to get rich more quickly, believed his stock was worth $4,500. He rejected the offer, traveled to New York City, and found a vessel in port which was sailing to China. Smith and the ship's captain signed an agreement authorizing the skipper to serve as Smith's agent.

Meanwhile, Stevens, who had learned of Joseph's plans, booked his adult son on the same vessel to supervise his own load of ginseng. In her pained account of this venture, Lucy Smith later alleged that the captain sold the entire lot "to good advantage, or at a high price." But fraud was afoot and

48. John Stewart Massey, "Ginseng," 105.

49. This account of Smith's ginseng venture is based on Anderson, *Lucy's Book,* 281-86.

Joseph was the unfortunate mark. The captain reportedly entrusted young Stevens with Joseph's proceeds; and instead of giving Smith the money, Stevens kept it, palming off a story about the captain's failure to obtain a good price. Smith's profit amounted to nothing more than a small chest of tea, said the swindler. Then, no doubt using the proceeds, young Stevens rented a house from Stephen Mack and hired eight to ten men to renew his ginseng crystallization. Mack, visiting his property on an evening when the young entrepreneur was drunk, asked him bluntly, "How much did brother Smith's adventure bring?" Stevens took Mack by the hand, led him to a trunk, and threw it open revealing a large amount of silver and gold. "There, sir, are the proceeds of Mr. Smith's gensang [sic]!"

As soon as Mack could disengage himself from Stevens, he returned home, ordered his horse, and started at 10:00 p.m. to locate his brother-in-law. Once Stevens's head cleared, he realized he was in trouble. He went to the hostler who told him that Mack had gone to the Smith place. Stevens immediately went to his place of business, dismissed his hands, called for his carriage, and fled with the cash for Canada. Smith pursued him for a while, but the thief's head start was too great. The dispirited Joseph returned home, no doubt contemplating his financial ruin.

Smith launched an examination of his fiscal records to "see how he stood with the world." The answer was grim. In addition to the China fiasco, his shelves were empty, his books confirmed $2,000 of uncollectible debt, and his note to the Boston merchants was past due. All he had left was the Tunbridge farm, valued at $1,500, where the family now lived, and where daughter Sophronia had been born on May 17, 1803. To retire his Boston debt, Smith was forced to sell his property for $800, a little more than half its estimated value. But this was still insufficient to satisfy his creditors. Lucy rescued the family by contributing her $1,000 dowry.[50] She and her husband placed the $1,800 payment in Stephen Mack's hands, and he returned from Boston "with the receipts which set us free from embarrassment of debt but not from the embarrassment of poverty."

While still living in Tunbridge, Lucy once again became distressed about her religious life. The ongoing anxiety she attributed to "my singular experience during my sickness at Randolph."[51] She began attending local Methodist class meetings, and Joseph initially accompanied her. But he "had

50. John Mudget, who gave Lucy half of her dowry, had died at age twenty-nine on January 27, 1801, and was buried in the local cemetery.

51. For Lucy's religious experience, see Anderson, *Lucy's Book,* 291-94.

so little faith in the doctrines taught by them," Lucy remembered, that "my feelings were the only inducement for him to go." Nevertheless, the couple was stirred by the idea that the primitive Christian church had been lost, and they readily saw themselves as seekers—anxious souls looking for truth.[52] The Methodist Connection had begun in England in 1729, not as a new church, but as a "Holy Club," a renewal movement initiated by brothers Charles and John Wesley within the Anglican Church.[53] American Methodism had begun in the 1760s as a tiny seed that quickly sprouted in the fertile soil of the emerging nation. The denomination, a blend of New Testament Christianity, Protestant Reformation, and the influence of the Wesley brothers, organized for one reason: to bring people to an awareness of the Lord Jesus. Church leaders believed that a spiritually transformed people would make America a great nation. They purposed to spread scriptural holiness over the land. Nineteenth-century Methodist Bishop Holland McTyeire observed: "It was not new doctrine but new life the first Methodists sought for themselves and for others. ... The Methodists came forth as evangelists. ... Their controversy was not with Church or State authorities, but with sin and Satan; and their one object was to save souls."[54] In 1784, the movement was organized as the Methodist Episcopal Church in America.

Methodism was "a church of the poor, of plain people, where the 'mighty impulses' of God's Spirit were expressed through 'strong emotion' and preaching in 'thunder tones.'"[55] Methodist clergymen learned to produce in vivid pictures a hell of endless torments and of endless remorse. In 1798, American Methodist Bishops Thomas Coke and Francis Ashbury instructed evangelists:

> The preacher must ... Convince the sinner of his dangerous condition. He must "break up the fallow ground." "Cry aloud, spare not," says the Lord to his prophet, "Lift up thy voice like a trumpet, and shew my people their transgression, and the house of Jacob their sins.["] ... He must set forth the depth of original sin, and shew the sinner how far he is gone from original righteousness; he must describe the vices of the world in their

52. The Smiths were Seekers, aspirants who "waited for the reestablishment of the visible church, the return of authority to perform the ordinances, and the Coming of Christ to destroy the ungodly and establish the political kingdom of God" (Vogel, *Religious Seekers and the Advent of Mormonism,* 10).

53. Leo Rosten, *Religions in America,* 122.

54. Kenneth Cain Kinghorn, *The Heritage of American Methodism,* 152.

55. Kathryn Long, Associate Professor of History at Wheaton College, qtd. in Ann Taves, *Fits, Trances, and Visions,* 233.

> just and most striking colours, and enter into all the sinner's pleas and excuses for sin, and drive him from all his subterfuges and strongholds. He must labour to convince the formalist of the impossibility of being justified before God by his ceremonial or moral righteousness. Myriads are continually perishing. ... He must set forth the virtue of the atoning blood. He must bring the mourner to a present Saviour; he must shew the willingness of Christ this moment to bless him, and bring a present salvation home to his soul.[56]

Early American Methodists faced opposition and persecution. The majority of their preachers were neither culturally refined nor well educated—both marks against them. Often, the college-educated clergy of other denominations denounced Methodist preachers for "preaching delusions," "working to deceive others," "spouting heretical doctrines," and "promoting wild singularities."[57] These latter included dramatic preaching, exuberant worship, and weekly class meetings wherein members shared their innermost selves. Informal Methodist worship found expression in extemporaneous prayer, preaching without notes, outdoor meetings, lay involvement in worship services, and a variety of spontaneous expressions of worship. Despite Methodism's unassuming start, however, it grew steadily and eventually became a dynamic force in American religion.

Although Joseph and Lucy's brief passage through the Methodist Episcopal Church would later influence the religious bearing of son Joseph, they never become members. Their disengagement may have been primarily due to pressure from Joseph Sr.'s family. Asael and Jesse Smith, promoters of the local Universalist Society, were apparently infuriated by their brother's lapse into conventional Christianity. Reportedly, Asael knocked on Joseph and Lucy's cabin door, tossed a copy of Thomas Paine's *Age of Reason* to his son, and "angrily bade him read that untill he believed it."[58] In further confron-

56. Qtd. in Kinghorn, *The Heritage of American Methodism,* 152-53.

57. Ibid., 38.

58. Anderson, *Lucy's Book,* 291. At some point while Joseph Smith was living in Vermont, he delivered a tirade against organized religion that included this comment: "Voltairs writings was the best bible then extant, and Thomas Paines age of reason, the best commentary" ("Green Mountain Boys to Thomas C. Sharp"). Voltaire (1694-1778) was the pen name of Francois Marie Arouet, a French author and philosopher whose best known work, *Candide,* is a philosophical inquiry into the nature of good and evil. Voltaire fought religious intolerance and aided victims of religious persecution. The essence of deist Thomas Paine's *Age of Reason,* written in the 1790s, was: "All national institutions of churches, whether Jewish, Christian, or Turkish, appear to me no other than human inventions set up to terrify and enslave mankind, and monopolize power and profit." He saw "the exceeding probability" of a religious revolution in America where "human

tations, Asael and Jesse told Joseph that he "ought not to let his wife go to the meetings and it would be far better for him to stop going." Intimidated, Joseph asked Lucy to discontinue her affiliation with the Methodists.

Lucy did not argue, but emotionally devastated, she "retired to a grove of handsome wild cherry trees" and pled with God, on behalf of her man, "that the true Gospel might be presented to him, and that his heart might be softened so as to receive it, or that he might become more religiously inclined." Returning to her cabin "much depressed in spirit," Lucy tucked her babes in and retired to her bed where her turmoil soon evoked a dream she recalled in exquisite detail more than forty years later, when her husband was five years dead:

> I thought that I stood in a large and beautiful meadow, which lay a short distance from the house in which we lived, and that everything around me wore an aspect of peculiar pleasantness. The first thing that attracted my special attention in this magnificent meadow, was a very pure and clear stream of water, which ran through the midst of it; and as I traced this stream, I discovered two trees standing upon its margin, both of which were on the same side of the stream. These trees were very beautiful, they were well proportioned, and towered with majestic beauty to a great height. Their branches, which added to their symmetry and glory, commenced near the top, and spread themselves in luxurious grandeur around. I gazed upon them with wonder and admiration; and after beholding them a short time, I saw one of them was surrounded with a bright belt, that shone like burnished gold, but far more brilliantly. Presently, a gentle breeze passed by, and the tree encircled with this golden zone, bent gracefully before the wind, and waved its beautiful branches in the light air. As the wind increased, this tree assumed the most lively and animated appearance, and seemed to express in its motions, the utmost joy and happiness. If it had been an intelligent creature, it could not have conveyed, by the power of language, the idea of joy and gratitude so perfectly as it did; and even the stream that rolled beneath it, shared, apparently, every sensation felt by the tree, for, as the branches danced over the stream, it would swell gently, then recede again with a motion as soft as the breathing of an infant, but as lively as the dancing of a sunbeam. The belt also partook of the same influence, and as it moved in unison

---

inventions and priestcraft would be detected; and man would return to the pure, unmixed, and unadulterated belief of one god, and no more" (Thomas Paine, *Age of Reason,* edited by Moncure D. Conway, 2).

> with the motion of the stream and of the tree, it increased continually in refulgence and magnitude, until it became exceedingly glorious.
>
> I turned my eyes upon its fellow, which stood opposite; but it was not surrounded with the belt of light as the former, and it stood erect and fixed as a pillar of marble. No matter how strong the wind blew over it, not a leaf was stirred, not a bough was bent; but obstinately stiff it stood, scorning alike the zephyr's breath, or the power of the mighty storm.[59]

When she awoke the next morning, Lucy pondered the meaning of the experience, which she came to believe was an answer to her prayers. She interpreted the two trees as representing the "stubborn and unyielding" Jesse Smith and his "more pliant and flexible" brother Joseph. The "breath of heaven" which had passed over the men she interpreted as "the pure and undefiled Gospel of the Son of God." Jesse would always resist this good news, she believed, but Joseph, "when he was more advanced in life, would hear and receive with his whole heart, and rejoice therein; and unto him would be added intelligence, happiness, glory, and ever lasting life."

After the Tunbridge farm was sold, the Smiths moved in the spring of 1804 to Royalton, where Lucy discovered she was once again pregnant. The family remained here just a few months before moving again, this time to nearby Sharon Township, Windsor County, Vermont, which adjoined Royalton on the east. There they rented a 68-acre portion of Solomon Mack's hundred-acre farm. Lucy's father had purchased this acreage, straddling Sharon and Royalton townships, for $800 on August 27, 1804. The Macks located their home on Old Turnpike Road, in the northeast section of the property, while Joseph and Lucy took up residence to the southwest in a log cabin, on a prominence known as "Dairy Hill." Here Joseph Jr., child of promise, was born. Dr. Joseph Denison of South Royalton delivered the newborn. Years later, reflecting on Joseph Smith's controversial religious career, Denison reportedly wrote in an account book, "If I had known how he was going to turn out I'd have smothered the little cuss."[60]

The family then consisted of thirty-four-year-old Joseph, thirty-year-old Lucy, and children Alvin (seven), Hyrum (five), and Sophronia (two). Presumably, the new baby was showered with love and affection. Lucy, devoted to her children, was the family keystone, a loving mother, a primary source of their nurturing, their religious orientation, and their flair for the

59. Anderson, *Lucy's Book,* 292-94.
60. Dr. John D. Spring, qtd. in Porter, "A Study of the Origins of the Church," 13.

beauty and eloquence of the King James Bible. William Buchan's *Advice to Mothers,* published a year before Joseph Jr.'s birth, captures what may have been Lucy's essence:

> Everything great or good in future life, must be the effect of early impressions; and by whom are those impressions to be made but by mothers, who are most interested in the consequences? Their instructions and example will have a lasting influence and of course, will go farther to form the morals, than all the eloquence of the pulpit, the efforts of the schoolmasters, or the corrective power of the civil magistrate, who may, indeed, punish crimes, but cannot implant the seeds of virtue.[61]

While Joseph Jr. always referred to his pious, courageous, and benevolent mother with great affection, he probably had no memory of his first home, since the family moved before he was two. Sharon had been named for Sharon, Connecticut, from which many of the township's earliest settlers had originated. In biblical times, the Holy Land's Plain of Sharon was celebrated for its fertility and as the location where David tended his sheep. Sharon, Vermont, bisected by the White River, is a community of fertile intervale lands, suited to farming. Writing in 1905, Mormon Junius F. Wells, who oversaw the construction of the Joseph Smith memorial in Sharon, captured the pastoral nature of the Smith property, little changed since the preceding century:

> The foundation stones of the farmhouse are still in place, also the walls of the cellar and the hearthstone and door stone. Some of the stable foundation and much of a stone wall that enclosed the barnyard and extended far beyond to fence off the orchards, are yet visible. The old well, now filled with boulders, contains water. The orchard of apple trees was quite extensive and many of the old trees, the trunks of some of them two feet in diameter, are standing and bearing fruit. The blossoms were just beginning to burst forth from the most forward while I was there. Dimly marked on the hillside is the grass covered road that formerly led down from the farmhouse to the old Sharon road, along the right bank of the White brook, a beautiful little stream, abounding in trout, that flows through the property, and about equally divides the land of the old Mack farm.
>
> The hill, so largely covered with apple trees in bloom, surmounted by the ruins of the farm house, is very picturesque and beautiful. It is an isolated, quiet, lovely sylvan spot, surrounded by some of the most charming

61. Qtd. in Ruth R. Bloch, "American Feminine Ideals in Transition," 112.

scenery of the Green Mountains, of which varied and extensive views are obtained from many points of vantage on the premises.[62]

While living on his hilltop acreage, a hundred miles northwest of Boston, Joseph Sr., chastened by his recent economic reversals, concentrated on feeding his family by farming in the summer and teaching school during the winter. According to Lucy, "our circumstances gradually improved, until we found ourselves quite comfortable again." Just how secure the Smiths were during these years is a matter of perspective. The family moved frequently, were tenants who owned no property, and seemed continually impoverished and debt ridden until Joseph Jr., years later, rescued them from financial despair. Lucy, in her retrospective account, sometimes tended to overstate the family's financial status. For example, on October 15, 1807, when the family had packed up and returned to Tunbridge, Joseph Sr. petitioned the Vermont Assembly for an exemption from military obligations because of poverty.[63] Also during this time, the family continued to increase. Joseph Jr. was two when Samuel Harrison (who often went simply by Harrison) was born on March 13, 1808.

At some point after baby Joseph's birth, the family moved from Tunbridge and settled in nearby Royalton where they stayed for three years. Two more sons arrived. Ephraim, born on March 13, 1810, lived only eleven days, and his passing was probably four-year-old Joseph's first encounter with the reality of death. Even though Joseph never referred to the loss of his baby brother, Ephraim was not forgotten; and Joseph Sr., twenty-five years later, mourned the deaths of his three sons: his unnamed firstborn, Ephraim, and later Alvin: "I look round upon you before me and I behold a lack: three seats are, as it were, empty. The Lord, in his just providence has taken from me, at an untimely birth, a son … My next son, Alvin … and another [Ephraim] … taken also in his infancy. I pray that my loss may be abundantly supplied, and made up in additional blessings."[64]

William, who ultimately lived to be eighty-two, was born in Royalton on March 13, 1811.[65] Here young Joseph apparently started his formal education in a one-room schoolhouse on "Dewey Hill," where he learned his letters from Deacon Jonathan Rinney, the local schoolmaster.[66]

62. Junius F. Wells, "The Birthplace of the Prophet Joseph Smith," 461.

63. "To the Honorable General Assembly … Oct. 15, 1807," 1.

64. Joseph Smith Sr., Introductory Comments.

65. He had no middle name but added "Bunnell" during the Civil War to distinguish himself from the vast number of William Smiths. His name frequently appears as "William B. Smith."

66. Anderson, *Lucy' Book,* 169.

Within months of Ephraim's death, Lucy's father, Solomon, then living a mile or two away on his Sharon farm, experienced what he called an extraordinary conversion to the "Christian Faith." Miserable and arthritic, the seventy-six-year-old reprobate, on a fall evening in 1810, finally petitioned God. The response was life-changing: "It seemed to me that I saw a bright light in a dark night ... which I could not account for, but I thought I heard a voice calling to me again. I thought I saw another light of the same kind, all which I considered as ominous of my own dissolution." He became convinced that his Universalist faith was wrong but that he had been "reconciled to God." He published his experiences in a chapbook that he sold throughout the Vermont countryside, riding painfully in a woman's side saddle. The benediction of his memoir, after inviting all to "come to Jesus," was: "Take no pattern from me for I would not harken until I arrived to advanced age ... I have a love for your souls now listen to me, though like a child, but shun that path that I used to walk in—this is the prayer of SOLOMON MACK."[67]

Solomon's "change of heart" may have influenced the religious equilibrium of his son-in-law. Within months of her father's transformation, Lucy Smith recalled that her husband's mind "became much excited upon the subject of religion." He did not "contend" for any of the existing sects but, like his wife, became a Seeker after "the ancient order, as established by our Lord and Saviour Jesus Christ, and his Apostles." During his religious quest, Joseph Sr. began to have a series of dreams that Lucy called visions. His "1st vision"[68] evidently occurred in April 1811, the month after William was born, when Joseph Jr. was five. Joseph Sr. had retired for the night "in a very thoughtful state of mind," contemplating the discord that reigned in the religious world. As Lucy later quoted him, when he awoke the next morning, he related to his wife and family:

> I seemed to be travelling in an open, barren field, and as I was travelling, I turned my eyes towards the east, the west, the north, and the south, but could see nothing save dead fallen timber. Not a vestige of life, either animal or vegetable, could be seen; besides, to render the scene still more dreary, the most deathlike silence prevailed; no sound of anything animate could be heard in all the field.
>
> I was alone in this gloomy desert, with the exception of an attendant spirit, who kept constantly by my side. Of him I inquired the meaning

67. Solomon Mack, *A Narraitve [sic] of the Life of Solomon Mack,* 25.
68. Anderson, *Lucy's Book,* 295.

> of what I saw, and why I was thus travelling in such a dismal place. He answered thus: "This field is the world, which now lieth inanimate and dumb, in regard to the true religion, or plan of salvation; but travel on, and by the wayside you will find on a certain log a box, the contents of which, if you eat thereof, will make you wise, and give unto you wisdom and understanding."
>
> I carefully observed what was told me by my guide, and proceeding a short distance, I came to the box. I immediately took it up, and placed it under my left arm; then with eagerness I raised the lid, and began to taste of its contents; upon which all manner of beasts, horned cattle, and roaring animals, rose up on every side in the most threatening manner possible, tearing the earth, tossing their horns, and bellowing most terrifically all around me, and they finally came so close upon me, that I was compelled to drop the box, and fly for my life. Yet, in the midst of all this I was perfectly happy, though I awoke trembling.[69]

Over the next two decades, Joseph Sr. reportedly experienced seven visions, of which Lucy recalled and summarized five in her memoir. There appears to be a deep-rooted pattern to the reflections. In each, just beyond an obstacle, lay the promise of healing or salvation. In several visions, eternal life seemed just beyond reach. The implication was that something more was needed. At the same time, the visionary portrayal of the "barrenness" and "desolation" that surrounded him became, in Joseph Sr.'s interpretation (according to Lucy), the unsatisfactory nature of organized religion, thus solidifying his determination to remain free from any sect. Collectively, the visions convinced him that no spiritual guide knew "any more concerning the Kingdom of God, than those of the world … such as made no profession of religion whatever."[70]

Joseph was convinced that organized religion, as it stood, could not offer redemption. Hence, he looked forward with a primitivist's hope and a millennialist's anticipation to the future restoration of Christ's true church, which he believed would occur in his lifetime. This assurance helped the Smiths to endure the adversity the family encountered during Joseph Jr.'s boyhood.

Meanwhile, elsewhere in America news of events on the frontier inflamed anti-Indian and anti-British sentiments. General William H. Harrison, governor of Indiana Territory, advancing with a thousand men upon a hostile Shawnee stronghold at Tippecanoe in November 1811, forced

69. Ibid., 295-96.
70. Ibid., 296.

Tecumseh's tribesmen to retreat. In the aftermath, Harrison's men captured British-made guns and ample supplies of British powder. Harrison and other Americans became convinced that England was plotting with the Indians to reconquer the United States. The solution of many land-hungry Americans was to take "the whole of Canada," an action many believed would be absurdly simple, a mere "frontiersman's frolic."[71]

The thought of Indian war parties under the direction of British officers, raiding from nearby Canada, a day or two north of Royalton (which had suffered an atrocious Indian attack in 1780), must have caused considerable anxiety for Joseph and Lucy Smith. As war escalated during the summer of 1812, the couple, seeking a safer locale and greater economic security, descended the White River to its junction with the Connecticut in neighboring New Hampshire, the land where Lucy had entered onto the world's stage thirty-seven years earlier.

---

71. David M. Kennedy, Thomas A. Bailey, and Mel Piehl, *The Brief American Pageant,* 146.

2 | CRISIS IN LEBANON

A whole life can be shaped by an old trauma, remembered or not.

—Lenore Terr (a psychiatrist specializing in children's mental health), *Unchained Memories,* xiii

"Ye Mighty River," known to local native indigenous peoples as *Quenticut* or *Quinnehtukqut* ("long tidal river"), the Connecticut serves as the boundary between New Hampshire and Joseph Smith's native Vermont. Coursing 410 miles southward through Massachusetts and Connecticut, the waterway—New England's largest—carves a sinuous pathway past forests of white pines stretching 200 feet or more into the sky, small hamlets, and energetic cities to empty into the Atlantic at Long Island Sound.

A tributary feeding into the Connecticut, the Mascoma, bisects present-day West Lebanon, New Hampshire. In 1812, the small township was simply Lebanon. Sometime between May of that year, when taxes were assessed, and the end of July, when baby Katharine joined the household, the Smith family relocated there. Lebanon, then home to approximately 1,600, was an agricultural and light industrial area. A union meetinghouse, used by all denominations, graced the town, as did two school houses, three stores, two taverns, several grist and lumber mills, a brickyard, and a library housing some 300 books.[1] The town lies five miles south of Hanover's Dartmouth College, forty-nine miles from Concord (New Hampshire state capital since 1808), 90 from the genteel coastal town of Portsmouth, and 110 from Boston.

New Hampshire is pristine and picturesque. An early admirer of the Granite State claimed that its wilderness and snow-covered mountains gave "a keenness to the air, as a cake of ice to a quantity of liquor in which it floats."[2] Ralph Nading Hill, another booster, praised the area's air as "pure and salubrious."[3] Into that rarefied atmosphere came the Smiths, a move of

1. John Farmer and Jacob Moore, *Gazetteer of the State of New Hampshire,* 172.
2. *Early New Hampshire Belknap,* qtd. in Ralph Nading Hill, *College on the Hill,* 89.
3. Ibid.

twenty miles down the White River from South Royalton. Too poor to own a horse and wagon,[4] the family likely moved their meager belongings by engaging a teamster and conveyance, or perhaps had help from more prosperous Smith or Mack family members. When the group crossed the Connecticut River at Lyman's Bridge[5] into New Hampshire, it was young Joseph's first move out of the land of his nativity. In addition to his parents, six-year-old Joseph's immediate kin now consisted of fourteen-year-old Alvin, twelve-year-old Hyrum, nine-year-old Sophronia, four-year-old Harrison, and baby William. Lucy Mack Smith was at least seven months pregnant—possibly more—with Katharine, born on July 28, 1812.[6]

As backdrop to the Smiths' move, the U.S. Congress, at the urging of President James Madison, declared war against Great Britain on June 18, 1812. Unresolved hostility between the two nations had existed for years. Most Americans believed the British were behind the frontier warfare with Native Americans, hindering western expansion. Some wanted all English in North America driven back to London. To make matters worse, for decades aggressive British men-of-war, plying the Atlantic off the eastern seaboard, had forcibly seized an estimated $30 million worth of commercial U.S. shipping. Furthermore, the English had impressed between 6,000 and 8,000 Americans into the Royal Navy. During the summer and fall of 1812, the exploits of American heroes Commodore John Rodgers, Captain Stephen Decatur, and General William Hull were talked about wherever Mascoma Valley citizens gathered. Joseph Smith Sr., past forty, was too old for military service, and Alvin too young. But twenty-eight local men joined the Lebanon militia organized to guard against possible attack by the British from Canada.[7]

Although New England shipping was seriously affected by the war, no

---

4. The 1813 tax assessment shows the family owning only three milk cows and a beef animal (Dan Vogel, *Early Mormon Documents,* 1:664-65).

5. This privately built toll bridge linking Vermont and New Hampshire replaced a rope ferry. The bridge joined the Fourth New Hampshire and the White River Turnpikes. The structure was replaced in 1836 by a three-span covered bridge and in 1895 by one of steel ("Historic Lebanon NH").

6. Katharine's personal affidavit and tombstone both give her birth date as July 28, 1813 (Katharine Smith Salisbury, Affidavit; Kyle R. Walker, *Katharine Smith Salisbury,* 167). But Lucy Mack Smith and Don Carlos Smith, Katharine's younger brother, give the birth year as 1812 (Lavina Fielding Anderson, *Lucy's Book,* 266; Don Carlos Smith, "Smith Family Genealogy"). I favor 1812, as well, for another reason. Lucy says that one of her husband's visions occurred "soon after arriving here (in Lebanon)," in which he saw seven living Smith children, which had to include Katharine.

7. "Historic Lebanon, NH."

land campaign reached the Lebanon region. Thus, despite the ebb and flow of war news, New Hampshire revitalized the Smith family's hopes as they settled into the small frame home on the farm they rented on what is now West Lebanon's South Main Street,[8] a stone's throw from the Mascoma River.

The Lebanon area and Mascoma Valley had been the hunting territory of the Squakheag (Mascommah or Masscommah) band, from whose name Mascoma is derived. They had vacated the area as early as 1700, however.[9] Benning Wentworth, royal governor of the province of New Hampshire, had issued a charter on July 4, 1761, for a township six miles square to be known as Lebanon. A committee representing the original fifty-two proprietors came to the area shortly after to survey the first division of property. The baseline was the King's Highway, a road eight rods (132 feet) wide. Sections of this early road still survive, marked by its original stone walls.

In the spring of 1762, the William Downer family became the first Euro-Americans to settle in the Lebanon area. They traveled up a wilderness trail known as the "Horse Road," from Fort No. 4 in Charlestown, New Hampshire, a half-century before the Smith family moved into the district. As other pioneering families arrived, a small settlement took root on the Connecticut River flood plain south of the Mascoma River, and settlers quickly determined that their destiny would be linked to the Mascoma. The first sawmill was built on the river that year by Oliver Davison. His mill sawed trees felled in the old growth forests into lumber for frame houses.

Three years before the Smiths' arrival, Joseph Amsden, David Anderson, Brackett Greenough, and Joseph Wood Jr. built and operated a sawmill and gristmill at the mouth of the Mascoma. Simeon and Eliel Peck operated a clover seed and sawmill along what is now Mechanic Street, and Howard Phelps opened a sawmill on the bank of the Connecticut between Lebanon and Hanover. Dr. Phineas Parkhurst also invested heavily in mills in the area. Joseph's eldest brother Alvin, then a sturdy fifteen-year-old whose home schooling was essentially completed before the move to New Hampshire, may have found work in one of these many mills when not helping his father. Alvin may also have worked in the local brickyard owned by Comfort

8. Russell R. Rich determined the house's location as the southeast corner of Main and Benning Streets (197 S. Main), demolished in 1967. His source was Dehlia Edson of West Lebanon. Her daughter Louise had learned of the Smiths' residence while visiting with Fannie Alden, who lived past the century mark. Alden's parents had owned an inn near the farm which the Smiths rented in Lebanon township. A KFC/Pizza Hut occupied the site in 2005. (Larry C. Porter, "A Study of the Origins of the Church," 7-8, 14.)

9. "Historic Lebanon, NH."

Goff, who dug a clay pit on the north end of what is now Hanover Street. Another possible employer was Samuel Barrows, who arrived in Lebanon in 1806 and went into business as a cooper. Coopering—the fabrication of wooden barrel and barrel-type containers—was a traditional Smith family occupation, with Joseph Sr. learning the trade from his father, Asael.

In addition to providing employment, these mills played a social role in early Lebanon. Colbee C. Benton recalled in an 1872 article in the *Granite State Free Press* that the mill "was something like the bar-room. ... Each were happy meeting places for a social class of kindred spirits, and everybody was social then. Hard labor during the day was sweetened with jovial recreation in the evening. Feats of strength, pulling sticks, telling marvelous stories, singing songs and sometimes a [card] game of 'high-low jack' were among the amusements."[10]

Such gatherings may have been young Joseph's introduction to the rough-and-tumble world of nineteenth-century American masculinity. The Smith residence, about 500 feet south of the Mascoma, was a short walk from the mill sites. Joseph's occasional rambunctious behavior as a young man and adult evidences a love for the sporting life: stick pulling, wrestling, fisticuffs, boisterous claims of physical prowess, and the telling of tall tales.

Although the Smith home was demolished in 1967,[11] many early Lebanon structures that would have been part of the Smith environs still exist. The oldest surviving house in the area, built in 1766, became Dr. Ziba Hall's home in 1780. The Smith family physician, Dr. Phineas Parkhurst, later owned it. Now known as the "Dana House," it was moved to Seminary Hill in 1988 for preservation. Dana's Tavern, built in 1787, was one of the town's first public houses, augmented by nearby stables. It was a common sight in the 1800s to see Main Street lined with teams of horses while their drivers were inside drinking. The inn prospered for more than 150 years. Hough's Tavern, perhaps frequented by Joseph Sr., was built west of the common in 1804, and also housed the village's post office. The inn was described as "a haven for the neighbors, as well as travelers, a central depot for receiving and distributing the latest news; a place where men congregated for social enjoyment ..."[12]

That first summer in Lebanon must have been an exciting one for six-year-old Joseph. Crops had to be sown, but that was most likely done by

10. Qtd. in Roger Carroll, *Lebanon, 1761-1994,* 45.
11. LaMar C. Berrett, *Sacred Places: New England and Eastern Canada,* 70-71.
12. Carroll, *Lebanon, 1761-1994,* 46.

his father and older brothers. The monetary standard then was a bushel of wheat, which equaled a day's work. Most of the grain harvested was bartered for family needs. Corn, cabbage, peas, turnips, potatoes, squash, flax, and grain grew well in the area. During the years the Smiths lived in Lebanon, subsistence farming was the order of the day but was slowly being transformed into commercial farming as transportation along the Connecticut River was supplemented by the completion of the Fourth New Hampshire Turnpike, which linked Lebanon to the coast, and by the opening of the Croydon Turnpike in 1804.

The nearby Mascoma River, bordered by stands of white pine, oak, sugar maple, birch, beech, bass, ash, and hemlock, was a fisherman's paradise. Joseph, an angler throughout his life,[13] probably learned to fish in its fruitful waters. Old-timers recalled that, when fish migrated up the Connecticut to spawn—salmon in the White River, shad in the Mascoma—the rivers were "almost solid with fish."[14]

The Smiths probably explored several areas of interest in their new surroundings. Perhaps Joseph Sr. took Alvin, Hyrum, Sophronia, and young Joseph to the top of Mount Tug, the area's highest elevation, to view Mascoma Lake and the ridge lines surrounding the Mascoma basin. Veterans of the Revolutionary War would have pointed out that atop Signal Hill, east of the Great Hollow or Etna Road Valley, was a colonial signal post still anchored to the granite ledge by chains. Featuring a semaphore system by day and a fire basket at night, it was one of a series of signal hills from inland forts to the coast. A geographical feature of the area likely to capture the imagination of any six-year-old was "Devil's Kitchen," a deep gorge in the Mascoma Valley. Its high water-worn walls and large potholes, which may still be examined high above the river, were produced by an immense waterfall at the outflow of the ancient glacial Lake Mascoma.

The nearby Connecticut River was a beehive of activity. The river's Olcott Locks had been built just four years before the Smiths' arrival. Two years later, a $40,000 dam and diversion canals were constructed below present Wilder Dam. These locks were a busy place, resounding with the shouts of rivermen and loggers. River boats, loaded with supplies, were propelled upstream by poles, oars, or sails. Barges then floated downstream loaded with

13. For evidence of Joseph's fishing, see Stephen S. Harding to Thomas Gregg, Feb. 1882, qtd. in Gregg, *The Prophet of Palmyra,* 35; Michael Morse, Interviewed by William W. Blair, May 22, 1879.

14. Carroll, *Lebanon, 1761-1994,* 46.

produce for Hartford or other coastal markets. One account noted that, during the period the Smiths lived in the area, "a hundred boats were often tied up at one time on the river bank near Lebanon."[15]

As fall approached in 1812, the Smiths made arrangements for their children's education. According to Lucy's recollections, "our children had, in a great measure, been debarred from the privilege of schools" up to that point. The parents therefore "began to make every arrangement to attend to this important duty."[16] Nine-year-old Sophronia and six-year-old Joseph likely attended school less than a mile from home in the area's oldest schoolhouse, built in 1768 on the King's Highway. This log structure, the town's first public building, survived for more than a century. Another schoolhouse within walking distance of the Smith home was on Poverty Lane.

Dennis A. Wright and Geoffrey A. Wright write:

> The typical New England school building was small, typically less than twenty feet square, with a very low ceiling. The walls were of rough construction sometimes plastered with lime. If the building had windows, they were too small to allow much light into the room. A large fireplace or Franklin stove heated the room in the winter. There were no traditional desks, but planks were fixed to the walls for use as writing surfaces. The children sat on backless benches pulled up to the planks. The schoolmaster stood at a large table at one end of the room.[17]

The daily routine of the school day usually began with a reading of New Testament verses followed by writing, then arithmetic. While older students studied the Bible, younger ones repeated and recited sentences from their primers or spelling books.[18] An 1807 *New-England Primer* provides a window into typical maxims the boy Joseph might have been taught:

> MORAL PRECEPTS FOR CHILDREN
>
> Speak the truth and lie not.
> Live well that you may die well.
> Use no ill words, for they breed strife.
> Be not proud. Scorn not the poor.
> Give to all those who want.
> A good boy will be a good man.

---

15. "Historic Lebanon, NH."

16. Anderson, *Lucy's Book,* 301.

17. Wright and Wright, "The New England Common School Experience of Joseph Smith Jr., 1810-16," 242.

18. *The New-England Primer, Improved.*

DUTY TO GOD AND OUR NEIGHBOR

Love God with all your soul and strength,
With all your heart and mind.
And love your neighbor as yourself,
Be faithful, just and kind.
Deal with another as you'd have
Another deal with you;
What you're unwilling to receive,
Be sure you never do.[19]

Alvin Smith had probably finished his schooling. Hyrum, age twelve, was admitted to Moor's Indian Charity School on the campus of nearby Dartmouth College. His admission to the boarding school as an "indigent worthy scholar" not only indicates financial hardship, but considerable potential.[20] Originally established in 1754 by Congregationalist minister Eleazar Wheelock as an Indian missionary school, the institution was funded principally by grants from the English Company for Propagation of the Gospel in New England, and the Society in Scotland for Propagating Christian Knowledge.[21] "An honorable chapter in the dishonorable book of the white man's relations with the Indians," as one historian notes,[22] the academy was initially devoted to the civilization and education of American Indian youth.

Youths like Hyrum Smith were accepted, according to need and academic potential. The organization's philosophy, as expounded by Wheelock and his successors, was that Christians had the duty of preaching Christianity to Indians "from a belief or hope that they are the descendants of Abram."[23] Accordingly, promising Indian children were removed from tribal life and transported to the residential school "where they would be free during their formative period from the evil example of travelers, the lure of the hunt or of warfare or of wandering, and where they would be exposed to the better example of the religious community."[24] Hyrum mingled on the Dartmouth campus with more than fifty Charity School students, including

19. Ibid., 15, 20.

20. "Account of Monies Received in Tuition in Moor's I.C. School from Aug. 1814 to Aug. 1815." See also Richard K. Behrens, "Hyrum Smith," 4.

21. Hill, *College on the Hill,* 25.

22. Ibid., 27.

23. Qtd. in David M'Clure and Elijah Parish, *Memoirs of the Rev. Eleazar Wheelock, D.D.,* 106.

24. James D. McCallum, "Eleazar Wheelock," 79.

Native American classmates: sixteen-year-old Noel Annance, twelve-year-old Ignatius (no surname), and Louis Langford.[25]

Because the mission of Wheelock and his successors was also to "educate a number of promising English youth, who would devote themselves to the service of the Redeemer, in the capacity of missionaries,"[26] chapel attendance was compulsory, a common requirement for boarding schools. Roswell Shurtleff (Dartmouth class of 1801) was appointed professor of divinity in 1804. He and school president John Wheelock, Eleazar's son, usually preached the sermons Hyrum Smith would have heard daily in the White Church.[27] Shurtleff, steeped in guilt during a period of solemn reflection, had experienced a "road to Damascus" religious awakening earlier in his life.[28] His powerful testimony and interest in revival activity, theological questions, and the origin of the American Indians must have had a profound impact on the student body. Young Hyrum was technically unchurched, although later, in New York in the mid-1820s, he became a Presbyterian along with his mother and sister Sophronia, a commitment he subsequently rejected in 1829 to espouse the religious work of young brother Joseph. "It would have been difficult if not impossible," writes Richard Behrens, a historian of Hyrum's months at Dartmouth, to "avoid exposure to a spectrum of religious ideas while on campus especially when chapel was mandatory for everyone."[29]

Although Joseph and Lucy Smith were likewise unchurched, religious issues occupied an important place in their thought during their sojourn in New Hampshire. Shortly after their arrival in the area, according to Mother Smith, Joseph Sr. "received another very singular vision" which she recalled with great clarity in 1845:

> I thought, said he, I was travelling in an open, desolate field, which appeared to be very barren. As I was thus travelling, the thought suddenly came into my mind that I had better stop and reflect upon what I was doing, before I went any further. So I asked myself, "What motive can I have in travelling here, and what place can this be?" My guide, who was by my side, as before, said "This is the desolate world; but travel on." The road was so broad and baren [sic] that I wondered why I should travel in it; for, said I to myself, "Broad is the road, and wide is the gate that leads

25. "Chronological List of Students: Moor's Charity School and Dartmouth College."
26. M'Clure and Parish, *Memoirs of the Rev. Eleazar Wheelock, D.D.,* 20.
27. Richard K. Behrens, "Hyrum Smith," 7.
28. Clement Long, *Serving God with the Mind,* 28.
29. Behrens, "Hyrum Smith," 8.

to death, and many there be that walk therein; but narrow is the way, and straight is the gate that leads to everlasting life, and few there be that go in thereat."[30] Travelling a short distance further, I came to a narrow path. This path I entered, and, when I had travelled a little way in it, I beheld a beautiful stream of water, which ran from the east to the west. Of this stream I could see neither the source nor yet the termination; but as far as my eyes could extend I could see a rope, running along the bank of it, about as high as a man could reach, and beyond me was a low, but very pleasant valley, in which stood a tree such as I, had never seen before. It was exceedingly handsome, insomuch that I looked upon it with wonder and admiration. Its beautiful branches spread themselves somewhat like an umbrella, and it bore a kind of fruit, in shape much like a chestnut bur, and as white as snow, or, if possible, whiter. I gazed upon the same with considerable interest, and as I was doing so, the burs or shells commenced opening and shedding their particles, or the fruit which they contained, which was of dazzling whiteness. I drew near, and began to eat of it, and I found it delicious beyond description. As I was eating, I said in my heart, "I cannot eat this alone, I must bring my wife and children, that they may partake with me." Accordingly, I went and brought my family, which consisted of a wife and seven children,[31] and we all commenced eating and praising God for this blessing. We were exceedingly happy, insomuch that our joy could not easily be expressed. While thus engaged, I beheld a spacious building standing opposite the valley which we were in, and it appeared to reach to the very heavens. It was full of doors and windows, and they were all filled with people, who were very finely dressed. When these people observed us in the low valley, under the tree, they pointed the finger of scorn at us, and treated us with all manner of disrespect and contempt. But their contumely we utterly disregarded. I presently turned to my guide, and inquired of him the meaning of the fruit that was so delicious. He told me it was the pure love of God, shed abroad in the hearts of all those who love him, and keep his commandments. He then commanded me to go and bring the rest of my children. I told him that we were all there. "No," he replied, "look yonder, you have two more, and you must bring them also."[32] Upon raising my eyes, I saw two small children, standing some distance off. I immediately went to them, and

30. This portion of the dream is an allusion to Matthew 7:13-14.

31. The seven living children were Alvin, Hyrum, Sophronia, Joseph, Samuel Harrison, William, and Katharine.

32. A likely reference to the two deceased Smith children, the unnamed first child, born ca. 1797, and Ephraim who died eleven days after his birth on March 13, 1810 (Anderson, *Lucy's Book,* 871).

> brought them to the tree; upon which they commenced eating with the rest, and we all rejoiced together. The more we eat, the more we seemed to desire, until we even got down upon our knees, and scooped it up, eating it by double handfuls. After feasting in this manner a short time, I asked my guide what was the meaning of the spacious building which I saw. He replied, "It is Babylon, it is Babylon, and it must fall. The people in the doors and windows are the inhabitants thereof, who scorn and despise the Saints of God, because of their humility." I soon awoke, clapping my hands together for joy.[33]

The first religious meeting place in Lebanon had been under a gigantic elm tree in West Lebanon in 1768, at a site now marked by a stone tablet. Here was ordained the first settled pastor, Isaiah Potter (d. 1817), who served the community until 1813. In 1772, the town's first meetinghouse was built on Seminary Hill. This 34-feet-by-48-feet rectangular building was relocated to Farnam Hill about a decade later. It served as the place of worship for Congregationalists, Presbyterians, Baptists, and Methodists, who sent circuit riders to town in 1810, held classes in the schoolhouse, and conducted Lebanon's first baptism by immersion in a brook on Hardy Hill. In keeping with his 1797 declaration, Joseph Sr. paid no minister's tax.[34] He likely was a founding member of the Lebanon Universalist Society when it formed in 1813.[35] One of the interesting elements in Lebanon society from 1799 to 1845 was the "tything man," a town officer who was elected annually to "maintain order in the church, and to enforce observance of the Sabbath—no labor or travel except of necessity, no games, no play, no recreation."[36]

Lucy recalled of their first months in Lebanon: "[H]ere we settled ourselves down, and began to contemplate, with joy and satisfaction, the prosperity which had attended our recent exertions; and we doubled our diligence, in order to obtain more of this world's goods."[37] She personally contributed to the family income by purchasing 100 pounds of candles for the family to use after dark while transforming 200 yards of cloth into homemade clothing. The 1813 tax assessment records show that the family owned three milk cows and a three-year-old beef animal.[38] "Myself and companion," Lucy added, "were doing all that our abilities would admit of for the

33. Ibid., 297-98.
34. "List of the Polls and Rateable Estate of the Town of Lebanon."
35. Farmer and Moore, *Gazetteer of the State of New Hampshire,* 173.
36. "Historic Lebanon, NH."
37. Anderson, *Lucy's Book,* 299.
38. Vogel, *Early Mormon Documents,* 1:664-65.

future welfare and advantage of the family, and we were greatly blessed in our labours."[39]

But bad luck seemed forever destined to upend Smith family fortunes. An epidemic—cited in various accounts as typhous fever,[40] spotted fever,[41] meningococcic meningitis,[42] or typhoid fever[43]—began to spread throughout the upper Connecticut River valley in 1811, even though Dr. Nathan Smith, the area's foremost physician and founder of Dartmouth Medical School in Hanover, had noted his first case in 1798.[44] Typhus fever, spotted fever, and *Rickettsiae*-engendered meningitis are a family of diseases transmitted by lice, chiggers, and fleas.[45] Typhoid fever, though similar sounding in name, is an entirely different multisystemic disease caused by a bacterium, *Salmonellae typhi.* While typhoid fever results from poor sanitation and contaminated food and water, typhus fever is a disease of filth.[46] The confusion between the two contagions was not resolved until 1837 when physician William Wood Gerhard confirmed the distinction.[47]

Along with smallpox, scarlet fever, dysentery, and cholera, typhous fever, as the Smith family and their physicians termed the typhoid fever that afflicted the Smith children, was a major factor in keeping life expectancy low in the Connecticut Valley. Joseph A. Gallup, author of *Sketches of Epidemic Diseases,* notes that 6,000 people died during the three-year epidemic.[48] Lebanon had built a "pest house" near Storrs Hill in which to quarantine the

---

39. Anderson, *Lucy's Book,* 1:300.

40. By Lucy Mack Smith, Anderson, *Lucy's Book,* 300-303, and by Joseph Smith Jr., Dean C. Jessee, *The Papers of Joseph Smith,* 1:268; and by Nathan Smith, M.D., *Practical Essay on Typhous Fever.*

41. Carroll, *Lebanon, 1761-1994,* 24. See also Ebenezer Price, "Remarkable Deaths," in his *A Chronological Register,* 106-8.

42. Hayward and Putnam, *Improve, Perfect, and Perpetuate,* 135. On March 31, 1813, Dr. Nathan Smith wrote to Benjamin Silliman: "[W]e were visited by a very fatal epidemic and instances of sickness and mortality became so frequent that I was afraid to leave my family in such perilous times; and my fears were not groundless,—four of my children have lately been visited by sickness" (Emily A. Smith, *The Life and Letters of Nathan Smith,* 85.). Dr. William Wood Gerhard, however, in his classic 1863 paper, called it "Spotted Fever, or Cerebro-Spinal Meningitis" ("William Wood Gerhard," *Famous Americans).* Also see meningitis entry in Laurence Finberg and Ronald E. Kleinman, *Saunders Manual of Pediatric Practice,* 387.

43. Hayward and Putnam, *Improve, Perfect, and Perpetuate,* 135. Also see LeRoy S. Wirthlin, "Nathan Smith," 326.

44. Hayward and Putnam, *Improve, Perfect, and Perpetuate,* 159.

45. See "Rocky Mountain Spotted Fever"; "Typhus" in Wikipedia; "Typhus Patient Information"; "Typhus" and "Insects and Disease."

46. "Talk: List of Infectious Diseases"; Eugene Beauharnais Nash, "Leaders in Typhoid Fever"; David W. Tschanz, "Typhus Fever on the Eastern Front in World War I."

47. See "William Wood Gerhard (1809-1872)," and "William Wood Gerhard," Famous Americans website.

48. Qtd. in Richard L. Bushman, *Joseph Smith and the Beginnings of Mormonism,* 32.

seriously ill. "The spotted fever is still ravaging various parts of the country," wrote Nathan Smith in 1811. To a Yale professor in March 1813, Dr. Smith added that the epidemic was still raging:

> [F]our of my children have lately been affected by the prevailing epidemic, but by the Divine Goodness have nearly recovered. I believe this country has never before been visited by sickness which has carried off so great a number of adult persons in so short a time. In some towns of this vicinity which contain perhaps from 1000 to 1500 inhabitants they have buried over 50 persons since last January. The disease has not yet much abated either in its violence or frequency of attack. We hear of new cases every day, and almost ever day brings me an account of the death of some friend or acquaintance.[49]

Medical studies have shown that the incidence of typhoid worldwide is generally highest in children ages three to nine.[50] The first of the Smith youngsters to be struck down by the pestilence was Joseph's nine-year-old sister, Sophronia, who became ill in late 1812 or early 1813. The disease's incubation period is ten to twenty days, following ingestion of contaminated matter, during which time approximately 10-20 percent of patients suffer transient diarrhea. As the infestation increases, patients experience the onset of fever, which typically intensifies for the next two or three days, resulting in a severe, unrelenting headache. Other symptoms include chills, prostration, general malaise, constipation, mild nonproductive cough, and severe muscular pain. After seven to ten days, the patient may be relatively comfortable but apathetic and weak. Small pink papules (rose spots) that fade with pressure develop on the upper abdomen and lower chest. During the second week, the abdomen distends as the spleen enlarges. By the third week, the patient has usually lost weight and may become delirious. Abdominal distension becomes worse, followed by green-yellow diarrhea. While fatality rates of 10 to 50 percent have been noted in untreated typhoid victims, some patients become well in two weeks, the majority in four to six. A few cases, like Sophronia Smith's, may last as long as six months.[51]

Within days after Sophronia's outbreak, Hyrum fell ill in Hanover, where the disease was rampant, and returned home.[52] Lucy Smith remembered

49. Qtd. in Carroll, *Lebanon, 1761-1994,* 24.

50. "Typhoid Fever." This same report also notes that approximately 12.5 million worldwide annually still become infected with typhoid fever.

51. Charles Phillips Emerson Jr. and Jane Sherburn Bragdon, *Essentials of Medicine,* 767-68.

52. Samuel Farnsworth, "Account of the Typhous Fever."

that Alvin was stricken next. Then "one after another was taken down, till all of the family, with the exception of myself and husband, were prostrated upon a bed of sickness."[53] Joseph Sr. and Lucy had most likely developed an immunity to the disease. The contagion may have been spread by Joseph's or Lucy's failure to adequately wash his or her hands or safely dispose of Sophronia's infected waste.

The Smith family physician was Dr. Phineas Parkhurst,[54] who lived nearby in the Dana House on South Main. A successful farmer, industrialist, breeder of blue-ribbon mules, and founding president of the town's first bank, Parkhurst was a local legend. In 1780, after being wounded in an Indian attack at nearby Royalton, Vermont, he rode, Paul Revere-like, to warn Lebanon citizens of approaching danger. No stranger to family desolation, Parkhurst saw only one of his seven children reach age forty. Despite their father's medical training, the others died of consumption (tuberculosis).[55]

Initially, Sophronia was the most critically ill of the Smith family. For nearly three months, Parkhurst supervised medical treatment and experimented with hydrotherapy. A coffin-like tub made of pine boards was carried from house to house in which patients were submerged, first, in hot water in which a "concoction of hemlock boughs" had been steeped, then in cold water.[56] Sophronia remained ill. The mortality rate from typhoid in nineteenth-century America was estimated as high as 18 percent,[57] higher among some families. In the fall of 1814, for example, the Samuel Jackman family in nearby Merrimack County, New Hampshire, lost five of seven children, all under age nine, within a week.[58]

Dr. Parkhurst, believing that Sophronia would not survive, discontinued his treatment after three months. That very night, however, as the gravely ill girl lay on her bed in a stupor, "with that peculiar aspect which bespeaks the near approach of death," Lucy Smith "gazed upon her as a mother looks

53. Anderson, *Lucy's Book,* 300. Nash, "Leaders in Typhoid Fever," noted that he "once had five cases of typhoid fever in one family, all in bed at the same time."

54. In an 1842 dictated memoir, Joseph incorrectly recalled Parkhurst as "Dr. Parker." Jessee, *The Papers of Joseph Smith,* 1:268.

55. Carroll, *Lebanon, 1761-1994,* 15.

56. Dr. Nathan Smith describes this technique in Hayward and Putnam, *Improve, Perfect, and Perpetuate,* 159; see also Berrett, *Sacred Places: New England and Eastern Canada,* 71.

57. This early estimate, made by Charles Murchison, M.D. (1830-79), is cited in "Typhus." Prior to 1910, when prophylactic vaccination became available, as many as 35,000 Americans died from typhoid fever each year. During the Civil War, more than 80,000 cases of the disease were recorded, 37 percent of them fatal. Great epidemics continued worldwide until the epidemiology was discovered in the last half of the nineteenth century (Wirthlin, "Nathan Smith," 327).

58. Price, *A Chronological Register,* 106.

upon the last shade of life in a darling child." She and her husband clasped hands, "fell upon our knees by the bedside, and poured out our grief to God, in prayer and supplication, beseeching him to spare our child yet a little longer." As they arose from their appeal, the couple simultaneously received "a testimony that she should recover."

By this time, to all appearances, Sophronia seemed dead. But filled with hope, Lucy grabbed a blanket, wrapped the apparently lifeless girl, and paced the floor with the emaciated child in her arms. Neighbors admonished, "Mrs. Smith, it is all of no use; you are certainly crazy, your child is dead." But the indomitable Lucy refused to accept death. Suddenly the child sobbed, then gasped for air and began to breathe normally. Exhausted, Lucy lay her daughter on the bed, then collapsed beside her. From that moment, Sophronia's health improved until she recovered fully, living to age seventy-three.[59]

An adult Joseph Jr., writing to brother William, reflected on "the care and ... unremi[t]ting diligence [with which] our parents, have strove to watch over us, and how many hours, or sorrow, and anxiety, they have spent over our cradles and bedsides, in times of sickness."[60] He no doubt had Sophronia's illness in mind, as well as his own. Young Joseph, who turned seven in late December 1812, likely became infected from either Sophronia or Hyrum. His illness lasted only for a fortnight, and may not even have required medical treatment. Nathan Smith, who would soon become one of Joseph's physicians, later wrote in his treatise *A Practical Essay on Typhous Fever* that although the disease was more formidable than measles or whooping cough, it does not follow "that this disease in all cases requires remedies, or that a patient should necessarily take medicines because he has the disease. ... In fact, I feel well convinced, that all powerful remedies or measures, adopted in the early stage of Typhous Fever are very liable to do harm, and that those patients, who are treated with them in the beginning, do not hold out so well in the latter stages of the disease."[61]

After his two-week siege, Joseph, along with everyone else except Sophronia, was thought to have recovered. But one day, while sitting in a chair, he screamed in agony, complaining of intense pain in his left shoulder. The

59. For Sophronia's illness and recovery, see Anderson, *Lucy's Book,* 300-3. Sophronia Smith Stoddard McCleary died in 1876. (Ibid., 842.) In Father Smith's deathbed blessing to Sophronia in September 1840, he declared, "My oldest daughter, thou hadst sickness when thou was young, and thy parents did cry over thee, to have the Lord spare thy life" (ibid., 720).

60. Joseph Smith Jr. to William Smith, Dec. 18, 1835, in Dean C. Jessee, *The Personal Writings of Joseph Smith,* 114.

61. Hayward and Putnam, *Improve, Perfect, and Perpetuate,* 155.

discomfort was so great that his parents, fearing that "the consequence would prove to be something very serious,"[62] sent for Parkhurst. After the boy was examined, the doctor asserted he was suffering from a sprain, although Joseph protested that he had not been injured in any way. Joseph later recalled that the doctor "anointed [the tenderness] with bone ointment, & freely applied the hot shovel."[63] The anguish continued to escalate for two weeks. Ultimately, a large abscess gathered near the armpit. Parkhurst lanced this fever sore, which reportedly discharged a quart of purulent pus. "The disease [then] removed," Joseph later recalled, and "des[c]ended into my left Leg & an[k]le & terminated in a fever sore of the worst kind."[64] "My poor boy, at this was almost in despair," wrote Lucy. "Oh, father!" Joseph cried in anguish, "the pain is so severe, how can I bear it!" For nearly two more weeks, the leg continued to fester and swell.

Young Joseph's illness likely occurred simultaneously with Sophronia's three-month siege. The responsibility for Joseph's nursing fell to Lucy, who, in addition to Sophronia, also had four-year-old Harrison, toddler William, and newborn Katharine to attend to. Although the Smiths hired nursing care, for a fortnight the overburdened mother carried young Joseph almost constantly in her arms to ease his discomfort. The stress and anxiety proved "too much for my constitution," Lucy remembered, "and my nature sunk under it."

To the rescue came Hyrum, who would turn thirteen in February 1813, healthy again after his own bout. Tender and sympathetic, he volunteered to care for Joseph. "As he was a good, trusty boy," Lucy said, "we let him do so." Joseph, who by now could not walk, was laid on a low bed, and Hyrum sat by him almost constantly, grasping the painful part of his leg and squeezing it when the pain became too great. "In this manner," explained Lucy, "the little sufferer was enabled the better to bear the pain which otherwise seemed almost ready to take his life."

The pain in Joseph's leg resulted from acute osteomyelitis, which, along with the abscess under his arm, are common complications of unresolved typhoid fever.[65] Osteomyelitis, an inflammation of the bone and marrow, is almost always associated with an infectious microbe. The disease migrates

62. Unless otherwise stated, the account of Joseph's illness is from Anderson, *Lucy's Book,* 303-10.

63. Jessee, *The Personal Writings of Joseph Smith,* 268. This treatment evidently referred to a shovel being warmed in embers, then wrapped in cloth and placed on the afflicted area, creating a warm compress.

64. Ibid.

65. Thomas McCrae, "Typhoid Fever," 2:74.

usually from a distant infective focus—in Joseph's case, his armpit. Severe pain from osteomyelitis typically arises abruptly, "like lightening," as Joseph later affirmed.[66]

In children, the long leg bones, especially the femur and tibia, are most frequently affected because bacteria are deposited in the relatively slow blood flow through the capillary bed in these bones. The growing bacteria and accompanying inflammatory material usually migrate into the periosteal space. This leads to necrosis, or bone death.[67] Even modern antibiotics rarely cure these infections alone. Surgical removal of necrotic bone and tissue is necessary.[68]

Parkhurst had studied medicine under Dr. Ziba Hall, Lebanon's first physician. He had not attended medical school, and was not a skilled surgeon. Evidently, he turned Joseph's case over to a colleague, Dr. Stone,[69] who had trained under Nathan Smith at nearby Dartmouth Medical School, one of only seven medical schools in the United States.[70] Stone made a painful eight-inch superficial incision on the shin of Joseph's leg. The infected matter drained, providing relief from the building pressure. But within two weeks, as surface healing commenced, the pain returned because the deep tissue and bone were still infected. The surgeon returned and this time incised the wound bone-deep, from ankle to knee. But again, external healing led to more swelling and pain. At this point, Stone, discouraged with his progress, "deemed it wisdom to call a council of surgeons," as Lucy Smith wrote. Stone called in the two staff physicians from nearby Dartmouth Medical School, Harvard-trained Nathan Smith, president of the New Hampshire Medical Society, and his partner, Cyrus Perkins. Based on Stone's observations, and his assessment of Joseph's deteriorated leg, the medical team leaned toward amputation. This approach was standard procedure for treating this condition in America and England. Modern textbooks note that

66. Jessee, *The Personal Writings of Joseph Smith,* 268.

67. Finberg and Kleinman, "Osteomyelitis and Septic Arthritis," *Saunders Manual of Pediatric Practice,* 384-87.

68. Kurt J. Isselbacher et al., *Harrison's Principles of Internal Medicine,* 1889-90.

69. Although Joseph later noted, "I endured the most acute suffering for a long time under the care of Drs [Nathan] Smith, Stone & [Cyrus] Perkins of Hanover" (Jessee, *The Personal Writings of Joseph Smith,* 268), Dr. Stone has never been fully identified. LeRoy S. Wirthlin, who made an in-depth study of the question, noted that Smith and Perkins were the only physicians at Dartmouth Medical School. Although he found no Stones in the contemporary records of other New England Medical schools, Wirthlin noted that "class rolls of the Dartmouth Medical School list several Stones." See LeRoy S. Wirthlin, "Joseph Smith's Boyhood Operation," 149, and "Joseph Smith's Surgeon," 59.

70. "Changing Medical Practices in Early America."

even in the twenty-first century "sometimes the location or extent of osteomyelitis makes surgical cure short of amputation impossible."[71]

Amputation was a terrifying procedure in early America. Only when death was the alternative would a patient willingly submit to it. And whereas orthopedic surgeons today spend an hour or more on an amputation, in the nineteenth century, prior to the use of anesthesia, a skilled surgeon needed only forty or fifty "long, shriek-filled seconds."[72] When word of a potential amputation spread, the entire neighborhood gathered. Some onlookers were drawn by sympathy, others by curiosity. Farmers often dropped by as observers to improve their veterinary skills.

It was no surprise when the entire Dartmouth Medical School rode into the Smiths' front yard to participate in what they thought would be a leg amputation. But dauntless Lucy, protective of her children, was not about to accept this verdict tamely. When the medical team arrived, she ushered the group[73] into a room where young Joseph could not overhear the conversation. "Gentlemen, what can you do to save my boy's leg?" she asked. Stone replied, "We can do nothing we have cut it open to the bone [twice] and find the bone so affected that it is incurable."[74] "This was like a thunderbolt to me," Lucy recalled. But she evidently knew of another surgical option. "Can you not," she pled, "by cutting around the bone, take out the diseased part, and perhaps that which is sound will heal over, and by this means you will save his leg?" Not waiting for a reply, she exclaimed, "You will not, you must not, take off his leg, until you try once more. I will not consent to let you enter his room until you make me this promise."

The Smiths had evidently heard of Nathan Smith's reputation for repeatedly saving legs from amputation. This information possibly came from Hyrum, who had attended school with several of Dr. Smith's children at Hanover.[75] Perhaps the foremost expert in America on necrosis, Nathan

71. Isselbacher et al., 1990. "Amputation continued to be the treatment during the Civil War, the Crimean War, and even into the First World War" (Wirthlin, "Joseph Smith's Boyhood Operation," 135).

72. Hayward and Putnam, *Improve, Perfect, and Perpetuate,* 8.

73. Mother Smith reported seven doctors; Joseph remembered eleven (Anderson, *Lucy's Book,* 306; Jessee, *Personal Writings of Joseph Smith,* 268).

74. According to a student's lecture notes, Dr. Smith lamented that "persons often prefer their family physician although ignorant of surgery and therefore a surgeon is not usually called till the bone is dead and there is foreign matter in the place of it." Samuel Farnsworth, Lecture Notes, Oct. 20, 1812, Rauner Special Collections Library, Dartmouth College, Hanover, New Hampshire, qtd. in Wirthlin, "Nathan Smith," 333.

75. Hyrum was a year younger than his fourteen-year-old classmate, Malvina Smith, two years older than Gratia Eliza Smith, three years older then Mary Amanda Smith, and five years

Smith for nearly fifteen years had been aggressively treating osteomyelitis. His surgical technique for sequestrectomy was pioneering, especially without anesthetic, and would not be employed throughout America for nearly a century. He lectured regularly on the topic to Dartmouth medical students and within a few years authored what was then considered the most important essay on the topic: "Observations on the Pathology and Treatment of Necrosis." Furthermore, Smith amputated only to save life. Lecture notes from one of his medical students quotes him as saying: "I mentioned Necrosis [osteomyelitis] as a disease which frequently was the cause of amputation; true it is a lamentable fact. This is the cause of many limbs being taken off. When in all cases there is hardly need of a single operation of this kind."[76] Another of his students noted in an 1810 letter that "I went to Concord with Doct. Smith and upward of twenty of his students to see a limb taken off but when he got there he concluded that he could cure it without taking off the limb."[77]

Nathan Smith needed little persuasion to attempt the limb-saving procedure. The effect on seven-year-old Joseph is easy to envision. "Fear had by now certainly driven rational understanding of these terrible events from the child's mind," writes physician William D. Morain, who served his surgical residency at Harvard's Peter Bent Brigham Hospital and Children's Hospital Medical Center: "The repressed fears would likely have been erupting with waves of terror as fantasy and reality converged in the sleep-deprived chaos of his psyche. Something inside him—something of which he, at age seven, was but vaguely aware—must have known his father's companions could exact the ultimate punishment. His assaulted leg at some level of consciousness would become a powerful symbol for the terrible conflict of childhood fantasy that he would never resolve. Had they come to cut it off?"[78]

"My poor boy, we have come again," exclaimed the surgeon. "Yes," said the polite lad, "I see you have; but you have not come to take off my leg, have you, sir?" "No," the doctor replied, "it is your mother's request that we make one more effort, and that is what we have now come for." Father Smith,

older than James Morven Smith (Hayward and Putnam, *Improve, Perfect, and Perpetuate,* 274). Morven Smith, who became a physician like his father, published an article in the 1838 *American Journal of Medical Science* called: "Cases of Necrosis Illustrating the Practice of Exposing and Perforating the Diseased Bone at an Early Period in the Progress of the Malady" (Hayward and Putnam, *Improve, Perfect, and Perpetuate,* 257).

76. J. S. Goodwin, "Dartmouth Medical School Lecture Notes," 71.

77. Alexander Boyd to William Boyd, Nov. 26, 1810.

78. William D. Morain, *The Sword of Laban,* 19.

who young Joseph later remembered "d[e]spaired of my life" and recently had remained constantly with the boy, turned "to contemplate my countenance," as Lucy described the moment. Then looking at his sick son, the tender-hearted father "burst into a flood of tears, and sobbed like a child."

The surgeons ordered Joseph Jr. bound to the bedstead with ropes, but he refused. "No, doctor, I will not be bound," Lucy recalls the precocious lad saying. "I can bear the operation much better if I have my liberty." He was offered brandy or wine to dull his senses,[79] but again refused. "I will not touch one particle of liquor, neither will I be tied down," he responded. "I will have my father sit on the bed and hold me in his arms, and then I will do whatever is necessary in order to have the bone taken out." Cognizant of his mother's fragile state, the youngster then said, "Mother, I want you to leave the room, for I know you cannot bear to see me suffer so; father can stand it, but you have carried me so much, and watched over me so long, you are almost worn out." His eyes filling with tears, he continued, "now, mother, promise me that you will not stay, will you? The Lord will help me ... I shall get through with it; so do leave me, and go away off till they get through with it."

Lucy next brought a number of folded sheets, placed them under Joseph's leg, then left the house and walked several hundred yards distant. Although it cannot be affirmed which of the surgeons actually performed the procedure, it was Nathan Smith's signature sequestrectomy, as the technique ultimately was named. Describing his approach, Smith wrote that in the "third stage of the disease," the stage young Joseph suffered from, "the operation cannot save the bone entire; a portion must necessarily be cast off. The bone should then be perforated and a portion sawed out, so as to give free vent to the matter contained within it. ... If a portion of bone should be cast off, the perforation will enable the operator ... to break it the more easily, which is often a necessary part of the operation in removing large sequestra."[80]

79. Anesthetic for surgical procedures did not come into use until after 1842, when Crawford W. Long, an American physician, performed an operation after making his patient unconscious with ether vapor. Mary Karp, "Anesthesia," 1:436.

80. Nathan Smith, "Observations on the Pathology and Treatment of Necrosis," in Nathan R. Smith, *Medical and Surgical Memoirs,* 114-15. Samuel Farnsworth, one of Dr. Smith's medical students, described this disease process in his class notes:

> *Necrosis,* mortification or death of the bones. Subjects of this disease are generally young, oftenest boys, and attacked before the age of puberty. ... The death of bone commences by severe pain, and inflamation [sic] of it, and febrile symptoms are coexistent with the pain and inflamation. A common error of the present day is that matter forms in the soft parts over the bone, and thence corrupts the bone, but not usually so ... the disease terminating with the

Smith's prognosis for all his suffering necrotic patients, including young Joseph, was: "If the whole of the sequestra is removed, the cure will be perfect; but if any portion of it is left, it will keep up a discharge, somewhat in proportion to the quantity of dead bone left in the limb."[81] After the necessary instruments, consisting of "probe, knife, round saw, and one of more of Heys saws,[82] several pair of strong forceps and a pair of cutting forceps,"[83] were laid out, the procedure began. Working quickly, the surgeon drilled openings on the margins of the necrotic bone, a comparatively painless part of the procedure, then connected these holes with a small Heys saw. Using the bone-grasping forceps, the surgeon then broke loose two chunks of bone.

When the first fragment was detached, Joseph shrieked so loudly his mother came rushing into the house.[84] "Oh, mother, go back, go back," the boy cried out, "I do not want you to come in—I will try to tough it out, if you will go away." But when a third piece was broken off, Joseph's screams again drew his mother back into the room. "Oh, my God! What a spectacle for a mother's eye!" Lucy wrote. "The wound torn open, the blood still gushing from it, and the bed literally covered with blood." Her son "was as pale as a corpse, and large drops of sweat were rolling down his face, whilst upon every feature was depicted the utmost agony!"

Lucy was removed from the room until the surgery was completed. Afterwards, Joseph, "in a measure, free from pain; although pale as a corpse from exhaustion, and loss of blood," was dressed in a clean nightgown and placed on fresh sheets. The surgical team cleared away the instruments and the blood-splashed surgical garb.

Although the surgery effectively removed the majority of the dead bone, the exposed wound was horrific. The medical world would not standardize

death of the bone. … The pain in these cases is often first felt in the joint below the inflamed bone, as in the ankle if the tibia be affected. … A fluctuation circumscribed by hardness is easily found [in] the tibia. … This inflamitory [sic] affection has its seat between the periosteum and bone. In the long bones both between the external and internal periosteum and the intermediat[e] bone. Medullary substance is often destroyed. In this case there is bone between the collections of matter and circulation to it being cut off, it must die. (Samuel Farnsworth, "Nathan Smith's class notes, Lecture 2." Dartmouth Medical School, Oct. 20, 1812.)

81. Ibid., 116, 121.

82. Named for their inventor, William Heys, M.D.

83. Nathan Smith, "Observations on the Pathology and Treatment of Necrosis," 118-19.

84. Dr. William Heys noted the reaction of the first patient on whom he performed this procedure: "The pain was so great during this operation … that my patient assured me … she had not suffered more pain during the whole of the six weeks … than I had caused during the operation necessary for removing the unsound bone" (William Heys, "Abscess in the Tibia with Caries," 25, cited in Wirthlin, "Nathan Smith," 335).

treatment for these incisions with exposed bone until after World War II. But Nathan Smith's follow-up care consisted of dressing the wound with a bandage and irrigating it with a strong disinfectant as needed. Given his "unusual appreciation for the natural reparative process," as one modern physician has noted,[85] Smith was in no hurry to see the wound close. Commenting on his success in treating patients like Joseph, Smith wrote in his treatise on necrosis:

> When I first began to perform operations of this kind, I was under the apprehension lest so much bruising and handling of the soft parts, as is sometimes necessary, to dislodge a large sequestra unfavorably situated, might be followed with bad consequences, and some of these operations have been most laborious and tedious, both to myself and the patient, which I have ever performed, yet I have never known any untoward circumstances to follow such operations, of which I have performed a great many.[86]

Although Smith's sequestrectomy techniques were not accepted by the American medical community for generations, the Smith family was grateful to the doctor and to God for young Joseph's deliverance. Three decades later, Joseph remarked that fourteen additional slivers of bone ultimately worked themselves out of the wound.[87] Aside from that predictable occurrence, his recovery was essentially unremarkable. Although Joseph required crutches for three years and manifested a slight but life-long limp, his mother reported that, in the fall of 1813, he was able to accompany Uncle Jesse Smith to Salem, Massachusetts. This journey was "for the benefit of his health hoping that the sea breezes might help him[.] [I]n this we were not disappointed for he soon became strong and healthy."[88]

Years later, Joseph reported that his lameness made him "clear from Military duty by law"[89] (in other words, unfit for active service). Still, his

85. Wirthlin, "Joseph Smith's Boyhood Operation," 144.

86. Nathan R. Smith, *Medical and Surgical Memoirs,* 120-21. Difficulty in locating bone abscesses and fear of drilling into the bone and carrying out radical debridement prevented Dr. Smith's technique from finding acceptance in American medicine for nearly a century. Amputation continued to be the treatment for chronic osteomyelitis until 1874 when the surgical principles described by Nathan Smith in 1827 were independently rediscovered and applied (Wirthlin, "Nathan Smith," 330).

87. Jessee, *The Papers of Joseph Smith,* 1:268. In the chronic stages of osteomyelitis, like Joseph's, it was common for pieces of bone to work to the surface and protrude through the skin where they could be plucked out (Wirthlin, "Joseph Smith's Boyhood Operation," 135).

88. Anderson, *Lucy's Book,* 310.

89. Wilford Woodruff, Journal, July 4, 1843, qtd. in Andrew F. Ehat and Lyndon W. Cook, *The Words of Joseph Smith,* 227.

reported physical prowess in adulthood did not seem impaired by the osteomyelitis of his childhood. One wonders how differently Joseph's life would have unfolded had he been an amputee. Hanover physician Laban Gates (1753-1836), despite his profession, was sometimes mocked as he hobbled about town on a wooden leg.[90] Such an image is foreign to that evoked by stories of Joseph's robust adult persona.

90. Hill, *College on the Hill,* 103.

3 | IMPOVERISHED IN NORWICH

To either constable of Norwich in the county of [W]indsor[:] Greetings you are here by Required to Summon Joseph Smith & family now Residing in Norwich to depart Said town[.]

—Selectmen for Norwich, "A Record of Strangers Who Are Warned Out of Town," 53

The aftermath of Joseph's leg operation "must have doubled the hurt," speculates William D. Morain, a plastic surgeon with decades of experience dealing with traumatized children:

> As soon as Joseph could travel, his parents sent him away! Probably never having been separated from his parents and siblings before in his life, he was now to be deprived of his family's reassurance at the worst possible moment. During this time, when he could have been comforted by those whose understanding and caring he so desperately needed, he would instead be sent off with his Uncle Jesse to Salem, Massachusetts. ... Since the fear of dismemberment is invariably associated with the fear of abandonment in a boy's mind, this reinforcement of his conflict must have been doubly devastating. Whether his parents sent him away for his health or theirs, one might expect the effect to have been the same on this brutally traumatized boy. The absence of the familiarity and affection of his family was to be one more crashing blow that his mortally wounded psyche would have to endure.[1]

Jesse Smith, young Joseph's imposing uncle, was Joseph Smith Sr.'s eldest brother. "He was a man of good education, and had considerable display," remembered nephew George A. Smith (1817-75), and "being the elder of the family, he naturally elicited from us more or less respect."[2] Jesse may have lived briefly in Salem, Massachusetts, in 1790.[3] Though many writers

1. William D. Morain, *The Sword of Laban,* 26.
2. George A. Smith, Aug. 2, 1857, JD 5:103.
3. "Salem Heads of Household." In 1791, however, Jesse accompanied his father and Joseph

indicate that he, wife Hannah, and their eleven children[4] were residing in Salem in 1813-14,[5] the God-fearing and opinionated Calvinist was actually in Tunbridge, Vermont, where he had held many local offices, including selectman and town clerk.[6] Comments in his "Protest of Brother Jesse Smith against a Vote of the Ch[urc]h passed June 25th 1813" confirm that he was then residing in Tunbridge rather than in Salem.[7]

Uncle Jesse could be a difficult, obstinate man. These traits became particularly evident years later when Joseph Jr. began to make his religious claims. One account calls Jesse "prickly,"[8] another "frenzied and recusant," "censorious," a man possessing a "violent and acerbic tongue."[9] In 1830, when Joseph Sr. traveled to his brother's New York home to tell him of the Book of Mormon and organization of the new Church of Christ, an enraged Jesse threatened to strike his brother "with my broad axe" if he continued to talk of his son's new religion.[10] But in 1813, the boy Joseph was seven years old, eager for some bonding with his forty-five-year-old uncle.

Jesse and Joseph Jr. likely traveled eastward by Concord coach on the Fourth New Hampshire Turnpike, which led to the seacoast at Portsmouth, then on to Boston with connections to Salem. The roadway, completed in 1804, "was heavily traveled by two-, four- and eight-horse teams, stage coaches and post riders."[11] The trip must have been awe-inspiring to the young boy who had never been more than twenty-five miles from his birthplace. Joseph had not even visited the Smith family homestead in Essex County, nine miles from Salem, let alone experienced a cosmopolitan atmosphere.

Salem, the heart of Puritan America since the end of the American Revolution, had grown into a substantial metropolis. By 1790, it was the sixth

---

Smith Sr. to Vermont looking for inexpensive and uncleared land to develop into a farm. Jesse married in Danvers in 1792 but lived in Tunbridge until the late 1820s, when he moved to New York (Richard L. Anderson, *Joseph Smith's New England Heritage,* 127, 147).

4. For genealogical details on this family, see "The Riddel and Orn Family Tree Pages."

5. B. H. Roberts, *A Comprehensive History of the Church,* 1:30; LaMar C. Berrett, *Sacred Places: New England and Eastern Canada,* 26.

6. The Tunbridge Town Record from 1796 to 1810 contains numerous references to Jesse Smith. The majority of these entries note positions to which he was elected (Anderson, *Joseph Smith's New England Heritage,* 273).

7. John W. Welch, "Jesse Smith's 1814 Protest," 131-44.

8. Richard L. Bushman, *Joseph Smith and the Beginnings of Mormonism,* 151.

9. Mark L. McConkie, *The Father of the Prophet,* 11, 59, 121.

10. Lucy Mack Smith quotes John Smith's account in Lavina Fielding Anderson, *Lucy's Book,* 481. John, another of Asael's sons, accompanied Joseph Sr. on this mission.

11. "Historic Lebanon, NH."

largest city in the country, and the wealthiest per capita.[12] Rich in maritime history and graced with architectural splendor, the port city must have been a wonder to Joseph. Jesse had grown up in Essex County on Smith ancestral lands a few miles away at Topsfield. He and wife Hannah Peabody were wed in adjacent Danvers, which until 1752 was Salem Village.[13] The Smith family also had connections to the infamous 1692 witch hunts in the area which had resulted in the hangings of nineteen men and women, the demise of another man, crushed to death under the weight of stones, and still more fatalities of those being held in prison. In addition, the lives of hundreds had been irrevocably affected by the hysteria.[14] During the witch trials, Joseph's great-great-grandfather, Samuel Smith, and Samuel's father-in-law, John Gould, testified against Mary Towne Easty and Sarah Wilds, respectively.[15] Both women were subsequently hanged on Gallows Hill. A century later, Asael Smith, Jesse's father and Joseph Jr.'s grandfather, was still trying to mend the breach between the Smith and Towne families.[16] In 1834, Joseph Jr., commenting on religious persecution in New England without mentioning his own ancestor's role, wrote that "the Fathers of Salem, from 1691 to 1693, whipped, imprisoned, tortured, and hung many of their citizens for supposed witchcraft."[17]

Joseph Jr. had family connections to the town of Salem other than the witchcraft trials. His maternal grandfather, Solomon Mack, who spent years at sea, often weighed anchor in Salem Harbor. Occasionally two of his sons, Joseph's uncles Jason and Stephen Mack, were with him.[18] During the American War for Independence, Salem was a prominent privateering port. Privately owned warships had government permission to attack English

---

12. "The Great Age of Sail."

13. "The Riddel and Orn Family Tree Pages."

14. This heinous chapter in American history began when a West Indian slave girl named Tituba told voodoo tales to a group of young girls. The girls became so excited by her stories that they shivered and screamed at night. The village doctor, steeped in fervent fear of the Puritan devil, affirmed that the girls were bewitched.

15. Mary Easty was Samuel Smith's aunt by marriage. At the trial, he testified that five years previously he had been "to[o] rude in discourse" at the Easty house, likely at the wedding supper for his sister. Mary had warned him that he "might Rue it hereafter." Later that night, while riding past a stone wall, he "Received a little blow to my shoulder with I know not what and the stone wall rattled very much which affrighted me[,] my horse was also affrighted v[e]ry much but I cannot give the re[a]son of it" (qtd. in *Smith Family of New England,* 3).

16. Asael Smith to Jacob Towne Jr., Jan. 14, 1796. Asael was Mary Easty's great-great-great nephew. Anderson, *Joseph Smith's New England Heritage,* 154-56.

17. Qtd. in Joseph Smith III and Heman C. Smith, *History of the [Reorganized] Church of Jesus Christ of Latter Day Saints, 1805-1890,* 2:81.

18. Solomon Mack, *A Narraitve,* 12-13.

sloops, schooners, and row-galleys, then split the spoil with their benefactor(s). Merchants and private citizens bought shares from prospective privateers, who would use the funds to outfit ships. Seamen like the Macks served for a share of the money acquired from the auction of captured ships and cargo. Salem's fleet captured or sank 455 British vessels during the war.[19]

Solomon Mack, who experienced several close encounters with British ships, published his adventures in 1811 while living on the Mack homestead at Royalton where six-year-old grandson Joseph Jr. was also living. Joseph later wrote in his diary of the teachings "diffused into my soul by my grandfathers while they dandled [i.e., bounced] me on their knees."[20] One envisions young Joseph and his kin gathered around the fireside while the old mariner narrated quixotic tales of sailing escapades, even perhaps exploits of such men of fortune as Blackbeard and Captain William Kidd, a Scottish-born minister's son.[21] In the late 1600s, such pirates hoisted the skull and crossbones and plundered the New England coast in the temperate months while wintering in the West Indies. According to folktale circulating in Joseph's day, Captain Kidd and his crew had ascended the Connecticut River to Clarke's Island near Northfield, Massachusetts, where they buried a chest of gold. Lots were drawn to see which of their number would be slain and his body left atop the chest to hex treasure hunters. The legend attested that the gold could be recovered "only by three people at midnight when the full moon was directly overhead." To counteract the enchantment, treasure hunters were required to "form a triangle around the exact spot and work in absolute silence, words would break the charm!" On contemporary maps the place is named "Kidd's Island."[22]

Much of Solomon Mack's salty ventures were coastal vending in the same waters plied a century before by Captain Kidd. One historian has noted that "Salem's trade is remarkable not merely for the ingenious ways in which its merchants turned a profit, but also for the relative smallness

19. "The Great Age of Sail."

20. Scott H. Faulring, *An American Prophet's Record,* 395, July 9, 1843.

21. From the West Indies to New England, Blackbeard (Edward Teach), for twenty-seven months (1716-18), was known as the most diabolic villain in the New World. To many, he seemed the Devil personified. "Long, black hair covered his head and face, curling into small loops which, in time of battle, he stuck lighted matches into so as to light up his face and dark eyes. With a bandolier holding six pistols slung over his equally hairy chest, it seemed as though he might have stepped directly from the pits of hell" (Norman C. Pendered, *Blackbeard).* Kidd was born in Scotland around 1655. By 1689, he was in command of the *Blessed William,* operating as a privateer in the West Indies. He was tried and hanged in London in 1701.

22. "Captain Kidd—Pirate's Treasure Buried in the Connecticut River."

of the vessels that carried Salem cargoes."[23] These transports, like Captain Mack's, displaced less than a hundred tons, were only sixty to eighty feet in length, and had a crew of fewer than half a dozen men. Solomon's seagoing life ended in Salem in 1788.[24] While working in the "coasting trade," Solomon landed in town and "was taken very [s]ick," he later wrote. "I lay there [s]ome weeks when I recovered and returned to my family after an ab[s]ence of four years, in which time I had not heard from them."[25]

Trading may have also fetched Jesse Smith to Salem in 1813, acting in his own interests or perhaps as an agent. It is possible his commercial activities in Massachusetts were linked to the ongoing War of 1812, a misnomer for hostilities that lasted until 1815. British men-of-war patrolled the seaboard, blockading American ports and seizing Yankee vessels foolhardy enough to venture into the unfriendly Atlantic. The citizens of seaports like Salem feared a Redcoat invasion. The town was in a state of high anxiety in the fall of 1813 when the Smiths arrived.

Whatever Jesse Smith's interests in Salem, it may be more than coincidence that Joseph's surgeon, Dr. Nathan Smith, was also in Salem at this time. Young Joseph may have had a post-operative visit with the surgeon, although no documentation exists on that point. Tired of political infighting at Hanover, Nathan Smith had resigned from Dartmouth College on July 12, 1813. By mid-November, he commenced his new position with the Medical Institute of Yale College at New Haven, Connecticut.[26] Between July and November, he was in Salem consulting with his former student and respected Salem physician Reuben D. Mussey, who, later that year, would replace his mentor at Dartmouth. Smith also consulted on some of Dr. Mussey's cases. One was a nine-year-old Salem schoolboy named Nathaniel Hawthorne, later to become the novelist and Salem's most famous son. Hawthorne had injured his foot while playing what his sister called "bat and ball."[27] Fearing an incurable deformity, the family consulted a series of doctors. "Under the guidance of Dr. Smith of Hanover, New Hampshire," his sister Elizabeth ("Ebe") noted, the family tried to invigorate the child by "dousing his foot with cold water,"[28] the hydrotherapy for which Dr. Smith

23. K. David Goss, "The Maritime History of Salem," 10.

24. Anderson, *Joseph Smith's New England Heritage,* 19.

25. Mack, *A Narraitve,* 16.

26. Oliver S. Hayward and Constance E. Putnam, *Improve, Perfect, and Perpetuate,* 201.

27. Brenda Wineapple, *Hawthorne,* 26.

28. Ibid., 26-27. See also Terry Whitney, "Nathaniel Hawthorne's Early Life"; K. David Goss, "Hawthorne's Salem"; and Margaret B. Moore, "Salem and Hawthorne."

was noted.[29] Young Hawthorne, like his contemporary Joseph Smith, spent 1813 to 1816 on crutches.[30]

The known writings of Joseph and his mother Lucy offer no clue respecting how long he and his uncle remained in Salem. The trip probably lasted a few weeks, possibly a month. Whatever the duration, Joseph almost certainly exulted in sea breezes, admired the tall sailing ships, and relished Salem's historical ambience, conceivably while riding about town on his uncle's shoulders. Salem was then at the peak of its economic success as a shipping port. During the eighteenth century, the city became America's first boom town, one of the chief ports on the eastern seaboard, challenging Boston for dominance in fishing, shipbuilding, and maritime trade. The largest and busiest of Salem's wharves in the pre-Revolutionary era was Union Wharf. Constructed in the 1720s as a cooperative venture by a group of merchants, it was known as Pickering Wharf when Jesse and Joseph visited in 1813. Salem Harbor wharf was not only a privateering and East India trade center, but home to numerous sailmakers, coopers, carting services, and stores.

In addition to the wharves, Joseph and Jesse likely visited Winter Island, the site of one of Salem's earliest fortresses. Frequently rebuilt, repaired, and renamed, the bastion was Fort Pickering during the War of 1812 when the Smiths were in town. Winter Island was also the birthplace of the *Essex,* the famed 850-ton frigate built as Salem's contribution to the U.S. Navy. More than 12,000 people witnessed its 1799 launching. Commanded by Captain David Porter, the ship took ten British prizes during the first year of the war. During 1813, when the Smiths were visiting, the *Essex* was achieving remarkable success against the English in Pacific waters, capturing thirteen vessels.[31]

29. In his memoirs, Nathan Smith described his use of "cold-water therapy" on a young man suffering from typhoid: "stripped him naked as he lay on a straw mattress, and poured [a] gallon of [cold] water over him from head to foot. He seemed to feel the shock, but did not speak. ... The affusion of cold water was renewed as the day grew warm and the heat was kept down. ... Before night, the patient recovered so as to speak" (Hayward and Putnam, *Improve,* 159).

30. Joseph Smith and several other Mormon Church leaders returned to Salem in 1836 to search for buried treasure in the cellar of a "widow's house" on Union Street. In 2003, I walked down this block-long, alley-like access linking Essex and Derby Streets. Nathaniel Hawthorne was born in a home at 27 Union Street on July 4, 1804. Four years later, his sea captain father died. The house of the widow Hathorne (Nathaniel added a "w" to his name) remained on Union Street until 1958 when it was relocated to 27 Hardy Street, adjacent to the House of the Seven Gables.

31. "War of 1812." The *Essex* was captured by the British in Valparaiso, Chile, on March 28, 1814, after sustaining a loss of 155 fighting men. Repaired by the British, the ship was sent to England. In 1833, it served as a prison ship at Kingston, Jamaica and, in 1837, was sold at public

During the war, much of Salem's merchant fleet remained in port, paralyzed by the threat of British capture, but at least forty Salem privateers preyed upon the shipping lanes. The most acclaimed sea wolf of the day was the Crowninshield ship *America* which, during 1812, captured six British merchant ships, prizes that sold at Salem auction for $158,000. Later, during *America*'s second voyage under the command of Captain John Kehew, it seized ten more trophies while narrowly escaping capture by the British warship *La Hogue.*[32]

It is not known if *America* was docked in Salem when the Smiths visited the wharves, but they would have been filled with merchant ships. Written upon their mainmasts, jibs, booms, gaffes, and hulls was an exotic chapter of the young nation's maritime epic. "To the endmost port of the East," wrote one author,[33] journeyed the tall-masted ships with billowing sails, groaning under the weight of dried codfish, lumber, saddlery, shoes, furniture, and bales of tobacco. They returned months later freighting riches from the East Indies (Indonesia), China, the Mediterranean, the South Pacific, Africa, and the Baltic. Holds were stacked deep with barrels, crates, bags, and chests bulging with chinaware, tea, silks, spices, nuts, ivory, indigo, and the most lucrative of all the port's trade goods, Sumatran pepper. This highly profitable trading made Salem wealthy.[34]

To an enlightened man like Jesse Smith, the looming decline of Salem's Golden Age must have been apparent. Shortly after Joseph Smith's birth, Napoleon's France and Great Britain were clenched in a struggle for European dominance. U.S. President Thomas Jefferson's government kept the United States neutral by passing three Embargo Acts in 1807 and 1808. These embargos, aimed against Britain and France, proved disastrous to the American economy. Forests of dead masts gradually filled once-flourishing harbors. Docks that had bustled with activity were nearly deserted. Between December 1807 and March 1809, when Jefferson repealed the Embargo Acts, more than a hundred Salem ships lay idle. Thousands who depended on maritime commerce for subsistence sank into economic malaise, which only worsened when trade was further curtailed during the War of 1812-15.

---

auction. "Dictionary of American Fighting Ships." Salem's *Essex* should not be confused with Nantucket's whaleship *Essex*, which in 1820 was sunk by a sperm whale and subsequently became Herman Melville's inspiration for *Moby-Dick.*

32. Joseph Flibbert et al., *Salem,* 32.

33. Wineapple, *Hawthorne,* 14.

34. Goss, "Hawthorne's Salem."

Thus, Joseph and Jesse's 1813 visit to Salem came near the end of an era of prosperity. Nathaniel Hawthorne, who spent half of his life in the town, described Salem as a dark, somber place, perhaps the grimmest of all seventeenth-century Puritan communities. And although both Hawthorne and Joseph Smith shared a thirst for fame and immortality, their temperaments were vastly different. Hawthorne was "a pleasant child," remembered his sister, but as a man he was "studious, solitary, and introspective, ... of exquisite sensibility and melancholic temperament."[35] A nineteenth-century encyclopedia entry added that "the austere family tradition, the melancholy temperament of his taciturn father, the secluded widowhood of his mother, the decaying old seaport of witch-haunted memories in which he lived, impressed profoundly the imagination of the solitary boy."[36] Although Salem gripped his imagination, Hawthorne acknowledged no great affection for the town, noting that he was "invariably happier elsewhere."[37] Joseph Smith, in contrast, was usually gregarious, of sunny disposition, and not inclined to carry solitude with him. It seems probable that Joseph's brief Salem experience was more optimistic than Hawthorne's lengthier tenancy.[38]

Joseph's Salem excursion may have been the high point of his early life, his painful illness the low. Aside from the tales of witchcraft and sorcery, the allure of the sea, and Joseph's improving health, Salem streets were lined with impressive architecture and unique museums, a legacy of America's first millionaires. The mystery of such picturesque structures, many dating from the mid-seventeenth century, must have tantalized the boy. Many of the structures still extant in Salem would have caught Joseph's attention in 1813. The Pickering House, the oldest surviving dwelling, had sheltered ten successive generations of Pickerings since 1651. Also standing were the John Ward House (after 1684) and the Jonathan Corwin House (ca. 1675), known as the Witch House because preliminary hearings for the trials were held in it. With its multi-gabled roof and rambling floor plan, the Turner-Ingersoll house, the oldest of Salem's merchant mansions, was built in 1668 for Captain John Turner. It was the impetus for Hawthorne's *House of the Seven Gables,* and is now an American icon. Many stately houses from the Federalist period (1780-1830), designed by Salem carver, designer, and

35. Flibbert, "Nathaniel Hawthorne," 91, in Flibbert et al., *Salem,* 91.

36. "Nathaniel Hawthorne," 1.

37. Flibbert, "Nathaniel Hawthorne," in Flibbert et al., *Salem,* 88.

38. Hawthorne noted having "a home-feeling with [Salem's] past" that he did not have toward the Salem of his day. Flibbert et al., *Salem,* 88.

builder Samuel McIntire, were constructed on Chestnut Street, praised by some scholars of American architecture as the most beautiful residential street in the world situated in "one of the country's most noteworthy and magnificent residential districts."[39]

Jesse may have taken the boy Joseph to visit the collections at East India Marine Hall. The facility, now the Peabody Essex Museum, was originally created as a forum in which Salem's sea captains could share their adventures and explorations with residents and visitors. Joseph again visited the museum during the summer of 1836 when he, brother Hyrum, and friends Sidney Rigdon and Oliver Cowdery were in town searching for buried treasure in the cellar of a home on Union Street.[40]

Although there is no known information about the date of Jesse and Joseph's departure, the boy likely celebrated his eighth birthday on December 23, 1813, back in Lebanon. His mother reported that after the Salem trip her son "soon became strong and healthy" again, although he would continue to use crutches for three more years.[41] All family members had regained their health through the year of "sickness and distress." But medical expenses had reduced them to "very low circumstances."[42] The May 1814 Lebanon tax assessment records bear out Lucy's statement. With ownership of only two cows, assessed at 83 cents, Joseph Sr. was too poor to be levied a poll tax and therefore could not vote.[43] A change in the family's financial status was necessary, and so was changing residence again. Arrangements were made for "going into some kind of business," Mother Smith reported in 1845, "to provide for present wants rather than future prospects as we had previously contemplated."[44] This enterprise was evidently fruit peddling, and perhaps maple sugaring, to complement their subsistence tenant farming. The Smiths relocated, probably in autumn 1814 to one of Constant Murdock's farm properties, the 140-acre "Smith farm," approximately ten miles to the northwest in Norwich, Vermont. The move probably occurred after August 28, 1814, because, on that date, Hyrum appears on the rolls of Moor's Indian Charity School in Hanover as still living in Lebanon.[45]

---

39. Bryant F. Tolles Jr., "The Historic Architecture of Salem," 59-82, in Flibbert et al., *Salem;* see also "Houses in Salem."

40. For an account of this unsuccessful adventure, see Richard S. Van Wagoner, *Sidney Rigdon,* 180-81.

41. Anderson, *Lucy's Book,* 310.

42. Ibid., 310.

43. "List of the Polls & Rateable estate of the Town of Lebanon."

44. Anderson, *Lucy's Book,* 310-11.

45. "Account of monies received in tuition in Moor's I.C. School from Aug. 1814 to Aug. 1815."

New Hampshire and Vermont produce an unsurpassed display of fall colors; a wide variety of tree types turn at different times and provide a range of what writer Bernard De Voto called "intolerable beauty, an ecstasy of color, a splendor too great for the frail senses of mankind."[46] Swamp maples are one of the first tree species to change from summer greens to fall hues. Oak, poplar, and tamarack are among the last. With luck, the Smith family could admire the glorious foliage under the bright sun of Indian summer rather than the chilling drizzle of a New England fall day as they crossed the Connecticut River into Vermont, probably by the Norwich/Hanover Bridge built a decade earlier. Looking back on the family's New Hampshire years, Lucy Smith reflected, "I believe [we] felt more to acknowledge the hand of God in preserving our lives through such a desperate siege of disease pain and trouble than if we had enjoyed health and prosperity during the interim."[47]

Originally spelled *Norwhich,* the village of Norwich lies in the Upper Valley of the Connecticut, twenty-five miles southeast of Joseph Jr.'s birthplace in Sharon, and eight miles from Uncle Daniel Mack's where the boy's grandparents, Solomon and Lydia Gates Mack, lived. Norwich's town charter had been granted as early as July 4, 1761, by Benning Wentworth, royal governor of New Hampshire. The first families immigrated to the area in 1766. Initially part of New Hampshire, the town was returned to Vermont by a rebellion in 1783. The village population at the time the Smiths arrived was approximately 1,900.[48]

Constant Murdock, from whom the Smiths sublet their new farmstead, was one of Norwich's most prosperous citizens. Son of Revolutionary War hero Major Thomas Murdock, Constant was called "Squire Moredock" by Mother Smith in her writings, a designation attained when he served as village selectman in 1808 and as grand juror in 1814.[49] Tax records for 1813 show that the well-to-do, fifty-two-year-old landlord owned three farms, and possibly part of a fourth. Local tradition and an examination of tax and probate records point to the northernmost parcel of land on Bloody Brook as the farm that the Smiths rented in 1814.[50] It came with a house, a

46. Qtd. in Hardwick Moseley, *The Romance of North America,* 291.

47. Anderson, *Lucy's Book,* 310.

48. M. E. Goddard and Henry V. Partridge, *A History of Norwich, Vermont,* 129.

49. Ibid., 271. In the United States, the title "squire" is "commonly given in courtesy to lawyers and justices of the peace" ("Esquire: Dictionary Entry and Meaning").

50. Murdock purchased this land from Phillip Smith on September 10, 1810. The Murdock properties have been well researched by LaMar and Agnes Garrard in Norwich Village land deed records and tax records and Windsor County probate records. This research is cited in Berrett, *Sacred Places: New England and Eastern Canada,* 95-96.

still-extant two-story clapboard. The Murdock family lived farther south in the "home farm," designated in Norwich's history as "a fine residence ... on the hill a little north of Norwich village."[51]

To reach their new abode, the Smiths traveled north on Main Street through the village. En route young Joseph, still using crutches and likely riding in a slow-moving wagon, would have seen many of the homes and buildings still preserved today in the Norwich Village Historic District. A mile north of town, the travelers would have turned left onto Turnpike Road. This intersection was dominated by the Elisha Partridge home, built on the southwest corner in 1777 and complemented with a large wooden barn in 1780. Two and a half miles farther north, up Bloody Brook's vale, bypassing hill farms and hay meadows, the Smiths would have turned right on Upper Turnpike Road, crossed the stream, and come to a stop in the yard of their new place. They were tenants, not freeholders, but it was still a fresh and hopeful beginning.

The first item of business after the Smiths unpacked and settled in was likely sowing a crop of winter wheat. United Empire Loyalists from upstate New York had been successfully growing varieties of winter wheat there since the 1780s.[52] The seed, best planted mid-September, sprouts, grows a bit before the ground freezes, then falls dormant. If the wheat survives the winter, spring temperatures spur rapid growth, followed by heading out and ripening in July or early August. Winter and spring moisture normally makes winter wheat a more productive yield than spring-seeded grain. Regardless of the type of wheat sown, however, Vermont was not good grain country. The cold, hilly countryside and close-hemmed valleys were better suited to raising Merino sheep, dairy cattle, apples, and meadow hay. It is barely conceivable that the hill farms, many now reclaimed by forests, were once grain country; and the Smiths, despite their best efforts, were never able to successfully harvest a wheat crop while in Norwich. Fortunately, previous owners had planted and cultivated fruit orchards on the property, most likely apples and plums. Lucy noted that even when crops failed, "by selling fruit which grew on the place, we succeeded in obtaining bread for the family, and by making considerable exertion, we were enabled to sustain ourselves."[53]

---

51. Goddard and Partridge, *A History of Norwich, Vermont,* 227.

52. Lucy Smith's account, the only one known for the Norwich period, does not say what crops the family planted. An account of Norwich agriculture two decades later lists oats, Indian corn, buckwheat, and potatoes as being more abundantly harvested than wheat (ibid., 153). See also "Winter Wheat."

53. Anderson, *Lucy's Book,* 311.

Vermont's cool nights and warm days produce good apples to this day. But as early as 1810, "there were immense quantities of apples produced." Most were manufactured into cider, which was "drunk as freely as water."[54] They were also good for drying, cooking, pickling, mashing into applesauce, apple butter, or jelly, and giving at Christmas. Vermonters of Joseph Smith's day harvested a rich variety. Although the three most important apple stocks were Baldwin, Northern Spy, and Rhode Island Greening, one account also lists Honeygold, Summer Rambo, Tompkins County King, Cox Orange Pippin, Pound Sweet, Nonesuch, Wolf River, Wealthy and Winter Banana, Bethel, Roxbury Russet, St. Johnsbury Sweet, Sheepnose, Sops of Wine, Red Astrachan, Yellow Transparent, Peach, Seek-No-Further, Duchess of Oldenberg, King David, Black Gilliflower, Lady, and, best known of all, McIntosh.[55]

Despite the bounty of the orchards, farming was not easy. Bernard De Voto, commenting that New England geography seemed to "put a curse on the Yankee farmer," added that "work has always been too hard here and solvency too hard to maintain."[56] Successful farming required the combined efforts of every family member. The resulting lifestyle was characterized by industry, frugality, and mutual dependence. Vermont farm boys like Joseph Smith usually assisted with family chores by the age of seven or eight, and Alvin and Hyrum would have been in the fields laboring beside their father. Still, Joseph Jr.'s weakened leg and crutches would have confined him to comparatively sedentary chores where he did not have to walk and work simultaneously, such as gathering eggs, churning butter, chopping kindling, drawing water, and tending geese, while helping with his three younger siblings. Joseph, like the others, would have awakened at daybreak, then joined the family at the long wooden table in the kitchen for prayer and possibly scripture reading by their God-fearing father. The breakfast would have consisted of cornmeal mush, or perhaps a hearty meal of homemade cheese and rye or bran bread and butter, and occasionally smoked ham and eggs. Milk was consumed seasonally, as it could not be preserved in hot weather except when made into butter, buttermilk, or cheese. The Smiths, for the most part, likely drank cider made from their own apples, weak tea, or sometimes coffee, if they could afford it. Penurious New Englanders like the Smiths, whose meals were often unsatisfying, would have used these store-bought items sparingly.

---

54. Qtd. in *Report of the Vermont Board of Agriculture,* 37.
55. "A History of the Vermont Apple Industry," 1.
56. Qtd. in Moseley, *The Romance of North America,* 282-83.

Religious ardor prevailed in Norwich while the Smiths were there. Reverend James W. Woodward presided over the 300-member Congregationalist assembly which met in the town's meetinghouse. A few years before the Smiths' arrival, Methodist circuit preachers had begun to build up a local class. In 1815, the Methodists built a meetinghouse, "a wooden structure of modest dimensions, which stood near the forks of the highway leading from Union village to Norwich Plain."[57] But Joseph and Lucy, who relied on the scriptures to mediate life's crucial decisions, had not yet embraced organized religion. Bible study, morning and evening prayers, grace at the table, and observance of the Lord's Day were family rituals. "Father and Mother[,] pour[e]d out their Souls to God the don[o]r of all Blessings," wrote son William, "to keep and g[u]ard their children & keep them [from] sin and from all evil works."[58] "We always had family prayers," William commented on another occasion. "I well remember father used to carry his spectacles in his vest pocket ... and when us boys saw him feel for his specs, we knew that it was a signal to get ready for prayer." After the prayer's conclusion, the still-kneeling family would join in song, and perhaps scripture reading.[59]

The family devotional was a daily ritual repeated in thousands of Christian households throughout America in the early nineteenth century. Henry Clark Wright (1797-1870) recalled in his 1849 memoir: "The children were called in, before breakfast, wherever they were, if within hailing distance." The father's summons was, "Come to duty" or "Come to prayers." Everyone then gathered into the kitchen:

> After we were all seated, and my father had taken down and opened the great family Bible, and adjusted his spectacles, he began to read from the sermon on the mount; or about the killing of Achan and his little children, or the men, women, and infants of Jericho; or Samuel hewing Agag to pieces before the Lord; or Samson killing the Philistines; for he read chapter after chapter, verse after verse, in course; believing every verse and chapter to be the word of God, and given for instruction and edification. After reading the chapter, he stood up, and we all arose, each in his place; and he, generally standing in the same spot, began to pray. His prayer was the same, morning and evening, with slight alterations, and uttered in a deliberate and solemn tone and manner. He ended, and we at once

57. Goddard and Partridge, *A History of Norwich, Vermont,* 79.
58. William Smith, "Notes Written on 'Chambers' Life of Joseph Smith,'" 28.
59. "Another Testimony, Statement of William Smith," Jan. 20, 1894.

became as usual. We began to talk and busy ourselves about ordinary avocations, as though no extraordinary thing had been transpiring before us.[60]

Prayer and devotion to God were components of Smith family tradition. Mother Smith recorded numerous instances of how faith preserved them during adversity. That spirituality and an abundance of apples in the fall of 1814 warded off starvation. But 1815 crops, which may have included spring wheat, Indian corn, and field peas, failed as badly as the 1814-15 winter wheat. Young Joseph, with the other children, would have been aware of his parents' anxiety as the family sank deeper into insolvency. Resolutely, Joseph Sr. asserted that "he would plant once more on this farm," but if crops failed again, "he would go to New York where the farmers raised wheat in abundance."[61]

Originally, the western New York region from Seneca Lake to the Genesee River was called "Genesee Country," *Genesee* meaning "Pleasant Valley." This fertile region was heavily promoted by real estate agents. Father Smith had likely seen such advertisements as this 1810 notice: "Agriculture, already very respectable, is rapidly improving under the general and progressive exertions of hardy industry, and the enlightened and patriotic exertions of men of wealth, talents, and influence. There are but few portions of this State that display more of agricultural opulence than the country between Canandaigua and Genesee river, a tract of country abounding alike with superior richness and fertility of soil."[62]

Western New York crop lands were not only flat, blessed with deep loam, and generally free of stones, but also "well-timbered, well-watered, easily accessible and undeniably fertile—all to be had on long-term payments for only two or three dollars an acre."[63] One young settler enthusiastically wrote to his father in 1795 from Canandaigua that the surrounding country was "the most fertile I ever beheld, and probably the most fertile yet explored in America." It was common, he added, "to have thirty bushels of wheat and sixty bushels of corn to the acre."[64] With seed borrowed against his future crops, Joseph Sr. again sowed winter wheat in the fall of 1815 and with it the last of his hopes. But even before the seeds struck the ground, fate decreed

60. Qtd. in Louis C. Jones, *Growing Up in the Cooper Country,* 142-43.

61. Anderson, *Lucy's Book,* 311.

62. "Spafford" (name not complete) in 1810, quoted without further identification in W. H. McIntosh, *History of Ontario Co.,* 48.

63. Lewis D. Stilwell, *Migration from Vermont,* 135.

64. D. Saltonstall to Captain Dudley Saltonstall, Oct. 10, 1795, qtd. in McIntosh, *History of Ontario Co.,* 47.

failure. Neither the Smiths nor thousands of other hardscrabble Yankee planters had heard of Mount Tambora in the Dutch East Indies. Starting on April 5, 1815, a series of massive eruptions shook the mountain. Five days later, the summit exploded into the stratosphere, releasing 6 million times more energy than the atomic bomb dropped on Hiroshima in 1945. The boom of its detonation was recorded as far away as 1,118 miles to the west and 870 miles to the east.[65] About 92,000 people died as a direct result of the worst volcanic eruption in recorded history. The U.S. Geological Survey assigned Mount Tambora a VEI (Volcanic Explosivity Index) of 7, the highest rating ever given. In comparison, Krakatoa (1883) and Mount St. Helens (1980) received VEIs of 6 and 5, respectively.[66] "The darkness occasioned in the daytime by the ashes in Java," noted geologist Charles Lyell, was so profound that "nothing equal to it was ever witnessed in the darkest night."[67] The 1.5 million tons of volcanic ash and sulfuric acid spewed into the upper atmosphere spawned a volcanic winter. The debris cloud spread worldwide, reducing the amount of sunlight reaching the ground over the northern hemisphere and reducing global temperatures by 3-6 degrees Celsius.[68]

New England and eastern Canada were hit hardest by the unseasonably cool weather. Daily temperatures were abnormally low from the latter part of spring through late fall, resulting in what is known as the "Year without a Summer," or, more colorfully, "eighteen-hundred-and froze-to-death." The cold in May and June 1816 ruined most of the just-planted crops, including the Smith family's wheat. Vermonter Zadock Thompson (1796-1856) described the period as "the coldest, and perhaps the dryest during the early part of summer, ever known."[69] The abnormally cold and dry season created "nigh a famine," remembered Mother Smith.[70] Some families scraped by on "hedgehogs, boiled nettles and clover heads."[71]

Vermont clergyman Hosea Beckley wrote of the weather: "The summer

65. Richard B. Stothers, "The Great Tambora Eruption," 1191-98.

66. Ray L. Huntington and David M. Whitchurch, "Eighteen Hundred and Froze to Death," 90.

67. Charles Lyell, *Principles of Geology or the Modern Changes of the Earth and Its Inhabitants,* 104-5.

68. American climatologist William Humphreys in 1920 determined the cause of the 1816 year without summer, after reading an earlier treatise written by Benjamin Franklin. Franklin correctly determined that the unusually cool summer of 1783 was caused by volcanic dust drifting from Iceland. For details on the Mount Tambora eruption, see "Year without a Summer," in Face-Index website; and "Year without a Summer," on Wikipedia website.

69. Zadock Thompson, *Natural History of Vermont,* 20.

70. Anderson, *Lucy's Book,* 311.

71. Stilwell, *Migration from Vermont,* 129-30.

of 1816 was remarkably cold; and corn in this and other New England states was cut off by frost. It was a gloomy season; snow and frost in June, and drying winds shortening much the crop of hay. It was so cold about the tenth or twelfth of September, that the water in ponds and rivers froze to some thickness."[72] Zadock Thompson added:

> Snow is said to have fallen and frosts to have occurred at some places in this State in every month of that year. On the 8th of June, snow fell in all parts of the State, and upon the high lands and mountains, to the depth of five or six inches. It was accompanied by a hard frost, and on the morning of the 9th, ice was half an inch thick on shallow, standing water, and icicles were to be seen a foot long. The weather continued so cold that several days elapsed before the snow disappeared. The corn, which was up in many places, and other vegetables, were killed down to the ground, and upon the high lands, the leaves of the trees, which were about two thirds grown, were also killed and fell off. The summer was not only excessively cold, but very dry. Very little Indian corn came to maturity, and many families suffered on account of the scarcity of bread stuffs and their consequent high prices.[73]

Sometime during March 1816,[74] Joseph Sr. experienced another of his visionary dreams, so memorable in Smith family lore that his wife could recall it in detail three decades later:

> I dreamed that I was travelling on foot, and I was very sick, and so lame I could hardly walk. My guide, as usual, attended me. Travelling some time together, I became so lame that I thought I could go no further. I informed my guide of this, and asked him what I should do. He told me to travel on till I came to a certain garden. So I arose and started for this garden. While on my way thither, I asked my guide how I should know the place. He said, "Proceed until you come to a very large gate; open this, and you will see a garden, blooming with the most beautiful flowers that your eyes ever beheld, and there you shall be healed." By limping along with great difficulty, I finally reached the gate; and, on entering it, I saw the before-mentioned garden, which was beautiful beyond description, being filled with the most delicate flowers of every kind and colour. In the garden were walks about three and a half feet wide, which were set on both

72. Huntington and Whitchurch, "Eighteen Hundred and Froze to Death," 90.

73. Thompson, *Natural History of Vermont,* 20.

74. Lucy Smith dated this dream by noting that it was the same month that son Don Carlos was born—March 25, 1816 (Anderson, *Lucy's Book,* 319, 266).

sides with marble stones. One of the walks ran from the gate through the centre of the garden; and on each side of this was a very richly-carved seat, and on each seat were placed six wooden images, each of which was the size of a very large man. When I came to the first image on the right side, it arose and bowed to me with much deference. I then turned to the one which sat opposite me, on the left side, and it arose and bowed to me in the same manner as the first. I continued turning, first to the right and then to the left, until the whole twelve had made their obeisance, after which I was entirely healed. I then asked my guide the meaning of all this, but I awoke before I received an answer.[75]

The significance of this dream in the Smith family catalogue of dreams and their meanings is unknown.[76] For some, dreams are meaningless manifestations of subconscious energy. For others, dreams are visions, heaven-sent impressions on the sleeping mind. For example, in relating another of her husband's dreams, Lucy quoted Joel 2:28, "Your old men shall dream dreams," and added that it was fulfilled "in the case of my husband, for, about this time, he had another vision."[77] Joseph and Lucy's interest in dreams may have been initially kindled by their flirtation with Methodism where dreams were taken seriously. "What I have to say touching visions or dreams is this," wrote John Wesley, the founding spirit of that movement, in a letter to his brother:

> I know several persons in whom this great change [the new birth] was wrought, in a dream, or during a strong representation to the eye of their mind, of Christ either on the cross or in glory. This is the fact; let any judge of it as they please. And that such a change was then wrought appears (not from their shedding tears only, or falling into fits, or crying out: these are not the fruits, as you seem to suppose, whereby I judge, but) from the whole tenor of their life, till then many ways wicked; from that time holy, just, and good.[78]

The Smiths, no doubt like many others, also seemed not to differentiate between dreams and visions. In the Book of Mormon, which Joseph Jr. dictated a few years later, one of the characters tells his family: "I have dreamed a dream; or, in other words, I have seen a vision" (1 Ne. 8:2, 36).

75. Ibid., 319-20.

76. For instances of dream lore in the Smith family, see ibid., 323; Elizabeth W. Kane, *A Gentile Account of Life in Utah's Dixie,* 74; and *History of the Church,* 5:254-55, 6:194.

77. Anderson, *Lucy's Book,* 323.

78. Rupert E. Davies, *The Works of John Wesley,* 19:59-60.

This time of spiritual anxiety and economic hardship for the Smith family was paralleled by the changing American political panorama. Until 1815, it was not clear that the United States would survive. Wars in Europe and unrest at home threatened the republic. By 1815, however, Americans had won what some called a "Second War of Independence." This war gave rise to a growing spirit of nationalism and patriotic pride. There was a growing belief that Americans were unique and did not have to follow the lead of European powers. As this spirit spread, people's focus changed to the nation as a whole. In 1816, Jeffersonian Republicans swept to an easy victory when James Monroe was elected to the presidency. In Monroe, as one account noted, "the man and the times auspiciously met." The last president to wear an old-style cocked hat, he straddled two generations: the fading age of the Founding Fathers and the emergent age of nationalism.[79] In 1817, the newly elected president made a goodwill tour of New England to usher in the "Era of Good Feelings," as his administration was commonly called. He arrived in Norwich on July 22, remained for two hours, and visited with numerous children who had gathered to see him.[80]

Neither Joseph Smith nor any of his family members was at this gathering. Two days after the birth of Joseph's brother Don Carlos on March 25, 1816, Constable John Brown appeared at the door, with a warning-out notice in hand. Recently elected selectmen Don J. Brigham, Elijah Yemans Jr., and Daniel G. Baker had issued the citation, ordering "Joseph Smith [Sr.] & family now Residing in Norwich to depart Said town[.]"[81] The family had now been officially "warned out" out of the community.

Warning out, derived from English "Settlement" and "Poor Laws," existed because there was no centralized system of welfare to rescue the indigent. Although New Englanders generally embraced an "each for all and all for each" approach to life, they made notable exceptions to men not owning property and who therefore could not vote. In the nomenclature of the day, these folks, who had no voice in local affairs, were considered to be strangers, or transients, not legal residents. English common law governing inhabitancy was usually interpreted to mean that, if towns were "established by free consent, then it was the right of these free inhabitants to deny residency to those that were not considered desirable."[82] By sending needy people

79. David M. Kennedy, Thomas A. Bailey, and Mel Piehl, *The Brief American Pageant,* 156.

80. Goddard and Partridge, *A History of Norwich, Vermont,* 159.

81. "A Record of Strangers Who Are Warned Out of Town," 53.

82. "The History and Mystery of Old Cape Cod"; "Inhabitancy and Warning Out"; and Ruth Wallis Herndon, *Unwelcome Americans,* chap. 1.

elsewhere, presumably to their hometowns or legal domiciles, the law put the poor "in their place," as some viewed it, and prevented any single locality from becoming a gathering spot for those seeking poor relief.[83]

America's first warning-out law was passed in Plymouth, Massachusetts, in 1671. Vermont passed "An Act providing for and ordering transient, idle, impotent and poor persons" in 1787. This directive required each town to "take care of, support, and maintain its own poor." Amended by legislation on November 6, 1801, its new Section 1 directed: "That whenever any person, or persons, shall come and reside within any town in this state, the select men of such town, may at their discretion, warn such person, or persons, to depart said town, which warning shall be directed to either constable of said town."[84]

By law, then, Norwich's selectmen and overseers of the poor[85] were required to care for the destitute and infirm within the village boundaries. They were also required to determine who was not legally entitled to relief and to send them away. If the town treasury became depleted, property owners (by definition legal settlers) were required to levy taxes on themselves to replenish the coffers. Thus, a get-out-of-town warning like that delivered to the Smiths was a legal if callous means of protecting the township against incurring debt in supporting "strangers," "transients," or others for whom property owners did not wish to become responsible.

"A Record of Strangers Who Are Warned Out of Town" notes that between 1813 and 1818 Norwich Village warned out 98 individuals or families. The law was then repealed under the Vermont Settlement Act of 1817. Town officials had to have credible reasons for focusing on the general population of "transients" who resided in every town. In most cases, officials were responding to reports made by land-owners, employers, or landlords. Perhaps Constant Murdock, who would be elected an overseer of the poor in 1817, alerted the newly elected selectmen that the Smiths were not prospering on his farm and, furthermore, had just added an eighth child to the family.

It would have been customary first to summon Joseph Sr. to a council meeting where town officials would question him about his financial status.

83. Richard Burn, *The Justice of the Peace, and Parish Officer,* 3:272-520; William Blackstone, *Commentaries on the Laws of England,* 1:347-48; "Poor Laws," *The Dictionary of English History,* 857-59.

84. Qtd. in Benton, *Warning Out in New England,* 106.

85. On March 5, 1816, Joseph Howes, Elisha Burton, and Paul Brigham were elected "to settle the accounts of the overseers of the poor" in Norwich.

Such appearances were typically "permeated with tension and frustration," notes New England historian Ruth Wallis Herndon:

> On one side of the council table sat people who, in the eye of the law, truly belonged to the community: well-to-do leaders charged with maintaining order, trying to keep track of the many poor and troublesome people living under their jurisdiction, protecting the peace and property of the taxpaying inhabitants who elected them to office. On the other side of the table stood people, who, in the eye of the law, did not belong, however deep their attachments in the community: unpropertied people with few advocates, few advantages, and few prospects, struggling to maintain a place in the towns where they lived.[86]

After Joseph Smith's interrogation, the selectmen could have made one of two decisions: the family might be allowed to remain within the community for a limited time with the decided expectation that their financial situation would improve, or they would be given a deadline to leave. That the Smiths were warned out is evidence they were among the hamlet's most impoverished souls. Norwich issued only twelve other warnings-out that year despite the ruin of every crop in the village by the wintery weather.[87] The public rebuke to the poverty-stricken Smiths was undoubtedly a humiliating incident. Those who had been warned out were considered comparative lowlifes by property-owning "good and industrious citizens." No wonder property ownership became the paramount goal for the Smiths once they moved to New York.

A dejected Joseph Sr. soon gathered his family and lamented, "could he so arrange his affairs, he would be glad to start soon for New York with a Mr. Howard, who was going to Palmyra." The choice of location was based on reports circulating about the rich wheat lands of Ontario County, New York, and possibly even rumors of the impending construction of the future Erie Canal then being championed by New York City Mayor DeWitt Clinton. But Joseph was concerned how his family could survive without him. He also wondered how they could resolve their indebtedness, woven as it was into the intricate local network of bartered debts and credits. Indefatigable Lucy seemed confident her husband could bring his creditors and debtors together and "arrange matters between them in such a way as to give satisfaction to all parties concerned." She affirmed that though she

86. Herndon, *Unwelcome Americans,* 4.

87. See "A Record of Strangers," 50-55.

had a newborn babe, she would, with help from the children and her eighty-four-year-old mother, organize family matters so they could leave that land of woe on a moment's notice.[88]

Joseph followed his wife's counsel and, according to her, settled the ledger with his creditors, although one wonders how, with meager resources, he was able to do so.[89] Worried, though eager to put the stark Vermont years behind him, he and Howard then left Norwich to begin the westward trek. Eighteen-year-old Alvin and sixteen-year-old Hyrum tagged along for some distance before returning home. Ten-year-old Joseph Jr. did not accompany them on this farewell walk, no doubt because of his crippled leg.

The Smiths were not the only warned-out Yankees to abandon hope in the unforgiving climes of unpredictable New England. Thousands of others made the same choice. One account estimates that 10,000-15,000 Vermonters quit the state following the cold summer of 1816.[90] In nearly every town, in every season, worn-out and warned-out men, women, and children packed up their belongings, however meager. The great tide of western emigration from country districts like Norwich continued for nearly a century as men and their families chased their dreams to horizon's end.

---

88. See Lucy Smith's account in Anderson, *Lucy's Book,* 312.

89. Being literate and numerate people, early New Englanders generally kept written accounts of what monies were owed them, and what monies they owed others. Cash values in the bartering economy were assigned to all goods and services to make an exchange of dissimilar goods and services possible. After a transaction was made, people transferred these cash values to an account book or ledger arranged with an account for each trading partner on a separate page. Historian Tom Kelleher has written that accounts often "ran for years or appear never to have been balanced. A new exchange, a move, the necessity for money, or a death and the settlement of an estate often prompted the parties to 'settle accounts.' Debts and credits were added and compared, and the parties signed the book as an acknowledgment. Small amounts were sometimes simply carried forward to begin a new account. Larger differences were settled by a promissory note (IOU), even a third party's note, or cash when the creditor demanded payment" (Tom Kelleher, "The Debit Economy of 1830s New England").

90. Henry Stommel and Elizabeth Stommel, *Volcano Weather,* 12.

4 | THE ROAD TO PALMYRA

When the glaciers came they left in their wake a realm of gentle hills. And when the sun rose for the first time upon the new land, a spirit of the earth saw it, and thought it so beautiful that he laid his hands upon the ground to bless it. When his hands were moved, the hollows left by his fingers were filled with water.

—"Legends of the Lakes," 6

In 1816, New York—the Empire State—was populated primarily in the east: the Catskills, Lake George, and the Mohawk and Hudson River Valleys. The western portion remained mostly unsettled; the six large counties lying between Pennsylvania's northern border and Lake Ontario counted a mere 23,148 people. No town had more than 6,000 residents; most were less than half that size.[1] The west was served by small, poor roads, which did not advance far into the wilderness. When Joseph Smith Sr. and his traveling companion journeyed westward into New York, the settlements they encountered were small and widely separated. Roads on the 250-mile route could be difficult. Dry, they were rutted and the source of choking dust. When roads were wet, wagons often sank to their axles in mud. Crossing the Hudson River, likely north of present Troy, New York, the men would have followed the Mohawk Valley west to reach their destination.

Palmyra is located on the Great Lakes Plain, at the northern end of the Appalachian Plateau. Glacial erosion and gouging shaped the country, creating a picturesque landscape dominated by a dozen slender lakes, which reminded early map makers of colossal fingers. Early New Yorkers named this land of many waters the Finger Lakes Region. Fanciful names were given to the five largest lakes. Seneca Lake, named for one of the five branches of the powerful Iroquois nation, is thirty-six miles long and, like Cayuga Lake, more than 600 feet deep. The Canandaigua, sixteen miles long, translates to "Chosen Spot" in the Seneca language. Honeoye, a mere

1. "Shaping the Age of Expansion."

five miles long, in Seneca means "Lying Finger," in reference to its shape. Canadice, the Seneca's "Long Lake," actually stretches only three miles in length. Hemlock Lake, one of the few to receive an English name, was eight miles long and surrounded by pines. The area's rich soil supports luxuriant forests and undulating grasslands. Unlike Vermont, western New York was well suited for agriculture, particularly grain raising.

The land was originally inhabited by two of the largest and most powerful Native American groups. These were peoples Joseph Smith Jr. would later call Lamanites. One alliance included the Delaware, Mohican, Montauk, Munsee, and Wappinger, tribes of the Algonquin family. The other was the fierce and greatly feared clans whom the French called the Iroquois. Named the Five Nations by the British, this Haudenosaunee confederacy, founded in the fifteenth century, consisted of the Cayuga, Mohawk, Oneida, Onondaga, and Seneca tribes. Western New York was also claimed by both Dutch and English settlers during America's colonial period. The site of numerous battles, New York played a vital role in the American Revolution.

Following the war, the government made these western lands, including the Palmyra area, available for settlement, a situation promptly exploited by land speculators. When wealthy speculators Oliver Phelps and Nathaniel Gorham first sought to purchase land in this area, they discovered conflicting assertions of ownership. Massachusetts, New York, and the Iroquois all laid claim to the acreage. Ultimately, Phelps and Gorham claimed title to 6 million acres, the largest land purchase in the world to that date, which cost them approximately 2½ cents per acre.[2]

Agents John Swift and John Jenkins returned to Canandaigua and contracted to buy Township 12. Swift moved his family into the township in September 1790. Initially, his settlement along Mud Creek was called Swift's Landing. For a time, the area was known as Tolland, but in 1797 the name was changed to Palmyra. Daniel Sawyer, Swift's brother-in-law, was engaged to Dosha Boughton, the town's schoolmistress. He had been studying ancient history and had concluded: "[I]f Zenobia had a Palmyra his queen should dwell there, too." Therefore, he proposed the name which was later officially adopted.[3] By 1800, the population of Palmyra reached 986. Within a decade, Main Street, running east and west, boasted a business district and one intersecting north-by-south street which was known south of Main as

2. W. H. McIntosh, *History of Wayne County,* 138; "A Brief History of Palmyra"; Woman's Society of the Western Presbyterian Church, comp., "Palmyra, New York."

3. "Palmyra, New York"; see also "A Brief History of Palmyra."

Canandaigua Road and north of it as Church Street. By 1810, the town had advanced from log cabins to frame houses. Census records indicate that the 350 families in the area constituted 2,187 inhabitants—most of them, like Smith and Howard, New Englanders. The settlers had a gristmill, a tavern, a printing press, a distillery, and a "household manufacturing" establishment, which, in that year, turned out nearly 3,400 yards of cloth.[4]

Yankees exerted a powerful influence upon the regions where they settled. Farmers like Joseph Smith Sr., weary of trying to wrest a living from infertile soil; seamen displaced by Jefferson's Embargo Acts, the War of 1812, and the Tariff of 1816; the poor but ambitious; dissenters, resenting the restrictions upon their political freedom—all worked to create in the west a new New England. Palmyra was a modified New England village. Joseph Sr., taken with "Genesee Fever," liked the looks of the flourishing community surrounded by rich land, new farms, and timbered hills. As historian Whitney Cross notes, many, like Smith, "shunned the rugged pioneering life demanded by the more primitive regions in Ohio or west of the Genesee in New York, in favor of a community of some age, respectability, and commercial prospects," even though "they would have a greater struggle to pay for their land."[5]

Joseph Sr.'s principal interest, after finding lodging in either the Ensworth or Phelps tavern, was to size up the town and assess the opportunities. Palmyra itself was a "place of considerable business," noted an 1813 gazetteer. Weaving seemed to be the main commercial activity—the town boasted a yearly output of 53,719 yards of cloth,[6] mostly woven on handlooms in homes. Looking down Main Street, a contemporary account noted, "[T]he eye rested upon small one-story frame houses, with a few two-story exceptions." There were no log houses, "as their day was past." Joseph would have noted "spacious lots fenced with picket and board fences." The sidewalks "were of rude character," but a row of Lombardy poplars created an orderly aspect.[7] The business district was situated entirely along Main Street. A scan of advertisements in the 1817 *Palmyra Register,* a year after the Smiths settled, shows five general stores, a sign-painting and gilding firm, a coopering business, two tailors, a saddle and harness shop, two cabinet factories, a tannery, a boot and shoe-making shop, a wagon and sleigh-making concern,

4. John Henry Evans, *Joseph Smith,* 30.
5. Whitney R. Cross, *The Burned-Over District,* 139.
6. Horatio Gates Spofford, *A Gazetteer of New York,* 27.
7. McIntosh, *History of Wayne County, New York,* 142.

a bookstore, and a store vending paints, oils, dye-stuffs, drugs, medicines, snuff, and other notions. Dr. Gain Robinson, soon to become a friend to the Smiths, maintained a drugstore there, and nephew Alexander McIntyre had a second. Other establishments included Levi Daggett's blacksmith shop, Hurlbut's distillery, Blackman's blacksmith shop, and the law office of Abner Cole, a man with whom the Smiths would tangle several years later. At the corners stood the Ensworth Tavern. Nearby was Phelps Tavern.[8]

It is not known precisely how, in the summer and fall of 1816, Joseph Sr. earned the $210 or $230 he gave Lucy to transport the family westward.[9] William Smith later wrote: "[H]ere my father engaged in a coopering business for a livelyhood[.]"[10] Perhaps he worked in Joseph D. Hayward's cooper shop, and supplemented his earnings as a farm hand. Maybe he built rock walls, dug cisterns, or curbed wells. It is not implausible that, with his merchandising experience, he clerked for merchant Samuel Jennings, his future landlord. Regardless of how he obtained the money, within a matter of months Joseph had enough cash to lease or purchase a team of horses and wagon, and to lease a small home. One traditional but late account locates the Smiths' first Palmyra home in a "small rented frame building on the eastern outskirts of the village near where Johnson Street takes off Vienna."[11] Palmyra Road District 26 records, however, show that from 1817 to 1819, the Smiths lived in a small frame building owned by merchant Samuel Jennings that stood on the west end of the Main Street business district and north side of the street.[12]

Given these preparations, Joseph wrote to his wife, telling her to prepare to leave Norwich. Pragmatic Lucy had started her own preparations soon after his departure. Young Joseph and his siblings, "who were of much size," Lucy wrote, "toiled faithfully, until we considered ourselves fully prepared to leave at a moment's warning."[13] It is unlikely that Lucy and Joseph

8. Ibid., 142.

9. For this specific amount, see Lavina Fielding Anderson, *Lucy's Book,* 313.

10. William Smith, "Notes on 'Chambers' Life of Joseph Smith,'" 34.

11. Willard Bean, *A.B.C. History of Palmyra,* 19. The address of this site, near the town cemetery, is 212 Vienna. The original home no longer stands.

12. "A Copy of the Several Lists of the Mens [sic] Names Liable to Work on the Highways." New York state law required each township to maintain its own roads. Accordingly, each road district within the township required all able-bodied males, twenty-one years or older, to devote at least one day per year to keeping district roads in repair. For discussions on the location of the Smiths' first home in Palmyra, see Dan Vogel, *Early Mormon Documents,* 3:412; H. Michael Marquardt and Wesley P. Walters, *Inventing Mormonism,* 10.

13. Anderson, *Lucy's Book,* 313.

had many possessions other than bedding, clothing, and cooking and eating utensils. A contemporary account describes the meager goods of poor people like the Smiths:

> [M]en's possessions were seldom plows, livestock, and other farm goods, and women's were seldom feather beds, silver spoons, and other items of dowries. Instead, warned-out people's goods tended to be the bare essentials, movable and few: a change of clothing that by make and material announced the wearer's low rank; a cup, a bowl, and other household utensils with which to make and eat a small meal; knitting needles or a razor; a knapsack or bag for transporting the whole.[14]

The Smiths' ordeal of moving from Vermont to New York was commonplace. Lewis D. Stilwell, writing of the typical migration pattern, noted that the head of the household would start out "frequently on foot, for the long hike" to the Genesee Country, the name given to the area bounded by Seneca Lake and the Genesee River. Once the family heads arrived, continued Stilwell, they typically

> selected lands, began a clearing, and erected enough of a cabin to keep out of the weather. Then back again on foot to Vermont to get their families. ... Usually the women-folk and children were loaded into a sledge in midwinter along with a jumble of food and furniture, farewells were said, and a pair of stout oxen started dragging the whole load through the drifts. The entire journey took about a month. The idea seems to have been to start in February, arriving at the new home before the snow went off and in time for the spring plowing. Sometimes the snow failed and a wagon had to be bought en route. Once they arrived, the old, brave story of pioneering began again. ... More than one Vermonter arrived in such a state of complete poverty that he was forced to buy his land on credit and pay for it by his own day-labor.[15]

This account is similar to the Smiths' experience. It was during the winter of 1816-17, possibly early in 1817, by the time teamster Caleb Howard,[16] whom Joseph had hired in Palmyra, arrived in Norwich with the Smiths' team, wagon, and travel funds. As word spread that Lucy and her clan were preparing to depart, several men came forward with promissory

14. Ruth Wallis Herndon, *Unwelcome Americans,* 180.

15. Lewis D. Stilwell, *Migration from Vermont,* 140-41.

16. Lucy Smith notes that Caleb Howard was a cousin to the Mr. Howard who accompanied her husband to Palmyra (Anderson, *Lucy's Book,* 314).

notes bearing her husband's signature and demanded payment. According to Lucy, she was under the impression that Joseph had cleared all claims before he left. She argued that the ledgers had been balanced, before witnesses, and that no debts were owed. The note holders disagreed. Teamster Howard was "waiting on expense," Lucy wrote, so she paid the men the demanded $150, leaving her less than $100 in traveling monies.

When word of the family's plight spread, two of her husband's friends, Lucy wrote, feeling that she had been defrauded, asked that she allow them to try to recover the money. But Lucy feared that further delays would deplete her funds, preventing the family from reaching New York. Her two advocates then offered to raise money by subscription to help the impoverished family. "We know the people feel as we do concerning this matter," the gentlemen reportedly explained, and "if you will receive it we will make you a handsome present." But independent Lucy refused, explaining that "the idea of receiving assistance in such a way as this was indeed very repulsive to my feelings."[17]

So Joseph Jr., who turned eleven during that winter, his mother, his siblings, and his eighty-four-year-old grandmother, Lydia Mack, left Norwich with the few worldly goods they still possessed. The weather was frigid, but Joseph and the others were outfitted in woolen clothing, handmade by their mother and Sophronia. The first two days' travel brought them to nearby Royalton. En route the sleigh in which Grandmother Mack was riding turned over, injuring the elderly woman.[18] The frail victim was taken to Willard Pierce's tavern and made comfortable, her care transferred to Lucy's brother Daniel. As their departure drew near, young Joseph and the others gathered at her bedside. It was a cheerless farewell. Joseph saw his grandmother weep "long and bitterly," lamenting that she would probably never see them again. But "[my] Dear Child," she said to her forty-one-year-old daughter, "I have lived long[,] my days are nearly numbered I must soon exchange the things of Earth for another state of existence where I hope to enjoy the society of the Blessed and now as my last admonition I beseech [you] to continue faithful in the exercise of every religious duty to the end of your days that I may have the pleasure of embracing you in another fairer World above."[19]

17. Ibid., 314.

18. Lucy Smith wrote that the accident involved a wagon (ibid., 314). But Joseph later said that the injury occurred in an overturning sleigh. See Dean C. Jessee, comp. and ed., *The Papers of Joseph Smith,* 1:269.

19. Anderson, *Lucy's Book,* 315. Mother Mack was transported to the nearby home of her son, Daniel Mack, where she died two years later.

It seems foolhardy to undertake a 250-mile winter trip, in a wagon whose covering consisted of linen stretched over bent poles, and filled with children, including the lame Joseph. But circumstances left no alternative for the Smiths, and the frozen roads actually facilitated their travel. One traveler noted that, during the wet season, "it was a common sight to see 10 or 15 horses drawing a single wagon from its fastness in the mud."[20] Another noted that in springtime progress was "slow and tedious," averaging "only eight to ten miles a day."[21]

The family's route through Vermont lay southwesterly, passing through Bennington, where John Stark's Vermont militia routed the British on September 16, 1777, and then into Hoosick, New York. The Smiths likely crossed the Hudson River at its confluence with the Mohawk River near Half Moon or present-day Waterford. This site was the northern apex of explorer Henry Hudson's 1609 sail up the river that bears his name in his Dutch East India Company sponsored vessel, the *Half Moon*. The Smiths may have crossed the Hudson on the Union Bridge, a covered toll bridge 800 feet long and 30 feet wide.[22]

As far as can be determined, the Smiths traveled the "Genesee Road" up the Mohawk Valley on the north bank of the fabled Mohawk River. This route was the "great central trail" of the Iroquois.[23] At the beginning of the eighteenth century, this gateway between the Adirondacks and the Allegheny Plateau was a near-impenetrable forest of spruce, fir, larch, and pine, traversed by Indian trails alone. At first, the Mohawks refused to let white settlers ascend the valley, although they welcomed traders and their goods. Eventually, the English convinced the Mohawk to abandon their villages on the north side of the river and build stronger fortresses on the south side. The English then enlarged the Mohawk trail on the north side of the river into a wagon road. Initially known as the King's Highway, this road became the preferred route of thousands of Iroquois and Algonquin warriors, Dutch patroons, German Palatines, French Jesuits, and Walloons, as well as patriots of both the French and Indian and Revolutionary Wars.

With its *bowlands, hoeks,* and graceful sweeps, the valley of the Mohawk is rich in Native American lore, a subject of life-long interest to Joseph Smith. To this valley, the Mohawks came, seeking a haven after being driven

20. Jeptha R. Simms, *The Frontiersmen of New York,* 2.
21. "Roads."
22. Don Rittner, "Crossing That Bridge When You Come to It!"
23. McIntosh, *History of Ontario County, New York,* 54.

from their northern homes by the Algonquin. In 1634, an estimated 7,740 Mohawks and 2,000 Oneida lived in the valley in palisaded villages, called castles by the English.[24] The Smith family would have passed through Schenectady, the traditional home of the legendary Hiawatha, an Onondaga chief, who founded the Iroquois Confederacy or League of Five Nations. Anciently, Schenectady was called *Con-nugh-harie-gugh-harie,* which meant "a great multitude collected together." Constructed by a band of Mohawks, the forest-city could, at its peak, field 800 warriors. In 1690, a terrible massacre of Iroquois and settlers by the French bloodied the ground here. The Indian settlement was abandoned before the American Revolution, but it still existed, essentially a ghost town, when the Smiths passed through.[25]

Continuing their westward trek on the eighty-mile-long Mohawk Turnpike,[26] Joseph Jr. and his family traversed Amsterdam, Caughnawaga, Fort Plain, and then East Canada Creek, where they crossed the Mohawk and continued their voyage on the river's south bank. Here the Smiths would have seen evidence of the major eighteenth-century Mohawk Indian community of Canajoharie, or Upper Castle. This large village stretched for a mile and a half along the Mohawk from a point opposite the mouth of East Canada Creek west to the Nowadaga Creek outlet. Here had lived the Mohawk leader Thayendanegea who, using the anglicized name Joseph Brandt, became the most effective Indian military commander in the Revolutionary War. Fighting on the British side, Brandt, commanding Indian and non-Indian Loyalist troops, wreaked havoc on the Mohawk Valley. This dead leader's home and the Anglican meetinghouse he helped to build were still standing when the Smiths passed through the area.

The Mohawk Turnpike was heavily traveled. Depending on the weather, Joseph and his family would have seen hundreds of sleighs gliding along the packed snow. There were "horse- and ox-teams, wagons covered with canvas, marked Ohio or other Western points," noted one early account, "men on horseback and on foot, singly and in parties, flocks of sheep, droves of cattle, and a caravan whose tolls and tavern bills made many rich."[27] Writer Elkanah Watson described immigrants wending their way into western New York or Ohio as "swarming into these fertile regions in shoals, like the

24. "Iroquois Landscape."
25. John C. Devendorf, "Battles of New York."
26. This roadway was constructed in 1802-1803. "The Old Mohawk-Turnpike Book."
27. McIntosh, *History of Ontario County,* 54.

ancient Israelites, seeking the land of promise."[28] A highlight would have been the mammoth freighting rigs—huge blue or slate-gray wagons, with tires measuring six to twelve inches in width, and pulled by six to eight work horses. Year-round they transported produce, wheat, whiskey, and potash eastward to Albany, then returned to the interior filled with merchandise. Capable of hauling a hundred or more bushels of wheat, the conveyances were slow moving. The teamsters usually walked beside them, whip in hand; their constant travel wore a noticeable footpath along each side of the turnpike near the fence lines.[29]

At Little Falls, New York, the waters of the Mohawk formed a cataract, likely frozen during the Smiths' journey. The road then led on to Herkimer, named for Nicholas Herkimer, a war hero killed while trying to relieve Fort Stanwix during "the bloodiest battle of the Revolution" at Oriskany.[30] Near Utica, the roadway was rocky and uneven. One traveler noted: "We had jolting enough not only to have broken our vehicle, but almost to have dislocated every bone in our bodies."[31]

En route, the Smiths stopped nightly at roadhouses or taverns, which in some areas were located every mile or so along the wayside. The inns were equipped with a bar, a few beds, and large sheds. Teamster Caleb Howard developed the habit, after stabling the horses and stowing the gear, of finding his place in the barroom where, according to Joseph's later reminiscence, he spent much of Joseph Sr.'s advance "drinking & gambling."[32] Lucy made arrangements for the family's accommodations. The quality of the lodgings and meals varied. John Fowler, a Englishman traveling the same route, left a colorful portrayal of an inn along the way. "Look for no bowing landlord or obsequious waiter at the door to welcome your arrival," he warned, "neither expect to find any snug parlour ... to retire to; the bar seems the only inhabited apartment about the house, and there, upon arrival, the company immediately proceed: within it are always to be met with conveniences for washing—the very first operation—and a comb and a brush attached together by a string, suspended most likely from the ceiling ... and used ... by all comers and goers."[33]

Wayfarers like Fowler and the Smiths were bombarded nightly by news

28. Qtd. in John H. Thompson, *Geography of New York State,* 143.
29. Max Reid, *The Mohawk Valley.*
30. "History of the Mohawk Palatines."
31. John Fowler, *Journal of a Tour,* 69.
32. Jessee, *The Papers of Joseph Smith,* 1:268.
33. Fowler, *Journal of a Tour,* 72-73.

and rumors. "You would suppose that all the news and affairs of the commonwealth … had gained access to this place," Fowler wrote. Newspapers, "daily, and weekly, local, and from different parts of the Union, are strewed about." And "the merits of all persons and all things are discussed by all present," he added. Eleven-year-old Joseph would have found the profusion of posted fliers entertaining. "The walls are covered with advertisements of elections, fares of stages and steamboats—when and where running," Fowler noted. Other broadsides announced "auctions—sales of land—sales of stock—sales of merchandise—sales of everything that can be sold—quack medicines without end": "Wadsworth's cheese," "New shad," "Antibilous Pills," "Cash for corn and rye," "Cash for wheat," and the patriotic "American independence for ever."[34]

The multitude of inns along the Mohawk Turnpike were "not the comfortable, do-as-you-like public or private sort of places," Fowler observed in his account:

> A roomy bar, full of strangers, and residents of the town, who half live at the hotels, standing about, ten minutes before dinner, as impatient as a throng at a theatre, until the ringing of a bell announces the repast ready to be pounced upon. Forthwith one simultaneous rush takes place to the … eating room, and each … seating himself in the vicinity of his favourite dish, the dire attack commences.[35]

After the meal—which usually consisted of "soup, fish, flesh, pudding, pastry, and dessert"—the men adjourned to the nearby barroom where they smoked, chewed, and spat everywhere "with most perfect freedom," Fowler noted. Travelers like the Smiths who could not afford the few somewhat private chambers had to sleep rolled up in blankets on the barroom floor amid the fresh tobacco quids.

Ninety-four miles west of Albany, the Smiths arrived in Utica, on the south bank of the Mohawk. With an 1816 population of 2,828, the town was one of the larger stops en route. Here young Joseph saw the remains of old Fort Schuyler, where a garrison of troops had been kept prior to the Revolutionary War. Just west of Utica, tensions erupted with the Smiths' teamster. Howard had proven himself to be, according to Lucy, in addition to a drinker and gambler, an "unprincipled and unfeeling wretch."[36] He was

34. Ibid., 73.
35. Ibid., 120-21.
36. Anderson, *Lucy's Book,* 315.

also brutal to the young Joseph, just coming off his crutches. As they were traveling west through heavy snows, the Smiths fell in with another family by the name of Gates, who were riding in sleighs. Reportedly, two of the Gates girls caught Howard's eye. Instead of allowing Joseph to continue to ride, "Howard drove me from the waggon & made me travel in my weak state through the snow[,] 40 miles per day for several days," Joseph later stated. The boy "suffered the most excruciating weariness & pain."[37] Whenever Alvin or Hyrum, both in their late teens, tried to intervene, the more powerful Howard was reported to have knocked them to the ground with the butt of his whip. The family continued westward, patiently bearing "repeated aggravations," remembered Lucy, until events climaxed at a tavern approximately twenty miles west of Utica.[38] As the family was preparing to start in the morning, Alvin hustled inside to report that Howard had thrown the family goods from the wagon, hitched up the team, and was ready to depart without his passengers. Lucy asked Alvin to call Howard into the bar room where a large number of travelers were having breakfast. Confronting the teamster, Lucy demanded to know his intentions. He responded that the monies her husband had advanced for the trip had been spent, and he had no intent of conveying the family to Palmyra.

The irate mother, not about to be tyrannized, turned to the others in the room: "Now, as sure as there is a God in Heaven," she announced, "that team, as well as the goods, belong to my husband, and this man intends to take them from me, or at least the team, leaving me with eight children, without the means of proceeding on my journey." Turning to Howard with a touch of the iron of old New England in her rebuke, she added, "Sir, I now forbid you touching the team, or driving it one step further. You can go about your own business; I have no use for you. I shall take charge of the team myself, and hereafter attend to my own affairs."[39]

Mother Smith's can-do attitude recalls that of Mohawk Valley heroine Nancy Van Alstine of an earlier generation. Her mansion had been plundered by Indians who also stole the family's horses. Riding to the Indian village the following day, she found her husband's horses, cut their ropes, and returned with the animals. At daybreak the next day, a raiding party returned

37. Ibid., n67.

38. This is likely a reference to Vernon, New York, where taverns owned by the Williams, Graves, and Persons families are listed in an 1816 almanac (Andrew Beer, *Farmers' Calendar, or Utica Almanack, for the Year of Our Lord, 1816,* 36).

39. Anderson, *Lucy's Book,* 316-17.

to the Van Alstine estate and headed for the stables where they were met by the determined woman who demanded to know what they wanted. "Our horses," replied the marauder. "They are ours," she said boldly, "and we mean to keep them." When the leader reached out to open the door of the stable, Nancy pushed him away. Presenting his rifle, he threatened her with death if she did not move. Opening her neckerchief, she told him to shoot. The warriors retreated empty-handed. The leader later allegedly told a settler that if there "were fifty such women as she in the settlement, the Indians never would have molested the inhabitants of the Mohawk Valley."[40]

Lucy Smith was a like-minded defender when it came to her family. Howard evidently left without any further attempt to face her down, and the family followed her westward, likely with Alvin driving the team. Their route led them to New Hartford, then Auburn, Manchester, Hartsville, Fayetteville, and Syracuse, a town of approximately 1,500. A little west of Syracuse, the family would have seen a plain of 300 acres covered with vats for manufacturing salt by solar evaporation. Saline brought to the site from a spring at Salina was the strongest salt water yet discovered in the world, forty gallons yielding about a bushel of pure salt.

After Salina the road led to Onondaga Lake, then Marcellus and Skaneateles, where the family had a fine view riding the fifteen miles along the lake. At Cayuga, the wagon passed over a wooden bridge measuring a mile and eight rods long. John Fowler, who later crossed the same bridge, described it as "a most barbarous structure, built upon piles, and conveying the idea, if not the reality, of great insecurity; as the planks, or logs, upon which you pass, uncovered with gravel, soil, or other material, are of all shapes and sizes, heedlessly laid across from side to side, without nails or any kind of fastening whatever."[41] From there the group traveled through Seneca Falls, a town of 2,000, then Waterloo, where they would eventually live in 1829-30. Next was Geneva, a town of 3,000, then Canandaigua on the northwestern shore of the lake of the same name. The seat of Ontario County since 1790, Canandaigua was in 1816 a center of trade, serving as the principal provisioning center serving the stream of settlers into the west. As described a few years before the Smiths traveled through the village, Canandaigua sported a "handsome brick court-house in the center square, a jail, and on the most elevated ground in the village an elegant academy, exhibiting at a distance

40. William W. Fowler, "The Story of Mrs. Martin J. (Nancy) Van Alstine," 95.

41. Fowler, *Journal of a Tour*, 95.

a beautiful appearance."[42] Fifteen miles farther down the road, in Palmyra, Joseph Sr. awaited the arrival of his family.

The portion of the trip from Utica to Palmyra was the most difficult of the entire journey. The snow lay deep and the family was out of cash. Joseph Jr. later remembered that Lucy bartered for their lodging with pieces of cloth and items of homemade clothing. The last payment was made with his sister Sophronia's earrings. And although Howard was evidently no longer with the company, young Joseph was still bullied by one of the Gates boys. The eleven-year-old had been assigned to ride in the last sleigh, driven by the bully, but during an altercation with the older boy, Joseph was knocked to the ground and "left to wallow in my blood until a stranger came along, picked me up, & carried me to the Town of Palmyra."[43]

When the Smiths arrived in their new home after a twenty-four-day trip,[44] they were destitute. Aside from their team of horses, Lucy later narrated, they arrived with "a small portion of our effects, and barely two cents in cash."[45] Still, the family was overjoyed to be reunited. Joseph and the other children surrounded their father. They clung tightly to his neck, and "cover[ed] his face with tears and kisses that were heartily reciprocated by him."[46]

The Smiths had landed in a hotbed of religious enthusiasm. Western New York was so frequently ablaze with spiritual intensity that "New-light" revivalist preacher Charles Grandison Finney called the area the "burnt district."[47] For decades, Palmyra had been awash in the ebbs and flows of religious ebullience that swept western New York in the late eighteenth and early nineteenth centuries as a reaction to the apathy and indifference that had crept into the American psyche after the Great Awakening of earlier times. Major attacks on orthodox Christianity had been leveled during the American Revolution by men such as Thomas Paine (1737-1809), Ethan Allen (1738-89), and Elihu Palmer (1764-1806). Aggressive deism was rampant throughout the young nation. The spurts of nineteenth-century religious enthusiasm in Palmyra and elsewhere were manifestations of the so-called Second Great Awakening that had begun in Kentucky in 1800 but which spread throughout eastern America, lasting into the 1820s. Playing upon the emotions of the anxious, revivalistic fervor struck fear in the

42. John Melish, *Travels in the United States of America,* 519-20.

43. Manuscript History of the Church, Note A.

44. Bean, *A.B.C. History of Palmyra,* 19.

45. Anderson, *Lucy's Book,* 317.

46. Ibid., 317.

47. Cross, *The Burned-Over District,* 1.

hearts of restless souls not yet settled in the comfort of God's saving grace. As historian Richard L. Bushman notes, "The recurrence of revivals within a community meant that the urgent question, 'What must I do to be saved?' was on everyone's mind."[48]

At the turn of the nineteenth century, during a period of religious upheaval in Ontario County, a minister wrote in 1799 that "the seriousness" began in Palmyra.[49] But the zealous fires soon burned out, and a period of spiritual darkness ensued until 1816. In that year, as the Smiths settled into their new home, the embers of religious ardor burst into open flame once again. Palmyra was luminous with inspirited enthusiasm. Revivalist ministers like the Reverend Abner Chase, a Methodist circuit rider in Oneida County, were afire for the souls of displaced New Englanders like the Smiths who had been victimized by the "year without a summer." These religious workers used the catastrophe "to improve the providence, by impressing the minds of the people with a sense of their entire dependence on God, [who] could easily deprive them, not only of the comforts, but even of the necessaries of life."[50] By September, news of the successful, ongoing revival had reached the ears of many. Before the fervor waned, the Presbyterian church alone counted 120 new converts.[51] Predictably, however, the delirium subsided, and people returned to talking about secular things such as the upcoming construction of the Erie Canal.

Although Joseph later wrote that his parents "spared no pains to instructing me in [the] christian religion,"[52] none of the Smiths belonged to a church, nor did they join one during this 1816-17 revival. It was another reawakening, one that ignited in 1824, that left its indelible impression upon the Smith family. Like most of the townsfolk, they went about their daily affairs untroubled that many of the Sunday-go-to-meeting men and women thought they and their kind were surely doomed. Despite the lack of official church allegiance, the family was God-fearing. Mary Salisbury Hancock, a great-granddaughter of Joseph and Lucy, noted that "their simple lives were

48. Richard L. Bushman, *Joseph Smith and the Beginnings of Mormonism,* 52.

49. Rev. Seth Williston to C. Davis, Apr. 29, 1799.

50. Abner Chase, *Recollections of the Past,* 103. Joshua Bradley in his *Accounts of Religious Revivals in Many Parts of the United States from 1815 to 1818,* 130, added that in 1816 "Brandon [Vermont] trembled at the exhibitions of God's awful judgments that touched her mountains, and spread desolation through her fruitful vales."

51. James R. Hotchkin, *A History of the Purchase and Settlement of Western New York,* 130.

52. Jessee, *The Papers of Joseph Smith,* 1:5. This "History of the Life of Joseph Smith, Jr.," the earliest known autobiography of Joseph Smith, was written between the summer of 1831 and November 1832 (Jessee, "The Early Accounts of Joseph Smith's First Vision," 277).

one round of duty and devotion." She added that the family "loved their home life and usually spent their evenings together around the great fireplace, the mother and daughters knitting or sewing while Father Smith read from the Bible, explaining or extolling its passages until the children became quite proficient in their knowledge of its teachings. In this home atmosphere the girls and boys grew and formed their ideals of life."[53]

Joseph Jr. and his siblings scrupulously honored the Lord's Day. A New York contemporary, Henry Clarke Wright, later wrote of the strict observances of the pious. "Often have I been rebuked for laughing and merriment on Sunday," he noted, "and for looking out of the window." Children, according to Wright, were "[t]aught to reverence every chapter and verse in the bible as the Word of God, and to believe that when [they were] reading any part of it, [they were] conversing with the Deity."[54]

Sometime in the spring of 1818 (Lucy thought it was May), Joseph Sr. experienced another of his visions. "I thought I was walking alone," he recalled, according to Lucy.

> I was much fatigued, nevertheless I continued travelling. It seemed to me that I was going to meeting, that it was the day of judgment, and that I was going to be judged. When I came in sight of the meeting-house, I saw multitudes of people coming from every direction, and pressing with great anxiety towards the door of this great building; but I thought I should get there in time, hence there was no need of being in a hurry. But, on arriving at the door, I found it shut; I knocked for admission, and was informed by the porter that I had come too late. I felt exceedingly troubled, and prayed earnestly for admittance. Presently I found that my flesh was perishing. I continued to pray, still my flesh withered upon my bones. I was almost in a state of total despair, when the porter asked me if I had done all that was necessary in order to receive admission. I replied, that I had done all that was in my power to do. "Then," observed the porter, "justice must be satisfied; after this, mercy hath her claims."
>
> It then occurred to me to call upon God, in the name of his son Jesus; and I cried out, in the agony of my soul, "Oh, Lord God, I beseech thee, in the name of Jesus Christ, to forgive my sins." After which I felt considerably strengthened, and I began to amend. The porter or angel then

53. Mary Salisbury Hancock, "The Three Sisters of the Prophet Joseph Smith," pt. 1, 34. Mary was the granddaughter of Katharine Smith Salisbury, Lucy and Joseph's second oldest daughter, and was twenty-nine when the long-lived Katharine died in 1900.

54. Henry Clarke Wright, *Human Life,* qtd. in Louis C. Jones, *Growing Up in the Cooper Country,* 137, 141.

> remarked, that it was necessary to plead the merits of Jesus, for he was the advocate with the Father, and a mediator between God and man.
>
> I was now made quite whole, and the door was opened, but, on entering, I awoke.[55]

One imagines Joseph Sr. relating this dream at the breakfast table and young Joseph then pondering it as he went about his farm chores.

Aside from the daily religious training Joseph Jr. received from devout though unchurched parents, the boy ultimately sought enlightenment on his own terms, through Bible study and introspection. Although his mother later wrote that he "never read the Bible through by course"—meaning from start to finish—he spent a considerable portion of his youth from age twelve onward studying the scriptures and memorizing passages from his favorite chapters. He was essentially a non-denominational Christian. Although there is no record of his personality or temperament before the operation on his leg at age seven, afterwards, as he approached his teens, he was apparently a rather somber lad. One account reported that the boy "was said never to have been known to smile, but always wore a most serious expression."[56] "Remarkably quiet," "a well-disposed child," Joseph "always seemed to reflect more deeply than common persons of his age upon everything of a religious nature" and was "more given to meditation and deep study," than the rest of the children, according to Lucy.[57] His father added in an 1834 patriarchal blessing on twenty-nine-year-old Joseph: "Thou hast sought to know his [God's] ways, and from thy childhood thou hast meditated much upon the great things of his law."[58]

Joseph's retrospective accounts of his early years, which focused on his supernatural religious experiences, must be treated prudently. Although he had a vivid imagination and a nimble intellect, the adult Smith was sometimes less than forthright in discussing his past. Much of what he would later present as reality was wishful thinking or myth making. Aside from his reading of the Bible, and his own years-after-the-fact musings on the topic, there is little evidence that he gave serious thought to religious issues such as which church was true, or which denomination he should join, until after brother Alvin's death in 1823.

Years after the fact, Smith attested that his first spiritual awakening

55. Anderson, *Lucy's Book,* 324-25.
56. W. W. Miner, qtd. in "Visitor Tells of His Boyhood Days," B-2.
57. Anderson, *Lucy's Book,* 344.
58. Joseph Smith Sr., "Blessing on Joseph Smith, Jr."

occurred in 1817, when he was eleven. He wrote: "[M]y mind become Seriously imprest with regard to the all importent concerns for the well=fare of my immortal Soul."[59] This attention likely resulted from the contagion of revivalistic zeal that had been ongoing in Palmyra since the Smiths arrived in the area. The boy's absorption was the typical reaction of many impressionable youths. Adolescence, asserts an early twentieth-century psychologist, "lends itself readily to the excitement of revival."[60] Joshua Bradley, who published an account of revival activities in 1819, agreed: "The happy subjects of this work have been principally youths from 14 to 25." Furthermore, "some of the most giddy and thoughtless youths were arrested in their career of vanity. Their thoughts were turned upon the solemnities of death, judgment and eternity. Their eyes were opened to see their lost condition. Some were soon brought to an humble reliance on that Saviour who came not to call the righteous but sinners to repentance."[61]

Pioneering American psychologist William James describes the similarities between the conversion experience of youth, like Joseph Smith, in evangelical circles and the growth into a larger spiritual life common to every class of human beings. "The age is the same, falling usually between fourteen and seventeen. The symptoms are the same,—sense of incompleteness and imperfection; brooding, depression, morbid introspection, and sense of sin; anxiety about the hereafter; distress over doubts, and the like."[62] Joseph, in his own words, felt led to "searching the scriptures," believing, as taught by his parents, "that they contained the word of God thus applying myself to them." Convinced by the persuasions of his father, the budding enthusiast adjudged most congregants in the area to be hypocrites who did not observe "a holy walk and Godly conversation."[63] This observation, as sincere as it may have been arrogant, caused "grief to my Soul," he noted.

Accordingly, for the next three years, Joseph immersed himself in Bible studies, attended occasional camp meetings and nearby church services, and pondered "many things in my heart" respecting the contentions and divisions, the "wicke[d]ness and abominations and the darkness which pervaded

59. Jessee, *The Personal Writings of Joseph Smith,* 4.

60. Frederick Morgan Davenport, *Primitive Traits in Religious Revivals,* 290.

61. Bradley, *Accounts of Religious Revivals,* 25.

62. William James, *The Varieties of Religious Experience,* 171.

63. One of the basic rules for Methodist preachers, to whom Joseph often listened as a youth, was "Let your motto be 'Holiness to the Lord.' Avoid all lightness, jesting, and foolish talking" (Leigh Eric Schmidt, *Hearing Things,* 51). Other advice was "Withdraw thyself from superfluous talk and useless visits, as also from hearkening after news and rumours" (Thomas à Kempis, *An Extract of the Christian's Pattern,* 9).

the minds of mankind." His mind became "exceedingly distressed," he remembered, until he became fully "convicted of my sins."

Similar statements from youths like Joseph were common in his time and place. Stanford Fleming, who analyzed the place of children in New England Puritanism between 1620 and 1847, observed that they "were not infrequently tormented by a conviction of their own wickedness and a terror of damnation."[64] Not only did Joseph lament his sinful state, but he had also concluded that humankind "did not come unto the Lord" but had apostatized from the Christianity of the Bible. His judgment, one shared by his parents and many of his seeker ancestors, was that there was "no society or denomination that built upon the gospel of Jesus Christ as recorded in the new testament and I felt to mourn for my own sins and for the sins of the world."[65]

Joseph Sr.'s visionary dreams during this period also manifested spiritual tension. According to Lucy, he experienced his seventh vision in 1819:

> "I dreamed," said he, "that a man with a pedlar's budget on his back, came in, and thus addressed me: 'Sir, will you trade with me today? I have now called upon you seven times, I have traded with you each time, and have always found you strictly honest in all your dealings. Your measures are always heaped, and your weights overbalance; and I have now come to tell you that this is the last time I shall ever call on you, and that there is but one thing which you lack, in order to secure your salvation.' As I earnestly desired to know what it was that I still lacked, I requested him to write the same upon paper. He said he would do so. I then sprang to get some paper, but, in my excitement, I awoke.["][66]

Joseph Sr.'s spiritual anxiety was no doubt shared by most, if not all, family members. Lucy and he recounted these dreams to their children, probably more than once; and Joseph Jr., for one, later incorporated elements of the visions into his religious writings. His father's dreams were frequently similar: he was typically lame or ill and required a guide. Invariably, the scene was a desolate plain or desert. Joseph Sr. often seemed intent on achieving an ill-defined goal that lay beyond him in the distance. Many of his contemporaries also had dreams of religious import laced with symbols of hell and torment, suggesting unresolved inner conflicts. "Revolutionary and

64. Stanford Fleming, *Children and Puritanism,* 22.

65. Jessee, *The Personal Writings of Joseph Smith,* 5. For a discussion of Seekerism in the Smith and Mack families, see Dan Vogel, *Religious Seekers and the Advent of Mormonism.*

66. Anderson, *Lucy's Book,* 330.

postrevolutionary American revivalism," writes historian Jon Butler, "had a tendency to involve dreams, visions, apparitions, and physical manifestations of divine intervention."[67] Although skeptics might have scoffed at using prophetic dreams, visions, and supernatural impressions for guidance, the Smiths and many others did not.

While the Smiths continued their quest for primitive Christianity—the simple religion of the New Testament—it had become evident to all that Joseph Sr.'s meager earnings could barely sustain the family. "We were much reduced," wrote Lucy, "not from indolence, but on account of many reverses of fortune, with which our lives had been rather singularly marked."[68] Sometime in late 1817 or early 1818, twelve-year-old Joseph participated in a family council to discuss their finances. They had not owned property since 1803, two years before Joseph was born. His life had been circumscribed by poverty. The consensus of the destitute clan was to become freeholders, to pool their resources, purchase a plot of undeveloped land, then convert it through their own labor into a self-sustaining farmstead. Joseph Sr. was a well-worn forty-seven, and perhaps beyond developing a new farm through his own efforts. The work of hacking out an existence in heavily forested confines required years of strenuous labor. The young had the physical strength and sufficient life expectancy to attempt such a grueling project. Fortunately, the Smith family had an abundance of manpower. Alvin, their mainstay, was a powerful young man of twenty, Hyrum a brawny eighteen. Young Joseph's leg had almost healed, and two more sons, not counting toddler Don Carlos, would soon be coming along. These strapping sons provided the elemental ingredients needed to convert forest into farmland.

Although Lucy later noted that "this was then a raw country and land was low being in its rude state,"[69] prices were spiraling upward. In 1817, New York Governor DeWitt Clinton had announced the construction of the long-dreamed-about Erie Canal, a manmade waterway linking the Hudson River and the Great Lakes. The path of the 363-mile "Clinton's Ditch," an engineering marvel, cut directly through Palmyra, paralleling Mud Creek. Promoters portended vast prosperity. The public pronouncements, however, modified theories of land use and worth to include proximity to the canal. Real estate values along the route began to escalate, making it harder for poor families to buy new land.

67. Jon Butler, *Awash in a Sea of Faith*, 222-23.
68. Anderson, *Lucy's Book*, 317.
69. Ibid., 318.

One of the many sources of revenue to the Smiths was a small eatery that Joseph and Lucy established in their Main Street home. Although their meager resources did not allow them to advertise in the local *Palmyra Register,* they posted a sign above their doorway announcing it as a "Cake and Beer Shop." Palmyra neighbor Pomeroy Tucker recalled that the offerings included "gingerbread, pies, boiled eggs, root-beer, and other like notions" which were "popular with the juvenile people of the town and country, commanding brisk sales."[70] James G. Bennett (1795-1872), a New York newspaperman who visited upstate New York in 1831, wrote that "Old Joe Smith[,] ... a country pedlar," possessed "all the shrewdness, cunning and small intrigue which are generally and justly attributed to that description of persons." While living in Manchester, added Bennett, Joseph Sr. followed "a branch of the 'American System'—the manufacture of gingerbread and such like domestic wares [in which] he was a considerable speculator, having on hand during a fall of price no less than two baskets full."[71]

The "root-beer" Tucker recalled was likely Lucy's own brew of ginger beer or perhaps the more familiar concoction of sassafras bark and sarsaparilla. On holidays and "military training days," Tucker added, the Smiths peddled their wares about the streets from a handcart constructed by Joseph Sr.[72] Both parents also drew on natural lore with Joseph Sr. digging and selling "rutes and yarbs [roots and herbs]."[73] Anna Ruth Eaton (?-1910), wife of Horace Eaton, pastor of Palmyra's East Presbyterian Church for three decades, recalled in 1881 that Lucy "knew the virtues of remedial roots and herbs."[74] Great-granddaughter Mary Salisbury Hancock, no doubt passing on family tradition, wrote that "when called upon," Lucy "would ride for miles to administer her prayers or her herbs and home remedies to a sick child or to assist a mother in childbirth."[75] The roots could have been such wild tubers as leeks, ramps, goutweed, Solomon's seal, anise root, cow parsnip, curly dock, sassafras, and "evin root," which when

70. Pomeroy Tucker, *Origin, Rise, and Progress of Mormonism,* 4.

71. James Gordon Bennett, "Mormonism—Religious Fanaticism—Church and State Party," Pt. 1, in Vogel, *Early Mormon Documents,* 3:283. Bennett wrote this dispatch in Canandaigua on August 15, 1831; it was published in both the *New York Morning Courier* and *New York Enquirer,* Aug. 31, 1831.

72. Tucker, *Origin, Rise, and Progress of Mormonism,* 4.

73. Hamilton Child, *Gazetteer and Business Directory of Broome and Tioga Counties, N.Y. for 1872-3,* 53; "Palmyra," undated clipping from *Wayne County Journal.*

74. Anna Ruth Eaton, *The Origin of Mormonism,* 2.

75. Hancock, "The Three Sisters," pt. 1, 35.

boiled was a popular substitute for tea and coffee.[76] The edibles may have been domesticated turnips, yams, horseradish, beets, parsnips, or potatoes. Peddled herbs improve the flavoring of food, could be steeped as tea, and also served medicinal purposes. These would have been pepper, basil, mint, ginger, ginseng, catnip, parsley, sage, rosemary, and thyme, many of which are indigenous to eastern woodlands.[77]

In addition to baking the pies, cakes, and gingerbread sold in their shop, Lucy had, in her own words, "done considerable at painting oil cloth coverings for tables[,] stands[,] &c."[78] An area resident noted that Lucy "wove the threads and painted the cloths herself, and when a sufficient stock was found to be on hand, it was her custom to start out herself and hawk her wares from door to door."[79] She painted and sold enough of these oilcloths to provide an "abundance of good and wholesome provision," as well as "replenish my household furniture a fine stock of which I had sacr[i]ficed entirely in moving."[80]

Alvin's contributions to the common fund made the greatest impact. Energetic, motivated, and skilled, he became a carpenter's apprentice. Joseph Sr. was also an all-around handyman. He is known to have made split-wood chairs, black-ash baskets, and birch brooms, which he peddled.[81] He also constructed stone walls and rough fireplaces, witched for water, and dug and curbed wells and cisterns.[82] Hyrum and young Joseph helped their father in these tasks, and also worked as day laborers and field hands.

In the spring of 1818, Joseph Sr., Alvin, Hyrum, and Joseph Jr. engaged in a sharecropping venture with Palmyra farmer Jeremiah Hurlburt. Joseph Sr. and Alvin signed a promissory note for $65 "to be Paid in good Merchant Grain at the market Price by the first January next."[83] This arrangement soon led to discord, however, and both parties sued each other.[84] Arrangements

76. Levi Beardsley, *Reminiscences,* in *Growing Up in the Cooper Country,* edited by Louis C. Jones, 40.

77. Steve Brill et al., *Identifying and Harvesting Edible and Medicinal Plants in Wild (and Not So Wild) Places.*

78. Anderson, *Lucy's Book,* 318.

79. C. W. Brown, "Manchester in the Early Days," Mar. 11, 1904.

80. Anderson, *Lucy's Book,* 318.

81. William Alexander Linn, *The Story of the Mormons,* 182.

82. Bean, *A.B.C. History of Palmyra,* 19.

83. Joseph Smith Sr. and Alvin Smith, Promissory Note, Mar. 27, 1818, in Vogel, *Early Mormon Documents,* 3:385.

84. *Joseph Smith, Sr., vs. Jeremiah Hurlburt,* Feb. 17, 1819; *Jeremiah Hurlburt vs. Joseph Smith Sr. and Alvin Smith,* June 26, 1819. See also Jeffrey N. Walker, "Joseph Smith's Introduction to the Law: The 1819 Hurlbut Case," *Mormon Historical Studies* 11, no. 1 (Spring 2010): 117-40.

were more cordial with Martin Harris and other prosperous farmers and landowners for whom the Smiths worked. "Whenever the neighbors wanted a good day's work," related Joseph's brother William, who turned seven in 1818, "they knew where they could get a good hand."[85] Neighbor Orlando Saunders (1803-89) seconded the assertion: "I knew all the Smith family well," he declared. "Young Joe (as we called him then), has worked for me, and he was a good worker; they all were."[86] At the time, contractors were paying laborers on the Erie Canal 50 cents a day, or $8 to $12 a month, a fact which drove up farm wages and wheat prices. Wheat harvesters in the Genesee Valley at that time were paid $1.50 a day.[87]

In addition to day labor for neighbors in the Palmyra area, young Joseph also may have found work farther afield in the early 1820s. Two accounts list a Joseph Smith as a woodcutter. According to an 1867 account in the *Rochester Daily Union and Advertiser,* he "worked through the winter in company with some twenty or thirty others, rough backwoodsmen." He and two others "built a rude cabin of poles and brush, covered with leaves and earth, in the woods open to the south, with a camp-kettle in front for cooking."[88] He also possibly found work in nearby Seneca County. When he was about sixteen or seventeen, according to local historian Ernest L. Welch, Joseph "located at Kingdom, a mile west of Seneca Falls, about 1821, or '22 as a general hand for any kind of work."[89] The Kingdom, short for Devil's Kingdom, midway between Waterloo and Seneca Falls, sprang up in 1808 astride the Cayuga/Seneca Canal, which connected the two finger lakes. The community "was the toughest spot on the Buffalo turnpike," noted one newspaper account:

> [I]t had a reputation for gangsters, gamesters, adventurers and fighters who made their headquarters at a tavern operated by Pontius Hooper, who arranged cockfights, fox chases, wrestling matches, prize fights and horse races.
>
> Canalers, stage drivers and other travelers knew the place. Over the canal and through the waterway that led to Cayuga and Seneca Lakes came travelers, who stopped for a bit of excitement. Stage coaches and

85. "Another Testimony, Statement of William Smith."

86. Orlando Saunders, qtd. in William H. Kelley, "The Hill Cumorah, and the Book of Mormon," 165.

87. Bushman, *Joseph Smith and the Beginnings of Mormonism,* 202.

88. "Joe Smith, the Mormon Prophet," 2. See also John B. Buck Account in Emily C. Blackman, *History of Susquehanna County, Pennsylvania,* 577.

89. Ernest L. Welch, *"Grip's" Historical Souvenir of Seneca Falls, N.Y.,* 26. See also Arnold H. Barben, *Notes on "The Kingdom,"* 1.

packet boats brought their quotas. Drivers of the stages changed horses at the tavern.

On the north side of the river in 1810 were the tavern, a red school house, grocery, blacksmith shop, flour mill, saw mill, cooper shop and a half dozen houses.

Across the river on the south side, a considerable settlement grew up around the canal block. Abundant water power afforded mill sites, which later were developed on both sides of the river.[90]

An 1876 history of Seneca County lists young Joseph as "a day-laborer" who sometimes worked "for old Colonel Jacob Chamberlain, and occasionally for others." Daniel S. Kendig added that Joseph started working for Chamberlain about 1820, when he was "an odd-looking boy, clad in tow frock and trousers, and barefooted." Chamberlain owned grist mills in the vicinity of Kingdom Lock on the Cayuga/Seneca Canal.[91]

While the Smiths worked to accumulate a down payment for new land, they inventoried the undeveloped property in the area. A well-informed farmer regarded the presence of deciduous hardwoods as a sure sign of fertile soil, especially if the trees were tall and the forest thick. Immigrants to western New York were prone to follow successful agricultural models such as that promoted by Tench Coxe, Supervisor of the Revenue under George Washington. Coxe recommended that settlers purchase "one hundred acres of sugar maple land." If this acreage were developed to standards of "ordinary American improvement," he added, two thirds should be cleared for the "culture of grass and grain" and one third left in "wood and timber." He suggested that the wooded areas should include about 1,500 maple trees, which in a good year could produce 1,000 pounds of maple sugar.[92]

The property the Smiths finally settled on was a "wild and unimproved place" on Farmington (now Manchester) Lot 1, known to locals as "North Woods."[93] Part of the original Phelps and Gorham acquisition, the property had passed through the hands of several speculators before being purchased by Nicholas Evertson of New York City. Evertson, who bought 3,000 acres in 1798, began selling the land in farm-size parcels. After Evertson's death in 1807, the unsold portions of the property remained unattended for thirteen years. It was not until June 1820 that Evertson's

90. Charles F. Hulbert, Scrapbook, undated newspaper clipping.
91. Daniel S. Kendig, Statement, in McIntosh, *History of Seneca Co., New York,* 129.
92. Trench Coxe, *A View of the United States of America,* 69.
93. Milton V. Backman, *Joseph Smith's First Vision,* 40.

executors conveyed to Caspar W. Eddy, a New York City physician, power of attorney to sell the property.[94]

This period of neglect had been long enough that the Smiths probably thought they could exercise preemption or squatter's rights. Throughout American history, squatters often asserted rights over unclaimed or neglected properties by virtue of occupation rather than ownership. It was generally understood at that time that squatters were allowed to make valid claims to land, particularly public land, if no one else stepped forward with a legal claim. Palmyra newspaperman Pomeroy Tucker seemed to think that this was the case with the Smiths. "In 1818 they settled upon a nearly wild or unimproved piece of land," he wrote, "mostly covered with standing timber, situate[d] about two miles south of Palmyra. … The title of this landed property was vested in non-resident minor heirs; and the premises being uncared for by any local agent or attorney, the Smiths took possession of it by the rights of 'squatter sovereignty.'"[95]

The tract the Smiths occupied was situated about two miles south of Palmyra on a rutted wagon trail through the trees, a track which later became Stafford Street. The fertile, well-drained soil, which promised crops of wheat, Indian corn, buckwheat, oats, and beans, had a briary cloak of red raspberry, black raspberry, service berry, or shadbush, and blackberry bushes. Near the ground grew red and white trillium, adder's tongue or dogtooth, poison ivy, Virginia creeper, moonseed (climbing ivy), grape vine, spice bush, white snakeroot (upland boneset), spleenwort white baneberry or doll's eyes, red baneberry, skokeweed, and much goldenrod. Overhead rose majestic copses of beech, butternut hickory, shagbark or sweetnut hickory, catalpa, white oak, flowering dogwood, white elm, white ash, basswood (American linden or American whitewood), tulip, wild black cherry, and other hardwoods.[96] Especially valuable were the 1,200 to 1,500 sugar or rock maples from which the family would later harvest syrup. Crooked Creek, lined with willows and tall grasses, meandered through the property, furnishing a year-round supply of water for farm and domestic needs. Trout and even salmon spawned in the stream. The Smith men planned meadowlands, hayfields, and winter pasturage along the stream's banks once the dense forest was cleared.

94. Marquardt and Walters, *Inventing Mormonism,* 4.

95. Tucker, *Origin, Rise, and Progress of Mormonism,* 12-13.

96. This list of fourteen varieties of trees and twenty shrubs, flowers, and vines is found in a 1944 study of the Smith farmstead (John D. Giles, "Survey Made of Flora of Sacred Grove," 6, 12).

Rising along the hills on the eastern side of the property, towards the Mason Chase farmstead, lay grazing ground.

Two centuries later, one envisions the Smiths' enthusiasm as the family visited the picturesque wilderness rich with promise. "I shall never forget the freshness and beauty of the forest, after winter had passed away," wrote New Yorker Levi Beardsley, "the spring flowers were everywhere in bloom, the herbage high and luxuriant covered the ground." Only those "who have resided in a new country," he added, "where forest scenery in all its richness and beauty is presented to the view, can realize how strongly those recollections are impressed on the mind."[97]

The Smiths' first task was selecting a home site, typically a small clearing. Once the spot was chosen, young Joseph and his older brothers began, under their father's direction, to clearcut the underbrush and small trees, called straddles. The larger trees, those needed for construction, were felled outward to enlarge the clearing. Once the timber was down, it was customary to arrange a house-raising bee, calling in the help of neighbors. Lucy wrote of friends and neighbors: "Never have I seen more kindness or attention shown to any person or family than we received from those around us."[98] One of Lucy's great-granddaughters, drawing on a general knowledge of how such house-raises were conducted, described it: "The neighbors brought teams, axes, and saws. Huge logs were rolled in cut, hewn, and notched to fit one upon the other. In a short time the frame of a new house of the size desired by the family was erected."[99]

The most common dwelling built by pioneer settlers in wilderness areas of western New York was horizontal log construction with notched and fitted corners. This method, first introduced to America by Swedish settlers on the Delaware River in 1638, became universal in the great westward expansion after 1765. Few tools were needed, usually only an axe or adz and an auger. All fastenings were of wood. The spaces between the logs were chinked, or filled in, usually with clay or lime mortar. Sometimes logs were sculpted to produce a smoother exterior and tighter fitting walls.[100]

William, Joseph's younger brother, remembered that the improvements made on the farm were "first commenced by building a log house at

97. Beardsley, in Louis C. Jones, *Growing Up in Cooper County,* 38.

98. Anderson, *Lucy's Book,* 321.

99. Hancock, "The Three Sisters," pt. 1, 35.

100. Fred B. Kniffen and Henry Glassie, "Building in Wood"; "Log Cabin."

no small expense."[101] Lucy added that they had achieved the move in just "two years from the time we entered Palmyra."[102] Willard Bean, a Mormon who collected Palmyra incidents and artifacts during the 1920s and 1930s, described the house as being "nestled among the trees of the forest."[103] Thomas Cook, who published a history of Palmyra in 1930, states that it was 1818 when the Smiths "moved to this tract of wild land to occupy it" but provided no source for his information.[104] An earlier historian, George W. Cowles writing in 1895, agreed, although again without citing a source, that "in 1818 the family moved to a wild farm, two miles south of the village, and lived in a log house about twelve years."[105] Neighbors Joshua Stafford, Barton Stafford, and Henry Harris all remember the Smiths "in Manchester" by 1819 or 1820.[106] Orsamus Turner, an apprentice printer at the local newspaper, later recalled that he first saw the Smith family in the winter of 1819-20 living "in a rude log house, with but a small spot underbrushed around it" near the town boundary.[107] The most contemporary document is a report of a Palmyra road survey, dated June 13, 1820, and authored by Commissioners of Highways Isaac Durfee and Lumon Harrison. It locates the center of Stafford Road "three rods fourteen links southeast of Joseph Smith's dwelling house."[108]

Lucy Smith recalled the home a quarter-century later, with satisfaction and affection, as "a snug comfortable though humble habitation built and neatly furnished by our own industry."[109] Pomeroy Tucker thought it less inviting: "a small, one-story, smoky log-house ... divided into two rooms, on the ground-floor" with "a low garret [attic], in two apartments. A bedroom wing, built of sawed slabs, was afterward added."[110] Into this unpretentious dwelling crowded not only the ten Smiths and their furniture, but also the wide variety of implements required for the numerous domestic manufactures of the farm family.[111]

---

101. William Smith, "Notes Written on 'Chamber's Life of Joseph Smith,'" 27.

102. Anderson, *Lucy's Book,* 321.

103. Bean, *A.B.C. History of Palmyra,* 21.

104. Thomas L. Cook, *Palmyra and Vicinity,* 219.

105. George W. Cowles, *Landmarks of Wayne County,* 182.

106. See their accounts in Eber D. Howe, *Mormonism Unvailed,* 250, 251, 258.

107. O[rsamus] Turner, *History of the Pioneer Settlement of Phelps and Gorham's Purchase, and Morris's Reserve,* 212-13.

108. Isaac Durfee and Lumon Harrison, "Minutes of the Survey of a Public Highway," June 13, 1820.

109. Anderson, *Lucy's Book,* 321.

110. Tucker, *Origin, Rise, and Progress of Mormonism,* 13.

111. Several recent studies, based on the speculations of Wesley P. Walters, have reasoned

Aerial photography and archaeological excavations by Brigham Young University in the 1970s and 1980s identified the site where the Smith log house stood. Forensic examination determined that the structure measured approximately twenty by thirty feet, with a second half-story or loft. The dwelling was more than a mere log cabin or shanty. Folks living in log cabins typically had dirt floors, oiled paper or cloth for windows, and animal hide coverings for doors. They used earthenware, wooden utensils, crudely constructed furniture, and owned few other possessions. In contrast, the dig at the Smith site produced evidence of "furniture with hinges, brass fittings in their home, and a door with a metal key hole."[112] The home was evidently constructed of hewn logs, notched and fitted with the openings between chinked and plastered with clay. The floor was puncheon—split logs with the flat sides up. The second-story loft was divided into two sleeping compartments, one for the daughters and the other for the sons. They most likely reached this crowded upper room, roughly twelve by twelve feet, with a center height of a mere four to six feet, by ladder.[113]

The roof was covered with "bark shingles," laid on the rafters, then lashed to a ridgepole.[114] The house had several windows of flat glass panes, probably the standard size of eight by ten inches. Although the builders did not construct a rock foundation, inside the house was a large fireplace built of mortared cobble stones, each approximately six inches in diameter. "The large opening," wrote Dale Berge, principal archaeologist, "allowed the cook to reach food being prepared in blackened pots hanging on rods. The firebox was lined with brick and the hearth constructed of large flat stones. There

---

that the Smiths lived in two different log homes south of Palmyra, one on Samuel Jennings's property, the other on the Smiths' Farmington/Manchester acreage. See Wesley P. Walters, "Joseph Smith's Move to Palmyra and Manchester, N.Y."; Marquardt and Walters, *Inventing Mormonism,* 4; Vogel, *Early Mormon Documents,* 1:278; Anderson, *Lucy's Book,* 321. Despite these impressive arguments, I believe that all references to a log home in the area point to a single structure. I base my belief on the fact that none of the ten accounts, including testimony from two Smith family members, describe the dwelling as "the first" or as "the second" log home. Pomeroy Tucker, however, noted the family "remained unmolested in [the property's] possession for some twelve years, occupying as their dwelling-place, *in the first instance,* a small, one-story, smoky log-house, which they had built prior to removing there. ... Shortly before quitting the premises," Tucker added, "they erected a small frame-house thereon, partly enclosed, and never finished by them ... using their original log hut for a barn" (Pomeroy Tucker, *Origin, Rise and Progress of Mormonism,* 13; emphasis mine). In addition, several accounts note that the family lived in the home for "a dozen years," meaning essentially from 1818 to 1830 (Pomeroy Tucker, "Mormonism and Joe Smith," *Wayne Democratic Press,* May 26, 1858; George W. Cowles, *Landmarks of Wayne County,* 182).

112. Dale L. Berge, *Archaeology at the Boyhood Home of Joseph Smith, Jr., Palmyra, New York,* 75.

113. Dale L. Berge, "Archaeological Work at the Smith Log House," 26.

114. Berge, *Archaeology at the Boyhood Home*, 68.

was no iron stove, because of the freight expense."[115] While the lower part of the chimney was rock, the upper was likely of mud-plastered sticks.

The interior of the two-room home was basic. The "keeping room" served as kitchen, dining room, and common area for the family's home industries. The kitchen table was probably pine, with a drawer underneath for cutlery. The homemade chairs were either bottomed with flags, split ash (called "basket stuff"), or woven elm bark. This multi-use area contained a clutter of pots, kettles, dishes, carpentry tools. One corner, likely serving as a scullery or buttery, would have contained a jumble of barrels, cheese presses, and a churn. Another nook would have accommodated spinning wheels for flax and wool, a carder, winder, and perhaps loom. Nearly all of the Smiths' clothing, as well as bedding and toweling, was homemade. The exposed beams overhead had hooks or nails driven into them from which hung strings of red peppers, festoons of dried apples, bundles of dried herbs, and ears of curing seed corn. A visitor might have seen in the rafters different sorts and sizes of implements, bags, lengths of cord and twine, and skeins of yarn waiting for the busy hands of Lucy Smith and her daughters. The keeping room floor, typically scoured with clean white sand, was a source of pride for the mistress of the house.

The best room contained the family's finest furniture, perhaps a couple of chests, a few chairs, and Joseph and Lucy's bed. There were likely no carpets or curtains, and no painted floors or wall paper. The family's poverty did not permit frills. A log home like the Smiths' in the early 1820s would have been valued at approximately $100, "at the bottom of the upper range of homes in the United States at that time."[116] In addition to the house itself, other improvements detected on the property during the Brigham Young University reconnaissance survey included an uncurbed surface well approximately fifty feet from the house, a nearby barn, a cooper shop with floor and loft, an apple orchard of three dozen trees, and other outbuildings.[117]

Palmyra tax records suggest that the family, except Alvin, likely relocated from their storefront home to the farmstead between April 1819 and April 1820.[118] Joseph Jr.'s sister Lucy, the eleventh child and third daughter of Jo-

115. Ibid., 68.

116. Ibid., 72.

117. Donald L. Enders, "The Joseph Smith, Sr., Family," 219. In the 1990s, the Church of Jesus Christ of Latter-day Saints announced plans to restore the Smith farm. Subsequently, based on details found during the archaeological dig and other historical information, the log house, barn, and cooper's shop, were reconstructed in the late 1990s, and the frame home was preserved.

118. One may surmise that Alvin, who turned twenty-one on February 11, 1819, listed in

seph Sr. and Lucy, was born in this log cabin on July 18, 1821.[119] Unknown to virtually everyone, including themselves, the Smiths had inadvertently constructed their log home on Samuel Jennings's property in Palmyra, fifty-nine feet north of the Palmyra/Farmington survey line, although the farm itself was in Farmington. When the mistake was discovered, the family arranged payment with Jennings, a merchant who died on September 1, 1821, to purchase the property on which their home had been built.[120] Jennings's 1822 estate papers show Joseph Smith as owing $11.50, the possible price of the small piece of property.[121]

---

the April 1820 Road Tax List is still residing at the Main Street address. "A Copy of the Several Lists of the Mens [sic] Names ...," in Vogel, *Early Mormon Documents,* 3:411-14.

119. Anderson, *Lucy's Book,* 845-46.

120. Undated newspaper clipping from the Willard Bean Collection, cited in Rand Hugh Packer, "History of Four Mormon Landmarks in Western New York," 43.

121. "An inventory of the property of Samuel Jennings Deceased," June 5, 1822, cited in Vogel, *Early Mormon Documents,* 3:448.

5 | FARMING IN FARMINGTON

The poor man, and his class is the most numerous, will generally undertake about one hundred acres. The best mode of dealing with him, is to grant him the fee-simple by deed, and secure the purchase money by a mortgage on the land conveyed to him. ... His spirit is enlivened; his industry is quickened; every new object he attains brings a new ray of hope and courage: he builds himself a barn and a better habitation; plants his fruit-trees, and lays out his garden: he clears away the trees, until they, which were the first obstacles to his improvement, becoming scarcer, become more valuable, and he is at length as anxious to preserve, as he was at first to destroy them: he no longer feels the weight of debt, for having the fee, he can sell at an improved value, nor is he bound to remain against his will.

—Judge William Cooper (1754-1809), qtd. in William Cooper, *A Guide in the Wilderness,* 10-11

In writing years afterwards of her son Joseph's boyhood, Lucy Smith commented that "nothing occurred during his early life, except those trivial circumstances which are common to that state of human existence."[1] This observation was made after Joseph's death in 1844, when his mother, nearing seventy, was intent on enshrining the religious life of her adored son, whose followers she depended on for her own sustenance. The osteomyelitis surgery, his parent's religious differences, the family's poverty, and the harrowing trip from Vermont to New York impacted Joseph in ways neither he nor his mother fully appreciated. Robert D. Anderson, a psychiatrist, speculates that the cumulative effect of these and similar early events may have resulted in "problems with identity and an absence of life direction." He also suggests that "Joseph's self-esteem must have been low; he had to deal with a lifestyle of moves, intermittent failures, and the amiable contempt of others." As a result, Anderson wonders if Joseph "was probably engaging in

1. Lavina Fielding Anderson, *Lucy's Book,* 329.

a fantasy compensation for personal inferiority, for his family's low social importance, and his own unpromising future."[2]

Others writing about Joseph's early years noted aspects of his development not mentioned by his mother. Anna Ruth Eaton, wife of minister Horace Eaton of Palmyra's Western Presbyterian congregation, the church Lucy and some of her children attended, saw Joseph as possibly acting out Lucy's own ambitions: "Even in Vermont, before moving to New York, while Joe was a child, Mrs. Smith's mind was made up that he should be a prophet."[3] Clark Braden and E. L. Kelley also stated that a minister employed by the Home Missionary Society in Vermont from 1809 to 1813 observed: "[I]n 1812 a religious imposter created an excitement in the neighborhood of the Smith's. ... [Lucy] prophesied at the time, that Joe, then seven years old, would be a prophet, and give to the world a new religion. Joe was raised with this idea before him. All the family used to speak of Joe as the 'gen[i]us,' ... of the family."[4]

Much has been made of Joseph's limited formal education. But despite such shortcomings, he possessed considerable natural ability. Early Mormon convert Orson Hyde noted that "Nature had endowed him with a keen critical intellect."[5] That Joseph became the center of a movement attracting millions of followers seems to be evidence of this. And he, like many of his disciples, tended to understate the boyhood schooling he was able to obtain. Joseph, in common with nineteenth-century contemporaries Andrew Jackson, William Lloyd Garrison, Abraham Lincoln, Thurlow Weed, and Brigham Young, accomplished much despite limited formal education. In addition, William Shakespeare, who like Joseph participated irregularly in a rural grammar school, is universally recognized as a creative genius. The Bard's "brilliance and his inventiveness," writes Marjorie Garber, professor of English and director of the Humanities Center at Harvard University, were "the results of attributes and resources that were innate rather than learned."[6]

"Being in indigent circumstances," Joseph recalled of his New York years, the Smiths "were obliged to labour hard for the support of a large Family." This adversity "deprived [me] of the bennifit of an education suffice it to say I was mearly instructid in reading writing and the ground rules

2. Robert D. Anderson, *Inside the Mind of Joseph Smith,* 38.
3. Anna Ruth Eaton, *The Origin of Mormonism,* 3.
4. Clark Braden and E. L. Kelley, *Public Discussion,* 46.
5. Orson Hyde, *Ein Ruf aus der Wuste,* 14.
6. Marjorie Garber, "Our Genius Problem," 68.

of Arithmatic which constituted my whole literary acquirements."[7] Joseph's younger brother William, however, tempered this personal assessment by noting: "[T]hat he was illitterate to some extent is admitted but that he was [entirely] unlettered is a mistake. In Sintax, Mathamatics[,] grammar[,] geography[,] with other studies in the Common Schools of his day he was no novice and for writing he wrote a plain intelegable hand[.]"[8] Historian Dale Morgan, after reading several of Joseph's early letters, concluded that there was "evidence of a flair for words, a measure of eloquence, and a sufficient degree of schooling."[9]

A common school education (as contrasted to a classical education) was the norm during Joseph's adolescence in early America, where sheer survival was the prevailing ambition of all. "In the winter nearly all the boys went to school," reminisced Joseph's New York contemporary, Levi Beardsley.[10] But they were there just ten to twelve weeks a year, when they were not needed at home, and seldom remained in school past the age of fourteen. That young Joseph attended school in Palmyra before the family moved from Main Street is certain. The village schoolhouse, a frame structure built in 1801, was used for both educational and religious purposes.[11] Isaac Butts and Christopher Stafford both attended school there with Joseph. Stafford remembered Smith as a "dull scholar,"[12] while his brother John recalled Joseph as "quite illiterate." He added, however, that after the Smiths began to have school in their house where they used the Bible for a text, "he improved greatly."[13]

Three textbooks Joseph used during this period still exist.[14] *The First Lines of Arithmetic,* "for the use of Young Scholars, adapted to the capacities of children," was published in Hartford, Connecticut, in 1818. Another of his school books is *The English Reader* (ca. 1799). It contains selections

7. Joseph Smith [Jr.], "History, 1832."

8. William Smith, "Notes Written on 'Chambers' Life of Joseph,'" 26.

9. John Phillip Walker, *Dale Morgan on Early Mormonism,* 147.

10. Levi Beardsley, *Reminiscences,* 62, 70.

11. Hamilton Child, *Gazetteer and Business Directory of Wayne County, N.Y. for 1867-8,* 52.

12. Isaac Butts, Statement, 2; Christopher M. Stafford, Affidavit, 1.

13. John Stafford, Statement, qtd. in William H. Kelley, "The Hill Cumorah, and the Book of Mormon," 167.

14. In 1990, these three books were donated by representatives of the Wilford C. Wood family to the LDS Museum of Church History and Art in Salt Lake City. Wood had obtained the books at a public auction in New York in the early twentieth century. As Dennis A. Wright and Geoffrey A. Wright note, the collection in the museum "consists of a copy of *First Lines in Arithmetic* (1818), access no. LDS 90-12-3, *English Reader* (ca. 1799), access no. LDS 90-12-4, and a book of gospel sonnets of an unknown title and date, access no. LDS 90-12-5" (Wright and Wright, "The New England Common School Experience of Joseph Smith Jr., 1810-16").

of prose and verse: "narrative, didactic, descriptive, conversational, and promiscuous," wrote one biographer.[15] Among its moral precepts were "The Pious Sons," "Filial Sensibility," "Cruelty to Insects Condemned," "Tenderness to Mothers," "Respect and Affection Due from Pupils to Their Tutors," and "To a Young Woman with a Watch." The third book was a 264-page religious reader containing scores of "Gospel Sonnets" arranged in six parts: "Believer's Espousals," "Believer's Jointure," "Believer's Riddle," "Believer's Lodging," "Believer's Soliloquy," and "Believer's Principles." Years later, while in Nauvoo, Illinois, Smith gave these books to Richard Bush, a young farmhand in his employ.[16]

Early American educators stressed patriotism. American schools also used their influence to give children a sense of their nation's greatness and destiny. Young Joseph's teachers would have exposed him to the prevailing concept, arising from the Second Great Awakening, that good Americans were deeply religious Protestants. Such folk were honest, thrifty, hard-working, and courageous. Students were taught that the English, Scottish, German, and Swiss peoples were similar to themselves and thus admirable. But people whose way of life differed considerably from their own were viewed unfavorably. The prevailing opinion of most educators of Joseph's youth was that Native American Indians, though noble and possessing some merit in their own group, were nonetheless savages and could not be civilized.

One description of Joseph as a schoolboy in Palmyra calls him a "big-bodied, flaxen-haired youth, with small hands for his size, large feet, prominent frontals covered with a heavy growth of very light hair, and striking blue eyes, half hidden by long light lashes." To distinguish him from his father, everyone called him "Young Joe Smith," whereas his father was "Old Joe Smith."[17] Orsamus Turner, four years older than young Joseph, retained clear memories of him. Turner, an apprentice printer at the *Palmyra Register* newspaper in 1818-19, frequently saw Joseph in the village "with little jags of wood, from his backwoods home; sometimes patronizing a village grocery too freely; sometimes find[ing] an odd job to do about the store of Seymour Scovell." Once a week, Joseph came into town to check the mail and pick up his father's newspaper at the *Register* office. Turner and the other printers sometimes bullied young Joseph by "blacken[ing] the face of the then meddling inquisitive lounger—but afterwards Prophet, with the old fashioned

15. John Henry Evans, *Joseph Smith,* 35.
16. Ibid., 35.
17. Ibid., 37.

[ink] balls."[18] Other young rogues, noted Pomeroy Tucker, "used to delight in obtaining the valuable goods intrusted to Joseph's clerkship" in the family eatery "for worthless pewter imitation two-shilling pieces."[19]

Several individuals, interviewed years later, included descriptions of Joseph's homespun clothing and "vagabondish appearance."[20] "Clothing poor," added Philetus B. Spear.[21] "I can see him now, in my mind's eye," remarked Daniel Hendrix, "with his torn and patched trousers, held to his form by a pair of suspenders made out of sheeting, with his calico shirt as dirty and black as the earth, and his uncombed hair sticking through the holes in his old battered hat." But he had a "jovial, easy, don't-care way about him that made him a lot of warm friends," Hendrix added.[22]

Other interviewees corroborated Joseph's essentially pleasant disposition. Benjamin Saunders, who said he knew Joseph "as well as I did my own brothers," recalled that young Smith and his brothers "were big stout men but never was quarrelsom[e]. [W]ould put up with any thing and every thing rather than have a quarrel."[23] Saunders's brother Orlando opined that although young Smith by nature "was peaceably disposed ... when he had taken too much liquor he was inclined to fight, with or without provocation."[24] But Stephen Harding, Joseph's boyhood acquaintance, later appointed territorial governor of Utah, added that Joseph "was noted as never having had a fight or quarrel with any other person."[25] And Pomeroy Tucker remembered his peer as "proverbially good-natured, very rarely if ever indulging in any combative spirit toward any one, whatever might be the provocation."[26] Joseph's mother described him as a "remarkably quiet, well disposed child," against whom no one "had aught."[27]

Elsewhere, Mother Smith added: "We always had a peculiar anxiety about this child for it seemed as though something was alw=ays occurring to place his life in jeopardy and if he was absent ½ <an> hour unexpectedly we were apprehensive of some evil befa=lling him."[28] Evil nearly did befall him

18. Orsamus Turner, *History of the Pioneer Settlement of Phelps and Gorham's Purchase,* 212-13.

19. Pomeroy Tucker, *Origin, Rise, and Progress of Mormonism,* 14.

20. Pomeroy Tucker, "The Mormon Imposture."

21. Jan Shipps, "Joseph Smith and Mormonism."

22. Daniel Hendrix, qtd. in "Origin of Mormonism," May 14, 1893.

23. Benjamin Saunders, Interviewed by William H. Kelley, in Dan Vogel, *Early Mormon Documents,* 2:140.

24. Orlando Saunders, qtd. in Frederick G. Mather, "The Early Days of Mormonism," 198.

25. Thomas Gregg, *The Prophet of Palmyra,* 39

26. Tucker, *Origin, Rise, and Progress of Mormonism,* 4.

27. Anderson, *Lucy's Book,* 329.

28. Ibid., 373.

one night in 1820, when he was fourteen; someone apparently attempted to harm, or at least scare, him. The lad was returning home from an errand one evening near dark. As he came into the clearing of the family home, a shot evidently rang out. It was a load of buckshot perhaps intended for him. He "sprang to the door much frightened," said his mother. Family members immediately fanned out to look for the culprit, but nothing was found in darkness. The next morning tracks were found under a wagon. And the following day some of the discharged lead was found embedded in the head and neck of one of the family's cows. The Smiths were never able to discover "the man who made this attempt at murder," wrote his mother, neither could they "discover the cause thereof."[29]

Much later, when reeling from religious persecution, Joseph offered this self-portrait of youthful maltreatment: "Though I was an obscure boy, only between fourteen and fifteen years of age, and my circumstances in life such as to make a boy of no consequence in the world, yet men of high standing would take notice sufficient to excite the public mind against me, and create a bitter persecution."[30] Joseph in later years chalked up the assault to religious harassment, stating that "several times I was shot at, and very narrowly escaped."[31] But oppression linked to his religious claims came later, and his mother, in her account, did not attribute this incident to persecution over his spiritual claims. Moreover, there are no other shootings involving Joseph that he or anyone in his family mentioned.

"My father was a farmer and taught me the art of husbandry," wrote Joseph.[32] Boys of that era typically began helping with heavy chores when they were seven or eight. Raking and pitching hay during the rush of harvest was common for youngsters. At ages ten to twelve, they were scything, threshing, and shocking grain, splitting wood, and carting hay. By adolescence, sons shouldered basically any farm job, working beside their fathers. Skills that Yankee farm boys like Joseph acquired as they grew to manhood included building log houses, clearing land, providing an adequate water supply, fencing fields and pastures, and planting, tending, and harvesting crops. Boys were also adept at threshing grain, mowing and putting up field hay, and raising and slaughtering animals. Fourteen-year-old Joseph and twelve-year-old Harrison are not listed in the Smith family census of Farmington, New York, which was

29. Ibid., 329.

30. *History of the Church,* 1:7.

31. Joseph Smith to John Wentworth, 708.

32. Ibid., 706.

taken between August 7, 1820, and February 5, 1821.[33] Presumably, they were boarding elsewhere, having been "hired out" for the fall harvest.

Much of U.S. President James Monroe's Era of Good Feelings began to diminish during this period. In 1819, a paralyzing economic panic descended upon the country. Currency deflation, depression, bankruptcies, bank failures, unemployment, soup kitchens, and overcrowded pesthouses called debtors' prisons became the order of the day. Lucy noted that "it was almost a time of famine[—]wheat was $2.50 per bushel and other things in proportion."[34] Although many factors contributed to the catastrophe of 1819, much of the economic damage was caused by over-speculation in frontier lands. The Bank of the United States, through its various branches, had become deeply involved in this popular type of outdoor gambling. The Smiths were drawn into this web of speculation in the summer of 1820 when the non-resident heirs of Nicholas Evertson conveyed to Casper W. Eddy, a New York City physician, the right to sell their Ontario County land holdings. Eddy transferred his power of attorney to Zachariah Seymour, a land agent living nearby in Canandaigua, the Ontario County seat.

No doubt Joseph, like the rest of his kin, had saved every bit of money he earned over a two-or-three-year interval. After a period of "the strictest kind of economy and labor," wrote Lucy, the family had saved money enough to make a down payment on the land on which they were squatting.[35] Sometime after July 14, 1820, Joseph Sr. and Alvin arranged for the purchase with Seymour, an associate of Oliver Phelps, who with partner Nathaniel Gorham had initiated the practice of "articling" for real estate. "Articling was a way for hard-working but cash-poor pioneers to obtain possession of land by buying on an installment plan," explained a study of the concept. "Articles of Agreement" were compacted between the two parties. The contract stipulated that "the deed was held by the seller until the final payment was made; if the buyer defaulted he lost all right to the land as well as to any improvements, and the seller could then resell it."[36] Terms of the articling required the Smiths to pay for the property in installments, each due on the anniversary of the contract signing. Although William Smith, as an elderly man, thought the property value was $300 at the time of purchase,

33. U.S. Bureau of the Census, Farmington, Ontario County, New York, 1820, p. 318.

34. Anderson, *Lucy's Book,* 318.

35. Ibid.

36. For details on this articling, see John W. Barber and Henry Howe, *Historical Collections of the State of New York,* qtd. in H. Michael Marquardt and Wesley Walters, *Inventing Mormonism,* 5.

with the payments being $100 each, the land was actually assessed at $700 when it was first placed on the tax assessment roll in July 1821.[37] The title, as mutually agreed upon, would remain with the Evertson agent until the purchase was complete.[38]

Once Joseph Sr. and Alvin signed the contract, they continued the arduous task of clearing trees from the property and enlarging their cropland. "What a noble gift to man are the forests! What a debt of gratitude and admiration we owe for their utility and their beauty!" wrote Susan Fenimore Cooper, in her 1850 reminiscence. Like Joseph, she had spent many hours amid imposing woodlands in Cooperstown, New York, and described them romantically:

> How pleasantly the shadows of the wood fall upon our heads, when we turn from the glitter and turmoil of the world of man! The winds of heaven seem to linger amid these balmy branches, and the sunshine falls like a blessing upon the green leaves; the wild breath of the forest, fragrant with bark and berry, fans the brow with grateful freshness; and the beautiful woodlight, neither garish nor gloomy, full of calm and peaceful influences, sheds repose over the spirit. The view is limited, and the objects about us are uniform in character; yet within the bosom of the woods the mind readily lays aside its daily littleness, and opens to higher thoughts, in silent consciousness that it stands alone with the works of God.[39]

But beauty was not provender. Grandeur could not pay the mortgage. Acreage had to be cleared as quickly as possible to ready the ground for crops. The stands of old-growth timber were immense. Many of the hardwoods soared more than a hundred feet skyward. Felling them by axe, one tree at a time, was a formidable task. And once down, many, with diameters up to six feet, were impossible to cut with a cross-cut saw and had to be slowly burned, noted Joseph's younger brother William.[40] "The whole scenery cannot be described in words that can convey an adequate description nor can it be conceived by those, who have not witnessed it," wrote an Englishman describing an old-growth New York forest:

---

37. Marquardt and Walters, *Inventing Mormonism,* 7. The remaining 200 acres of Lot No. 1 were taxed to the Evertson heirs at a value of $1,400.

38. The "Articles of Agreement," drawn up to bind the two parties, has not been discovered, and the exact date the papers were prepared is unknown. Because the Smiths eventually lost the property, they did not obtain the deed nor was it recorded in county records. See Larry C. Porter, "A Study of the Origins of the Church," 139.

39. Susan Fenimore Cooper, *Rural Hours,* 125. She was the daughter of American novelist James Fenimore Cooper and granddaughter of William Cooper, founder of Cooperstown.

40. William Smith, "The Old Soldier's Testimony," 634.

> Over our heads stretched a vast dome of vegetation. ... Below this thick veil and amid the damp depths of the forest, there lay one vast confusion, a sort of chaos. Trees of all ages, foliage of all colours, plants, fruits and flowers of a thousand species, entangled and intertwined. Generations of trees have succeeded one another there through uninterrupted centuries and the ground is covered with their debris. ... Amid them a thousand different plants press in their turn towards the light. They glide between these immobile corpses, creep over their surface and under their decaying bark raise and disperse their powdered debris. It is like a fight between death and life.[41]

Yankee settlers like the Smiths were legendary woodsmen. "They had earned a collective reputation as the most skilled handlers of the axe in America," notes New York historian Alan Taylor. "They were simply less daunted by the hard work of felling extensive tracts of hardwoods and hemlocks than were most."[42] The five-step Yankee system consisted of "felling, logging, drying, burning, and ash-gathering."[43] Prosperity for a family required at least twenty acres of cleared land, equally subdivided into grain tillage, hay fields, and pastures. Lucy noted that during their first year of residence on their new farm, the Smiths cleared thirty acres of forest.[44] An additional thirty acres were cleared within a few years. Responding to accusations that the Smiths were indolent folk, William Smith pointed out: "If you will figure up how much work it would take to clear sixty acres of heavy timber land ... trees you could not conveniently cut down, you can tell whether we were lazy or not."[45] Horticultural studies confirm that approximately a hundred trees per acre typically flourished in old-growth timber like the Smiths'. Clearing thirty acres in one year represents the felling of approximately 3,000 trees, or twenty-five trees per month.[46] Levi Beardsley, a contemporary of Joseph Smith living in Otsego County, near Cooperstown, New York, reminisced: "A good chopper would cut his acre and pile the brush in seven or eight days ... but at the age of twenty-two years I could cut an acre in seven days, seven to ten days, particularly if several worked together."[47]

No doubt Alvin and Hyrum Smith were "good choppers," each capable of hewing down an acre of trees per week. Father Smith was getting a

41. William Strickland, *Journal of a Tour,* 139.
42. Alan Taylor, "The Great Change Begins," 278.
43. Ibid., 279.
44. Anderson, *Lucy's Book,* 319.
45. William Smith, *William Smith on Mormonism,* 11.
46. Donald L. Enders, "The Joseph Smith, Sr., Family," 219.
47. Beardsley, *Reminiscences,* 44.

little old for such strenuous labor. But he and fifteen-year-old Joseph ("large and strong," according to boyhood friend Orlando Saunders) probably could clear an acre per week together between them.[48] A conservative estimate is that the Smiths, working six days a week chopping three acres, could have cleared thirty acres in ten to twelve weeks or essentially one summer.

"Chopping is hard, but clean work," wrote Levi Beardsley. "A man going into the woods with his axe soon makes an opening, which being enlarged daily, serves to encourage and stimulate him to vigorous action."[49] The first step in clear cutting a forest is to trim out the brush and small trees and pile them in heaps, with dead, fallen tree limbs. Even the best timber of the largest trees was only an obstacle to be removed. There were no nearby sawmills. William Smith, recalling his boyhood years, said, that if a visitor came to the Smith farm during this period you would find Joseph and his brothers "rolling logs or carrying brush."[50] The work was hard, the hours long. Even during the dog days of summer, the family arose before sunrise, then worked until dark. "Being in indigent circumstances," Joseph later wrote, "[we] were obliged to labour hard for the support of [our] large Family having nine children and ... it required the exertions of all that were able to render any assistance for the support of the Family."[51]

Skilled woodsmen using the "driver tree" method would chop half-way through the same side of a line of trees. The axeman then felled the rearmost tree, which crashed into the next one, forcing it down in a domino effect that brought down the whole row. Once the toppled trees were cut into manageable lengths of fourteen-to-sixteen feet by the Smith men, the logs were rolled together into the brush pile.

At this point, tradition usually mandated a "logging bee," as much a social event as a work project. The neighboring farmers would arrive on the specified day with their ox teams. Three men and a yoke of oxen could log an acre per day. The heaps of logs and brush, with commingled branches and limbs, were allowed to dry for several months, then torched. William Smith remembered that their land clearance was "mostly done in the form [of] fire."[52] The fires were immense. Levi Beardsley recalled this labor, unlike the chopping, as

48. Orlando Saunders, interview qtd. in Frederick G. Mather, "The Early Days of Mormonism," 198.

49. Beardsley, *Reminiscences*, 44.

50. Smith, "The Old Soldier's Testimony," 644.

51. Dean C. Jessee, *The Personal Writings of Joseph Smith*, 4.

52. Smith, "Notes Written on 'Chambers' Life of Joseph Smith,'" 34.

"dirty, smoky, disagreeable work."[53] Tourist Uriah Edward, visiting friends in New York, noticed many with smudged faces and soot-covered clothes. Asking about their welfare, Edward was greeted with: "I am well but I am Black."[54] Another contemporary account commented that "the traveler among the settlements in those spring days found the woods darkened by smoke, and the fires by night conveyed a strong impression of a camp. The men, rude in dress, blackened with the handling of charred timber, and perspiring at their labor, would deceive a novice as to their character and ability, and it was hard to realize that these men so engaged were well calculated to lead in council, preside at assembly, and conduct with credit business of moment."[55]

In typical farms of western New York, the log home, barnyards, hay meadows, orchards, and cultivated fields seldom required more than fifty acres. Of the remaining land, less than half was pasture, the rest woods. As the Smiths cleared their eventual sixty acres, they gathered up the rock from the area and built stone walls to keep deer and livestock out of the fields. Rocks remained in the meadows and pastures, which were enclosed with split-rail fences that could be easily taken down and relocated. These portable zig-zag barriers were made of stacked rails, braced at their junctures by stakes. Each section of rail was about fourteen feet long and stood five or six feet high.

Coin and currency were scarce in early New York. Most exchanges were made by bartering. Pomeroy Tucker recalled that the Smiths' chief industry while living on the farm lot was retailing cord wood, which they exchanged "in the village for tobacco, whiskey, or other notions of trade."[56] He also listed, among the Smiths' economic activities, the "raising and bartering of small crops of agricultural products and garden vegetables, the manufacture and sale of black-ash baskets and birch brooms, the making of maple sugar and molasses in the season for that work, and in the continued business of peddling cake and beer in the village on days of public doings."[57]

About the only farm product in the early 1820s that constituted a cash crop was ashes, which seemed a godsend to early settlers with timberlands. In the words of one 1883 New York pioneer autobiography, "*ashes* were silver and gold to the young or poor farmer."[58] An acre of New York hardwood

53. Beardsley, *Reminiscences,* 44.
54. Uriah Edward, qtd. in Ross McGuire and Nancy Grey Osterud, *Working Lives,* 16.
55. W. H. McIntosh, *History of Ontario Co.,* 29.
56. Tucker, "The Mormon Imposture."
57. Tucker, *Origin, Rise, and Progress of Mormonism,* 13.
58. Harriet A. Weed, *Autobiography of Thurlow Weed,* 1:11; emphasis his.

yielded 60 to 100 bushels of ash.[59] In some cases, the sale of ash could pay for clearing the land. Joseph and his brothers would rake together the burning fragments in their bonfires until the wood was entirely consumed, leaving mounds of ashes rich in potassium salts. The cooled debris was scooped into baskets and carted into Palmyra, where merchants paid as much as twelve cents per bushel, half in cash and the remainder in trade goods. Some farmers, apparently including the Smiths, boosted profits by leaching their ashes, drenching them with water, then boiling the lye residue in large kettles, creating what New Yorkers called "black salts," potash darkened by carbon residue. Asheries bought the salts for as much as $3.00 per hundred weight. In the ashery's brick kiln, the black salts were burned at a high temperature to reduce the impurities. The result was a white residue called pearl ash. Potash and pearl ash, important trade items between America and Europe, were used in dyeing cloth and in the manufacture of glass, soap, and saltpeter. "Nothing else the family produced yielded such a good price and ready credit," noted one study.[60] The proceeds of their ashes or black salts likely sustained the Smiths until their first crops came in.

New clear-cut lands were rich in vegetable mold. Farmers with any thrift raised enough vegetables for their own consumption in a large kitchen garden near the house where the women could readily tend it. Potatoes, peas, cabbages, carrots, beets, turnips, parsnips, onions, beans, and pumpkins grew well in the area. Indian corn (maize) and cucumbers were considered indispensable at the table. "Americans of all classes eat as much maize as their Indian predecessors," wrote Joseph's contemporary, Susan Fenimore Cooper, "and as for cucumbers, they are required at every meal of which a thorough going Yankee partakes, either as salad in summer, or pickled in winter. We sometimes see men about the villages eating them unseasoned like apples."[61]

Many families like the Smiths positioned near their back door what they called a samp mortar, an implement developed by the Iroquois. A hard log with the end cut off square was set on end and hollowed out. Dried corn was dumped into the hollow mortar and pounded, until pulverized, by a pestle. "I have had many a good supper of samp [corn mush] and milk, made in this way," wrote Joseph's contemporary Levi Beardsley.[62]

Mush was a common breakfast dish of the area. Most families ate

59. Taylor, "The Great Change Begins," 280.
60. Ibid.
61. Cooper, *Rural Hours,* 78.
62. Beardsley, *Reminiscences,* 58.

buckwheat cakes with maple syrup for breakfast every winter day, since it was the only way to use their buckwheat flour. Aside from eating roasted corn, the Smiths would have enjoyed a variety of cornmeal dishes including sampaen, or hasty pudding; griddle cakes, made with eggs and milk; hoe-cake, or Indian bread; hominy, corn coarsely broken and boiled; or johnnycake, thin, wafer-like sheets, toasted, and eaten with butter. New corn, mixed with beans, formed the common Indian dish of succotash. There were also Indian puddings and dumplings. Stephen Harding recalled a supper in the Smith home of "brown bread, milk, and abundance of fine raspberries," but that Mother Smith apologized for serving "ryn' Injun" instead of "table flour bread."[63]

Cattle, pigs, and sheep were the principal livestock on the Smith farm. The family probably had two or three dairy cows from which they obtained milk, cheese, and butter. The herd was allowed to graze on the mowing fields along Crooked Creek until June. During summer, the Smith boys turned their cows into the wood lots to browse. In late autumn, Joseph and his younger brothers herded the animals into the barnyard, where they were kept until spring. Hogs, which required less care than cattle, were common on every farm. Sheep supplied the women with wool. Only when the flock was sufficient for this need did families butcher any sheep to provide mutton. Chicken and geese were also a familiar sight on the Smith farm. But struggling settlers like the Smiths rarely ate poultry. Hens were kept for eggs, geese for feathers. Nearly a hundred fragments of eggshells were unearthed during the archaeological dig at the Smiths' log house. The evidence of bones also indicated that the family ate beef, pork, rabbit, deer or elk, grouse, and duck or goose.[64]

Wheat was an important crop in the Palmyra area at this time, raised mostly for personal consumption. In the earliest years of the Smiths' grain operations, there was little domestic market for wheat because of the high transport costs. Prior to the opening of the Erie Canal, grain was hauled to Albany and goods brought back in the same wagon. The cost of transportation being deducted from the market price left little for the grower. When the canal became fully operational, the price of shipping grain from Buffalo to New York City dropped from $100 per ton to $5.00. It was such a difficult commodity to sell that merchants frequently stipulated they be paid in any grain except wheat. So the Smiths also grew barley, oats, rye, and

63. Stephen Harding, qtd. in Gregg, *The Prophet of Palmyra,* 42.

64. Dale L. Berge, *Archaeology at the Boyhood Home of Joseph Smith, Jr., Palmyra, New York,* 56.

buckwheat. The family was not known to own a plow. Nor could one have been used on the burned-over crop lands for several years because of the profusion of charred stumps.[65] Young Joseph likely helped his brothers harrow between the stumps, sow the grain by hand, then harrow a second time for good measure. The average yield of a new grain field during this period was twenty-five bushels an acre.[66]

The Smiths' lives, like the lives of farmers everywhere, were governed by the natural calendar of the seasons and the incessant clock of the sun. They usually rose at dawn and went to bed at dark. Chores could be done after nightfall only if they were worth the burning of the laboriously hand-manufactured candles. Young Joseph's spring farm calendar began with the late February/early March thaw when sugar maple buds began to swell and sap began to flow in the family's stand of 1,200 to 1,500 trees. It was a time of exhilaration. "The sugar-making session was always hailed with rapture by the boys," remembered one New Yorker. "No one, brought up in a new country, but can realize how exciting it was, and how eager and industrious the boys were to commence tapping the trees."[67] "The persons at work there," added Susan Fenimore Cooper, "usually eat and sleep on the spot until their task is done; and it is a favorite rallying place with the children and young people of the farms, who enjoy vastly this touch of camp life, to say nothing of the new sugar."[68]

A typical sap run lasts only three or four weeks. In Joseph's generation, sugar-bush (or camp) duty was a labor-intensive process. Brother William recalled, "To gather the sap and make sugar and molasses from [1,200-1,500 sugar] trees was no lazy job."[69] The mature sugar maples, at least twenty years old, were ten to twelve inches in diameter. A notch was first cut in each tree, one to three feet above the ground. A sharp instrument called a tapping gouge was then driven into the trunk below the notch, then removed and replaced with a small hollow spout or spile, made of an alder or sumac twig, sharpened at one end. This process let sap drip down into troughs of basswood or linden or oaken buckets, which the Smiths could have also made.

65. After five or six years, the stumps would rot sufficiently for settlers to plow about them. John Harriott, a traveler in upstate New York, saw "ploughs, always drawn by oxen, making their sturdy way amongst the stumps like a ship navigating through coral reefs, a difficult and tiresome operation. After about ten years, farmers could begin to pull the rotting stumps up and away with oxen and chains" (qtd. in Taylor, "The Great Change Begins," 284).

66. McIntosh, *History of Ontario County,* 29.

67. Beardsley, *Reminiscences,* 63.

68. Susan Cooper, *Rural Hours,* 14.

69. J. W. Peterson, "Another Testimony," 11.

The collection buckets or troughs were emptied into larger buckets, carried by yoke to the sugar camp centralized in the woods. The sap was poured into large kettles hung from pole tripods and boiled down day and night until it "aproned" from the ladle or "threaded" from the stirring stick. The thickened syrup was then poured into jugs or the sugar into wooden cake molds, depending upon the consistency. From two to five pounds of maple sugar could be made from each tree. The process required four or five gallons of sap to make a pound of sugar.[70]

While many people could make maple syrup, much skill was required to make high-quality sugar. Lucy wrote that the family produced an average of 1,000 pounds of sugar per year during their residency in Farmington/Manchester.[71] Neighbor Lorenzo Saunders remembered that the Smiths "were great sugar makers; they had a large bush and sugared off every day at their house." He added that the family "made seven thousand lbs. one year and took the bounty in the County—of $50.00."[72]

"Many a farmer's son has found his best opportunity for mental improvement in his intervals of leisure while tending sap-bush," wrote Thurlow Weed (1797-1882), a prominent Joseph Smith contemporary who also grew up in western New York's woodlands, and who later achieved fame as a newspaperman in Rochester, New York. "At night you had only to feed the kettles and keep up your fires, the sap having been gathered and the wood cut before dark."[73] It was a period of rewarding introspection for Weed, who tended sugar bush fires throughout his youth. Contemporary Henry Clark Wright (1797-1870), who grew up near Cooperstown, New York, and later became a fiery minister and follower of prominent abolitionist William Lloyd Garrison, found maple sugaring a quasi-religious experience: "In the sugar camp, or 'sugar bush,' I used, as a child, to enjoy this feeling of deep solitude, of stern desolation, and proud independence, which comes over the mind when surrounded by a thick and extensive forest." In the midst of the woods deep in the sugar bush, Wright added, he "was a child—my thoughts and feelings were those of a child; but then and there I received impressions of God, and of my self, and my destiny, more cheerful, more purifying,

70. Chris Granstrom, "Sweet Taste of Spring," 22; Goddard Space Flight Center, "Science Question of the Week"; J. M. Hirsch, "Tapping into a Sweet Success Story," B2.

71. Anderson, *Lucy's Book,* 322.

72. Lorenzo Saunders, interviewed by William H. Kelley, Sept. 17, 1884. Experts have determined that for each 1,000 pounds of maple sugar produced, one would need 5,000 gallons of sap and 32,000 cubic feet of firewood to boil it down ("Making 1,000 Pounds of Maple Sugar").

73. Weed, *Autobiography,* 1:16.

ennobling, and life-like, than I ever received in a meeting-house, or theological seminary, or from catechisms or ministers."[74] Perhaps the sugar-bush experience of young Joseph Smith paralleled those of Weed and Wright.

In addition to maple sugaring, the Smiths continued fencing the perimeter of their farm, a distance of nearly two miles. To fence this distance with a standard ummortared stone fence, determined Donald L. Enders of the LDS Church's Historic Sites, "required moving tons of stone from fields to farm perimeter, then cutting and placing about 4,000 ten-foot rails." This estimate did not include the labor and materials "involved in fencing the barnyard, garden, pastures, and orchard, which, at a conservative estimate, required an additional 2,000 to 3,000 cut wooden rails."[75]

In April or May on the Smith farm, sowing began. Hanging a seed sack about their necks, the men and boys walked slowly among the blackened stumps, broadcasting the rye, flax, barley, wheat, and peas by hand with long, sweeping motions. Potatoes were planted in late April or May, at the same time that Lucy and her daughters planted the family vegetable garden. Once the danger of frost ended in May, the Smiths planted corn, the importance of which stood next to wheat and hay. Near the end of May, the corn required its first hoeing, much of it likely done by Joseph and Harrison. Neighbors also recall that young Joseph spent some time trapping chipmunks and ground squirrels on the property to prevent damage to the sprouting corn. Levi Beardsley noted that "we had to trap and shoot the striped squirrels [chipmunks] to protect the corn, as those little animals have an inveterate desire to dig it up, to obtain the grain at the root."[76] In swampy areas, young Joseph and others trapped small game, mostly muskrats (which they called "mushrats"), and bartered their pelts in town. Joseph and his brothers also gathered cattails, which were used as gasket materials for barrels made in the family cooper shop.

Summertime for the Smiths afforded virtually no leisure. The first hay mowing began in mid-July. They scythed by hand, raked it into rows to dry, heaped it, then carted it to stacks in the barnyard. If it rained at any time during this process, the hay had to be shaken out by hand, spread out to dry, then collected again. Flax was also pulled in late July and stored until September, when it would be spread to rot so that its fibers could be used for linen making.

74. Henry Clarke Wright, *Human Life,* 108.

75. Enders, "The Joseph Smith, Sr., Family," 219.

76. Beardsley, *Reminiscences,* 45.

Late July or early August saw the harvest of rye, barley, wheat, and oats. Again, it was all hand-labor. They cut the grain with a sickle, then bundled it into shocks which stood upright until dry. Haying was second-cropped in late August. By mid-September, both the haying and the grain-reaping were completed, and the farmer began to prepare for fall planting. After broadcasting the winter wheat and rye, they would harrow it in, then harvest the ears of corn from the stalks, by now dead and dry. "The farmers are busy with their later autumn tasks, closing the work of the present year," wrote Susan Fenimore Cooper, "while, at the same time, they are already looking forward to another summer. There is something pleasing in these mingled labors beneath the waning sun of November. It is autumn grown old, and lingering in the field with a kindly smile, while they are making ready for the young spring to come."[77]

When the family had their harvest safely under cover in the barn, the slow process of thrashing and husking began, a process which would continue throughout the winter as time permitted. The butchering of the winter's meat was usually accomplished in November or early December to coincide with the sharp frosts. The women's soap- and candle-making were also timed for the same season, since both tasks used rendered animal tallow. The Smith women would have spent their late summer and early autumn preserving and storing enough food to last until the following summer. They pickled vegetables in large crocks, and dried peas and beans for soup. They dug up potatoes, onions, turnips, parsnips, and carrots from the garden, storing them in a root cellar that archeologists have since determined was under the floor of their log home.

When the first serious snows of winter fell in late November or early December, the demands on the Smiths' time changed but did not lessen. The livestock could no longer be pastured once the snow was too deep or too hard to paw through, but had to be housed and tended in the barn. Snow permitted the use of sleds for heavy hauling, so Joseph Sr. and his boys began their major winter work, cutting and hauling wood. Firewood required a year's seasoning, so the family's entire supply for the following year had to be gathered. Seventy loads probably comprised the annual minimum required for a family like the Smiths, who used an open fireplace for both heating and cooking. Joseph and brother Harrison seem to be the likely candidates for maintaining the firewood required indoors. Every evening, the boys would

77. Susan Cooper, *Rural Hours,* 230.

pull a hand sled to the wood pile and roll onto it a four-foot-long back log, one-and-a-half-to-two feet in diameter. They would open the kitchen door, then drag the loaded sled across the floor to the fireplace, off-load, then bring in two or three more loads of split wood and kindling. They would probably do this before supper, since it would be difficult to work in the darkness that would fall while they ate.

After supper, Joseph Sr. would rake forward the coals and ashes from the back of the fireplace, roll in the back log, then bank up the front with ashes. The split wood and kindling would be piled atop and the fire would soon burst into lavish flame. After supper, things were put away, and the family would gather around the fire for the evening devotional and socialization.

"A fine, open, wood fire is undeniably the pleasantest mode of heating a room," wrote Susan Fenimore Cooper.

> The very sight of a bright hickory or maple fire is almost enough to warm one; and what so cheerful as the glowing coals, the brilliant flame, and the star-like sparks which enliven the household hearth of a bracing winter's evening as twilight draws on! Such a fire helps to light as well as heat a room; the warm glow it throws upon the walls, the flickering lights and shadows which play there as the dancing flames rise and fall, express the very spirit of cheerful comfort. The crackling, and rattling, and singing, as the flame does its cheerful work, are pleasant household sounds.[78]

Lucy would have needed a brisk but steady fire for cooking. Pots and kettles hung suspended from a metal crane on hooks and trammels, swinging forward to the hearth to be stirred and to have ingredients added, then swung backward to center over the hot coals. From childhood, the Smith girls learned caution as they leaned over their cooking so keep their skirts away from the fire that could set the cloth alight. Potatoes roasted in the embers on the hearth. Bread, biscuits, and short cake were either baked in tins facing the fire, or in a Dutch oven, with hot coals under the kettle and on top.

Apparently during the first year they moved onto their farm, the Smiths built a threshing barn and nearby a cooper shop. A barn was essential to the success of any farmer, and their structure was the board-and-batten barn common to the area. The battens, or exterior planking nailed over the vertical boards on the sides, kept out gusts of wind. Inside, the space was crowded with livestock, equipment, and crops. On the wooden floor of the central bay, they threshed wheat, barley, rye, buckwheat, and oats. In a loft overhead,

78. Ibid., 269.

on poles and scrap lumber that provided a flooring across the barn's interior beams, was sheltered storage for the bound sheaves of various grains awaiting threshing. Only a small amount of hay was likely stored inside, with the main haystack outside, well-mounded to shed rain and snow.

A side bay in the barn would have provided storage for the freshly harvested shocks of grain. Another probably housed grain bins. Hanging from nails and pegs on the end walls would have been the scythes, sickles, adzes, rakes, shovels, axes, mallets, and other hand tools. Beneath these on the floor no doubt stood assorted wooden barrels, tubs, and crates. The larger pieces of farm equipment, which conceivably included a two-wheeled ox cart and sledges and sleds used for hauling during the winter, leaned against the barn's exterior, exposed to the elements.

The Smith family, like others in the area, grew flax to provide raw materials for making linen, linsey-woolsey, and linseed oil. But processing flax was labor-intensive compared to wool, which therefore remained the major fiber for the family's clothing. Most households had spinning wheels to process both materials into thread and yarn; not all also had looms to weave the thread into cloth, but those who did frequently contracted or traded their services to neighbors. The Smiths' clothing was mostly homespun and homemade by Lucy and her daughters. Great-granddaughter Mary Salisbury Hancock passed on the family tradition that Lucy "saw that there was no frivolity" in the lives of her three daughters: Sophronia, Katharine, and Lucy. The girls, who had inherited the "severely chiseled Smith features," did not lead the "easy, flirtatious way of life fashionable among the young people in some parts of the United States," said Katharine's granddaughter.[79] From March through July, the principal labor of the Smith women was hackling, carding, and spinning flax fiber taken from the plant's rotted stems. From July to January, the women were daily employed in spinning and weaving, frequently carding by hand, and dying the wool or linen with butternut bark. The evenings were spent sewing and mending clothes by the light of a candle or fire. They used pieces of fabric from worn-out clothing to mend damaged clothing, pieced together the tiniest scraps of discarded clothing for patchwork quilts, and braided cloth too worn for quilts into rag rugs.

The crops and livestock grown by farm families provided most of their food and clothing but could not be relied upon as sources of cash income. To produce the earnings needed for store-bought items, most farmers like

79. Mary Salisbury Hancock, "The Three Sisters," pt. 1, 34.

Joseph Sr. had one or more secondary occupations. These nonfarming ventures occupied his time when the weather did not permit farm work and during seasonal lulls in the farm routine. As already noted, coopering was Father Smith's secondary livelihood, and most of the boys learned rudimentary coopering skills. Coopers were skilled at crafting barrels, casks, kegs, funnels, churns, tubs, and buckets from wood and repairing them when needed. Craftsmen like Smith used adzes, jointers, draw knives, and shaving benches to shape long chunks of wood into staves. The staves were held together with a windlass or truss hoops to form barrel sides while iron or wooden hoops were driven into place. Crozes and howels cut channels for lids and the rims were shaped with chamfer knives. The Smiths found a ready market for their wares, particularly in the local maple sugar and apple cider industries.

Despite the heavy labor required during these six or seven years to pull a farm out of the forest, life was not all work for Joseph Jr. The family was close knit. According to Mary Salisbury Hancock, who must have heard the stories from Grandmother Katharine, the Smiths "usually spent their evenings together around the great fireplace, the mother and daughters knitting or sewing while Father Smith read from the Bible, explaining or extolling its passages until the children became quite proficient in their knowledge of its teachings. In this home atmosphere the girls and boys grew and formed their ideals of life."[80]

Young Joseph also loved trapping and fishing. Stephen Harding remembered seeing the "long-legged, tow-headed" Joseph, in his early teens, "generally fishing in the mill-pond at Durfee's grist-mill, on Mud Creek, when my elder brother and I went to mill."[81] Other amusements included neighborhood corn huskings, log rollings, house-raising bees, annual harvest fairs, and public holidays flavored with races, contests, and feats of strength. Joseph Sr. and his boys were a rough, hardy lot. They enjoyed the wrestling, stick pulling, running, jumping, and hopping contests which excited rugged men of their day. Joseph's limp may have prevented him from being a strong competitor in races; but wrestling and stick pulling were favorite sports, passions which survived into adulthood. At nearly every public gathering in the Palmyra/Manchester area, individual wrestling and stick pulling contests usually commenced with young lads like Joseph pairing off, while the men

80. Ibid.

81. Stephen Harding, qtd. in Gregg, *The Prophet of Palmyra,* 36. Harding and his family moved from Palmyra in 1820 (Stephen S. Harding to Pomeroy Tucker, June 1, 1867, in ibid., 34).

looked on. Losers would bring in a willing contender to face the victor. The matches would advance through the bigger and stronger men until one man was left standing.

While Joseph was busy swinging the axe or plying the hoe, his mind no doubt sometimes drifted elsewhere. The country was new and handsome. The farmstead abounded with marvels. The woods and wayside fluttered with goldfinches, wrens, song-sparrows, and bluebirds. Wild flowers grew in abundance in sun-drenched openings among the trees. Larkspur, honeysuckle, foxglove, night-shade, buttercups, cowslips, bachelor's buttons, snowdrops, traveler's joy, spicy gilliflowers, daffadowndillies, shepherd's purse, and pennyroyal were vivid blooms of the day. Autumn on the Smith farmstead would have been particularly spectacular. Susan Fenimore Cooper painted a word image of the scene young Joseph would have enjoyed:

> How rapid are the changes in the foliage at this season! One can almost see the colors growing brighter. The yellows are more decided, the scarlet and crimson spreading farther, with a pink flush rising on many trees where yellow prevails, especially among the maples. Still there is a clear vein of green perceptible; not the verdure of the pine and hemlock, but the lighter greens of the aspens and beeches, with some oaks and chestnuts not yet touched. Indeed, the woods are very beautiful today; the general effect is charming, while here and there we note a scarlet maple, a golden birch, so brilliantly vivid that we are really amazed of the richness and beauty of their coloring.[82]

In many ways, Joseph's life on the farm between ages thirteen and twenty, despite the poverty, was idyllic. "The experience of a young man who commences life in a wild, new country," wrote Thurlow Weed, "shows how very little of the world's wealth is necessary to secure happiness."[83] Joseph and his family, for the most part, were likely content on their farm. "We began to rejoice in our prosperity and our hearts glowed with gratitude to God for the manifestations of his favor," remembered Lucy of this period.

As late as 1830, at least six families in the Smith neighborhood still lived in log homes.[84] But the ambition of nearly all settlers was a framed house. "Ladies of piety and culture never visited Mrs. Smith in her home in a sequestered neighborhood," wrote minister's wife Anna Ruth Eaton, they

82. Cooper, *Rural Hours,* 196.
83. Weed, *Autobiography,* 3.
84. Thomas L. Cook, *Palmyra and Vicinity,* 24-56.

"never sat down by her side, and in an unpatronizing manner, sympathized with her in her many cares and labors."[85] This was not entirely true. Lucy, on at least one occasion, accepted an invitation to "take tea" with "some wealthy merchants wives and the minister's lady." After exchanging polite pleasantries, one woman reportedly commented: "Well I declare Mrs. [Smith] Ought not to live in that log house of her's any longer she deserves a better fate and I say she must have a new house." "So she should," added another, "for she is so kind to every one[.] She ou[gh]t to have the best of every thing." But Lucy, though accepting of the compliments, took umbrage at the ladies' judgments. "I am the wealthiest woman that sits at this table," she said. "How so?" one of the women asked. "I have never prayed for riches [of the world] as perhaps you have," she began,

> but I have always desired that God would enable me to use enough wisdom and forbearance in my family to set good precepts & examples before my children[,] whose lives I always besaught to spare[,] as also to secure the confidence and affection of my husband that we acting tog[e]ther in the education and instruction of our children that we might in our old age reap the reward of circumspection joined with parental tenderness viz the Pleasure of seeing our children dign[i]fy their Fathers name by an upright and honorable course of conduct in after life I have been gratified so far in all this and more[.] I have tis true suffered many disagre[e]able disap[p]ointments in life with regard to property but I now find myself very comfortably situated[.][86]

Only when sufficient woodlands were cleared, fields fenced, and livestock sheltered could the Smiths contemplate constructing a larger frame residence. Such an undertaking required years of effort, since the demands of livestock and crops frequently interrupted each day's labors. Building permanent homes also demanded a substantial investment for milled lumber and other building supplies. But completion of a substantial home marked the end of the frontier stage of farming and was seen as a necessary step toward a better lifestyle. It would be 1823 when the Smith family, under Alvin's management, was able finally to turn their efforts toward this quintessentially American aspiration.

---

85. Anna Ruth Eaton, *The Origin of Mormonism,* 3.
86. Anderson, *Lucy's Book,* 322.

6 | MONEY DIGGING

I know more about money digging, than any man in this generation, for I have been in the business more than thirty years.

—Joseph Smith Sr., qtd. in James Colin Brewster, *Very Important!*, 1

In 1819, U.S. senators and representatives gathered in Washington, D.C., for a new session of Congress. For five years, they had been unable to meet in the Capitol because the British had burned it during the War of 1812. Now a rebuilt Capitol stood ready for occupancy. Thick red curtains hung in the Hall of Representatives. Red silk draped above the Speaker's desk. As the session began, it became clear that the mood of the Congress was also new. The Era of Good Feelings was ending. Tensions were growing that would set the country's course for years to come. The financial panic of 1819, which fell most heavily on the poorer classes, the so-called "one-suspender men" like Joseph Smith Sr., should have dimmed the political star of President James Monroe. But the politician was so popular and the Federalist opposition so weak that Monroe received every electoral vote but one in the election of 1820. The Federalist Party was all but dead, leaving the field to the Republicans. This and other news filtered into the Smith family home through the local Palmyra newspapers.[1] Newspaperman Orsamus Turner remembered that, once a week, young Joseph "would stroll into the office of the old Palmyra Register, for his father's paper."[2] It may be difficult today to imagine with "what avidity the little weekly messenger was sought after, and how thoroughly it was read among the neighbours," wrote one of Joseph's New York contemporaries.[3]

1. Local papers available to the Smiths from 1816 to 1830 included the *Palmyra Register* (1817-21), *Western Farmer and Canal Advocate* (1821-22), *Palmyra Herald and Canal Advertiser* (1822-23), *Wayne Sentinel* (1823-63), *[Palmyra] Reflector* (1828-31), *Palmyra Freeman* (1828-29), and *Western Spectator & Public Advertiser* (1830-31). See "New York State Newspaper Project," and "History of the Newspapers of Palmyra Briefly Told."

2. Orsamus Turner, *History of the Pioneer Settlement*, 214.

3. Levi Beardsley, *Reminiscences*, 67.

In mid-1822, a Palmyra newspaper reprinted a feature from Vermont's *Montpelier Watchman* bearing the eye-catching headline, "Money Diggers."[4] Vermont acquaintances of the Smiths affirm that Father Smith hunted for buried treasure in the Granite State.[5] And he must have been intrigued by the report of diggings near the family's former home in the White River Valley. "Each country has its money-diggers," the news story began,

> who are full in the belief that vast treasures lie concealed in the earth. So far from being a new project, it dates its origin with the first man who ever wielded a spade. 'Tis as old as Adam. Even in these latter days, we find men so much in love with the "root of all evil," and so firm in the belief that it may be dug up, that they will traverse hill and dale, climb the loftiest mountain, and even work their way into the bowels of the earth in search of it. Indeed, digging for money hid in the earth, is a very common thing; and in this state it is even considered an honorable and profitable employment.[6]

From the early years of European history, many country folk assumed that the land abounded with treasure caches where people had buried their valuables for safekeeping. To this day, Roman coins are still being unearthed in rural England. In New England, buried treasure is most often linked to Spanish legends, plundering pirates, or burial mounds of American Indians, often filled with mortuary goods. Some early Americans became grave robbers, removing valuable articles from Indian graves.[7] Nineteenth-century archaeologist Ephraim G. Squier lamented in 1851 that most of the burial mounds in western New York "have been excavated, under the impulse of an idle curiosity, or have had their contents scattered by 'money diggers.'"[8]

Treasure seekers in New England, for more than two-and-a-half centuries, have been enthralled by the possibility of finding buried booty from an October 4, 1759, raid on a Jesuit mission at the Abenaki village of St. Francis near present-day Pierreville, Quebec. Eight rangers from an elite force of American frontiersmen attached to the British army during the French and Indian War disappeared with stolen treasure including a ten-pound silver

4. "Money Digging," *Palmyra Herald and Canal Advertiser,* July 24, 1822.

5. See the four documents in the section titled "Mormon Origins in Vermont and New Hampshire," in Dan Vogel, *Early Mormon Documents,* 1:595-628.

6. "Money Digging," *Palmyra Herald and Canal Advertiser,* July 24, 1822.

7. James Adair, *The History of the American Indians,* 178; Thaddeus Mason Harris, *The Journal of a Tour,* 165.

8. Ephraim G. Squier, *Antiquities of the State of New York,* 97.

statue of the Virgin Mary and baby Jesus, a ruby ring "as big as your eye," a stash of coins, a gold calf, and other priceless religious artifacts.[9]

In addition to the possibility of finding buried goods, some New Englanders visualized an additional prospect in this transcendental land of milk and honey: riches that were metaphysical, invisible to the natural eye. Most traditional accounts allege that magic and occultism were curtailed in the eighteenth century. Historian Jon Butler summarizes this view of inevitable "progress": "The rise of Enlightenment philosophy, skepticism, and evangelical Christianity, the continuing opposition from English Protestant denominations, the rise in literacy associated with Christian catechizing, and the cultural, economic, and political maturation of the colonies simply destroyed the occult practice and belief of the previous century in both Europe and America." Given these forces, the assumption goes, the arcane practices of village wise men and women essentially dissolved before the secularism of scientific progress. But, continues Butler, significant evidence demonstrates that, in both Old England and New England, "colonial magic and occultism did not so much disappear everywhere as they disappeared among certain social classes and became confined to poorer, more marginal segments of early American society."[10]

In a society where "individual expectation often outran contemporary economic prosperity," Butler adds, "it is not surprising that seekers attributed other treasures to divine action, part of the supernatural's influence on the world."[11] These arcane hoards, folk tales asserted, could only be obtained by following special occult formulae of the magic world. "Divination and spirit-raising to locate buried treasure and to compel its surrender by supernatural guardians," writes W. R. Jones, "has a history extending from antiquity to the modern age and from Europe to the Americas."[12] George Kittridge's study of occult activities in Britain and early New England notes that "spells and incantations ... are needful in the quest for buried riches. Indeed, they are doubly necessary: first to call up a spirit who shall disclose the right spot; and second, to control the demon who keeps the hoard."[13]

Divination, a form of folk magic used in attempts to foretell the future or to discover hidden knowledge, has long manifested itself in hundreds

9. Wilson Ring, "Mystery Treasure Still Tempting N.H. Searchers," A14.
10. Jon Butler, *Awash in a Sea of Faith,* 83.
11. Ibid., 231. Also see Alan Taylor, "The Early Republic's Supernatural Economy."
12. W. R. Jones, "'Hill-Diggers' and 'Hell-Raisers,'" 97.
13. George Lyman Kittridge, *Witchcraft in Old and New England,* 205.

of assorted forms.[14] Anthropologists have concluded that divination is a universal phenomenon present in virtually every age and culture including the Egyptian, Chaldean, Hindu, Roman, Greek, and Mayan. Divination in Judeo-Christian culture, however, has traditionally been viewed as evil, being condemned in the Bible. As the Hebrews departed from Egypt—legendary font of occult wisdom—and reached Canaan, a region inhabited by superstitious tribes, they would have their natural taste for foreknowledge intensified by the environment. So God forbade his chosen ones to have anything to do with charmers, wizards, diviners, familiar spirits, and necromancers—an "abomination in His sight" (Deut. 18:10-12; Num. 23:23; Lev. 20:6, 27; Isa. 44:25). Despite these warnings, occult handbooks instructing readers in folk magic, including divination tactics for seeking buried treasure, have existed in nations dominated by Judeo-Christian traditions since the 1600s, if not earlier.

For more than four centuries, seekers after the riches of enchanted treasure have been guided by diviners, seers like the Smiths. In "Money Diggers," the 1822 article published first in the *Montpelier Watchman* and then in the *Palmyra Herald and Canal Advertiser,* searchers were advised that success depends "on the skillful use of the genuine mineral rod" in the diviner's hands. "Countless treasures yet remain hid in the earth," readers were promised, "speed the plough—ply the hoe—'twill all come to light."[15] Another article published in an early Palmyra newspaper describing money-digging activities asserted: "Men and women without distinction of age or sex became marvellous wise in the occult sciences, many dreamed, and others saw visions disclosing to them, deep in the bowels of the earth, rich and shining treasures, and to facilitate those mighty mining operations, (money was usually if not always sought after in the night time,) divers devices and implements were invented." The paper also commented that mineral rods and (crystal)

14. Some of these are *aalomancy:* divination by table salt; *anthropomancy:* divination by interpreting the organs of newly sacrificed humans; astrology: divination using celestial bodies—the sun, moon, planets, and stars; *cartomancy:* fortune telling using cards such as the Tarot; *chiromancy:* divination from the lines on people's hands; *lampadomancy:* interpreting the movements of the flame of a lamp; *omphalomancy:* interpretation of the belly button; *oneiromancy:* the interpretation of dreams; *onychomancy:* interpreting the reflection of sun rays off fingernails; *palmistry:* divination through interpretation of the lines and structure of the hand; *phrenology:* divination through study of head formations; *pyromancy:* divination by fire; and *uromancy:* divination by reading bubbles made by urinating in a pot. Robert Todd Carroll, "Divination (Fortune Telling)." See also "Types of Divination," BoxArt, "A Glossary of Divination"; and "Divination."

15. "Money Digging," *Palmyra Herald and Canal Advertiser,* July 24, 1822.

balls along with "peep stones" were "supposed to be infallible guides to these sources of wealth."[16]

Some early Americans saw money-digging as a potential source of wealth. "The settlers of Maine, like all the other settlers in New England," noted adventurer Edward Augustus Kendall, "indulge an unconquerable expectation of finding money buried in the earth." Kendall added that money-chests "have been dug for in all parts of the United States; and, as the history further goes, they have not unfrequently been found."[17] Mormon historian Ronald W. Walker has observed that in Vermont "the embrace of the cunning arts probably exceeded any other region."[18] The money-digging heart of the state was the fabled Green Mountains. Within this area, twenty-seven towns, representing 10 percent of Vermont municipalities, evidenced treasure-digging activities.[19] Vermont Judge Daniel Pierce Thompson, whose dramatic *May Martin, and Other Tales of the Green Mountains* was a popular work of the day, wrote that money-digging seers with the "faculty of discovering things hidden or unknown to them ... prevailed to some extent in many parts of this country."[20]

Joseph Smith Sr., who spent twenty-five years in this area of Vermont, was an occasional diviner. His daily life, wrote western historian Dale Morgan, was vividly colored "by that common heritage of his society, the tenuous but ineluctable realities of magic, witchcraft, and demonology the *Mayflower* and the *Arbella* had disgorged so long ago into the gray mists of Massachusetts shore. Good fortune or bad, as Joseph well understood, was not an affair of Providence only; man had to contend with the dark world of the supernatural, penetrable or governable only by the most potent of ritual and incantation."[21] A judge visiting Sharon and Royalton, Vermont, after the Smiths had moved to New York, heard the rumor that "Joseph Smith, Sr., was at times engaged in hunting for Captain Kidd's buried treasure."[22] By

16. "GOLD BIBLE NO. 3," *The Reflector* (Palmyra, NY), Feb. 1, 1831.

17. Edward Augustus Kendall, *Travels through the Northern Parts,* 3:84, 87-88.

18. Ronald W. Walker, "The Persisting Idea of American Treasure Hunting," 447.

19. Ibid.

20. Daniel Pierce Thompson, *May Martin,* 46-47.

21. Qtd. in John Phillip Walker, *Dale Morgan on Early Mormonism,* 220-21.

22. Daniel Woodward, "Birthplace and Early Residence of Joseph Smith, Jr.," 316. According to George Francis Dow and John Henry Edmonds, *The Pirates of the New England Coast 1630-1730,* iii, "There is scarcely a sandy beach on New England's long and deeply indented coastline that has not connected with it some traditionary tale of the landing of pirates or their buried treasure."

his own statement, Joseph Sr. became involved in the money-digging culture about the time young Joseph was born.[23]

Fayette Lapham, in an interview with Father Smith about the time the Book of Mormon was published (1830), noted that he "was a firm believer in witchcraft and other supernatural things; and had brought up his family in the same belief." Smith also reportedly told Lapham that he "believed that there was a vast amount of money buried somewhere in the country; that it would some day be found; that he himself had spent both time and money searching for it, with divining rods, but had not succeeded in finding any, though sure that he eventually would."[24]

Newspaperman James Gordon Bennett, after an 1831 excursion to western New York, wrote: "A few years ago the Smith's and others … caught an idea that money was hid in several of the hills which give variety to the country between the Canandaigua Lake and Palmyra on the Erie Canal. Old Smith had in his peddling excursions picked up many stories of men getting rich in New England by digging in certain places and stumbling upon chests of money. The fellow excited the imagination of his few auditors, and made them all anxious to lay hold of the bilk axe and the shovel."[25] Roswell Nichols, a neighbor of the Smiths in Manchester, claimed that Joseph Sr. informed him that "the ancients, half of them melted the ore and made the gold and silver, while the other half buried it deeper in the earth, which accounted for these hills."[26] Father Smith also allegedly told neighbor William Stafford that "nearly all the hills in this part of New York, were thrown up by human hands, and in them were large caves" filled with treasure.[27] Contrary to such notions, the hills surrounding Palmyra are not man-made burial mounds, like many in the Ohio and Mississippi Valleys, but rather drumlins, piles of glacial debris left behind when massive ice sheets had retreated thousands of years earlier.

Joseph Sr., like other transplanted New Englanders, grew up in the maritime districts of the republic hearing that "large sums of money and masses of bullion were there buried in the earth by the buccaneers, as well

23. Brewster, *Very Important!,* 1.

24. Fayette Lapham, "Interview with the Father of Joseph Smith, the Mormon Prophet, Forty Years Ago," 306.

25. James Gordon Bennett, "Mormonism—Religious Fanaticism—Church and State Party," Pt. 1.

26. Roswell Nichols, in Eber D. Howe, *Mormonism Unvailed,* 257-58.

27. William Stafford, in ibid., 237.

as, more recently, by persons concerned in the revolution."[28] B. H. Roberts, prominent early twentieth-century Mormon historian and president of the third-ranked body of LDS Church leaders, the Council of Seventy, agreed that the Smith family had some seemingly gullible traditions: "It may be admitted that some of them believed in fortune telling, in warlocks and witches. ... Indeed it is scarcely conceivable how one could live in New England in those years and not have shared in such beliefs. To be credulous in such things was to be normal people."[29]

An absorbing anecdote from Stephen Harding, later appointed Utah territorial governor by Abraham Lincoln, provides a window into the Smith family's beliefs. Invited to stay overnight with the family in Manchester in 1829, Harding, then a young lawyer, settled back in his chair after dinner to hear Oliver Cowdery, Joseph Jr.'s amanuensis, read portions of the newly completed Book of Mormon. "The reading had proceeded for some time," Harding remembered, "when the candle began to spit and splutter, sometimes almost going out, and flashing up with a red-blue blaze." The fact that the "blaze had been interrupted by the flax shives that remained in the tow wicking, would not do," Harding recalled. Instead Martin Harris, the prosperous farmer who had financed the first printing of the Book of Mormon, looked at Lucy Smith and commented, "Do you see that ... I know what that means; it is the Devil trying to put out the light, so that we can't read any more." "'Yes,' replied the old lady; 'I seed 'im! I seed 'im as he tried to put out the burnin' wick, when the blaze turned blue.'" Mother Smith then lit her clay pipe and puffed away as the conversation turned to dreams and their significance. "You'll have visions and dreams, mebby, to-night," she told Harding, "but don't get skeered; the angel of the Lord will protect you."[30] Skeptical, Harding later said that the experience "increased my desire to make further experiments in this wild fanaticism."[31]

Ronald Walker, in his study of American and Smith family treasure hunting, notes that "from colonial times to at least the Age of Jackson, Americans dug for magical treasure." Thousands of diggers sought "troves of fabled coins, mines, jewels, and other valued prizes." Despite the labor, however, riches "were as rare as Merlin's transmuted gold."[32] But this fact did not prevent

28. "Some Account of Joseph Smith and the Mormon Imposture."

29. *History of the Church,* 1:26-27.

30. Thomas Gregg, *The Prophet of Palmyra,* 42-43.

31. Ibid., 48.

32. Ronald W. Walker, "The Persisting Idea of American Treasure Hunting," 430.

many like the Smiths from seeking their fortunes in such projects. In the minds of many, money digging fused supernatural belief with American materialism. It seemed a perfectly acceptable way of life. The author of "Money Digging" claimed that he could name "at least five hundred respectable men, who do, in the simplicity and sincerity of their hearts, verily believe that immense treasures lie concealed in the Green Mountains, many of whom have been industriously and perseveringly engaged in digging it up."[33] But many sincere folk have believed in the powers of gnomes, fairies, sylphs, witches, ghosts, devils, goblins, enchantment, divining rods, and peep stones. Tales of such things, notes historian Jon Butler, "became the social foundation of the supernaturalist literature of Irving, Poe, Hawthorne, Melville, and James that typified American letters throughout the nineteenth century."[34]

Benjamin Franklin discounted money digging. "Great Numbers of honest Artificers and labouring People ... voluntarily endure abundance of Fatigue in a fruitless Search after Imaginary hidden Treasure," he complained in 1729. "They wander thro' the Woods and Bushes by Day, do discover the Marks and Signs; at Midnight they repair to the hopeful Spot with Spades and Pickaxes."[35] And a Lutheran minister in New York, Frederick Quitman, protested in his 1810 *Treatise on Magic* that occult belief was running wild in that state: The "government ou[gh]t to stop such fatal practices, whereby the lives of many are put in jeopardy."[36]

The January 17, 1825, *Windsor* [Vermont] *Journal* lamented, "We are sorry to observe even in this enlightened age, so prevalent a disposition to credit the accounts of the Marvellous. Even the frightful stories of money being hid under the surface of the earth, and enchanted by the Devil or Robert [sic] Kidd, are received by many of our respectable fellow citizens as truths."[37] Prominent New York newspaperman and politician Thurlow Weed, a contemporary of Joseph Smith, described an incident from his boyhood that was very similar to Joseph's money-digging experiences. "In those days," Weed wrote,

> there was a delusion among poor but credulous people about the buried treasure of Captain Kidd. I remember to have been as a boy permitted to

33. "Money Digging," *Palmyra Herald and Canal Advertiser,* July 24, 1822.

34. Butler, *Awash in a Sea of Faith,* 229.

35. Leonard W. Larabee, *Papers of Benjamin Franklin,* 1:136-37.

36. Frederick H. Quitman, *A Treatise on Magic,* 73.

37. "Money Digging," *Windsor Journal,* Jan. 17, 1825. This article, reprinted in the *Wayne Sentinel,* Feb. 16, 1825, related the ill-fated adventures of "[a] respectable gentleman in Tunbridge" who in a dream saw a chest of money buried on a small island in Agre's brook, in Randolph. One of the diggers broke silence, "the chest moved off through the mud, and has not been seen or heard of since."

> accompany a party on an expedition which was supposed to be pregnant with golden results. Upon reaching the mysterious locality, the throat of a black cat was cut, and the precise spot was indicated by the direction the blood spurted. And there the digging commenced with an energy worthy of Dousterswivel, in the "Antiquary," but it was not rewarded by even so much as the discovery of "Search No. 1."[38]

Susan Fenimore Cooper, eight years younger than Joseph Jr., decried a failed money-digging operation near her Cooperstown home. A singular tree growing tall and conspicuous nearby was thought to mark the treasure trove. A group of diggers from another valley came "with pick and spade and laid bare its roots, digging for buried treasure," killing the tree. "Who would have thought that this old crazy fancy of digging about remarkable trees for hidden treasure should still exist in this school-going, lecture-hearing, newspaper-reading, speech-making community?" asked Cooper. She explains the strength of this "crazy fancy": "They were digging for Captain Kidd's treasure" and "men will seek for gold everywhere, and in any way."[39]

As the wave of early nineteenth-century emigration from New England swept the Smith family and thousands of others into western New York, money-digging and occult tradition followed. Henry Clark Wright, who like Cooper and Joseph Jr. grew up in New York, wrote that the state abounded in superstitious beliefs: "Such a region was the fit place for supernatural agents to come and work their pleasure. ... [G]hosts appeared there, to reveal some appalling murder, some hidden treasure, or to give warning of some death or some approaching calamity."[40] "Such superstition was frequent in the new settlements," one of James Fenimore Cooper's characters in *The Pioneers* (1823) acknowledged.[41] The February 1, 1831, [Palmyra] *Reflector* labeled the New York treasure seeking a "*mania,*" and attested that "men and women without distinction of age or sex became marvellous[l]y wise in the occult sciences, many dreamed, and others saw visions disclosing to them, deep in the bowels of the earth, rich and shining treasures."[42]

While some treasure-seeking activities were merely prospecting, not

38. Harriet A. Weed, *Autobiography of Thurlow Weed,* 1:7. "Herman Douster-swivel" was a character in Sir Walter Scott's 1816 novel *The Antiquary* who, through trickery, tried to convince people he could find hidden treasure.

39. Cooper, *Rural Hours,* 232.

40. Henry Clarke Wright, *Recollections,* in Louis C. Jones, *Growing Up in the Cooper Country,* 111.

41. James Fenimore Cooper, *The Pioneers,* 415.

42. "GOLD BIBLE, NO. 4.," *The Reflector* [Palmyra, NY], Feb. 1, 1831.

fueled by divination or other occult practices, most money diggers sought their troves through the magic lore of dreams, conjured spirits, blessed amulets, divining rods, and seer stones. Some diggers were thought by their peers to be endowed with "the spirit of truth, prophecy, or the power of speaking in tongues."[43] Many Palmyra area friends, neighbors, and acquaintances of the Smiths testified that Joseph Sr. was a rodsman who conveyed divining lore to his sons Alvin, Hyrum, and young Joseph. Father Smith acquired his divination techniques through a long history of oral and written traditions imported from Europe into New England culture.

Use of the divining or mineral rod to locate water or find buried or hidden objects had spread to all regions of America by 1800. "As with astrology," comments Butler, "its theoretical and theological underpinnings could be exceptionally elusive. Its effectiveness was variously attributed to 'natural' sympathies between water and the metal or wooden rod, secret properties of the rod, secret knowledge possessed by the practitioner, or ritual magic utilized by the practitioners."[44] While certainly a colorful chapter in the history of folklore, dowsing is not based upon any known scientific or empirically verifiable forces of nature. An official 1938 publication of the U.S. Department of the Interior's Geological Survey notes: "The use of a forked twig, or so-called divining rod, in locating minerals, finding hidden treasure, or detecting criminals is a curious superstition that has been a subject of discussion since the middle of the sixteenth century, and still has a strong hold on the popular mind." This report continues: "It is doubtful whether so much investigation and discussion have been bestowed on any other subject with such absolute lack of positive results. It is difficult to see how for practical purposes the entire matter could be more thoroughly discredited."[45]

Still, as one form of the hundreds of variations of divination, the lore is ancient and persistent.[46] Although a divining rod can be a stick, staff, or other device, its most familiar traditional form is a forked branch. Usually cut from a witch hazel or willow, the Y-shaped twig is traditionally inverted and the forked parts grasped, one in each hand, palms up, usually with the thumbs pointing away from the body in opposite directions and the elbows drawn in tightly against the body. Historically, divining rods have been used to search

43. Aaron C. Willey, "Observations on Magical Practices," 378-80; see also Early W. Hayter, *The Troubled Farmer, 1850-1900,* 6-7.

44. Butler, *Awash in a Sea of Faith,* 229

45. O. E. Meinzer, U.S. Geologic Survey, qtd. in Arthur J. Ellis, *The Divining Rod,* 1, 5.

46. Charles Mackay, psychologist, qtd. in James Randi, *An Encyclopedia of Claims, Frauds, and Hoaxes,* 75-76.

for water, ore deposits, buried treasure, lost landmarks, property boundaries, lost farm animals, or, as the U.S. Geological Survey publication noted, criminals. Some have used a rod to ascertain the quality of fabrics, to distinguish genuine coins from counterfeit, to analyze personal character, to cure diseases, to insure immunity against ill fortune, to determine the direction of cardinal points, and to determine distances and heights of trees and structures.[47]

A form of rhabdomancy (from the Greek for "rod" and "divination"), dowsing is mentioned in several books of the Hebrew Bible, including Hosea 4:12, Psalms 125:3, Numbers 17, 20:9-11, and Ezekiel 21:21. Some hypothesize that Moses used this lore in such miraculous feats as twice striking a rock to produce enough water to satisfy his multitude of followers and their cattle. Rods were considered acceptable in the Old Testament only if they were used to promote God's work, however, and the Catholic Church for years disapproved of any kind of divination. Dowsing was considered the work of the devil.

Despite the condemnation, divining rods were used routinely in sixteenth-century Germany as a means to locate mines and to discover secret treasure when the practice of burying valuables for safekeeping was commonplace. The use of the dowsing rod may have been first described in print by Georgius Agricola (pen name for Georg Bauer), a mining camp doctor in northern Bohemia. His treatise, *De re Metallica [On the Nature of Metals/ Minerals]* published in 1556, explained, in part:

> The wizards, who also make use of rings, mirrors, and crystals, seek for [ore] veins with a divining rod shaped like a fork; but its shape makes no difference in the matter—it might be straight or of some other form—for it is not the form of the twig that matters, but the wizard's incantations. ... The ancients, by means of the divining rod, not only procured those things necessary for a livelihood or for luxury, but they were also able to alter the forms of things by it; as when the magicians changed the rods of the Egyptians into serpents, as the writings of the Hebrews relate. ... Therefore it seems that the divining rod passed to the mines from its impure origin with the magicians. Then when good men shrank with horror from incantations and rejected them, the twig was retained by the unsophisticated common miners, and in searching for new veins some traces of these ancient usages remain.[48]

47. Ibid., 8; Grillot de Givry, *Witchcraft, Magic, and Alchemy,* 316.

48. Qtd. in Ellis, *The Divining Rod,* 11. *De re Metallica* was first translated into English in 1912 by Herbert Hoover (later U.S. President) and his wife, Lou Henry Hoover.

The divining rod was introduced into England by German dowsers helping to prospect for tin during the reign of Queen Elizabeth I (1558-1603). Before the end of the seventeenth century, dowsing had spread throughout Europe. Its champions explained dowsing as being like magnetism, an act of attraction and repulsion. Opponents condemned its use as a superstitious and vain practice. A third view was that rodsmen were under demonic influence. To counter this, the rod was often anointed or Christianized through incantation. "I conjure thee," one enthusiast prayed over his rod, "by the power of God, by the obedience of Jesus Christ of Nazareth, God and Mary's own son, who died on the cross, and by the power of God, by the truth of God arose from the dead; God the Father, Son and Holy Ghost, who art the very truth thyself, that thou showest me where silver and gold is hidden."[49] Another laid his newly cut switch in the bed with a newly baptized child. The rod was then addressed in the new Christian name of the infant: "In the name of the Father and of the Son and of the Holy Ghost, I adjure thee, Augusta Carolina, that thou tell me, so pure and true as Mary the Virgin was, who bore our Lord Jesus Christ, how many fathoms is it from here to the ore?" The wand was then expected to reply by dipping a certain number of times corresponding to the number of fathoms.[50] An example of a consecration prayer, purportedly translated from a manuscript of Johannes Trithemius (a German Benedictine abbot and occultist, 1462-1516), is: "Oh, God! Who art the author of all good things, strengthen, I beseech thee, thy poor servant, that he may stand fast, without fear, through this dealing and work; enlighten I beseech thee, oh Lord! The dark understanding of thy creature, so that his spiritual eye may be opened to know and see the angelic spirits descending here in this crystal."[51]

Rhabdomancy in one form or another is prevalent in essentially every

49. Albertus Magnus, *Egyptian Secrets,* 76.

50. Moriz Ferdinand Gaetzschmann, qtd. by Rossiter W. Raymond, "The Divining Rod," *Transactions of the American Institute of Mining Engineers* 11 (Feb. 1883): 411-46, qtd. by Ellis, *The Divining Rod,* 14. There is some evidence that Father Smith and others may have anointed their divining tools in the Kirtland temple in the 1830s. Charismatic young Mormon seer James Colin Brewster alleged that "to prevent the Devil deceiving" Smith and others, the gentlemen "anointed the mineral rods and seeing stones with consecrated oil, and prayed over them in the house of the Lord in Kirtland" (Brewster, *Very Important!,* 3).

51. Theodore Besterman, *Crystal Gazing,* 49. A few years earlier in New York, Father Smith's elder brother, Jesse, in a hostile 1829 letter to Hyrum Smith, complained that a messenger from the Smiths, evidently Martin Harris, had told his elderly father, Asael Smith, that Joseph Smith Sr. "has a wand or rod like Jannes & Jambres who withstood Moses in Egypt—that he can tell the distance from India to Ethiopia" (Jesse Smith to Hiram [sic] Smith, June 17, 1829; he is alluding to Exodus 7:10-12 and 2 Timothy 3:8).

branch of the occult. "The staff or sceptre is the emblem of power," notes one sixteenth-century treatise, "the bishop has his pastoral staff, and the magician the enchanted wand with which he rules nature, the elements, and the beings of darkness and infernal creatures. The magic wand is necessary for tracing the circle in which the sorcerer shuts himself to call up spirits."[52] First-person references from Smith family members themselves on the use of divining rods are sparse, but the Smiths used such tools for several purposes, primarily as a hydroscope, to aid them in locating water. Water witching, as it is traditionally called, evolved in England near the end of the eighteenth century and quickly spread to New England, where the Smiths and other diviners used the technique to locate sites for wells. Thomas De Quincey, known for his literary associations with Coleridge and Wordsworth, included an interesting account of witching for water in his 1822 memoirs:

> In Somersetshire, which is a county the most ill-watered of all in England, upon building a house, there arises uniformly, a difficulty in selecting a proper spot for a well. The remedy is to call in a set of local rhabdomantists [dowsers]. These men traverse the adjacent ground, holding the willow wand horizontally: wherever that dips, or inclines itself spontaneously to the ground, there will be found water. I have myself not only seen the process tried with success, but have witnessed the enormous trouble, delay, and expense, accruing to those of the opposite faction who refused to benefit by this art.[53]

Despite the enthusiasm, every scientifically controlled study of divining rods has concluded that "dowsers do no better than chance in finding what they are looking for."[54] Noted skeptic James Randi[55] tested a group of dowsers using a protocol they all agreed upon. If they were successful in locating water 80 percent of the time in a given area, they would be awarded $10,000. All the dowsers failed.[56] The 1938 U.S. Geological Survey warned: "Anything … deeply veiled in mystery affords a good opportunity for swindlers, there can be no reasonable doubt that many of the large group of professional finders of water, oil, or other minerals who take pay for their 'services' or for the sale of their 'instruments' are deliberately defrauding the people."[57]

52. de Givry, *Witchcraft, Magic, and Alchemy,* 311.
53. Thomas de Quincey, *The Confessions of an English Opium-eater,* 63.
54. Robert Todd Carroll, "Dowsing (a.k.a. Water Witching)," 1-2.
55. Randall James Hamilton Zwinge (1928-) is a professional magician, author, and lecturer.
56. Qtd. in Carroll, "Dowsing," 2.
57. Qtd. in Ellis, *The Divining Rod,* 6.

Peter Ingersoll, a neighbor and later critic of the Smiths, noted that on one occasion about 1822-23, Joseph Sr. and Alvin walked with him a short distance from the Smith log home to see "whether a mineral rod would work in my hand, saying at the same time he [Father Smith] was confident it would." Joseph cut a switch from a witch hazel bush and showed Ingersoll how to hold it. He added that his apprentice should simultaneously whisper, "Work to the money." Joseph then watched, contorting his body "into various shapes," while Ingersoll, noting that "this was rare sport for me," continued chanting, "work to the money." But nothing happened, and Ingersoll soon tired of the dowsing.

As he was walking away, Ingersoll picked up a smooth stone and began tossing it from one hand to another. Joseph Sr. asked what he intended to do with it. When Ingersoll replied that he was going to throw it at birds, Smith responded that the stone was of great worth and asked to borrow it. "If you only knew the value there is back of my house[!]" exclaimed Joseph. He pointed eastward toward a drumlin and announced that it contained "one chest of gold and another of silver." Ingersoll handed over the stone, Smith put it into his hat, "and stooping forward, he bowed" looking into the hat and "made sundry maneuvers, quite similar to those of a stool pigeon." After a few moments, he lifted his face from the hat and said, in a faint voice, "[I]f you knew what I had seen, you would believe." Father Smith then handed the stone to his son Alvin who "went through with the same performance."[58] Ingersoll was not convinced.

Others also attested to the family's involvement in magic. Mrs. S. F. Anderick, who as a young girl lived across Stafford Street from the Smiths, noted that Joseph Jr. often claimed "he could tell where lost or hidden things and treasures were buried or located with a forked witch hazel."[59] Isaac Butts, a schoolmate, noted that "Young Joe had a forked witch-hazel rod with which he claimed he could locate buried money or hidden things. Later he had a peep-stone which he put into his hat and looked into it. I have seen both."[60] Pomeroy Tucker wrote that Joseph used both a divining rod and seer stone in treasure quests.[61]

That Joseph Jr. used divining rods in his divination should not be surprising. In fact, the practice is described in a Book of Mormon passage that

58. Peter Ingersoll, Affidavit.

59. Mrs. S. F. Anderick, Affidavit.

60. Isaac Butts, Statement.

61. Pomeroy Tucker, *Origin, Rise, and Progress of Mormonism,* 21-22.

most followers believe refers to Joseph. Father Lehi, the book's earliest patriarch, while giving a blessing on his deathbed to his youngest son Joseph, prophesied:

> I am a descendant of Joseph who was carried captive into Egypt. ...
>
> ... Joseph truly saw our day. And he ... truly testified, saying: A seer shall the Lord my God raise up, who shall be a choice seer unto the fruit of my loins.
>
> And thus prophesied Joseph, saying: Behold, that seer will the Lord bless; and they that seek to destroy him shall be confounded. ...
>
> And his name shall be called after me; and it shall be after the name of his father. And he shall be like unto me; for the thing, which the Lord shall bring forth by his hand, by the power of the Lord shall bring my people unto salvation. ...
>
> And the Lord hath said: I will raise up a Moses; and I will give power unto him in a rod; and I will give judgment unto him in writing. Yet I will not loose his tongue, that he shall speak much, for I will not make him mighty in speaking. (2 Ne. 3:4-6, 14-15, 17.)[62]

Smith family members were not alone in the Palmyra/Manchester area in embracing a magical world view. According to a 1831 story in a local newspaper:

> Men and women without distinction of age or sex became marvelous wise in the occult sciences, many dreamed, others saw visions disclosing to them, deep in the bowels of the earth, rich and shining treasures, and to facilitate those *mighty* mine operations, (money was usually if not always sought after in the night time) divers devices and implements were invented.
>
> Mineral rods, (as they were called by the imposters who made use of them,) were supposed to be infallible guides to these sources of wealth—*"peep stone"* or pebbles, taken promiscuously from the brook or field, were placed in a hat or other situation excluded from the light, when some *wizard* or *witch* (for these performances were not confined to either sex) applied their eyes, and nearly staring their [eye]balls from their sockets, declared they saw all the wonders of nature, including of course, ample stores of silver and gold.[63]

Peep or seer stones like those used by the Smiths have long been used as catalysts in an ancient branch of divination known variously as seeing,

62. This passage in the 1981 edition is identical to the 1830 first edition.
63. "GOLD BIBLE NO. 3," emphasis in original.

peeping, glass looking, or gazing, but is perhaps most suitably called "scrying."[64] This word has drifted into near-oblivion in English vernacular. One current definition reads: "To scry or descry is to spy out or discover by the eye objects at a distance."[65] "Scrying," in its metaphysical sense, is "a method of bringing into the consciousness of the scryer by means of a speculum through one or more of his senses the content of his subconsciousness."[66] In occult literature, "scrying" is the faculty of discerning things in the past and future by gazing at a shiny stone, mirror, or crystal ball. Concentrated gazing enables the seer to still the conscious self, to "envision" with the spiritual or mind's eye.

The history of gazing on a shiny or reflecting object as an aid in prophecy had a long history and was known at least as early as the Greeks. Nostradamus (the Latinized name of Michel de Nostredame, a French physician and astrologer who lived from 1503 to 1566), used a bowl of water on a brass tripod and a black mirror to scry his prophecies. Queen Elizabeth I at times consulted Dr. John Dee on matters of state. Dee, a Cambridge-educated alchemist, astrologer, and mathematician, while kneeling in prayer in 1581 received a heavenly manifestation. "There suddenly glowed a dazzling light," he reported, "in the midst of which, in all his glory, stood the great angel, Uriel." The spirit handed Dee a crystal "most bright, most clear and glorious, of the bigness of an egg" and informed him that, if he gazed into the stone, he could communicate with otherworldly spirits.[67] Despite the promise, Dee was unable to see in the stone but employed others who could. For his own part, he constructed a lamine or breastplate with an arrangement of several seer stones (he called them "shewstones") by which he conversed with angels. He considered this device the equivalent of the biblical Urim and Thummim that ancient Hebrew priests and prophets used in their divination (Ex. 28:15-30; Lev. 8:8; Num. 27:21). Dee's young assistants were not mediums in the Victorian sense of the term. Spirits of the dead did not speak through them, and the angelic conversations cannot properly be called seances. But Dee's scryer Edward Kelley claimed to raise through the shewstone a host of spiritual beings who conveyed, among others things, a new

64. If the scrying stone is clear or transparent, the process is called crystallomancy. If the pebbles are opaque, like Joseph Smith's known seer stones, the scrying process is more correctly known as lithomancy.

65. Robert Todd Carroll, "Scrying," *The Skeptic's Dictionary,* 1.

66. Besterman, *Crystal Gazing,* 160.

67. "John Dee, "Astrologer to the Queen," 2-3.

language, "Enochian," supposedly the language spoken by angels, Adam and Eve, and inhabitants of the city of Enoch.[68]

Joseph Smith Jr., who like Dee linked his scrying to the biblical Urim and Thummim, was referring to himself as Enoch by 1835 (D&C 78). And also like Dee, Smith used several seer stones in his scrying activities. In 1826, while giving testimony before Justice Albert Neely of South Bainbridge, New York, Joseph reported that "when he was a lad, he heard of a neighboring girl some three miles from him, who could look into a glass and see anything however hidden from others."[69] This seer, Sarah (Sally) Chase, daughter of Clark Chase and Phebe Mason Chase, was five years older than young Joseph.[70] Sally's brother Willard later recalled that the families became acquainted in 1820.[71] If this was also the year when Joseph met Sally, he would have been fifteen, she twenty. As soon as he heard of her clairvoyant ability, young Joseph, in his words, was "seized with a strong desire to see her and her glass."

Other Palmyra residents also remembered Sally and her stone. According to Lucy Smith, it was "a green glass, through which she could see many very wonderful things."[72] Lorenzo Saunders added, "It was a little bit of a stone & it was green & she would hold it before light."[73] Benjamin Saunders, Lorenzo's brother, remembered it as "about the Size of my thumb. She had it fit in to a paddle."[74] Orrin Porter Rockwell's sister, Caroline Rockwell Smith, also remembered that "Sallie Chase, a Methodist, had [a seer stone] and people would go for her to find lost and hidden or stolen things."[75] Mrs. Anderick, who grew up in the Smith/Chase neighborhood, recalled its color as "gray" and its texture as "smooth," and also remembered differently how Sally used it. Rather than holding it before a light source, Sally would put it "in a hat and hold it to her face, and claimed things would be brought to her

68. Ibid., 3.

69. My narrative is based on Purple, "Joseph Smith," 3.

70. Sally, born October 26, 1800, never married (Clark Chase Family Group Records). She is listed on the 1860 New York census as "sewing machine operator." The 1870 census lists her as a "Tailoress." In 1870, she and her elder brother Willard, then a widower, who was classified in the census as an "invalid," lived in the same Palmyra home. Willard, who died on March 10, 1871, had been incapacitated since 1855 ("Rev. Willard Chase Departed This Life"). Sally died on April 7, 1880 (Palmyra, NY, Cemetery File).

71. Willard Chase, Affidavit, 240.

72. Anderson, *Lucy's Book,* 393

73. Lorenzo Saunders, Interview, Nov. 12, 1884, 8.

74. Benjamin Saunders, Interview, Sept. 1884, 29.

75. Caroline Rockwell Smith, Statement, Mar. 25, 1885.

view."[76] Sally's brother Abel, as late as 1881, confirmed that she had "a stone that she could see in."[77] John Stafford (1805-1904), also of Palmyra, knew the rumors but passed them on without personally vouching for them: people in the neighborhood "use[d] to Claim Sally Chase Could look through [a] stone she had & find money."[78]

A 1923 history of clairvoyance noted that "usually a boy or a virgin was employed as scryer," qualifications that both Sally and Joseph met.[79] An 1849 account specified that a scryer was expected to remain "a pure virgin, a youth who had not known woman, or at least a person of irreproachable life and purity of manners."[80] Still another account recommended exploring the future by having "a pure boy" look for it "in a crystal, in a glass, or in the transparency of water."[81] Psychologist Northcote Thomas, writing in 1905, acknowledged that "young children" were often "use[d] as scryers in mediaeval times" because of their talent at "visualizing (or calling up the image of the object of which one is thinking)." He dismissed "a crystal vision" (or crystal gazing) as "simply a day-dream."[82]

William Morain writes that Joseph shared "an additional trait in common with other victims of childhood trauma suffering with dissociative symptoms: the belief that he was 'psychic,' or had paranormal gifts of clairvoyance." Morain, citing child psychiatrist Lenore Terr, explains that there is often a "reordering of events in a traumatized child's mind" that gives rise to a "sense of the ability to predict the future." This may be observed, Morain writes, in Joseph's "practice of crystal gazing—the ability to stare at a fixed point or object until consciousness is altered and vivid hallucinations supervene. ... Traumatized children typically possess an illusory sense of being gifted."[83]

When fifteen-year-old Joseph Jr. asked his parents for permission to visit Sally the seer, they at first refused. He finally convinced them "after much effort."[84] Mormon historian Mark Ashurst-McGee proposes that Joseph Sr.'s reluctance may have stemmed from Sally's gender. "Until the second decade of the nineteenth century," he notes, "treasure was located primarily by adult

76. Anderick, Affidavit.
77. Abel D. Chase, Interviewed by William H. Kelley and Edmund L. Kelley, 9.
78. John Stafford, Statement.
79. Lynn Thorndike, *A History of Magic and Experimental Science,* 2:364-65.
80. John Brand, *Observations on the Popular Antiquities of Great Britain,* 3:60.
81. J. von Goores, *Die Christliche Mystik,* 3:600.
82. Northcote W. Thomas, *Crystal Gazing,* 8.
83. William D. Morain, *The Sword of Laban,* 35
84. Purple, "Joseph Smith," 3.

males with divining rods."[85] Father Smith may have preferred that his son's apprenticeship be under his or another adult male's supervision. However, it was "a neighboring adolescent female [who] provided Joseph Junior with his first experience of supernatural vision and also provided him a role model of the village seer."[86]

It was relatively common knowledge among Smith family acquaintances that both young Joseph and his father believed that everyone who could find a personal seer stone was entitled to it. For example, Joseph Sr. told Fayette Lapham: "There is a stone of this quality, somewhere, for every one."[87] According to Christopher Stafford (1808-92), a Smith friend, young Joseph told him "there was a peepstone for me and many others if we could only find them."[88] And neighbor Lorenzo Saunders remembered young Joseph saying, "men can pick stones out of this Earth. ... [A]ny one can get a stone, & see knowledge of futurity."[89] As an adult, Joseph Jr. assured other Mormon Church leaders in Nauvoo, Illinois, of the same universality. Brigham Young recorded Joseph's statement that "every man who lived on the earth was entitled to a seer stone."[90]

When Joseph Jr. visited Sally Chase, the scryer permitted him to "look in the glass, which was placed in a hat to exclude the light." When he gazed into the darkened hat, Joseph reportedly "was greatly surprised to see but one thing, which was a small stone, a great way off." As he later told the story, the pebble quickly "became luminous, and dazzled his eyes, and after a short time it became as intense as the mid-day sun." He could see the stone's location, buried under the roots of a tree or shrub about a mile upstream from a creek entering Lake Erie, not far from the New York and Pennsylvania border, many miles west of his Manchester home.[91]

Astounded by his ability to see in Sally's stone, Joseph returned to the Chase home frequently to gaze into the magical stone. During each scrying,

85. Mark Ashurst-McGee, "A Pathway to Prophethood," 210.

86. Ibid.

87. Lapham, "Interview with the Father of Joseph Smith," 306.

88. Christopher M. Stafford, Statement. Born in Manchester, New York, Stafford married Emily Rockwell, sister of Orrin Porter Rockwell, on January 7, 1830.

89. Lorenzo Saunders, Interview, 9-10.

90. "History of Brigham Young," 118-19.

91. Purple, "Joseph Smith," 3. Early Mormon convert Edward Partridge, who later became a Presiding Bishop of the Church, related in 1835 that in Kirtland a young woman seer, Sarah Alley, looked in her stone and "told me she saw a seer's stone for me, it was a small blue stone with a hole in one corner, that it was 6 or 8 feet in the ground, nor far from the lake shore a little west of Buffalo on a hill, a tree growing near the spot" *(An Account of a Trance or Vision of Sarah Alley).*

he had the same vision. "The singular circumstance occupied his mind for some years," he noted in his 1826 court hearing.[92] Finally, most likely in 1821 or 1822, Joseph decided to obtain the luminous pebble and make it his personal speculum, the stone his father, at the time young Joseph was born, had told Vermont friends "he intended to procure" for his boy "to see all over the world with."[93]

It was a larger-than-life journey: leaving his home and setting out on a quest for a desired, even essential, object. The distance did not intimidate. An anonymously written article on "Palmyra" that was published in an unidentified newspaper noted that "Joseph, the boy, was fond of strolling about the country."[94] Another added that "Jo traveled about the country considerable and was well known."[95] Accordingly, with little cash and only a small bundle of provisions, he began walking westward. En route he worked three days for a farmer to replenish his supplies. Eventually, he reached the mouth of the creek he had envisioned in Sally's glass. After borrowing an ax and hoe from nearby settlers, he dug until he uncovered the mineral.

After he had recovered the prized stone, Joseph carried it to the creek, washed it, carefully dried it, then knelt and placed it in the crown of his hat. As soon as he lowered his face into the hat, he "discovered that time, place and distance were annihilated; that all intervening obstacles were removed, and that he possessed one of the attributes of Deity, an All-Seeing-Eye."[96] The diviner arose to his feet "with a thankful heart," he reported, "carried his tools to their owner, turned his feet towards the rising sun, and sought with weary limbs his long deserted home." Joseph's long walk was no doubt an important step in his rite of passage from farm boy to prophet. Evan M. Zuesse comments:

> Divination requires the radical submission of the diviner and indeed the client to the transcendental sources of truth, before their lives can be transformed and set straight, before they can be reincorporated harmoniously

92. Purple, "Joseph Smith," 3.

93. "Green Mountain Boys to Thomas Sharp."

94. "Palmyra," undated clipping from *Wayne County Journal,* Willard Bean Scrapbook.

95. Joseph Rogers (1805-?), Statement. Rogers, born in western Oneida County, New York, ten months before Joseph Smith, lived in Phelpstown, a few miles south of Palmyra from 1815 to 1842. In his statement, Rogers added that he was "well acquainted with Jo Smith, who became the Mormon Prophet."

96. Purple, "Joseph Smith," 3. In 1816, treasure seekers in Dresden, Maine, consulted a seer who used a stone in which "he could see everything that existed, or was transacted in any part of the world" *(Newburyport [MA] Herald,* Nov. 21, 1816, qtd. in George G. Carey, "Folklore from the Printed Sources of Essex County, Massachusetts," 30).

into the world. In short, divinatory rites follow the pattern of all rites of passage. The client, having learned in the course of the rite to offer up to the divine all egocentric resistance, ends the session reoriented to the world and able to take positive and confident action in it.[97]

There has been some confusion about what Joseph's *first* seer stone—the one he found near the creek bed—looked like.[98] During his 1826 court examination, he was asked to display it. William Purple, a physician who made a memorandum of the proceedings, recorded that the stone was "about the size of a small hen's egg, in the shape of a high instepped shoe. It was composed of layers of different colors passing diagonally through it. It was very hard and smooth, perhaps by being carried in the pocket."[99] On another occasion, Purple noted that the rock was a "fine-grained, reddish sandstone, curiously striped, originally hardened from a sandy sediment, broken into a fragment and rounded by natural attrition." (Later observers corroborated the shape but not the color.) Purple added that the seer stone's "power arose from the fact that its layers, or stripes, corresponded with the number of weeks in the year."[100] David Whitmer, who watched Joseph Smith scry in 1829, recalled that the rock was "a strange, oval-shaped, chocolate-colored stone, about the size of an egg, only more flat."[101] After using it during the dictation of the Book of Mormon text, Smith gave the stone to his cousin and scribe Oliver Cowdery in 1830. In 1850, after Cowdery's death, Phineas Young, Oliver's brother-in-law, acquired the stone from Cowdery's widow, Elizabeth, and later that year gave it to Brigham Young in Utah Territory.[102] "Oliver sent me Joseph's *first* Seer stone," Young said in 1855.[103] On February 25, 1856, Brigham showed it to the University of Deseret Board of Regents. Hosea Stout described it as "a selecious granite dark color almost black with light colored stripes some what resembling petrified poplar or cotton wood bark. It was about the size but not the shape of a hen's egg."[104] Samuel Bateman, a bodyguard to LDS Church president John Taylor, saw the stone in 1887. "It was a dark color," Bateman wrote, "not round on one side. It was shaped

97. Ashurst-McGee, "A Pathway to Prophethood," 225.

98. See Michael Hubbard MacKay and Nicholas J. Frederick, *Joseph Smith's Seer Stones* (Provo, Utah: Religious Studies Center, Brigham Young University/Salt Lake City: Deseret Book Co., 2016), pp. 65-88.

99. Purple, "Joseph Smith," 3.

100. "Joseph Smith—His Early Attempts at Imposture," 3.

101. David Whitmer, Interview, June 1, 1881, *Kansas City Journal.*

102. David Whitmer, Interview, Oct. 10, 1886, *Omaha Herald.*

103. Ashurst-McGee, "" Pathway to Prophethood," 230; emphasis mine.

104. Hosea Stout, *On the Mormon Frontier,* 2:593.

like the top of a baby's shoe, one end like the toe of the shoe [square], and the other round."[105] In 1966, Grant Palmer, an employee of the LDS Church Educational System, handled the stone, now in possession of the LDS First Presidency. "It was a shiny or polished stone," he wrote, "shaped somewhat like a hen's egg only larger (between a chicken egg and a handball). It was dark brown, almost black and had several whitish stripes running through it."[106] Hugh B. Brown, a member of the First Presidency, showed the stone to his daughter, Mary Brown Firmage. She described it as "3-4 inches long, 2 inches wide, and had a hump in the middle which made it perhaps 2 inches thick at the thickest point." In addition, it had "three black, concentric circles on the top ½ inch. Below the circles were many small black circles."[107] The stone remains in the possession of the LDS Church.[108]

Joseph acquired a second seer stone in Manchester in the spring or summer of 1822. Pomeroy Tucker noted that this stone "was of a whitish, glassy appearance, though opaque, resembling quartz."[109] Mrs. Anderick, who grew up in the Smith neighborhood, described it as "a gray smooth stone about the size and shape of an egg."[110] Another account called it a "semi-transparent quartz ... a curious looking white stone."[111] Palmyra historian Thomas L. Cook called it a "stone of vitreous [glassy] though opaque appearance and in form like an infant's foot."[112]

Joseph was not the rock's original owner. This distinctive stone was discovered in 1822 on the nearby Chase farm, possibly in the same general locale as Sally's stone. Sometime between 1811 and 1813, Clark Chase and Phebe Mason Chase moved to Palmyra from Rutland, New York, with their children.[113] They relocated to a farm on Canandaigua Road less than a mile from the Smith place. The two families became acquainted in 1820, probably when the Smiths moved just north of the Palmyra/Farmington township line. Shortly afterwards, on July 27, 1821, fifty-one-year-old Father Chase died, leaving his widow with ten children, ranging in age from twenty-seven

105. Samuel Bateman, Diary, 69.

106. Grant H. Palmer, "My Recollection of Viewing Three 'Seer Stones.'"

107. Mary Brown Firmage, Interview.

108. See the color photograph in Richard E. Turley Jr., Robin S. Jensen, and Mark Ashurst-McGee, "Joseph the Seer," *Ensign* 35 (October 2015): 53.

109. Tucker, *Origin, Rise, and Progress of Mormonism,* 18.

110. Anderick, Statement, 2.

111. A. W. Cowles, "The Mormons," 3.

112. Thomas L. Cook, *Palmyra and Vicinity,* 221.

113. Son Henry S. Chase was born April 9, 1811, in Rutland, New York (Clark Chase Family Group Record). The earliest entry for Clark Chase in the Account Book of his brother-in-law, Palmyra grocer Lemuel Durfee, is April 25, 1813.

to three.[114] Their eldest son, Durfee, was a physician. The next two sons, twenty-six-year-old Mason and twenty-three-year-old Willard (1718-1871), assumed management of the farm. Willard and sister Sally were both stalwart Methodists.[115] Yet Willard and Sally, like the Smiths, believed in magic. In addition to Joseph's scrying experiences with Sally, Willard dug for treasure with Alvin Smith. When neighbor Lorenzo Saunders asked Chase how he broke his shovel, Chase told him that the men had located a large buried iron treasure chest: "Alvin & I went down & found that chest."[116] There is no evidence, however, that they recovered the treasure. Finding and getting were two completely different operations in the magic world of the money diggers.[117]

In 1822, a year after Clark Chase's death, Mother Chase and Willard evidently hired Alvin and Joseph Jr. to help dig a surface well on the family's property. Such wells were typically five to six feet in diameter, the depth determined by the water table. While Willard was taking a digging turn approximately twenty feet down, he saw in the semi-darkness a whitish, "singularly appearing stone."[118] Curious, he pocketed the object and, leaving the well, showed it to the Smiths. Sixteen-year-old Joseph dropped the stone into his battered stovepipe, then buried his "face into the top" of the hat, telling the men "he could see in it." Joseph wanted the stone, but Chase "did not wish to part with it on account of its being a curiosity, but would lend it," which he did for approximately two years.

According to Lorenzo Saunders, the purpose of the excavation was not to discover water: "They dug that hole for money."[119] And Joseph Sr. told Fayette Lapham that his boys found the stone "under the pretense of digging a well."[120] Wilford Woodruff, who became a Mormon in 1833, recalled when he was president of the Church: "the seer stone known as 'Gazelem,' which was shown of the Lord to the Prophet Joseph to be some thirty feet

---

114. By 1824, Phebe Chase owned a millinery shop in Palmyra ("Millinery," *Wayne Sentinel,* July 28, 1824). For a listing of her children, see Clark Chase Family Group Record.

115. Willard was a Weslyan Methodist minister, and a Methodist minister delivered both his and Sally's funeral sermons.

116. Lorenzo Saunders, Interview, Nov. 12, 1884.

117. An example of this occurred in New London, Connecticut, in 1827 when a woman discovered "by the aid of a crystal pebble" a legendary Spanish treasure buried by the port. Unfortunately, "the pebble was not clear enough to reveal the exact place of the box" (Charles M. Skinner, *Myths and Legends of Our Own Land,* 282-83).

118. This discussion of the Chase seer stone discovery comes from Willard Chase's December 11, 1833, affidavit in Howe, *Mormonism Unvailed,* 241.

119. Lorenzo Saunders, Interview, Nov. 12, 1884.

120. Lapham, "Interview," 305.

under ground, and which he obtained by digging under the pretense of excavating for a well."[121] Danish Mormon Jens Weibye also reported:

> [T]he Prophet Joseph Smith had a Peepstone (Cal[l]ed in the Book of Doc[trine]. & Covenant[s] Gaslum) that he got by digging in a Ladies Garden 25 feet down in the Ground. The Lord [revealed] to Joseph Smith that such a Stone was 25 feet down in the Ground but he (J. Smith) did not know how to get it; but he went to the Lady there [who] owned the Garden and asked her if she did not wish to have a Well dug in her Garden, she said yes … and Joseph Smith the Prophet found the Peepstone 25 feet down he could see many thing[s] in that Stone.[122]

After the Smiths had Chase's whitish seer stone for two years, Willard asked for its return. As he related, he had heard that Joseph Jr. was "publishing abroad what wonders he could discover by looking in" his stone and was angry that Smith was profiting from "the credulous part of [the] community." Joseph returned it; but about a year later in 1825, Hyrum again borrowed it for Joseph, who kept it the remainder of his life, using it in many different circumstances.[123]

---

121. "No author, untitled, and undated statement," George A. Smith Papers.

122. Jens Weibye, "6th Daybook," 143-44.

123. In November 1830, after Joseph gave his first stone, the brown one, to Oliver Cowdery, he dictated a revelation for a recent convert (D&C 34), using his whitish stone. Five years later, he pronounced a blessing "according to the Spirit of prophecy and revelation" upon a married couple through the "Urim and Thummim," his term for the white stone. He later used the same stone to help "translate" some ancient Egyptian papyrus (Woodruff, *Wilford Woodruff's Journal,* 2:155). Joseph showed the white stone to some associates in 1841, telling them "every man who lived on the earth was entitled to a seer stone, and should have one, but they are kept from them in consequence of their wickedness" ("History of Brigham Young," 118-19). In 1843, Hyrum asked Joseph to use the white stone to dictate a revelation on plural marriage, but Joseph said he already "knew the revelation perfectly from beginning to end" (Roberts, *Comprehensive History of the Church,* 2:106). A recent convert said in Nauvoo that Lucy Smith allowed her to feel the white stone through its cloth wrapping (see Jane Manning James, Autobiography, 19). After Joseph's death, both stones came into Brigham Young's possession. At his death, they were part of Young's estate. One of his daughters later told a cousin:

> There is a matter that I wish to lay before you, that weighs upon my mind, and seems very important to me. I refer to some very sacred articles I bought at the sale of my father's personal effects,—articles that never should have been given up to the idle gaze; but being brought out, my mother and myself felt it a wish of our hearts to get them, that their sacredness might not be sullied.
>
> They are: two sear-stones and an arrow point. They are in the possession of President Woodruff now, and very properly too, but I feel dear cousin, that they should ever be the property of the President of the Church, and not of individuals; that at his demise, they are not retained as they were before among "personal effects," but considered ever the legitimate property of God's mouth-piece. (Zina Young Williams Card to Franklin D. Richards, July 31, 1896.)

In 1888, Wilford Woodruff carried the white stone to the dedication of one of the Church's

The physical composition of a seer stone is irrelevant to the rational mind because it has no power of its own. The scrying experience is a fundamentally psychological one. The scryer looks within to find the answers he or she seeks. The degree of success depends upon the scryer's ability to concentrate. The stone merely serves as a catalyst. "By using or attuning to an external source or object," notes psychologist Stuart Waldron, "one can enhance the stillness and peace needed to start the visions rolling."[124] John L. Walters, a behavioral scientist, agrees: "Scrying helps a person access his own subconscious mind or unconscious mind."[125] The perceptions that arise are projections of images, sounds, and sensations from the subconscious mind to the conscious mind. Leonardo Da Vinci often gazed at a familiar stone wall to visualize new ideas for his paintings.[126] Poverty-stricken scryers like Joseph Smith, who could not afford a quartz crystal (crystallomancy), instead used a solid stone (lithomancy).

Scryers who have used techniques similar to those used by Joseph report that, after a few moments of resting one's gaze on the speculum, the eyes will want to close about half way as vision softens and goes out of focus.[127] Small flickers of light appear, and from that light shapes or images emerge. Once the visions begin to form in the mind, the scrying tool is no longer necessary. Whether the eyes are open or closed is immaterial.[128] Those mental pictures may relate to the past, the present, or the future.[129]

---

temples. "Before leaving," he wrote, "I Consecrated upon the Altar the seers stone that Joseph Smith found by Revelation some 30 feet under the Earth Carried by him through life" (Woodruff, *Wilford Woodruff's Journal,* 8:500, emphasis mine). In 1900, Church President Lorenzo Snow showed the stone to a recently returned missionary, and his wife, who described it as "the shape of an egg though not quite so large, of a gray cast something like granite but with white stripes running round it. It was transparent but had no holes, neither in the end or in the sides" ("The History of a Nephite Coin"). More than a half-century later, when Grant Palmer saw both stones (as well as a third of unknown origin), he described the white stone as "opaque, a milky-white coloration ... round, sort of like an egg only smaller." He added that "from a top or above view [the stone] was indeed shaped like a baby's footprint" (Palmer, Interviewed by Richard S. Van Wagoner, Sept. 12, 2004; Palmer to Van Wagoner, Oct. 4, 2004).

124. Stuart Waldron, "Scrying."

125. John L. Waters, "Using Scrying to See How a Genius Works," 3.

126. Ibid.

127. This phenomenon, called the Ganze Field Principle, is the same technique that allows one to interpret computer-generated "3-D" hidden pictures using unfocused vision.

128. For a sampling of techniques currently being used by scryers who have made their techniques available on the internet, see http://w3.one.net/~browe/ashort.htm; www.mindweaver.co.uk/page_21.htm; www.sophiaswisdom.com/art_scrying.shtml; www.jaguarmoon.org/public/Scry/Methods.htm; and www.silverhoofs.com/c-steps.htm. *Ganze,* a German word meaning "whole," may best be understood through Edmund Husserl's "Phenomenology."

129. "Scrying," and "The Wonderful World of Scrying."

However irrational nineteenth-century money-digging culture may seem to many men and women today, some people then and since have embraced it as a natural way of life. Despite the fact that most sought treasure in vain, "what made them persist?" wonders Ronald Walker:

> Relying on an immemorial but now forgotten world view, the money diggers placed faith in conjuring, elemental spirits, thrice-spoken dreams, seeric gifts, and enchanted treasure that could slip and rumble through the earth as easily as a fish moving through the deep. The modern age will probably never fully understand the diggers' strange compound of treasure seeking, religious feeling, and intense psychological devotion to an old but fading way of life. Theirs was another world which we can speak of but hardly enter.[130]

In this difficult-to-enter other-worldly environment, Joseph would evolve from a boy with a scrying stone in a battered hat to a charismatic visionary, a man with a mission that he—and others—were convinced was divinely inspired.

130. Walker, "The Persisting Idea of American Treasure Hunting," 430-31.

7 | VILLAGE SCRYER

[T]he picture of Joseph, his family, and their friends as indefatigable searchers after buried treasure, limned in contemporary newspapers and the recollections of their neighbors, stands forth clearly after every discount has been made for malice and dislike.

—Dale Morgan, in John Phillip Walker, *Dale Morgan on Early Mormonism*, 218

The township of Farmington, New York, where the Smith family farm was located, was settled in 1789 and experienced most of its growth before the Smiths arrived.[1] In March 1821, the township was divided into Farmington, on the west, and Burt, on the east. A year later, Burt became Manchester, named after the principal village. Although the Smiths' acreage was in Manchester township, most family business was conducted in nearby Palmyra, then a thriving town on the survey line of the Western or Grand (later Erie) Canal. As historian Donald Cannon observes, "In a real sense Palmyra and the Erie Canal grew up together."[2] Without the canal Palmyra would likely have remained an obscure village straddling Mud Creek in the middle of virtually nowhere.

In 1724, half a century before the American Revolutionary War, surveyor Cadwallader Colden realized the benefits of a waterway linking the Hudson River with Lake Erie.[3] However, most Americans, including Thomas Jefferson, thought the idea was "little short of madness."[4] Daring miller and flour merchant Jesse Hawley, while living a few miles from Palmyra in Geneva, New York, envisioned shipping by waterway great quantities of grain grown

1. A town or township—a large division within a county—may include several villages or cities. For example, the village of Palmyra, where the Smiths lived when they moved to New York, is included in the larger town or township of Palmyra, but their Manchester farm was not located in the village of Manchester.

2. Donald Q. Cannon, "Palmyra, New York," 3.

3. Helen Walker, "We Remember … the Erie Canal."

4. Qtd. in "Erie Canal."

in upstate New York to markets on the eastern seaboard. In 1806, he published a proposal in the *Pittsburgh Commonwealth* to construct a waterway connecting Lake Erie and the Mohawk and Hudson Rivers. While serving a sentence in the Ontario County debtors' prison at Canandaigua, Hawley sent a series of fourteen essays to the *Genesee Messenger*, noting that shipping by water cost only an eighth as much as by land.

DeWitt Clinton, convinced of the value of a western canal, soon became its champion and was elected New York governor in 1817 on a build-the-canal platform. An adherent of practical republicanism, he held that the nation's common good depended on prosperity and unfettered individual opportunities. Practical men like Clinton believed that morality and wealth sprang from the same source of virtue. By improving their physical surroundings through such projects as the Erie Canal, Americans could realize their special destiny of universal moral and material prosperity. By combining natural simplicity with human genius, the canal would fill the country's dream to finish God's work, which many believed would hasten the return of Jesus and the onset of the Millennium.[5]

In 1816, the same year Joseph Smith Sr. arrived in New York, the state government approved the construction of the Erie Canal, later appropriating $7 million. At daybreak, July 4, 1817, cannons thundered as a large crowd gathered near Rome, New York, seventy-five miles east of the Smith home, to watch the turning of the first spadeful of canal dirt. Construction proceeded immediately—eastward toward Albany, westward toward Utica, and ultimately to Palmyra. The canal's trenching required a four-foot-deep cut. The excavated soil was heaped on the downhill slope to form a walkway which eventually became the towpath for horses, mules, and oxen piloted by youthful drivers called hoggees.

The success of the canal's construction depended on the sheer strength and backbreaking labor of its thousands of diggers. According to Carol Sheriff, a historian of the canal, these men "felled forests, shoveled and piled dirt, picked away at tree roots, blasted rock formations, heaved and hauled boulders, rechanneled streams, and molded the canal bed."[6] Some New Yorkers thought of the construction workers as a "drunken and boisterous lot."[7] Three-fourths were native-born Americans, and most of the rest were Irish

5. F. H. Cuming, *An Address, Delivered at the Laying of the Cap-Stone, of the Ten Combined Locks*, 8.

6. Carol Sheriff, *The Artificial River*, 36.

7. Ibid., 49.

immigrants from New York City, rough-and-tumble lads with short tempers. Diggers engaged in so many fisticuffs in Palmyra that the intersection of Canal and Market Streets became known as Bloody Corners.[8] Perhaps it was here that Joseph Smith Jr. and others witnessed a slugging match between two Irishmen. Years later, Joseph told the story, adding that when one of the rowdies tried to "gouge the other's eyes," Alvin leaped into the fray, grabbed the unfair fighter "by his collar and breeches, and threw him over the ring, which was composed of men standing around to witness the fight."[9]

The presence of such an unruly gang of itinerants helped to make the region ripe for religious revival. Josiah Bissell, a merchant in nearby Rochester, bemoaned canal workers' depravity. In a single season, he complained, one canal line "dismissed nine women from their boats in a stage of pregnancy." He added that a boat captain, discussing the plight of young drivers, lamented that the boys "might as well be sent to the state prison as to the Canal. … [T]hey are sometimes diseased by their unlawful lives—these are only specimens of a large budget of evil rolling thro our land & among us."[10] Religious advocates warned that to neglect the spiritual welfare of canal men and boys would have far-reaching effects. "It is high time," one reformer wrote, that something should be done "upon the lines of our canals, particularly the great Western Canal [i.e., the Erie]." He warned that inaction would result in vices that "will soon become too firmly rooted to be eradicated, except by the destruction and perdition of one whole generation."[11] In a millennial age, when many Christians thought they could usher in the Lord's kingdom on earth by converting fellow sinners, the possibility of losing an entire generation of God's common men was of great consequence.

The religious revivals of the 1820s in western New York ignited a concerted effort to convert wayward canal workers as well as villagers. An interesting account of a revival that flared up after Christmas 1821 in nearby Lyons, New York, provides background to the religious enthusiasm that gave rise to the area's colorful nickname "The Burned-Over District." A local newspaper reported:

> A most extraordinary change within two or three weeks past, has taken place in regard to the religious state of this village. This change from one

8. Bonnie Hays, "Palmyra, Believe It or Not."

9. *History of the Church,* 5:247.

10. Josiah Bissell to Charles G. Finney, Sept. 15, 1829. Bissell was a Rochester merchant and land speculator; Finney was one of the era's prominent revivalist preachers.

11. "Boatmen's Friend Society to the Forwarders, Merchants, and Others," *Rochester Daily Advertiser,* Aug. 20, 1830.

> extreme to another, has been so powerful, and universal as scarcely to admit of a precedent in all this western region. Such hath been and is still the manifest power of God, through the overwhelming influence of the Divine Spirit, that the whole place exhibits the aspect of a house of mourning. Large collections assemble every evening in the week at the house of God for worship and various religious exercises. These meetings are solemn beyond description. Persons who had formerly opposed awakenings, and persons of every other character are struck with amazement—and exclaim, this must be the work of God. A large number of [hopeful] converts are now rejoicing in the Saviour, and scarcely an individual can now be found in the place whose mind is not, in a considerable degree, solemnized.[12]

Such outpourings during this period were part of what has become known as the Second Great Awakening. The phenomenon began in England as the Wesleyan revival of holiness in 1792, the year after John Wesley died, and quickly reached American shores. In New England, Baptist leader Isaac Backus addressed an urgent plea for revival to pastors of every Christian denomination in the United States in 1794. American churches adopted the plan until the new nation, like Britain, was interlaced with a network of prayer meetings.[13]

The first revivals sprang up in Kentucky where James McGready, a Presbyterian minister, pastored three small congregations in Muddy River, Red River, and Gasper River in the Bluegrass region. In June 1800, nearly 500 members of McGready's three congregations and several other ministers gathered at Red River for a camp meeting which lasted several days. On the final day of the religious celebration, "a mighty effusion of [God's] Spirit" came upon the crowd and the ground was soon "covered with the slain; their screams for mercy pierced the heavens."[14] Convinced that God was manifesting himself, McGready and his associates planned another camp meeting to be held the following month at Gasper River. A huge crowd of 8,000, many from as far away as a hundred miles, gathered at the Gasper. During an evening meeting illuminated by flaming torches, a Presbyterian pastor delivered a fiery sermon. "The power of God seemed to shake the whole assembly," wrote McGready. Toward the end of the sermon, "the cries of the distressed arose almost as loud as his [the preacher's] voice." After the

12. "A Most Extraordinary …," *Western Farmer,* Jan. 30, 1822.
13. "Nineteenth Century Revivals."
14. Frederick Morgan Davenport, *Primitive Traits in Religious Revivals,* 70.

congregation was dismissed, "the solemnity increased, till the greater part of the multitude seemed engaged in the most solemn manner." No one wanted to leave, "hunger and sleep seemed to affect nobody—eternal things were the vast concern. Here awakening and converting work was to be found in every part of the multitude."[15]

Revivalistic fervor spread like wildfire. Barton Stone, a Presbyterian minister, organized similar camp meetings at Cane Ridge, near Lexington, Kentucky. A crowd of more than 12,000 enthusiasts gathered. James Finley, a visiting Methodist circuit rider, described it: "The noise was like the roar of Niagara [Falls]. The vast sea of human beings seemed to be agitated as if by a storm. I counted seven ministers, all preaching at one time, some on stumps, others in wagons and one standing on a tree which had, in falling, lodged against another." Finley climbed atop a log to get a better view and beheld an "indescribable" scene: "I saw at least five hundred swept down in a moment as if a battery of a thousand guns had been opened upon them, and then immediately followed shrieks and shouts that rent the very heavens."[16]

The Rev. Moses Hoge, also present at Cane Ridge, recorded the same scene: "The careless fall down, cry out, tremble, and not infrequently are affected with convulsive twitchings. … [N]othing that imagination can paint, can make a stronger impression upon the mind, than one of those scenes. Sinners dropping down on every hand, shrieking, groaning, crying for mercy, convulsed; professors praying, agonizing, fainting, falling down in distress, for sinners or in raptures of joy!" As to the work in general, continued Hoge, "There can be no question but it is of God. The subject[s] of it, for the most part are deeply wounded for their sins, and can give a clear and rational account of their conversion."[17]

The fires of enthusiasm spread from Kentucky to Virginia, to Vermont, Maine, and soon to Palmyra, New York. Most of America, particularly rural areas, seemed ablaze. The Smiths likely attended many of the revivals and camp meetings within walking distance during summer months when they could peddle their wares from Joseph Sr.'s handcart. Young Joseph's experience with Methodist camp meetings would probably have been similar to that of his contemporary, New Yorker Henry Clarke Wright (1797-1870), who, as a young boy, attended a Methodist camp meeting near his father's Otsego County farm. In his 1849 autobiography, Wright recalled:

15. James McGready, qtd. in "Nineteenth Century Revivals."
16. James Finley, qtd. in "Nineteenth Century Revivals."
17. Moses Hoge, qtd. in "Nineteenth Century Revivals."

> The camp was formed in a beautiful spot—in a forest of tall trees, and at the foot of a high hill. The underbrush and bushes were cleared away from about an acre—the trees were left standing. The old logs and brushwood were taken away; and the clear spot was enclosed by a brush fence, not easily penetrated by man or beast. There were two gates, one for the public to enter,—and the other for private entrance, and retirement of the preachers. A high scaffolding was erected near the entrance gate, for the preacher's stand. In front of it was a platform; before the platform was a little pen or fold, into which the anxious inquirers were put.
>
> To this meeting came the Methodists from thirty or forty miles around; bringing their tents, beds and provisions with them. The tents were put up around inside the enclosure; and sometimes several families were in a tent. Here they remained in the camp, men, women and children—singing, praying, preaching, shouting, exhorting, day and night, for a week; having several sermons every day and every night.
>
> I was there two days and one night; spending the night in the tent of some friends. It was the first I ever attended. What I there saw and heard deeply affected my spirit. Within the camp, convictions and conversions were going on night and day. The singing, by night, was most impressive, as it rose and died away in those dark woods; but all around the camp, outside of the enclosure, was carried on every species of wickedness, Gingerbread and whiskey carts, and shows of various kinds, were there, and the noise of revelry, drunkenness and blasphemy mingled with the singing, praying, and preaching.[18]

Although the Smiths may have been entertained by the camp meetings they visited, they apparently were not "wounded in their hearts" (a common nineteenth-century term for conversion).[19] None of them affiliated with a

---

18. Henry Clarke Wright, *Human Life,* 148-49. Not all religionists approved of camp meetings. Dr. Samuel Miller observed:

> I confess I deeply regret that the use of camp meetings should be resumed in our body. To say nothing of the irregularities and abuses which it is difficult, if not impossible, in ordinary cases, wholly to avoid, on the skirts, and sometimes in the interior, of such camps; they have always appeared to me adapted to make religion more an affair of display, or impulse, of noise, and of animal sympathy, than of the understanding, the conscience, and the heart. In short, they have always struck me as adapted, in their ordinary forms, to produce effects on our intellectual and moral nature analogous to strong drink on the animal economy; that is, to excite, to warm, and to appear to strengthen for a time but only to pave the way for a morbid expenditure of "sensorial power," as we say concerning the animal economy, and for consequent debility and disease. (Qtd. in Lewis Bevens Schenck, *The Presbyterian Doctrine of Children in the Covenant,* 78.)

19. Joshua Bradley, *Accounts of Religious Revivals in Many Parts of the United States from 1815 to 1818,* 24.

congregation at the time. And while a small number of local farmers labored on the Erie Canal project during lulls in the agricultural cycle, none of the Smiths evidently worked on the huge enterprise, even though laborers were paid well. A Welsh worker in nearby Utica reported in 1818 that "wages on the canal are one dollar a day and thirteen to fourteen dollars a month with food and washing and half a pint of whisky a day. Those who provide their own food, wet and dry, get twenty-two to twenty-three dollars."[20] Average wages in Philadelphia during this time ranged from seventy-five cents to a dollar a day.[21]

The first section of the canal to be completed was a fifteen-mile stretch between Rome and Utica. After it opened in October 1819, contracts were let, and construction commenced in Palmyra.[22] A series of celebrations marked the canal's progress. Rochester newspapers noted the ceremonies held at Rome, Utica, Palmyra, and other eastern ports. By spring 1822, canal boats plied the waterway from Hartwell's basin, east of Rochester, to Little Falls, east of Palmyra. The *Palmyra Herald* noted on June 19, 1822: "[O]ur village has assumed an appearance which may be justly considered characteristic of the elevated rank to which it is destined. The canal crosses Main St. at the Eastern end where there is a large and commodious basin (Jessup) and nearly opposite the center of the village, another basin (Rogers) is now nearly completed plus at the west end of the Village is a third basin (Aldrich), directly opposite to which there is an elegant dry dock."

No doubt Joseph Jr. paused to watch the construction when he was in Palmyra on family business. Of particular interest would have been the building of the Mud Creek (officially Ganargua Creek) Aqueduct, and adjacent Canal Lock No. 29, both on the west end of town.[23] The stonework on these and other massive rock forms was done by hundreds of German masons who later constructed many of New York's famous buildings.

During the 1820s, at least fifty-two different kinds of commercial establishments found success in Palmyra.[24] In addition to general stores, other emporiums sold books, cabinets, crockery, dry goods, groceries, hardware, hats, meat, medicine, shoes, stoves, and wagons. One of the larger estab-

20. David Richard to his brother, Dec. 11, 1818, in Alan Conway, *The Welch in America,* 62.

21. Donald R. Adams Jr., "Wage Rates in the Early National Period: Philadelphia, 1785-1830," 406.

22. Blake McKelvey, "Rochester and the Erie Canal," 4.

23. This beautifully restored aqueduct in 2008 is located in Aqueduct Park.

24. Lisa Riddle compiled this listing of Palmyra businesses from Palmyra newspapers and Thomas L. Cook, *Palmyra and Vicinity,* Mar. 1988, qtd. in Cannon, "Palmyra, New York," 7-8.

lishments in the village, S. L. Thompson & Co., advertised the following dry goods: black lace veils, blankets, broadcloth, calicoes, cashmere, cotton, flannel, furniture prints, handkerchiefs, lambs' wool, merino shawls, ostrich feathers, shirtings, and tartan plaids.[25] A bookstore in the same advertisement proffered Bibles, *Child's Instructor, Dabolls Arithmetic, English Readers, Morse's Geography, Murray's Grammar, Wall's Psalms and Hymns, Walker's Dictionary,* and *Webster's Spelling Book.*

The Smiths and other Palmyra area residents had access to many services including asheries, bakeries, blacksmiths, breweries, cobblers, coopers, dentists, foundries, gristmills, lawyers, livery stables, lumber yards, pharmacists, physicians, saddle and harness shops, sawmills, sign painters, bankers, tailors, tanneries, tin smiths, and wagon and sleigh shops. Palmyra's economic success, although it may have done little to bolster Smith family fortunes, was based on the prosperity of the Erie Canal—which proved to be one of the most profitable ventures in American history. The canal opened new markets for the port of New York, and manufactured products and commodities were shipped inland on the canal. Approximately 70 percent of the freight headed toward New York consisted of agricultural products, mostly grain and flour. Some 14 percent of the cargo was forest products, including "barrels of potash and great bundles of staves."[26]

A puzzling question is why Joseph Sr., who learned coopering from his father, did not attempt to profit from the high demand for wooden staves in the Eastern market. He built a cooper's shop, with a wood floor and loft, on his Manchester property, and taught barrel-making skills to Alvin, Hyrum, and Joseph Jr.[27] The Smith farm had thousands of hardwoods—oak, beech, and chestnut—the very woods used to manufacture staves. With the Erie Canal only a few miles away, transportation would have been easy. In retrospect, coopering was a neglected opportunity that could have lifted the family from poverty, and possibly have saved the farm from eventual foreclosure.

Coopering, the trade of making wooden containers for various uses, is

---

25. *Wayne Sentinel,* Jan. 5, 1827, qtd. in Cannon, "Palmyra, New York," 8.

26. "Shaping the Age of Expansion," 5; McKelvey, "Rochester and the Erie Canal," 9.

27. Lavina Fielding Anderson, *Lucy's Book,* 392; Donald L. Enders, "The Joseph Smith, Sr., Family," 222. Several sources mention young Joseph's coopering skills. For example, Wallace Miner reminisced that "Joseph could make good sap buckets" (qtd. in Cook, *Palmyra and Vicinity,* 222). George Edward Anderson, after interviewing Jason Estey, a resident of Manchester, New York, in 1907, noted in his diary that Estey had a "cedar tub said to have been made by Joseph Smith Jr. before he was twenty-one years or when he was a big boy or minor. Made for Mrs Balinda White Sa[u]nders, wife of Orlando Sa[u]nders, one of Mr. Smith's near neighbors" (Richard Neitzel Holzapfel and Ted D. Stoddard, *Church History in Black and White,* 181).

a difficult and exacting occupation, particularly if the vessel is intended to hold liquid. The craft dates to at least as early as 2690 B.C.E.[28] With the passing of time, three divisions of skill levels evolved. White coopering, the oldest form, refers to fabricating buckets, tubs, butter churns, casks, and vats commonly used in the home or on the farm. Dry coopering, which is less demanding, manufactures boxes and casks to hold small items such as grain, flour, apples, grease, lard, and nails. Dry coopers used the poorest quality of wood since the containers were usually discarded after shipping. The most difficult form was wet coopering, which required the construction of air-tight containers to hold liquids, such as beer, wine, or spirits, under pressure and for extended period of time.

The 1820 census for Farmington, New York, lists the occupations of three adult (over age sixteen) males in the Joseph Smith Sr. family, although the census identified only the head of the household by name. Two appear in the "agriculture" column, the third in "manufactures." Census takers were instructed that "in the column of manufactures will be included not only all the persons employed in what the act more specifically denominates manufacturing *establishments,* but all those artificers, handicrafts men, and mechanics, whose labor is preeminently of the hand, and not upon the field."[29] This suggests that Alvin and Hyrum, then twenty-one and twenty, probably farmed, while Joseph Sr. coopered.

The level of Joseph Sr.'s expertise is unknown. Samples of his work have not survived, although he is known to have made dye tubs, barrels, buckets, split-wood chairs, baskets, sap-bowls, and "bee-gums." He also repaired leaky barrels for neighbors at cidering time.[30] However, neighbor and frequent visitor Benjamin Saunders commented that although "they were coopers by trade. Did not like to make steady busines[s] of it."[31] Another neighbor noted that Father Smith and Hyrum "worked some at coopering."[32] Christopher Stafford, who lived on a farm just south of the Smiths, reported that "Old Jo claimed to be a cooper but worked very little at anything. He was intemperate."[33] By 1822, however, Joseph Sr., was fifty-one, which was

28. Dan Zaroski, "Research on Coopering," 1.

29. Carroll D. Wright, *History and Growth of the United States Census,* 135.

30. Willard Bean, *A.B.C. History of Palmyra,* 27; Donald L. Enders, "'A Snug Log House,'" 17; Enders, "The Joseph Smith, Sr., Family," 222.

31. Benjamin Saunders, interviewed by William H. Kelley, ca. Sept. 1884, 20.

32. Mrs. S. F. Anderick, Statement.

33. Christopher M. Stafford, Statement, Mar. 23, 1885. "Intemperate": "2. Addicted to an excessive or habitual use of spirituous liquors"(Noah Webster, *American Dictionary of the English Language* [1828], s.v. "Intemperate").

considered old by nineteenth-century definition and was beginning to slow down, although he would live another eighteen years.[34]

Father Smith's sometimes melancholic disposition may have caused him periodically to skid into depression and excessive drinking in New York. Sylvia Butts Walker, who grew up in Manchester, close enough that the "Smith family lived in sight of my parents' house," later described him as "very intemperate."[35] Mrs. S. F. Anderick, while living with her uncle Earl Wilcox "nearly opposite old Jo Smith's," observed that "Old Jo was dissipated."[36] Another Manchester neighbor, Barton Stafford, likewise described Father Smith as "a noted drunkard."[37] Cornelius R. Stafford added that "father and son [Joseph Jr.] were frequently drunk."[38] Still another Palmyra resident, Hiram Jackway, "[s]aw Joe and his Father Drunk in a hay field."[39] Sylvia's brother Isaac Butts, a schoolmate of young Joseph, reported he had "frequently seen old Jo drunk."[40] And Lorenzo Saunders, who knew the Smiths well, recalled how Joseph Sr. "would go to Turkey shoots and get drunk; pretend to enchant their guns so that they could not kill the Turkey. ... He would blow in the gun and feel around the lock then tell them it was charmed and they could not kill the turkey."[41]

Martin Harris, who financed the publication of the Book of Mormon, told an 1859 interviewer how some Palmyra residents "put whiskey into the old man's cider and got him half drunk."[42] In the summer of 1830, Joseph Sr. traveled to nearby Victor with a basket of copies of the Book of Mormon to sell. Stopping at William C. Dryer's tavern, he "sought entertainment in exchange for a book," pleading that he was "out of money." Dryer agreed to the trade and the next morning paid his penniless guest "three shillings as balance of account." Smith used the money to purchase some whiskey,

34. Lucy Smith, working on her biography in 1845, refers to her husband in the 1820s as an "old man" and both herself and husband as "persons in advanced life" (Anderson, *Lucy's Book,* 323, 326). In Joseph Sr.'s funeral eulogy, Robert B. Thompson noted that he "was already in the wane of life, when the light of truth broke in upon the world" (R. B. Thompson, "An Address," 171). Alvin Smith, on his deathbed in 1823, when his father was fifty-two, admonished his brother Hyrum to "take care of [our parents] in their old age, and do not any more let them work hard, as they are now in old age" (Anderson, *Lucy's Book,* 352).

35. Sylvia Walker, Statement.

36. Anderick, Statement, 2.

37. Barton Stafford, Statement.

38. Cornelius R. Stafford, Statement.

39. William Kelley, Notebook, No. 5, 11.

40. Isaac Butts, Statement.

41. Lorenzo Saunders, Interviewed by William H. Kelley, Sept. 17, 1884.

42. Martin Harris, qtd. in Joel Tiffany, "Mormonism—No. II," *Tiffany's Monthly.*

and when he left the place, "he couldn't navigate." Some mischievous boys grabbed the man, tipped him into a horse watering trough, and pumped water on his head until he sobered up.[43] Even one of the Smith family's physicians, Dr. Alexander McIntyre, reportedly referred to Father Smith as "a drunkard" (as well as a "liar and a thief").[44]

Later, on December 9, 1834, during a family celebration in Joseph Jr.'s home in Ohio, Oliver Cowdery recorded that "Joseph Smith, senior, a Patriarch, and President of the high priesthood in the church of the Latter Day Saints," pronounced patriarchal blessings upon the heads of each of his family members.[45] While blessing Hyrum and Joseph Jr., Father Smith acknowledged his excessive drinking during their boyhood. In reference to Hyrum's enduring support, the elder Smith pronounced: "Thou has always stood by thy father, and reached forth the helping hand to lift him up when he was in affliction; and though he has been out of the way through wine, thou has never forsaken him nor laughed him to scorn."[46] While blessing his son Joseph, Patriarch Smith added: "Thou hast stood by thy father, and like Shem, would have covered his nakedness, rather than see him exposed to shame: when the daughters of the Gentiles laughed, thy heart has been moved with a just anger to avenge thy kindred."[47]

Joseph Sr. was by no means an exception. Many men of the period drank to excess on occasion. Early Americans were fond of what they called "ardent spirits." Beer, ale, wine, rum, gin, cider, and whiskey were the "good creatures of God." In 1830, Americans annually consumed nearly four gallons of alcohol per person, the highest rate in recorded history.[48] Gain Robinson, another local physician, was a blue-ruin Thompsonian (herbalist) who routinely made his rounds while inebriated. He "was a successful doctor," wrote one Palmyra historian judiciously, "but at times rather intemperate." On one occasion, he made a house call "in no condition to examine." When the concerned family suggested he lie down on the couch, he replied, "I will when it comes around again."[49] In 1828, a committee of local Presbyterian elders suspended Robinson's church membership for "an immoderate and

43. "In the Summer of the Year," *Syracuse Journal,* Feb. 16, 1867.

44. Qtd. by Clark Braden in Clark Braden and E. L. Kelley, *Public Discussion of the Issues between the Reorganized Church of Jesus Christ of Latter Day Saints and the Church of Christ (Disciples),* 350.

45. Joseph Smith Sr., Introductory Comments: Patriarchal Blessing Book, 1:1-2.

46. Joseph Smith Sr., "Blessing on Hyrum Smith."

47. Joseph Smith Sr., "Blessing on Joseph Smith, Jr." See Genesis 9:18-29.

48. W. J. Rorabaugh, *The Alcoholic Republic,* 10.

49. Cook, *Palmyra and Vicinity,* 125.

in=temperate use of spiritous liquors to the great injury of his christian character and usefulness."[50]

"They had no temperance societies, in those days," explained Levi Beardsley, a New York contemporary of the Smiths, "and no one, whether he drank or not, deemed it sinful or improper to refresh the inner man when the needful could be had."[51] Most Americans began their day with a tumbler of "ardent spirits"—"taking our bitters," they termed it. "Spirit in some form was upon the breakfast table, carried into the field at eleven o'clock, at every training, raising, husking, log rolling bee, and sheep washing," added a Vermont chronicler in 1954. "It was as free as water."[52] The age was noted for its marathon drinking bouts. Rare indeed was the funeral, wedding, birth, or christening that was not celebrated with alcohol, fermented or distilled. Henry Clarke Wright observed that chopping, logging, and husking bees were sources of a "vast amount of drunkenness." He lamented that, although there were "great outcryings against excessive drinking, not a word was ever uttered against the drinking custom. He would have been counted a fool or a madman, who should have declared all drinking, distilling, and vending of alcoholic liquor to be wrong and ruinous."[53]

Joseph Jr. as a confident twenty-seven-year-old would announce his interpretation of God's will that "inasmuch as any man drinketh wine or strong drink among you, behold it is not good," and that "strong drinks are not for the belly, but for the washing of your bodies" (D&C 89:5-7). But in the early 1820s, his voice had not yet been sufficiently stimulated by the then-emerging American Temperance Movement, and other influences, and the young seer may have imbibed as much as the average American youth of the day.

As an adult, Joseph sometimes sounded vainglorious. In 1843, he wrote: "I combat the errors of ages: I meet the violence of mobs; I cope with illegal proceedings from executive authority; I cut the Gordian knot of powers; and I solve mathematical problems of Universities: WITH TRUTH, *diamond truth, and God is my 'right hand man.'*"[54] A year later, he announced: "I have more to boast of than ever any man had. I am the only man that has ever been able to keep a whole church together since the days of Adam. A

50. "Records of the Session of the Presbyterian Church," 2.

51. Levi Beardsley, *Reminiscences,* 59.

52. "Fifty Years of Farming in Vermont," 5.

53. Wright, *Human Life,* 155-56.

54. Joseph Smith Jr., "To the *Times and Seasons,*" 375. For a further discussion of Joseph's boasting, see Richard Lyman Bushman, *Joseph Smith,* 483-86.

large majority of the whole have stood by me. Neither Paul, John, Peter, nor Jesus ever did it. I boast that no man ever did such a work as I. The followers of Jesus ran away from him, but the Latter-day Saints never ran away from me yet."[55] But as a boy, Joseph was quiet and reserved. "Taciturnity was among his characteristic idiosyncracies," wrote Palmyra newspaperman Pomeroy Tucker, "and he seldom spoke to any one outside of his intimate associates except when first addressed by another." Joseph's reserve concealed an intense curiosity, however, and from his early adolescence on, he "read comprehensively, in which qualification he was far in advance of his elder brother and even his father."[56]

Joseph honed his developing intellectual skills by joining the local debating club. The January 23, 1822, *Western Farmer,* a Palmyra newspaper, announced: "The young people of the village of Palmyra and its vicinity are requested to attend a Debating school at the school house near Mr. Billings' on Friday next." Orsamus Turner, also a member of the club, thought that "Joseph had a little ambition; and some very laudable aspirations; the mother's intellect occasionally shone out in him feebly, especially when he used to help us solve some portentous questions of moral or political ethics, in our juvenile debating club, which we moved down to the old red school house on Durfee street, to get rid of the annoyance of critics that used to drop in upon us in the village."[57]

Joseph sought self-improvement through various religious activities as well. Although he joined no church, he said he "attend[ed] their several meetings as often as occasion would permit."[58] Pomeroy Tucker added, "Protracted revival meetings were customary in some of the churches, and Smith frequented those of different denominations, sometimes professing to participate in their devotional exercises."[59] Organized in 1797, the Presbyterian Church was the oldest denomination in Palmyra. The sect was in a favorable position to expand into the Finger Lakes region because its theology was similar to New England Calvinism, the religion with which many New York immigrants, including Lucy Smith, was most familiar. For twenty years, Presbyterian ministers in Palmyra preached on alternating Sundays in the east and west ends of town. The first meetinghouse in western Palmyra was

55. *History of the Church,* 6:408-9.
56. Pomeroy Tucker, *Origin, Rise, and Progress of Mormonism,* 16, 17.
57. Orsamus Turner, *History of the Pioneer Settlement of Phelps and Gorham's Purchase,* 214.
58. *History of the Church,* 1:3.
59. Tucker, *Origin, Rise, and Progress of Mormonism,* 17-18.

erected in 1811 on the west side of Church Street on land donated by General John Swift, a prominent citizen killed in the War of 1812.[60]

Despite most churchgoers in the area being Presbyterians, the meeting hall was non-denominational. The forty-by-fifty-foot wooden structure, surmounted with a steeple, also served as the town hall until it burned in 1838.[61] Lorenzo Saunders recalled: "[T]he first time I ever went to Sabbath School I went with young Joe Smith at the old Presbyterian Church."[62] Joseph's youngest brother, William, added that it was there that he "spent much of my boy-hood days, especially the Sabbath in the Sunday Schools of that day."[63] Joseph may have attended some services in the union meetinghouse, and Lucy and three of her children—but not Joseph—joined the Western Presbyterian Church in the mid-1820s.[64]

At the same time, Joseph Sr. in the early 1820s was probably a Methodist, or at least Methodist-inclined,[65] and Joseph Jr. at this time was evidently more interested in the Methodist Episcopal Church than in Presbyterianism. His involvement in Methodism was likely due, in part, to the early influence of both parents, who attended a Methodist church in Vermont before Joseph was born. No doubt the church's focus on ordinary folk also impressed him. "The movement eroded patterns of difference to established authority and tradition," write Nathan O. Hatch and John H. Wigger, historians of Methodism, "and dignified the convictions of ordinary people on important matters—religious, political, or economic. It elicited choice and participation by people long ignored, and bound them together in disciplined and supportive groups."[66]

The first Methodist class in Palmyra, under the direction of itinerant circuit preachers connected with the Ontario circuit of the Geneva Conference, initiated meetings in Palmyra in 1811, five years before the Smiths

---

60. Woman's Society of the Western Presbyterian Church, comp., "Palmyra, New York."

61. Cook, *Palmyra and Vicinity,* 247.

62. Lorenzo Saunders, interviewed by Kelly, Sept. 17, 1884.

63. William B. Smith, "Sermon by Elder Wm. B. Smith."

64. Anderick, Statement, June 24, 1887. On February 13, 1817, the Presbytery divided the church of Palmyra into the Presbyterian Church of East Palmyra, and the Western Presbyterian Church of Palmyra under successive pastors Reverend Stephen M. Wheelock (Apr.-Aug. 1817), Jesse Townsend (Aug. 1817-Jan. 1822), Daniel C. Hopkins (Jan. 1822-Feb. 1824), Benjamin B. Stockton (Feb. 1824-Oct. 1827), Stephen Porter (Oct. 1827-Nov. 1828), and Alfred D. Campbell (Nov. 1828-Sept. 1831). See Woman's Society of the Western Presbyterian Church, "Palmyra, New York," 7.

65. W. H. McIntosh, *History of Ontario Co.,* 42; "Mormonism in Its Infancy," 2. Although young Joseph was frequently involved in Methodist activities in Palmyra, there is no evidence that he joined the church here.

66. Nathan O. Hatch and John H. Wigger, *Methodism and the Shaping of American Culture,* 16.

arrived. Prior to its incorporation as "the first Methodist Episcopal Church of Palmyra" on July 3, 1821, the Methodist Society met in barns, homes, tents, and schoolhouses.[67] On July 7, 1821, prominent Palmyra resident Durfee Chase deeded to the Methodist Church property on Vienna Road where a campground was established.[68] The organization built its first meetinghouse the next year on the corner of Vienna and Johnson Streets.[69]

For reasons both complex and controversial, Joseph Jr. did not formally join a church in his youth. Years after the fact, as an adult, he said that Jesus, appearing in vision with the Father, told him in 1820 not to unite with any church because "they were all wrong." But this particular reminiscence does not match the reality of Joseph's life during that earlier time. For example, Lucy, Hyrum, Harrison, and Sophronia all joined the Western Presbyterian Church in 1824 or 1825 and remained members of record until as late as March 1830.[70] And Joseph himself on several occasions after 1820 participated in various Methodist ventures, particularly camp meetings.

These "brush arbor" meetings constituted one of Methodism's most effective means of evangelism and mark the beginning of what historians called the Second Great Awakening in America. As noted above, Henry Clarke Wright described in detail the surroundings of a Methodist camp meeting held during his boyhood in Hartwick township in Otsego County that would have been similar to the kinds of meetings Joseph Smith was exposed to.[71] Many people attended the camp meetings for entertainment. Sermonizing was a kind of performance art, and the enthusiastic "shout tradition" was a lively practice dating back to the revivals of the late eighteenth century.[72] Preachers whooped, waved copies of the Bible, thumped pulpits,

67. Ontario County Clerk's Office, Miscellaneous Records, Book C, pp. 385-88.

68. Ontario County, Deeds, Book G, p. 345. Durfee Chase (1793-1872), a successful Palmyra physician, was Willard and Sally Chase's eldest brother. A Grand Master of Palmyra's Mount Moriah Masonic Lodge in 1822 and 1823, he, along with fifty other prominent Palmyra men, signed an 1833 statement declaring, in part: "We, the undersigned, have been acquainted with the Smith family, for a number of years, while they resided near this place, and we have no hesitation in saying, that we consider them destitute of that moral character, which ought to entitle them to the confidence of any community. They were particularly famous for visionary projects, spent much of their time in digging for money which they pretended was hid in the earth" (Eber D. Howe, *Mormonism Unvailed*, 261).

69. Woman's Society of the Western Presbyterian Church, comp., "Palmyra, New York," 10.

70. On March 3, 1830, a committee from Palmyra's Western Presbyterian Church was assigned to visit the Smiths to determine why they had not attended church the previous eighteen months ("Records of the Sessions of the Presbyterian Church in Palmyra").

71. Wright, *Human Life*, 148-49.

72. For an excellent treatment of the Methodist "shout" tradition, see Ann Taves, *Fits, Trances, and Visions*, 76-117.

and threatened hell-fire and damnation as they delivered their extemporaneous sermons. Abraham Lincoln, Joseph's contemporary, commented, "When I see a man preach I like to see him act as if he were fighting bees."[73] Parishioners were part of the drama as well. The association of weeping, crying out, falling to the ground, and shouting for joy as the power of God was said to descend on the gathering made preaching and worship interactive. One observer described "[m]en and women pray[ing] at the top of their voices ... persons [falling] to the ground ... [and hours] sometimes elaps[ing] before they awoke to consciousness."[74]

Beyond the emotional extravagance lay the serious business of salvation—the experience of what participants believed was the overshadowing of God's presence. For believers, the camp was sacred space. Both in terms of layout and rituals, the organization of camp meetings was drawn from biblical accounts of Israelites encamped about the tabernacle in the wilderness. The camp-meeting ground was the new public place of worship where the heavenly presence was expected and where believers gathered to glorify God. The heart of the campground was the stand or stage from which ministers preached.[75] One campground in Pennsylvania probably resembled the Methodist campground in Palmyra that Joseph Jr. and his family would have visited:

> A rough board stand was constructed, which was occupied by the preachers during Divine service, and a circle of tents was formed round about, composed of wagon and bed covers stretched over hooped saplings. The floors of the tents were the bare ground concealed by a sprinkling of straw, while the beautiful green foliage of the forest was spread out above them. Multitudes of people collected from far and near, attracted, many by novelty, and some by a desire to do good and to get good. The tremendous emotions of the speaker were communicated to his audience, and

---

73. Qtd. in John H. Wigger, *Taking Heaven by Storm,* 48.

74. Galusha Anderson, *When Neighbors Were Neighbors,* 106.

75. The Book of Mormon would subsequently include a description of a public address by King Benjamin that recalls a Methodist camp meeting:

> And it came to pass that when they came up to the temple, they pitched their tents round about, every man according to his family, consisting of his wife, and his sons, and his daughters, and their sons, and their daughters, from the eldest down to the youngest, every family being separate, one from another; and they pitched their tents round about the temple, every man having his tent with the door thereof towards the temple, that thereby they might remain in their tents, and hear the words which king Benjamin should speak unto them; for the multitude being so great, that king Benjamin could not teach them all within the walls of the temple; therefore, he caused a tower to be erected, that thereby his people might hear the words which he should speak unto them. (Book of Mormon [1830], 156.)

> an excitement was produced of which we in this day can have but a faint conception. The cries of the penitent, and the shouts of rejoicing Christians, mingled with the deep tones of the preacher, produced a marked effect even on the most obdurate infidel.[76]

Jesse Lee described a typical day at a camp meeting in an unspecified location and year: "Soon after the dawn of day," he narrated, "a person walks all round the ground in front of the tents, blowing a trumpet as he passes." A few minutes after this reveille, another trumpet call sounded at which time "the people in all their tents begin to sing, and then pray, either in their tents, or at the door of them, as is most convenient." At sunrise, a sermon was preached. "We have preaching again at 10 o'clock, and dine about one," continued the report. "We preach again at 3 o'clock, eat supper about the setting of the sun, and have preaching again at candle light."[77]

Pomeroy Tucker wrote that Joseph Jr. "made some active demonstrations of engagedness [in Methodism], though his assumed convictions were insufficiently grounded or abiding to carry him along to the saving point of conversion."[78] In the Methodist tradition, class meetings were the basic units of the faith. Originating under John Wesley in the 1740s, these gatherings were essentially patterned after late seventeenth- and early eighteenth-century Church of England groups, and the communal piety of the Moravian Bands which so impressed Wesley. Christian nurture began prior to one's conversion to Christ. When seekers, like Joseph Smith, were "awakened" to God's claim on their lives, they typically joined a class on a six-month probationary basis. The groups gathered weekly under a class leader, often a lay person like Willard Chase. In 1856, an anonymous chronicler, without citing his source, claimed that Joseph "had previously professed religion at a camp meeting, and was quit[e] an exhorter at evening meetings."[79] Orsamus

76. Stewart Pearce, *Annals of Luzern County,* 294.

77. Jesse Lee, *A Short History of the Methodists,* 366-67.

78. Tucker, *Origin, Rise, and Progress of Mormonism,* 18.

79. "Mormonism in Its Infancy," 2. A Methodist exhorter, following the minister's sermon, engaged in an earnest conversation with the audience, underscoring the minister's message and admonishing listeners to follow the clergyman's teachings. John H. Wigger, a historian of Methodism, explains: "In theory, exhorting consisted of simply telling one's testimony of conversion or relating life experiences in the faith, with the goal of imploring one's listeners toward greater holiness and fuller service" *(Taking Heaven by Storm,* 29). "To commence speaking by exhortation," added Methodist itinerant Charles Giles in his 1844 autobiography, "is doubtless the best mode of procedure for a young man who is intending to preach extemporaneously." He added: "To declaim, to advise, to warn, to persuade, to entreat with tears, all are comprised in the ample range of exhortation. And, in doing this awfully sublime work, the depths of human learning may be opened, the wide field of revelation explored, its doctrines brought up, its promises spread out,

Turner also remembered Joseph's involvement with the Methodist Church in the early 1820s. "After catching a spark of Methodism in the camp meeting, away down in the woods, on Vienna road," Turner wrote, Joseph became a "very passable exhorter in evening meetings."[80] This grove, where Vienna and Johnson Streets intersected near the Palmyra Cemetery, was the site of camp meetings during 1821-22, a year or more after Joseph later said he received a visitation from the Father and the Son informing him that all Christian churches were "wrong."

In 1838, Joseph began working out a detailed recital of his early visionary experiences. (At least twice before, in 1832 and in 1835, he had produced somewhat abbreviated narratives.)[81] At this later date, Joseph was under siege in Ohio. To escape creditors and the taint of a failed financial institution, he left the state with counselor and friend Sidney Rigdon. The beleaguered pair landed on their feet at a safe distance in Far West, Missouri, hoping to refurbish their tarnished images. Each began dictating personal histories to correct "the many reports which have been put in circulation by evil disposed and designing persons."[82] Virtually all information then circulating about Joseph related not to religious activities but to what former neighbors said

---

together with the rousing of Sinai's thunder, and the blood and groans of Calvary" *(Pioneer,* 84-85). Charles Chauncy, an eighteenth-century American Congregational minister, believed that exhorters, more often than ministers, were able to impact audiences. The exhorters, he wrote, were "[m]en of all Occupations … who, though they have no Learning, and but small Capacities, yet imagine they are able, and without Study too, to speak to the spiritual Profit of such as are willing to hear them: Nay, there are among these Exhorters, *Babes in Age,* as well as Understanding." He added that the exhorters, like Joseph Smith, were "chiefly … *young Persons,* sometimes *Lads,* or rather *Boys" (Seasonable Thoughts on the State of Religion,* 226).

80. Turner, *History of the Pioneer Settlement of Phelps and Gorham's Purchase,* 214. Palmyra Methodists did not purchase this property in the woods on the Vienna road until July 1821 (Wesley P. Walters, "New Light on Mormon Origins from the Palmyra Revival," 99). They constructed a meetinghouse in Palmyra in 1822.

81. In 1832, Joseph wrote an earlier version of this epiphany, one less polished and somewhat different from the 1838 account. This earlier sketch notes, in part:

> while in <the> attitude of calling upon the Lord <in the 16th year of my age> a piller of light above the brightness of the sun at noon day come down from above and rested upon me and I was filled with the spirit of god and the <Lord> opened the heavens upon me and … he spake unto me saying Joseph <my son> thy sins are forgiven thee. [G]o thy <way> walk in my statutes and keep my commandments … <behold> the world lieth in sin at this time and none doeth good no not one they have turned asside from the gospel and keep not <my> commandments they draw near to me with their lips while their hearts are far from me and mine anger is kindling against the inhabitants of the earth[.] (Dean C. Jessee, *The Personal Writings of Joseph Smith,* 5-6.)

82. Rigdon's narrative was never published. A summary and analysis is in Richard S. Van Wagoner, *Sidney Rigdon,* 214-15. My narrative of Smith's 1838-39 history is taken from the original Manuscript History of the Church, Book A-1, Joseph Smith Papers. For convenience, see Jessee, *The Personal Writings of Joseph Smith,* 196-210; or *History of the Church,* 1:5-6.

was "money digging" in affidavits published in book-form in 1834. Joseph did not directly address these accusations in his 1838-39 history, but the context is unmistakable. Joseph began by relating a miraculous incident he said had unfolded on "the morning of a beautiful clear day early in the spring of Eighteen hundred and twenty," when he was fourteen and had been swept up in "an unusual excitement on the subject of religion."

He said that as he prayed "I saw a pillar <of> light exactly over my head above the brightness of the sun, which descended gradually untill it fell upon me." Two angelic "personages (whose brightness and glory defy all description) standing above me in the air" addressed him. Though they did not say who they were, one spoke Joseph's name, pointed to the other, then announced in the language of Matthew 3:17, Matthew 17:5, Mark 1:11, and Luke 3:22: "This is my beloved Son, Hear him." Seeking answers, Joseph asked: "Which of all the sects [is] right?" and which "should [I] join?" Joseph said that the speaker advised him against uniting with any of the churches "for they were all wrong." He elaborated that "all their Creeds were an abomination in his sight," that their professors were all corrupt, that "they draw near to me with their lips but their hearts are far from me, They teach for doctrines the commandments of men, having a form of Godliness but they deny the power thereof."

"When I came to myself again," Joseph continued, he was lying on his back "looking up into Heaven." The typical Methodist would probably have interpreted Joseph's experience as a "falling down" or "lying slain in the Spirit" episode (see chap. 9). Joseph later said that he related the story to a local Methodist preacher and was shocked when he "treated my communication ... with great contempt, saying it was all of the Devil, that there was no such thing as visions or revelation in these days."[83] Recounting the experience in 1838,

83. On the contrary, willingness to accept divinely inspired impressions, dreams, and visions as evidence of the work and call of God were hallmarks of the Methodist connection. Charles Chauncy, a New England Congregationalist minister and a somewhat jaundiced observer of the Great Awakening in the 1740s, wrote: "Visions now became common, and Trances also, the Subjects of which were in their own Conceit transported from Earth to Heaven, where they saw and heard most glorious Things; conversed with Christ and Holy Angels" (Charles Chauncy, "A Letter from a Gentleman in Boston to Mr. George Wishart," 118-19). Wigger, in his history of Methodism and rise of popular Christianity in America, states: "A great many early Methodists believed in the efficacy of prophetic dreams, visions, and supernatural impressions and were not afraid to base day-to-day decisions on such phenomena. Examples of this kind of supernaturalism abound in the journals and autobiographies of Methodist preachers and lay men and women" *(Taking Heaven by Storm,* 106). George Peck, writing just before the Civil War on "early Methodism" in the Genesee country, noted that visions of God and other heavenly beings were common during the revivalistic era: "Men and women, old and young, dreamed dreams, saw visions, and were filled

Joseph stressed that "telling the story had excited a great deal of prejudice against me among professors of religion and was the cause of great persecution which continued to increase and though I was only an obscure boy."

Joseph's 1838-39 narrative has become part of the official founding story of most groups based on his restorationist message. Yet not a single witness, friend or foe, mentions in the dozens of contemporary sources that survive an 1820 visionary experience instructing Joseph that all churches were an abomination before God.[84] There were documented persecutions. But these arose from conflicts with Joseph's money-digging associates and unresolved Smith family debts, not from any religious claim. Other than Joseph's own remembered testimony, there is no documentary evidence that a visionary experience occurred in the "15th year of my age," as he stated in the 1830s.[85] The principal minister in the area in 1820, Presbyterian Reverend Jesse Townsend, whom the editor of *Sackets' Harbor Courier* characterized

---

with the spirit of prophecy" *(Early Methodism,* 187). Joshua Bradley published in 1819 the account of a fifteen-year-old girl:

> whose distress for sin had been deep and affecting for several weeks, without obtaining any hope of pardoning mercy. At length, her whole life appeared unveiled to her view; and she seemed placed on the verge of destruction. ... With her sins pressing her down, and the flaming gulf of eternal misery before her, she cried aloud for mercy, mercy, mercy, to her compassionate Saviour, or she must perish for ever. ... At the close of this awful scene, which struck horror through the whole family, she suddenly burst out in raptures of joy and praise, that she had obtained deliverance. ... It was a sight of the Lord Jesus, she said, the almighty Saviour of sinners, that gave her instant relief. He was present to her view in all his mediatorial glory, as able and willing to save to the uttermost; and her shuddering soul clasped him in the arms of faith, and he bore her away as a brand from the everlasting burning. *(Accounts of Religious Revivals,* 176.)

84. Historian Dale Morgan, in a August 13, 1948, letter to Samuel A. Burgess, a member of the Reorganized Church of Jesus Christ of Latter Day Saints in Missouri, wrote:

> I have made a most determined search for evidences that would support Joseph Smith's claims in this respect, the most thorough search, I believe, that anyone has ever made, and this evidence does not exist. I have examined all the surviving newspapers published in Palmyra and Canandaigua during the time of the Smith residence in that neighborhood, as well as fragmentary files of the papers published in the Susquehanna Valley—I spent months on this research—and in none of them is there anything to bear out Joseph Smith's later portrait of himself as a person who had had spiritual experiences of overwhelming import (that is to say, one to whom God the Father had shown himself). Mr. [Francis W.] Kirkham, who did much research in the same field, was not able to demonstrate anything in this respect either; on the contrary, the stories he found and published present quite another picture of the young Joseph Smith. If you had to go into a court and present a case for Joseph Smith that hinged upon establishing the fact that his spiritual claims were common knowledge during the seven years before 1830, not to speak of the period before that, you could present no evidence except that of an obviously interested witness, himself. ... I have found no evidence whatsoever—in newspaper, religious periodical, court record, or private journal—that the First Vision was talked about or even known among the church members before 1840. (Walker, *Dale Morgan on Early Mormonism,* 160-62.)

85. Jessee, *The Personal Writings of Joseph Smith,* 6.

as "a gentleman of the first respectability in Palmyra,"[86] wrote two letters in 1833 and 1834 summarizing Joseph's character without mentioning a vision. "A person of questionable character, of intemperate habits," wrote Townsend in late 1833—"[a] noted *money-digger,*" who lived "in a sequestered neighborhood, where, with his dupes, his impostures and low cunning gave him a reputation for being 'smart.'"[87] To an 1834 correspondent, Townsend reported that Joseph claimed he "had been directed by the Spirit of the Lord to dig [the golden plates of the Book of Mormon] from the earth," and nothing else. "The founders & propagators of the Mormon imposition are here [in Palmyra] considered as not uttering the truth in any of their sectarian assertions, & as wholly unworthy of public & individual confidence," Townsend concluded.[88]

"It is notorious," an English critic of Methodism lamented as early as 1747, "that the Methodist writings abound with intimations of divine communications, prophetic whispers, and special guidances."[89] Nathan Hatch adds that the Methodist Episcopal Church empowered "ordinary people by taking their deepest spiritual impulses at face value rather than subjecting them to the scrutiny of orthodox doctrine and the frowns of respectable clergymen."[90] The Methodist system, according to Wigger, encouraged both preachers and congregants to "use their imaginations and creative resources to extend the movement and to evangelize those within their reach."[91] Certainly, if Joseph had reported a vision to a Methodist minister, Willard Chase,[92] a Smith family neighbor, fellow money digger, and loyal Methodist, would have heard about it. Chase served as class leader, or lay pastor, in the local Palmyra congregation.[93] When the Methodist Episcopal Church

86. James Howe, editor of *Sackets' Harbor Courier,* rpt., clipping from undated and unidentified newspaper, Jonathan B. Turner Papers, Illinois Historical Society Library, Springfield.

87. Jesse Townsend to Phineas Stiles, Dec. 24, 1833, qtd. in Tucker, *Origin, Rise, and Progress of Mormonism,* 288.

88. Jesse Townsend to Elisha Camp, Aug. 16, 1834, in Vogel, *Early Mormon Documents,* 3:24-27.

89. "John Smith" to John Wesley, Aug. 21, 1747, in Frank Baker, *The Works of John Wesley,* 259.

90. Nathan O. Hatch, *The Democratization of American Christianity,* 10.

91. Wigger, *Taking Heaven by Storm,* 22.

92. Chase was born at Swansea, Bristol County, Massachusetts, on February 1, 1798 (Clark Chase Family Group Record).

93. Anderson, *Lucy's Book,* 381. The class meeting was the "fundamental institutional building block of American Methodism" (Wigger, *Taking Heaven by Storm,* 80). After the circuit preacher, the next most important worker in early Methodism was the class leader. From the 1740s, the class meeting was the "foundation of both Methodist finances and Methodist corporate piety and discipline" (ibid., 80). Class leaders were responsible for receiving financial contributions and watching over the souls of their brethren. The majority of class leaders "were

gained prominence in southern states, many members were slave holders. At nearby Utica, New York, on May 31, 1843, Methodists opposed to slavery organized the Wesleyan Methodist Connection, a forerunner of the Wesleyan Methodist Church.[94] Chase, at that point a minister, became affiliated with this anti-slavery body, chairing its Niagara District in the Rochester Conference from 1846 until 1853.[95] He was then assigned as minister in Peruville and Harford, Cortland County.[96] Poor health forced his retirement in 1855.[97] He subsequently died in Palmyra on March 10, 1871.[98] Chase, in 1820 among the most prominent Methodists in a Palmyra congregation of fewer than 200, left no record of Joseph's hostile reception from a Methodist preacher. In fact, in an 1833 affidavit, highly critical of Joseph, Chase affirmed: "I became acquainted with the Smith family ... in the year 1820. At that time, they were engaged in the money digging business, which they followed until the latter part of the season of 1827."[99]

Dozens of other witnesses, many of them exemplary citizens, including some long-time neighbors and acquaintances of the Smith family, provide testimony that, during the early 1820s, the family's most conspicuous focus was treasure seeking. Religious activities are hardly mentioned in the contemporary record, and never a vision of the Father and the Son.[100] As

---

the more successful members of their peer groups, in terms of both worldly accomplishments and spiritual progress" (ibid., 98). Their responsibilities included visiting new families, sick people, and those "whose spiritual zeal began to cool" (Kenneth Cain Kinghorn, *The Heritage of American Methodism,* 70).

94. Brief histories of the Wesleyan Methodist Church may be found in "Our History" and "Wesleyan Church." The definitive treatment is Ira F. McLeister and Roy S. Nicholson, *Conscience and Commitment.*

95. Chase had direct ministerial responsibility for Somerset (McLeister and Nicholson, *Conscience and Commitment,* 543).

96. Ibid., 546.

97. Lorenzo Saunders, Chase's brother-in-law, said that Chase "had the poralisis [paralysis]" (Lorenzo Saunders, interviewed by William H. Kelley, Sept. 17, 1884, 5 [back]). The 1870 federal census lists seventy-two-year-old "Will Chase" in Palmyra as an "Invalid" under the care of his sixty-nine-year-old sister, Sally (U.S. Bureau of the Census, New York, 1870, film #1113, p. 365).

98. Willard Chase, Obituary, *The American Wesleyan,* Apr. 10, 1871, courtesy Bill Clark; see also Willard Chase, Obituary, *Palmyra Courier,* Mar. 17, 1871.

99. Willard Chase, Affidavit, Dec. 11, 1833.

100. Dan Vogel, "The Locations of Joseph Smith's Early Treasure Quests." D. Michael Quinn's "Joseph Smith's *Experience* of a Methodist 'Camp-Meeting' in 1820" treats Methodist Camp Meetings, weather patterns, and what he calls Joseph's "anachronistic conflation of memory and narrative" in an attempt to prove that Smith, in fact, experienced his "first vision," a theophany of the Father and Son, in June 1820. I remain unconvinced. Lucy Smith remembered that her son's "first" visionary experience occurred during the fall harvest of 1823 when he was "pondering in his mind which of the churches [was] the true one" (Anderson, *Lucy's Book,* 335). And Joseph's cousin and friend Oliver Cowdery wrote in a history they compiled together in 1834-35 that Smith was

LDS historian James B. Allen concluded: during the early years of Joseph's church, at least, "the public image of Joseph Smith and his spiritual experiences did not include the story of the first vision. … belief in the vision was not essential for conversion to the Church, for there is no evidence that the story of told to prospective converts of the early 1830's."[101]

As intriguing as Joseph found Sally Chase, she was an amateur, often unsuccessful seer. Benjamin Saunders reported in 1884: "I have seen Sally (Sarah) Chase peep or look in her seer Stone a many a time. She would look for anything. … My oldest Brother had some Cattle stray away. She claimed she could see them but they were found right in the opposite direction from where she said they were."[102] Benjamin's brother Lorenzo added that Steve Mungou,[103] a Manchester resident, lost a pocket book which contained four promissory notes and some cash. Sally sought his lost pocketbook in her seer stone and announced that it "lays right at the side of a log in the woods were you loaded that wood." Despite extensive searching, the missing item was found elsewhere. Lorenzo recalled that Sally was also wrong when he asked her where to look for the drag tooth on his harrow.[104]

Although Sally Chase may have been one of Joseph's first contacts with practical occultism, his principal early mentor was folk magician Luman Walters. Young Joseph, according to his father, during his teen years "happened to be where a man was looking into a dark stone and telling people, therefrom, where to dig for money and other things."[105] The boy was impressed by the clairvoyant's charisma. Born in Connecticut in 1788, Walters

not even certain in 1823 that God existed. The account noted that Smith called "upon the Lord in secret" for an answer to the question: "if a Supreme Being did exist, to have an assurance that he was accepted of him" (Cowdery to Phelps, "Letter IV," 77). The answer to his prayer was the reported appearance of the angel Moroni, not God or Jesus (see Chap. 8). Furthermore, the Cowdery-Smith account and the published reminiscences of both Lucy and William Smith, as outlined herein in chapter 9, are clear that the family members who converted to Presbyterianism did so during the local religious revival prompted by Alvin's 1823 death, and not a June 1820 camp meeting.

101. James B. Allen, "The Significance of Joseph Smith's 'First Vision' in Mormon History," 44.

102. Benjamin Saunders, interviewed by William H. Kelley, ca. Sept. 1884, 29-30. Saunders's story is reminiscent of the 1827 tale of the New London, Connecticut, woman reportedly who discovered "by the aid of a crystal pebble" a legendary Spanish treasure buried by the port. (Charles M. Skinner, *Myths and Legends of Our Own Land,* 282-83).

103. Dan Vogel surmises that this individual may have been Stephen Lemunion who advertised the loss of his "red Morocco Pocket Book" in the *Wayne Sentinel,* Jan. 12, 1827 (Vogel, *Early Mormon Documents,* 2:155).

104. Lorenzo Saunders, interview, Nov. 12, 1884, 9. A drag tooth was like a metal spike fitted to the frame of the harrow.

105. Fayette Lapham, "Interview with the Father of Joseph Smith," 305.

was an eccentric conjurer and clairvoyant. After receiving a "scientific education" in Paris, according to Brigham Young, who had met him in New York, Walters returned to America to live "like a misanthrope." At that point, Walters was reportedly "an infidel, believing neither in man nor God. He used to dress in [a] fine broadcloth overcoat, but no other coat nor vest, his trousers all slitted up and patched, and sunburnt boots—filthy!"[106] On another occasion, Young called Walters a "fortune-teller, a necromancer, an astrologer, a soothsayer, and possessed as much talent as any man that walked on the American soil, and was one of the wickedest men I ever saw."[107]

Walters was smitten with the wizardry of hocus-pocus, the enchantment of legerdemain, the sleight-of-hand wiles of the sorcerer. In New Hampshire, however, a century-old statute outlawed "using any subtle Craft, Jug[g]ling ... Physiognomy, Palm[i]stry ... [to] discover where lost or stolen Goods may be found."[108] And in August 1818, Walters was jailed for being on the felonious side of this law. "A TRANSIENT person, calling himself LAMAN WALTER," announced a deputy sheriff, "has for several days past been imposing upon the credulity of people in this vicinity, by a pretended knowledge of magic, palmistry, conjuration, &c. and a corresponding conduct."[109] Walters soon escaped from jail and left the state.

In the early 1820s, Walters the Magician, for unknown reasons, showed up in Joseph Smith's neighborhood. The mountebank looked like a medieval enchanter with eccentric clothing, a magical seer stone, a desiccated toad, and rust-encrusted sword. Under his arm, he tucked mysterious books written in Latin from which he delivered incantations with a dramatic flair. Eventually, he found willing disciples. Credulous and easily exploitable people abound in every age. Our own time can easily produce any number who maintain that the earth is flat, that the Holocaust never occurred, that man did not walk on the moon, that Elvis still lives, etc. In the 1820s, these credulous souls believed in the posturings of Luman Walters and other tricksters like him. As Diedrich Willers Jr. of nearby Fayette, New York, wrote: "Fortune tellers are consulted as to the future, [and] many in this neighborhood, when they wish to find anything which is lost, or pry into hidden mysteries, will consult Dr. Walters."[110]

In an 1830 parody of the Book of Mormon and "Mormonite" culture,

106. Brigham Young, qtd. in Elizabeth Kane, *A Gentile Account of Life in Utah's Dixie,* 71.
107. Brigham Young, Feb. 18, 1855, JD 2:180-81; July 19, 1857, 5:55
108. Qtd. in Peter Benes, *Wonders of the Invisible World,* 137.
109. Ibid.
110. Diedrich Willers Jr., "Ambition and Superstition."

Palmyra newspaperman and lawyer Abner Cole claimed that some "Idle and slothful" locals decided:

> [L]et us send for Walters the Magician, who has strange books, and deals with familiar spirits. ... And the Magician led the *rabble* into a dark grove, in a place called *Manchester,* where after drawing a Magic circle, with a rusty sword, and collecting his motley crew of *latter-demallions,*[111] within the centre, he sacrificed a Cock (a bird sacred to Minerva[112]) for the purpose of propitiating the *prince* of spirits. ... And he took his *book,* and his rusty sword, and his *magic* stone, and his stuffed *Toad,* and all his implements of *witchcraft* and retired to the mountains near Great Sodus Bay, where he holds communion with the Devil even unto this day.[113]

Before departing, Walters left his mark on the Smiths and other money diggers in the Palmyra/Manchester area. Neighbor Lorenzo Saunders testified that he watched Joseph Sr. dig under the direction of "one Walters who pretended to be a conjurer." Saunders noted that after Walters was paid his conjurer's fee, he went through various incantations to sanctify the undertaking. The dig then commenced. "I seen the old man [Smith] dig there day in a[nd] day out," Saunders remembered.[114] On another occasion, Alvin Smith and Willard Chase worked together on a promising dig on property occupied by the Saunders family but owned by Abner Cole. The men paid Walters $3.00 per day for his services. According to Saunders: "At the time the big hole was dug in the hill they was duped by one Walters[,] who pretended to be a conjurer. I heard Willard Chase say that he was duped."[115]

Walters also convinced a few people that the most prominent hill in the area, one owned by the Robinson family, later called Mormon Hill (also Cumorah), concealed hidden treasure. As Brigham Young reported in 1872, Walters and a group of Manchester men, including Joseph Jr., gathered in a

---

111. Probably "tatterdemalions": persons dressed in ragged clothing.

112. Roman goddess of wisdom, war, art, schools, and commerce.

113. Obediah Dogberry (pseud. Abner Cole), "Book of Pukei," 36.

114. Lorenzo Saunders, interview, Nov. 12, 1884, 11.

115. Ibid., 11. Elsewhere, Cole, editor of the Palmyra *Reflector,* published in his February 28, 1831, issue:

> Walters assembled his nightly band of money diggers in the town of Manchester, at a point designated in his magical book, and drawing a circle around the laborers, with the point of an old rusty sword, and using sundry other incantations, for the purpose of propitiating the spirit, absolutely sacrificed a fowl, ("Rooster,") in the presence of his awe-stricken companions, to the foul spirit, whom ignorance had created, the guardian of hidden wealth; and after *digging* until day-light, his deluded employers retired to their several habitations, fatigued and disappointed. ("GOLD BIBLE, NO. 5," 108.)

local tavern to discuss enchantments and slippery treasure. Walters lamented that although "he couldn't get" the treasure, "there was one that could." He then dramatically pointed to Joseph, saying: "There was the young man that could find it."[116] In an earlier account, Young said that Walters insisted he "could tell that those plates were there, and that they were a treasure whose value to the people could not be told."[117] On yet a third occasion, Young remembered that Walters said, "I believe he [Joseph Jr.] will get the treasure after all."[118] Abner Cole's newspaper story jested that when Walters left town, "his *mantle* fell upon the *prophet* Jo. Smith Jun."[119]

Despite Walters's pronouncement on the head of the young prophet-to-be, not until 1823 did Joseph successfully overcome the power of enchantment and fully envision the hidden treasure that Walters had predicted.[120] The riches Joseph could see in his scryed visions would emerge as an ancient record of America's aboriginal peoples, engraved on golden plates—a treasure known today as the Book of Mormon.

---

116. Kane, *A Gentile Account of Life in Utah's Dixie,* 71.

117. Brigham Young, July 19, 1857, JD 5:55.

118. Brigham Young, Feb. 18, 1855, JD 2:181.

119. Dogberry, "Book of Pukei," 36; emphasis his.

120. Brigham Young later asserted that Walters "knew where those plates were hid. He went three times in the summer to get them—the same summer in which Joseph did get them. Baptist, Presbyterian, and Methodist priests and deacons sent for him to tell where those plates were, and to get them out of the hill where they were deposited; and he had not returned to his home from the last trip he made for them more than a week or ten days before Joseph got them" (qtd. in Richard S. Van Wagoner, *The Complete Discourses of Brigham Young,* 3:1300).

8 | THE VISION OF ANGELS

Even colonial New Englanders lived in an enchanted universe where ghosts visited people in the night and neighbors dreamed prophetic dreams.

—John H. Wigger, *Taking Heaven By Storm,* 111

The presence of men and women who seek out occult practitioners to "resolve, direct, and helpe," as Essex Puritan Thomas Pickering put it, is ubiquitous throughout history.[1] Believers place confidence in diviners to find lost or stolen clothing, buried treasure, household items, cattle, and even missing children. In early modern England, scryers traveled the country "making a living through their reputation for visions and trying to maintain a balance between the economic necessity of adopting a public persona as a practicing seer and an interest in maintaining secrecy for purposes of self-preservation."[2]

During the early years of young Joseph Smith's scrying activities, although his conjuring reputation began to escalate, he received only small recompense for his skills. A shilling for foretelling fortune, or a copper or two for locating lost objects, did not enrich the young seer to any noticeable degree in the purse-pinched New York farm countryside. In the 1820 Palmyra area, grain had no cash worth. It was valued only for subsistence use and as an exchange or bartering medium:

> When farmers did exchange goods and services with neighbors, these transactions rarely involved cash—not because cash was in short supply, but rather because they saw no use for assigning monetary values. Instead, they calculated value in terms of social worth, and simply kept accounts of what they owed and were owed. A farmer, for example, might work for two days in his neighbor's cornfield in exchange for five chickens, since that was what it would take to feed his family during the time he spent

1. Qtd. in Jon Butler, *Awash in a Sea of Faith,* 22.
2. Keith Thomas, *Religion and the Decline of Magic,* 215, 230.

away from his own farm duties. Or he might simply hold the neighbor accountable for two days' labor at some later time. These farmers sought, not to accumulate wealth, but to secure a "competency" that would allow their families to live a comfortable and independent existence in a community limited in geographic reach.[3]

In the barter-based economy, the Smiths, aside from the ongoing development of their farm, collectively did what they could to sustain the large family. "Anything to survive until tomorrow" seemed to be the family maxim in their hardscrabble existence. Even the very minor sums Joseph Jr. received from scrying would have been a welcome addition to the family purse. Recall that although Lucy Smith admonished readers of her autobiography that the family never "suffered one important interest to swallow up every other obligation," she did admit to their "trying to win the faculty of Abrac," "drawing of Magic circles," and "soothsaying," magic folklore practices that included money digging.[4]

There is little doubt that the farm came first on the Smiths' list of priorities, but theirs was essentially subsistence farming, and brought in virtually no income. An 1867-68 gazetteer of Wayne County, New York, stated that "[i]n 1819 or 20, [the Smiths] commenced digging for money for a subsistence." Word spread, "and not a few were credulous enough to believe that they were within reach of a 'chest of gold,' (which had repeatedly eluded their grasp,) and contributed money to the Smiths to enable them to continue their excavations." The Smiths, however, "used the money thus obtained for the support of the family," the writer insisted, and "in the meantime kept their friends in a fever of excitement while treasure hunting."[5]

Peter Ingersoll, who moved next door to the Smiths in 1822, later said that the "general employment of the family, was digging for money."[6] At least seventy-two other individuals made affidavits essentially corroborating this point. For example, neighbor Lorenzo Saunders reported that the Smiths "were pretty good fellows in their way, but they were shiftless and were in the money digging business."[7] Samantha Stafford Payne, three years younger than Joseph Jr., lived near the Smith farm on Stafford Street. She "attended

3. Carol Sheriff, *The Artificial River,* 11.

4. Lavina Fielding Anderson, *Lucy's Book,* 323. See also Samuel M. Brown, "Reconsidering Lucy Mack Smith's Folk Magic Confession," *Mormon Historical Studies* 13, nos. 1-2 (Spring/Fall 2012): 1-12.

5. Hamilton Child, *Gazetteer and Business Directory of Wayne County, N.Y. for 1867-8,* 53.

6. Peter Ingersoll, Affidavit, Dec. 2, 1833, 1.

7. Lorenzo Saunders, interviewed by William H. Kelley, Sept. 17, 1884, 7.

school with him [Joseph Jr.] for some time" and recalled that for about seven years he "was more or less of the time engaged in digging for money."[8] William Stafford lived a couple of miles south of the Smiths on Stafford Street and participated with them in several digs. He said that the Smiths believed "that nearly all the hills in this part of New York, were thrown up by human hands, in them were large caves, which Joseph Jr., could see, by placing a stone of singular appearance in his hat." Stafford continued that young Joseph "pretended all things within and under the earth,—that he could see within the above mentioned caves, large gold bars and silver plates—that he could also discover the spirits in whose charge these treasures were, clothed in ancient dress."[9] Stafford added that the Smiths spoke of "keys, barrels and hogsheads of coined silver and gold—bars of gold, golden images, brass kettles filled with gold and silver—gold candlesticks, swords, &c. &c." James H. Kennedy, who interviewed some of the Smiths' neighbors before writing his 1888 history of early Mormonism, noted that Joseph reportedly used his seer stone to discover where "the treasures of [Captain] Kidd and others lay concealed; locate the trail of wandering flocks; point out the deposits of stolen goods; and perform other wonderful things."[10]

Henry Harris reported that the family's chief occupation was "to dig for money" and that young Joseph "used to pretend to tell fortunes; he had a stone which he used to put in his hat, by means of which he professed to tell people's fortunes."[11] "Jo, the Prophet, pretended to tell fortunes for pay," said Joseph Rogers, another neighbor. "[H]e could read the character of men readily."[12] Fayette Lapham, who interviewed Joseph Sr. in 1829 or 1830, recalled him saying his namesake used his seer stone for "telling fortunes, where to find lost things, and where to dig for money and other hidden treasure."[13] E. W. Vanderhoof, in his 1907 *Historical Sketches of Western New York,* included the report that his own grandfather had visited Joseph "to learn what had become of a valuable mare stolen from his stable."[14] Another Manchester resident anonymously recalled in 1856 that "credulity seems to have been a pretty large ingredient in his [Joseph Sr.'s] composition, as he was a great money digger, always seeing 'sights;' but never realizing his expectations."[15]

8. Samantha Payne, Affidavit, June 29, 1881.
9. William Stafford, Affidavit, Dec. 8, 1833, in Eber D. Howe, *Mormonism Unvailed,* 237-38.
10. J. H. Kennedy, *Early Days of Mormonism,* 20.
11. Henry Harris, undated affidavit, in Howe, *Mormonism Unvailed,* 250.
12. Joseph Rogers, Statement, May 16, 1887, *Naked Truths about Mormonism* 1 (Apr. 1888): 1.
13. Fayette Lapham, "Interview with the Father of Joseph Smith," 305.
14. E. W. Vanderhoof, *Historical Sketches of Western New York,* 138.
15. "Mormonism in Its Infancy," 2. Not all money-digging anecdotes about the Smiths are

Joseph Rogers remembered years later that, as a young man, Joseph Jr. "claimed to receive revelations from the Lord where treasures were buried. He told Peter Rupert and Mr. Cunningham, a blacksmith (simple-minded old men), that there was a chest of gold buried on my brother-in-law, Henry Murphy's, farm, under a beech tree. ... He [Rupert] said he paid Jo for the information."[16] And in 1833, in an affidavit signed by fifty-one of the "best people living at that time"[17] in the Palmyra area, the consensus was that the Smiths "were particularly famous for visionary projects," and spent much of their time "digging for money which they pretended was hid in the earth."[18]

Joseph Sr., Alvin, and Joseph Jr. were apparently the only money diggers in the family. Perhaps because of their shared interest and talent, the two sons seemed to have been the favorites, even in the extended family. Grandfather Asael Smith had "predicted that there would be a prophet raised up in his family."[19] According to some observers, Joseph Jr. assumed the money-digger's role only after Alvin's death in 1823. Orsamus Turner wrote that Alvin "was originally intended, or designated, by fireside consultations, and solemn and mysterious out door hints, as the forth coming Prophet. The mother and the father said he was the chosen one; but Alv[in], however spiritual he may have been ... sickened and died. Thus the world lost a Prophet, and Mormonism a leader."[20] McIntosh's 1876 account likewise claimed that "Alv[in], sickened and died, and Joseph was designated as the coming prophet."[21] James Kennedy wrote that Lucy Smith had "announced the advent of a prophet in her family, and on the death of Alv[in], the first born, the commission that had been intended for him was laid upon Joseph."[22] However, no source within the family designates a similar sequence of seers.

The Smith family probably conducted its first treasure dig on their Farmington farm in 1820. According to Pomeroy Tucker: the "inauguration" of

---

solemn. Lorenzo Saunders relates: "We went to Smith['s] one day, it was a rainy day; We went into the old mans shop, he was a cooper, and the old man had a shirt on it was the raggedest & dirtyest shirt, and all full of holes. & we got Jo. Smith to look & tell us what color our Girls hair was. [W]ell you see by & by some of them says go to Jo. [S]ays he Jo. Come look into futurity & tell us how it is there? Jo. says I can not do that, I can not look into futurity I can not look into anything that is holy. The old man stood there and says: 'I guess he can not look into my shirt then[.]'" (Lorenzo Saunders, Interviewed by E. L. Kelly, Nov. 12, 1884, 11.)

16. Rogers, Statement, 1.

17. Vanderhoof, *Historical Sketches of Western New York,* 136.

18. "Palmyra Residents Group Statement," Dec. 4, 1833, in Howe, *Mormonism Unvailed,* 261.

19. Mary Duty Smith, Asael's wife, 1836, qtd. in *History of the Church,* 2:442-43.

20. Orsamus Turner, *History of the Pioneer Settlement of Phelps and Gorham's Purchase,* 212.

21. W. H. McIntosh, *History of Ontario Co.,* 42.

22. Kennedy, *Early Days of Mormonism,* 12.

young Joseph's money-digging ventures took place on a "then forest hill, a short distance from his father's house." Tucker reported the account of an anonymous participant in this dig: Joseph Jr. located the spot with his seer stone, then used his scrying powers to locate the treasure. He ordered silence, commenced a two-hour dig which was unsuccessful when a spoken word broke the enchantment, and the treasure slipped away deeper into the earth.[23]

William Stafford, who lived nearly two miles south of the Smiths, was invited by Joseph Sr. to participate in a treasure dig on the Smith farm. According to his sworn testimony, Stafford said that Joseph Jr. saw in his stone "two or three kegs of gold and silver" located near the Smith home. Despite Joseph's leading the participants through a menu of folk magic tasks, they failed to recover the treasure. Young Joseph, who had remained in the house during the operation, later explained that the treasure's guardian spirit had caused the money to slip away from their grasp. According to Stafford, Joseph Sr. added that they "had made a mistake in performing the exercises."[24]

For the most part, the Smith men were not pick-and-shovel laborers on these treasure digs. Their contributions were of an arcane nature. In nineteenth-century America, the use of divination and magic ritual to discover buried treasure was part of a comprehensive belief system. Hidden subterranean spirits were believed to control precious metals that could only be captured by a knowledgeable diviner, who assumed the role of soothsayer, scryer, and seer, claiming to view not only the location of the buried riches in a seer stone, but also the movements of the elemental spirits assigned to protect the hoard. The *Fourth Book of Occult Philosophy* vouches: "[T]here are Spirits of the earth, which inhabit groves, woods and wildernesses, and are the plague and mischief of hunters. ... There are also subterranean Spirits, which do inhabit in dens and caverns of the earth, and in remote concavities of mountains, that they might invade deep pits, and the bowels of the earth; these do dig up metals, and keep treasures, which oftentimes they do transport from one place to another, lest any man should make use thereof."[25]

"All substantial evidence reveals that occultism's appeal transcended class, age, and gender," wrote Yale historian Jon Butler. "Wise men and wise women drew clients from the wealthy, the middling, and the poor." These seers, he explained, were most often "illiterates who had learned their

23. Tucker, *Origin, Rise, and Progress of Mormonism,* 22-23.

24. William Stafford, Affidavit, in Howe, *Mormonism Unvailed,* 238-39.

25. Henry Cornelius Agrippa, *Fourth Book of Occult Philosophy,* 116. The unknown author is often referred to as pseudo-Agrippa. The book was first published in 1655 and reprinted in 1665 and 1783.

secrets from earlier practitioners." Success "lay in their appearance of precision, their intimate knowledge of their clients, and a certain gullibility in the public."[26] Even ostensibly commonsense men like Brigham Young could be persuaded by practitioners of magic arts. In a sermon delivered shortly before his death, Young stated:

> These treasures that are in the earth are carefully watched, they can be removed from place to place according to the good pleasure of Him who made them and owns them. ... Orin P. Rockwell is an eye-witness to some powers of removing the treasures of the earth. ... Porter was with them one night where there were treasures, and they could find them easy enough, but they could not obtain them. ... He said that on this night, ... they dug around the end of a chest. ... One man who was determined to have the contents of that chest, took his pick and struck into the lid of it, and split through into the chest. The blow took off a piece of the lid, which a certain lady kept in her possession until she died. *That chest of money went into the bank.* Porter describes it so [making a rumbling sound]; he says this is just as true as the heavens are. ... [T]o those who understand these things, it is not marvelous.[27]

In ancient European Celtic society, from where much of the magic world view originated, seers performed divinations and made prophecies, organized special ceremonies, and watched and interpreted the omens of the natural world. One tale describes a "store of gold in a hillock" near Arenig Lake, Wales. A young man named Silvanus Lewis one day took his pick-axe and shovel and set out to find the hidden treasure. "No sooner had he commenced to dig in earnest," the tradition states, "than he heard a terrible, unearthly noise under his feet."

> The hillock began to rock like a cradle, and the sun clouded over until it became pitch dark. Lightning flashes began to shoot their forked streaks around him and pealing thunders to roar over his head. He dropped his pickaxe and hurried helter-skelter homewards to Cnythog. Before he reached there everything was beautifully calm and serene. But he was so frightened that he never returned to fetch his tools. Many another man has been prevented in the same way from continuing his search.[28]

26. Butler, *Awash in a Sea of Faith,* 21.

27. Brigham Young, June 17, 1877, JD 19:36-39. Some have speculated that this "lady" was Lucy Mack Smith. Orrin Porter Rockwell was a Smith family acquaintance and one of the first baptized members of Joseph Smith's church.

28. Qtd. in "Treasure Seeking."

This treatment of Celtic magic warns that "there is no end of treasure hidden in the mountains of Wales, but if you are not the person for whom it is intended, you will probably not find it. Even if you do find it, you will not be able to secure it, unless it is destined for you."[29] Many ingenuous folk believed or at least told others that a buried treasure was an active, almost life-like force. Like a burrowing creature it could rise or fall, and move about beneath the earth's surface. It could emerge and "blossom" or "sun" itself. Joseph Sr. told neighbor Peter Ingersoll that "the best time for digging money, was, in the heat of summer, when the heat of the sun caused the chests of money to rise near the top of the ground."[30]

Scryers, to retrieve hidden treasure, needed to outwit the guardian spirit who maintained the enchantment. Sometimes the devil himself caused the treasure to slip away.[31] Many money diggers also believed that Satan could summon ghosts or spirits to thwart success, or could transform himself into a frightening toad, rooster, dog, bear, snake, or dragon.[32] Even when such apparitions did not deter the seekers, they ruined the moment by causing one of the diggers to break the necessary vow of silence, at which point all hopes for success ended. Benjamin Franklin, as early as 1729, described the terror under which some night-time digs were conducted. "Full of expectation they labor violently," he wrote, "trembling at the same time in every joint, through fear of certain malicious demons who are said to haunt and guard such places." Franklin added the widespread belief that "through some mistake in the procedure, some rash word spoke, or some rule of art neglected, the guardian spirit had power to sink [the treasure] deeper into the earth and convey it out of their reach."[33]

Some treasure seekers tried to narrow the odds in wrestling with the powers of enchantment. Since medieval times, the elemental or guardian spirits, commonly known as "familiars," were viewed as easy to conjure. Diggers sought out virginal seers who, they believed, had special powers of

29. Ibid.

30. Ingersoll, Affidavit.

31. The "slippery treasure" theme appears at two points in the Book of Mormon (Hel. 13:31-37; Morm. 1:18).

32. On February 1, 1831, Abner Cole published in his Palmyra *Reflector* an article claiming that Joseph Smith Sr. "propagated the vulgar, yet popular belief that these treasures were held in charge by some *evil* spirit, which was supposed to be either the DEVIL himself, or some one of his most trusty favorites." The paper clarified, however, that the idea did not originate with Joseph Sr.: "We find that the vulgar and ignorant from time immemorial," "both in Europe and America, have entertained the same preposterous opinion" ("GOLD BIBLE, No. 3," 91).

33. Leonard W. Larabee, *The Papers of Benjamin Franklin,* 1:137.

discerning and recovering hidden treasure. Using their divining rods or seer stones, the young practitioners tried to "bind to their service, and imprison in a ring, a mirror, or a stone, some fairy, sylph, or salamander, and compel it to appear when called, and render answers to such questions as the viewer should propose."[34]

As one recent study notes, the seer stone

> constituted only the mediating instrument between the seer and the seen, between nature and preternature. Seeing required not only a stone, but a seer. Only a person with a gift for seeing in stones could do so. Many posited the existence of a third necessity. If the querent had the gift of seeing, there must also exist a bestower of that gift. In this schema, supernatural vision required three components: a seer, a speculum, and the grace of God—or some other preternatural identity, either willing or coerced, but necessarily able to bring images into the stone. A gift given, a gift received, and the right stone: these were three ingredients of the scryer's science.[35]

Although scrying is often dismissed today, it does not lack adherents and practitioners. In some magical circles, writes Norman Cohn, once a caulbearer reached maturity, "it was only a matter of time before he or she would receive a summons in a dream." This supernatural vision could be revealed through an angel or "a real person, known to the dreamer."[36] It seems probable, according to the accounts left by both Joseph Jr. and his contemporaries, that in the fall of 1823, when money-digging enthusiasm had somewhat abated in his neighborhood, Joseph began to envision the same treasure that Luman Walters earlier had discerned. This unfolding vision revealed a golden record hidden in a nearby glacial drumlin since named the Hill Cumorah.

Several accounts reconstruct plausible scenarios of how this story may have evolved into the Angel Moroni narrative known today. One of the earliest, published in 1831 by David Staats Burnet (1808-67), maintained that, for a long time in the Palmyra area, there had "existed an impression, especially among certain loose classes of society, that treasures of great amount were concealed near the surface of the earth, probably by the Indians." This group of individuals "conjured up a ghost, who they said was often seen and to whom was committed the care of the precious deposit." The hidden

---

34. Sir Walter Scott, *Letters on Demonology and Witchcraft,* 295.
35. Mark Ashurst-McGee, "A Pathway to Prophethood," 182.
36. Norman Cohn, Review of Carlo Ginzburg's *The Night Battles.*

golden treasure was said to be a "gold bible and a new revelation." This ghost or angel purportedly showed this record to Joseph Smith and "informed him that he would be inspired to translate the inscriptions without looking at the plates, while an amanuensis would record his infallible reading."[37]

Neighbor Willard Chase's 1833 affidavit declared that Father Smith told him six year earlier, in 1827, that "some years ago, a spirit had appeared to Joseph his son, in a vision, and informed him that in a certain place there was a record on plates of gold, and that he was the person that must obtain them."[38] Joseph Sr., interviewed in 1829 or 1830 by Fayette Lapham, who recorded his memory of that encounter forty years later, told Lapham that his son had a "singular dream" in which "a very large and tall man appeared to him, dressed in an ancient suit of clothes, and the clothes were bloody." The personage told young Joseph of "a valuable treasure, buried many years since, and not far from that place." The time had now "arrived for it to be brought to light, for the benefit of the world at large"; and if the boy would strictly follow instructions, he would be directed "to the place where it was deposited, in such a manner that he could obtain it."[39] Elsewhere Father Smith reportedly declared

> that his son Jo had seen the spirit, (which he then described as a little old man with a long beard,) and was informed that he (Jo) under *certain* circumstances, eventually should obtain great treasures, and that in due time he (the spirit) would furnish him (Jo) with a book, which would give an account of the Ancient inhabitants (antideluvians) of this country, and where they had deposited their substance ... which had ever since that time remained secure in his (the spirits) charge, in large and spacious chambers, in sundry places in this vicinity.[40]

Lucy Smith, speaking of her son's first vision experience in her 1844-45 memoirs, placed the event in the religious context her son created after the fact. As with Swedish visionary Emanuel Swedenborg, a hallmark of young Joseph's sanctity was a near constant stream of communications with angels.[41] "Whether wrapped in clouds of glory or trailing clouds of sulphur,

37. David Staats Burnet, "Something New—The Golden Bible," 218-19.

38. Willard Chase, Affidavit, Dec. 11, 1833.

39. Lapham, "Interview with the Father of Joseph Smith," 305.

40. "GOLD BIBLE, NO. 4," 101; emphasis in original.

41. As early as 1766, Swedenborg's familiarity with angels was ridiculed. One of Swedenborg's staunchest defenders in antebellum America noted the common view that his revelations were either "designed imposture" or "unconscious illusion," while his spiritual musings were usually dismissed as "a strange medley of hallucinations," a product of "religious mania," or "the fruit

angels are an abiding presence in the lore of Western religion," states writer Jacqueline Carey:

> They preside over birth and death, hymns and battles, the rising sun and falling stars. To the righteous, they offer healing and comfort, courage, strength, and vision. To the wicked, they offer temptation and retribution. Bearing messages from on high, sacred wisdom, and profane knowledge, they break the plane of heaven to descend to earth. Their lineage is ancient, winged shadows stretching back through time to forgotten mythologies, born anew in the light of monotheism. From the past to the present, the mortal to the divine, angels bridge the voids of human existence. In them, the splendor of God is reflected to a lesser degree. In them, the failings of humanity are reflected on a grander scale.[42]

Angels, from the Greek *angelos,* meaning messenger, are typically non-human "spirit beings" whose office is "to do [God] service in heaven, and by his appointment to succour and defend men on earth."[43] The concept of angels evolved primarily in Zoroastrianism, Judaism, Christianity, and Islam. In the Hebrew Bible, angels are often called the "hosts of heaven" or the "company of divine beings" (1 Kgs. 22:19; Isa. 6:13). In apocalyptic literature, seven angels, sometimes called archangels, lead the heavenly hosts. These seven, noted in the noncanonical First Book of Enoch, are: Uriel, leader of the heavenly hosts and guardian of *sheol* (the Underworld); Raphael, guardian of human spirits; Raguel, avenger of God against the world of lights; Michael, guardian of Israel; Sariel, avenger of the spirits who "sin in the spirit"; Gabriel, ruler of paradise, the seraphim, and the cherubim; and Remiel, also called Jeremiel, guardian of the souls in *sheol.*[44]

Christianity developed a hierarchy of angels based on the Judaic tradition from the Hebrew Bible. As objects of devotion, the archangels Michael, Gabriel, and Raphael have received special attention in both the Catholic and Mormon traditions. The *Catholic Encyclopedia* (1912) developed a complex view of how corporeal apparitions or visions might arise. It explains that, in a vision,

---

of a distempered brain." No matter how liberal the religious world of the new republic claimed to be, communicating with angels carried a heavy price (George Bush, *The Memorabilia of Swedenborg,* iii, vii-viii; George Bush, *Statement of Reasons for Embracing the Doctrines and Disclosures of Emanuel Swedenborg,* 69). Benjamin Rush (1745-1818), the most prominent physician of his day, specifically pathologized those who "see and converse with angels" (*Medical Inquiries and Observations upon the Diseases of the Mind,* 138).

42. In Jacqueline Carey, *Angels,* 127.

43. *A Concise Bible Dictionary Based on the Cambridge Companion to the Bible,* 8.

44. Qtd. in ibid., 56.

> either a figure really present externally strikes the retina and there determines the physical phenomenon of the vision; or an agent superior to man directly modifies the visual organ and produces in the composite a sensation equivalent to that which an external object would produce. … Sometimes the very substance of the being or the person will be presented; sometimes it will be merely an appearance consisting in an arrangement of luminous rays. The first may be true of living persons, and even, it would seem, of the now glorious bodies of Christ and the Blessed Virgin, which by the eminently probable supernatural phenomenon of multilocation may become present to men without leaving the abode of glory.[45]

Lucy Smith remembered that Joseph's first vision experience occurred during the fall harvest of 1823 as the Smith men reaped grain. After the day's labor, the Smith family gathered at the fireside to converse late into the night. Lucy said that the subject of the family's discussion that evening was "the diversity of churches that had risen up in the world." Later that night, after he had gone to bed in the small loft he shared with his five brothers, seventeen-year-old Joseph, according to his mother "was in a serious and contemplative state of mind."[46] According to Joseph's cousin, friend, and confidant Oliver Cowdery's account, Joseph "was unusually wrought up on the subject which had so long agitated his mind—his heart was drawn out in fervent prayer, and his soul was so lost to every thing of a temporal nature, that earth, to him, had lost its charms, and all he desired was to be prepared in heart to commune with some kind messenger who could communicate to him the desired information of his acceptance with God."[47] Although Lucy wrote that her son "was pondering in his mind which of the churches [was] the true one,"[48] Cowdery wrote that Joseph was not even certain in 1823 if God existed. The youth called "upon the Lord in secret," wrote Cowdery, for an answer to the question: "if a Supreme Being did exist, to have an assurance that he was accepted of him."[49]

Near midnight, after Joseph's brothers had fallen asleep, "while continuing in prayer for a manifestation," wrote Cowdery, "on a sudden a light like that of day, only of a purer and far more glorious appearance and brightness, burst into the room." Joseph later told Cowdery that it seemed to him

45. "Vision," in Charles Herbermann et al., *The Catholic Encyclopedia,* 50.

46. Anderson, *Lucy's Book,* 336.

47. Oliver Cowdery to W. W. Phelps, "Letter IV," 77. Unless otherwise noted, Cowdery's narrative here is taken from this letter (pp. 77-79).

48. Anderson, *Lucy's Book,* 335.

49. Cowdery to Phelps, "Letter IV," 77.

"as though the house was filled with consuming and unquenchable fire." At first, the appearance of such luminous splendor "occasioned a shock or sensation, visible to the extremities of the body," remembered Joseph, but that impression was soon followed by a "calmness and serenity of mind, and an overwhelming rapture of joy that surpassed understanding." In a moment, a personage stood before him floating in mid-air. Although the room had previously been filled with light "above the brightness of the sun," Cowdery wrote, there seemed to be an "additional glory surrounding or accompanying this personage, which shone with an increased degree of brilliancy." Though the countenance of the messenger was "as lightening," it was of such a "pleasing, innocent and glorious appearance," that all fear was banished from the boy's heart and "nothing but calmness pervaded [his] soul."

The being declared himself to be a messenger "sent by commandment of the Lord." Joseph's "sins were forgiven," and "his prayers were heard." The envoy, according to Cowdery, told Joseph that he was chosen to fulfill the scriptures which say "God has chosen the foolish things of the world to confound the things which are mighty; and base things of the world, and things which are despised."[50] Furthermore, Joseph learned that the Lord was about "to do a marvelous work among this people, even a marvelous work and wonder; the wisdom of their wise shall perish, and the understanding of their prudent shall be hid: for according to his covenant which he made with his ancient saints, his people, the house of Israel, must come to a knowledge of the gospel, and own that Messiah whom their fathers rejected, and with them the fulness of the Gentiles be gathered in, to rejoice in one fold under one Shepherd" (Isa. 29:14).[51]

Joseph learned that God's plan for humankind could not be fully enacted without his participation. "He has chosen you as an instrument in his hand," he was told,

> to bring to light that which shall perform his act, his strange act, and bring to pass a marvelous work and a wonder. Wherever the sound shall go it shall cause the ears of men to tingle, and wherever it shall be proclaimed, the pure in heart shall rejoice, while whose who draw near to

50. This statement is a truncated version of I Cor. 1:27-28. A month later, Cowdery added: "Not many mighty and noble were called in ancient times, because they always *knew so much* that God could not teach them; and a man that would listen to the voice of the Lord and follow the teachings of heaven, always was despised, and considered to be of the foolish class" (Cowdery to Phelps, "Letter V," Mar. 1835, 95; emphasis Cowdery's).

51. Cowdery to Phelps, "Letter IV," Feb. 1835, 78.

> God with their mouths, and honor him with their lips, while their hearts are far from him, will seek its overthrow, and the destruction of those by whose hands it is carried. Therefore, marvel not if your name is made a derision and had as a by-word among such, if you are the instrument in bringing it, by the gift of God, to the knowledge of the people.[52]

This personage, whom Joseph called Nephi in his 1838-39 autobiography but later identified as Moroni,[53] was said to be an angel, defined as a resurrected being who had been born and died on the American continent some four centuries after the death of Jesus.[54] In a multitude of religious traditions, when God has business with people on earth, he sends an emissary to act on his behalf. As Jacqueline Carey notes: "The Almighty Lord of Hosts seldom descends from His throne to terra firma; it is His angels

52. Ibid.

53. Dean C. Jessee, *The Papers of Joseph Smith,* 277; D&C 27:5, 128:20. Moroni is the largest city of the Comoro (historically *Camora* or *Comora)* Islands, located in the Indian Ocean, an area swarming with pirates, including Captain Kidd, in the seventeenth century. The Hill Cumorah, where Moroni's father Mormon reportedly hid the golden plates, is consistently spelled "Camorah" in the first (1830) edition of the Book of Mormon. Perhaps Joseph retained a memory of the names *Moroni* and *Camorah* from stories he heard in boyhood from Grandfather Solomon Mack, a retired sea captain, who plied the same New England waters once haunted by Kidd, or from Joseph Sr. who, while living in Vermont, was "at times" reportedly engaged in hunting for Kidd's buried treasure (Kennedy, *Early Days of Mormonism,* 8). While in Lebanon, New Hampshire, young Joseph no doubt heard of "Kidd's Island," located downstream on the Connecticut River. According to local tradition, Kidd and one of his crew had buried treasure on the island, along with the body of a Creole girl they had kidnaped, "covering in one grave their gold and their victim; setting as a watch over their pirate treasure, the spirit of her who was once a guileless maiden on the earth" ("Kidd's Island," 430). According to J. H. Kennedy, who published a biography of Joseph Smith in 1888, Smith admitted that Kidd's autobiography "made a deep impression upon him" *(Early Days of Mormonism,* 13; Kennedy does not cite a source for this statement). Palmyran Philetus B. Spear recalled in 1873 that Joseph, as a boy, "had for a library a copy of the 'Arabian Nights,' stories of Captain Kidd, and a few novels" (Dan Vogel, *Early Mormon Documents,* 3:94). In 1857, British convert John Hyde Jr., who did not know Joseph personally, wrote: "It was quite common in the western part of New York, about thirty years ago [1827] for men to dig for treasure which they supposed had been hidden by Captain Kidd and others" *(Mormonism,* 263). Orrin Porter Rockwell, Joseph's neighbor in Manchester, New York, told Elizabeth W. Kane in the early 1870s that "[n]ot only was there religious excitement, but the phantom treasure of Captain Kidd were sought for far and near, and even in places like Cumorah" *(A Gentile Account of Life in Utah's Dixie,* 73). And both William R. Hine and Ketchel E. Bell gave affidavits that young Joseph searched for Kidd's buried treasure on the Susquehanna River. For other Captain Kidd/Joseph Smith connections, see Ronald V. Huggins, "From Captain Kidd's Treasure Ghost to the Angel Moroni." See also Noel A. Carmack, "Joseph Smith, Captain Kidd Lore, and Treasure-Seeking in New York and New England during the Early Republic," *Dialogue: A Journal of Mormon Thought* 46, no. 3 (Fall 2013): 78-153.

54. Joseph later said that "Spirits can only be revealed in flaming fire, or glory. Angels have advanced farther—their light and glory being tabernacled, and hence appear in bodily shape" (Joseph Smith, qtd. in "Minutes of a Special Conference of the Church ... in ... Nauvoo, ... 6th of October 1843," 331).

who get the dust of the mundane world on their celestial feet."[55] An "angel or some other mediator is necessary, in the biblical view," writes theologian Susan R. Garrett, "because no mortal can look upon God's face. God is too vast, too holy, for our feeble human minds fully to comprehend." Hence, as John Calvin argued, continues Garrett, "God relates to us in ways appropriate for us. Angels are divine messengers in whom the full power and glory of God are tempered so as not to overwhelm us. The angels convey that God is present with us finite human creatures, concerned about our welfare, and willing to intervene to set persons on the right path. They demonstrate God's willingness to meet us where we are."[56]

Joseph's Moroni, like the angel Gabriel of Islamic and Jewish tradition,[57] served as an angel of annunciation. He and the other "aborigines of this country," as Cowdery paraphrased Joseph's version of Moroni's words, were remnants of Israel, "literal descendants of Abraham." The American Indians, Moroni said, were once "enlightened and intelligent" Christians who had come to this continent as a civilized people who possessed the true religion and enjoyed God's favor. Prophets and inspired men had once existed among them. But ultimately they ceased to walk in the ways of the Lord, engaged in all kinds of wickedness, and massacred one another in endless wars. The survivors degenerated into the savage tribes whom the Europeans found. The angel further revealed that the ancient records of this people, kept by their prophets and seers, were, at that very moment, in a secure depository, hidden in a nearby hill. If Joseph remained "obedient to the commandments of the Lord," the angel added, he could obtain the record and translate it into English.[58]

Tales of buried treasure and the discovery of great wealth are among

55. Carey, *Angels,* 49.

56. Susan R. Garrett, "Messengers of God," 4.

57. Gabriel is the angel who revealed the words of the holy Koran to the prophet Mohammed. He is acclaimed in some sources as the Angel of the Lord who appeared to Hagar, maid to Abraham's wife Sarah, and pronounced her pregnant with Ishmael. Hagar is revered as the mother of Islam. In addition to announcing to Mary the glad tidings that forever after changed the world, Gabriel appeared before the elderly Zechariah, husband to Mary's kinswoman Elisabeth, and announced the impending birth of a son—John the Baptist. Earlier, Gabriel had appeared to the prophet Daniel, assuring him that he was beloved of God. Jewish folklore maintains that Gabriel appeared to the biblical Joseph after his brothers threw him in the pit. Gabriel not only protected the young boy, but gave him the ability to interpret dreams—the gift that blesses him in Pharoah's sight. ("Gabriel," in Wendy Doniger, *Merriam-Webster's Encyclopedia of World Religions,* 56.)

58. Cowdery to Phelps, "Letter IV," 79. Smith's exact wording, according to Cowdery, was: "Moroni, who deposited the plates in a hill in Manchester, Ontario County, New York, being dead and raised again therefore, appeared unto me, and told me where they were" *(History of the Church,* 3:28).

the oldest daydreams of human beings. The discovery of secret treasure is a common myth that appears in nearly all cultures. As psychoanalyst Selma Frailberg has written:

> Typically the treasure story follows this pattern: A poor boy or man accidentally discovers a secret which leads him to buried treasure or to the acquisition of great wealth. Usually the treasure is the stolen loot of a bandit, a pirate or an evil sorcerer; it may be buried in the ground or in a mysterious cavern. The hero obtains secret knowledge of the treasure either through a conniving and evil person who wishes to use the innocent hero for a tool, or through the accidental "overhearing" or "overseeing" of an event which betrays the secret, or through the acquisition of a magic formula or device or a map or code. Usually, too, the hero must overcome an evil opponent who seeks the treasure. The treasure is successfully won by the hero who vanquishes his enemies, marries a beautiful princess, or brings wealth and prestige to his mother, elevating her from her humble and impoverished station.

The secret hiding place is often a "mysterious cavern which has no door, the hidden place deep under ground," continues Fraiberg. And there is the "unwavering belief of the child that if he should have the magician's magic lamp, the pirate's map, the key to the treasure, the knowledge of 'the place,' he could win for himself this treasure of treasures. In this ageless daydream of childhood, the poor boy who has nothing steals the magician's secret, the pirate's map, and outwits the powerful opponent who stands between him and the treasure."[59]

As Joseph's angel described the record's location to him, Cowdery continued, "the vision of his mind being opened at the same time, he was permitted to view it critically; and previously being acquainted with the place, he was able to follow the direction of the vision."[60] The visitation was repeated twice more that night. Each time, Cowdery attested, the angel's conversation centered "upon the important fact of the blessings, promises and covenants to Israel, and the great manifestations of favor to the world, in the ushering in of the fulness of the gospel, to prepare the way for the second advent of the Messiah, when he comes in the glory of the Father with the holy angels."[61] Cowdery was careful to add that, although the vision

59. Selma Fraiberg, "Tales of the Discovery of the Secret Treasure," 239-41.
60. Cowdery to Phelps, "Letter VII," 156.
61. Ibid.

occurred in the dark of night, it was "an open vision." Joseph was awake, and in prayer, he told Cowdery.[62]

In 1838, Joseph, as previously noted, began to compose a history of the Church which was later canonized as scripture.[63] "[T]he vision was opened to my mind," Joseph said of his early spiritual experience, "that I could see the place where the plates were deposited, and that so clearly and distinctly that I knew the place again when I visited it" (JS-H, 1:42). The adult Joseph does not say how the vision was opened to his mind. Parallel accounts, however, suggest that it may have been scryed through his seer stone. Martin Harris, an early benefactor, recalled in 1859: "Joseph had before this described the manner of his finding the plates. He found them by looking in the stone found in the well of Mason Chase. The family had likewise told me the same thing."[64] Willard Chase added that "if it had not been for that stone, he [Joseph] would not have obtained the book [of Mormon]."[65] Henry Harris, Martin's brother-in-law and an acquaintance of the Smith family, confirmed that Joseph "said he had a revelation from God that told him they [the plates] were hid in a certain hill and he looked in his stone and saw them in the place of deposit."[66] Further corroboration is provided by Dr. W. D. Purple, who took notes during Joseph Smith's 1826 trial as a "glass looker": "Smith, by the aid of his luminous stone, found the Golden Bible, or the book of Mormon."[67] And in 1856, after attending a meeting of the Board of Regents of the University of Deseret, longtime Mormon convert Hosea Stout recorded that "President [Brigham] Young exhibited the 'seer's stone' with which the Prophet Joseph discovered the plates of the Book of Mormon."[68]

Joseph's 1838 account of discovering the plates, though it makes no mention of a seer stone, does not preclude its use: "Moroni, the person who deposited the plates, from whence the Book of Mormon was translated, in a hill in Manchester, Ontario County, New York, being dead, and raised again therefrom, appeared unto me, and told me where they were; and gave

---

62. Ibid.

63. For details surrounding the production of this early history, see *History of the Church,* 3:25-26, and Dean C. Jessee, *The Papers of Joseph Smith,* 1:230-31.

64. Martin Harris, qtd. in Joel Tiffany, "Mormonism—No. II," *Tiffany's Monthly,* Aug. 1859, 169.

65. Willard Chase, in Howe, *Mormonism Unvailed,* 246-47.

66. Henry Harris, Affidavit, in ibid., 252.

67. W. D. Purple, "Joseph Smith, the Originator of Mormonism," 3.

68. Juanita Brooks, *On The Mormon Frontier,* 2:593.

me directions how to obtain them."[69] The seer stone could have been the medium through which Joseph envisioned his instructions. There is never any mention that the Smith brothers who shared the room in which Joseph claimed to receive Moroni's night-long visitations were disturbed by the blazing radiance that surrounded him or by Moroni's voice. This fact supports a vision received through Joseph's stone.

Lucy Smith noted that the emissary cautioned her son to "beware of covetousness, and he must not suppose the Record was to be brought forth with the view of getting gain." The angel further warned that, when Joseph went to get the plates, "he must be on his guard, or his mind would be filled with darkness." Finally, the angel instructed Joseph to tell his father "all which he had both seen and heard."[70] The next day, the Smith men continued harvesting grain. Joseph stopped in the midst of the heavy work. Alvin, thinking his younger brother was idling, urged him to get back to work. Joseph resumed cutting a swath with his sickle, but within moments again stopped. Joseph Sr., noticing that his son had turned pale, ordered him to the house to have his mother "doctor" him. En route, Joseph came to an apple tree. Feeling faint, he lay down in the shade. Within minutes, the messenger reappeared and demanded, "Why did you not tell your father that which I commanded you to tell him?" Joseph excused himself: "I was afraid my father would not believe me," he replied. The angel then reassured him: "He will believe every word you say to him."

Joseph returned to the field. In the meantime, his father had gone to the house. Joseph asked Alvin to fetch him, saying he had "something of great importance to communicate to him." When Joseph Sr. returned, Joseph told him of the night before. His father told him "not to fail in attending strictly to the instruction which he had received from this heavenly messenger." Heeding the advice, Joseph traveled to the nearby drumlin, owned by the Robinson family, and found the spot he had seen in vision. On the west side of the hill, not far from the top, he saw with his spiritual eyes the record "under a stone of considerable size." He further explained that "this stone was thick and rounding in the middle, on the upper side, and thinner towards the edges, so that the middle part of it was visible above the ground; but the edges all round were covered with earth."

The anxious adolescent reported that he perceived the treasure, a golden

69. Joseph Smith, "Answers to Questions," *Elder's Journal* 1 (July 1838): 43.

70. The ensuing narrative is based on Lucy Mack Smith's account in Anderson, *Lucy's Book,* 338-43.

record laying in the bottom of a stone box, cemented together on the sides and bottom. The angel, who now was present, showed him the "difference between good and evil, and likewise the consequences of both obedience and disobedience" to God's commandments in "such a striking manner," wrote his mother, "that the impression was always vivid in his memory until the very end of his days." In addition, the angel told him he could not get the plates until "he had learned to keep the commandments of God—not only till he was willing, but able, to do it." The angel then instructed Joseph to visit the same site at the same time each year, where he would meet him and give further instructions.

That evening the family gathered around the fireside listening to Joseph recount his story of angelic visitation. Alvin, noticing that Joseph seemed tired, proposed that they all go to bed, rise early the next morning, "in order to finish our day's work at an hour before sunset." After supper that next evening, the family was prepared to "give our undivided attention to Joseph[']s recitals," said his mother. The boy began by cautioning them not to tell others what he was about to relate to them. He explained that "the world was so wicked" that others would attempt to secure the plates for their monetary value. Furthermore, "our names would be cast out as evil by all people," added Joseph. From that time forth, by Lucy's account, the family gathered around the fireside nightly to listen to Joseph's stories. "I presume our family presented an aspect as singular as any that ever lived upon the face of the earth," stated Mother Smith, "all seated in a circle, father, mother, sons, and daughters, and giving the most profound attention to a boy, eighteen years of age."

Joseph told his family "some of the most amusing[71] recitals that could be imagined," Lucy added. The boy described "the ancient inhabitants of this continent, their dress, mode of traveling, and the animals upon which they rode; their cities, their buildings, with every particular; their mode of warfare; and also their religious worship. This he would do with as much ease, seemingly, as if he had spent his whole life with them." Listening to Joseph's stories, the family became "confirmed in the opinion that God was about to bring to light something upon which we could stay our minds, or that would give us a more perfect knowledge of the plan of salvation and the redemption of the human family," as Lucy recalled. It was the beginning of

71. Probably "Entertaining; giving moderate pleasure to the mind, as to engage it; pleasing" (Noah Webster, *American Dictionary of the English Language* [1828], s.v. "Amusing").

the revelation for which Joseph Sr. and Lucy had been seeking their entire lives, and seemed perfectly to satisfy their spiritual yearnings. "This caused us greatly to rejoice," remembered Mother Smith; "the sweetest union and happiness pervaded our house, and tranquility reigned in our midst." But as soon as the Smith family managed to find some contentment, dark clouds began to threaten fresh misery on the frequently unfortunate family.

9 | A BROTHER'S DEATH

Ye doctors all of every rank
With their long bills that break the bank.
Of wisdom's learning, art, and skill
Seems all composed of calomel.

Since calomel has been their toast,
How many patients have they lost,
How many hundreds have they killed,
Or poisoned with their calomel. ...

The man grows worse, grows bad indeed
"Go call the doctor, ride with speed."
The doctor comes, the wife to tell
To double the dose of calomel.

The man begins in death to groan,
The fatal job for him is done,
The soul must go to heaven or hell,
A sacrifice to calomel.

—"Calomel", from *American Ballads and Songs* (to the tune of "O Tannenbaum")[1]

The Smith family's efforts, particularly Alvin's, raised enough cash to make both the 1820 and the 1821 payments on their farm.[2] The third and final

1. American lexicographer Noah Webster defined calomel in 1828 as follows: "A preparation of mercury, much used in medicine. It is called the submuriate or protochloride of mercury, and is prepared in various way, by sublimation or precipitation, and also in the dry way. The following are the directions given in the last *London Pharmacopoeia.* Take of muriated quicksilver one pound, and of purified quicksilver, nine ounces; rub them together or till the globules disappear; then sublime, and repeat the sublimation twice more successively" (Noah Webster, *American Dictionary of the English Language* [1828], s.v. "Calomel").

2. Alvin had earlier told his father that "he should take the buisness [sic] at home in his entire charge whilst I said <I> will go abroad <to> see if I cannot make the second payment and the remainder of the first" (Lavina Fielding Anderson, *Lucy's Book,* 320-21).

payment was due on August 1, 1822. But fate intervened—Zechariah Seymour, the land agent in Canandaigua to whom the Smiths paid their mortgage payments, died in July 1822. Rather than retain the money until a new agent was appointed, the Smiths diverted their funds to purchase building materials needed to complete a new frame home on the property. Lucy, the last of Joseph and Lucy's children, born on July 18, 1821, increased the size of the family to eleven. More room was needed. The Smiths became convinced that by the time the Evertson heirs appointed a new land agent, they would be able to raise enough additional capital to cover the final payment. This error in judgment ultimately cost the family their farm.

An apprentice carpenter, Alvin spearheaded construction of a new frame home several hundred yards south of the log home. By November 1822, a month before Joseph Jr. turned seventeen, the frame of the new home was raised and all the materials needed to complete the project were stored on the property. "This opened to Alvin's mind," his mother later wrote, "the pleasing prospect of seeing his father and mother once more comfortable and happy." The dutiful son announced: "I am going to have a nice pleasant room for father and mother to sit in, and everything arranged for their comfort, and they shall not work any more as they have done."[3] But fate once again intervened to disappoint Smith dreams.

Around ten o'clock on the morning of November 15, 1823, shortly after the family had moved into the shell of their frame home,[4] Alvin came in from work extremely ill with what his mother called "the bilious colic," a nineteenth-century term that, according to Noah Webster's 1828 *Dictionary,* meant a severe stomach ache. Eventually, it would be shown that Alvin was manifesting acute appendicitis, a bacterial inflammatio,n or viral infection in the digestive tract.[5] Typical symptoms of appendicitis include intense pain radiating to the lower right section of the midriff, abdominal cramps and swelling, nausea or vomiting, and elevated temperature.[6] By the time pain manifests, the appendix has usually filled with pus. Left untreated, the

3. Ibid., 349.

4. On May 2, 1917, LDS Church member Willard Bean interviewed a Dr. Pratt, a Palmyra physician, who said that "the Smith family had moved into their new house shortly before Alvin's death." Pratt was a boy at the time and sat in a buggy outside the Smith home while his father, also a physician, attended the patient. (Qtd. in Rand Hugh Packer, "History of Four Mormon Landmarks in Western New York," 47).

5. The highest incidence of appendicitis occurs during the "second and third decades of life." The incidence is twice as high in males as in females ("Appendicitis Symptoms," 3).

6. Ibid.

infection spreads through the wall of the appendix, becomes gangrenous, then ruptures. The ensuing peritonitis may cause death within forty-eight hours.

So it went with Alvin. The brawny twenty-five-year-old, "a youth of singular goodness of disposition—kind and amiable," according to his mother, in extreme pain, asked his father to summon a doctor as quickly as possible. Alexander McIntyre, Smith family physician, was unavailable at his storefront office on Palmyra's Main Street.[7] Evidently, the former family physician, Dr. Gain Robinson, and other local doctors were also unavailable. Father Smith hurried to an adjoining village, possibly Macedon, returning with Dr. Greenwood,[8] a practitioner of "heroic medicine," who used purges, bleeding, and large dosages of toxic drugs like calomel to treat nearly every condition. After examining the suffering patient, the doctor administered a measure of calomel, a heavy, soft, white, sweetish-tasting halide mineral that is not easily swallowed. The mercurous chloride compound was also known as sweet sublimate "until the Civil War when its use was discontinued."[9] An 1848 compendium commented that calomel was "perhaps more frequently used, and in a greater variety of complaints than any other medicine."[10] A medical textbook published in 1845 noted that as a purgative, or vermifuge, it was particularly useful with bilious fevers, hepatitis, jaundice, bilious colic.[11] The appropriate dosage of a calomel treatment was arguable. One nineteenth-century prescription recommended: "[T]en grains of calomel,

---

7. Alexander McIntyre, the son-in-law and nephew of Gain Robinson, was president of the county medical association. An early source identifies McIntyre as an allopath (Woman's Society of the Western Presbyterian Church, comp., "Palmyra, New York," 1907, 2-3). Allopathy attempts to "produce a condition of the system either different from, opposite to, or incompatible with the condition essential to the disease" (Virginia S. Thatcher and Alexander McQueen, *The New Webster Encyclopedic Dictionary,* s.v. "allopathy"). Allopathic physicians "used plenty of calomel," noted "The Family Journal of the Horton Family of Iowa," 2.

8. No researcher has found additional information on this individual. Neither U.S. censuses nor medical registers name him. It is possible that Mother Smith may have confused the doctor's name with the Smith family's new land agent, John Greenwood. See Dan Vogel, *Early Mormon Documents,* 1:300n97.

9. Cathartic mercury compounds such as calomel were taken out of the U.S. Medical Department's pharmacopoeia in May 1863 during the Civil War. Surgeon General William A. Hammond ordered calomel and tartar emetic removed because he believed that Union physicians were using them indiscriminately and excessively, thereby causing profuse salivation, loss of teeth, and sometimes mercurial gangrene. Ultimately, the majority of physicians under his command defied this order and what was known as the "calomel war" began. Hammond was court-martialed and fired because U.S. Secretary of War Edwin M. Stanton took sides against him (G. H. Brieger, "Therapeutic Conflicts," 215; Janet King, "Vermont Civil War Medicine," 9; John V. Norris, "Many Medical Advances in Last Half-Century"; George E. Omer Jr., "An Army Hospital," 7).

10. Arnold James Cooley, *A Cyclopaedia of Six Thousand Practical Receipts,* 156.

11. George B. Wood and Franklin Bache, *The Dispensatory of the United States,* 988.

combined with a portion of jalap, may be given in molasses, and repeated or followed by a saline purgative, until copious evacuations are produced."[12] Another prescription noted that the "normal dose of calomel for constipation in those days was one quarter of one grain."[13]

At first, Alvin refused to take the remedy with its metallic aftertaste but eventually relented. In 1843, his brother Joseph told a boatload of new English converts: "Calomel doctors will give you calomel to cure a sliver in the big toe; and they do not stop to know whether the stomach is empty or not; and calomel on an empty stomach will kill the patient."[14] Was he remembering Alvin's condition? Perhaps the young man had vomited, or not eaten for several hours, since it probably took Father Smith until late afternoon to find the doctor.

After three days of unremitting misery, unable to purge his bowels because of the festering gangrene in his intestines, Alvin seemed to accept his doom. Dr. McIntyre and four other physicians finally arrived on the 17th with $12.76 worth of what Mother Smith called "the most efficient and powerful medicine"[15] from Gain Robinson's drugstore.[16] But "it was all in vain," she continued. "[T]heir exertions proved unavailing, just as Alvin had said would be the case."[17] Once the physicians left the household, peace descended on the dying man. He called twenty-three-year-old Hyrum to his bedside to admonish him: "Hyrum, I must die. Now I want to say a few things, which I wish to have you remember. I have done all I could to make our dear parents comfortable. I want you to go on and finish the house, and take care of them in their old age, and do not any more let them work hard, as they are now in old age."

Next he beckoned Sophronia, a "serious, modest, and shy" twenty-year-old who had "grown into a tall and delicate-looking young lady with soft brown hair and big dark-brown eyes that seemed to look into one's very soul."[18] "You must be a good girl," he told her, "and do all you can for father

12. Jalap is a purgative, principally obtained from the tuberous root of a climbing plant of the convolvulus family, a native of Mexico. Quotation from *The Household Cyclopedia,* 4.

13. Ben Weider, "The Assassination of Napoleon," 12.

14. "Remarks of the Prophet to the Saints Newly Arrived from England," *History of the Church,* 5:357.

15. Anderson, *Lucy's Book,* 351n64.

16. "Gain C. and Caius C. Robinson Invoice Book, 1819-1831," entry for Nov. 17, 1823. It is listed as a bad debt; the Smiths never paid this bill.

17. Unless otherwise stated, all quotations related to Alvin's illness and death are from Anderson, *Lucy's Book,* 351-56.

18. Mary Salisbury Hancock, "The Three Sisters," pt. 1, 35.

and mother—never forsake them; they have worked hard, and they are now getting old. Be kind to them, and remember what they have done for us."

The following night, realizing death was near, he summoned all the children to advise them separately. When it was eighteen-year-old Joseph's turn, Alvin said: "I am now going to die, the distress which I suffer, and the feelings that I have, tell me my time is very short. I want you to be a good boy, and do everything that lies in your power to obtain the Record. Be faithful in receiving instruction, and in keeping every commandment that is given you. Your brother Alvin must leave you; but remember the example which he has set for you; and set the same example for the children that are younger than yourself, and always be kind to father and mother."

Finally, Alvin called for little Lucy, the two-year-old baby of the family who had been put to bed for the night. "He was extremely fond of her," Mother Smith later wrote, "which naturally attached her to him." As Lucy woke her sleeping namesake, the baby "screamed out Oh! Amby[,] Amby." When she was taken to Alvin's bedside, she sprang from her mother's arms, caught him around the neck, and cried out, "Oh My Amby & kissed him again and again." His parting words to this favorite child were: "Lucy, you must be the best girl in the world, and take care of mother; you can't have your Amby any more. Amby is going away; he must leave little Lucy."

By this time, Alvin had likely developed large, mercurial ulcers in his mouth with their coppery taste. "Take her away, I think my breath offends her," said the dying man. "We took hold of her to take her away," recalled Mother Smith, "but she clinched him with such a strong grasp, that it was with difficulty we succeeded in disengaging her hands." As little Lucy left the room, Alvin exclaimed, "[F]ather, mother, brothers, and sisters, farewell! I can now breathe out my life as calmly as a clock." He then closed his eyes in death. The baby cried out to be returned, but someone in the room, possibly Father Smith, said, "Alvin is gone; an angel has taken his spirit to heaven."[19]

Until the body was removed from the house, the distraught toddler continued to cry, "and to manifest such mingled feelings of both terror and affection at the scene before her, as are seldom witnessed," said her mother. The child dragged in a board from outside, laid it beside the corpse, then wrapped herself in a white cloth and lay down. The next morning an autopsy was performed at Dr. McIntyre's request to determine the exact cause of

19. Joseph, writing later of this incident, added: "[W]hen he died the angel of the Lord visited him in his last moments" *(History of the Church,* 5:126-27).

death. In addition to McIntyre, his uncle Gain Robinson, then nearing seventy,[20] participated, as did a Dr. Pratt.[21] Robinson, a Thomsonian physician,[22] was trained in the use of emetics (lobelia), rather than using the bleedings and calomel treatments of "heroic medicine."[23]

The philosophy of homeopathic physicians like Robinson was that doctors tended to give patients too much medicine. They believed that "tiny amounts of drugs should be diluted in water before being given to a patient."[24] The Smiths could only interpret the heavy dose of calomel as medical malpractice, and Robinson agreed. Lucy Smith recounted that "he spoke long and earnestly to the younger physicians" during the autopsy "upon the danger of administering powerful medicines without a thorough knowledge of [the practice of] physic [i.e., medicine]."[25] He commented on Alvin's character: "[H]ere is one of the loveliest youths that ever trod the streets of Palm[y]ra destroyed[,] murdered as it were by him at whose hand relief was expected—cut off from the face of Earth by a careless quack." Robinson's remarks resonated in the Smith family psyche. Seventy-one years later, sister Katharine recalled that "my brother [Alvin] took sick, and through the ministering of medicine by the doctors he passed away."[26] In 1875, William related that Alvin "died of an over dose of Calo=mill [sic], while having a Sick spell of the Billious cholic."[27] William also wrote in his Nauvoo newspaper, *The Wasp*, on August 4, 1842: "We will not say that he that gives Calomel murders, nor he that takes it commits suicide, but we will say ... that he that uses the least medicine lives longest in nine cases out of ten." Joseph Sr. reminisced in 1835: "Alvin, as you all are aware, was taken from us in the vigour of life, in the bloom of youth: my heart often mourns his loss, but I have no disposition to complain against the Lord." While conferring a blessing on Hyrum's head, the patriarch gave voice to

20. Dr. Robinson's November 20, 1823, day book notes that he received $3.00 for "Joseph Smith visit" ("Gain C. and Caius C. Robinson Invoice Book, 1819-1831").

21. Dr. Pratt's involvement was related to Willard Bean by Pratt's son. "When they opened [Alvin] up they observed a ruptured intestine. Country doctors knew little or nothing about appendicitis in those days" (Willard Bean, "Report of 2 May 1917 interview of Dr. Pratt conducted by Willard Bean," 47).

22. Followers of Samuel Thomson, a New Hampshire practitioner who wrote *The New Guide to Health.* Thomsonian practitioners used a variety of botanicals to treat disease.

23. "Changing Medical Practices in Early America."

24. Ibid.

25. Anderson, *Lucy's Book,* 355.

26. Kyle R. Walker, "Katharine Smith Salisbury's Recollections of Joseph's Meetings with Moroni," 16.

27. William Smith, "Notes Written on 'Chambers' Life of Joseph Smith,'" 31.

the perceptions of persecution then espoused by the Smith family: "Wo be to the man who sought [Alvin's] fall by which means he was deprived of leaving seed to rise up in his inheritance to call him blessed. … God is just and he will reward the enemy of my son four fold."[28]

Young and possibly inexperienced, the physician identified in Lucy's narrative as Dr. Greenwood was not the murderer Robinson and Joseph Sr. seem to have implied. Robinson's opinion may merely have reflected the quarrel in American medical circles at the time between homeopaths like Robinson and allopaths like Greenwood, most of them poorly trained, who thought that disease was the result of poison and that the poison should be removed by bloodletting and purging. Ultimately, no physician alive at the time could have saved Alvin. Appendectomy, the only cure for acute appendicitis, was beyond any medical skills of the day. Brigham Young died of appendicitis fifty-four years later in 1877 because the surgical remedy would not be developed for another twenty years.[29]

Word of Alvin's death spread quickly throughout the area. In that period, "inviters" or "warners" were sent from door to door to notify friends and neighbors of a loved one's death. Mortuary science had not yet developed, and a neighbor with experience in "laying out" the dead helped to prepare Alvin's body for burial.[30] "Alvin was a youth of singular goodness of disposition," his mother said, "so that lamentation and mourning filled the whole neighborhood."[31] He was engaged to be married in the near future, although the name of his fiancée has not survived. According to Lucy, this young woman "was rendered most desolate by his unexpected Death and as long as we knew her she never recovered her wonted animation and Good spirits." Funerals were an occasion for social intimacy, being one of the few times large numbers of people got together. Mother Smith related that "the inhabitants of the surrounding country gathered to gather [sic] and during the funeral obsequies they gave the most affectionate manifestations of th[e]ir sympathy." The funeral was held in Palmyra's union meetinghouse,

28. Joseph Smith Sr., "Blessing on Hyrum Smith."

29. Reginald H. Fitz, a Harvard University anatomopathologist who advocated early surgical intervention, first described appendicitis in 1886. Because he was not a physician, however, his recommendations were virtually ignored. The first successful appendectomy in a patient with acute appendicitis was accomplished by Dr. H. Hancock, an English surgeon near the end of the nineteenth century. "Appendicitis."

30. For a treatment of funerary practices of the day, see Loretta M. Alirangues, "Funerary Practices in Early and Modern America."

31. This narration of Alvin's death and burial, unless otherwise noted, is taken from Anderson, *Lucy's Book,* 354-56.

also called the Western Presbyterian Church, on cemetery hill, a stone's throw from the new Erie Canal.

Funerals in nineteenth-century America were often gloomy and distressing for the bereaved. Alvin's eulogy was delivered by the Reverend Benjamin Stockton, who had been ministering in the area for some time and who, within three months, on February 18, 1824, would be appointed the regular minister of Palmyra's Western Presbyterian congregation.[32] Conservative Calvinistic theology in the 1820s offered no salvation to unbaptized persons like Alvin. Neither of Joseph and Lucy's two other deceased children had experienced conviction and conversion.[33] Even the "offspring of the godly," wrote one scholar of Presbyterian theology, "were born enemies of God and must await the crisis of conversion."[34] The Westminster Confession of Faith, which infused Stockton's theology, held that Adam's transgression and corrupted nature were transferred to everyone. Thus, all humanity sins and only the elect can be saved:

> By the decree of God, for the manifestation of his glory, some men and angels are predestinated unto everlasting life, and others fore-ordained to everlasting death. ... These angels and men, thus predestinated and fore-ordained, are particularly and unchangeably designed; and their number is so certain and definite that it cannot be either increased or diminished. ... Wherefore they who are elected being fallen in Adam are redeemed by Christ, are effectually called unto faith in Christ by his Spirit working in due season; are justified, adopted, sanctified, and kept by his power through faith unto salvation. Neither are any other redeemed by Christ, effectually called, justified, adopted, sanctified, and saved, but the elect only. ... The rest of mankind, God was pleased ... to pass by.[35]

Joseph's younger brother William later remembered: "Reverend Stockton had preached my brother's funeral sermon and intimated very strongly

---

32. Woman's Society of Western Presbyterian Church, "Palmyra, New York," 9.

33. Later, in an 1836 vision, Joseph said he saw "the celestial Kingd=om of God." Therein "I saw father Adam, and Abraham and Michael and my father and mother, my brother Alvin, that has long since slept, and marv[e]led how it was that he had obtained an ineritance <in> that Kingdom, seeing that he had departed this life, before the Lord <had> set his hand to gather Israel the <second time> and had not been baptized for the remission of sins." The prophet reported that the Lord told him that "all who have died with[out] a knowledge of it, who would have received it, with all their hearts, shall be heirs of that Kingdom, for I the Lord <will> judge all men according to their works according to the desires of their hearts" (Dean C. Jessee, *The Personal Writings of Joseph Smith,* 146).

34. Lewis Bevens Schenck, *The Presbyterian Doctrine of Children in the Covenant,* 153.

35. "The Westminster Confession of Faith," 6.016, 6.017, 6.019, 6.020.

that he had gone to hell, for Alvin was not a church member, but he was a good boy, and my father did not like it."[36] Joseph Sr., suffused with Universalist beliefs, considered such doctrine uninspired by a God who extended love and opportunity to all. It was obviously an angry father who saw his exemplary and beloved son lowered into a cold grave without any promise of salvation.[37] The despondent Smith family returned home that dreary November day to the bleakness of the frame home that Alvin's hands had erected.

The impact on the family of the loss of Joseph's eldest brother is beyond easy understanding. As with all premature or unnatural deaths, the grief was deeper, the disbelief more profound. "Our happiness [was] blasted in a moment when we least expected the blow," remembered Mother Smith, "it came upon us[,] the poisoned shaft entered our very heart['s] core[,] and diffused its deadly effect throughout our veins." The gloom overshadowed all the family's interests. "We were for a time almost swallowed up in grief," Lucy remembered, "so much so that it seemed impossible for us to interest ourselves at all about the concerns of life."

Alvin was a role model for younger brothers Hyrum and Joseph. "Thy next brother," Father Smith recalled in Hyrum's 1834 patriarchal blessing, "whom thou didst love, around whose heart thine affections were twined, has been taken in the vigor of youth, even in the morning of his days."[38] Joseph Jr. felt a heavy grief. His loneliness, which no kindness could completely cheer, persisted until he married three years later. He would say a full two decades afterwards, "I remember well the pangs of sorrow that swelled my youthful bosom and almost burst my tender heart when he died."[39]

Lucy Smith noted in her memoirs that "Alvin manifested, if such could be the case, greater zeal and anxiety in regard to the Record [i.e., Book of Mormon] that had been shown to Joseph, than any of the rest of the family." As a result, the Smiths "could not bear to hear anything said upon the subject" because it would bring Alvin to their minds, "with all his zeal, and with all his kindness; and, when we looked to this place, and realized that he was gone from it, to return no more in this life, we all with one accord wept over our irretrievable loss, and we could not be comforted, because he was not."

"Christianity is essentially a social religion," pronounced Methodist

36. J. W. Peterson, "Another Testimony."

37. Years later, Joseph considered relocating Alvin's remains from Palmyra to a new tomb he had built in Nauvoo, Illinois. This was never done, however *(History of the Church,* 5:127).

38. Joseph Smith Sr., "Blessing on Hyrum Smith."

39. *History of the Church,* 5:126-27. Joseph added that Alvin "was the noblest of my father's family" and "in him there was no guile."

John Wesley in 1789.[40] A church was the one social organization outside the family that could provide meaning to the Smiths' struggles. Not only did it extend the promise of eternal salvation, but it also provided a social network to buffer crises. The circumstance of Alvin's death, remembered Mother Smith, "aroused the neighborhood to the subject of religion."[41] About this same time, she later reported, "[T]here was a great revival in religion and the whole neighborhood was very much aroused to the subject and we among the rest flocked to the meeting house to see if there was a word of comfort for us that might rel[i]eve our overcharged feelings."[42]

In other words, they came to church with hopes that their needs would be met. Not surprisingly, they encountered a slightly different agenda. Many Protestant denominations during this period put aside their differences and united to promote Christianity. Mother Smith recalled, without naming him, that "a man [was] then laboring in that place to effect a union of all the churches that all denominations might be agreed to worship God with one mind and one heart."[43] Joseph Jr. remembered that this resurgence "commenced with the Methodists, but soon became general among all the sects."[44] Oliver Cowdery's account of this period, based on information supplied by Joseph, added that the revival was spearheaded by "Mr. Lane, a presiding Elder of the Methodist church ... a talented man, possessing a good share of literary endowments, and apparent humility."[45] William Smith

40. John Wesley, from "Upon Our Lord's Sermon on the Mount," qtd. in John H. Wigger, *Taking Heaven by Storm,* 80.

41. Anderson, *Lucy's Book,* 355. On August 15, 1840, Joseph made the first known public mention of the doctrine of baptism for the dead at the funeral of Seymour Brunson *(History of the Church,* 4:179, 231.) Father Smith died the following month. On his deathbed, he requested that Alvin be baptized vicariously. In his last moments, the senior Smith's eyes brightened and before dying he said, "I see Alvin." In accordance with his father's request, Hyrum Smith was baptized for Alvin by proxy in 1840 and again in 1841 in the Mississippi River at Nauvoo ("Nauvoo Baptisms for the Dead," 145, 149).

42. Anderson, *Lucy's Book,* 357.

43. Ibid.

44. *History of the Church,* 1:2. Joseph's memory of the revival starting among the Methodists is verified in a local newspaper account: "A reformation is going on in this town to a great extent. The love of God has been shed abroad in the hearts of many, and the outpouring of the Spirit seems to have taken a strong hold. About twenty-five have recently obtained a hope in the Lord, and joined the Methodist Church, and many more are desirous of becoming members" ("Communication," *Wayne Sentinel* 1 [Sept. 15, 1824]: 3).

45. Oliver Cowdery to W. W. Phelps, "Letter III," *Latter Day Saints' Messenger and Advocate* 1 (Dec. 1834): 41. According to Dan Vogel, "In 1835 Cowdery's eight letters to Phelps were copied into Joseph Smith's 'large journal' by Frederick G. Williams and Warren Parrish. These letters received wide circulation during Smith's lifetime, being published in the *Times and Seasons* (Nauvoo, Illinois), in the *Gospel Reflector* (Philadelphia, Pennsylvania), in the *Prophet* (New York, New York), and as a pamphlet in 1844 (Liverpool, England)" (Vogel, *Early Mormon Documents,* 2:418).

corroborated: "[T]he people in our neighborhood were very much stirred up with regard to religious matters by the preaching of a Mr. Lane, an Elder of the Methodist Church, and celebrated throughout the country as a great revival preacher."[46] The Puritan tradition of religious revival as manifest in both Great Awakenings expected individuals to experience a conversion, in which God was omnipotent judge and humans were entirely sinful, helpless to save themselves. It was common in Joseph's lifetime for spiritually lethargic congregations, particularly among the Methodists who were more inclined to revivalistic urges, to call in evangelists to instill new life into their members' commitment to the Lord.

In July 1824, Methodist minister George Lane (1784-1859) was assigned to preside over the Ontario District which comprised the circuits of Lyons, Ontario (which included Palmyra), Seneca, Crooked Lake, Canandaigua and Geneva, Canisteo and Bath, and Prattsburgh.[47] He held the position for twelve months, until July 1825.[48] Lane was cast in the mold of John Wesley, founding spirit of Methodism, and was acclaimed for his "catholic spirit" and "willingness to maintain fellowship with all Christians."[49] Such unselfishness, as Mother Smith noted, was manifestation of a broader religious phenomenon that transcended sectarian and denominational boundaries. Most clergymen and communicants belonged to specific sects, but the Second Great Awakening promoted a sense of direct connection to the ultimate theological goal of Christian history: advancing the Millennium.

The religious intensity of Joseph's boyhood, a counter-offensive to flourishing deistic thinking, religious rationalism, and other forms of iconoclasm that many linked with the French Revolution and the Enlightenment, had roots in an earlier period of revivalism which had ignited the spiritual landscape of Smith's grandparents. This Great Awakening, as it was subsequently

46. William Smith, *William Smith on Mormonism,* 6.

47. *Minutes of the Annual Conferences of the Methodist Episcopal Church, 1824,* 52. The responsibility of Presiding Elders was to manage quarterly and camp meetings in the district, collect receipts from the sale of books, handle the toughest disciplinary cases, administer the sacraments, and recruit and evaluate candidates for the ministry (Wigger, *Taking Heaven by Storm,* 36). Another New York Presiding Elder, Rev. Charles Giles, in 1818 supervised eleven circuits, eighteen traveling preachers, and more than 4,500 members. From 1818 to 1822, he supervised 164 quarterly conferences (Charles Giles, *Pioneer,* 283).

48. Larry C. Porter, "Reverend George Lane," 336. Because of the declining health of Lane's wife, Sarah, he relocated to Pennsylvania where he worked as a merchant until 1834. He then moved to New York City after the General Conference of the Methodist Church elected him assistant book agent for the Methodist Book Concern in 1836. He died in Wilkes-Barre, Pennsylvania, on May 6, 1859.

49. Kenneth Cain Kinghorn, *The Heritage of American Methodism,* 15.

called, was part of the religious ferment that swept western Europe in the latter part of the seventeenth and early eighteenth centuries. In Europe, among Protestants and Catholics, the movement was referred to as Pietism or Quietism. Under John Wesley's leadership in England, the effort became known as Evangelism. Historians consider the Great Awakening to be the primal religious event of America between 1740 and 1760. Whole regions of the American colonies were consumed by intense emotional fervor. The ensuing crusade awoke many from religious slumber and reinvigorated congregations. This enthusiastic phenomenon began in the Middle Colonies, then swept into New England in the 1730s, where fire-and-brimstone preaching typically drew large crowds wherever and whenever passionate evangelists discoursed. In the 1740s and 1750s, revivalistic influences reached as far as the southern seaboard.

The Great Awakening caused a substantial reformation of thought and action before it lost momentum. At the time of the American Revolution, the emerging country could count approximately 3,000 churches. The majority of these were Calvinist Presbyterians and Congregationalists. The roots of Congregationalism may be traced to English Protestants who resented bishops and any controlling influences on the local body of Christians—except those arising from God. These worshippers believed they had covenanted with God and that each local congregation could best interpret the terms of this testament. The first American Congregationalists came to New England as Separatist Pilgrims in 1620, and Puritans in 1630, establishing their churches by decree. In 1776, there were 749 Congregational churches in the country and 495 Presbyterian.

But as early as the 1790s, Protestant leaders took the view that the masses were backsliding into apathy. Laymen seemed restive, uninterested in the old doctrines. By 1800, fewer than 10 percent of the population on the eastern seaboard were either Congregationalists or Presbyterians. These Calvinist groups had not kept their finger on the secular, optimistic, republican pulse of America. Defections to the "boiling hot" Methodists and Baptists began to erode the older, more staid churches. Simpler, more emotionally engaging versions of Christianity were better adapted to the spiritual needs of frontier settlers.

The earliest outbreak of new American fervor occurred in 1799-1800 among Scotch-Irish immigrants in Tennessee. These "sinewy men thrust in between the people of the seaboard and the red warriors of the wilderness" had settled in the Green River, Tennessee, and Cumberland Valleys of

Kentucky and Tennessee.[50] The epicenter of this turn-of-the-century revival, the advent of the Second Great Awakening, was Logan County in southwestern Kentucky, a geographical area then called the Cumberland Country, which, according to Frederick Morgan Davenport, professor of sociology at Hamilton College, was viewed by many as a sordid region overrun with "murderers, horse-thieves, highway robbers and counterfeiters, fugitive bond servants and runaway debtors, who fled there from all parts of the Union to escape the clutches of the law."[51] (See also chap. 7.)

The pioneer preachers who initiated the Second Great Awakening were mainly Presbyterians of the Transylvania presbytery and the synod of Kentucky. Rev. James McGready, minister of the Gasper River, Muddy River, and Red River societies, was the key spirit in this small confederation of modified Calvinists—"New Side men," as they were called—who emphasized the importance of a religious experience as proof of conversion and, hence, as qualification for salvation.[52] Finis Ewing, a friend of McGready, praised his ability to "so array hell before the wicked that they would tremble and quake, imagining a lake of fire and brimstone yawning to overwhelm them and the hand of the Almighty thrusting them down the horrible abyss."[53] Another contemporary recorded that "the fierceness of [McGready's] invective derived additional terror from the hideousness of his visage and the thunder of his tones."[54]

During fervent preaching in Red River in the summer of 1799, a vocal woman in the congregation, "unable to repress the violence of her emotions, gave vent to them with shoutings loud and long," wrote John McGee, a Methodist minister present on the occasion. Her outburst created a contagion of weeping that spread throughout the hall. McGee arose and exhorted the audience "to let the Lord God Omnipotent reign in their hearts, and submit to Him, and their souls should live." Shouting and rejoicing erupted. McGee left the pulpit and "went through the audience shouting and exhorting with all possible ecstasy and energy, and the floor was soon covered with the slain."[55]

50. Frederick Morgan Davenport, *Primitive Traits in Religious Revivals,* 61.

51. Ibid., 69.

52. New Side Presbyterians were "experientialists," who "retained the New England Puritan assumption that a unique experience is the mark of salvation and the basis for assessing one's status as a saint" (Gary North, *Crossed Fingers,* 104).

53. Anonymous, qtd. in Davenport, *Primitive Traits in Religious Revivals,* 67.

54. (First name not given) Davidson, "History of the Presbyterian church in Kentucky," qtd. in ibid.

55. John McGee to Thomas L. Douglas, Presiding Elder of Nashville District, Tennessee Conference of the Methodist Episcopal Church, qtd. in ibid., 70. The revivalistic terms "slain

The Red River parishioners leaving this service were like sparks in dry stubble: "They rushed into the arms of their friends shouting and telling what wonderful things God had done for their souls."[56] The conflagration spread as McGready and Barton Stone, in particular, preaching a vivid religion of hellfire, rigid morality, and salvation, attracted huge crowds. During a camp meeting at Cane Ridge, Kentucky, in 1801, between 10,000 and 20,000 people listened to forty evangelists preach over a six-day period. One account of this "Great Revival" recorded that "boisterous emotion, loud ejaculations, shouting, leaping, falling and swooning were in vogue, and were regarded as the *true criteria of heartfelt religion.*"[57] Another minister preaching before the Kentucky Synod in 1803 lamented that these excesses "have no relation to religion."[58] But the enthusiasm spread rapidly. This intense, experiential element of conversion became permanently associated with American religious revivals. The embers of this fervency, smoldering from the earlier outbreak in Joseph Smith's neighborhood in 1817, burst into a firestorm after Alvin Smith's death.

"At this time of which I am speaking," said William Smith of that revival, "one of the most extraordinary reformations was being had all over the country." Residents gathered in schoolhouses and homes as well as in meetinghouses. "Many claimed to be converted to God and professed religion," described William, who would have been thirteen.[59] Mother Smith was "a very pious woman," as William described her, "and much interested in the welfare of her children, both here and hereafter." As a result, she "made use of every means which her parental love could suggest, to get us engaged in

---

of the Lord" or "slain by the Spirit," also known as the "falling down exercise," were inspired by Ezekiel 21:7: "[A]nd every heart shall melt, and all hands shall be feeble, and every spirit faint, and all knees shall be weak as water." These dramatic manifestations had been noted as early as 1739 among the Methodists. John Wesley recorded in his journal on January 1, 1739: "About three in the morning," while he and five other clergymen were engaged in prayer with sixty others, "the power of God came mightily upon us, insomuch that many cried out for exceeding joy, and many fell to the ground. As soon as we were recovered from shock and amazement at the presence of his majesty, we broke out with one voice, 'We praise thee, O God; we acknowledge thee to be the Lord.'" On April 21, 1739, "a young man was suddenly seized with violent trembling all over, and in a few minutes, 'the sorrows of his heart being enlarged,' sunk down to the ground." Five days later, Wesley wrote again: "Immediately one and another and another sunk to the earth: they dropped on every side as thunderstruck" (Rupert E. Davies, *The Works of John Wesley,* 19:29).

56. "History of the Cumberland Presbyterian Church," cited in Davenport, *Primitive Traits in Religious Revivals,* 71.

57. Unnamed observer, qtd. in Schenck, *The Presbyterian Doctrine of Children in the Covenant,* 77; emphasis his.

58. Unnamed individual, qtd. in ibid., 78.

59. William B. Smith, "Sermon by Elder Wm. B. Smith," 82.

seeking for our souls' salvation, or (as the term then was) 'in getting religion.'" She took her children to the interdenominational revivals in the Western Presbyterian church at the Union Meeting House where Alvin's funeral had been the year before. "Almost the whole family became interested in the matter," wrote William, and became "seekers after truth." The excitement "prevailed not only in our neighborhood but throughout the whole country. Great numbers were converted." Mother Smith continued her "importunities and exertions" to interest family members in "the importance of seeking for the salvation of our immortal souls, until almost all of the family became either converted or seriously inclined."[60] Joseph Jr. was also "thought to be what was called under concern of mind."[61]

After the initial excitement waned, the local sects began to "beat up for volunteers." A war of words among the various factions ensued. Oliver Cowdery, using information provided by Joseph Jr., wrote that for a time the "reformation seemed to move in a harmonious manner, but as the excitement ceased, … a general struggle was made by the leading characters of the different sects, for proselytes." Instead of the "union and harmony" which had previously prevailed, strife arose, and "a cry—I am right—you are wrong—was introduced in their stead."[62] William Smith also remembered that Methodist, Presbyterian, and Baptist factions each began to proclaim: "We are right," or "Come and join us," or "Walk with us and we will do you good."[63] Whitney Cross, in his history of the "Burned-Over District," observed, "It is paradoxical that purportedly nonsectarian revivalism and benevolence should encompass much of the spirit they professed and yet engender inter-denominational strife of a bitterness scarcely to be paralleled."[64] Joseph Smith, in his 1838-39 account of his life, lamented:

> [N]otwithstanding the great love which the converts to these different faiths expressed at the time of their conversion, and the great zeal manifested by the respective clergy, who were active in getting up and promoting this extraordinary scene of religious feeling, in order to have everybody converted, as they were pleased to call it, let them join what sect they pleased; yet when the converts began to file off, some to one party and some to another, it was seen that the seemingly good feelings

60. Smith, *William Smith on Mormonism*, 6.
61. Smith, "Sermon by Elder Wm. B. Smith."
62. Cowdery to Phelps, "Letter III," Dec. 1834, 41.
63. Smith, *William Smith on Mormonism*, 6.
64. Whitney R. Cross, *The Burned-Over District*, 40.

> of both the priests and the converts were more pretended than real; for a scene of great confusion and bad feeling ensued—priest contending against priest, and convert against convert; so that all their good feelings one for another, if they ever had any, were entirely lost in a strife of words and a contest about opinions.[65]

Benjamin Stockton, the New Light Presbyterian minister who delivered Alvin Smith's funeral sermon, was president of the affiliated sects at the Palmyra interdenominational revival. Stockton suggested that Palmyrans join his flock because "it was their meeting and under their care," and in their sanctuary as well. Mother Smith, Hyrum,[66] Sophronia, and Harrison, who turned sixteen on March 13, 1824, agreed, for they joined the Presbyterian Church at this time. Katharine (age eleven), Don Carlos (eight), and Lucy (three) were probably considered too young to join.[67] Although at thirteen he was probably too young as well to join, William later wrote that "it was in this church presided over by the Rev. Stockton that I spent much of my boy-hood days."[68]

In his 1838-39 narrative, Joseph Smith said that his first vision experience occurred in "my fifteenth year" during fervent religious activity in the Palmyra/Farmington area where his family resided. He claimed that "early in the spring" of 1820 an "unusual excitement on the subject of religion" occurred and that "great multitudes united themselves to the different religious parties."[69] The June 23, 1820, *Palmyra Register* does report that during the last week of June a forty-year-old Irishman essentially drank himself to death at the "[Methodist] Camp-ground" outside the village of Palmyra,

---

65. *History of the Church,* 1:5-6.

66. Another source confirming Hyrum's conversion was Willard Chase, class leader in the local Methodist church. In 1825, when Hyrum asked to borrow his seer stone, Chase, though reluctant, complied because Smith "had made a profession of religion" and could, he felt, be trusted to return the stone (Chase, Affidavit, in Eber D. Howe, *Mormonism Unvailed,* 241).

67. Kenneth J. Ross, Reference Librarian of the Presbyterian Historical Society, wrote an explanation, quoting the 1822 *Book of Discipline,* Book 2 of the "Form of Government," and part of the Constitution of the Presbyterian Church in the USA: "All baptized persons are members of the church, are under its care, and subject to its government and discipline: and when they have arrived at the years of discretion, they are bound to perform all the duties of church members." Furthermore, Ross continues quoting: "The years of discretion, in young Christians, cannot be precisely fixed. This must be left to the prudence of the eldership. The officers of the church are the judges of the qualifications of those being admitted to sealing ordinances; and of the time when it is proper to admit young Christians to them" ("Directory for Worship," in *Constitution of the Presbyterian Church in the USA,* chap. 9, sec. 2).

68. Smith, "Sermon by Elder Wm. B. Smith," 81.

69. *History of the Church,* 1:3

deep in the woods, on the road running southeast to Vienna.[70] Methodist meetings in Palmyra during hot summer months were typically held outdoors at the cooler campgrounds, deep in the woods, about a mile outside the village on Vienna Road. But these gatherings did not often spark the significant revival of religious enthusiasm Joseph remembered. When they did, results were usually reported in the *Methodist Magazine.*

The small Methodist Society of Palmyra was not incorporated as the Methodist Episcopal Church of Palmyra until July 3, 1821, and did not build a meeting house until 1822, necessitating many outdoor gatherings.[71] Furthermore, records of the Baptist, Methodist, and Presbyterian churches for 1820 do not suggest "great multitudes" joining these small congregations during that year. Membership rolls of the "first Baptized [sic] Church in Palmyra," for example, show that during all of 1820 only eight people joined.[72] Methodist membership records for the Ontario circuit, on which Palmyra was located, constantly lost members from 1819-21: twenty-six in 1819, six in 1820, and forty-nine in 1821.[73]

In his 1838-39 history, Smith further added that "great multitudes" joined the Baptist, Methodist, and Presbyterian churches during the revival. In its details, however, Joseph's reminiscent account more closely matches records for the period 1824-25, after Alvin's death, not 1820. Membership rolls of the first Baptist church, which had a meetinghouse west of Palmyra village in Macedon township, report that, between October 1824 and April 1825, 94 persons were added to the membership roll by baptism. The revival's influence in the local Baptist congregation manifested itself on October 20, 1824, when eight people "told their Christian experience to the Church and were fellowshiped by the Church and on Thursday following were Baptized by Elder Bradley and Received into the Church." From October 1824 to the end of September 1825, Baptist membership jumped from 132 to 219, an increase of 65 percent.[74]

The Methodists were the third denomination to benefit from this jointly

70. "Effects of Drunkenness," *Palmyra Register,* June 23, 1820, 2; and "Plain Truth," *Palmyra Register,* July 5, 1820, 2.

71. "Palmyra Village," *Palmyra Herald,* June 19, 1822, 2.

72. Marquardt and Walters, *Inventing Mormonism,* 17.

73. *Minutes of the Annual Conferences of the Methodist Episcopal Church [1773-1828],* published in 1840, report: 330 [1819], 345 [1820], and 366 [1821], qtd. in Marquardt and Walters, *Inventing Mormonism,* 34.

74. See *Minutes of the Ontario Baptist Association,* 5, for 1824-25 membership figures; also minutes of Oct. 16; Nov. 20, 24; 24; Dec. 4, 5, 18, 1824; and Jan. 1, 15, 29; Feb. 19; Mar. 5, 19, and Apr. 3, 1825. Records of "The First Baptized [sic] Church in Palmyra" may be found in the

sponsored revival. The Ontario Methodist circuit, in which Palmyra was located, had consistently shown a decrease in membership from 1819 to 1821. But from 1824 to 1825, it gained 208 new members.[75] The same pattern appears in records of the Presbyterian church for the Geneva Presbytery to which the Western Presbyterian Church of Palmyra belonged. "[B]less the Lord," began the February 1825 report

> for the displays of sovereign grace which have been made <within our boundaries> during the past year. In the congregation of Palmyra, the Lord has appeared in his glory to build up Zion. More than a hundred have been hopefully brought into the kingdom of the Redeemer. The distinguishing doctrines of grace have proved eminently the sword of the Spirit, by which the rebellion of man's heart has been slain. The fruits of holiness in this revival even now are conspicuous. The exertions for the promotion of divine knowledge are greater than formerly. Sabbath Schools, Bible classes. Missionary & Tract Societies are receiving unusual attention, & their salutary influence is apparent.[76]

Rev. James Hotchkin, who later catalogued the revivals in the churches of Geneva Presbytery, wrote of the Palmyra area: "[A] copious shower of grace passed over this region in 1824 under the labors of Mr. Stockton, and a large number were gathered into the church, some of whom are now pillars in Christ's house."[77] Mother Smith, one of this number, wanted her husband

---

American Baptist Historical Society in Rochester, New York, qtd. in Marquardt and Walters, *Inventing Mormonism,* 17.

75. *Minutes of the Annual Conferences of the Methodist Episcopal Church* (1773-1828), published in 1840, report membership as follows: 446 (1824), 471 (1825), 330 (1819), 345 (1820), and 366 (1821), qtd. in Marquardt and Walters, *Inventing Mormonism,* 34. Records of the Palmyra Methodist congregation were lost in a fire in Rochester, New York, in 1933.

76. Geneva Presbytery "Records," Feb. 2, 1825, Book D:27-28, Presbyterian Historical Society, Philadelphia, qtd. in Marquardt and Walters, *Inventing Mormonism,* 34.

77. James H. Hotchkin, *A History of the Purchase and Settlement of Western New York, and the Rise, Progress, and Present State of the Presbyterian Church in That Section,* 378. On November 9, 1824, a newspaper, the *Western Recorder,* noted: "A revival of religion has lately commenced in the town of Palmyra, N.Y. It is stated by one of the subjects of this glorious work, that one hundred or more persons, it is thought, have lately been brought out of darkness into marvelous light.—Persons of all ages and classes are the subjects of this work of grace" (qtd. in Marquardt and Walters, *Inventing Mormonism,* 24). One month later, Rev. Reuben Winchell wrote in a letter: "In Palmyra, a town about 30 miles North East of this, God has triumphed gloriously. About 200, as I am informed, are sharers in this great and precious work" (in *American Baptist Magazine* 5 [Feb. 1825]: 61-62, rpt. in Marquardt and Walters, *Inventing Mormonism,* 25). "Religious," *Wayne Sentinel,* March 2, 1825, 3-4, reported that "in Palmyra and Macedon, including Methodist, Presbyterian and Baptist churches, more than 400 have already testified that the Lord is good. The work is still progressing. In the neighboring towns, the number is great and fast increasing. Glory be to god on high; and on earth, peace and good will to all men." Methodist Rev. Abner Chase who was

to join her and the three children who helped to swell the ranks of Presbyterianism, but Joseph Sr.'s dislike of Stockton and his rigid Calvinism was too great an obstacle. After two or three meetings, Lucy noted, Joseph Sr. "peremptorily refused going any more, either for my gratification, or any other person's."[78] And although young Joseph "had become seriously inclined," said William, he was not "brought out" but remained in his father's corner, holding Presbyterianism at arm's length.[79]

It seems natural that Lucy should have espoused Scotch-Irish Presbyterianism. Her parents, Solomon Mack and Lydia Gates, were married at the Second Congregational Church in East Haddam, Connecticut. And although her father was a religious backslider until the autumn of his life, Lucy's mother was a staunch Congregationalist. In 1801, the Calvinistic American Presbyterian and Congregationalist churches adopted the Plan of Union. Both groups agreed to combine their efforts, particularly in western New York, and transform what they viewed as an uncivilized American frontier into a pious region. In this "presbygational" arrangement, as it came to be known, each sect agreed to recognize the other's ministry and polity. The plan allowed Congregational and Presbyterian adherents in a given community to combine into a single congregation employing a minister of either denomination.[80] Relationships between the two groups were enhanced under the Accommodation Plan of 1808, which made the confederation the most influential religious organization in western New York, and made it possible for Lucy Smith to savor the Congregationalism of her youth while worshipping in a Presbyterian assembly.

When Lucy pressed young Joseph to join the Presbyterian Church, she did so without any opposition from her husband who had told her that he

---

appointed presiding elder over the Ontario District (which included Palmyra township), Lyons circuit, in July 1820 summarized his four-year term on July 1, 1824: "The Lord has been pleased to visit this District (Ontario) in mercy the present year [July 1823-July 1824]. ... Though for two or three years [July 1820-July 1823] we saw no great awakenings, yet we saw that truth and rational scriptural piety were evidently gaining ground. ... The present year [July 1823-July 1824] we have had some glorious revivals" (in *Methodist Magazine* 7 [Nov. 1824]: 435-36, qtd. in Marquardt and Walter, *Inventing Mormonism,* 31-32).

78. Anderson, *Lucy's Book,* 358.

79. Smith, *William Smith on Mormonism,* 6.

80. Although the first Presbyterian clergy in America were Scots and Scotch-Irish ministers, this tie eventually became too difficult to maintain. An insufficient number of ministers from Scotland and Ulster were willing to be recruited to America. This circumstance "compelled the Presbyterians to accept Congregational clergy, principally from New England, who differed from the immigrant ministers over the degree of adherence to the Westminster Confession of Faith" (A. C. Guelzo, "New Side Presbyterians," in Daniel G. Reid, *Dictionary of Christianity in America,* 821).

did not object to her "and such of the children as chose <going or becoming> church members <if we wished>."[81] Joseph Jr., age nineteen or twenty, took the same stance: "Mother," he told her, "I do not wish to prevent you from going to meeting or joining any church you like, only do not ask me to <do so>." His reason was as much dissatisfaction with organized religion as it was confidence in his own spiritual powers. "I can take my Bible, and go into the woods, and learn more in two hours than you can learn at meeting in two years, if you should go all the time," he told his mother.[82] Adding that there would be no harm in joining them, he added that she would "not stay with them long for you are mistaken in them[,] you do not know the wickedness of their hearts." As an example, he asked her to look at Henry Jessup, a wealthy local Presbyterian elder who was one of the original trustees of the Western Presbyterian Church of Palmyra and who had served several terms as "overseer of the Poor."[83]

> [Y]ou hear him talk very piously. Well, you think he is a very good man. Now suppose that one of his poor neighbours should owe him the value of a cow, and that this poor man had eight little children; moreover, that he should be taken sick and die, leaving his wife with one cow, but destitute of every other means of supporting herself and family—now I tell you, that Deacon Jessup, religious as he is, would not scruple to take the last cow from the poor widow and orphans, in order to secure the debt, notwithstanding he himself has an abundance of everything.[84]

Years later, in retrospective accounts, Joseph stated that during this intense religious period he experienced a vision that drained his energy but filled his mind and heart with new possibilities. Joseph reported the effects, but not the cause, to his mother when he staggered into the house and "leaned

81. Anderson, *Lucy's Book,* 358.

82. Ibid., 357. Joseph's words on this point are reminiscent of the philosophy of prominent New York evangelist Charles Grandison Finney (1792-1875). "I read my Bible on my knees a great deal during those days of conflict," wrote the lawyer-turned-minister, "beseeching the Lord to teach me his own mind on those points. I had nowhere to go but directly to the Bible, and to the philosophy or workings of my own mind. I gradually formed a view of my own mind, as revealed in consciousness" (qtd. in Nathan Hatch, *The Democratization of American Christianity,* 199).

83. Jessup, with his partner George Palmer, owned a prosperous tannery in Palmyra from 1814 to 1828 (Thomas L. Cook, *Palmyra and Vicinity,* 16-17). On December 4, 1833, Jessup signed an affidavit, along with other Palmyra residents, declaring the Smith family "entirely destitute of *moral character, and addicted to vicious habits*" (Howe, *Mormonism Unvailed,* 261; emphasis Howe's).

84. Anderson, *Lucy's Book,* 358. Mother Smith added: "At that time this seemed impossible to us, yet one year had scarcely expired when we saw Joseph's supposition literally fulfilled" (ibid., 359).

up to the fire p[lace]" to support his weakened limbs. Lucy "Enquired what the matter was. I replied never mind all is well.—I am well enough off. I then told my mother I have learned for myself that Presbyterianism is not true."[85] Lucy, Hyrum, and Sophronia Smith stopped attending Palmyra's Western Presbyterian Church in about September 1828, which suggests that this is may have been about the time, if not sometime before, when Joseph told his mother that her church was not of God. As Joseph's later reports make clear, Presbyterianism was not the only religion he made this decision about, but he singled it out, not only because of the affiliations within his own family but also because he seemed to harbor a certain animosity toward Presbyterianism. For the rest of his life, he saw much of his religious persecution originating in that sect. For example, he recorded in his diary on February 21, 1843: "I was ground in Ohio & [New] York States [in] a Presbyterian smut machine."[86] Twelve of the forty-five prominent Palmyra area men who signed an affidavit in 1833 describing the Smith family as "destitute of that moral character, which ought to entitle them to the confidence of any community," were members of the town's Western Presbyterian Church, the same congregation where the Smith family worshipped.[87] This stinging rebuke, which had been published four years earlier, may have prompted Smith to begin his 1838 history: "Owing to the many reports which have been put in circulation by evil disposed and designing persons ... I have been induced to write this history."[88]

In contrast, despite Joseph's contempt for the doctrines and outward manifestations of Calvinism as embodied in American Presbyterianism, he was personally inclined toward Methodism. Its priests were common folk like him, not college-educated, stiffed-neck "hirelings" like the erudite Presbyterian clergymen he resented.[89] Furthermore, most representatives of the Methodist Episcopal church, following the lead of founder John Wesley,

85. Dean C. Jessee, *The Papers of Joseph Smith,* 1:273n1.

86. Scott H. Faulring, *An American Prophet's Record,* 257. By means of rapidly rotating brushes, a smut machine removed smut-contaminated wheat from non-contaminated wheat.

87. See brief biographical sketches on these forty-five men in Vogel, *Early Mormon Documents,* 2:48-55.

88. Manuscript History of the Church, Book A-1, 1.

89. Public New Side opinion during the Presbyterian schism of 1741-58 held that many Old Side ministers were not converted. Gilbert Tennent, a New Side leader and son of William Tennent, founder of the famous theological "Log College," which espoused Pietist principles, emphasized this point in "The Danger of an Unconverted Ministry." He charged that many Old Side men were at worst "hireling, murderous, Hypocrites," and at best only "letter-learned Pharisee teachers" (qtd. in Archibald Alexander, *Sermons of the Log College,* 375).

embraced the belief that Christ's atonement was potentially universal, available without restriction to all who would repent and surrender to God. This concept was a key belief in the Church of Christ which Joseph would found in 1830. He also incorporated into his organization the Methodist practice of opening a wide variety of lay leadership positions to ordinary men. A third appeal was the euphoria of Methodist exuberance. Methodists revivals with their emphasis on conversion after an intense and doleful struggle were praised as the surest road to Christian discipleship. The physically and emotionally intense experience he had reported so briefly to his mother had left him shaken but also exultant.

While Methodists made much of conversion, revivals, and testimonials of religious experience, many antagonists were critical of the drama and emotional outbursts of common folk who claimed they were under the influence of the Holy Ghost. Virginian Devereaux Jarratt (1733-1801), an evangelical Anglican, lamented that the denomination was controlled by "tinkers and taylors, weavers, shoemakers and country mechanics of all kinds," men who were prone to "jargon," "wild notions," and "furious gestures" in their preaching.[90]

Other critics suggested that revivalists were "unrestrained enthusiasts and disturbers of both God and man ... [and] were wildly emotional, irresponsibly unconcerned with the objective order and truth of Christian doctrine, and ... poorly educated and ill-equipped to understand and interpret the scriptures rightly."[91] Despite such disapproval, Methodism offered ordinary Americans the opportunity to determine their own religious destiny in the same way they were trying to control their social and economic fate. "Look at the Methodists," observed New York Presbyterian evangelist Charles Grandison Finney, early in his preaching career. "Many of their

90. Devereaux Jarratt, *The Life of the Reverend Devereaux Jarratt,* 36. Thomas Wallcut, another Methodist critic, after observing many Methodist gatherings, recounted that they were "attended with all that confusion, violence and distortion of the body, voice & gestures that characterizes such a boiling hot religion. No Jack Tar in his cups appears to me more irreverent in profaning the name of the Deity than these noisy bellowers when they call upon him" (Thomas Wallcut to James Freeman, Oct. 31, 1789). John Fanning Watson, a lay Methodist and contemporary of Joseph Smith, wrote in 1814 that, although he was "not opposed to extravagant emotions and bodily exercises at the time of conversion or in private devotion," he was "on the part of converted Christians in the context of public worship" (James Fanning Watson, *Methodist Error; or, Friendly Christian Advice to Those Methodists Who Indulge in Extravagant Emotions and Bodily Exercises,* 10). Methodist itinerant George Roberts stressed as early as 1807 that what many found most offensive about this style of worship was not "the involuntary loud hosannas of ... pious souls," but the "jumping, dancing, shouting ... and pushing our social exercises into those extremes" (George Roberts, *The Substance of a Sermon ...* , 29-30).

91. Summarized in Douglas Sloan, *The Scottish Enlightenment and the American College Ideal,* 45.

ministers are unlearned, in the common sense of the term, many of them taken right from the shop or the farm, and yet they have gathered congregations, and pushed their way, and won souls every where. Wherever the Methodists have gone, their plain, pointed and simple, but warm and animated mode of preaching has always gathered congregations."[92]

Much of the early prosperity of the Methodist Episcopal Church in America resulted from the same source as the success of Joseph Smith's brand of Christianity: group focus on the witness of the Spirit. Devotees of both persuasions hungered for the Holy Ghost and were desperate to see God move in their midst. John Wesley defined witnessing as "an inward impression on the soul whereby the spirit of God immediately and directly witnesses to my spirit that I am a child of God ... that all my sins are blotted out and I am reconciled to God."[93] On his death-bed in 1735, Samuel Wesley said to his son John: "The inward witness, son, the inward witness, this is the proof, the strongest proof of Christianity."[94] The witness of the Spirit remained central to Wesley's understanding of what was distinctively Methodist. In *The Character of a Methodist* (1742), he wrote that the Methodist is "one who has 'the love of God shed abroad in his heart by the Holy Ghost given unto him.'"[95] Hymn 93, in the 1780 Methodist *Collection of Hymns,* rhapsodized:

> We by his Spirit prove
> And know the things of God; ...
> His Spirit to us he gave,
> And dwells in us, we know;
> The witness in ourselves we have,
> And all his fruits we show.[96]

Visions, healings, deliverance from demons, and commotion marked Wesley's ministry—people weeping, violently shaking, crying out, losing consciousness, falling down, and occasionally becoming uncontrollably agitated. Wesleyan evangelism was a conspicuous part of almost every type

---

92. Charles Grandison Finney, qtd. in Hatch, *The Democratization of American Christianity,* 199.

93. John Wesley, qtd. in Leo Rosten, *Religions in America,* 129.

94. Samuel Wesley, qtd. in Alan C. Clifford, "Charles Wesley," 1.

95. Davies, *The Works of John Wesley,* 9:35. Elsewhere Wesley explained that "a man should be filled with this peace and joy and love by the inspiration of the Holy Ghost without perceiving it, as clearly as he does the light of the sun. This is (so afar as I understand them) the main doctrine of the Methodists. This is the substance of what we all preach. And I will still believe, none is a true Christian till he experiences it" (ibid., 26:181-82).

96. Qtd. in Ann Taves, *Fits, Trances, and Visions,* 55-56.

of Methodist gathering. Methodist clergymen, for the most part, preached Arminianism,[97] a traditional philosophy which emphasized the duty and ability of sinners to repent and desist from sin and, hence, the responsibility of priests to prepare the hearts of devotees to put them in a spiritual frame of mind. The witness of the Holy Ghost, claimed the clerics, manifests itself in a profound, unnerving, and frighteningly disturbing conviction of sin. The process characteristically started when a person became directly concerned with the state of his or her soul and seriously inquired, "What can I do to be saved?" This agitation led to a state of emotional upheaval, a spiritual dismay marked by deep concern about God's wrath, which in turn burgeoned into a heartfelt realization that one stood justly condemned for one's sins and deserved damnation. At this point, the distraught soul usually came to the terrifying conclusion that no matter how much he or she might desire it and despite his or her most strenuous efforts, there was nothing he or she could do to earn salvation except to repent and surrender unconditionally to God's will, pleading for mercy. The emotions of this conversion experience were often so intense that sinners felt entirely under the control of forces beyond their power. Many were compelled to cry out, groan loudly, or shout. Others saw visions or received revelations from angels, God, or Jesus. Methodist journals and histories recorded scores of gatherings where such manifestations were observed.

Conversion in Joseph Smith's day was typically called a Christian or "religious" experience. Often accompanied by tears, the process provoked a deep sense of humility, relief, and peace, an upwelling of love toward God, and the belief that one had entered a new state of being. Conversion *was* belief, although faith was essential to it—a profound psychological transformation that left the disciple with a fundamentally altered sense of self. The convert entered a new spiritual state referred to as regeneracy—that is, regenerated—and sanctification in which the paramount desire was to do God's will, a desire expressed almost immediately in active concern for the transformation of family, friends, and even strangers.

To lead congregants to conversion, ministers of Joseph Smith's youth performed the gospel as much as proclaimed it. Methodist itinerant ministers observed that, even though adherents may once have feared God, they

97. Jacobus Arminius (1560-1609) was a Dutch theologian strongly opposed to the Calvinistic doctrine of predestination. He rejected the doctrine that men lack free will and therefore cannot help themselves attain salvation through faith. His followers published a *Remonstrance* on his views in 1610. His ideas profoundly influenced Methodist theology.

tended to backslide and needed to be occasionally aroused anew to build up churches and maintain high moral standards. To re-inspire slackers, early Methodist evangelists fashioned a dramatic language that appealed to the common folk. Above all else, what characterized this evangelicalism was its dynamism, the pervasive sense of energy it released.[98] Ministers spoke in emotional terms of the terrible bleakness of life without God and how crucial conversion was. This fear-based preaching usually plummeted worshippers into the conviction/conversion cycle. Boston Congregationalist minister Charles Chauncy, an early observer of Methodist enthusiasm, quoted an account published in a 1742 Boston newspaper where itinerant preachers were declaring to congregations "that God is doing *extraordinary* Things in other Places, and that they are some of the last hardened Wretches that stand out; that this is the last Call that ever they are likely to have; that they are now hanging over the Pit of Destruction, and just ready, this Moment, to fall into it; that Hell-fire now flashes in their Faces; and that the Devil now stands ready to seize upon them, and carry them to Hell!" The writer concluded that the preachers would often repeat the words *"Damn'd! Damn'd! Damn'd* three or four Times over."[99]

Those who were brought out, or convicted, of their sins by these techniques often moaned, cried, laughed, swooned, and shouted. Chauncy listed some of the "Strange Effects upon the Body" of such preaching: *"swooning away* and *falling to the Ground,* where Persons have laid, for a Time, speechless and motionless; bitter *Shriekings* and *Screamings; Convulsion-like Tremblings* and *Agitations, Strugglings* and *Tumblings."* He added that these effects were not "peculiar to some particular Places or Constitutions; but have been common all over the Land." Even more dramatic corporeal displays consisted of dancing with joy, jerking, and "the singing exercise."[100] A spectator at one of these Methodist meetings (time and place not specified) left this description:

> On the one hand you would have seen a poor sinner leaning with his head against a tree, with tears running from his eyes, and somebody going and pointing him to the Lamb of God upon the cross. On the other hand you would have seen a whole group of people, and from the midst of them you would have heard the piercing outcries of the broken-hearted penitent;

98. An excellent treatment of the "Methodist shouting tradition" is Taves, *Fits, Trances, and Visions,* 76-117.

99. Charles Chauncy, *Seasonable Thoughts on the State of Religion in New England,* 96.

100. Ibid.

> and to turn your eyes in another direction you would see a gray-headed father and his children crying to God to have mercy on their souls. ... I could have led you to a place where the divine blessing was manifested, similar to the glory which appeared in the tabernacle of the congregation when the wandering Israelites fell upon their faces and shouted.[101]

Although these emotional displays were not unique to Methodism, "boiling hot religion," as some observers then called it, was a trademark of the faith. Methodists, as Winthrop Hudson described them, were "like Augustus Longstreet's 'honest Georgian' who preferred his whiskey straight and his politics and religion red hot."[102] Chauncy included additional examples of this exuberance in the influence of George Whitefield's preaching in which the "*sensible Perceptions* [of the "Multitudes"] arose to such a Height, as that they *cried out, fell down, swooned away,* and, to all Appearance, were like Persons in Fits." Chauncy explained to a 1742 correspondent:

> The *Speaker* delivers himself, with the *greatest Vehemence* both of *Voice* and *Gesture,* and in the most *frightful Language* his Genius will allow of. If this has its intended Effect upon *one* or *two weak Women,* the Shrieks catch from one to another, till a great Part of the Congregation is affected; and some are in the Thought, that it may be too common for those *zealous in the new Way to cry out themselves,* on purpose to move others, and bring forward a *general Scream.* Visions now become common, and Trances also, the Subjects of which were in their own Conceit transported from Earth to Heaven, where they saw and heard most glorious Things; conversed with *Christ* and *Holy Angels;* had opened to them the *Book of Life,* and were permitted to read the names of persons there, and the life.[103]

New Englander Jesse Lee, who published a history of American Methodism in 1810, was both a participant and observer in many colorful emotional outpourings. He wrote: "Many sinners were powerfully convinced,

---

101. Kinghorn, *The Heritage of American Methodism,* 160. Faultfinders objected to excitement and emotion as violating "dignity and order." In 1805, the General Assembly of another denomination summarily denounced camp meetings: "God is a God of order and not of confusion, and whatever tends to destroy the comely order of his worship is not from him." These critics charged Methodism with promoting "intemperate zeal" (ibid., 159).

102. Winthrop Hudson, qtd. in George C. Bedell, Leo Sandon Jr., and Charles T. Wellborn, *Religion in America,* 159. Longstreet (1790-1870), southern lawyer, educator, and humorist; author of *Georgia Scenes* (1835).

103. Charles Chauncy, "A Letter from a Gentleman in Boston to Mr. George Wishart," 118-19.

and cried for mercy. The news of convictions and conversions were common; and the people of God were inspired with new life and vigour, by the happiness of others. ... Numbers of old and gray-headed, of middle-aged persons, of youth, yea, of little children, were the subjects of this work. ... This out-pouring of the spirit extended itself, more of less, through most of the circuits."[104]

American psychologist William James, reflecting in 1901-1902 on conversion experiences, linked them particularly, but not exclusively, to Methodism. He thought the average Protestant set little store by "instantaneous conversion," allowing "ordinary religious duties ... to suffice for his salvation." For Methodists, he said, this was "not enough." For them, there must be an "acute crisis of self-despair and surrender followed by relief." Without this, "salvation is only offered, not effectively received, and Christ's sacrifice is incomplete."[105]

This revivalist fervor was the background to the 1817-28 religious ambiance of Joseph Smith's formative years in western New York. As Mark Thomas, a scholar of the Book of Mormon's cultural context, observes: "[T]he evangelical churches were the mainstream of nineteenth century religion, and *as such they served as Joseph Smith's primary exposure to institutional religion.*"[106] Joseph noted that he "attended various meetings <as often> as occasion would permit." During this period, he says, "my mind became somewhat partial to the Methodist sect, and I felt some desire to be united with them."[107] Palmyra newspaperman Pomeroy Tucker, in his 1867 book on Mormonism, wrote that "at one time [Joseph Jr.] joined the probationary class of the Methodist church in Palmyra, and made some active demonstrations of engagedness, though his assumed convictions were insufficiently grounded or abiding to carry him along to the saving point of conversion."[108] Orsamus Turner, another newspaperman who lived in Palmyra until 1822, also remembered Joseph's involvement with the Methodist Church in the early 1820s.[109]

---

104. Kinghorn, *The Heritage of American Methodism,* 153.

105. William James, *Varieties of Religious Experience,* 186.

106. Mark Thomas, "The Meaning of Revival Language in the Book of Mormon," 20; emphasis his.

107. Manuscript History of the Church, Book A-1, 2.

108. Pomeroy Tucker, *Origin, Rise, and Progress of Mormonism,* 18.

109. Orsamus Turner, *History of the Pioneer Settlement of Phelps and Gorham's Purchase,* 214. Despite his youthful exuberance for Methodism, the mature Joseph Smith viewed the denomination's religious enthusiasm with less ardor. "A Primitive Methodist will shout under the influence of that spirit, until he will rend the heavens with his cries," said Smith in 1842. "Is God the author

Despite his early interest in Methodism, and participation in the 1824 revivals during which his mother and three siblings were converted, Joseph did not experience a conversion to any of the religious denominations he investigated. Although there was no prerequisite for Methodist membership other than a desire for salvation, New England and New York churches traditionally expected novices to give an account of God's saving action in their lives as part of being accepted to full membership in a congregation.[110] Alexander Neibaur, Joseph's dentist in Nauvoo, Illinois, wrote that young Smith yearned for the Methodist promise of a witness of the Spirit. "Br[other] Joseph tolt us the first call he had [at] a Revival Meeting his Mother & Br[other] & Sist[er] got Religion." The young enthusiast "wanted to get Religion too," Neibaur continued. He "wanted to feel & shout like the Rest"—to be overshadowed by the power of God, to be quickened, to be created anew. But, as he lamented to Neibaur, he "could feel nothing."[111]

Many more Americans attended Methodist gatherings than actually

---

of all this?" he queried his audience. "If not of all of it, which does He recognize? Surely, such a heterogeneous mass of confusion never can enter into the kingdom of heaven" *(Times and Seasons* 3 [Apr. 1, 1842]: 744).

110. Robert Ellis Thompson, in his *History of the Presbyterian Churches in the United States,* commented: "Instantaneous, conscious conversion, preceded by an overwhelming sense of personal guilt, and followed by a joyful assurance of acceptance with God, was the only *ordo salutis* [order of salvation] recognized" in the Great Awakening. "Religion must thus come into the man like 'a bolt from the blue,' and with no conceivable relation to the past providences of his life, the human relationships in which he had been placed by God, and the Christian nurture in divine things he had received from his childhood" (qtd. in Schenck, *The Presbyterian Doctrine of Children in the Covenant,* 72).

111. Alexander Neibaur, Journal, May 24, 1844. Psychologist George Coe wondered, as did Joseph Smith, "[W]hy is it that of two persons who have had the same bringing up, and who seek conversion (or sanctification) with equal earnestness, one is ushered into the new life with shoutings and blowing of trumpets, as it were, while the other, however earnestly he may seek such experiences, never attains them at all[?]." Coe's research found that those "for whom emotion was the predominant faculty and those whose mental processes were melancholic or sanguine were likely to have dramatic conversion experiences. Those for whom intellect was the predominant faculty and those whose mental processes were oriented toward practical action were not. Those least likely to experience a sudden conversion, in other words, were intellectuals with an orientation toward practical action" (qtd. in Taves, *Fits, Trances and Visions,* 267-68).

Although young Joseph may have wanted to "feel & shout like the Rest," his adult perspective was quite different. "One great evil," he opined in 1842,

> is that men are ignorant of the nature of spirits; their power, laws, government, intelligence, &c., and imagine that when there is anything like power, revelation, or vision manifested, that it must be of God. Hence the Methodists, Presbyterians, and others frequently possess a spirit that will cause them to lie down, and during its operation, animation is frequently entirely suspended; they consider it to be the power of God, and a glorious manifestation from God—a manifestation of what? Is there any intelligence communicated? Are the curtains of heaven withdrawn, or the purposes of God developed? Have they seen and conversed with an angel—or have the glories of futurity burst upon their view? No! But their body has been inanimate, the operation of their spirit suspended, and all the intelligence that can be

joined the church. Methodist Bishop Francis Ashbury, John Wesley's representative in the United States, estimated that in 1805, the year Joseph was born, Methodist membership in America was approximately 100,000, but that "up to one million people regularly attend our ministry."[112] Much of Joseph's veneration for Methodism came from the influence of the Palmyra area's Presiding Elder, George Lane, a spiritual descendant and emulator of John Wesley. In many respects, Lane's boyhood was similar to Joseph Smith's. Although Lane was two decades older than Smith, they both grew up poor in new country, nurtured by pious mothers. George Peck, friend and fellow preacher, wrote that Lane's early history "was marked by the toils, hardships, and exposure common to the life of a boy in a new country. The simple food, [was] often deficient in quantity, and few of the means and appliances of intellectual improvement [existed]. In those disadvantages our subject shared a common lot with his fellows. The Puritan morals, piety, books, and reading of his excellent mother exerted a strong moral influence upon his mind while very young."[113]

Coincidentally, Lane grew up in Windsor, New York, about ten miles north of what is now Harmony, Pennsylvania, where Joseph Smith's future wife, Emma Hale, also a Methodist, resided.[114] Lane, who subsequently awakened Joseph spiritually, experienced religion himself, and joined the Methodist Church when he was a young school teacher in 1803. "The fervor of his spirit," wrote the admiring Peck, "and his gifts in prayer and exhortation, soon indicated that he was a chosen vessel, destined to be heard at the division of God's sacramental host, then doing battle valiantly upon the frontiers."[115]

Revivalists like Lane often assumed a paternalistic attitude towards their listeners. They saw themselves as shepherds leading followers through the emotional labyrinth from conviction to conversion. Lane was a powerful and persuasive preacher. "The exhortations of the presiding elder, George Lane," wrote Peck of an 1819 camp meeting, "were overwhelming. Sinners

---

obtained from them when they arise, is a shout of "glory," or "hallelujah," or some incoherent expression; but they have had "the power." (*Times and Seasons* 3 [Apr. 1, 1842]: 744.)

112. Qtd. in Nathan O. Hatch and John H. Wigger, *Methodism and the Shaping of American Culture,* 15.

113. George Peck, qtd. in Larry C. Porter, "Reverend George Lane," 322.

114. Isaac and Elizabeth Hale, Emma's parents, were members of the first Methodist Class at Lanesboro, Pennsylvania, a small hamlet just two miles from their Harmony home (George Peck, *The Life and Times of Rev. George Peck,* 68). Emma's uncle, Nathaniel Lewis, an ordained Methodist minister, also lived in the vicinity.

115. Peck, *Christian Advocate and Journal,* qtd. in Porter, "Reverend George Lane," 322.

quailed under them, and many cried aloud for mercy."[116] "As a preacher," continued Peck,

> [Lane] was thoroughly orthodox, systematic, and earnest. His sermons exhibited a thorough acquaintance with the Scriptures and with the human heart. In the palmy days of his itinerancy he was often overwhelmingly eloquent. Sometimes under his powerful appeals vast congregations were moved like the trees of the forest before a mighty wind. Many a stout-hearted sinner was broken down, and cried aloud for mercy under his all but irresistible appeals. His language was unstudied, but chaste, correct, simple, and forcible.[117]

Oliver Cowdery, recalling Joseph's description of Lane's preaching, noted that it "was peculiarly calculated to awaken the intellect of the hearer, and arouse the sinner to look about him for safety—much good instruction was always drawn from his discourses on the scriptures, and in common with others, our brother's [Joseph's] mind became awakened."[118] Joseph himself said that "during this time of great excitement my mind was called up to serious reflection and great uneasiness, but though my feelings were deep and often [poignant], still I kept myself aloof from these parties."[119]

Reportedly, both Presbyterian and Methodist congregations sought Joseph's allegiance. "After strong solicitations to unite with one of those different societies," wrote Cowdery, "and seeing the apparent proselyting disposition manifested with equal warmth from each," Joseph's mind was "led to more seriously contemplate the importance of a move of this kind."[120] In his 1838-39 autobiography, which reworked his earlier accounts of a personal experience of forgiveness of sin into a prophetic call, Joseph said: "[I]n the midst of this war of words, and tumult of opinions, I often said to myself, what is to be done? Who of all these parties are right? Or are they all wrong together? And if any one of them be right which is it? And how shall I know it?"[121] He received guidance, younger brother William recalled, when Rev.

116. Peck, *Life and Times of Rev. George Peck,* 108-9.

117. George Peck, *Early Methodism within the Bounds of the Old Genesee Conference,* 494.

118. Cowdery to Phelps, "Letter III," 41. Cowdery had written in an earlier installment of letters: "That our narrative may be correct, and particularly the introduction, it is proper to inform our patrons, that our brother J. SMITH jr. has offered to assist us. Indeed, there are many items connected with the fore part of this subject that render his labor indispensible [sic]" ("Letter I" to Phelps, Sept. 7, 1834).

119. Dean C. Jessee, *The Papers of Joseph Smith,* 1:270.

120. Cowdery to Phelps, "Letter III," 42.

121. Joseph's personal narrative in this section is taken from Jessee, *The Papers of Joseph Smith,* 1:270-75.

Lane sermonized on "What church shall I join?" His text was James 1:5, which in essence captured the heart of Methodism and its emphasis on the witness of the Spirit: "If any of you lack wisdom," this verse reads, "let him ask of God, that giveth to all men liberally, and upbraideth not; and it shall be given him." According to Orson Pratt, a founding member of Smith's Quorum of Twelve Apostles, this quotation was "cheering information" to Joseph—"tidings that gave him great joy. It was like a light shining forth in a dark place, to guide him to the path in which he should walk. He, now, saw that if he inquired of God, there was, not only, a possibility, but a probability; yea, more, a certainty, that he should obtain a knowledge, which, of all the doctrines, was the doctrine of Christ and, which, of all the churches, was the church of Christ."[122]

Joseph, according to his account, went home and repeatedly read the verse in the family Bible. "Never did any passage of scripture come with more power to the heart of man than this did at this time to mine," he remembered, "it seemed to enter with great force into every feeling of my heart. I reflected on it again and again, knowing that if any person needed wisdom from God, I did, for how to act I did not know and Unless I could get more wisdom than I then had would never known." At length, he concluded: "I must either remain in darkness and confusion or else I must do as James directs, that is, Ask of God." William Smith added to an 1894 interviewer that his brother was "impressed to do just what the preacher had said, and going out in the woods with child like, simple trusting faith believing that God meant just what He said, he kneeled down and prayed; and the time having come for the reorganization of His church, God was pleased to show him that he should join none of these churches but if faithful he should be chosen to establish the true church."[123]

In 1844, Joseph told Alexander Neibaur that he went into the wood to pray; but as he knelt, his tongue cleaved "to his roof—could utter not a word, felt easier after a while—saw a fire towards heaven came near & nearer saw a personage in the fire." This being, reported Smith, had "a light complexion[,] blue eyes[, and] a piece of white cloth drawn over his shoulders[,] his right

122. Orson Pratt, *An Interesting Account,* 3-4. About a decade earlier, Solomon Mack, Joseph Smith's maternal grandfather, had achieved Christian conversion in 1810: "I rejoiced in the God of my salvation, and found Christ's promises verified that what things fo[r]ever ye ask in prayer, believing, ye shall receive, and found that Christ would fulfill all his promises" (Solomon Mack, *A Narraitve [sic] of the Life of Solomon Mack,* 23). He is alluding to Matt. 21:22: "And all things, whatsoever ye shall ask in prayer, believing, ye shall receive."

123. J. W. Peterson, "Another Testimony."

arm bear." Within moments, another "person came to the side of the first [and] Mr Smith then asked must I join the Methodist Church[?]" He was told, "No—they are not my People, [they] have gone astray there is none that doeth good[,] no not one."[124]

Although Joseph said he gave several accounts of this epiphany, no contemporary record of such an encounter has ever been discovered. Smith did not share his recollections widely with others until a few years before his 1844 death. In the earliest written accounts, Joseph claimed that his vision was inspired by religious revival activity. His 1832 version contains such typical revival language as "the wicke[d]ness and abominations and the darkness which pervaded the minds of mankind," "my mind became excedingly [sic] distressed for I become convicted of my Sins," "I felt to mourn for my own Sins and for the Sins of the world," "I cried unto the Lord for mercy," "thy sins are forgiven thee," "mine anger is kindled," and "my soul was filled with love." As years passed, and Joseph met others who recounted an array of visionary experiences, the theological significance of his youthful visions solidified in his mind.[125] Ultimately, the revival language in the earliest tellings was muted, while the restorative elements were enhanced. As Mark Thomas notes, "The developed first vision account bears the markings of a revival vision remodeled into a prophetic calling after later theological reflection."[126]

When Joseph arranged the elements of his spiritual journey in retellings from 1832 to 1844, he sometimes edited events to portray himself in favorable terms. Although he always included a foundational vision, it is not always clear that it included a visitation from God and even less clear when the event occurred.[127] Joseph's friend Josiah Stowell Jr. (1809-75), who met

124. Neibaur, Journal, May 24, 1844.

125. For accounts of others who also claimed visions of God or Jesus, see Appendix A.

126. Thomas, "The Meaning of Revival Language in the Book of Mormon," 20.

127. The concept of Christian Experience is a controversial notion. From the psycho-physiological vantage point, such enthusiasm is viewed as merely the result of an overactive imagination. Charles Chauncy, an observer of the Great Awakening, wrote that "the enthusiast mistakes the workings of his own passions for divine communications, and fancies himself immediately inspired by the Spirit of God, when all the while, he is under no other influence than that of an over-heated imagination." Following the example of preachers they admire, Chauncy continued, the common people often mistook "the Motions of their own Minds for divine Suggestions." Many developed a "low Opinion of *studied Sermons* … while gladly hear[ing] any who will venture to speak to them without *previous Preparation,* whether *learned or unlearned* (if converted)." Not only did they "see Visions and hear voices," they were able to discern "the *internal* State of others … whether *Ministers,* or *People,* and speak of them, and act towards them accordingly" (Chauncy, *Seasonable Thoughts on the State of Religion in New England,* 216). Jonathan Edwards wrote that the common people often viewed impressions upon their minds or "imaginary ideas" as "spiritual discoveries" (C. C. Goen, *The Works of Jonathan Edwards,* 4:48).

him in 1825, later reported that "at that time [i.e., 1825] [Joseph] did not Profess religion,"[128] implying that Joseph made no claims of a visitation from God and Jesus, though he related his visits from the angel. Michael Morse, who later married Emma Hale's sister Tryphenia, first met Joseph in 1825 when the young seer "was a green, awkward, and ignorant boy of about 19 yrs of age. ... [H]e made no pro=fession of religion."[129] The next year, when a hearing before a Bainbridge, New York, judge probed whether Smith was guilty of "glass looking," Father Smith "trusted that the Son of righteousness would some day illumine the heart of the boy, and enable him to see His will concerning him."[130] In other words, irrespective of formal religious affiliation, Joseph's own father in 1826 seems not to have considered him as having had a significant spiritual experience. Six months after Joseph Jr. organized his new church in 1830, Peter Bauder of Albany, New York, came to Fayette and spent a day with Joseph "for the purpose of seeing Smith, and searching into the mystery of his system of religion." Four years later, Bauder recalled: "He could give me no [C]hristian experience." Instead, the head of the newly organized Church of Christ related to Bauder only the story of Moroni's visitations. He "told me that an angel told him he must go to a certain place in the town of Manchester, Ontario County, where [there] was a secret treasure concealed," Bauder wrote, "which he must reveal to the human family."[131]

On January 25, 1825, Rev. George Lane, in a letter to the *Methodist Magazine,* outlined the unusual successes of his district within the previous six months: "I found that the work which had for some time been going on in Palmyra," he wrote, "had broken out from the village like a mighty flame, and was spreading in every direction. When I left the place, December 22nd, there had, in the village and its vicinity, upward of one hundred and fifty joined the [Methodist] society, besides a number that had joined other churches, and many that had joined no church."[132] Nineteen-year-old Joseph Smith placed himself in the second category. "To say that a man is 'converted,'" wrote psychologist William James, "means in these terms, that religious ideas previously peripheral in his consciousness now take a central place and that religious aims form the habitual centre of his energy."[133] Al-

128. Josiah Stowell Jr. to John S. Fullmer, Feb. 17, 1843.

129. Michael Morse, Interviewed by William W. Blair, *Saint's Herald,* June 15, 1879, 52-56.

130. William D. Purple, "Joseph Smith, the Originator of Mormonism," 3.

131. Peter Bauder, *The Kingdom and Gospel of Jesus Christ ...*, 36.

132. Rev. George Lane, "Revival of Religion on Ontario District," 160.

133. James, *The Varieties of Religious Experience,* 162.

though in 1832, Joseph would record "his marvilous experience and of all the mighty acts which he doeth in the name of Jesus Ch[r]ist,"[134] seven years earlier, his Palmyra neighbors remembered him not as having been spiritually reborn but primarily as a money digger, seer, and originator of the "Gold Bible business."[135]

134. Joseph Smith Jr., "History, 1832," in Joseph Smith Letterbook, 1:1. Although this autobiography is in his own handwriting, Smith refers to himself in third person.

135. Joseph Smith used this term in a letter to Oliver Cowdery, Oct. 22, 1829, Joseph Smith Letterbook, 1:9.

10 | THE GLASS LOOKER

[I]t is immaterial what the finding of the court was on the technical charge of being "a disorderly person and an impostor;" what is important is the evidence adduced, and its bearing on the life of Joseph Smith before he announced his claim to be a prophet of God.

—Dale Morgan, in John Phillip Walker, *Dale Morgan on Early Mormonism,* 373

"Convenient to the village of Manchester, Ontario County, New York," Joseph stated in his history, "stands a hill of considerable size, and the most elevated of any in the neighborhood."[1] Lying east of the Smith farm and three to four miles south of Palmyra, this large knoll in the 1820s was skirted on the west by the mail road connecting Palmyra with Canandaigua. "The north end rises quite sudden until it assumes a level with the more southerly extremity," Oliver Cowdery wrote. "[A]s you pass toward Canandaigua it lessens gradually until the surface assumes its common level, or is broken by other smaller hills or ridges, water courses and ravines. I think I am justified in saying that this is the highest hill for some distance round, and I am certain that its appearance, as it rises so suddenly from a plain on the north, must attract the notice of the traveller as he passes by."[2]

The hill, Cowdery continued, presents

> a varied appearance … forming a promontory without timber, but covered with grass. … As you passed to the south you soon came to scattering timber, the surface having been cleared by art or by wind. … The part cleared was only occupied for pasturage, its steep ascent and narrow summit not admitting the plow of the husbandman, with any degree of ease or profit. … There were several trees standing; enough to cause a shade in summer, but not so much as to prevent the surface being covered with grass which was also the case when the record was first found.[3]

1. *History of the Church,* 1:15.
2. Oliver Cowdery to W. W. Phelps, "Letter VII," July 1835, 157.
3. Oliver Cowdery to W. W. Phelps, "Letter VIII," Oct. 1835, 195.

This prominence is one of approximately 11,000 formations oriented in a north-south axis between Rochester and Syracuse, lying north of the Finger Lakes in western New York. Flowing ice from early glaciers deposited these compact piles of debris into "elongated half-egg shaped forms, the most symmetrical of which are called drumlins."[4] This fabled promontory has been called Ramah, Bible Hill, and Mormon Hill. Now revered by millions, the site is known today as the Hill Cumorah. Cowdery reported in 1835 why Cumorah and the surrounding area would become so esteemed by Latter-day Saints. "In this valley [between Cumorah and another hill one mile west]," he began,

> fell the remaining strength and pride of a once powerful people, the Nephites [of the Book of Mormon]—once so highly favored of the Lord, but at that time in darkness, doomed to suffer extermination by the hand of their barbarous and uncivilized brethren [the Lamanites]. From the top of this hill, Mormon [a leader in the Book of Mormon], with a few others, after the battle, gazed with horror upon the mangled remains of those who, the day before, were filled with anxiety, hope, or doubt. A few had fled to the South, who were hunted down by the victorious party, and all who would not deny the Savior and his religion, were put to death. Mormon himself, according to the record of his son Moroni, was also slain.
>
> ... [Mormon] abridged from those records, in his own style and language, a short account of the more important and prominent items ... after which he deposited, as he says ... all the records in this same hill, Cumorah, and after gave his small record to his son Moroni, who, as appears from the same, finished, after witnessing the extinction of his people as a nation.
>
> ... This hill, by the Jaredites [also of the Book of Mormon], was called Ramah: by it, or around it, pitched the famous army of Coriantumr their tents. Coriantumr was the last king of the Jaredites. The opposing army were to the west, and in the same valley, and near by, from day to day, did that mighty race spill their blood, in wrath, contending, as it were, brother against brother, and father, against son. In this same spot, in full view from the top of this same hill, one may gaze with astonishment upon the ground which was twice covered with the dead and dying of our fellow men. Here may be seen where once sunk to nought the pride and strength of two mighty nations; and here may be contemplated, in solitude, while

4. "Drumlin" derives from the Gaelic words for "ridge or summit of a hill" or "little hills" (Francis Smith, "Americana in Drumlin Square").

nothing but the faithful record of Mormon and Moroni is now extant to inform us of the fact.[5]

On September 22, 1823, the fall equinox, seventeen-year-old Joseph Smith walked two to three miles eastward from his Manchester farmstead to this Hill Cumorah, then owned by Robert Robinson.[6] This was the place where young Smith had envisioned golden plates while gazing into his seer stone the night before. His scrying led him to a spot near the summit, on the west side of the hill, near a "lone, solitary, sugar maple tree … a clumpy sort of a tree, about two feet in diameter."[7] Although his hopes for retrieval were high, they were soon dashed by the golden treasure's angel guardian.

In his earliest known account of the day, written in 1832, Joseph said that he "straightway made three attempts" to get the record, but was not successful. He became "exceedingly frightened," supposing that he had merely dreamed the golden plates. "[W]hy can I not obtain them?" he cried in frustration. "[Y]ou have not kept the commandments of the Lord which I gave unto you," replied the messenger who materialized beside him, "therefore you cannot now obtain them for the time is not yet fulfilled." The messenger further explained: "Thou wast left unto temptation that thou mightest be made acquainted with the power of the advisary [sic] therefore repent and call on the Lord thou shalt be forgiven and in his own due time thou shalt obtain them." Joseph's 1832 account added that he "had been tempted of the advisary and saught the Plates to obtain riches and kept not the commandment that I should have an eye single to the glory of God."[8]

Other sources provide additional information about this 1823 visit. Joseph Sr. told neighbor Willard Chase that when he attempted to remove "the

5. Cowdery to Phelps, "Letter VII," 157-58.

6. George Albert Smith, Journal, June 1907, 179. My thanks to H. Michael Marquardt, who drew this source to my attention.

7. Edward Stevenson, *Reminiscences of Joseph, the Prophet, and the Coming Forth of the Book of Mormon,* 11.

8. Joseph Smith Jr., History, 1832, in Dean C. Jessee, *The Papers of Joseph Smith,* 8. Cowdery's 1835 version of this incident, based on Joseph's account to him, relates that, when Joseph could not get the plates, he began to pray. Then

> darkness began to disperse from his mind and his soul was lit up as it was the evening before, and he was filled with the Holy Spirit; and again did the Lord manifest his condescension and mercy: the heavens were opened and the glory of the Lord shone round about and rested upon him. While he thus stood gazing and admiring, the angel said, "look!" and as he thus spake he beheld the prince of darkness, surrounded by his innumerable train of associates. All this passed before him, and the heavenly messenger said, "All of this is shown, the good and the evil, the holy and impure, the glory of God and the power of darkness, that you may know hereafter the two powers and never be influenced or overcome by that wicked one." (Cowdery to Phelps, "Letter V," Oct. 1835, 197.)

book of gold" from the stone box that contained it, he was hindered. "He saw in the box something like a toad, which soon assumed the appearance of a man, and struck him on the side of his head." Not "discouraged at trifles," the boy "again stooped down and strove to take the book, when the spirit struck him again, and knocked him three or four rods [i.e., 49½ -66 feet], and hurt him prodigiously." After recovering, Joseph asked why he could not obtain the plates. "Come one year from this day," he was told, "and bring with you your oldest brother, and you shall have them." This guardian, Father Smith told Chase, "was the spirit of the prophet who wrote this book, and who was sent to Joseph Smith, to make known these things to him."[9]

Another Smith neighbor, Benjamin Saunders (1814-93), reported hearing young Joseph tell Benjamin's mother and sister that an angel directed him to the site where the records were hidden. "When he took the plates," Saunders recalled, "there was something down near the box that looked some[thing] like a toad that rose up into a man which forbid him to take the plates."[10] Years later, Saunders's nephew Orson (1838-189?) related a colorful, second-hand story of this event told to him in 1891 by his uncle Benjamin. Under the headline "How Joe Smith Fought Devils," Orson Saunders alleged, in what he claimed were Smith's own words, uttered six decades earlier:

> I forced the crowbar under the stone and raised it without difficulty. There I beheld a casket of golden plates, on which were inscribed the new gospels. The glory of heaven shone around them and upon them. The place seemed on fire. I was about to remove the plates when an enormous toad appeared, squatting upon the pages.
>
> Instantly it was revealed to me that I had forgotten to carry out some request made by the angel in digging for the plates. I had forgotten to give thanks to God, and I knew what was passing in the toad's mind. Instantly the beast arose and expanded as large as a dog, then as a bullock, then it rose far above me, a flaming monster with glittering eyes, until it seemed to fill the heavens, and with a blow like lightning it swept me from the mountain into the valley beneath.[11]

The tale obviously became inflated in the retelling. Mother Smith's less flamboyant account is probably more reliable. She reported in 1844 that the

9. Willard Chase, Affidavit, 241.

10. Benjamin Saunders, Interview, ca. Sept. 1884, 21-22.

11. Printed as "Mormon Leaders at Their Mecca. ... Joe Smith's Life at Palmyra," 12.

messenger first told her son that "the churches that are now upon the Earth are all man made." Then, Joseph said, the messenger added:

> There is a record for you ... but you cannot get it untill you learn to keep the commandments of God <For it is not to get gain> But it is to bring forth that light and intelligence which has been long lost in the Earth[.] Now Joseph beware <or> when you go to get the plates your mind will be fill[e]d with darkness and all manner of evil will rush into your mind[.] To <prevent> you from keeping the commandments of God <that you may not succe[e]d in doing his work> ... [T]he record is on a side hill on the Hill of Cumorah 3 miles from this place[. R]emove the Grass and moss and you will find a large flat stone[.] Pry that up and you will find the record under it laying on 4 pillars—<of cement> then the angel left him.[12]

Recall that Fayette Lapham in 1870 reported that Joseph Sr. had told him about a dream of Joseph Jr. in which "a very large and tall man appeared to him, dressed in an ancient suit of clothes, and the clothes were bloody." The man told young Joseph about "a valuable treasure, buried many years since, and not far from that place" but the time "had now arrived for it to be brought to light, for the benefit of the world at large." As Joseph attempted to retrieve the promised record, "he felt something strike him on the breast, which was repeated the third time, always with increased force, the last such as to lay him upon his back." Coming to his senses, he looked up and "saw the same large man that had appeared in his dream, dressed in the same clothes." The personage said to him that when the treasure had originally been deposited, "he was sworn to take charge of and protect that property, until the time should arrive for it to be exhibited to the world of mankind; and, in order to prevent his making an improper disclosure, he was murdered or slain on the spot, and the treasure had been under his charge ever since." Although this version does not differ substantially from standard folk-magic accounts, it corroborates other versions of this 1823 visitation in rebuking Joseph because "he had not followed his directions; and, in consequence of laying the article down before putting it in the napkin, he could not have the article now; but that if he would come again, one year from that time, he could then have them."[13]

Cowdery, using information he learned from the Smith family, provided more detail: "[N]o motive of a pecuniary, or earthly nature, was to be

12. Lavina Fielding Anderson, *Lucy's Book,* 335-36.
13. Fayette Lapham, "Interview with the Father of Joseph Smith," 305-306.

suffered to take the lead of the heart of the man thus favored." Yet Joseph could not easily control his materialistic thoughts. The boy who had known nothing but poverty remembered that those "who had acquired a little of this world's goods" passed by virtuous folks like himself "with a stiff neck and a cold heart," scorning them "because they were poor" and lording their own status over those who, like his own family, "were subjected to suffer the miseries of this life."[14] No sooner had the thought that he was entitled to wealth because of his family's circumstances entered into his mind than the messenger's words followed: "Remember, that he who does this work, who is thus favored of the Lord, must do it with his eye single to the glory of the same." Joseph's mind must have juggled differing thoughts as he walked through woods and fields to his rendezvous with the golden plates. "Here was a struggle indeed," penned Cowdery, "for when he calmly reflected upon his errand, he knew that if God did not give, he could not obtain; and again, with the thought or hope of obtaining, his mind would be carried back to his former reflection of poverty, abuse,—wealth, grandeur and ease." His musings ultimately tilted toward wealth. "This wholly occupied his desire," wrote Cowdery, and when Joseph "thought upon the fact of what was previously shown him, it was only with an assurance that he should obtain, and accomplish his desire in relieving himself and friends from want." The thought of a "history of the inhabitants who peopled this continent," previous to its discovery by Columbus, was something that "must be interesting to every man," imagined Smith. Furthermore, such a work would disclose the fact "that the present race were descendants of Abraham, and were to be remembered in the immutable covenant of the Most High to that man, and be restored to a knowledge of the gospel, that they, with all nations might rejoice, seemed to inspire further thoughts of gain and income from such a valuable history." Surely, thought Joseph, "every man will seize with eagerness, this knowledge, and this incalculable income will be mine."

Adding weight to the pressures of poverty, Cowdery wrote, were the facts that Smith "was young, and his mind easily turned from correct principles, unless he could be favored with a certain round of experience."[15] As Joseph reached the envisioned spot on the west side of the hill, then, his mind had fixed on becoming rich. "After arriving at the repository," said Cowdery, "a little exertion in removing the soil from the edges of the top

14. Unless otherwise stated, I have taken Cowdery's narrative from Cowdery to Phelps, "Letter VII," 156.

15. Cowdery to Phelps, "Letter VIII," Oct. 1835, 196.

of the box, and a light pry, brought to his natural vision its contents. No sooner did he behold this sacred treasure than his hopes were renewed, and he supposed his success certain." But as he leaned down to take possession of the record, "a shock was produced upon his system, by an invisible power, which deprived him, in a measure, of his natural strength." Astounded, Joseph reached a second time only to be "more sensibly shocked than before."

Supposing that "physical exertion and personal strength" were enough to "enable him to yet obtain the object of his wish," Smith tried a third time. "Why can I not obtain this book?" he asked. "Because you have not kept the commandments of the Lord" was the answer. Joseph then saw the same messenger he had seen the previous night:

> In an instant, all the former instructions, the great intelligence concerning Israel and the last days, were brought to his mind: he thought of the [night before] when his heart was fervently engaged in prayer to the Lord, when his spirit was contrite, and when his holy messenger from the skies unfolded the wonderful things connected with this record. He had come, to be sure, and found the word of the angel fulfilled concerning the reality of the record, but he had failed to remember the great end for which they had been kept, and in consequence could not have power to take them into his possession and bear them away.[16]

Joseph's friend and employer, Joseph Knight Sr., also later wrote of the boy's attempt to recover the golden record. He explained that Joseph

> took it out and laid [it] Down By his side and tho[ugh]t he would Cover the <place> over again [thinking] there might be something else here But he was told to take the Book and go right away and after he had Covered the place he turned round to take <the> Book and it was not there and he was astonished that the Book was gone[17] he tho[ugh]t he would look in the

16. Ibid., 196.

17. Lucy Smith wrote that the "divine messenger" told Joseph he "must take [the plates] into your hands and go straight to the house without delay <and put them in immediately and lock them up>." But when he lifted the places from their place, "the thought flashed across his mind that there might be something more in the box that would be a benefit to him in a pecuniary point of view." In the excitement of the moment, Joseph "laid the record down in order [to] cover up the box lest some one should come along and take away whatever else might be deposited there." In that moment, the elusive plates slipped away. Alarmed, Joseph began to pray. "The angel appeared to him and told him that he had not done as he was commanded in that he laid down the record in order to secure some imaginary treasure that remained." Joseph once again lifted up the stone lid and saw the plates in their original location. He reached down to pick them up, his mother said, "but was <thrown> to the ground—when he recov<ered the angel was gone and he arose and returned to the house>" (Anderson, *Lucy's Book,* 346-47).

> place again and see if it had not got Back again[. H]e had heard People tell of such things and he opened the Box and Behold the Book was there[.][18] [H]e took hold of it to take it out again and Behold he Could not stur the Book any more than he Could the mount[a]in[. H]e exclaimed why Cant I stur this Book[?] and he was answere[e]d you have not Done rite you should have took the Book and a gone right away you cant have it now[.] Joseph says when can I have it[?] the answer was the 22nt Day of September next if you Bring the right person with you[.] Joseph Says who is the right person[?] the answer was your oldest Brother [Alvin].[19]

Fayette Lapham's recollections of Father Smith's version corroborates these details: "Joseph asked when he could have them; and the answer was, 'Come in one year from this time, and bring your oldest brother with you; then you may have them.'"[20] Neighbor Willard Chase also recalled the same detail: "[C]ome one year from this day, and bring with you your oldest brother, and you shall have them"; while according to another Smith neighbor, Lorenzo Saunders, the messenger told Joseph to "take his oldest Brother with him in a year from that time and go and get them."[21] Joseph's sister Katharine likewise verified that the messenger instructed Joseph: "Come here the next year at this time and bring your oldest brother with you, and you can receive the records."[22]

Mother Smith remembered that when Joseph returned to his house on September 22, 1823, without the plates, he was "weeping for grief and disappointment,"[23] a reaction shared by the family. Joseph also had a keener worry: "fearing that we might doubt his having seen them." As soon as Joseph entered the house, his father asked if he had the plates. "No father, I could not get them," Joseph replied. "Did you see them?" asked his father. "Yes," answered young Joseph, "I saw them, but could not take them." "I would have taken them," responded his father, "if I had been in your place." "You do not know what you say," his son reportedly responded; "I could not get them, for the angel of the Lord would not let me."[24]

---

18. Cowdery's account also stressed the supernatural power that kept the plates from Joseph. "[H]e had heard of the power of enchantment, and a thousand like stories, which held the hidden treasures of the earth, and supposed physical exertion and personal strength was only necessary to enable him yet to obtain the object of his wish" (Cowdery, "Letter VIII," 196-97).

19. Joseph Knight Sr., Reminiscence, 1.

20. Lapham, "Interview with the Father of Joseph Smith," 305.

21. Chase, Affidavit, 241; Lorenzo Saunders, Interview, Sept. 17, 1884, 8.

22. Katharine Smith Salisbury, "An Angel Told Him."

23. Anderson, *Lucy's Book,* 348.

24. Ibid.

Two months later, on November 19, Alvin Smith died. The angel's directive to bring him to the September 22, 1824, meeting atop the hill could not be met. During that week in 1824, however, Alvin's grave was mysteriously disturbed. Rumors circulated that his corpse had been removed. On September 25, 1824, Joseph Sr. published an announcement in the local newspaper:

> Whereas reports have been industriously put in circulation, that my son *Alvin* had been removed from the place of his interment and dissected, which reports, every person possessed of human sensibility must know, are peculiarly calculated to harrow up the mind of a parent and deeply wound the feelings of relations—therefore, for the purpose of ascertaining the truth of such reports, I, with some of my neighbors, this morning repaired to the grave, and removing the earth, found the body which had not been disturbed.
>
> This method is taken for the purpose of satisfying the minds of those who may have heard the report, and of informing those who have put it in circulation, that it is earnestly requested they would desist therefrom; and that it is believed by some, that they have been stimulated more by a desire to injure the reputation of certain persons than a philanthropy for the peace and welfare of myself and friends.[25]

It was relatively common for professional grave robbers, also known as "resurrectionists" or "sack-'em-up men," to steal bodies for medical schools. Students needed to be able to perform dissections and to practice surgical techniques, but cadavers were difficult to obtain. Dr. Nathan Smith, the Dartmouth Medical School professor who had operated a decade earlier on young Joseph's leg, stressed in lectures at Yale the importance of dissections: "It is of little consequence that a man read anatomy if he cannot have demonstrations. He must have demonstrations to have correct knowledge of the parts. It cannot be obtained from partings, drawings, or reading books."[26] The public, however, generally opposed disturbing the dead. Professors of

---

25. "To the Public," *Wayne Sentinel* 2 (Sept. 29, 1824): 3; emphasis in original. The notice, dated Sept. 25, 1824, also appeared in the issues of Oct. 6, 13, 20, 27, and Nov. 3.

26. Worham L. Fitch, "Extracts From Lectures on Surgery," 389, qtd. in Oliver S. Hayward and Constance E. Putnam, *Improve, Perfect, and Perpetuate,* 82. "The difficulty and danger of procuring subjects for dissection is another consideration which induced Dr. Smith to remove from [Dartmouth Medical School]," wrote medical student Timothy J. Gridley to Jonathan Knight on November 20, 1810. "Without these, you may know," he continued, "the study of anatomy is but trifling with time and expense, to say nothing of the danger to [which] the patient of the merely descriptive anatomist is subject in cases of difficult appreciation. ... But the inhabitants within forty or fifty miles of this place are constantly on the watch, lest the silent repose of their departed friends be disturbed by the nocturnal visitations of medical students" (qtd. in ibid., 199).

anatomy in nearly every eighteenth- and early nineteenth-century American medical school "had to face charges, usually verbal but sometimes delivered by armed mobs, that he engaged in grave-robbing to get materials for classroom dissections."[27] Bodies of young people were difficult to obtain because "grave watchers" were often hired to guard new burials in cemeteries.[28] In the aftermath of one early 1824 grave-robbing episode in New Haven, a search warrant was served on a Yale professor of anatomy. When the remains of the young woman were found in the basement of the medical school, "public outrage expressed itself in nightly rioting for much of a week."[29] Nathan Smith wrote that the unruly mob "broke more than 100 panes of glass in the building before they could be dispersed."[30]

Although these "anatomy riots," which occurred only a few months prior to Alvin's death, may have precipitated rumors about his grave being pillaged, resurrectionists did not usually steal corpses that had been decomposing for ten months. Perhaps more likely, the disturbance of Alvin's grave was linked to tales of necromancy, a mode of divination based on the evocation of the dead. Through magical ritual, some believed, Alvin's spirit, like the biblical prophet Samuel's,[31] could be beckoned back briefly into the body for interrogation. Another speculation was that Joseph, or some other interested party, may have tried to excavate the grave to retrieve a part of Alvin's body which could serve as a talisman to overcome the enchantment that guarded the record.

Necromancy in early America evolved from the occultism of ancient Persia, Chaldea, Babylonia, Etruria, Greece, and Rome. The Israelites may have borrowed the practice from the Persians; certainly they sometimes engaged in it, although the Hebrew Bible forbids it (Lev. 19:31, 20:6, 27; Deut. 18:11; Isa. 8:19). In Europe during the Middle Ages, necromancy was reportedly practiced by magicians, sorcerers, soothsayers, and others. The Catholic Church condemned it as the "agency of evil spirits."[32] In the time

27. Whitfield J. Bell Jr., *The Colonial Physician and Other Essays,* 228.

28. Martin Kaufman, *American Medical Education,* 30.

29. Suzanne M. Schultz, *Body Snatching,* 30.

30. Hayward and Putnam, *Improve, Perfect, and Perpetuate,* 101.

31. In 1 Samuel 28, King Saul, who was afraid of the armies of the Philistines, prayed for God's advice. But "the LORD answered him not, neither by dreams, nor by Urim, nor by prophets." The frustrated monarch ordered his servants: "Seek me a woman that hath a familiar spirit, that I may go to her, and inquire of her. And his servants said to him, Behold, there is a woman that hath a familiar spirit at Endor." The woman, at Saul's request, summoned the spirit of the deceased Samuel to advise him.

32. The Catholic Church's current position is: "Any method of divination with direct

of Elizabeth I, the Witchcraft Act of 1604 outlawed the practice.[33] Despite Old World decrees, however, various manifestations of necromancy were practices of the money-digging folk culture of America during colonial and early republic times.

Necromancy supposes three elements: belief in the soul's survival after death, its possession of superior knowledge, and the possibility of communication between the living and the dead. The spirits of the dead were sought for consultation. Not possessing a body, spirits no longer had earthly limitations; hence, a returned spirit ostensibly had access to past and future information that was unavailable to the living. The Ritual of Necromantic Evocation, as explained in various magical texts of Joseph Smith's day, summoned the soul back into the body so that information could be extracted and power gained.[34] Typically, participants fasted and spent the night in a cemetery, "some private detached churchyard," or another "solemn, melancholy place between the hours of twelve and one in the night, either when the moon shines very bright, or else when the elements are disturbed with storms, thunder, lightning, wind, and rain."[35] The ritual was initiated with prayer. "While making this prayer," described one account,

> we must identify ourselves with the evoked person, speak as he spoke, believe in a sense as he believed; then, after a silence of fifteen minutes, we must speak to him as if he were present, with affection and with faith, praying him to manifest to us. Renew this prayer mentally, covering the face with both hands; then call him thrice with a loud voice; tarry on our knees, the eyes closed and covered, for some minutes; then call again thrice upon him in a sweet and affectionate tone, and slowly open the eyes. Should nothing result, the same experiment must be renewed in the following year, and if necessary a third time, when it is certain that the desired apparition will be obtained, and the longer it has been delayed the more realistic and striking it will be.[36]

---

invocation of spirits is grievously sinful, and worse still if such intervention ensues; with tacit invocation divination is in itself a grievous sin, though in practice, ignorance, simplicity, or want of belief may render it venial" ("Necromancy," entry in *New Advent Catholic Encyclopedia).*

33. "Necromancy," entry in *Occultopedia.*

34. See D. Michael Quinn, *Early Mormonism and the Magic World View,* 161, for a discussion of these magical texts.

35. "Necromancy: Or Divination by Means of the Spirits of the Dead." Folklore decreed that "the shade of the departed lingered in the vicinity of its grave for a period of 12 months" (Arthur E. Waite, *Book of Ceremonial Magic,* 324).

36. "Necromancy: Or Divination By Means of the Spirits of the Dead," 4.

Whatever the reason for the possible disturbance of the grave that precipitated Joseph Sr.'s notice in the *Wayne Sentinel,* young Joseph was prevented again in September 1824 from retrieving the golden plates from their guardian. Family friend Willard Chase said that when the nineteen-year-old seer arrived at his rendezvous on the hill "to demand the book," the guardian "enquired for his brother." When informed "he was dead," the guardian told him to "come again, in just one year, and bring a man with him." When Joseph asked which man, "he was answered that he would know him when he saw him."[37]

Months passed, and Joseph apparently searched in his stone for the mystery man. He finally decided that it must be another local seer and money-digger, Samuel Tyler Lawrence (1786-1847).[38] Joseph persuaded Lawrence to accompany him to the hill in the fall of 1825, where together they envisioned the gold plates in their seer stones, but the guardian did not appear, possibly because they were not there on the equinoctial date of September 22, or Lawrence was not the man the guardian wanted. As the seers huddled atop the hill, Lawrence asked if Joseph had seen anything else with the plates. When Joseph said no, Lawrence urged him to "look into his stone, to see if there was any thing with them." Joseph dropped his stone into his hat and began to scry. Initially, no other artifacts appeared. "[L]ook again and see if there was not a large pair of specks with the plates," prompted Lawrence. Encouraged, Joseph "soon saw a pair of spectacles." Although the seers still could not overcome the enchantment, Lawrence reportedly warned Joseph that "it would not be prudent to let these plates be seen for about two years, as it would make a great disturbance in the neighborhood."[39]

Joseph's future employer, Joseph Knight Sr., knew that Lawrence "had Bin [been] to the hill and knew about the things in the hill and he was trying to obtain them." Ultimately, Joseph worried that Lawrence might try to keep him away from the hill so that Lawrence himself could overcome the enchantment and retrieve the plates. So Joseph told the older man he "was not the right man, nor had he told him the right place."[40] Meantime, other

37. Chase, Affidavit, 243.

38. Lorenzo Saunders corroborates that "Joseph chose Samuel Lawrence." Saunders also said that Lawrence was a "very intimate acquaintance" of Joseph (Lorenzo Saunders, Interview, Sept. 12, 1884, 10, qtd. in Vogel, *Early Mormon Documents,* 2:148). For an overview of the several Samuel Lawrences who were Joseph Smith's contemporaries, see Rich Troll, "Samuel Tyler Lawrence: A Significant Figure in Joseph Smith's Palmyra Past," *Journal of Mormon History* 32, no. 2 (Summer 2006): 38-86.

39. Chase, Affidavit, 243.

40. Ibid., 242.

events were in train, bringing Joseph to the woman whom he would marry and who would enable him to obtain the treasure.

In October 1825, New York Governor DeWitt Clinton and other dignitaries, celebrated the grand opening of the full length of the Erie Canal. The party left Buffalo on a packet boat, the *Seneca Chief*, traveling eastward. Their departure was marked by a relay of cannon fire along their route through Rochester, Palmyra, Syracuse, and ultimately Albany and the Hudson River. It took an hour and twenty minutes for all cannons along the 363-mile route to fire. Clinton, traveling at three miles per hour, arrived later and ceremoniously poured a barrel of Lake Erie water into the Hudson River, symbolically wedding the Great Lakes with the Atlantic Ocean.

Celebrations erupted en route as the company was slowly towed toward its destination. In towns like Palmyra, bisected by the Western Canal, as it was first called, there were "combinations of speeches, prayers, songs, parades, theatrical performances, and artillery salutes."[41] The citizenry, presumably including the Smiths, participated in the festivities. One of the faces in the Palmyra crowd was likely Josiah Stowell, an old Vermonter then living in the township of South Bainbridge, New York. A well-to-do farmer seeking to purchase grain in the area, he was staying with his oldest son, Simpson Stowell of Manchester.[42] According to William D. Purple,[43] an early historian of Afton (South Bainbridge), New York, the elder Stowell was "a man of much force of character, of indomitable will. ... He was a very industrious, exemplary man, and by severe labor and frugality had acquired surroundings that excited the envy of many of his less fortunate neighbors." But Stowell, added Purple, since 1825 had taken "upon himself a monomaniacal impression to seek for hidden treasures which he believed were buried in the earth" and, in the grip of this obsession, had allowed the money-digging culture to attain "entire control over his mental character."[44] Like Lucy Smith, Stowell

---

41. Carol Sheriff, *The Artificial River*, 27-28.

42. Simpson, also known as Simeon, son of Josiah Stowell and Miriam Bridgman Stowell, was born July 29, 1791 (William Henry Harrison Stowell, *Stowell Genealogy*, 229-30). Dan Vogel noted that his presence in the area is confirmed by a real estate purchase he made January 29, 1827 (Vogel, *Joseph Smith*, 592).

43. Purple practiced medicine in the area from 1824 to 1830 and served as town clerk in 1829.

44. W[illiam] D. Purple, "Joseph Smith, the Originator of Mormonism," 3. Brothers Joseph and Hiel Lewis, Emma Hale Smith's first cousins, in 1879 recounted Stowell's treasure-digging ventures in Harmony township:

> [S]ome time previous to 1825, a man by the name of Wm. Hale, a distant relative of our uncle Isaac Hale, came to Isaac Hale, and said that he had been informed by a woman named Odle, who claimed to possess the power of seeing under ground, (such persons were then commonly

was a staunch puritan, "strait and strong in dogma," described N. E. Barton, a member of South Bainbridge's Presbyterian congregation.[45] Despite admonishment from family, neighbors, and fellow churchgoers, Deacon Stowell "took his [hired] help and provisions from home, and camped out on the black hills of that region [Lanesboro] for weeks at a time."[46]

Orson Pratt reported that the catalyst for Stowell's interest in buried treasure was "an old document [that] had fallen into his possession, in some way or other, containing information of silver mines being somewhere in the neighbourhood in which he resided."[47] Joseph Smith's grandson, Heman C. Smith, wrote that it "was rumored that in or near to Harmony, Pennsylvania … there had been found at some time in the past, rich silver deposits, from which the discoverers had taken fabulous sums, considerable portions of which had been coined, and left in safe places waiting the convenience of its owners to remove it; that owing to the uncertain and shifting nature of the times these hidden treasures had not been removed, that the secret of their places of deposit and the mines whence they were taken had been lost."[48] Oliver Cowdery asserted in October 1835:

> [I]n the town of Harmony, Susquehannah county, Pa. is said to be a cave or subter[r]raneous recess, whether entirely formed by art or not I am uninformed, neither does this matter; but such is said to be the case,—where a company of Spaniards, a long time since, when the country was uninhabited by white set[e]llers, excavated from the bowels of the earth ore, and coined a large quantity of money; after which they secured the cavity and evacuated, leaving a part still in the cave, purposing to return at some distant period. A long time elapsed, and this account came from one of the individuals who was first engaged in this <mining> buisness [sic]. The country was pointed out and the spot minutely described. … Enough however, was credited of the Spaniard story, to excite the belief of

---

> called peepers) that there was great treasures concealed in the hill north-east from [Hale's] house. By her directions, Wm. Hale commenced digging, but being too lazy to work, and too poor to hire, he obtained a partner by the name of Oliver Harper, of [New] York state, who had the means to hire help (Joseph Lewis and Hiel Lewis, "Mormon History," 1).

After Harper was murdered in 1824, according to an 1880 newspaper article, which reproduced the 1825 Articles of Agreement that Joseph Sr. and Jr. and others signed, the money diggers returned to Harmony and "work[ed] during a considerable part of the past summer [of 1825]" ("An Interesting Document").

45. N. E. Barton, "Joe Smith's Youthful Days."

46. Purple, "Joseph Smith, the Originator of Mormonism," 3.

47. Qtd. in Anderson, *Lucy's Book,* 360n82.

48. Ibid.

many that there was a fine sum of the precious metal lying coined in this subter[r]aneous vault.[49]

Stowell had spent the summer of 1825 with a group of men in northeastern Pennsylvania digging for a lost "Spanish mine" which a woman named Odle had envisioned.[50] As was common in money-digging ventures of the day, however, the "power of enchantment" prevented recovery of the treasure. Although neither a mine nor a cache of silver coins was uncovered during the digging in Harmony, Stowell remained convinced that the treasure could be located if only the proper seer were employed. According to Presbyterian N. E. Barton, Stowell had heard reports that nineteen-year-old Joseph Smith "could see objects which lay fifty feet below the surface of the earth with entire distinctness."[51] William Purple corroborated: Stowell had heard of Joseph, who "by the aid of a magic stone had become a famous seer of lost or hidden treasures." These tales of young Joseph's divination skills "were fully received into [Stowell's] credulous mind, and kindled into a blaze his cherished hallucination" with the result that "visions of untold wealth appeared through this instrumentality, to his longing eyes."[52] Lucy Smith's account reinforces the main point: Stowell sought out son Joseph "to assist him in digging for a silver mine … on account of having heard that he possessed certain keys, by which he could discern things invisible to the natural eye."[53] Fayette Lapham recalled Joseph Sr. saying that Joseph Jr. went to Harmony "at the request of some one who wanted the assistance of his divining rod and stone in finding hidden treasure."[54]

Although Joseph later portrayed himself as a reluctant participant, he apparently went willingly and convinced the older man of his abilities through a demonstration. According to Stowell, Joseph, gazing into his stone, accurately

49. Cowdery to Phelps, "Letter V," 200.

50. Joseph Lewis and Hiel Lewis, "Mormon History," 1. D. Michael Quinn speculates that this seeress may have been "Clary Odell," who was listed in the 1820 census for Harpersfield, Delaware County, New York (Quinn, *Early Mormonism and the Magic World View,* 49).

51. Barton, "Joe Smith's Youthful Days," 2.

52. Purple, "Joseph Smith, the Originator of Mormonism," 3.

53. Anderson, *Lucy's Book,* 360. Swedenborgian convert Elizabeth Jones used similar language in an 1818 letter to her Presbyterian pastor in Newburgh, New York. "[Swedenborg] will furnish you with a *key* to unlock the holy treasures of Divine Wisdom contained in the written Word of the Lord" (John Johnson and Elizabeth Jones, *An Interesting Discussion of the Fundamental Doctrine of the Christian Religion,* 15).

54. Lapham, "Interview with the Father of Joseph Smith," 307.

described Josiah's farm, house, various outbuildings, and a "painted tree with a man's hand painted upon it" that was familiar to the farmer.[55]

Stowell was impressed, hired Joseph on the spot, and pressed him to come immediately to Pennsylvania. Mother Smith later said that her son "endeavoured to divert [Stowell] from his vain pursuit, but he was inflexible in his purpose, and offered high wages."[56] Joseph's acquiescence in response to the promise of "high wages" is plausible considering the financial pressures on the family. In May 1824, John Greenwood, a lawyer from New York City, had received power of attorney from the Evertson Land Company, which owned the Smith farm. Soon after his arrival in Ontario County, Greenwood informed the Smiths that their final mortgage payment was more than eighteen months in arrears. Legally, Greenwood could have foreclosed and laid claim not only to the property, but also any improvements. The Smiths, however, reached "an understanding with the agent." The family, according to Mother Smith, arranged a contract with Josiah Stowell and Joseph Knight. "[W]e agreed to deliver a certain quantity of flour to them the ensuing fall, for which we were to receive a sufficient amount of money to make the final payment on our farm."[57] Greenwood allowed the family until December 25, 1825, to come up with the final payment, which would have been about $200.

Mother Smith later claimed that the frame house on their farmstead had been paid for prior to construction. However, the principal carpenter on the project, Russell Stoddard, sued Joseph Sr. on February 18, 1825, for $66.59 for "work & labour & lumber … in building a dwelling house."[58] Stoddard

---

55. Daniel S. Tuttle, "A Document Discovered," 1. In speculating how one might have envisioned New York/Pennsylvania scenery more than a hundred miles from his home, Vogel suggests: "A skeptic can only suggest that among the possible methods would be those used by present-day psychics in what is called a 'cold reading.' This involves moving gradually from general to more specific statements based on educated guesses and reactions from the client. … If Smith provided descriptions that were rather unspecific and then let Stowell provide the details, this would have been consistent with the tradition of palm readers and others" (Vogel, *Joseph Smith,* 70).

56. Anderson, *Lucy's Book,* 360. Joseph later admitted in 1838 that he had been "a money digger … but it was never a very profitable job to him, as he only got fourteen dollars a month for it" (Joseph Smith, "Answers to Questions," 43). By comparison, Erie Canal workers received only eight to twelve dollars per month (Richard L. Bushman, *Joseph Smith and the Beginnings of Mormonism,* 47).

57. Anderson, *Lucy's Book,* 362.

58. Mother Smith noted that Stoddard offered her husband $1,500 for the house. "But that was no temptation," she added. "[N]othing could persuade Mr. Smith to abandon the scene of his labor and the toiling of his family for here they had borne the burden and heat of the day and we contemplated much happiness and great enjoyment with the fruit of our labors" (Anderson, *Lucy's Book,* 359).

was awarded judgment, and the Smiths paid the debt.[59] So it seemed good fortune to the Smiths to have Josiah Stowell arrive on the scene when they were only a few months away from defaulting on their property. As an additional incentive, Stowell may have suggested to the Smiths that his friend Joseph Knight, who owned a grist mill in Colesville, New York, could buy their grain futures to prevent the foreclosure.

Both Joseph Sr. and young Joseph agreed to accompany Stowell to South Bainbridge. Before they left, however, Father Smith sent Hyrum to Canandaigua to consult with Greenwood. The land agent confirmed that he would not sell the Smith farm before Christmas Day. With that assurance, the father-and-son treasure hunters climbed into Josiah Stowell's rig on a late October day, convinced they would soon have sufficient monies to redeem their farm.

The trio probably headed directly for the Stowell place on the Susquehanna. This route would have taken them easterly along the well-maintained turnpike to Syracuse, then directly southward through Onondaga, Cortland, and Broome Counties. After stopping at Stowell's farm in South Bainbridge for provisions, to gather digging tools, and to conscript several of Stowell's farm hands, the treasure hunters rolled south another thirty miles, following the Susquehanna to Harmony (now Oakland) Township in Great Bend country. The ride would have been picturesque, the scenery ablaze with fall colors. "From its source in Otsego Lake [Cooperstown] to its union with the Chesapeake," wrote local historian Julia Anna Shepherd Perkins in 1906, "every mile of the Susquehanna is beautiful."[60] And historical too. From this ancestral home of the Delaware, the Iroquois Confederation drove their Algonquian enemies out—"clothed them in petticoats"[61]—and the Susquehanna Valley was repeopled by the Seneca, Cayuga, and Oneida.

Stowell was acquainted with pioneer settlers Isaac and Elizabeth Hale, who maintained a well-reputed boarding house beautifully situated near Harmony, Pennsylvania, south of the Oquago Mountains. Isaac had been born at Waterbury, Connecticut, in 1763. An adventurer at heart, the Revolutionary War veteran traveled to the Great Bend of the Susquehanna River in the fall of 1787 to assess the area's hunting potential. Pleased with its herds of deer and elk, Hale returned to Vermont, and married Elizabeth

59. *Russell Stoddard v. Joseph Smith,* Feb. 18, 1825, Common Pleas Transcripts, Ontario County Record Center and Archives.

60. Mrs. George A. Perkins, *Early Times on the Susquehanna,* 195.

61. Ibid., 2.

Lewis. The newlyweds moved to Harmony Township, accompanied by Elizabeth's brother Nathaniel and his bride, in 1790. Hale quickly established a reputation as a prodigious hunter. Methodist minister George Peck, who boarded with the Hales whenever he was in the area, remembered: "Hale was a mighty hunter. In fact, he came from Vermont, and fixed his home in this new region for the purpose of pursuing game in the Harmony Woods—the great forest which then stretched from the Susquehanna to the Delaware. He slaughtered about a hundred deer annually, most of which he sent to the Philadelphia market. He often killed bears and elks, as well as a great variety of smaller game, of the flesh of which I often partook at this table."[62]

Hale was also a rational-thinking, hard-working farmer. Between 1809 and 1833, he purchased 623 acres of property locally, converting most of it into farmland, which he and his five boys worked.[63] Lucy Smith, who visited the Hales in 1828, described their holdings as a large, neatly framed "mansion" situated "on an extensive and well cultivated farm," which did "honor to the good taste of the intel[l]igent proprie<tor>."[64] It was here, on November 1, 1825, that the two Joseph Smiths and their money-digging associates stepped from Stowell's transport. The Smiths were not particularly prepossessing. According to William Purple, Father Smith was "a wandering vagabond ... lank and haggard ... his form very poorly clad."[65] An account published in Palmyra's *Reflector* in February 1831 described young Joseph as "tall and slender—thin favored."[66] Contemporary Daniel Hendrik remembered young Joseph's "torn and patched trousers," suspenders, his blackened calico shirt, disheveled hair, and "old battered hat."[67] Another acquaintance, William R. Hine, in 1885, remembered Joseph as "miserably clad, coarse and awkward."[68] Isaac Hale's initial impression recalled in 1834, was likewise not favorable. "His appearance at this time," said Hale of the young scryer, "was

62. Rev. George Peck, *The Life and Times of Rev. George Peck,* 67-68. For more on the Hales, see Mark Lyman Staker, "Isaac and Elizabeth Hale in Their Endless Mountain Home," *Mormon Historical Studies* 15, no. 2 (Fall 2014): 1-105.

63. Larry C. Porter, "A Study of the Origins of the Church of Jesus Christ," 46.

64. Anderson, *Lucy's Book,* 430.

65. Purple, "Joseph Smith, the Originator of Mormonism," 3.

66. "GOLD BIBLE, NO. 3," *[Palmyra] Reflector,* Feb. 1, 1831.

67. "Origin of Mormonism: Joe Smith and His Early Habits," 12.

68. William R. Hine, Affidavit, ca. Mar. 1885, 2.

that of a careless young man, not very well educated, and very saucy and insolent to his father."[69]

Appearances aside, Joseph Jr. was in Harmony hoping to improve his life. He intended not to blister his hands digging, but rather labor in the "capacity of Glass Looker or fortune tel[l]er," wrote Joel K. Noble in 1842.[70] Joseph's aim was to get enough money to save the family farm by putting his seer stone to work. The money-digging consortium got busy right away. The very day the New Yorkers arrived, the eleven stockholders apparently drew up "Articles of Agreement," detailing how they would divide the treasure. The eleven included Josiah Stowell, his brother Calvin, and William Hale, a relative of Isaac Hale, who had unsuccessfully been working the diggings since 1822. As principal shareholders, these men were jointly entitled to two-thirds of the find. The remaining third was to be divided among Charles Newton, William I. Wiley, and the unnamed widow of Oliver Harper, who prior to his May 1824 murder was a major contributor to the Stowell/Hale company. These six individuals were considered "proprietors." The remaining five—the two Joseph Smiths, John F. Shephard, Elihu Stowell, and John Grant—were seers, laborers, and minor stockholders. The agreement stipulated that "Joseph Smith, Sen. and Joseph Smith Jr. shall be considered as having two shares, two elevenths of all the property that may be obtained, the shares to be taken equally from each third." Isaac Hale and son David witnessed the signing of the document.[71]

From dawn to dusk for the next seventeen days, the boarders labored. The household buzzed with activity, feeding and bunking at least eight money diggers. The Hales were devout Methodists who had opened their doors to itinerant preachers in the Broome County circuit so often that, according to Rev. George Peck, "Father Hale's house was the preacher's home."[72] Probably Stowell, as a deacon, also wished to board his crew in a God-fearing home, one in which morning prayers preceded breakfast. An early history of Susquehanna County describes the type of food Elizabeth Hale and her daughters probably served their guests. First, she "filled the tea-kettle and hung it over the fire, or set it on fresh coals, drawn from the wood fire, on the hearth to boil; she then put her meat to frying in a spider,

69. Isaac Hale, "Statement."

70. Joel King Noble to Jonathan B. Turner, Mar. 8, 1842, qtd. in H. Michael Marquardt and Wesley P. Walters, *Inventing Mormonism,* 70.

71. "An Interesting Document," 4.

72. George Peck, "Mormonism and the Mormons," 112.

having legs about three inches long, by setting it on fresh coals; her potatoes, if boiled, were put in a pot and hung over the fire; if she desired pancakes they were baked on a round griddle, suspended over the fire."[73]

Once the crew had eaten, they headed up into the foothills above Isaac's farm. Their destination was Joseph McKune Jr.'s property. As the men ascended the rocky slope, they could see evidence of Stowell's earlier diggings. Near the pathway was a pit twenty feet deep and approximately 150 feet in circumference.[74] Although Father Smith's role in the diggings is not clear, there is no question about what his son was doing. Hale, who probably climbed up the slope to inspect the project, later said that young Joseph's job "was that of seeing, or pretending to see, by means of a stone placed in his hat, and his hat closed over his face. In this way he pretended to discover minerals and hidden treasure."[75]

Although Stowell's treasure hunters may have embraced the project with enthusiasm, another strand of the tradition emphasized its riskiness. "Distinct from fiery spirits," wrote Ebenezer Sibly in his 1787 book, *A New and Complete Illustration of the Occult Sciences,*

> are a species which properly belong to the metallic kingdom, abiding in mountains, caves, dens, deeps, hiatas or chasms of the earth, hovering over hidden gold, tombs, vaults, and sepulchers of the dead. These spirits are termed by the ancient philosophers "protectors of hidden treasure," from a principle of quality in their nature whence they exceedingly delight in minds of gold and silver, and places of hidden treasure; but are violently inimical to man ... every [sic] haunting those places where money is concealed, and retaining malevolent and poisonous influences to blast the lives and limbs of those who attempt to make such discoveries; and therefore extremely dangerous for magicians to exorcise or call up.[76]

After first examining the diggings on November 2, Joseph gazed into one of the two seer stones he carried in his pockets and saw what Odle had earlier seen. The Spanish had indeed visited the site many years before, Smith reported, leaving behind about a "ton of silver bars." But after the crew had dug for several days, Joseph informed Stowell that the enchanted

73. Blackman, *History of Susquehanna County,* 59. A "spider" is a forerunner of a modern frying pan.

74. For the location and nature of the diggings in Harmony Township, see Dan Vogel, "The Locations of Joseph Smith's Early Treasure Quests."

75. Blackman, *History of Susquehanna County,* 578.

76. Ebenezer Sibly, *A New and Complete Illustration of the Occult Sciences,* 1,074.

treasure had moved elsewhere. During the next two weeks, the crew dug four more holes, three smaller pits to the south and another to the east.[77] Again, no cache yielded riches to their spades. Joseph and Hiel Lewis, Hale's nephews, recalling the digging many years later, remembered that the money diggers dug in several places "in compliance with peeper Smith's revelations." The brothers remembered that Joseph would "attend with his peep-stone in his hat, and his hat drawn over his face." The seer would "tell them how deep they would have to go; but when they would find no trace of the chest of money, he would peep again, and weep like a child, and tell them the enchantment had removed it on account of some sin or thoughtless word; finally the enchantment became so strong that he could not see, and so the business was abandoned."[78] According to Isaac Hale, "Young Smith gave the 'money-diggers' great encouragement, at first, but when they had arrived in digging, to near the place where he had stated an immense treasure would be found—he said the enchantment was so powerful that he could not see. They then became discouraged, and soon after dispersed. This took place about the 17th of November, 1825."[79]

In recounting the Harmony experience later, Joseph downplayed his role. After "nearly a month without success in our undertaking," he said in 1838, "finally I prevailed with the old gentleman to cease digging after it. Hence arose the very prevalent story of my having been a money digger."[80] Actually, Joseph refused to give up, telling Stowell of other treasures he envisioned near the old Vermonter's property along the Susquehanna, and securing an invitation for him and his father to join Stowell there. They were at Stowell's when they learned of trouble brewing back at the Smith farmstead in Manchester.

Mother Smith was enjoying an "exceedingly fine" day in her newly completed frame home. As she stood at a window, "musing, among other things, upon the prospect of a quiet and comfortable old age,"[81] she saw three men approach the house. She recognized one as Russell Stoddard, her neighbor to the south. Stoddard, the carpenter who had finished her home after Alvin's death, had not yet been paid in full. After inviting the trio in, Lucy became agitated when they started to ask questions she thought were

77. Blackman, *History of Susquehanna County,* 581-82.

78. Joseph Lewis and Hiel Lewis, "Mormon History," 1.

79. Isaac Hale, "Statement."

80. Joseph Smith, Manuscript History A-1, 8, in Vogel, *Early Mormon Documents,* 1:68.

81. My narrative of this incident, unless otherwise stated, is based on Anderson, *Lucy's Book,* 365-72.

impertinent. Had the family made its final payment on the property? If not, did they want to sell the house? Where had Father Smith and young Joseph gone? Lucy politely repelled any possibility of selling: "No, sir," she replied, "we have no occasion for that, we have made every necessary arrangement to get the deed, and also have an understanding with the agent. So you see we are quite secure, in regard to this matter."

As the group was conversing, Hyrum, who would marry in a few months and set up housekeeping in the family's log home, arrived. The visitors began to ask him the same questions. When Hyrum gave them the same answers as Lucy, the men blurted out that Hyrum need not worry about the farm in the future. "We have bought the place," they announced, "and we now forbid your touching anything on the farm; and we also warn you to leave forthwith, and give possession to the lawful owners." Thunderstruck, Lucy kept asking Hyrum what they meant. She quickly recovered enough to try to persuade the men to "change their vile course." But the only answer they gave was reportedly: "well, we've got the place, and d[am]n you, help yourselves if you can." When the full gravity of the situation sank in, Lucy slumped into her chair "almost deprived of sensibility."

Panic-stricken, Hyrum immediately went into Palmyra to seek the family physician, Gain Robinson—"a man of influence and notoriety," said Lucy, and like them a Presbyterian. Hyrum anxiously recounted the unfortunate events of the day. The doctor sat at his desk and, according to Lucy, "wrote at some considerable length the character of the family—our industry, and faithful exertions to secure a home, with many commendations calculated to beget confidence in us with respect to business transactions." Robinson then walked about the village seeking petitioners to verify his sentiments. Within an hour, Lucy alleged, he had "procured sixty subscribers." Likely many of them would have been members of the Western Palmyra Presbyterian Church. Hyrum then rode to Canandaigua with the petition and presented it to John Greenwood, the family's land agent. According to Lucy, Greenwood was shocked and explained to Hyrum that the men had earlier come to him with the tale that Father Smith and young Joseph had run away, abandoning their farm, and that Hyrum was cutting down valuable sugar maples on the property, burning fence rails for firewood, and "doing all manner of mischief to the farm." Duped, Greenwood felt he had no choice but to sell them the place. He had the money, he told Hyrum, and had already surrendered the property deed.

Hyrum explained why his father and brother were still "detained on the road," although they were expected back before Christmas. Greenwood advised him to write to his father and have letters deposited in every public house on the road his father Smith traveled. Greenwood also dispatched a messenger with a request for the three swindlers to come to his office. They ignored him until Greenwood sent a second message threatening to "fetch them with a warrant." "To this," Mother Smith said, "they gave heed," and came without delay. Despite the agent's efforts to convince the men "of the disgraceful and impolitic course which they were pursuing," they refused to change course. "We've got the land, sir, and we've got the deed," the men said, "so just let Smith help himself." Then Stoddard, who knew of Joseph's treasure-seeking activities, told Greenwood not to worry about Smith because "he had gold plates, gold bibles, he is rich—he don't want anything." Finally, the men agreed to sell the property to Hyrum provided he raise $1,000, the full value of the property, within three days.

Hyrum made the nine-mile ride back to Manchester with a heavy heart, "supposing it impossible to effect anything towards redeeming the land." But when he arrived, Father Smith and Joseph had returned and were waiting for him. The next day, Joseph Sr. asked his wife to seek financial help from an "old Quaker" the family had known since they settled in the area. Probably at the same time, he rode to Canandaigua to talk with Greenwood. Lucy asked the Quaker, evidently George Crane of nearby Macedon,[82] if he was interested in buying their farm and letting them "have the benefit of the crops that were upon the ground." Unfortunately, she was thirty minutes too late. Crane had just paid $1,500 to his land agent and had no money left to spare, but told Lucy he would look into other options and get back to her as quickly as he could. Within a few hours, Crane arrived at the Smith home and referred them to another wealthy Quaker, Lemuel Durfee Sr., an early Palmyra settler and merchant, who lived a few miles away.[83] Joseph Sr.

82. "Poor Masters," *Western Farmer* (Palmyra), Apr. 3, 1822, 3, lists George Crane along with Henry Jessup, another wealthy local man, as the local poor masters.

83. Durfee, father of six sons and five daughters, immigrated to the Palmyra area in 1798, and with "indomitable energy and unwearied industry," according to his son's obituary, "set about making a house" (Lemuel Durfee Jr., "Obituary," *Palmyra Courier,* Apr. 21, 1871). On December 4, 1833, Lemuel Durfee Jr., a prominent Palmyra physician, was one of fifty-one local residents who signed an affidavit attesting that the Smiths, because of their "visionary projects" and money-digging, were "considered entirely destitute of moral character, and addicted to vicious habits" (in Eber D. Howe, *Mormonism Unvailed,* 261-62). After Lemuel Sr.'s death on August 8, 1829, Lemuel Jr. sued Joseph Smith Sr. and Abraham Fish for $39.92, to recover a note to his father that they had consigned ("Lemuel Durfee Probate Papers").

immediately started for the Durfee home, arrived before daylight, and awakened the old gentleman, who sent him three miles down the road to bring back one of his sons, a county sheriff.

After discussing business over breakfast, the three rode together to the Smith farm, examined the premises, then continued to Canandaigua. "What I felt and suffered in that short day no one can imagine who has not experienced the same," remembered Lucy years later. "I now looked upon the proceeds of our industry, which smiled around us on every hand, with a kind of yearning attachment that I never before had experienced." Heartbroken, she foresaw a dismal future: "I now felt that all must go at one fell swoop if this last resort failed, and we be left in the decline of life destitute[,] a burden upon our children[']s hands."

Father Smith and his companions arrived in Canandaigua at 9:30 p.m., just thirty minutes before the payment deadline was to expire. Despite some initial resistance, the men handed the deed over to Durfee who bought the Smith farmstead for $1,135. The date was December 20, 1825, five days before what may have been a cheerless Christmas.[84] Durfee agreed to let the Smiths stay on the farm for one year in exchange for six months of son Harrison's labor.

The loss of the farm, so near to Alvin's death, was certainly one of the most severe setbacks the Smith family had yet endured. "I did not feel our early losses so much," Lucy recalled, "for I realized that we were young and might by exertion better our situation and I further had not felt the inconvenience of poverty so much as I had now done, and consequently did not appreciate the value of property justly."[85] It was no consolation that others experienced the same financial disaster. "[Few know] of the ceaseless round of hard labor which was the price of all improvement," wrote New Yorker W. H. McIntosh in his *History of Ontario County:*

> And were all that was done so much for the future, the prospect was not so dark; but however small the price, whatever the time given, a day of judgment ultimately came, and by default the land often reverted to the original owner. ... There is a talk of pioneer privation, as though the language used were cheap of utterance; but when the settler toiled hard and late, saw sickness and death enter the cabin, incurred indebtedness he

84. Deed Liber 44:232-34, Dec. 20, 1825, Ontario County Records Center and Archives, Canandaigua, New York, qtd. in Marquardt and Walters, *Inventing Mormonism,* 82.

85. Anderson, *Lucy's Book,* 371.

> could not meet, and finally abandoned to some other the place he longed to call home, there was that in it which must be experienced to be felt.[86]

In the quest for independence in early America, owning a farm outright, being free from indebtedness (and thus free from the whims of a creditor), was the dream of most people. The Smiths' fellow New Yorker, widow Mary Ann Archbald, wrote of her own experiences in 1828 when debt shadowed the family's farm: "There was also a considerable debt on the farm which [her son Jamie] had been paying as he earned it & expect to have it all cleared off this fall ... now, as being out of debt is, in my estimation, being rich I trust that I will in my next [letter] be able to tell you *positively* that I am *rich.*"[87] Unlike Archbald, the Smiths were positively poor—literally "dirt poor"—at Christmas 1825, again slapped down by cruel fate. One wonders why, following the death of their land agent in 1822, the Smiths chose to invest their savings in the new frame house instead of putting it in escrow until a new agent was appointed. And why did Joseph Sr. not contact the Evertsons by mail, perhaps even making the payment directly to his landlords rather than their agent? A related issue is Joseph Sr.'s economic insouciance following Alvin's death. He had nearly two years to come up with the final payment. Surely his coopering skills and other efforts could have accumulated the needed $200. But instead of working in Manchester, he turned to the get-rich-quick dream of treasure hunting. While he was digging in Pennsylvania, his New York property, the fruit of seven years' hard work, was essentially stolen from under him.

Shortly after Christmas 1825, young Joseph and his father returned to Stowell's home in South Bainbridge to continue their pursuit of buried treasure. According to William Purple's 1877 recollections, Jonathan Thompson testified in 1826 that "Smith had told the Deacon [Stowell] that very many years before a band of robbers had buried on his flat a box of treasure, and as it was very valuable they had by a sacrifice placed a charm over it to protect it, so that it could not be obtained except by faith, accompanied by certain talismanic influences."[88] This treasure too slipped into oblivion. Book of Mormon benefactor Martin Harris told Joel Tiffany in 1859 about an "old Presbyterian," a reference to Stowell, who told him that "on the Susquehannah flats he dug down to an iron chest, that he scraped the dirt off with

86. W. H. McIntosh, *History of Ontario County, New York,* 29.

87. Mary Ann (Wodrow) Archbald Papers, Sophia Smith Collection, Smith College, qtd. in Sheriff, *The Artificial River,* 11.

88. Purple, "Joseph Smith, the Originator of Mormonism," 3.

his shovel, but had nothing with him to open the chest; that he went away to get help, and when they came to it, it moved away two or three rods into the earth, and they could not get it."[89] William Hine added that Joseph Jr. reportedly said he "saw Captain Kidd sailing on the Susquehanna River during a freshet, and that he buried two pots of gold and silver. He claimed he saw writing cut on the rocks in an unknown language telling where Kidd buried it, and he translated it through his peep-stone."[90]

Ever optimistic, Stowell sponsored another money-digging effort near his farm. New Yorker Smith Baker (1796-1897) told historian Frederick Mather the tale in 1880, nearly a half century after it allegedly occurred. Baker said that Joseph Smith saw in his stone "an extensive and rich silver mine on the farm of Abraham Cornell, at Bettesburgh ... and a hole was dug there to the depth of over thirty feet, but no silver was found except what was contributed by Josiah Stowell to provide for the expenses of the diggers."[91]

Though marvelous to some, Joseph's treasure-seeking activities consistently came up empty. There was always a reason: a mistake in the procedure, an uncontrollable spirit, or impenetrable enchantment. By the spring of 1826, members of Stowell's extended family had lost patience with the lack of success. Some, including Stowell himself, believed Joseph to be a genuine seer. Others saw him as more of a confidence man. Those subscribing to the second view, according to Purple, thought that Stowell was "squandering his property in the fruitless search for hidden treasures, and saw that the youthful seer had unlimited control over the illusions of their sire."[92] The disillusioned who saw Stowell throwing good money after bad probably included his wife, Miriam Bridgman Stowell, since it was her twenty-two-year-old nephew, Peter G. Bridgman,[93] who in 1826 swore out a written

89. Martin Harris, qtd. in Joel Tiffany, "Mormonism—No. II," *Tiffany's Monthly* 5 (Aug. 1859): 166.

90. Hine, Affidavit, ca. Mar. 1885, 2.

91. Frederick Mather, "The Early Days of Mormonism," 203.

92. Purple, "Joseph Smith, the Originator of Mormonism," 3.

93. Wesley P. Walters has suggested:

> Apparently [Bridgman] became deeply concerned when he saw his uncle's money being transferred bit-by-bit into the pockets of a young "glass-looking" confidence man named Joseph Smith. To safeguard the fortune of his aunt and cousins he took vigorous action by swearing out the warrant, something that would have been difficult for either Mrs. Stowell or her sons to do without raising an internal family argument. Everything we know about this crusading young 22-year-old Bridgman suggests that he had just the determined personality that would do such a thing. Within a month after the trial he was licensed as an exhorter by the Methodists and within three years had helped establish the West Bainbridge Methodist Church. Upon his death in 1872 his fellow ministers characterized him as "an ardent Methodist and any attack upon either the doctrines or the polity of the M.E. Church, within his field of labor,

complaint that "one Joseph Smith of Bainbridge was a disorderly person and an Impostor."[94] New York law grouped various vagrancies into a broad category which included, along with beggars, prostitutes, and men who neglected their families, "persons pretending ... to discover where lost goods may be found."[95] Since Smith had never led Stowell to any item of value, Bridgman and the others believed that he merely pretended to discover lost treasure and thus was a fraud.

Constable Philip DeZeng arrested Joseph Jr. and duly charged the county for fees, including "[a]ttendance with Prisoner two days & 1 night."[96] On March 20, 1826, the twenty-year-old Joseph appeared in an "examination" or "preliminary hearing" before Judge Albert Neely, a pioneer merchant who also served the town as justice of the peace.[97] The purpose of the inquiry

---

was sure to be repelled by him with a vigorous hand." (Walters, "Joseph Smith's Bainbridge, N.Y. Court Trials," 141-42.)

94. As Gordon A. Madsen has pointed out, the term "Impostor," under New York state law, did not describe a criminal offense (Madsen, "Joseph Smith's 1826 Trial," 94). But "disorderly person" points to a specific section of the New York statute that describes various offenses. The section applicable to Peter Bridgman's charge states: "All jugglers [deceivers], and all persons pretending to have skill in physiognomy, palmistry, or life crafty science, or pretending to tell fortunes, or to discover where lost goods may be found ... shall be deemed and adjudged disorderly persons" *(Laws of the State of New York,* 1:114, sec. 1).

95. *Laws of the State of New York,* 1:114, 410.

96. In Vogel, *Early Mormon Documents,* 4:265.

97. This narrative is based on *People of State of New York, vs. Joseph Smith,* qtd. in Tuttle, "A Document Discovered," 1. As Vogel notes in *Early Mormon Documents,* 4:239, the original record made in the Bainbridge court on March 20, 1826, has evidently not survived. Researchers have relied on three separate printings of the document. The first appeared in 1873, in English journalist Charles Marshall, "The Original Prophet," 479-88. Marshall attested that:

> During my stay in Salt Lake permission was courteously accorded me to copy out a set of such judicial proceedings not hitherto published. I cannot doubt their genuineness. The original papers were lent me by a lady of well-known position, in whose family that had been preserved since the date of the transactions. I reproduce them here, partly to fulfill a duty of assisting to preserve a piece of information about the prophet, and partly because, while the charges are less vehement than some I might have chosen, the proceedings are happily lightened by a touch of the ludicrous.

The "lady of well-known position" was Emily Pearsall. The identical record was published again in 1883 by Episcopal Bishop Daniel S. Tuttle. He later explained: "The [manuscript] was given me by Miss Emily Pearsall who, some years since, was a woman helper in our mission and lived in my family, and died here. Her father or uncle was Justice of the Peace in Bainbridge, Chenango Co., New York, in Jo[seph] Smith's time, and before him Smith was tried. Miss Pearsall tore the leaves out of the record found in her father's house and brought them to me" (Tuttle, "Mormons," 1). Pearsall (1833-72) was the niece of Justice Albert Neely, who presided over the hearing.

Given the absence of the original court document, some writers have questioned the authenticity of the Pearsall manuscript (Francis W. Kirkham, *A New Witness for Christ in America,* 1:475-92; 2:354-68, 470-500; Hugh Nibley, *The Myth Makers,* 139-58). But Wesley P. Walters's discovery of Neely's 1826 bill of costs in the basement of the Chenango County Jail in the summer of 1971 has laid to rest most objections. As Walters noted,

was to determine if Joseph should be discharged as innocent or if the evidence was sufficient to bring him to trial. During the examination, the young "glass-looker," as court documents brand him, testified that while living in Stowell's home he had some of the time "been employed in looking for mines,—but the major part had been employed by said Stowel[l] on his farm, and going to school."[98] Joseph attested that "he had a certain stone, which he had occasionally looked at to determine where hidden treasures in the bowels of the earth were, that he professed to tell in this manner where gold mines were a distance under ground, and had looked for Mr. Stowel[l] several times and [had] informed him where he could find those treasures, and Mr. Stowel[l] had been engaged in digging for them." While living in Palmyra, he had "pretended[99] to tell by looking at this stone, where coined money was buried in Pennsylvania" and, for the previous three years, while in Palmyra, had "frequently ascertained in that way where lost property was of various kinds." But recently, Joseph continued, he had "pretty much given it [scrying] up on account of injuring his Health, especially his eyes, made them sore." Furthermore, the witness said that he "did not solicit business of this kind," implying that others sought him out, "and had always rather declined having anything to do with this business." At the court's request, Joseph took his dark-colored seer stone from his pocket and allowed the judge and others to examine it. Purple described it as "about the size of a small hen's egg, in the shape of a high instepped shoe. It was composed of layers of different colors passing diagonally through it. It was very hard and smooth, perhaps by being carried in the pocket."

Joseph Sr., according to Purple, was the next witness examined although his testimony does not appear in the court record. This is not unusual for

---

The discovery of the 1826 bills ... establishes the Neely record beyond any further doubt because the official record and the trial bills corroborate each other so precisely. The Neely trial record and the bill submitted by him to the county both place the date of the trial on March 20, 1826. Both also agree exactly on the total costs to Mr. Neely of $2.68. Both are also in agreement on the nature of the charge, the bill listing it as a "misdemeanor" and the trial record defining it as "a disorderly person and an Impostor" (Walters, "Joseph Smith's Bainbridge, N.Y., Court Trials," 137).

98. Both Josiah Stowell Jr. and Asa B. Searles mentioned that Joseph Smith Jr. attended school while living with the Stowell family (Josiah Stowell Jr. to John S. Fullmer, Feb. 17, 1843; Asa B. Searles, "Reminiscence," 397).

99. The current use of "pretend" implies: "To hold out falsely; to allege falsely; to use as a pretext; to make false appearance or representation of." But the nineteenth-century meaning, as in this court language, lies closer to the definition "to put in a claim, truly or falsely." Virginia S. Thatcher and Alexander McQueen, *The New Webster Encyclopedic Dictionary of the English Language,* 658, s.v. "pretend." See also Noah Webster, *American Dictionary of the English Language* (1828), s.v. "Pretend."

the time—the court was required to "put in writing" only as much of the testimony "as shall be material to prove the offence."[100] Purple described him as raggedly dressed, but also called him "old man eloquent," "long-faced," and "sanctimonious seeming." Father Smith "swore that both he and his son were mortified that this wonderful power which God had so miraculously given him should be used only in search of filthy lucre, or its equivalent in earthly treasures." The elder Joseph said it was his "constant prayer" that "the Son of Righteousness would some day illumine the heart of the boy, and enable him to see His will concerning him."

The next witness was Stowell who testified that the young seer had been living at his home for approximately five months—in other words, since January, which overlooks their association dating from the previous October—and that he had hired him to work on his farm part of the time. Stowell described Smith's work as a scryer:

> [H]e pretended to have skill of telling where hidden treasures in the earth were by means of looking through a certain stone—that Prisoner had looked for him some times[:] once to tell him about money buried on Bend Mountain in Pennsylvania,[101] once for gold on Monument hill,[102] and once for [a] Salt Spring[103] and that he positively knew that the Prisoner, could tell and possessed the art of seeing those valuable treasures through the medium of said stone—that he found the digging part at Bend and Monument Hill, as prisoner represented it—that prisoner had looked through said stone for Deacon Attl[e]ton—for a mine[;] did not exactly find it but got a (piece) of ore which resembled gold, he thinks; that Prisoner had told by means of this stone where, a Mr. Bacon had buried money, that he and prisoner had been in search of it; that prisoner said that it was on a certain Root of a stump 5 feet from surface of the earth, and with it would be found a tail feather[;] that said Stowel[l] and prisoner thereupon commenced digging, found a tail feather, but [the] money was gone, that he supposed that [the] money moved down.

100. *Laws of the State of New-York, Revised and Passed,* 2:507.

101. This is likely Oquago Mountain, which lies in the Great Bend of the Susquehanna River and covered one-half of Harmony Township. Near Isaac Hale's home on the south slope of the peak were the diggings on the McKune/Skinner property described by Emily Blackman in her *History of Susquehanna County,* 579-82.

102. A notable elevation in the hills on the west side of the Susquehanna River in northern Windsor township ("Historical Sketch of Windsor, Broome County, New York," 3). William R. Hine also mentioned these diggings on Monument Hill (William R. Hine, Affidavit, ca. Mar. 1885, 2).

103. Hine, who was born in Colesville, New York, said that Smith "dug for salt two summers, near and in sight of my house" (William R. Hine, Affidavit, ca. Mar. 1885, 2).

Although no treasure was discovered in any of these digs, Stowell swore that Joseph "possessed all the power he claimed." The young visionary could see things just as clearly fifty feet below the surface of the earth, said Stowell, as he could see what was on Neely's table. "Deacon Stowell," Neely responded, "do I understand you as swearing before God, under the solemn oath you have taken, that you *believe* the prisoner can see by the aid of the stone fifty feet below the surface of the earth, as plainly as you can see what is on my table?" "Do I *believe* it?" answered the old Presbyterian, "do I believe it? no, it is not a matter of belief: I positively know it to be true."

Jonathan Thompson, a member of Stowell's money-digging crew, was the fourth witness. He and another employee "always attended the Deacon and Smith in their nocturnal labors," although they never obtained anything of value. On one occasion, Joseph Jr. was requested to look in his stone for a chest of money, and did so. When Thompson and another Stowell employee accompanied Smith to the site, darkness had fallen. Joseph began to scry in the usual fashion—placing his stone into his hat—and told the men how the envisioned chest was situated. After shoveling for several feet, the diggers "struck upon something sounding like a board or plank," said Thompson. They looked at Joseph, who, "pretending that he was alarmed on account of the circumstances," refused to gaze into his stone again, stating that he had envisioned "two Indians who buried the trunk, that a quarrel ensued between them, and that one of said Indians was killed by the other, and thrown into the hole beside the trunk, to guard it, as he supposed." Thompson "believe[d] in the prisoner's professed skill; that the board which he struck his spade upon was probably the chest, but on account of an enchantment the trunk kept settling away from under them when digging."[104]

The outcome of Joseph Smith's 1826 examination has long been debated. Nine years later, Oliver Cowdery, narrating what was probably Joseph's version of the story, recounted that "some very officious person complained of him as a disorderly person, and brought him before the authorities of the county; but there being no cause of action he was honorably acquitted."[105] Purple added: "It is hardly necessary to say that, as the testimony of Deacon Stowell could not be impeached, the prisoner was discharged, and in a few weeks left the town."[106] But Cowdery's and Purple's accounts are contradicted by the record. Neely concluded that there was sufficient evidence that Smith asserted he

104. Daniel S. Tuttle, "A Document Discovered," 1.
105. Cowdery to Phelps, "Letter V," Oct. 1835, 201.
106. Purple, "Joseph Smith, the Originator of Mormonism," 3.

could discover lost goods, a misdemeanor under the Vagrant Acts because no treasure had been found and "therefore the Court find the Defendant [Joseph Smith] guilty." Neely ordered Constable DeZeng to notify two other justices to prepare for trial and put three unnamed material witnesses under recognizance to appear at the forthcoming Court of Special Sessions.

The trial never materialized. Another local justice of the peace, Joel Noble, wrote that Joseph, because of his youth, took "Leg Bail," meaning he "escape[d] from custody."[107] Abram W. Benton, a Bainbridge resident, said in 1831 that Joseph was "condemned" by Neely but that "considering his youth, (he then being a minor) and thinking he might reform his conduct, he was designedly allowed to escape."[108] Although this account tidily concludes the hearing, Joseph in fact returned to South Bainbridge several times. One of Joseph's biographers, Dan Vogel, wonders: "There must have been more involved than an escape from custody because, if this had been the case, he probably would not have been so bold in returning to South Bainbridge."[109] Vogel hypothesizes that Neely released Smith on his own recognizance with instructions to appear at the forthcoming trial. But when Neely learned that Smith had unlawfully crossed the county line to stay with Joseph Knight in Colesville, he might have issued a *mittimus* to have the young seer returned to his court. After being reprimanded, Joseph, "understanding that a formal trial would likely result in his conviction and possible imprisonment," could have worked out an off-the-record agreement. Neely may have imposed a fine "not exceeding twenty-five dollars, or imprisonment in the common jail of the county not exceeding six months, or both." In court cases involving non-locals, the same statute stipulated that upon payment of the fine and/or release from jail, the "offender shall be immediately ordered or transported out of the said county to his last place of settlement or abode if known; and if any person so ordered or transported shall remain in the said county for forty-eight hours, or return thereto within six calendar months after such order of transportation, he shall be again fined as aforesaid, or confined as aforesaid."[110]

No record of such an arrangement exists, but Neely may have stipulated that the young seer leave the county for at least six months and may also have stipulated that he refrain from scrying. Thus, when Joseph returned to

107. Noble to Turner, Mar. 8, 1842; for "leg bail," see Eric Partridge, *A Dictionary of Slang and Unconventional English,* 476.

108. [Abram W. Benton], "Mormonites," 120.

109. Vogel, *Joseph Smith,* 85.

110. *Laws of the State of New-York, Revised and Passed,* 2:508, sec. 4.

South Bainbridge in November 1826 to seek more work with Stowell, and again in January 1827 to be married to Emma Hale by Justice Zechariah Tarbell, he did not fear arrest and incarceration.

Lucy Mack Smith does not mention the 1826 hearing in her memoir. In fact, in 1829 when Martin Harris's wife, Lucy, brought charges against Joseph, Lucy Smith stated that it was "the first time that a suit was ever brought before any court which affected any of my children."[111] Had she forgotten her son's South Bainbridge arrest? Did she intentionally omit any reference to the event? Or did father and son conceal it from her?

The embarrassment that ensued from this arrest and questioning may have caused or intensified conflict with Joseph's future in-laws. Isaac Hale "was a little deluded at first," noted Emily Blackman, a regional historian, "in regard to Joe's prophecy of the existence of precious minerals, when the digging was progressing in the vicinity ... but his common sense soon manifested itself, and his disapproval of Joe was notorious."[112] One easily imagines Hale reacting angrily all over again as each wave of news about his son-in-law reached Harmony from Ohio, Missouri, and Illinois.

The fact of Joseph's trial, as much as the outcome, must have shaken the young seer. Yet despite the humiliation, he could not have failed to notice that no matter how many Peter Bridgmans challenged his claims, he was also hedged by true believers—like his father, like Josiah Stowell, and later like Joseph Knight and Martin Harris. Such men would never abandon their belief in what others dismissed. Joseph's power of persuasion was one of many gifts that would serve him throughout his life.

---

111. Lucy Smith also apparently forgot that in 1819 Jeremiah Hurlburt had jointly sued her husband and eldest son, Alvin *(Jeremiah Hurlburt v. Joseph and Alvin Smith).*

112. Blackman, *History of Susquehanna County,* 103. The November 7, 1832, issue of the *New England Christian Herald,* published by the Boston Wesleyan Association, declared that Smith was "disowned by his pious father-in-law" ("Mormonism," 22).

New England communities, including those in which Joseph Smith Jr. lived from birth until his relocation to Ohio. (Map by Ken Gross, Rustbelt Cartography, Akron, Ohio.)

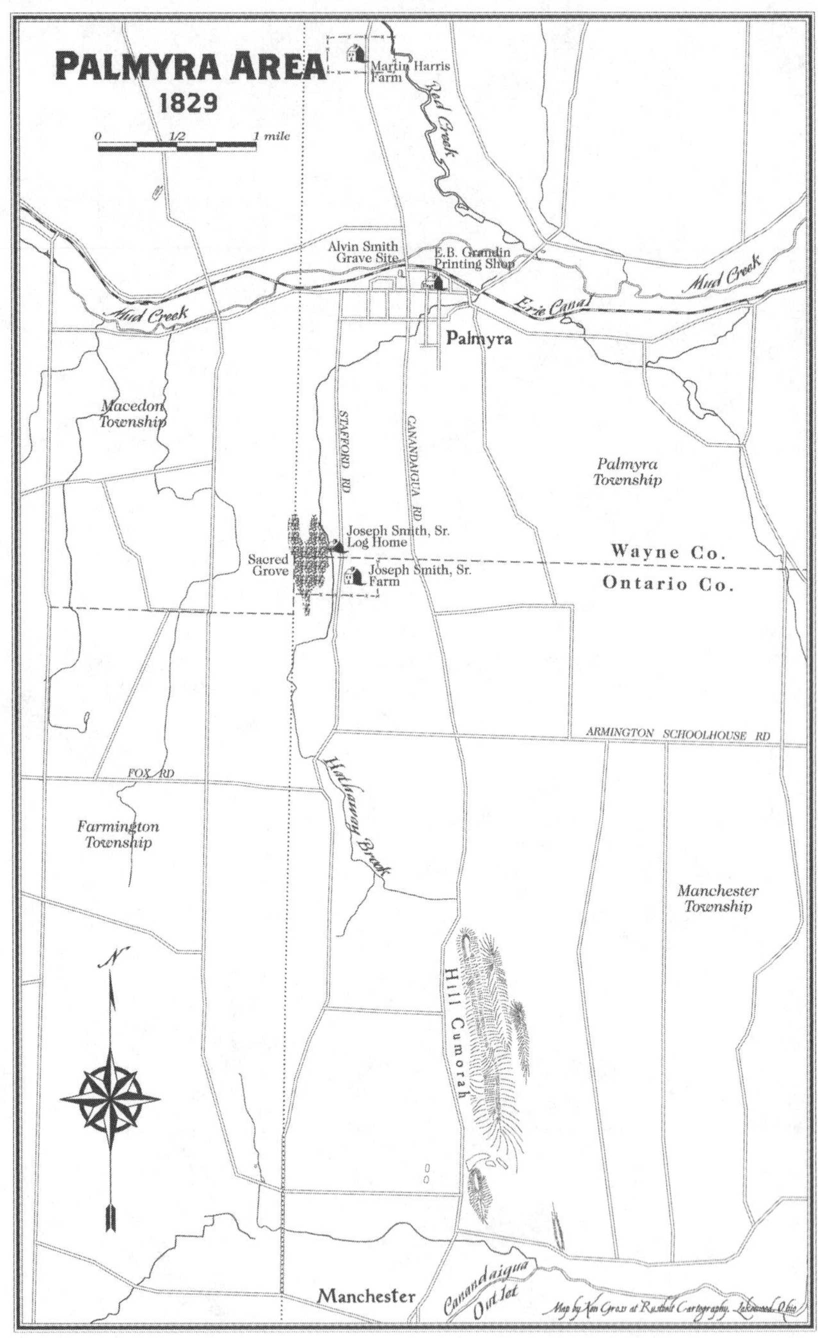

Important Smith family historical sites in the Palmyra-Manchester, New York, area. (Map by Ken Gross, Rustbelt Cartography, Akron, Ohio.)

The "verts monts" (green mountains) surrounding Tunbridge, Vermont.

The Joseph Smith family farm and memorial obelisk mark the birthplace of Joseph Smith Jr. in Sharon, Vermont (ca. 1907).

The Joseph Smith Sr. family Norwich, Vermont, home (ca. 1908).

Palmyra, New York, looking east (ca. 1840).

Joseph Smith Jr., by Sutcliffe Maudsley (ca. early 1840s).

Hyrum Smith, by Sutcliffe Maudsley (ca. early 1840s).

Lucy Mack Smith.

Tombstone of Alvin Smith, Joseph Smith Jr.'s oldest brother.

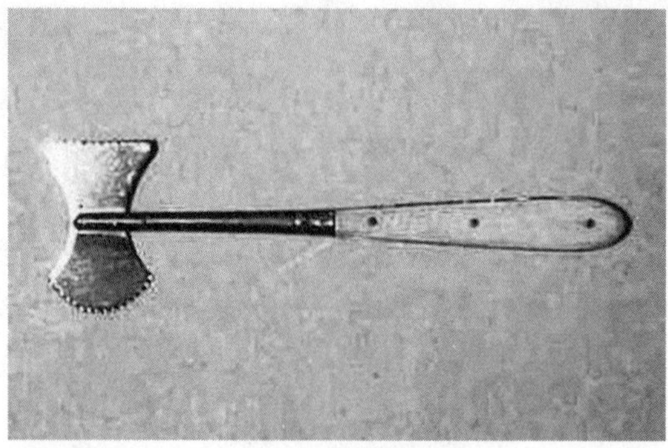

A Heys saw, similar to the kind used to extract diseased portions of bone from Joseph Smith Jr.'s left leg, 1812.

Jesse Smith gestures to eight-year-old nephew Joseph Smith Jr., on crutches, as the two tour Salem, Massachusetts, in 1813-14. (Illustration by Kurt Gray.)

Portrayals of various religious revivals and camp meetings during the early 1800s.

Young Joseph Smith, older brother Hyrum, and their father sell refreshments and oilcloths painted by their mother at a religious camp meeting in Palmyra, New York. (Illustration by Kurt Gray.)

The Joseph and Lucy Smith family: Alvin (left), daughter Lucy, William, Mother Lucy, Joseph Sr., Joseph Jr., Sophronia, Hyrum, Don Carlos on Samuel Harrison's lap, and Katharine. (Illustration by Kurt Gray.)

A sixteenth-century German woodcut showing dowsers seeking wealth with divining rods. Joseph Smith, his father, and Oliver Cowdery are all reported to have worked with the rod.

Joseph Smith Jr.'s chocolate-colored seer stone.
(LDS Church Newsroom)

Miner's Hill, where a man points to presumed location (a cave) of one of Joseph Smith Jr.'s treasure digs (ca. 1907).

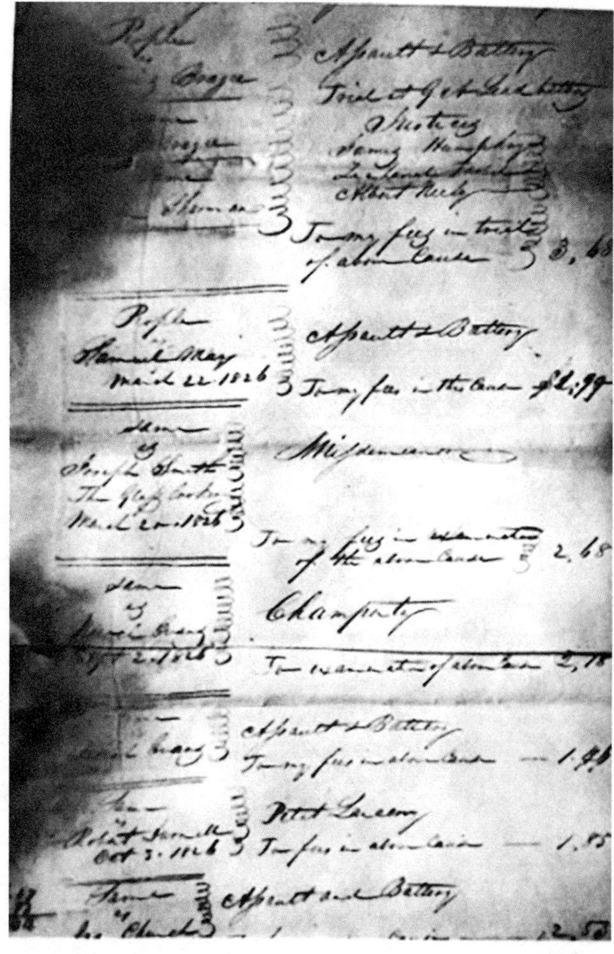

1826 court record identifying Joseph Smith Jr. as a "Glass looker."

Close-up of entry on Joseph Smith from the 1826 court record.

In this 1791 engraving, printed for John Hagerty, a Methodist preacher, the Tree of Life brings forth, under the redemptive rays of the tri-une God, twelve fruits of salvation. A crowd strolls by the narrow gate of salvation along the Broad Way to the Devil as "babylon Mother of Harlots" beckons. The sinners are stigmatized with labels indicating: "pride," "chambering [indulging in lewd or immodest behavior] & wantonness," "Quack," "usury," and "extortion." These and similar images may also be found in Joseph Smith's and his father's accounts of dreams and visions.

Emma Hale Smith (ca. 1844-45).

Joseph Smith and Emma Hale were married in this South Bainbridge (later Afton), New York, home on January 18, 1827.

The house of Emma Hale Smith's parents, Isaac and Elizabeth Hale, Harmony, Pennsylvania (ca. 1907).

The Joseph Smith Sr. family log home, Palmyra, New York (reconstructed).

The Joseph Smith Sr. family frame home,
Manchester/Palmyra, New York (reconstructed).

Joseph Smith scries the Book of Mormon through his seer stone placed in a hat, while Oliver Cowdery records the dictation and Emma performs household tasks. (Illustration by Kurt Gray.)

Joseph Smith digs the grave of his firstborn son, Alvin, stillborn on June 15, 1828. Isaac and Elizabeth Hale, Joseph's in-laws, and two of his brothers-in-law watch. (Illustration by Kurt Gray.)

Road leading to the Sacred Grove (ca. 1907).

The Sacred Grove (ca. 1920s).

The Hill Cumorah (ca. 1907).

View from the summit of the Hill Cumorah.

Samuel L. Mitchill (also Mitchell).

Charles Anthon.

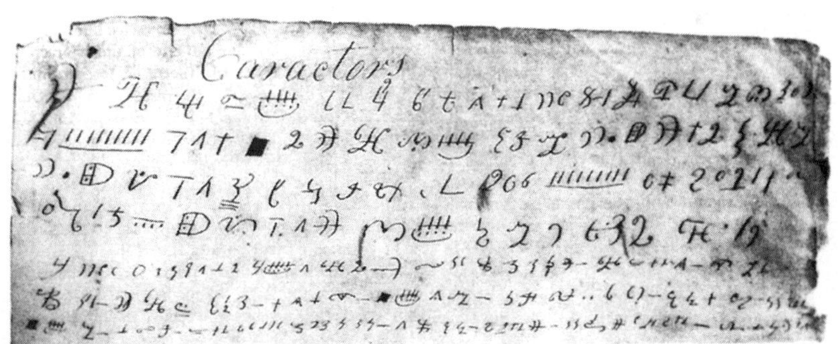

A sample of characters said to have been transcribed from the gold plates of the Book of Mormon.

Egbert B. Grandin,
Palmyra, New York, printer.

E. B. Grandin's bookstore and printing office, downtown Palmyra, New York (ca. 1907).

THE

BOOK OF MORMON:

AN ACCOUNT WRITTEN BY THE HAND OF MOR-MON, UPON PLATES TAKEN FROM THE PLATES OF NEPHI.

Wherefore it is an abridgment of the Record of the People of Nephi; and also of the Lamanites; written to the Lamanites, which are a remnant of the House of Israel; and also to Jew and Gentile; written by way of commandment, and also by the spirit of Prophesy and of Revelation. Written, and sealed up, and hid up unto the LORD, that they might not be destroyed, to come forth by the gift and power of GOD unto the interpretation thereof; sealed by the hand of Moroni, and hid up unto the LORD, to come forth in due time by the way of Gentile; the interpretation thereof by the gift of GOD; an abridgment taken from the Book of Ether.

Also, which is a Record of the People of Jared, which were scattered at the time the LORD confounded the language of the people when they were building a tower to get to Heaven: which is to shew unto the remnant of the House of Israel how great things the LORD hath done for their fathers; and that they may know the covenants of the LORD, that they are not cast off forever; and also to the convincing of the Jew and Gentile that JESUS is the CHRIST, the ETERNAL GOD, manifesting Himself unto all nations. And now if there be fault, it be the mistake of men; wherefore condemn not the things of GOD, that ye may be found spotless at the judgment seat of CHRIST.

BY JOSEPH SMITH, JUNIOR,

AUTHOR AND PROPRIETOR.

PALMYRA:

PRINTED BY E. B. GRANDIN, FOR THE AUTHOR.

1830.

Title page from the 1830 edition of the Book of Mormon.

Oliver Cowdery, Joseph Smith's scribe and Book of Mormon witness.

Martin Harris, Joseph Smith's benefactor and Book of Mormon witness.

David Whitmer, Joseph Smith's supporter and Book of Mormon witness.

Joseph Knight Sr., Smith family friend and supporter.

Said to be a baptismal pool on the Joseph Smith farm, Palmyra, New York.

Dirt road through the Joseph Smith farm, Palmyra, New York.

Seneca Lake, New York, site of early baptisms into the Church of Christ (ca. 1907).

Susquehanna River, Pennsylvania (ca. 1907).

11 | COURTING EMMA HALE

He must first go on a journey into Pennsylvania—and there among the mountains, he would meet with a very lovely woman, belonging to a highly respectable and pious family, whom he was to take for his wife. As a proof that he was sent on this mission by Jehovah, as soon as he saw the designated person, he would be smitten with her beauty, and though he was a stranger to her, and she was far above him in the walks of life, she would at once be willing to marry him and go with him to the ends of the earth.

—Martin Harris, qtd. in John A. Clark, *Gleanings by the Way*, 222

During the holiday season of 1825, shortly after his twentieth birthday, Joseph visited his family in Manchester, where his thoughts turned to marriage. Alvin had been engaged at the time of his death, and Hyrum was courting Jerusha Barden, a local girl known for her beauty and character, whom he would marry a year later on November 2, 1826.[1] While he was not traditionally handsome, Joseph was "a fine man, no doubt of it," recalled his Nauvoo associate and counselor in the First Presidency, William Law, more than forty years later.[2] Another close friend, Parley P. Pratt, who met Joseph in 1830, described him as

> tall and well built, strong and active, of light complexion, light hair, blue eyes, very little beard, and of an expression peculiar to himself, on which the eye naturally rested with interest and was never weary of beholding. His countenance was very mild, affable, beaming with intelligence and benevolence; mingled with a look of interest and an unconscious smile, or cheerfulness, and entirely free from all restraint or affectation of gravity; and there was something connected with the serene and steady penetrating glance of his eye, as if he would penetrate the deepest abyss

1. Lavina Fielding Anderson, *Lucy's Book*, 364; Pearson H. Corbett, *Hyrum Smith, Patriarch*, 37-38.
2. William Law, "Dr. Wyl and Dr. Wm. Law."

> of the human heart, gaze into eternity, penetrate the heavens and comprehend all worlds.[3]

In western New York, Joseph's name, as far as is known today, was never romantically linked with anyone. But during the seventeen days he worked in Harmony, Pennsylvania, boarding with the Isaac Hale family, he became smitten with the charms of twenty-one-year-old Emma Hale. Standing five feet nine inches to Joseph's six feet, Em, as she was known to family members, had "very black and piercing" eyes and "hair of the same color"[4]—the inverse of blue-eyed and ruddy-complexioned young Joseph. Joseph would later say that Emma was "of Indian descent, in a line from one of the tribes of Israel."[5] "[A]s pretty a woman as I ever saw," averred Joseph's Manchester friend and neighbor Lorenzo Saunders, who remembered that Emma was "an awful fine pretty girl ... an intelegent [sic] woman."[6] A local Illinois historian, writing fourteen years after Emma's death in 1879, described her as "well turned, of excellent form ... with splendid physical development."[7] Rhamanthus M. Stocker, a lawyer and historian, who interviewed many of Joseph's and Emma's acquaintances in Susquehanna County, Pennsylvania, noted she was "quite tall, of comely form and feature, well educated, a fine singer and very social."[8] "Emma is naturally a very smart woman," Brigham Young would later say. "[S]he is subtle and ingenious."[9] Emma Hale was a woman capable of inciting ardent passion and intense interest.

Back home in Manchester at the end of 1825, 130 miles away from the Hales, Joseph confided to his parents that he "had felt so lonely" since Alvin's death. If they had no objections, he continued, "he though[t] that no young woman that he ever was acquainted with was better calculated to render the man of her choice happy than Miss Emma Hale a young lady whom he had been extremely fond <of> since his first introduction to her."[10] Though Lucy Smith had not yet met Emma, she told her son that she and her husband "were pleased with his choice, and not only consented to his marrying her,

---

3. Parley P. Pratt Jr., *The Autobiography of Parley Parker Pratt,* 45.

4. "Mrs. Joe Smith. An Interview with the Widow of the Noted Mormon Leader," *Wellsville [New York] Daily Reporter,* Oct. 27, 1884.

5. George T. M. Davis, *An Authentic Account of the Massacre of Joseph Smith ...,* 6, excerpted in John E. Hallwas and Roger D. Launius, *Cultures in Conflict,* 103-107.

6. Lorenzo Saunders, Interviewed by E. L. Kelley, Nov. 12, 1884, 12.

7. Inez A. Kennedy, *Recollections,* 96.

8. Rhamanthus M. Stocker, *Centennial History of Susquehanna County,* 554.

9. Brigham Young, Unpublished discourse, Oct. 7, 1866.

10. Anderson, *Lucy's Book,* 362.

but requested him to bring her home with him, and live with us. Accordingly he set out with his father for Pennsylvania."[11]

At some point during this period, Joseph felt divine confirmation that Emma was not only his destiny, but also the crucial element to overcome Cumorah's enchantment. Identifying one's future spouse supernaturally was a common theme in early American folklore. "A maiden should go down the cellar-stairs backwards looking all the time into a mirror, in which she will see the face of her future husband," avowed one account.[12] "Take a candle, and go alone, to a looking glass," advised another, "eat an apple before it ... comb your hair all the time ... the face of your conjugal companion, to be, will be seen in the glass, as if peeping over your shoulder."[13] Still another promised that "any single person who holds a mirror over a well on the 1st of May, will see reflected in it the likeness of the future wife or husband."[14] A further bit of folklore advised the seeker to walk backwards to a well, circle it "three times," still backward, then look into the water "in which will then appear the face of [the] future lover."[15]

Joseph did not foresee his wife by gazing into a well or mirror. Instead, he used the same seer stone in which he had scryed for hidden treasure and envisioned the golden plates of Cumorah. According to Joseph Knight Sr., Joseph explained that an angel had said that on the next September 22 he "mite have the Book if he Bro[ugh]t with him the right person[.] Joseph says who is the right Person? The answer was you will know. Then he looked in his glass and found it was Emma Hale, daughter of old Mr. Hail of Pensylvany, a girl that he had seen Before, for he had Bin [been] Down there Before with me."[16] Lorenzo Saunders remembered: "Joseph said that he saw the angel again; The Angel told him he must go & get him a wife & then he could take his wife & go & get the plates."[17] New York neighbor Henry Harris told Doctor Philastus Hurlbut in about 1833, more than forty years before Saunders's interview, that an angel told young Smith "he could not

11. Ibid., 312.

12. F. D. Bergen, "Current Superstitions," 56.

13. Theodore Besterman, *Crystal Gazing,* 59.

14. Bergen, "Current Superstitions," 58.

15. E. Gutch and Mabel Peacock, *Examples of Printed Folk-Lore Concerning Lincolnshire,* 9.

16. Joseph Knight Sr., "Reminiscence." Dan Vogel believes that Knight's statement is somewhat problematic because Smith did not meet Stowell and Knight until 1825: "As some versions have it, in 1824 [Smith] saw Samuel Lawrence, who turned out to be the wrong person. More likely, after Emma became the person in 1827, she became part of the earlier story" (Vogel, Statement to Van Wagoner, July 16, 2008).

17. Lorenzo Saunders, Interview, Nov. 12, 1884, 16.

get the plates until he was married, and that when he saw the woman that was to be his wife, he should know her, and she would know him."[18]

Manchester informant Sylvia Walker remembered in 1885: "It was freely talked among the neighbors that Jo Smith said he had a revelation to go to Pennsylvania and get him a wife."[19] Another neighbor recalled, again in 1885, that "Jo told Emma he had a revelation about the plates, but that he could not obtain them until he had married her."[20] Emma's cousins also reported that Joseph stated, "in our hearing," that Emma was the person who "must come with him" to obtain the golden plates, according to the requirement of "the ghost."[21] Among others familiar with this requirement was the McKune family in Harmony. "Until he obtained [a wife]," said Sally McKune, "there was no use in trying to get certain buried treasures at Palmyra."[22] Katharine Smith Salisbury, Joseph's youngest sister, provided the best summary of this requirement. When Joseph asked, "What shall I do?" the angel said, according to Katharine:

> "Come here the next year at this time and bring your oldest brother with you, and you can receive the records."
>
> In November my brother took sick, and through the ministering of medicine by the doctors he passed away. Joseph went to the place and inquired of the angel what he should [do] now. The angel said: "you must bring some person with you."
>
> And Joseph said: "Who shall I bring? My oldest brother is gone."
>
> The angel said: "You will know her when you see her."
>
> That fall he went down to Pennsylvania and became acquainted with his wife, Miss Hale, and he knew when he saw her that she was the one to go with him to get the records.[23]

These half-dozen accounts make it clear Joseph believed that marrying Emma was a requirement for obtaining the golden plates. If he were not married by September 22, 1827, the angel warned, he "never would" recover the record.[24] But Joseph also truly loved Emma. Marrying her was

18. Henry Harris, Affidavit, in Eber D. Howe, *Mormonism Unvailed,* 252. "Doctor" was Hurlbut's given name and not a title.

19. Sylvia Walker, Statement, Mar. 20, 1885, 1.

20. William R. Hine, "Affidavit."

21. Joseph and Hiel Lewis, "Mormon History," 1.

22. Sally McKune, qtd. in Mather, "The Early Days of Mormonism," 200.

23. Kyle R. Walker, "Katharine Smith Salisbury's Recollection of Joseph's Meetings with Moroni," 16-17. Salisbury made this statement in 1895, when she was eighty-two.

24. Knight said that Joseph "told me the Conversation he had with the personage which

much more than an expedient. She was, Joseph would later say, the "choice of my heart."[25]

Emma Hale was born on July 10, 1804, in the Susquehanna Valley township of Harmony. The seventh of nine children, she was a pragmatic, hard-working, happy girl, contented in a thriving family and a comfortable home. She attended school whenever she could, including a year beyond the common grammar school education of her brothers and sisters. An occasional school teacher, Emma was well read, and possessed both common sense and a broad view of life. Although her mother, Elizabeth Lewis Hale, was a life-long Methodist, Elizabeth's husband (and Emma's father), Isaac, like Joseph Smith Sr., was a deist in the early years of his marriage. According to testimony from family members, Isaac's return to the fold was affected by young Emma's piety. Walking through the woods near his home, Hale came upon his seven-year-old daughter, in a small clearing, pleading on her knees for her father's return to orthodox Christianity. Reportedly moved by the simple faith of his beloved Em, Hale embraced the Methodism of his wife.

The Methodist Episcopal Church played a more compelling role in young Emma's life than in Joseph's. Emma, unlike Joseph, apparently underwent a conversion experience or "change of heart" at an early age. According to neighbor W. R. Hine, Emma was "a good singer, and she often got the power."[26] Class meetings were frequently held in her girlhood home. Uncle Nathaniel Lewis was a lay minister, and Michael Morse, who had married her younger sister Tryal, was a class leader in the local assembly. A Methodist itinerant preacher who often stayed with the Hales when passing through remembered not her fine voice but her cooking: "In those old times [we] often partook of a good repast of venison, eels, and buckwheat cakes, prepared by her hands."[27]

By the time she first laid eyes on Joseph Smith, Emma Hale had lived nearly twenty-one years with nothing to distress or vex her that has made it into the records of the time. She loved riding horseback with family and friends. The Susquehanna, one of America's captivating rivers, coursed a mere stone's throw away from her doorstep. "[H]eaven and earth seemed never to

told him if he would Do right according to the will of God he mite obtain [the plates] the 22nt Day of Septem[b]er Next and if not he never would have them" (Joseph Knight Sr., "Reminiscence," in Vogel, *Early Mormon Documents,* 4:12).

25. *History of the Church,* 5:107.

26. Hine, "Affidavit."

27. George Peck, "Mormonism and the Mormons," *Methodist Quarterly Review* 3, no. 1 (1843): 112.

have agreed better to frame a place for man's commodious and delightful habitation," said Captain John Smith (1580-1631) of the river named after the fabled Susquehannocks.[28] The waterway dominated the valley of Emma's childhood, and she no doubt enjoyed the ebb and flow of the river, fishing, and canoeing in its emerald waters.

Although she reciprocated Joseph's affection, Emma's parents and several siblings took sharp exception to the young money-digger from New York. The custom of that day was that marriage proposals were broached first with the woman's father. Joseph followed the custom by asking Isaac for Emma's hand. "Old Hickory Hale," a "sturdy, honest, humbug-hating Pennsylvania farmer," as a nephew described him, turned the young seer down flat.[29]

As Joseph later narrated, Isaac's repugnance stemmed from Joseph's spiritual claims. "Owing to my continuing to assert that I had seen a vision," Joseph reported in the late 1830s, "persecution still followed me, and my wife's father's family were very much opposed to our being married."[30] But his religious beliefs were probably not the reason why the Hales objected. Joseph's friend and companion during this period, Josiah Stowell Jr., recalled a quarter century later that Joseph "did not Profess religion." Smith's brother-in-law, Michael Morse, interviewed in 1879, also remembered that during this period Joseph "made no pro=fession of religion."[31] Thus, while Joseph reported religious differences as the source of conflict, it seems more likely Isaac disapproved of the scryer's money-digging, an activity Hale viewed as humbuggery.

Writing under a pseudonym in 1886, Wilhelm Ritter Von Wymetal, who interviewed many of Joseph's early surviving associates, characterized Hale as preferring sons-in-law who were "steady-going, hardworking men, with 320 or at least 100 acres of good land, fine horses, cows, good house, barn and stables, a family Bible and good fences."[32] Joseph would never satisfy such expectations. In fact, Isaac took the then-drastic step of putting his disapproval on the record in an 1833 affidavit which was published the following year.[33] In this sworn testimony, Hale explained that he refused

---

28. "Captain John Smith Describes the Susquehanna." The Susquehanna meanders for 444 miles from its origin at Otsego Lake near Cooperstown, New York, until it empties into Chesapeake Bay at Havre de Grace, Maryland.

29. Hiel Lewis, qtd. in W. Wyl, *Joseph Smith, His Family, and His Friends,* 74.

30. *History of the Church,* 1:17.

31. William W. Blair, Journal, May 8, 1879, 52-56, Community of Christ Library-Archives, Independence, Missouri.

32. Wyl, *Joseph Smith, His Family, and His Friends,* 74.

33. Hale's scribe was his son Jesse. Isaac's brother-in-law, Nathaniel Lewis, a Methodist minister, attested: "I have been acquainted with Isaac Hale for fifty years, and have never known

Joseph's entreaties because "he was a stranger,[34] and followed a business that I could not approve." To avoid misunderstanding, Isaac specified: Joseph's "occupation was that of seeing, or pretending to see by means of a stone placed in his hat, and his hat closed over his face. In this way he pretended to discover minerals and hidden treasure."[35] Isaac's nephew, Hiel Lewis, later told Wymetal that Isaac would not hear of Emma "taking that slouching, shiftless feller from New York State."[36]

Emma did not share her family's opinion. Women eighteen and older were legally of age and could marry without parental consent. Moreover, Joseph was a persistent suitor and kept company with Emma for more than a year while he lived and worked upriver in South Bainbridge and Colesville, New York. Disregarding Emma's parents wishes, "young Smith made several visits at my house."[37]

For a time, Joseph continued to work for Josiah Stowell. But the old Presbyterian, who had spent much of his wealth on the unsuccessful money-digging ventures, reached the point where he could no longer employ the young scryer. He referred Joseph to his friend and fellow grain broker, Joseph Knight, who lived in Colesville, a small community on the east bank of the Susquehanna River. At this time, Knight owned four farms and, with his sons, operated the area's principal gristmill, plus two other works for carding wool. These enterprises often employed day workers, like Joseph Smith, on a seasonal basis. Knight later wrote that Joseph worked for him from November 1826 "until about the time that he was Married," three months later.[38]

Knight's youngest son, Joseph Jr., worked with Joseph Smith in farming

him guilty of wilfully, or deliberately telling a falsehood. His character for truth and veracity has never been questioned. He has been Supervisor, Assessor and collector, in this town—has kept his own accounts, and made his returns, to the satisfaction of all concerned" (Nathaniel Lewis, Statement, Mar. 20, 1834).

34. "Stranger" in the 1820s referred both to "one of another place" and an "unpropertied man." Virginia S. Thatcher and Alexander McQueen, *The New Webster Encyclopedic Dictionary of the English Language,* 828. See also Ruth Wallis Herndon, *Unwelcome Americans,* 5.

35. Isaac Hale, Statement.

36. Hiel Lewis, Statement, qtd. in Wyl, *Joseph Smith, His Family, and His Friends,* 74.

37. Isaac Hale, Statement.

38. Joseph Knight Sr., "Reminiscence," 2. Knight, born November 3, 1772, at Okham, Worcester County, Massachusetts, later lived at Bainbridge, New York (1808-10), then at Colesville, New York (1810-29). Knight's principal farmstead was "situated ... near the Colesville bridge—bounded on one side by the Susquehanna River, and containing about one hundred and forty two acres." Located on the property were "two dwelling houses, a good barn, and a fine orchard" *(Broome County Republican,* May 5, 1831, in Vogel, *Early Mormon Documents,* 4:11). Knight and his wife, Polly Peck Knight, were the parents of seven children. Knight later followed the Mormon migration westward, dying in Mount Pisgah, Iowa, on February 2, 1847.

and milling activities. The two became friends, and young Knight later remembered that his father praised Joseph as "the best hand he ever hired." Knight also recalled that soon after young Smith arrived at the Knight farm, he told the family in secret that "he had seen a vision" in which "a personage had appeared to him and told him where there was a gold book of ancient date buried, and if he would follow the directions of the angel he could get it."[39] Young Knight said that, although he and his father believed Smith's account, his brothers Nahum and Newel did not.

While living with the Knight family, Joseph Smith was involved in at least one treasure-seeking project. Emily Colburn Austin, sister of Newel Knight's wife, Sally, reported seeing holes where the money diggers had excavated for "pots of money" on Knight property. She also heard that the diggers had reportedly sacrificed a dog in a failed attempt to overcome an enchantment.[40] Joel K. Noble, a Colesville justice of the peace before whom Joseph Smith would appear in 1830, recalled the same tale: "Jo. and others were digging for a chest of money in [the] night [but] could not obtain it. They procured one thing and another, together with [a] *black bitch.* The bitch was offered a … sacrifice, [blo]od sprinkled, prayer made at the time. [But] (no money obtained). The above sworn to on trial."[41]

Despite Joseph's best efforts to win over Isaac Hale, the blunt hunter-farmer never accepted the impoverished money-digging youth as a suitable husband for his daughter. Nor, while courting Emma, did Smith show that he was capable of developing resources for sustaining a family. Neither he nor his father owned land; he was not established in a business; he knew no trade or profession. Emma was probably familiar with much of the advice literature for young women—self-help books and cautionary newspaper columns warning that "if a husband turned out to be intemperate, shiftless, or just unlucky, his wife and children would be vulnerable to poverty, social isolation, humiliation, even moral ruin."[42] Furthermore, conventional wisdom stressed the roles of prudent provider and hard-working helpmeet in seeking a mate. Yet love—physical attraction, in addition to emotional and, for some couples, spiritual compatibility—was at the center of early nineteenth-century marriage and courtship. Men and women of Joseph and Emma's generation were urged to choose cautiously but never to

39. Joseph Knight Jr., "Joseph Knight's Incidents of History from 1827 to 1844."

40. Emily M. Austin, *Mormonism,* 32.

41. Joel K. Noble to Jonathan B. Turner, Mar. 8, 1842, 2.

42. "An Overview of Courtship and Marriage in Early Nineteenth-century Rural New England," 1.

ignore the feelings of their hearts. The young couple did not. Local historian Emily Blackman, unable to explain how an intelligent schoolteacher like Emma could marry a seemingly ne'er-do-well like Smith, scoffed that "he had bewitched her," as he "afterwards bewitched the masses."[43]

No details have survived to explain precisely how Joseph and Emma engineered their elopement. Joseph Knight later wrote that in January 1827 he paid Smith his wages and furnished him "with a horse and Cutter to go and see his girl Down to Mr. Hails and soon after this he was Married."[44] In 1834, Isaac Hale averred: "while I was absent from home, [Smith] carried off my daughter, into the state of New York, where they were married without my approbation or consent."[45] "I was visiting at Mr. [Josiah] Stowell's, who lived in Bainbridge, and saw your father there," Emma told her eldest son years later, "I had no intention of marrying when I left home; but during my visit at Mr. Stowell's, your father visited me there. My folks were bitterly opposed to him; and, being importuned by your father, aided by Mr. Stowell, who urged me to marry him, and preferring to marry him to any other man I knew, I consented."[46]

The majority of young couples in the nineteenth century were married in the bride's home. But that was not possible for Joseph and Emma, since "<my wife's father's family was very much> opp=osed to our being married," Smith "was therefore under the necessity of taking her elsewhere, so we went and were married at the house of Squire Tarbill."[47] Again, this may put a better face on matters than the picture that emerges from those who recalled the incident. Emma apparently took advantage of her father's absence to receive a visit from Joseph, who asked her to accompany him to the Stowell home, ostensibly to call on Josiah's daughters Rhoda and Marion, ages twenty-five and twenty-three. There Emma easily yielded to the combined coaxing of Joseph and Josiah Stowell.

The ceremony took place in South Bainbridge, New York, in the home of justice of the peace Zachariah Tarbell/Tarble on January 18, 1827. Martha Carpenter, years later, wrote that she saw "Rhoda and Miriam [Stowell] take the young couple in a sleigh to the ferry ... cross on the ice, then go up the east side of the river to the home of Squire Tarbell who married them."[48]

43. Emily C. Blackman, *History of Susquehanna County, Pennsylvania,* 103.
44. Joseph Knight Sr., "Reminiscence," 2.
45. Hale, Statement.
46. Joseph Smith III, "Last Testimony of Sister Emma," 289.
47. Dean C. Jessee, *The Papers of Joseph Smith,* 1:283.
48. Martha Carpenter to Rev. Oscar Beardsley, n.d., qtd. in Nan Hill, "Joe Smith Lived and Married Here."

Perhaps the Stowell sisters witnessed the wedding take place. The event was a brief civil formality to meet the letter of the law.[49] Perhaps the newlyweds' sentiments compared to those of contemporary Elizabeth Ann Jennison of Massachusetts, who after her own wedding thought to herself: "From this hour of solemn union of our outward as well as inward lives, we begin to live a new life—and at this beginning implore His pleasure in our joy."[50] Presumably, the young couple returned to the Stowell home for a small celebration.

Joseph and Emma were slightly under the average age for marriage at the time in New England. He had just turned twenty-one, she was twenty-two. More typically for the era, most men married between ages twenty-four and thirty, while women usually married for the first time between the ages of twenty and twenty-seven.[51] In Joseph's immediate family, men generally married even later. Alvin died engaged but unmarried at twenty-five, Hyrum married at twenty-five, Joseph Sr. married at twenty-four, and three of Joseph Sr.'s brothers had married at twenty-eight, thirty-four, and thirty-eight.

Nothing is known of Joseph and Emma's honeymoon and little of the earliest months of their marriage. Neither provided much information about the interlude. Interviewed at age fifty-one when Joseph had been dead for a decade, Emma told Frank Stevens that, although "there always existed a feeling of perfect confidence between Joseph and me, he was often strange and incomprehensible to me."[52]

What is known is that the newlyweds left South Bainbridge promptly, their host and confidante, Josiah Stowell, driving the young couple on the two- or three-day trip to Joseph Sr. and Lucy's frame home in Manchester sometime between January 18-31, 1827.[53] It is also not known if Emma made any effort to inform her parents directly of the step she had taken or if she let rumor do that task. Certainly the prospect of returning to the Hale home for a wedding visit was not possible: "The Hale family was greatly exasperated," reported Hiel Lewis, Emma's cousin. "[P]erhaps it would not have been safe for Smith to have shown himself at his father-in-law's house.

49. Years later as an elderly woman, Emma noted: "My certificate of marriage was lost many years ago, in some of the marches we were forced to make" (Joseph Smith III, "Last Testimony of Sister Emma," 289).

50. "The Wedding of William Sumner Barton and Elizabeth Ann Jennison, 1849," 3.

51. "An Overview of Courtship and Marriage in Early Nineteenth-century Rural New England," 1.

52. Emma Hale Smith Bidamon, qtd. in Otto Reimherr, "The Susquehanna," 75-76.

53. Joseph's personal history notes: "Immediately after my marriage I left Mr. Stoals, and went to my father's and farmed with him that season" (in Manuscript History of the Church, Book A-1, 8).

Emma was or had been the idol or favorite of the family, and they all still felt a strong attachment for her."[54]

Stowell apparently had another motivation besides a generous heart in providing the newlyweds with transportation back to Manchester. Joseph reportedly told the Dutchman that he had discovered on the bank of the Black River in Watertown, New York, "a cave, in which he had found a bar of gold, as big as his leg, and about three or four feet long."[55] The find was too heavy for one man to remove, but "they would go together ... take a chisel and mallet ... get it ... [and] share the prize." Stowell jumped at the opportunity and drove the couple to their destination. But when he reminded Joseph about the treasure trove, another day's journey from Manchester, Joseph said that "he would not go, because his wife was now among strangers, and would be very lonesome if he went away." Stowell returned home "without any gold, and with less money than he came."[56]

Joseph and Emma were welcomed by the Smith clan with open arms. Lucy, who had not yet met her new daughter-in-law, had put her "House in order throughout" to welcome her. Mother Smith described Hyrum's new wife of nearly three months, Jerusha, as "one of the most excellent of women, with whom I had seen much enjoyment." I hoped for "as much happiness with my second daughter-in-law, as I had received from the society of the first, and there was no reason why I should expect anything to the contrary."[57] She described the newly arrived Joseph as "in fine health & spirits,"[58] but said nothing about Emma's demeanor. It is conceivable that Emma was disappointed at the Smiths' poverty and crowded home,[59] perhaps she was also feeling guilty and homesick. It would have been natural for her to want to talk to her mother and sisters about married life, but she was cut off from them. Neighbor Lorenzo Saunders asserted that when Emma "came to the Smiths she was disappointed and used to come to our place and sit down and cry. Said she was deceived and got into a hard place."[60]

Emma may have begun to wonder if her father's assessment of her

---

54. Hiel Lewis, qtd. in Wyl, *Joseph Smith, His Family, and His Friends,* 75.

55. Unless otherwise stated, my narrative at this point is based on Willard Chase's 1833 affidavit, 244.

56. Ibid., 243.

57. Anderson, *Lucy's Book,* 364.

58. Ibid., 373.

59. Although Hyrum and his new wife, Jerusha Barden Smith, were living in the Smiths' log house, Sophronia, Harrison, William, Katharine, Don Carlos, and Lucy were apparently still at home with their parents.

60. Saunders, Interview, Sept. 17, 1884, 9-10. Saunders's older sister, Melissa, who later

husband was perhaps correct. His occasional bouts of drinking and life-long inclination to get into fistfights may have raised cause for her concern.[61] David Stafford, who worked with young Joseph during this period, noted that alcohol often incited the budding seer to fight. "When intoxicated, he was very quarrelsome," said Stafford. "[W]hile at work at one time, a dispute arose among us, (he having drinked [sic] a little too freely) and some hard words passed between us, and as usual with him at such times, was for fighting. He got the advantage of me in the scuffle, and a gentleman by the name of Ford interfered, when Joseph turned to fighting him. We both entered a complaint against him and he was fined for the breach of the peace."[62] David's brother Barton recalled that while Joseph was employed as a laborer for his father, William Stafford, Smith became "quite drunk on a composition of cider, molasses and water." Young Stafford remembered that Joseph was so intoxicated, he could hardly stand and had to support himself by holding onto the rails of a fence. Joseph soon fell to fighting with another hand who "tore his shirt nearly off from him." Emma, who was visiting the womenfolk inside, came out and "appeared very much grieved at his conduct, and to protect his back from the rays of the sun, and conceal his nakedness, threw her shawl over his shoulders and in that plight escorted the Prophet home."[63] There was ample hard cider at the Smith home during the year that Joseph and Emma lived there. An account book of their landlord, merchant Lemuel Durfee, records the purchase of five barrels of "liquor cider" (meaning fermented) by Joseph Smith Sr. and Hyrum during the spring and summer of 1827.[64]

Hiram Jackway, who grew up on a farm about a mile and a half north of the Smiths on Stafford Road, when asked about the Smiths' drinking habits, described one incident (either before or after Joseph's marriage) in which

---

married Willard Chase, according to Lorenzo, was "very intimate" with Emma Smith after she moved to Manchester (Lorenzo Saunders, Interview, Nov. 12, 1884, 10).

61. For details of Joseph's fisticuffs with David Stafford, David Patten, an unnamed wife beater, an unnamed bill collector, and his brother William, see Kyle R. Walker, "The Joseph Sr. and Lucy Mack Smith Family," 156-74. For Joseph's fight with brother-in-law Calvin Stoddard, see Fawn M. Brodie, *No Man Knows My History,* 164. For his fight with Walter Bagby, see George D. Smith, *An Intimate Chronicle,* 113-14. For whipping a Baptist minister in Kirtland "till he begged [for mercy]" and assaulting Josiah Butterfield of the First Council of Seventy, see D. Michael Quinn, *The Mormon Hierarchy,* 636, 637.

62. David Stafford, Statement, Dec. 5, 1833, in Howe, *Mormonism Unvailed,* 249.

63. Barton Stafford, Nov. 3, 1833, in Howe, *Mormonism Unvailed,* 250-51. Barton's cousin, Christopher M. Stafford, Affidavit, mentioned what may be this same incident: "Jo got drunk while we were haying for my uncle, Wm. Stafford; also at a husking at our house, and stayed overnight. I have often seen him drunk."

64. Lemuel Durfee, Account Book, records the purchase of three barrels of hard cider on May 31, 1827, and two more barrels on September 1.

both father and son were drunk. Father Smith, like his son, prided himself on his prowess as a wrestler, willing and able to take on anyone at any time, with a fair prospect of success. Jackway remembered the intoxicated father and son grappling during a break in their haying labors. "Joe and his father wrestled," Jackway recalled, "and Joe threw the old man down, and he cried." When the interviewer asked why Father Smith cried, Jackway answered, "Because Joe was the best man I guess."[65]

Joseph Jr. probably spent the spring and summer of 1827 in farm work or other odd jobs for various local employers; but by the fall of 1827, he and his father had turned to another money-digging project near their Manchester farmstead. Both Martin Harris in 1859 and Lorenzo Saunders twenty-five years after that noted that shortly before he claimed to have recovered the golden plates of the Book of Mormon, young Joseph was scrying for a local treasure-digging company.[66] Prior to that September 22 milestone, however, Joseph and Emma returned to Pennsylvania to face her parents. Susquehanna County historian Emily C. Blackman wrote: "Poor Emma Hale Smith lived long enough to rue her 'inquiry into Joe's character'; the pretext she gave for leaving home the day she went with him to be married." Blackman added that Emma's mother, Elizabeth, had said of her behavior: "Don't you think Emma was such a goose as to go up to Joe's father's to find out his character?"[67] But Oliver Cowdery later said that Emma "most certainly evinced a decidedly correct mind and uncommon ability of talent and judgment, in a manifest willingness to fulfill, on her part, that passage in sacred writ.—'and they twain shall be one flesh,'—by accompanying her husband against the wishes and advice of her relatives, to a land of strangers."[68]

After six months of marriage, Emma, following receipt of a favorable letter from her sister Elizabeth Wasson, who lived in Bainbridge, New York, decided to communicate with her still incensed father.[69] Emma, who had eloped with nothing but the clothes she was wearing, now wrote to ask if she could retrieve the rest of her belongings. Hale replied that the property

65. Hiram Jackway, Interviewed by William H. Kelley, "The Hill Cumorah, and the Book of Mormon," 166-67.

66. Martin Harris, qtd. in Joel Tiffany, "Mormonism—No. II," 164-65, and Lorenzo Saunders, Interview, Nov. 12, 1884.

67. Calling someone a goose was a mild epithet, meaning "a silly, stupid person, from the popular notion as to the stupidity of the goose" (Thatcher and McQueen, *New Webster Encyclopedic Dictionary of the English Language,* 373); Blackman, *History of Susquehanna County, Pennsylvania,* 582.

68. Oliver Cowdery to W. W. Phelps, "Letter VIII," 200.

69. Wyl, *Joseph Smith, His Family, and His Friends,* 75.

was at her disposal. With this assurance, Joseph hired a Palmyra teamster, Peter Ingersoll, to transport Emma and him on a "down and back" (round trip) to retrieve her things in the summer of 1827.[70] Ingersoll's memory of this trip included what he called Joseph's "true [Y]ankee wit." When Ingersoll's wagon rumbled up to a toll gate near Ithaca, Joseph did not have exact change. But he assured the gate tender he would "hand" him the double toll on his return since he was coming back within days. Ingersoll said that on the return trip Joseph tendered the toll keeper "25 cents, the toll being 12 ½." But the official, who had forgotten Smith's promise, "accordingly gave him back 12 ½ cents." After they passed through the gate, Ingersoll asked Smith "if he did not agree to pay double gatage on our return?" "No, said he, I agreed to 'hand' it to him, and I did, but he handed it back again."[71]

Ingersoll also recalled a "truly affecting" reunion. Far from being either cold or stoic, Isaac Hale burst into "a flood of tears" as he confronted his unwanted son-in-law: "You have stolen my daughter and married her," he sobbed. "I had much rather have followed her to her grave. You spend your time in digging for money—pretend to see in a stone, and thus try to deceive people." According to Ingersoll, Joseph began to weep—perhaps the entire family by now was in tears—and humbly "acknowledged he could not see in a stone now, nor never could; and that his former pretentions in that respect, were all false." Smith then promised to give up his "old habits of digging for money and looking into stones."[72] Almost immediately, Hale warmed up to his son-in-law and promised that if Joseph would move back to Pennsylvania and "work for a living he would assist him in getting into business." Eager to accept this détente, young Smith agreed. In Hale's words, "Smith stated to me, that he had given up what he called 'glasslooking,' and that he expected to work hard for a living, and was willing to do so."[73]

On the return trip to New York, Smith told Ingersoll that "although he intended to keep the promise which he had made to his father-in-law," it would be difficult for him because the members of his money-digging company "will all oppose, as they want me to look in the stone for them to dig money." There was also the question of his family's response. They looked to him to retrieve their shattered fortunes. With their farm gone

70. Lorenzo Saunders noted that Ingersoll's land "joined the Smith farm on the north" (Saunders, Interview, Nov. 12, 1884, 6).

71. Peter Ingersoll, Statement, Dec. 2, 1833, in Howe, *Mormonism Unvailed,* 233.

72. Ibid.

73. Isaac Hale, Statement, 578.

and few prospects in sight, Joseph represented their only hope. As Ingersoll summed up the situation later, the pressures on Joseph to continue glass looking forced him back into the same patterns.[74]

Joseph's money-digging company in the Palmyra/Manchester area may have been financially underwritten by Abraham Fish, a neighbor with whom the Smiths had previous dealings. In a January 1832 letter, a group of leading citizens from nearby Canandaigua, including friends of Martin Harris, reported having heard that Joseph's money-digging company in Manchester was "for a time ... supported by a Mr. Fish an illiterate man of some property who was duped by them." When he found that the diggers were likely "to consume what he had gathered by his industry," Fish "turned them off." At this point, according to Fish, Joseph then said he found a box "digging in the woods, containing some gold plates with Characters upon them which none but himself could decypher."[75]

Not long after Joseph and Emma returned to Manchester in the fall of 1827, Father Smith sent Joseph into town to attend to some business. He left early in the day; and when he had not returned by dark, his family became anxious. "We always had a peculiar anxiety about this child," reported Lucy, "for it seemed as though something was always occurring to place his life in jeopardy." If he were an hour late, his folks worried "of some evil befalling him." It was 9:00 p.m. that fateful night in early 1827 when Joseph finally walked into the house as "pale as ashes" and threw himself into a chair "seemingly much exhausted," said his mother. Joseph Sr., whose worry had turned to anger, queried Joseph as to why he was three hours late. At first, Joseph refused to answer. His father insisted. "Now, father, let him rest a moment," Mother Smith intervened, "don't trouble him now—you see he is home safe, and he is very tired, so pray wait a little."[76]

In a few moments, "after Joseph recovered himself," he told his father, "I have had the severest chastisement that I ever had in my life." His father bristled: "Well upon my word I would like to [know] who has been takeing you to task and what their pretext was. Its pretty well too, if you are to be detained till this time of night to take lectures for your bad practi[c]es." A smile crept across Joseph's face as he saw his father "so hasty and indignant." The chastisement was from the "angel of the Lord," young Joseph added, "I have been negligent ... the time has now come when the record should be

74. Ingersoll, Statement, 233.

75. Nathaniel W. Howell et al. to Ancil Beach, Jan. 1832, 1-2.

76. Anderson, *Lucy's Book,* 374.

brought forth … I must be up and doing that[,] I must set myself about the things which God has commanded me to do. … I know what course I am to pursue and all will be well."[77]

Perhaps Joseph's mind had been jogged that morning as he walked down Canandaigua Road past the drumlin he would later call Cumorah en route to Manchester Village. He told others that the angel had urged him to make another attempt to obtain the golden plates on the upcoming September 22, the autumn equinox. LDS historian David J. Whittaker notes that September 22, 1827, was "both the autumnal equinox and a new moon, an excellent time [in astrology] to commence new projects."[78] "Whether by command of the treasure-guardian … or by Joseph Smith's own choice," adds historian D. Michael Quinn, "every circumstance of his September 1827 visit conformed to astrological traditions and to an occult handbook on sale in his neighborhood."[79]

Joseph wanted to be prepared with a storage chest for the treasure. Accordingly, he asked neighbor Willard Chase, a cabinet maker, to make a strongbox. Penniless as usual, Joseph offered him "a share in the book" he anticipated writing in exchange for the work. But Chase declined, telling him he was too busy. He did offer to lock up the record once Smith acquired it, however, but Smith told him "he was commanded to keep it two years, without letting it come to the eye of any one but himself." The skeptical Chase offered to make him a chest for free if he would "convince me of [the book's] existence," but Joseph said "that would not do, as he must have a chest to lock the book in, as soon as he took it out of the ground."[80] Chase demurred, and Joseph looked elsewhere.

Joseph was not the only diviner to envision treasure in Cumorah. Luman Walters, his former occult mentor, had recently been in town. According to Brigham Young, "a week or ten days" before Smith said he recovered the record, a "fortune-teller" from western New York had looked for the plates.[81] Samuel Lawrence, another of Joseph's acquaintances, was also reportedly trying to preempt the young seer. "Now Joseph was some affraid of [Lawrence] that he mite be a trouble to him," Joseph Knight wrote of September 21,

77. Ibid., 375.

78. David J. Whittaker, "Almanacs in the New England Heritage of Mormonism," 94.

79. D. Michael Quinn, *Early Mormonism and the Magic World View*, 167.

80. Willard Chase, Affidavit, 78.

81. Brigham Young, July 19, 1857, JD 5:55. Young's likely source was Artemisia Beman Snow, daughter of Alva Beman, who was involved with this group of money diggers (Elizabeth W. Kane, *A Gentile's Account*, 71-72).

1827. "He therefore s[e]nt his father up to Sams as he Called him near night to see if there was any signs of his going away that night. He told his father to stay till near Dark and if he saw any signs of his going you tell him if I find him [at Cumorah] I will thrash the stumps with him. So the old man came a way and saw no thing like it."[82]

Josiah Stowell and Joseph Knight, Joseph's former employers, who shared an affinity for Joseph's proposals, had arrived at the Smith home on September 20, perhaps anticipating a look at the much-rumored golden plates. According to Martin Harris, Stowell's appearance at Manchester was not coincidental: "Mr. Stowel was at this time at old Mr. Smith's digging for money."[83] Willard Chase, either in his conversations with Joseph about the strongbox or from other sources, had learned that Joseph was required to "repair to the place where was deposited this manuscript, dressed in black clothes, and riding a black horse with a switch tail, and demand the book in a certain name. ... They accordingly fitted out Joseph with a suit of black clothes and borrowed a black horse."[84] According to Fayette Lapham, Joseph Sr. told him that Joseph Jr. had to "get a certain coverlid [coverlet?] ... and an old-fashioned suit of clothes, of the same color, and a napkin to put the treasure in."[85]

The emphasis on the color black was also consistent with occult instructions in "Concerning the Convocation of the Good Spirits." One later occult manual specified that the supplicant should not wear ordinary clothing, but rather "a [black] Robe of Mourning ... [before] familiar conversation with your Guardian Angel."[86] Reginald Scot's works and Ebenezer Sibly's *Occult Sciences* provided similar instructions.[87]

The early hours of September 22, 1827, were astrologically favorable for overcoming the enchantment of the previously envisioned golden plates. The new moon, in its second night, its least visible phase, was a fitting interval for communing with good spirits.[88] In addition, the *Book of Fate,* first published

82. Joseph Knight Sr., "Reminiscence."

83. Martin Harris, qtd. in Joel Tiffany, "MORMONISM—No. II," 165.

84. Willard Chase, Affidavit, 241.

85. As D. Michael Quinn notes, in the 1820s "an 'old-fashioned suite of clothes' was black, a style popularized in 1821 when U.S. president James Madison attended his inauguration 'dressed in a plain suit of black broadcloth with a single-breasted coat and waistcoat with flaps, in the old fashion'" *(Early Mormonism and the Magic World View,* 165-66).

86. Abraham ben Simeon of Worms, *The Book of the Sacred Magic of Abra-Melin the Mage,* 81-85. Joseph Smith mentioned a guardian angel at least twice *(History of the Church,* 2:263; 6:461).

87. Reginald Scot, *Discovery of Witchcraft,* 215, 218-20, 226; Ebenezer Sibly, *A New and Complete Illustration of the Occult Sciences,* 1,102, 1,104.

88. Francis Barrett, *The Magus,* Book 2:110.

in New York in 1817 and advertised in the May 12, 1824, issue of the *Wayne Sentinel*, Palmyra's local newspaper, further specified that "the second day [of the new moon] is very lucky for discovering things lost, or hidden treasure."[89]

Near midnight on September 21, Joseph, who had been unable to obtain a container, asked his mother if she had a chest with a lock and key. "I knew in an instant what he wanted it for," she later said, "and not having one, I was greatly alarmed, as I thought it might be a matter of considerable moment." When Joseph saw his mother's dismay, he told her: "Never mind, I can do very well for the present without it—be calm—all is right." At that moment, Emma walked through the room wearing her bonnet and riding dress. A few minutes later, the two left, taking Knight's black horse and his wagon without explicit permission.

The man in black and his new wife drove south on Stafford Road before turning east on Armington Road, then turned right at the intersection of Canandaigua Road. They continued southward past the Chase family farm, where Joseph had obtained his white seer stone. They rolled past Miner and Arrington Roads, then crossed Hathaway Brook before arriving at their destination. At this time of night, they likely saw no one else on the road. After tethering the horse beside the quiet road, Joseph walked up the west side of Cumorah to a spot just below the hill's crest, which peaks at 117 feet above ground level.[90] According to Martin Harris, Emma "kneeled down and prayed," while Joseph was atop the hill. Harris added that, after Joseph wrapped the plates in a covering, "he hid them in an old black oak tree top which was hollow."[91] Emma never saw the record—then or ever.

The Smiths did not return home until early morning. Lucy Smith had spent the night in supplication, praying for her son's success. At daybreak, about 5:40 a.m., she began to prepare breakfast with her "heart fluttering at every footfall for I now expected Joseph & Emma every moment and was in dread of a second disap[p]ointment in his obtaining the plates."[92] When the men and boys in the household sat down for breakfast, Father

89. *The Book of Fate,* 149.

90. The height was determined using a Global Positioning System; LaMar C. Berrett, *Sacred Places: New York and Pennsylvania,* 155.

91. Martin Harris, qtd. in Joel Tiffany, "MORMONISM—No. II," 165. Father Smith, in conferring a patriarchal blessing on his daughter-in-law, alluded to this event: "Thou shalt ever remember the great condescension of thy God in permitting thee to accompany my son when the angel delivered the record of the Nephites to his care" (Joseph Smith Sr., "Blessing on Emma Smith," 1:472).

92. Unless otherwise stated, this portion of my narrative is taken from Anderson, *Lucy's Book,* 376-79.

Smith asked for Joseph. Only Lucy knew his whereabouts, and she implied that Joseph was sleeping late and would eat later with his wife. Then Joseph Knight, strolling outside, noticed that his horse was missing. "Never mind the horse," said the protective mother. "Mr. Knight does not know all the nooks and corners in the pasture[.] I will call [W]illiam ... he will soon bring him." Within minutes, Knight discovered his wagon was also gone and naturally suspected theft. Once again Mother Smith smoothed things over.

Knight must have been astonished shortly thereafter to see Joseph and Emma drive up in the wagon. Joseph turned the animal out to pasture, then entered the house with Emma. Lucy saw his empty arms. Fearing that "all might be lost ag[ain] by some small failure in keeping the commandments," she left the room in anguish. Her boy, witnessing the anxiety, followed her. "Do not be uneasy all is right," Joseph said, "I have got the key."[93] He placed in her hands a bundle, wrapped in a silk handkerchief, which he instructed her not to remove. She ran her fingers along the shapes within while he told her that she was holding "2 sm<ooth> 3 cornered diamonds[94] set in glass and the glass was set in silver bows stones connected with each other in the same way that old fashioned spectacles are made." Here were the spectacles that Samuel Lawrence had suggested he envision in his stone a few years earlier. Joseph took the bundle from his mother, making no mention of the record from Cumorah.

After breakfast, Joseph beckoned Knight into a bedroom. "[H]e set his foot on the Bed," Knight wrote, "and leaned his head on his hand and says, 'Well I am Dissopinted.'" Knight offered condolences, but Joseph rejoined:

93. In Lucy's recollection, dictated in 1844-45 in Nauvoo, Illinois, she explained: "The thing which spoke of that Joseph termed a Key was indeed nothing more nor less than a [U]rim and Thummim by which the angel manifested those things to him that were shown him in vision by the which also he could at any time ascertain the approach of danger either to himself or the record and for this cause he kept these things constantly about his person" (Anderson, *Lucy's Book,* 389). Also in Nauvoo, Lucy permitted Jane Manning James, a black Mormon, to handle objects concealed in a bundle: "One morning I met Brother Joseph coming out of his mothers room," James later wrote,

> he said good morning and shook hands with me. I went in to his mothers room she said good morning bring me that bundle from my bureau and sit down here. I did as she tole me, she placed the bundle in my hands and said, handle this and after I had done it she said sit down. Do you remember that I told you about the Urim and Thummim when I told you about the [B]ook of Mormon, I answered yes mam. She then told me I had just handled it, you are not permitted to see it, but you have been permitted to handle it. You will live long after I am dead and gone and you can tell the Latter-day Saints, that you was permitted to handle the Urim and Thummim. (Jane Manning James, "Autobiography," 19.)

94. As Quinn has noted, *diamond* in some folklore circles was a euphemism for seer stone *(Early Mormonism and the Magic World View,* 170-71).

"I am grateley Dissopinted; it is ten times Better then I expected." Joseph "went on to tell the length and width and thickness of the plates." According to Knight, Smith said "they appear to be Gold" but seemed to "think more of the glasses or the urim and thummem[95] [than] he Did of the Plates." "I can see any thing" in them, Joseph said, "they are Marvelus. Now they are writ[t]en in Caracters and I want them translated."[96]

Joseph later told his mother that, when he lifted the plates, "the angel of the Lord stood by and said now you have got the record into your own hands and you are but a man therefore you will have to be watchful and faithful to your trust or you will be overpowered by wicked men for they will lay every plan and scheme that is possible to get them away from you and if you do not take heed continually they will suceed." The angel, who had been in charge of the record for nearly fourteen centuries, told Joseph that "I [Joseph] could keep them and no man had power <to take> them away but now I [the angel] give them up to you[,] beware and look well to your ways—<and you shall have power to retain them until the time for them to be translated>."[97]

Despite the angel's warning, Joseph and other family members told friends and neighbors that he had finally unearthed the enchanted treasure, but Joseph made it clear he was operating under new rules. According to Martin Harris: "Joseph said the angel told him he must quit the company of the money-diggers. That there were wicked men among them. He must have no more to do with them."[98] In short, no one was entitled to a share in the find. Harris

---

95. "Urim and Thummim" refers to priestly objects used by Aaron and his successors to determine God's will in matters affecting the Israelites. See Cornelis Van Dam, *The Urim and Thummim.*

Use of "Urim and Thummim" in regards to Joseph Smith's divination practices is problematic. Smith and his contemporaries prior to 1833 called his scrying medium "spectacles," the term inspired by Manchester seer Samuel Lawrence. Moreover, the Book of Mormon does not contain the words "Urim and Thummin." Ammon, a warrior-missionary-leader, speaks of an individual who "can translate the records: for he hath wherewith that he can look, and translate all records that are of ancient date; and it is a gift from God. And the things are called interpreters; and no man can look in them, except he be commanded, lest he would look for that he had not ought, and he should perish. And whosoever is commanded to look in them, the same is called seer" (1830 Book of Mormon, 172-73.) At a later point in the narrative, the Book of Mormon states that records in foreign languages are translated "by the means of those two stones which was fastened into the two rims of a bow ... and was handed down from generation to generation, for the purpose of interpreting languages" (216). These Nephite interpreters were not publicly equated with the Urim and Thummim until W. W. Phelps, an eccentric Mormon newspaperman, did so in 1833. The Book of Mormon "was translated by the gift and power of God," Phelps wrote, "by an unlearned man, through the aid of a pair of Interpreters, or spectacles—(known, perhaps in ancient days as Teraphim, or Urim and Thumim [sic])" (Phelps, "The Book of Mormon," 58).

96. Joseph Knight Sr., "Reminiscence," in Vogel, *Early Mormon Documents,* 4:15.

97. Anderson, *Lucy's Book,* 388.

98. Martin Harris, qtd. in Tiffany, "Mormonism—No. II," 165.

made this statement in 1859, but almost thirty years earlier in 1830, anti-Mormon newspaperman Abner Cole had sarcastically proposed another version of the angel's instructions: "thou art greater than all the 'money-digging rabble,' and art chosen to interpret the book, which Mormon has written."[99]

As word spread, people began to clamor for a look at Joseph's treasure. According to Joseph Knight, Joseph told everyone, including his family, that "he was Commanded not to let [any] one see those things." Many of the curious "oferd money and Property to see them," said Knight, "but, for keeping them from the Peopel they persecuted and abused [him]."[100] At first, the young seer mentioned only the golden plates and spectacles; later, he included a large metallic breast-plate,[101] the "gold hilt and chain" of the fabled "sword of Laban," and a "gold ball with two pointers"—the compass ball or director referred to in the Book of Mormon as the Liahona (1 Ne. 16:10, Alma 37:38-40).[102] It was a fabulous collection, and Joseph's former money-digging companions wanted their fair share. David Whitmer, who made a business trip to Palmyra in 1828, staying with Oliver Cowdery, and who became one of the three witnesses to the Book of Mormon a year later, recalled in 1881: "I had conversations with several young men who said that Joseph Smith had certainly golden plates, and that before he attained them he had promised to share with them, but had not done so, and they were very much incensed with him."[103]

---

99. Obediah Dogberry (pseud. Abner Cole), "Book of Pukei," *[Palmyra] Reflector,* July 7, 1830, 60.

100. Knight, "Reminiscence," in Vogel, *Early Mormon Documents,* 4:16.

101. Lucy Smith claimed that Joseph showed her this breast-plate "wrapped in a thin muslin handkerchief, so thin that I could see the glistening metal, and ascertain its proportions without any difficulty. It was concave on one side and convex on the other, and extended from the neck downwards, as far as the centre of the stomach of a man of extraordinary size. It had four straps of the same material, for the purpose of fastening it to the breast, two of which ran back to go over the shoulders, and the other two were designed to fasten to the hips. ... The whole plate was worth at least five hundred dollars" (Anderson, *Lucy's Book,* 390).

102. Fayette Lapham, "Interview with the Father of Joseph Smith," 306. See also David Whitmer, Interviewed by Orson Pratt and Joseph F. Smith, Sept. 7-8, 1878, Richmond, Missouri, in Lyndon W. Cook, *David Whitmer Interviews,* 40. Joseph's sister, Katharine Smith Salisbury, said that her brother "went frequently to the hill, and upon returning would tell us, 'I have seen the records, also the brass plates and the sword of Laban with the breast plate and interpreters'" (Katharine Smith Salisbury, "Dear Sisters," 260). She told essentially the same story elsewhere. After describing how her brother gained access to the secreted plates, she said he "beheld the records that were to be translated, and the Urim and Thummim, and the sword and the breast-plate of Laban, and the brass plates Lehi brought from Jerusalem" (Kyle R. Walker, "Katharine Smith Salisbury's Recollections of Joseph's Meetings with Moroni," 12).

103. David Whitmer, Statement, June 5, 1881, in Lyndon W. Cook, *David Whitmer Interviews,* 60.

Once Smith told his family he had the plates, the question of a strongbox became pressing. Although he said he had secreted them in the woods, they could not remain there indefinitely. He consulted his mother, who suggested he commission another cabinet maker who had recently made some furniture for the soon-to-be married Sophronia. Tell him "we would pay him for making a chest as we did for the other things," meaning "half money and half produce."[104] Joseph agreed but worried about coming up with the cash, "for there was not a shilling in the house." The following day, a Mr. Warner came to him from nearby Macedon to hire him to dig a well for the "Widow Wells." Lucy considered this offer a "provision of Providence to enable us to pay the money we were owing the cabinet maker."

Joseph promptly left, no doubt equally relieved for the job and for the fact that it postponed, if only temporarily, further activity involving the plates. In his absence, however, Joseph Sr. learned that a dozen or so men, including Willard Chase, Lumen Walters, and Sam Lawrence, had "clubbed together" to "divine the place where the record was deposited by magic art," remembered Lucy. The Smiths' apprehension was these others seers might succeed, and then the plates would be like the infant "Moses who was hid in the bul[l]rushes." The morning after Father Smith heard of the money-diggers' plans, he "went over a hill that <lay> east of <us> to see what he could discover among the neighbors there" on a made-up errand. At Samuel Lawrence's place, he discovered "conjuror Willard [C]hase and the company all together" in the yard. Pretending to read a paper, he sat in a chair with the door ajar, listening carefully to the men. Determining that the group was "devising many plans and schemes to find Joe Smith[']s gold bible[,] as they termed it," Father Smith went home, remembered daughter Katharine, and asked Emma, who was at work on her weaving, "if she knew aught of the record whether Joseph had taken them out or where they were."[105] She said no, she knew nothing of the plates, but "<if> Joseph was to have the record he would <get it>." Yes, Father Smith replied, "but remmember [sic] that for a small thing Esau lost his blessing and birthright[—]it may be so with Joseph."

Emma volunteered to ride to Macedon to inform Joseph of the problem. The Smiths were too poor to own a horse, but Father Smith told her

---

104. My narrative at this point, unless otherwise stated, is based on Anderson, *Lucy's Book,* 380-85.

105. Katharine Salisbury also noted: "My father ... heard that they had got a conjurer, who they said would come and find the plates" (Walker, "Katharine Smith Salisbury's Recollections of Joseph's Meetings with Moroni," 17).

there was a stray on the premises. Young William caught the animal, put a green withe (a fastening of plaited or twisted twigs) about its neck to signify it was a stray, and the pregnant Emma rode hastily away. Arriving at the Wells home, she told Joseph what had transpired. He pulled his seer stone from a pocket, gazed into its depths, and scryed that "the record was perfectly safe for the present." But borrowing another horse from the widow, he returned home with Emma, promising to finish his work later. (Lucy does not record whether he kept this promise.) As Joseph and Emma neared the Smith home, they saw Father Smith "pacing back and forth in great anxiety of mind." Joseph Jr. reassured his father that there was "no danger[,] all is perfectly safe[,] there is no cause of alarm." Joseph then asked Hyrum for a chest "that had a good lock and Key," and set out on foot to retrieve the golden plates concealed in the woods three miles away near Cumorah.

According to his story, related by Lucy, Joseph arrived at the hollow tree, "took the plates from their place and wrapping them in his linen frock put them under his arm and started for the house." After walking a short distance north on Canandaigua Road, he deemed it safer to cut across lots through timber. He later told his mother that as he was jumping over a large windfall, "a man spran[g] up and gave him a heavy blow with a gun." Joseph "leveled [his assailant] to the ground" and ran at "the top of his speed" about another half mile where he claimed he was once again assaulted. Again, he succeeded in bringing "this one down also," and continued running. A third time, a man popped up before he got home and struck Joseph with his gun. During this final scuffle, Joseph dislocated his thumb, then reached home. His mother said he "arrived altogether speechless from fright and exhaustion." Sister Katharine added that he "threw himself on the bed and fainted, and when he came to he told us the circumstances; he had his thumb put out of place and his arm was very lame."[106] Soon reviving thanks to his mother and sister, Joseph asked Lucy to send eleven-year-old Don Carlos to find his father and Joseph Knight, who was still staying with the Smiths, to see if they could locate the assailants in the woods. Carlos then ran a second errand to Hyrum's place, who brought his lockable toolbox for the plates. Joseph Sr. and Joseph Knight returned without seeing anyone in the area. By this time, the plates were in a locked box.

106. Ibid., 17. Katharine's grandson, Herbert Salisbury, remembered his grandmother relating, "When [Joseph] came in the house ... he was completely out of breath. [Katharine] took the plates from him and laid them on the table temporarily, and helped revive him until he got breathing properly, and also examined his hand, and treated it for the bruises on his knuckles" (ibid).

The Smiths were naturally interested to see the plates. In fact, when Father Smith returned with Knight, Joseph announced: "Father I have got the Plates." The enthused father asked, "Joseph, can we not see them?" No, the young seer responded, "I was disobedient the first time, but I intend to be faithful this time; for I was forbidden to show them until they are translated, but you can feel them."[107] Joseph unlocked the box and handed over the wrapped bundle. Joseph's younger brother, William, during an 1884 interview, recalled: "We handled them and could tell what they were. They were not quite as large as this Bible. Could tell whether they were round or square. Could raise the leaves this way (raising a few leaves of the Bible before him). One could easily tell that they were not a stone, hewn out to deceive, or even a block of wood. Being a mixture of gold and copper, they were much heavier than stone, and very much heavier than wood."[108] Some skeptics have since speculated that Joseph had earlier fashioned a facsimile from scrap sheet metal or tin, which was available in Palmyra from North & Pierson's "Tin-Ware and Stove Pipe Factory."[109]

Convinced that Joseph had found a treasure, his former money-digging associates wanted to put their hands on the plates. Joseph later wrote that "I soon found out the reason why I had received such strict charges to keep them safe. … For no sooner was it known that I had them, than the most strenuous exertions were used to get them from me. Every stratagem that could be invented was resorted to for the purpose. The persecution became more bitter and severe than before, and multitudes were on the alert continually to get them from me if possible." Katharine Smith Salisbury corroborated: "[O]ur house was searched all around; and our field and our wheat stacks were searched. The mob was around our house nearly every night."[110]

One day Joseph rushed into the house and asked if a company of men

---

107. William Smith, "The Old Soldier's Testimony," 644.

108. Ibid., 643. When asked on this same occasion why he or other family members had not uncovered the plates to test Joseph's veracity, William responded, "The Lord knew he could trust Joseph and as for the rest of the family we had no desire to transgress the commandment of the Lord but on the other hand was exceeding anxious to do al<l> we were commanded to do" (643). Elsewhere, when interviewer Edmund C. Briggs asked William, "Didn't you want to remove the cloth and see the bare plates?" He replied, "No … for father had just asked if he might not be permitted to do so, and Joseph, putting his hand on them said, 'No, I am instructed not to show them to any one. If I do, I will transgress and lose them again'" ("W[illia]m B. Smith's Last Statement," 6).

109. See the firm's advertisement in the *Wayne Sentinel,* Apr. 7, 1824. One of Joseph Smith's self-claimed protégés, James J. Strang, also created a collection of metal plates, which he "translated," from scrap metal. See Chauncey Loomis, "Experience on Beaver Island with James J. Strang," 718.

110. Katharine Smith Salisbury, "An Angel Told Him," 1.

had been there. When his parents said no, he said that a mob would soon arrive to search for the record and that it must be moved. Then another seer and rodsman, Alva Beaman, "a man in whom we reposed much confidence," in Mother Smith's terms, came from the nearby village of Livonia.[111] When Joseph told him of his fears that his former money-digging associates were trying to steal the plates from him, the men decided to lift the hearthstone, bury the purported Nephite artifacts which by Joseph's account included the golden plates, enclosed in a box, the large metallic breast-plate, the "sword of Laban," and the Nephite director or Liahona. The "hearth was scarcely laid down," wrote Mother Smith, "when a large company of men came rushing up to the house armed with guns." Joseph reportedly threw open the door; and exhibiting the same Yankee pluck that had saved Grandfather Solomon Mack's life during the French and Indian War,[112] "hallooed [i.e., exclaimed] as if he had a legion at hand giving the word of command with great importance and in a tone like stentor,"[113] while the other males simultaneously raised a ruckus. The mob, reported a gleeful Lucy, "thought it best to give leg bail while they were able and fled <and were> pursued by our little spartan band away into the woods and dispersed themselves to their several homes."

Mother Smith reported that, after this incident, Joseph crossed the road and secreted the golden plates, wrapped in cloth, in a pile of flax, stored in the loft of the family's cooper shop. He then nailed shut the box the plates had been stored in, "tore up the floor[,] and put the box under it." Within days, the money-diggers were back, this time accompanied by seer Sally Chase, who had helped to stimulate Joseph's interest in scrying. Sally by looking in her "green glass," remembered Lucy, had found out the place where Joseph had hidden the box, although she overlooked the loft. The money-diggers "lay siege to the cooper shop," tore up the floor, smashed Joseph's box, but found nothing. Still the group did not lose faith in Sally. Lucy said "they still went from place to place by her suggestion determined to get possession of the object of their research."

Mary Salisbury Hancock, Katharine Smith's granddaughter, related

111. Joseph Knight, in contrast, aligned Alva Beaman—the description "a grate Rodsman" is Knight's—with the Smith family's money-digging persecutors. Knight related that Samuel Lawrence and Beaman came to visit with Joseph in the west room of the home and "Proposed to go shares with him and tried every way to Bargain with him But Could not." While they were wrangling, Beaman took out his "Rods and [held] them up and they pointed Dow[n] to the harth whare they ware hid. [T]here, says Beeman, it is under that harth. So they had to garde the house until some time in November" (Knight, "Reminiscence," in Vogel, *Early Mormon Documents,* 4:16).

112. For the full episode, see *A Narraitve [sic] of the Life of Solomon Mack,* 6.

113. Stentor was a Greek herald, known during the Trojan War for his resounding voice.

another instance when Joseph was chased by a mob. She recounted: "Hearing an unusual commotion outside Catherine flew to the door and threw it open just as Joseph came rushing up, panting for breath. He thrust a bundle into her arms, and in a gasping voice whispered hoarsely, 'Take these quickly and hide them,' then he disappeared into the darkness. Catherine closed the door, dashed into the bedroom she shared with Sophronia, and thrust them into the bed. Sophronia quickly climbed under the bedclothes, feigning sleep, while Katherine joined her. The mob, failing to find Joseph outside, returned to the house to search, but they did not disturb the girls since they appeared to be sleeping."[114]

One wonders why law enforcement officials were apparently never asked to investigate the incursions. The trespassing of an armed mob onto private property, the assault of a young man walking through woods, the ransacking of a family's home and cooper shop, were all criminal offenses. Yet local authorities evidently never intervened. Moreover, the Smith men, all six-foot or taller, as folklore has it, were reportedly among the toughest fellows in the area, fully capable of collectively thrashing their gang of tormentors. In addition, Joseph had apparently taken the treasure trove from the Robinson family's private property. It seems reasonable that they could have enforced a demand that Joseph hand the items over. But evidently no such summons was ever made, and none of the Robinsons are known to be associated with Smith's persecutors. The harassment, which would soon drive Joseph and Emma back to the Hale homestead in Harmony, can be traced to a handful of men, almost certainly fewer than a dozen. They were not cutthroats intent on mayhem, but a frustrated lot of inveterate get-rich-quick dreamers. As Martin Harris recalled: "[T]hey had as much right to the plates as Joseph had, as they were in company together. They claimed that Joseph had been traitor, and had appropriated to himself that which belonged to them."[115]

114. Mary Salisbury Hancock, "The Three Sisters of the Prophet Joseph Smith," Jan. 11, 1954, 36.

115. Martin Harris, qtd. in Tiffany, "Mormonism—No. II," 167.

12 | MARTIN HARRIS, MONEY MAN

The erratic enthusiasm Martin Harris brought to Joseph's tale of the golden plates was the fitful wind which fanned the smoldering spark of Mormonism into flame; and the money that was forthcoming from him over the next two and a half years was the tinder on which the fire fed until its hungry growth crowned in the inflammable popular will for a new revelation.

—Dale Morgan, in John Phillip Walker, *Dale Morgan on Early Mormonism,* 272

One of the hallmarks of Joseph's career as a religious innovator was his ability to sustain himself and his extended family by appealing to the sympathies of others. His Yankee ingenuity, charisma, and subtlety served him well in attracting benefactors willing to underwrite what he convinced them—and what they believed—was God's will. Like other creative individuals, Joseph availed himself of a type of patronage. This favoritism was not unlike that prevailing in and around Florence, Italy, during the Renaissance when men of various talents were supported by a deeply rooted system of patronage. It allowed gifted individuals to create while sustained by wealthier patrons. Galileo's lifelong career as a mathematician, scientist, and inventor was supported by both the Marchese del Monte and the Grand Duke of Tuscany, Cosimo II de Medici. Michaelangelo had his Pope, Julius II. Joseph Smith first had Josiah Stowell, then Joseph Knight, Martin Harris, Peter Whitmer, Newel K. Whitney, and ultimately, after 1830, contributions from the collective purses of members of his newly organized Church of Christ.

Martin Harris, like others with Quaker leanings in the Palmyra area, possessed good business sense, though later actions made many question his religious sensibilities. By the time his name became intertwined with Joseph Smith's, Harris was recognized as one of the more prosperous farmers and managers in Wayne County. Between 1813 and 1827, he accumulated 320 acres of beautifully situated, rich-loam farmland, much of it part of his father

Nathan's original estate, some of which Martin inherited, and paid more than $1,600 for the rest.[1] Well-to-do Martin also maintained a weaving establishment in an outbuilding on his farmstead where he and employees manufactured homespun fabric. He was frequently honored at local fairs for his cotton and woollen coverlets, bleached linen, worsted cloth, flannel, and bed ticking.[2] "None in the neighborhood were more promising in their future prospects," concluded Stephen Harding, who grew up near the Harris family and later became a governor of Utah Territory.[3] Lorenzo Saunders, a Manchester farmer, agreed. Harris "stood as well as anybody in ... town," he recalled, and with proper management of his assets could have become the area's richest citizen.[4] Harris's wife, Lucy (nicknamed Dolly), a spirited first cousin whom he had married when he was twenty-four and she not yet sixteen,[5] estimated their total wealth in the late 1820s as $10,000.[6] In 1827, when Martin was forty-six, he announced that he was in a position to enter semi-retirement. "My hands are altogether untied," he asserted, as he contemplated hiring a farm manager so he could travel for a year or two: "I can come and go and do as I please."[7]

In contrast, Joseph Smith Sr., twelve years older than Martin, was never financially successful nor well respected within his community. From 1830 until his 1840 death, Father Smith became a de facto ward of his son's church, pronouncing patriarchal blessings for what often amounted to pocket change. Due to his father's financial distress, young Joseph grew up dirt poor. The scramble-for-your-daily-bread feeling was never far from him. Harris frequently employed the Smiths as seasonal laborers on his large farmstead. Twenty-three years older than young Smith, the industrious Martin often hoed corn side-by-side with the adolescent, paying him fifty cents per day. During breaks in their field work, the two were sometimes said to tangle periodically in lively wrestling matches.[8] In the fall of 1824, Joseph Sr. and

1. Ronald W. Walker, "Martin Harris," 32; and Madge Harris Tuckett and Belle Harris Wilson, *The Martin Harris Story,* 10.

2. Walker, "Martin Harris," 32.

3. Qtd. in Thomas Gregg, *The Prophet of Palmyra,* 37.

4. Lorenzo Saunders, Interview, Sept. 17, 1884.

5. Palmyra historian James H. Reeves called Martin and Lucy's union "contrary to laws and customs" (James H. Reeves, *Palmyra Courier,* May 24, 1872, in Betty Troskansky, comp. *Writings of James Reeves, Palmyra's First Historian,* 148).

6. Lucy Harris, Affidavit, Nov. 29, 1833, in Eber D. Howe, *Mormonism Unvailed,* 254. Lucy, the daughter of Martin's paternal uncle, Rufus Harris, was nine years younger than Martin. Today, $10,000 would probably have a value approaching $200,000 or more.

7. Lavina Fielding Anderson, *Lucy's Book,* 397.

8. Martin Harris was born on May 18, 1783, in East Town, New York, the second of the

Hyrum walled up a basement and dug and curbed a well and cistern for Harris. During the course of their work, Father Smith confided to his employer the angelic manifestations young Joseph was experiencing and the golden record whose resting place he had seen in vision near their place in Manchester township. Like Josiah Stowell and the Smiths, Harris hungered after the marvelous. Palmyra newspaperman Pomeroy Tucker wrote that "his betrayal of vague superstitions, with a belief in 'special providences,' and in the terrest[r]ial visits of angels, ghosts, &c., brought upon him the imputation of being 'crazy'" on religious matters.[9] Harris was interested in young Joseph's exploits and told Father Smith to keep him posted on the young man's life. Father Smith did. Within three years, Harris became the first person outside the Smith family to accept Joseph's assertions that he was not only a seer of marvelous hidden things, but an emerging prophet of God as well.

Martin first heard rumors from his brother Preserved Harris in Palmyra that young Joseph had discovered golden plates or a "gold bible." Martin initially dismissed the report, thinking that the boy and his money-digging sidekicks had dug up an "old brass kettle, or something of the kind" from one of the many native Indian mounds in the area.[10] When Martin went into the village, however, he was surprised at the level of talk about the young farmhand. When someone asked what he thought of the stories, the Bible-thumping farmer replied: "The Scripture says, He that answereth a matter before he heareth it, it is foolishness unto him. I do not wish to make myself a fool. I don't know anything about it."[11] But when he inquired for further details, he found that the information had been coaxed out of an intoxicated Joseph Smith Sr. and was probably accurate. He decided to visit the Smiths as soon as possible.

Before Martin could travel to Manchester, however, Lucy Smith came on foot to visit him at young Joseph's request. The Smiths had not a penny in their pockets, yet young Joseph wanted to publish a book, a "translation" of the golden plates. Joseph, who would periodically use older women as messengers and advocates later in his life, asked his mother to convince Harris, a potential investor, that the plates were real and to solicit his assistance. Lucy was reluctant because Harris's "wife was a peculiar sort of a woman, one that

Harrises' eight children. For a review of Joseph's connections with Harris, see Stanley B. Kimball, "The Anthon Transcript," 325-52.

9. Pomeroy Tucker, "The Mormon Imposture," 2.

10. Qtd. in Joel Tiffany, "Mormonism—No. II," *Tiffany's Monthly,* 167.

11. Ibid. He is paraphrasing Proverbs 18:13.

was habitually of a very jealous temperament."[12] Dolly Harris, in addition to being reportedly jealous of her wealthy, older husband, was also hearing impaired, a condition that may have contributed to her irritability, frequent misunderstandings, and ill-conceived suspicions that people were talking about her behind her back. To placate his sometimes testy wife, Martin had allowed her a "private purse" to spend as she wished and, in 1825, arranged for her to own eighty acres in her name.[13]

Joseph and his mother mutually agreed she should visit Dolly first, to disarm her suspicions. When Lucy arrived at the Harris home, she explained Joseph's recovery of the golden plates "as far as wisdom dictated and necessity demanded." To Lucy's surprise, Dolly interrupted the conversation to offer a "substantial amount of money" toward the venture. She knew that Joseph would "want money and she could spare $200 as well as not." Dolly's widowed sister, Polly Harris Cobb, who was present, also wanted to invest $75. But Lucy Smith, according to her account, advised them that Joseph would handle his own business affairs. For the moment, she wanted only to talk further with Martin.

Harris, busy laying the stones of a new hearth, and not wanting his mortar to set up, told Lucy he would visit Joseph in a day or two. "I am coming to see him too," announced Dolly Harris. "I will be there [T]uesday afternoon and stop over night." As good as her word, she arrived punctually, accompanied by her teenage daughter, also named Lucy, and began to interrogate young Joseph about the golden plates, insisting on seeing them immediately. She offered, then and there, to help Smith publish his book as soon as she had eyewitness proof that the golden plates existed. Joseph replied that he was not permitted to show the plates to any one "except those whom the Lord will appoint to testify of them." Then, in what may have been a breach of politesse, he continued, "I always prefer dealing with men rather than their wives." Dolly, "who piqued herself upon her superiority to her husband," according to Lucy Smith, redoubled her insistence: "[W]ell now Joseph ... are you not telling me a lie[?] Can you look full in my eye and

12. My narration at this point, unless otherwise noted, is based on Anderson, *Lucy's Book,* 394-99. Lorenzo Saunders, during an 1884 interview, said of Lucy Harris: "Her face was on top of her head [i.e., haughty] and her combativeness was large and her cautiousness was not large enough to control them. She had an irritable temper and was a hard piece to live with. Martin used to whale [i.e., "hit, thrash, or trounce"] her" (Saunders, Interview, Sept. 17, 1884; Jonathon Green, *Green's Dictionary of Slang,* s.v. "whale v[erb].").

13. Ontario and Wayne County, New York Deeds, Nov. 29, 1825. The transaction was initiated by Martin first selling the acreage to his cousin, Peter Harris, who then transferred the land to his sister Lucy.

say before God that you have in reality found that record as you pretend[?]" Giving as good as he got, Joseph answered: "[W]hy yes Mrs. Harris[,] I would as soon look into your face and say so as not if you would be at all gratified by it."

Harris, a Quakeress attuned to the personal manifestations so valued in that faith, then replied, "Joseph, I will tell you what I will do, if I can get a witness that you speak the truth, I will believe all you say about the matter, and I shall want to do something about the translation—I mean to help you any way." That night, as Dolly slumbered in the Smith home, according to Lucy, she dreamed a remarkable dream, which Lucy interpreted as a divine rebuke. A personage appeared and admonished that she had done "that which was not right in the sight of God." Her sin was to dispute "the servant of the Lord." Now, said the messenger, "behold here are the plates[,] look upon them and believe[.]" Dolly, Lucy Smith elaborated, then described "the record minutely." She then offered Joseph $28, which he took, said his mother, "in order to get rid of her importunities,"[14] after allowing them to heft the wooden storage container.

After Dolly and her daughter returned home, Martin asked about their visit. "My daughter said [the plates] were about as much as she could lift," he recalled later. "They were now in the glass-box, and my wife said they were very heavy. They both lifted them."[15] Martin was intrigued by his wife's and daughter's descriptions but waited a few days before venturing to Manchester himself. Then, telling Dolly that he was visiting Palmyra on business, he set out for the Smith home. Since young Joseph was working for neighbor Peter Ingersoll, Harris cross-examined other family members to make sure their stories about the golden record concurred. All accounts agreed.

When Joseph returned home, Martin pressed him for more details. Although Harris had previously heard rumors of golden plates, he had assumed a money-digging context. But Joseph now told him a different story, a tale steeped in religious lore. An angel, young Smith reported, had ordered him to have nothing more to do with the money diggers. Additionally, the angel advised that he must observe high standards of moral rectitude: He "must not lie, nor swear, nor steal." The celestial visitor told Joseph to "look

14. This money had special significance to Lucy Harris. Because Lucy's mother bequeathed it to her just before her death on August 15, 1824, Lucy wanted the money used in a noteworthy manner. W. H. Homer Jr. to Cornelius Vander Does, Dec. 18, 1959, 4.

15. Unless otherwise noted, my narrative in this section is based on Martin Harris's interview with Joel Tiffany, "Mormonism—No. II," *Tiffany's Monthly*, 168-69.

in the spectacles, and he would show him the man that would assist him" in his marvelous work. "He did so," Harris continued, and "saw myself, Martin Harris, standing before him." Apparently not yet convinced, Harris advised Joseph to be "very careful about these things." Joseph replied, "I saw you standing before me as plainly as I do now." Harris answered, "Well, if it is the work of the devil I will have nothing to do with it; but if it is the Lord's, you can have all the money necessary to bring it before the world." Joseph testified to his future patron that "the angel told him that the plates must be translated, printed and sent before the world."

Then Harris, relying on his Quaker values, said: "Joseph, you know my doctrine, that cursed is every one that putteth his trust in man, and maketh flesh his arm; and we know that the devil is to have great power in the latter days to deceive if possible the very elect;[16] and I don't know that you are one of the elect. Now you must not blame me for not taking your word. If the Lord will show me that it is his work, you can have all the money you want." Returning home, Harris knelt in prayer, asking for God's witness: "I covenanted that if it was his work and he would show me so, I would put forth my best ability to bring it before the world. He then showed me that it was his work, and that it was designed to bring in the fullness of his gospel to the gentiles to fulfill his word, that the first shall be last and the last first. He showed this to me by the still small voice spoken in the soul. Then I was satisfied that it was the Lord's work, and I was under a covenant to bring it forth."[17]

Although Harris may have concluded that Smith's "Gold Bible business," as skeptics in the area sometimes dismissed it, was a God-inspired venture, he, like Joseph, also saw its potential financial benefits. Martin had the village silversmith give him an estimate of the value of the golden plates, taking as a basis Joseph's account of their dimensions.[18] He also no doubt listened intently to Lucy Smith's optimistic appraisals of the book's commercial potential "as it was something entirely new." Furthermore, Lucy Smith happily planned, "[t]he plates were to be publicly exhibited, admittance 25 cents."[19]

Despite investing his time and money, Harris, like everyone else, was not allowed to see the plates, the spectacles, or any of the other artifacts Joseph

16. This phrase is a approximation of Jeremiah 17:5 and Matthew 24:24.

17. Qtd. in Tiffany, "Mormonism—No. II," 169.

18. Orsamus Turner, *History of the Pioneer Settlement of Phelps and Gorham's Purchase,* 215.

19. Qtd. by Abigail Harris, Statement, Nov. 28, 1833, 253. Later, while living in Kirtland, Ohio, and Nauvoo, Illinois, Mother Smith exhibited Church-owned Egyptian mummies and other artifacts for a fee.

said he possessed. "[I]t would arouse the most terrible divine displeasure," Smith told Harris, "if he should attempt to draw near" the ancient record, "or look at Smith while engaged in the work of decyphering the mysterious characters."[20] Elsewhere Martin told an interviewer: "I was told by Joseph Smith that God would strike [me] dead if [I] attempted to look at them, and I believed it."[21]

But Smith's God was not opposed to letting Harris glimpse Joseph's prowess with a seer stone, and Joseph gave him a compelling demonstration. Smith had borrowed Willard Chase's stone again.[22] Interviewed in 1859, Harris testified that "to my certain knowledge" the young seer "could see many things." Not only had Smith "discover[ed]" the golden plates with this stone, but he also saw many other marvelous events.

Smith began by offering "to bind it [the seer stone] on his eyes, and run a race with me in the woods," Martin said, suggesting that Joseph would be able to avoid trees and other obstacles. A few days later, while visiting the Smith farm, Harris was sitting on a fence rail, visiting with young Joseph and Northrop Sweet, and picking his teeth with a pin.[23] "The pin caught in my teeth, and dropped from my fingers into shavings and straw," Harris later related. The three men hopped down and began to search for the prized object in the debris. Their hunt was fruitless. Harris, who had yet to see the seer stone, asked Joseph to retrieve the pin through its use. Joseph removed the stone from his pocket, dropped it in his upturned "old white hat"—a stovepipe—then "placed his face in his hat." Harris watched him closely. Smith "reached out his hand beyond me on the right, and moved a little stick, and there I saw the pin, which he picked up and gave to me. I know he did not look out of the hat until after he had picked up the pin."[24] Impressed, Harris became a believer.

---

20. "John A. Clark to Dear Brethren," 94. Two acquaintances of Joseph Smith—William T. Hussey and Azel Vandrover—later claimed that they went to Smith's house to inspect the "golden book," offering to "take upon themselves the risk of the death-penalty denounced." But Joseph would only permit them to view the plates covered by "a piece of thick canvas." Not satisfied, Hussey exclaimed, "Egad! I'll see the cri[t]ter, live or die!" and removed the cover to reveal a "large tile-brick." Joseph then reportedly admitted that "his friends had been sold by a trick of his," and the three men laughed off the incident (Pomeroy Tucker, *Origin, Rise, and Progress of Mormonism,* 31).

21. Anthony Metcalf, *Ten Years before the Mast,* 71. Metcalf interviewed Harris during the winter of 1873-74 when Harris was living in Smithfield, Utah.

22. Willard Chase, Affidavit.

23. Sweet, three years younger than Joseph, married Elathan Harris, the daughter of Martin's brother Emer. For other biographical details, see Dan Vogel, *Early Mormon Documents,* 2:303.

24. Qtd. in Tiffany, "Mormonism—No. II," 163.

Despite his newfound convictions of Joseph's abilities, Harris approached the Gold Bible business with some prudence for several months. Meanwhile, agitation in the Palmyra/Manchester area continued to grow primarily because Joseph would not show the golden plates to anyone even when money was offered. Emma, homesick and pregnant, "wanted to go to her Father[']s," recalled Joseph Knight.[25] In late fall, Smith wrote to his thirty-two-year-old brother-in-law, Alva Hale, that he and Emma were ready to relocate in Harmony. In December, Alva arrived from Pennsylvania with his wagon and team. But Joseph was still penniless. He could neither pay Hale's expenses nor settle his own local debts. "While preparing to start," Joseph later remembered, "being very poor, and the persecution so heavy upon us that there was no probability that we would ever be otherwise … we found a friend in a gentleman by the name of Martin Harris."[26]

There are several accounts of how Smith obtained the needed funds from Harris. Peter Ingersoll related that Joseph first asked him for a loan, promising that Alva would be his security. Ingersoll hesitated, then agreed to lend a sum, but only as a last resort. Joseph walked into town and, according to Ingersoll, "met that dam[n] fool Martin Harris, and told him that I had a command to ask the first honest man I met with, for fifty dollars in money, and he would let me have it. I saw at once … that it took his notion, for he promptly gave me the fifty."[27] Willard Chase's account of how Joseph obtained the fifty dollars, a sum then equal to more than two months of an average man's income, is similar to Ingersoll's. "I have a commandment from God to ask the first man I meet in the street to give me fifty dollars," Smith reportedly said, "to assist me in doing the work of the Lord by translating the Golden Bible."[28] Reverend Jesse Townsend, a former Palmyra Presbyterian minister, wrote to a friend that Smith told Harris that the Lord had advanced him a "revelation" to "call on him for fifty dollars to enable him to go to Pennsylvania and translate the contents of the plates." For good measure, Smith assured Harris that "the Lord had revealed to him that they (Smith and Harris) were the only honest men in the world. This at once took with the dupe, who had specially prided himself on his honesty; and the wily deceiver understood this fact; he knew this was the assailable point in his

25. "Joseph Knight, Sr., Reminiscence."
26. *History of the Church,* 1:19.
27. Peter Ingersoll, Affidavit, Dec. 2, 1833, 233.
28. Willard Chase, Affidavit.

victim's visionary mind. The delicious bait was greedily swallowed; and the fifty dollars was soon put into the hands of Smith."[29]

According to Harris's own account, Joseph and Alva met him on the street. Joseph first introduced Alva, then told Martin that, although the plates were in his possession, he could not translate them "because wicked men haunt me, day and night. And I can not begin the translation, and it hurts. Mr. Harris, I am a poor boy; my parents and family are poor, but we are honest. I have a letter in my possession, recently received from my father-in-law, stating that if I will come to his house, with my wife, Emma, he will let me have a room where I will be secluded—but I am poor, and have not the money to go there with." Harris reached into his pocket, pulled out some money, and said, "Take that ... I am not giving it to you, I am giving it to the Lord, for His Servant to do his bidding."[30] Lucy Smith tells a similar story: Harris walked into a public house where Smith and Hale were conducting business. Pulling a pouch of silver from his pocket, Harris handed it to Joseph and said, "[H]ere Mr. Smith is $50[.] I give it to you to do the Lord[']s work." Then he appended himself, saying, "No ... I give it to the Lord for his own work."[31]

This gift, the first of thousands of dollars Harris would contribute to Smith, was evidently in addition to paying off Joseph's debts. "I paid for him," Harris later recalled, "and furnished him money for his journey." Harris also ordered a black suit for Joseph to be made according to the best pattern available, remarking to Sexton and Butterfield clerk David S. Aldrich that Joseph should "appear comely before men."[32]

---

29. Jesse Townsend to Phineas Stiles, Dec. 24, 1833, 288. Harris's honesty was legendary in his hometown. A group of Palmyra residents in a December 4, 1833, statement, while criticizing Martin on "moral and religious subjects," said "in matters of business his word was considered good" (Howe, *Mormonism Unvailed,* 261). William H. Kelley collected comments on Harris, which he quoted in "The Hill Cumorah, and the Book of Mormon," 166: (1) John H. Gilbert, Palmyra newspaperman, said that Martin "was a very honest farmer, but very superstitious"; (2) Hiram Jackway, a neighbor of the Smith family, said that "Harris was an industrious, honest man"; and (3) Dr. John Stafford, who also lived near the Smiths, described Harris as an "honorable farmer." Another Smith family neighbor, Lorenzo Saunders, called Harris a "squaretoed [i.e., formal] up=right man" (Lorenzo Saunders, Interview, Sept. 20, 1884, 5). Orsamus Turner described Harris as "an honest worthy citizen; but especially given to religious enthusiasm, new creeds, the more extravagant the better; a monomanic" (Turner, *History of the Pioneer Settlement of Phelps and Gorham's Purchase,* 214), while Pomeroy Tucker wrote that Harris "was universally esteemed as an honest man" (Tucker, "The Mormon Imposture," 2).

30. William Pilkington, "Address Delivered in the Lewisville Ward," Apr. 23, 1939, 2. Pilkington heard this story from Harris when he (Pilkington) was thirteen years old. His memory and subsequent recall sixty-three years later, however, may have been shaped by Lucy Mack Smith's autobiography, which had been in print since 1853.

31. Anderson, *Lucy's Book,* 400-401.

32. Tucker, *Origin, Rise, and Progress of Mormonism,* 55. Comely: "handsome; graceful.

Given Alva Hale's presence, Harris's chattiness, the elaborate preparations including the new suit, and the public transfer of funds, Joseph's former money-digging associates—said by Lucy Smith to number nearly fifty—saw Joseph and their rightful treasure slipping out of their hands. Fortified by liquor, they approached Alexander McIntire, the Smiths' family physician and high-ranking Freemason, and asked him to lead them in a raid to "follow Joe Smith" and "take his Gold Bible away from him." McIntire admonished the miscreants that "they must be a pack of devilish fools" and advised them to go home and mind their own business.[33]

By now, the plates were reportedly being stored in a wooden Ontario glass box.[34] To prepare the box for transportation, it was placed in a large cask or barrel. The Smiths then filled it with concealing beans, nailed it shut, and hoisted it aboard Alva's wagon along with whatever personal possessions Joseph and Emma possessed and the items she had retrieved from her Harmony home the previous summer. Harris advised the two men to protect themselves with clubs, which they did. They slipped out of town under cover of darkness and made an uneventful trip to Harmony, arriving in late December 1827.

Trouble with Isaac Hale arose shortly after Joseph and Emma settled into an attic bedroom in their host's home. Alva apparently told him that Joseph and Emma had "brought a wonderful book of Plates down with them." When Isaac asked to see the items, Joseph showed him the "box in which it is said they were contained, which had, to all appearances, been used as a glass box of the common sized window-glass."[35] Isaac, like others, was allowed to heft the box, but not allowed to see the marvelous items Joseph claimed it contained. The first to see these, Smith assured him, would be "a young child."[36] This child was Joseph's own soon-to-be-born infant, since Sophia Lewis, the wife of Emma's first cousin, Levi Lewis, remembered Joseph saying that "the book of plates could not be opened under penalty of death by any other person but his (Smith's) first-born, which was to be a male."[37] Joshua McKune, a young Harmony resident, corroborated in a statement seven years later: Joseph "told him that Smith's first-born child

Applied to person or form, it denotes symmetry or due proportion, but it expresses less than *beautiful* or *elegant*" (Noah Webster, *American Dictionary of the English Language* [1828], s.v. "Comely").

33. Anderson, *Lucy's Book,* 401.
34. Martin Harris, qtd. in Joel Tiffany, "Mormonism—No. II," 167.
35. The common window pane of the day was ten by twelve inches.
36. Isaac Hale, Statement.
37. Sophia Lewis, Statement, May 1, 1834.

was to translate the characters, and hieroglyphics, upon the plates into our language at the age of three years."[38]

Isaac concluded that Joseph's reluctance was a delaying tactic. As historian Dale Morgan has written, "The sharp-eyed old bear-hunter was no swallower of marvels after the order of Martin Harris, and this business had too much the aspect of a piece of legerdemain."[39] Hale informed Smith that "if there was any thing in my house of that description, which I could not be allowed to see, he must take it away; if he did not, I was determined to see it." The old man added, "After that, the Plates were said to be hid in the woods."[40]

Despite his father-in-law's skepticism, and despite his own promise the previous summer to settle down, Joseph began work on the Book of Mormon as soon as he and Emma were situated in their room in the Hale household. "I copied a considerable number [of characters]," Joseph recalled a decade later, "and by means of the Urim and Thummim[41] I translated some of them, which I did between the time I arrived at the house of my wife's father, in the month of December, and the February following."[42]

"It was manifested to the Prophet," wrote Edward Stevenson, a close friend of Martin Harris in his later years, "that a facsimile of characters must be copied and sent to the most learned professors of the country, and that Martin Harris should be the bearer of them."[43] Lucy Smith also understood that "Mr. Harris was to take to the east and through the country in every direction to all who were professed linguists to give them an op[po]rtunity of showing their talents."[44] Submitting a transcription of the characters to eastern scholars for their inspection and comment would help to create and perpetuate a believable foundation for Smith and the book he was preparing to dictate.

38. Joshua McKune, Statement, May 1, 1834, 1.

39. John Phillip Walker, *Dale Morgan on Early Mormonism,* 277.

40. Isaac Hale, Statement.

41. Apparently, Joseph never used the term Urim and Thummim before 1833, when W. W. Phelps referred to it in the first issue of the *Evening and the Morning Star* (Kirtland, Ohio), which Phelps edited. There are no eyewitness accounts of Joseph using spectacle-like devices or twin seer stones. There is no good reason to think that Smith either had or used anything but a single seer stone during the production of his book. In Smith's accounts, including his 1832 history, he invariably used the term "spectacles."

42. *History of the Church,* 1:19. Joseph Knight, sometime between 1833 and 1847, remembered that "[Smith] Began to be anxious to git them translated. He therefore with his wife drew of[f] the Caricters exactley like the ancient and sent Martin Harris to see if he Could git them Translated" ("Joseph Knight's Recollection," 34).

43. Edward Stevenson, *Reminiscences of Joseph, the Prophet and the Coming Forth of the Book of Mormon,* 28-29.

44. Anderson, *Lucy's Book,* 402.

Samuel Latham Mitchill, a sixty-eight-year-old New York lawyer, professor, and physician, reportedly the nation's preeminent linguist, and a personal friend of Thomas Jefferson, was an obvious choice. The distinguished gentleman had served three terms in the New York Assembly and thirteen years in Congress during the Jefferson and Madison eras. As a politician, he played a significant role in the Louisiana Purchase, the Lewis and Clark Corps of Discovery, the embargo crisis, and the War of 1812.[45] After Benjamin Franklin's death, many Americans turned to Mitchill for the final word on everything from "ancient American ruins to natural history, medicine, or agriculture."[46] "If someone wanted publicity for a new discovery or even a harebrained scheme," wrote Richard Stout, a Mitchill biographer, "Dr. Mitchill's patronage could make him the talk of the town."[47] For example, John Symmes, a visionary and promoter of the "hollow-earth theory," sought Mitchill's backing for a polar expedition. At the North Pole, he expected to find the opening to a "warm and rich land, stocked with thrifty vegetables and animals, if not men." Mitchill had no trouble refusing to lend his sponsorship. His patronage of better-founded projects, such as the development of nitrous oxide as an anesthetic, Rutgers Medical School, and the New York State Society for the Promotion of Agriculture, carried considerable weight. Jefferson once referred to Mitchill as the "Congressional Dictionary," while colleagues in Congress called him the "talking library."[48] Linguistics scholar and colleague Charles Anthon, a devout Episcopalian and professor of classical studies at Columbia College, called him our "Magnus Apollo [My Leader/My Authority]."[49] Another colleague, Fitz-Green Halleck, penned:

Time was when Doctor Mitchill's word was law,
When monkeys, monsters, whales and Esquimaus
Asked but a letter from his ready hand,
To be the theme and wonder of the land[.][50]

---

45. Alan David Aberbach, *In Search of an American Identity,* cover.

46. Rick Grunder, "Martin Harris/Charles Anthon/Dr. Mitchell Story."

47. Richard B. Stout, "A Singular Discovery," 28.

48. Qtd. in Aberbach, *In Search of an American Identity,* 5. Through his study of American Indian culture, Mitchill came to the conclusion that "the identity, origin, and derivation of the natives of Asia and those of North and South America were identical," wrote Aberbach. And like Joseph Smith, Mitchill mistakenly believed that America, not Africa, was "the cradle of the human race" (ibid., 143-44).

49. Charles Anthon to Thomas Winthrop Coit, Apr. 3, 1841, 231.

50. Fritz-Green Halleck, *The Great Moral Picture,* qtd. in Courtney Robert Hall, *A Scientist in the Early Republic,* 14.

A possible origin for the plan of taking the copied characters to Mitchill may have been Joseph Smith's maternal uncle Stephen Mack, who had died in Detroit, Michigan, on November 11, 1826, fifteen months earlier.[51] In 1823, a few months before Joseph began to talk about the golden plates, Colonel Abraham Edwards, a prominent Detroit entrepreneur and Mack's business partner, had discovered an ancient manuscript written in hieroglyphics in the foundation of an old home. Edwards allowed the large manuscript, described as 300-400 pages long, to be displayed at the *Detroit Gazette* office for examination by the public. On March 14, 1823, the *Gazette* noted that the volume had been "compared with more than thirty different alphabets, ancient and modern, and although the characters in which it is written bear a slight affinity to several of them, it is very clear that they belong to neither [sic].—They bear more resemblance to the Ph[o]enician Alphabet than any other with which they have been compared, though a number of the letters differ but little from the Saxon."[52]

One of the *Gazette*'s reporters wrote that the manuscript had "travelled the round of the literary circle of this place for the last four or five days, and it still remains a mystery! The characters in which it is written are unknown; they are neither Hebrew, Greek, nor Saxon, and the only parts of it hitherto intelligible, are a few Latin quotations."[53] The uproar over the manuscript spread throughout the country as newspapers, including the *Ontario* [New York] *Repository* of April 15, 1823, published a few miles from the Smith home, carried accounts of it. The prominent feature of all commentaries in the press was the inability of anyone to decipher the strange symbols which appeared in the work.

According to an article in the *Detroit Gazette* on May 16, 1823, a partial transcript had been sent to various linguistic experts around the country, including Samuel Mitchill, to whom, reportedly, "[a]ncient and modern

---

51. Mack, born on June 15, 1766, was both Joseph Smith's maternal uncle and Oliver Cowdery's cousin. Cowdery's mother, Rebecca Fuller Cowdery, was the great-granddaughter of John Fuller and Mehitable Rowley Fuller, who were also the second great-grandparents of Lucy Mack Smith. In addition, Mary Gates, a cousin of Joseph's maternal grandmother, was married to Nathaniel Cowdery Jr., the brother of William Cowdery, Oliver's grandfather (Stanley R. Gunn, *Oliver Cowdery,* 33.) Mack lived in Gilsum, Vermont, from at least 1789 to 1793, then moved to Tunbridge, Vermont. He moved to northern Michigan, seeking new business opportunities in the Detroit/Pontiac area in 1810 (William L. Moore, "The 1823 Detroit Manuscript," 4). For Mack and Edward's business relationship, see Stout, "A Singular Discovery," 31.

52. "A Singular Discovery," *Detroit Gazette,* Apr. 16, 1823.

53. Ibid.

languages were unlocked."[54] According to the *Columbia Encyclopedia,* the former professor of natural history, chemistry, and agriculture at Columbia College was a "versatile scholar and student of science, who also dabbled in politics and philanthropy ... [and is] one of New York's most prominent and most eccentric characters."[55] Fluent in Spanish, German, Latin, Dutch, and Greek, with the further ability to "decipher ancient Oriental tongues,"[56] Mitchill was described by his contemporaries as both "a living encyclopedia" and "a chaos of knowledge."[57] A noted antiquarian, and student of American Indian lore, he was especially "drawn to the study of the ... speech of the American Indians."[58] His speculations on the origins of native indigenous peoples, published in various periodicals, were compiled in 1820 in *Archaeologia Americana,* the first collection published by the American Antiquarian Society of Worcester, Massachusetts. Mitchill theorized that a white race had met a dark race of pre-Columbian Americans in bloody conflicts in upstate New York, the precise area where, according to the Book of Mormon, white Nephites were finally destroyed by the "dark, filthy" and "loathsome" Lamanites (Mormon 5:15).

Mitchill examined the pages he received from Stephen Mack's partner and, after careful consideration, wrote to Edwards: "I have compared the writing with the *old black letter;* with the *engrossing character* of a deed of feoffment [i.e., the granting of a feudal fee], in my possession; with specimens of the *French palaeography,* in Pluche's Spectacle de la Nature; and with the *types* of various languages in the collection of the American Bible society, in this city. In these researches I was aided by James Smith and John Nitchle, Esquires." He then pronounced his (mistaken) conclusion: the language was a "scholastic or monastic" form of Latin, "not unfrequent about three centuries ago; that its age is perhaps a little anterior to the invention of printing, possibly subsequent; that it was carried to Detroit by one of the learned Jesuits, who when Canada was colonized, embarked in the missionary service

54. J. S. Francis, *Old New York,* qtd. in Stout, "A Singular Discovery," 19.

55. Qtd. in "Theodore Roosevelt." Mitchill, also spelled Mitchell, was appointed to the Columbia faculty as a professor of natural history in 1792. He taught geology, chemistry, mineralogy, zoology, and botany until 1801, when he was elected to Congress. While at Columbia, he edited *Medical Repository* (1797-1824), the first medical journal published in the United States. In 1826, he became vice president of Rutgers Medical College. Mitchill had the reputation as "perhaps the most versatile man of science in his time" (Robert A. McCaughey, "Columbia and Higher Learning in America," 2).

56. Stout, "A Singular Discovery," 18.

57. "Mitchell, Samuel Latham, 1764-1831."

58. Hall, *A Scientist in the Early Republic,* 11.

among the aborigines."[59] At the same time, scholars at Georgetown College in Washington, D.C., "immediately understood the whole affair" and trumped Mitchill when they examined four pages from the original manuscript. William Grace, a Hibernian scholar, announced that it was a Roman Catholic religious text written in "insular minuscule," an obscure form of Latin shorthand dating from the late Middle Ages and last used in remote Irish monasteries during the sixteenth and seventeenth centuries. The pages he examined primarily dealt with "the reasons for withholding the cup from the laity in the Catholic Church, and giving them only the bread, in administering the Eucharist."[60] Eventually, it was concluded that the manuscript had likely been brought to the area by a party of Catholic monks sent there to evangelize local Indians in the early eighteenth century.

The *Detroit Gazette* published Grace's findings on May 16, 1823, adding, with an apologetic tone, "It may be proper here to say, that the difficulty which the learned doctor [Mitchill] encountered, in his endeavors to dec[i]pher the *Irish* manuscript, does not at all derogate his reputation as a scholar; for it cannot be supposed, that in the many studies in which he has been engaged, he ever before met anything like it." In early 1828, however, while serving as vice president of Rutgers' Medical College,[61] Mitchill was again drawn into the quicksand of another mysterious manuscript, this one allegedly inscribed on golden plates in hieroglyphic-like symbols, and brought forth from its hiding place by a young man working "behind a curtain." Mitchill, a chronic alcoholic, was by this time locked in the downward dipsomaniac spiral which would end in his death three years later. Naturalist John James Audubon, a personal friend, wrote to his wife, Lucy, shortly before Mitchill's death: "'Doc' Mitchill is now lost to himself and to the world. I have seen him once half dead with drunken[n]ess."[62]

Martin Harris left western New York in a small wagon drawn by a team of mules in February 1828 when the dirt roads were rendered passable by freezing. Overnighting in taverns and inns while visiting scholars in Utica and Albany, including future Lieutenant Governor Luther Bradish,[63] whom

59. Samuel Mitchill to Col. Abraham Edwards, Apr. 16, 1823, rpt. in "The Manuscript," *Detroit Gazette,* May 16, 1823.

60. "William Grace to Maj. Roberdeau," *Washington Republican,* Apr. 23, 1823.

61. Founded as Queen's College in 1766, the school became the State University at Rutgers in 1825. Its main campus is in New Brunswick, New Jersey.

62. Qtd. in Fred Moreno, "Audubon's Friendship with Samuel Latham Mitchill."

63. Luther Bradish (1783-1863), a highly respected lawyer, diplomat, statesman, and student of languages, held the seat for Franklyn County in the New York state assembly from 1827 to 1830, was lieutenant governor from 1838 to 1842, and later was president of the New-York

he apparently knew personally, Harris hurried on to New York City. The earnest seeker traveled between 400 and 500 miles round trip, much of it on unimproved roadways. Mitchill, said Harris, received him "purlitely."[64] Presumably, the western New Yorker first explained the background of the document he wanted the linguist to examine. His work-calloused fingers removed from his wallet a strip of paper, unfolded it to its full size of 8 x 3¼ inches, then handed it to Mitchill. On it were copied seven lines of about 225 characters he claimed to have been transcribed from golden plates.[65] Mitchill, still smarting from his incorrect identification of the Detroit manuscript and "suspecting some trick,"[66] told Harris he could not decode it and instead referred Harris to his thirty-one-year-old friend and colleague, Charles Anthon (1797-1867), at nearby Columbia College in lower Manhattan. Mitchill drafted a note of introduction to Anthon, requesting him to decipher, if possible, the facsimile that Harris would show him.

Anthon, an antiquarian linguist, had joined the Columbia College faculty as an adjunct professor of Latin and Greek in 1820. Through his textbooks and translations published by Harper Brothers, he ultimately became one of the best-known American classicists of his day.[67] In his reminiscences

---

Historical Society. Bradish had occasionally lived in Palmyra. His parents, John Bradish Jr. and Hannah Warner Bradish, moved to the area in 1798. Pomeroy Tucker, founder, editor, and part owner of the *Wayne Sentinel,* published in Palmyra, reported that Harris "sought the interpretation and bibliological scrutiny of such scholars as Hon. Luther Bradish, Dr. Mitchell, Professor Anthon and others" (Tucker, *The Origin, Rise, and Progress of Mormonism,* 42). John H. Gilbert, the chief compositor of the Book of Mormon, said that Harris "stopped at Albany and called on Lt. Governor Bradish" (Gilbert, "Memorandum of John H. Gilbert, Esq., Sept. 8, 1892, Palmyra, NY," 3).

64. James Gordon Bennett, "Mormon Religion—Clerical Ambition—Western New York—The Mormonites Gone to Ohio."

65. This document is in the archives of the Community of Christ (formerly, Reorganized Church of Jesus Christ of Latter Day Saints), Independence, Missouri. Above the lines of characters is written the word *Caractors,* possibly in Joseph Smith's handwriting. Martin Harris, when examining a facsimile of this document for Edward Stevenson, specifically linked it to Smith. "Again you may see above the seven lines, written by him, 'caracters' instead of characters," he pointed out. "He was a poor speller and unlearned" (Stevenson, *Reminiscences of Joseph, the Prophet,* 32). For a history of this document, see Vogel, *Early Mormon Documents,* 4:415-17, and Kimball, "The Anthon Transcript," 346-50. David Whitmer, the source of this document in the Community of Christ Archives, wrote in 1887: "I have in my possession the original paper containing some of the characters transcribed from one of the golden plates, which paper Martin Harris took to Professor Anthon of New York, for him to read 'the words of a book that is sealed'" (David Whitmer, *An Address to All Believers,* 11).

66. Anthon to Coit, Apr. 3, 1841, 231.

67. "Columbia and Higher Learning in America," 2. For Anthon's background, see Kimball, "The Anthon Transcript," 331-32. Edgar Allan Poe described Anthon as "the most erudite of our classical scholars. ... There are few, if any, even in Europe, who surpass him in his peculiar path of knowledge." Commenting on Anthon's enemies, Poe added that the professor had "many little enemies, among the inditers of merely big books. He has not been unassailed, yet he has assuredly

six years later of the encounter with Harris, Anthon, who disdained interruptions to his schedule, remembered a "plain, and apparently simple-hearted farmer," who called on him with Mitchill's note and the request "to examine, and give my opinion upon, a certain paper, marked with various characters, which the Doctor confessed he could not dec[i]pher."[68] After glancing over the transcript for a few moments, Anthon said he came to the "conclusion that it was all a trick, perhaps a *hoax.*" When he asked Harris how he obtained the transcription, Harris told him that a "gold book" had been discovered in upstate New York along with an enormous pair of "gold spectacles" which were so large that "if a person attempted to look through them, his two eyes would have to be turned towards one of the glasses … the spectacles being altogether too large for the breadth of the human face." Whoever looked at the plates through the magic spectacles, Harris added, "was enabled not only to *read* them, but fully to *understand* their meaning." All this knowledge, Harris continued, was "confined at that time to a young man, who had the trunk containing the book and spectacles in his sole possession."

Harris also told Anthon that the young man worked behind a curtain, and "being thus concealed from view, put on the spectacles occasionally, or rather, looked through one of the glasses, dec[i]phered the characters in the book, and, having committed some of them to paper, handed copies from behind the curtain, to those who stood on the outside." Harris admitted that "no translation had been furnished at the time by the young man with the spectacles" but confirmed Anthon's suspicions by saying the young man had asked him to contribute a large sum of money toward the publication of the "golden book." Because Smith had assured Harris that the book will "produce an entire change in the world and save it from ruin," Harris intended "selling his farm and handing over the amount received to those who wished to publish the plates." As a last "precautionary step," however, Harris had

remained uninjured in the estimation of all those whose opinion he would be likely to value" (Edgar Allan Poe, "A Chapter on Autobiography [Part I]," 225). Alexander Campbell named Anthon as "one of the most distinguished Greek scholars in the Union. His long devotion to the study and teaching of this language is not the only reason [for] this superiority. His laborious researches in ancient literature, his critical collation of copies, various readings, marginal notes, general criticism, as editor of so many of the classics already in our colleges, and his excellent classical dictionary, have obtained for him this high reputation" (Alexander Campbell, *Christian Baptism, with Its Antecedents and Consequences,* 179). Although Anthon was a master of Greek, Latin, German, and French, there is little evidence that he was a scholar of ancient Near Eastern languages. See also Erin B. Jennings, "Charles Anthon—The Man Behind the Letters," *John Whitmer Historical Association Journal* 32, no. 2 (Fall/Winter 2012): 171-87.

68. Unless otherwise stated, my narrative in this section is based on Anthon's letter to Eber D. Howe, Feb. 17, 1834, 270-72.

made the long trip to New York in midwinter to obtain "the opinion of the learned about the meaning of the paper."

Anthon heard enough to convince him that the characters were "part of a scheme to cheat the farmer of his money" and warned the farmer to "beware of rogues." Harris, dismissing that part of the message, asked for a written opinion of the characters. Anthon wanted to tell the individual "behind the curtain" that his "trick was discovered." He wrote a note saying that "the marks in the paper appeared to be merely an imitation of various alphabetic characters, and had in my opinion no meaning at all connected with them."[69] In describing the transcription six years later, Anthon remembered the document as:

> The paper was in fact a singular scrawl. It consisted of all kinds of crooked characters disposed in columns, and had evidently been prepared by some person who had before him at the time a book containing various alphabets. Greek and Hebrew letters, crosses and flourishes, Roman letters inverted or placed sideways, were arranged in perpendicular columns, and the whole ended in a rude delineation of a circle divided into various compartments, decked with various strange marks, and evidently copied after the Mexican Calendar given by Humboldt, but copied in such a way as not to betray the source whence it was derived.[70]

In another letter written in 1841, Anthon concluded that "some cunning fellow had prepared the paper in question for the purpose of imposing upon the countryman who brought it, and I told the man so without any hesitation. He then proceeded to give me the history of the whole affair, which convinced me that he had fallen into the hands of some sharper, while it left me in great astonishment at his simplicity."[71]

---

69. Anthon to Coit, Apr. 3, 1841, 231. In "A Fact in the Mormon Imposture," a letter dated August 12, 1844, and printed May 3, 1845, in the *New-York Observer,* Anthon wrote:

> The Mormon story is complete falsehood. A person called upon me many years ago and showed me a pretended transcript of a page of the Golden Bible, desiring me at the same time to favor him with a translation. It required but a single glance to perceive that the whole affair was a sheer and very clumsy imposition. The paper contained in one or two parallel columns rude imitations of Hebrew and Greek characters together with various delineations of sun, moon, stars, &c. The man who handed me the scrawl had previously taken it to Dr. Mitchell and had been referred by that gentleman to me. He stated that he was about to engage in the affair of the Golden Book and (if my memory serve me right) intended to sell his farm and appropriate the proceeds to the publication of the volume.
>
> I told him very frankly that the whole matter was a hoax and cautioned him against being cheated out of his property. …

70. Anthon to Howe, Feb. 17, 1834, 270-71.

71. Anthon to Coit, Apr. 3, 1841, 231.

As historian Dale Morgan has observed, "Precisely what took place between Harris and Anthon has vexed Mormon history from the moment Anthon showed his visitor to the door."[72] One of Harris's versions, related second-hand by Joseph Smith in 1838, has become the accepted account among Smith's followers. In this version, Anthon classified the symbols as "Egyptian, Chaldaic, Assyric, and Arabic." Furthermore, Anthon reportedly praised the characters as translated correctly, "more so than any he had before seen translated from the Egyptian"—even though the transcription bore no English translation at all. By the time of this retelling, Harris had not only been expelled from the LDS Church but was living in Ohio, far away from Smith in Illinois, and therefore was unavailable to corroborate or deny this problematical second-hand description. Smith added that Anthon wrote out a deposition "certifying to the people of Palmyra that they were true characters, and that the translation of such of them as had been translated was also correct." But as Harris was leaving, Smith claimed, Anthon asked him how the young man had found the golden plates. When Harris said that an angel had revealed their existence, Anthon retrieved the certificate and tore it up, declaring that there is "no longer such a thing as ministering by angels." According to Joseph's account, Anthon told Harris to bring the golden plates to New York City where he would examine them. But when Harris replied that plates were sealed from view and that he was forbidden to even look at the book, Anthon ended the interview: "I cannot read a sealed book."[73]

Prior to his excursion eastward, Harris had visited with the Reverend John A. Clark, an Episcopal minister in Palmyra, in whose congregation he sometimes worshipped.[74] Harris assured the minister that "an important epoch had arrived—that a great flood of light was about to burst upon the world, and that the scene of divine manifestation was to be immediately around us." Baffled by these hints, Clark pressed for additional detail. A "GOLDEN BIBLE had recently been dug from the earth where it had been deposited for thousands of years," Harris explained, "and that this would be found to contain such disclosures as would settle all religious controversies and speedily bring on the glorious millennium."

Harris told Clark that Joseph had the golden record and some "sort of spectacles," which he had used to transcribe "one of the leaves of this book." Recalling this interview later, Clark reported: "His mind seemed to be quite as

---

72. Walker, *Dale Morgan on Early Mormonism,* 282.

73. *History of the Church,* 1:20.

74. My narrative in this section is based on John A. Clark, *Gleanings by the Way,* 222-30.

intent upon the pecuniary advantage that would arise from the possession of the plates of solid gold of which this book was composed as upon the spiritual light it would diffuse over the world." Moreover, Clark thought that Joseph had merely concocted a hoax to "practice upon [Martin's] credulity, or an artifice to extort from him money." However, Clark's "intimations to him, in reference to the possible imposition that was being practiced upon him," were "indignantly repelled," said Clark. Martin then took a narrow piece of paper from his pocket and carefully unfolded it to show, according to Clark, "three or four lines of characters." The minister studied the transcript, thought he saw one Hebrew-looking character in the grouping, then handed it back. "My ignorance of the characters in which the pretended ancient record was written," Clark summarized, "was to Martin Harris new proof that Smith's whole account of the divine revelation made to him was entirely to be relied on."

When Martin returned from his two-week trip in February, he pressed on to Harmony, where he reported his experience to Joseph. Then he went back to Palmyra. At home, he began to spread word about his adventure. He told John H. Gilbert, a typesetter in E. B. Grandin's Palmyra printshop, he was now satisfied that Joseph was a "little smarter than Professor Anthon."[75] He again called on Rev. Clark and reported that "among others he had consulted Professor Anthon, who thought the characters in which the book was written very remarkable, but he could not decide exactly what language they belonged to." The retired farmer had "become a perfect believer," wrote Clark. In fact, Harris had announced that he had no more doubt of Smith's divine commission than he did of the divine commission of the New Testament apostles. Clark summarized Harris's thinking: "The very fact that Smith was an obscure and illiterate man" was evidence that "he must be acting under divine impulses." Furthermore, he explained to his skeptical audience of one, "God had chosen the foolish things of the world to confound the wise, and the weak things to confound the mighty; and base things of the world, and things which are despised—yea, and things that are not to bring to nought—things that are—that no flesh should glory in his presence."[76] Clark's concern that Harris was being financially exploited was only confirmed by Harris's announced determination that the golden Bible should be published even if it "consumed all his worldly substance" and meant "the spoiling of his goods."[77]

75. Qtd. in Gilbert, "Memorandum," 4.

76. Harris was here quoting I Corinthians 1:27-29.

77. Clark, *Gleanings by the Way,* 230.

A year and a half later, in a feature on Smith and Harris's appearance in Rochester, New York, the *Rochester Advertiser and Telegraph* reported on August 31, 1829, that Harris "took some of the characters interpreted by Smith and went in search of someone, besides the interpreter, who was learned enough to English them; but all of whom he applied (among the number was Professor Mitchell of New York) happened not to be possessed of sufficient knowledge to give satisfaction." The *Rochester Gem* of September 5, 1829, reprinted the story and added: "Harris states that he went in search of someone to interpret the hieroglyphics, but found no one was intended to perform that all-important task but Smith himself."

Later, Harris, Smith, and newspaperman William W. Phelps, soon to be a Mormon, made retrospective comments about Mitchill's and Anthon's statements that were clearly intended to enhance the public image of the Book of Mormon, which by then had been in print for about a year and a half. Harris claimed that Mitchill "looked at his engravings—made a learned dissertation on them—compared them with the hieroglyphics discovered by [Jean-François] Champollion in Egypt—and set them more as the language of a people formerly in existence in the East, but now no more."[78] Phelps wrote in 1831 that "Dr. Mitchell ... referred [the characters] to Professor Anthon who translated and declared them to be the ancient short-hand Egyptian."[79]

Although Mitchill had died on September 7, 1831, and could not respond to these claims, Anthon was furious that Mormons were using his name to promote the Book of Mormon. "The whole story about my having pronounced the Mormonite inscription to be 'reformed Egyptian hieroglyphics' is *perfectly false,*" he wrote in 1834.[80] Moreover, prior to the publication of Champollion's work *Précis du Système Hiéroglyphique des anciens Egyptiens* in 1824, no one in the world could read Egyptian hieroglyphics.

Whatever the facts of his interviews with Mitchill and Anthon, Harris returned home with his faith in Joseph's book fully confirmed. The foremost linguists in America had admitted they could not translate the characters, while Joseph could. Anthon's ironic comment about the sealed portion of the plates struck Harris as especially significant. Thoroughly acquainted with the King James Bible, Harris saw the event as the fulfillment of Isaiah 29:11: "And the vision of all is become unto you as the words of a book that is sealed, which men deliver to one that is learned, saying, Read this, I pray

78. Harris, qtd. in Bennett, "Mormon Religion."
79. W. W. Phelps to Eber D. Howe, Jan. 15, 1831, in Howe, *Mormonism Unvailed,* 274.
80. Anthon to Howe, Feb. 17, 1834, emphasis his.

thee: and he saith, I cannot; for it is sealed. And the book is delivered to him that is not learned, saying Read this, I pray thee: and he saith, I am not learned." In 1835, as Oliver Cowdery was writing Smith's history, he made the connection explicit in recounting Moroni's instruction to Smith that "the scripture must be fulfilled before [the Book of Mormon] is translated, which says that the words of a book, which were sealed were presented to the learned; for thus has God determined to leave man without excuse."[81]

Both Martin and Joseph were impressed with what they saw as more than coincidence. Joseph took pains to improve upon this verse in the Book of Mormon. From a simple utterance, the passage became prophecy, perpetuating an interpretation that has become embedded in Mormon tradition:

> [I]t shall come to pass that the Lord God shall say unto him to whom he shall deliver the book: Take these words which are not sealed and deliver them to another, that he may shew them unto the learned, saying: Read this, I pray thee. And the learned shall say, Bring hither the book, and I will read them. ... And the man shall say: I cannot bring the book, for it is sealed. Then shall the learned say, I cannot read it. Wherefore it shall come to pass, that the Lord God will deliver again the book and the words thereof, to him that is not learned; and the man that is not learned, shall say, I am not learned. Then shall the Lord God say unto him, The learned shall not read them, for they have rejected them, and I am able to do mine own work; wherefore, thou shalt read the words which I shall give unto thee. (1830 Book of Mormon, 111; now 2 Ne. 27:15-20.)

Martin's obsession was eroding his marriage. As soon as Dolly caught wind of her husband's February plans to go to Harmony, she announced her intention to accompany him. But according to Lucy Smith, Martin "concluded that it would be better to go without her and left suddenly[,] not giving her any intimation of his intention." Instead Harris took Hyrum Smith. When Dolly realized that Martin was gone, she asked Lucy where her husband was. Lucy hedged: she had heard him say something about leaving, but knew nothing of his plans.

Enraged, Dolly accused Lucy of conspiring to circumvent her. The tiff ended when Dolly returned home "determined to have satisfaction in some way for the slight which she had received." Not only was Martin forever after denied access to his wife's affections, but within months she pirated away the first 116 manuscript pages of the Book of Mormon "translation."

81. Oliver Cowdery to W. W. Phelps, "Letter IV," Feb. 1835, 79.

Devastated, Joseph briefly considered abandoning the project. Had he done so, there very probably would have been no Mormonism, and the millions today who affirm their faith in the Book of Mormon would have had to look elsewhere for spiritual fulfillment. As for the Smith family, would this latest catastrophe have destroyed their family dream, driven Joseph Sr. permanently to alcoholism, and assured their financial destruction? Or would Joseph Jr. have settled in Harmony to work the fields, settle into the extended Hale family, raise his children as good Methodists, and give forum to his imagination in colorful tales to entertain neighbors?

13 | SCRYING THE BOOK OF MORMON

In writing for your father I frequently wrote day after day, often sitting at the table close by him, he sitting with his face buried in his hat, with the stone in it, and dictating hour after hour with nothing between us. ... The plates often lay on the table without any attempt at concealment, wrapped in a small linen table-cloth, which I had given him to fold them in.

—Emma Hale Smith Bidamon, in Joseph Smith III, "Last Testament of Sister Emma," 289

Early in the spring of 1828, as the cold weather began to lose its grip on Harmony, Joseph arranged with Isaac Hale to buy from him on credit a tract of 13.5 acres of drained farmland on Hale's property. Smith also purchased, on the same terms, a partially finished two-story frame home from Jesse Hale, Emma's oldest brother. Jesse and wife Mary had moved out of the house after two-year-old-daughter Nancy died there earlier on January 29, 1828.[1] Although Isaac had temporarily used the house to dress, tan, and store deer hides, Joseph and Emma embraced the opportunity to relieve the tensions of living with disapproving parents by moving into their own house. Smith and his brothers-in-law rolled the building on logs from its original location to a suitable spot on his new property, some 150 yards southeast of the Hale residence and about that far north of the small McKune family cemetery where little Nancy had been laid to rest.

An 1880 visitor to the Smiths' Harmony home a half-century later described it as a "partly-finished house, twenty-six feet broad, eighteen feet deep and fourteen feet in the posts."[2] Rex B. Hawes, who lived in it from

1. Nancy Hale's headstone, McCune Cemetery, Oakland (Harmony), Pennsylvania. In 1879, interviewed by her oldest son, Joseph III, Emma Smith said, "Your father bought your uncle Jesse's place, off father's farm, and we lived there till The Book of Mormon was translated; and I think published" (qtd. in Joseph Smith III, "The Last Testament of Sister Emma," 289).

2. Frederick G. Mather, "The Early Days of Mormonism," 201. "In the posts" refers to the building's height.

1896 to 1909, noted it was "built of lumber, having two rooms downstairs. The floor downstairs was of beautiful hardwood maple. When entering the house, one came into a hallway, and there a stairway led up to an attic or loft; the east end of this loft was boarded off into a room with a window looking toward the east. I was told that Joseph Smith did a lot of writing in this room. Another stairway, underneath the attic stairway, led down to the cellar underneath the house. There was a nice fireplace at the west end of the house."[3]

Here, beside the Susquehanna, Joseph and Emma, only a couple of months away from the birth of their first child, settled into the first home mostly of their own making. Emma, trained in her mother's boarding house, was a competent housekeeper and cook, although the Smiths' larder was frequently bare during this period. As was the case with many other settlers in the area, Joseph and Emma's meals consisted mainly of "meat, from the forest; bread, vegetables, short-cakes, johnny-cakes, and buckwheat pancakes," according to local historian Emily Blackman. "We used to eat our venison cooked in various ways. A venison steak is epicurean, and reckoned among the best of backwood dishes. Our bread was baked in a flat, shallow cast-iron kettle, set upon coals, with coals heaped upon the cover."[4] Emma had a reputation for being well-groomed, dressing her dark hair daily into an easy-to-care-for, tightly coiled bun.

Joseph had promised Isaac that he would work the land for a living, and the Smiths' acreage lay where Isaac could keep an eye on him.[5] Whatever Joseph's intentions, and Emma's hopes, facing the plodding, muscle-burning effort of plowing and planting that spring of 1828 made it plain to Joseph that farming was not in his future. Years of back-breaking labor had not only aged his father, it had brought him virtually nothing of lasting value—no real estate, no financial prosperity, and definitely no respect from the county's propertied men.

New York newspaperman Horace Greeley (1811-72) also grew up poor in New Hampshire and Vermont. In his 1868 memoir, he wrote of "genuine

---

3. The fireplace was opposite the front door. Rex B. Hawes, Statement to Abner H. Baird and Hazel H. Baird, "Harmony, Pennsylvania, Deeds, Wills, Maps, Pictures, and Historical Information of the Joseph Smith and Isaac Hale Farms."

4. Emily C. Blackman, *History of Susquehanna County, Pennsylvania,* 58

5. Joseph Smith did not secure title to this property until August 26, 1830, when he closed the transaction with a $200 payment (Deed Book 8, 290, Susquehanna County Courthouse, Montrose, Pennsylvania, cited in Porter, "A Study of the Origins of the Church," 65).

poverty,—not beggary, nor dependence, but the manly American sort," the type of impoverishment usually lived by farm families. Greeley deduced:

> Our farmers' sons escape from their fathers' calling whenever they can, because it is made a mindless, monotonous drudgery, instead of an ennobling, liberalizing, intellectual pursuit. ... In the farmer's calling, as I saw it followed, there was neither scope for expanding facilities, incitement to constant growth in knowledge, nor a spur to generous ambition. To preserve existence was its ordinary impulse; to get rich, its exceptional and most exalted aim. So I turned from it in dissatisfaction, if not in disgust, and sought a different sphere and vocation.[6]

As Joseph sent off Martin Harris with the strip of paper bearing the characters he said he had copied from the golden plates, he was envisioning an alternative future, even as he went through the motions of homebuilding and agricultural husbandry. Dissatisfied with his family's socio-economic status, tired of being dismissed by many Palmyra and Manchester folks, and convinced of his blossoming spiritual aptitude, he saw himself as someone capable of greater things. If all went well with Harris's mission, Joseph could prove his mettle as "author and proprietor" of a new book about ancient America, a book which would also resolve many of the religious contentions of the day. When Harris returned from his errand to the scholars, Joseph was eager to take the next step into that new future.

Joseph's mystique began to develop in Harmony. Some neighbors later recalled that he often "would sit for hours looking into his hat at the *round colored stone,* and tell of seeing things far away and supernatural. At times he was melancholy and sedate, as often hilarious and mirthful; an imaginative enthusiast, constitutionally opposed to work, a general favorite with the ladies."[7] Martin Harris may have been Joseph's first non-family disciple, but Smith's new wife was not far behind. Emma, who had gone with him to Cumorah and steadfastly prayed for him, willingly furthered his work by transcribing Joseph's first attempts at dictating the Book of Mormon text. Though her husband's handwriting was serviceable, his spelling was inconsistent. He knew that, when his manuscript went to the typesetter, a good, clear hand was essential. In 1879, at age seventy-four, Emma told her son, Joseph Smith III:

---

6. Horace Greeley, *Recollections of a Busy Life,* 60.
7. Blackman, *History of Susquehanna County, Pennsylvania,* 579.

> In writing for J[oseph] S[mith], I frequently wrote day after day, often sitting at the table close by him, he sitting with his face bu=ried in his hat, with the stone in it and dictating hour after hour, with nothing between us. He had neither mss [manuscript(s)] nor book to read from. If he had had any=thing of the Kind he could not have concealed it from me. The plates often lay on the table without any attempt at con=cealment, wrapped in a small linen <table> cloth, which I had given him to fold them in. I felt of the plates, as they lay on the table, tracing their outline and shape. They seemed to be pliable like thick paper, and would rustle <with a metallic sound> when the edges were moved by the thumb, as one does sometimes thumb the edges of a book.[8]

In Harmony, Joseph made no further allusions to using either magic spectacles or golden plates in his scrying and no longer concealed the process from family members. This change may have been prompted by charges that he used notes as well as in response to Emma's brothers, likely David and Isaac, who teased him, and, along with Isaac Hale, made life sometimes unpleasant. Brother-in-law Michael Morse, who married Emma's sister Tryal, remembered that "the sons of Mr. Hale seemed opposed to and at enmity with Joseph from the first, and took occasions to annoy and vex him."[9] Once, Morse said, "the Hale boys had a pique at Joseph and was Seeking to annoy him more or less, at different times."[10] Tormented by several of Emma's five brothers during a fishing trip, Joseph, who was also allegedly "pretty drunk,"[11] threw off his coat and "proposed to defend himself."[12]

In describing Joseph's scrying, Emma recalled in 1870 that his medium was "a small stone, not exactly black, but … rather a dark color."[13] Emma added that Joseph assured her that the plates "lay under our bed for a few months but I never felt the liberty to look at them."[14] She also refrained from unwrapping their covering when they were on a small table in her living room. "She would lift them," Joseph Smith III reported her saying, "and move them when she swept and dusted the room and furniture."[15]

8. Joseph Smith III, "Notes of Interview with Emma Smith Bidamon."

9. Qtd. in William W. Blair, "Letter to Editors," May 22, 1879, 191.

10. Qtd. in William W. Blair, Journal, May 8, 1879, 55.

11. Sally McKune and Jacob I. Skinner, Report, qtd. in Frederick G. Mather, "The Early Mormons."

12. Michael Morse, qtd. in Blair, "Letter to Editors," May 22, 1879, 191.

13. Emma Smith Bidamon to Emma S. Pilgrim, Mar. 27, 1870.

14. Nels Madsen, "A Visit to Mrs. Emma Smith Bidamon," 1877.

15. Joseph Smith III to Mrs. E. Horton, Mar. 7, 1900.

Emma's service as amanuensis, interrupted as it was by the need to put three meals a day on the table and perhaps complicated by her pregnancy, did not last long. Her handwriting does not appear on any original manuscript material now available.[16] The work also progressed slowly, perhaps only two pages per day.[17] On several occasions after her husband's death, Emma described how she and Joseph worked together on the book. "When my husband was translating the Book of Mormon," she said in 1856, "I wrote a part of it, as he dictated each sentence, word for word, and when he came to proper names he could not pronounce, or long words, he spelled them out." She specifically remembered his difficulty in pronouncing "Sariah," Father Lehi's wife, and had to spell it out, after which she pronounced it for him.[18]

On another occasion while Joseph's face was buried in his hat, he stopped mid-sentence and looked up as "pale as a sheet," according to Emma. "Did Jerusalem have walls around it?" he asked. When assured that it did, he replied, "Oh! I was afraid I had been deceived."[19] Emma believed that Joseph was infused by the spirit of God. "I am satisfied that no man could have dictated the [Book of Mormon] unless he were inspired," she told her oldest son, "for when acting as his scribe, your father would dictate to me hour after hour; and when returning after meals, or after interruptions, he would at once begin where he had left off, without either seeing the manuscript or having any portion of it read to him. This was a usual thing for him to do. It would have been improbable that a learned man could do this; and, for so ignorant and unlearned as he was, it was simply impossible."[20] Joseph assured family and friends early in his religious career that his scrying was divine. Brother-in-law Alva Hale was one of several intimates who recalled that Joseph said his "gift in seeing with a stone and hat, was a gift from God."[21]

Joseph was sometimes aided by Emma's seventeen-year-old brother, Reuben, the youngest of Isaac and Elizabeth's nine. Reuben later told a friend, Joseph Fowler McKune, that during the scrying process his

16. Dean C. Jesse, "The Original Manuscript of the Book of Mormon," 276-77.

17. Joseph stated that he and Harris began working together April 12, 1828, and continued until approximately June 14, just before Emma gave birth. During this sixty-four-working-day period, they produced approximately 116 manuscript pages, an average of 1.8 pages per day. Emma's brother Reuben Hale is also known to have scribed during this period (Dan Vogel, *Early Mormon Documents,* 1:71).

18. Qtd. in Edmund C. Briggs, "A Visit to Nauvoo in 1856," 454. *Sariah* is first mentioned in 1 Nephi 2:5, but this text was produced after the loss of the first 116 or so pages, discussed below.

19. Ibid.

20. Joseph Smith III, "Last Testimony of Sister Emma," 52.

21. Alva Hale, Affidavit, in Howe, *Mormonism Unvailed,* 268.

brother-in-law used the large hat commonly called a stove-pipe, later made famous by Abraham Lincoln. Reuben said that, while Joseph was scrying, "[t]he hat was on the table by the window and the stone in the bottom or rather in the top of the hat. Smith would bend over the hat with his face buried in it so that no light could enter it, and thus dictate to the scribe what he should write."[22]

Despite these exhibitions of Joseph scrying with his face in his hat while the golden plates were said to be in a box or in the woods, most of Joseph's in-laws concluded that the Book of Mormon, as David Hale put it, was "a humbug."[23] Father Hale, "a man of truth and good judgment," according to Elizabeth's brother, Nathaniel Lewis (1769-1860), was particularly opposed to what he thought of as his son-in-law's fraud.[24] After watching young Joseph in the earliest days of his work on the Book of Mormon, Isaac stated in 1834: "The manner in which [Joseph] pretended to read and interpret was the same as when he looked for the money-diggers, with the stone in his hat, and his hat over his face, while the book of plates was at the same time hid in the woods." Hale liked neither what he saw nor what he did not see. "I told them [Joseph and Emma]," he said, "that I considered the whole of it a delusion, and advised them to abandon it."[25] He was more specific: "I conscientiously believe," he wrote, "that the whole 'Book of Mormon' (so called) is a silly fabrication of falsehood and wickedness, got up for speculation, and with a design to dupe the credulous and unwary, and in order that its fabricators might live upon the spoils of those who swallowed the deception."[26]

Some others of Joseph's associates also believed that the Book of Mormon was originally a money-making scheme. "When this work was first brought forth by Joseph Smith," Palmyra neighbor Lorenzo Saunders remembered fifty-four years after the book's publication, "it was not claimed to be a religious thing at all; it was a money making <thing>."[27] Joseph

---

22. Joseph F. McKune, qtd. in Rhamanthus M. Stocker, *Centennial History of Susquehanna County, Pennsylvania,* 556.

23. David Hale, qtd. in Blackman, *History of Susquehanna County,* 104. For more on David Hale, see Mark Lyman Staker and Robin Scott Jensen, "David Hale's Store Ledger: New Details about Joseph and Emma Smith, the Hale Family, and the Book of Mormon," *BYU Studies Quarterly* 53, no. 3 (2014): 77-112.

24. Nathaniel Lewis, Statement, in "Mormonism," qtd. in Vogel, *Early Mormon Documents,* 4:288-89.

25. Isaac Hale, Statement, 578.

26. Ibid. From his affidavit, Hale saw not only his son-in-law as a "fabricator," but also Emma, Martin Harris, and Oliver Cowdery.

27. Lorenzo Saunders, Interview, Nov. 12, 1884, 2.

Capron (ca. 1792-1874), who lived near the Smiths on Stafford Road, noted that the Smiths were "daily harrassed [sic] by the demands of creditors" and "at length, Joseph pretended to find the Gold plates. This scheme, he believed, would relieve the family from all pecuniary embarrassment." Father Smith discussed the project with Capron, twenty-one years his junior, and referred to the Book of Mormon as "a speculation." He added: "[W]hen it is completed, my family will be placed on a level above the generality of mankind."[28] Stephen S. Harding, who grew up near the Martin Harris farm, was astounded that Harris, in becoming Joseph's disciple, ultimately abandoned "the cultivation of one of the best farms in the neighborhood" and changed "all his habits of life from industry to indolence and general shiftlessness." Unable to account for this change otherwise, Harding concluded that Harris became "absolutely infatuated, and believed that an immense fortune could be made out of the interprise."[29] And Emma's Uncle Nathaniel Lewis, who also lived in Harmony during this period, recalled the book as a money-making venture: "The first he [referring to himself in third person] heard of the matter, was a sort of vague representation from Joe and Em, that they knew of something that when carried out *would make them and all their friends rich.*"[30]

Nathaniel Lewis was a rock-ribbed Methodist, the local minister, age fifty-nine in 1828.[31] For a time after he returned to Harmony, Joseph hoped to draw the elderly minister into his camp, possibly seeing him as a balance against Isaac Hale. "The old gentleman heard his tale with due gravity," summarized Emily Blackman. He then asked, "Joseph, can anybody else translate strange languages by the help of them spectacles?" "O, yes," the young seer replied. "Well now," responded the minister, a man known for his wit, "I've got [Adam] Clarke's Commentary [on the Bible], and it contains a great many strange languages; now if you will let me try the spectacles, and if, by looking through them, I can translate these strange languages into

28. Joseph Capron, Statement, Nov. 8, 1833.

29. Stephen S. Harding to Thomas Gregg, Feb. 1882, 34.

30. Nathaniel Lewis, qtd. in "Mormonism and the Mormons," *Methodist Quarterly Review* 3, no. 1 (1843): 113.

31. Lewis, who owned 89 acres of land in Harmony, is credited with forming the first Methodist class there. William Thompson, an associate judge of Susquehanna County, described Lewis as "a respectable minister of the Methodist Episcopal Church, a man of veracity, and good moral character" (William Thompson, "Mormonism," *Susquehanna Register and Northern Pennsylvania* 8 [May 1, 1834]: 1). Albert Clark calls Lewis "an ordained preacher" (Clark, *Methodist Episcopal Church,* 11-12).

English, then I'll be one of your disciples." "This was a poser [i.e., a puzzle]," concluded Blackman, "and Joe had to run."[32]

Despite his failure to convince Nathaniel Lewis, Isaac Hale, and others that his work was divinely mandated, or even legitimate, Joseph still had the devotion of Martin Harris and a few others. As soon as he could arrange his affairs in Palmyra, Harris set out in April 1828 for Harmony, prepared to serve as Joseph's scribe in bringing the Book of Mormon to completion.[33] As delighted as Smith was to have Martin's assistance, his coming was not without problems. When the Harris wagon rolled up to Joseph and Emma's new home, Dolly Harris was perched aside her husband on the spring seat. Dolly, who had recently raised a ruckus back home, was ready to bring fresh hell to Harmony. Martin and Dolly's nineteen-year-old daughter Lucy was being courted by Flanders Dyke. Although Dolly did not like the young man, as Lucy Smith told the story, she was willing to barter her daughter's hand in exchange for a copy of the transcription Martin had taken east. Dyke successfully lifted the paper from Martin and made a copy, then sneaked the original back into Martin's pocket. Thereafter, whenever Martin produced his copy to show others, Lucy would promptly pull out her own copy and announce that "Joe Smith was not the only one that was in possession of this great curiosity that she herself had the same characters and they were quite as genuine as those displayed <to> them by Mr. H[arris]."[34]

Despite his misgivings, Martin had promised his wife—to the dismay of all around—that she could travel with him to Harmony for a couple of weeks. Dolly had scarcely alighted before she announced that her sole purpose was to see the golden plates and would not leave until her wish was fulfilled. Reportedly, she combed every corner of the small house, searching bureaus, chests, trunks, and cupboards. Joseph apparently did not protest since, according to what he later told his mother, he had buried both the record and the breastplate in the woods. When Dolly heard this, she simply transferred her search to the yard and surrounding forest. By mid-afternoon, she returned to the Smiths' house out of breath and "very ill natured," wrote Lucy Smith. As she had knelt to clear away snow and leaves from a suspected spot, she disturbed the hibernation of a "tremendous great black snake," which reared up and

32. Nathaniel Lewis, qtd. in Blackman, *History of Susquehanna County,* 104. Rev. Lewis and his family moved to Amboy, Lee County, Illinois, in the early 1840s where he continued his Methodist activities (Vogel, *Early Mormon Documents,* 4:293).

33. *History of the Church,* 1:20.

34. Unless otherwise stated, my treatment of this period is based on Lavina Fielding Anderson, *Lucy's Book,* 405-407.

"commenced hissing at me." Terrified, Dolly dashed back to the house and thereafter abandoned her intention of searching the woods.

Convinced the snake was an evil omen, Dolly refused continued residence with the Smiths. Instead she found lodging at the nearest inn, likely the Isaac and Elizabeth Hale place, from which she denounced Joseph to the neighbors, including his in-laws. According to Lucy Smith's second-hand account, Dolly "told them that he was a grand imposter that he had deceived her <husband with his> specious pretentions and was exerting all his deceptive powers in order to induce Mr. Harris to give his property into Joseph's hands that he might by robbing her Husband make to himself rich."[35] After two relentless weeks, Dolly finally agreed to let Martin take her home. "The peace that settled on Joseph's domicile," wrote historian Dale Morgan, "must have been like waking from a nightmare."[36]

The ride home for Martin, however, was anything but tranquil. More convinced than ever that Joseph was a fraud, Dolly must have repeatedly urged Martin to withdraw from the Gold Bible business. Back home, while Martin and Dolly visited her brother, Peter Harris, she begged Martin, in front of witnesses, to "leave the company of the Smiths, as their religion was false." But Martin, convinced that he was doing God's work and would get richer in the process, replied with what must have been a combination of irritation and placation: "[I]f you would let me alone, I could make money by it."[37]

Harris had promised Joseph before he left Harmony to return as scribe for a season. Rather than giving in to Dolly, he left within a few days for Harmony.[38] There he found a discouraged Joseph, still reeling from Dolly's attacks and their effect on Emma's family. Joseph had gone for a heart-to-heart-talk with Emma's Uncle Nathaniel. While still insisting that God had

35. Ibid., 406.

36. John Phillip Walker, *Dale Morgan on Early Mormonism,* 285.

37. Lucy Harris, Statement, Nov. 29, 1833, in Howe, *Mormonism Unvailed,* 254. Abigail Harris, who was married to Dolly's brother, Peter, later stated that she heard Dolly tell Martin she wished he would quit his association with the Smiths, believing "it was all false and a delusion," to which Martin reportedly replied: "What if it is a lie; if you will let me alone I will make money out of it!" (Abigail Harris, Statement, Nov. 28, 1833, 253). Eber D. Howe cited the understanding of some Palmyra residents when he said that Martin Harris "engaged in the new Bible business with a view of making a handsome sum of money from the sale of the books, as he was frequently heard to say" (Howe, *Mormonism Unvailed,* 13).

38. Dolly had her agenda as did Martin. As soon as he left their Palmyra home, she moved her furniture and belongings out of the house and stored them with friends. Though they verged on a full separation at this point, they did not reach that rupture until 1831 when Martin followed Joseph Smith to Ohio. Dolly remained in Palmyra, where she died, age forty-two, in 1836.

commanded him to "translate" the golden record, Smith said that he was "afraid of the people," then asked if he should keep on with the work. Nathaniel Lewis declined to advise him, but evidently others, including Emma, were not so reticent. Martin Harris in 1831 told Ezra Booth, briefly a Mormon convert in Ohio, that Joseph told him he was going to abandon the project "on account of the opposition of his wife and others." Harris was in no mood for vacillation. "I have not come down here for nothing," he retorted, "and we will go on with it."[39]

Reassured, Smith and Harris commenced a two-month labor on the Book of Mormon. It is not known how much of the book Joseph had already dictated to Emma and her brother Reuben. He later described this first portion as "the Book of Lehi ... an account abridged from the plates of Lehi, by the hand of Mormon."[40] But by mid-June 1828, no less than 116 foolscap pages had been penned as word after word of text fell from Joseph's lips as he continued his scrying.

Neither man left a detailed picture of how both spent their days, but there must have been some occasional tension. The spring plowing and planting were waiting outside for Joseph. His in-laws were just down the lane, displeased with the direction things seemed to be going. Emma had varied enough from her usual supportiveness to have pleaded, at least once, for Joseph to give up—or at least postpone—the project. It must have been troubling to her Methodist conscience that Joseph was breaking his promise to her father, even if she accepted, as Joseph no doubt urged, that the commandments of God took precedent. She was now in the final, uncomfortable stages of pregnancy and must have been worried about their future. Even though the disruptive Dolly Harris had been removed, far from having her husband to herself, Joseph was absorbed with Martin Harris in an activity that, by its nature, excluded Emma even while it required her to cook for a guest and clean around two men who were constantly underfoot.

Later, Harris ran afoul of some Church leaders in Ohio for once alleging that Joseph "drank too much liquor when he was translating the Book of Mormon."[41] And in 1870, Harris told Edward Stevenson that as the two once relaxed from their work by walking down to the river and skipping rocks across its surface, he picked up a river pebble and decided to test the seer's validity. Returning to the house, Harris substituted his stone for

39. Ezra Booth, "Mormonism No. II," *Ohio Star*, Oct. 9, 1831, 3.

40. Joseph Smith, "Preface," 1830 Book of Mormon; see also introduction to BC II:7.

41. "Kirtland Council Minute Book," Feb. 12, 1834, 28-29.

Joseph's. When they sat down to work, Joseph buried his face in his hat for a few moments, then sat up and exclaimed: "Martin! What is the matter. ... All is as dark as Egypt." Martin's expression must have given him away, and Joseph demanded why Martin had tried to trick him. Martin replied, perhaps to quell his own questions as much as others', "[T]o stop the mouths of fools" who had declared that he had memorized text and could not really "see by the seer stone." When Martin handed over the true stone, "the translation was resumed, as usual."[42]

According to Rev. John Clark, Joseph hung a blanket from the ceiling between Martin and himself and told his scribe that "it would arouse the most terrible divine pleasure, if he should attempt to draw near the sacred chest, or look at Smith while engaged in the work of dec[i]phering the mysterious characters."[43] Smith later changed his method, however. Other eye-witness accounts, and there are more than a dozen, do not support the view that Smith was behind a curtain. In an 1852 conversation with Reuben W. Alderman, in Ohio, Harris said he saw "Jo Smith translate the 'Book of Mormon,' with his peep-stone in his hat."[44] Elizabeth Ann Whitmer, who married Joseph's next scribe, Oliver Cowdery, in 1832, recorded in 1870 when she was fifty-five: "I cheerfully certify that I was familiar with the manner of Joseph Smith's translating the Book of Mormon. He translated the most of it at my Father's house. And I often sat by and saw and heard them translate and write for hours together. Joseph never had a curtain drawn between him and his scribe while he was translating. He would place the [stone] in his hat, and place his face in his hat, so as to exclude the light."[45]

Speaking at a Sunday meeting on September 4, 1870, in Salt Lake City, Harris, then eighty-seven, told attentive Latter-day Saints that Smith had both a seer stone and spectacles "by which he was enabled to translate," but for convenience he used the stone. He also explained his understanding of the scrying process: "By aid of the seer stone," sentences would appear (Harris did not specify if they appeared in the stone or in the darkness of the hat), and Joseph would read them aloud. When Joseph was finished, he would say, "'Written,' and if not written correctly it remained until corrected, so that

42. Edward Stevenson, "The Three Witnesses to the Book of Mormon," 389. Even if Joseph had not seen Martin make the substitution, he had had his original stone constantly in his possession for six years, and presumably would have noticed even minor differences.

43. Martin Harris, qtd. by John A. Clark, *Gleanings by the Way,* 239.

44. R. W. Alderman to Arthur B. Deming, Dec. 25, 1884, 3.

45. Elizabeth Ann Whitmer Cowdery, Affidavit, qtd. in William McLellan to "My Dear Friends," Feb. 1870.

the translation was just as it was engraven on the plates, precisely in the language then used."[46] Joseph Knight Sr.'s account, written between 1835 and 1847, gave a similar description of the process: "Now the way he translated was he put the urim and thummim into his hat and Darkened his Eyes then he would take a sentence and it would appear in Brite Roman Letters then he would tell the writer and he would write it then that would go away the next Sentence would Come and so on."[47]

David Whitmer, also an eye-witness, provides more specific information about the method. In 1887, at age eighty-two, he published a booklet in Richmond, Missouri, which includes a detailed description of what he remembered observing fifty-eight years earlier:

> Joseph Smith would put the seer stone into a hat, and put his face in the hat, drawing it closely around his face to exclude the light; and in the darkness the spiritual light would shine. A piece of something resembling parchment would appear, and on that appeared the writing. One character at a time would appear, and under it was the interpretation in English. Brother Joseph would read off the English to Oliver Cowdery, who was his principal scribe, and when it was written down and repeated by Brother Joseph to see if it was correct, then it would disappear, and another character with the interpretation would appear. Thus the Book of Mormon was translated by the gift and power of God, and not by any power of man.[48]

Whitmer reiterated that account on many occasions to many different audiences. In 1881, he told a reporter from a Kansas City newspaper: "Joseph did not see the plates in translation," he said, "but would hold the [stone] to his eyes and cover his face with a hat, excluding all light, and before him would appear what seemed to be parchment on which would appear the characters of the plates on a line at the top, and immediately below would appear the translation in English." He then added: "I, as well as all of my father's family, Smith's wife, Oliver Cowdery, and Martin Harris were present during the translation. ... [Smith] did not use the plates in the translation, but would hold the interpreters to his eyes and cover his face with a hat, excluding light."[49]

46. Martin Harris, qtd. in Stevenson, "One of the Three Witnesses."

47. "Joseph Knight, Sr., Reminiscence," in Vogel, *Early Mormon Documents,* 4:17-18.

48. David Whitmer, *An Address to All Believers in Christ,* 13.

49. David Whitmer, qtd. in "Mormonism. Authentic Account of the Origin of This Sect," 1. Alexander Campbell also noted in March 1831 that "the angel (ghost!) that discovered the plates

Whitmer explicitly tried to distinguish between the seer stone and the so-called Nephite interpreters (or Urim and Thummin), since confusion was general between them. He authorized his friend Edward Traughber to make the following statement:

> With the sanction of David Whitmer, and by his authority, I now state that he does not say that Joseph Smith ever translated in his presence by aid of Urim and thummim; but by means of one dark colored, opaque stone, called a "Seer Stone," which was placed in the crown of a hat, into which Joseph put his face, so as to exclude the external light. Then, a spiritual light would shine forth, and parchment would appear before Joseph, upon which was a line of characters from the plates, and under it, the translation in English; at least, so Joseph said.[50]

None of the eyewitnesses seems to have understood the scrying process beyond what Smith told them. One thing seems certain: The Book of Mormon is not a literal translation—at least not in any generally accepted definition of the term—of an ancient record. Whether golden plates actually existed, Smith seems not to have used or even needed them while dictating the text.

American novelist Nathaniel Hawthorne, writing in 1834, explained his own subconscious stirrings upon waking at midnight, "when the mind has a passive sensibility, but no active strength: when the imagination is a mirror, imparting vividness to all ideas, without the power of selecting or controlling them."[51] Although Joseph's scrying was a daytime activity, as writer G. St. John Stott observes, Smith "with his seer stone buried in his hat ... created his own midnight." Using his stone made it possible for him to "ignore the distractions of his environment," Stott theorizes, "still his thoughts, and let the translation that he had unconsciously studied out break into his mind."[52]

---

to [Smith], likewise informed him that he would be inspired to translate the inscriptions without looking at the plates" (qtd. in David Staats Burnett, "Something New—The Golden Bible").

50. John L. Traughber, *Saints Herald* 26 (Nov. 15, 1879): 341.

51. Nathaniel Hawthorne, "The Haunted Mind," qtd. in F. O. Matthiessen, *American Renaissance,* 232.

52. G. St. John Stott, "The Seer Stone Controversy," 47. Bertrand Russell (1872-1970), noted British mathematician and philosopher, and the author of more than forty books, explained a similar process of creativity which inspired his own writing:

> After first contemplating a book on some subject and after giving serious preliminary attention to it, I needed a period of subconscious incubation which could not be hurried and was if anything impeded by deliberate thinking. Sometimes I would find, after a time, that I had made a mistake, and that I could not write the book I had in mind. But often I was more fortunate. Having by a time of very intense concentration, planted the problem in my

For his part, Joseph was notably reticent regarding his scrying, did not encourage speculation from followers, and seems not to have attempted to analyze the inner workings that produced his dictations. He simply called what he "saw" as a product of "the gift and power of God."[53]

Joseph stopped dictating when Emma went into labor on June 14, 1828. The seer put away his stone and hat, Harris stoppered his inkwell and lay aside his quill. Martin had previously asked Smith if he could take home some manuscript as evidence to Dolly and his equally skeptical family that he was not on a fool's errand. Each time, however, Joseph had gazed into his stone, pondered for a moment, then answered no.[54] Now Harris again asked permission to take some 116 completed pages home. Despite the stormy relationship, Martin, as he told William Pilkington Jr., forty-two years later in Utah, "loved his wife and wanted to satisfy her in relation to the matter."[55]

Understandably, Smith hesitated. There was only one copy, which represented months of hard work. On the other hand, since Harris was the best (and at that point, the only) source of funding to publish the book, Smith did not want to alienate him. So he agreed, once again, to seek God's counsel through the seer stone. The conditional answer was yes, provided Martin let only five people examine the pages. Harris agreed to the demand, then left Harmony with a light heart.

The following day, June 15, after an extremely difficult delivery, Emma gave birth to the son whom Joseph had foretold. Neither he nor Emma, however, had anticipated that their first born, deformed, would live less than a day.[56] Emma received "but <small> comfort from the society of the dear little stranger," wrote Lucy Smith, perhaps recalling the stillbirth of her own first baby, "for he was very soon snatched from her arms."[57] A tiny grave was dug a stone's throw from their front door in the McCune cemetery.

---

subconscious, it would germinate underground until, suddenly, the solution emerged with blinding clarity, so that it only remained to write down what had appeared as if in a revelation. (Bertrand Russell, "How I Write," 195.)

53. "History of the Church," *Times and Seasons* 3 (Mar. 1842): 707. For a use of scrying today that seems to reflect elements of Joseph's practice, see the instructions issued by the Fellowship of the Inner Light in "Scrying."

54. William Pilkington, "A Biography [Autobiography] of William Pilkington, Jr.," 11.

55. Ibid.

56. Sophia Lewis, "Statement," in Vogel, *Early Mormon Documents,* 4:298. The infant was delivered by midwife Rhoda Skinner, wife of neighbor Jacob Skinner. After the death of her first husband, Rhoda married Emma's brother, David Hale (Linda King Newell and Valeen Tippetts Avery, *Mormon Enigma,* 314n13).

57. Anderson, *Lucy's Book,* 412.

Joseph, after weeks of being absorbed in the challenging project of dictating his text to the accommodating Martin, suddenly found his attention refocused on his wife. While her mother, sisters, and the midwife attended the agonizing delivery, Joseph probably hovered in the background or in the dooryard until he was allowed back inside. Seeing his pale, exhausted wife and the baby, struggling for breath, must have been a profound shock, emphasized by the death of the newborn. Almost certainly, the Hale men pitched in at that point, constructing a little coffin, helping to dig the grave, and standing solemnly around it while a local Methodist minister likely presided at the brief service. Most likely Emma, hemorrhaging and semi-conscious, did not hear the shovelsful of earth thud upon the remains of her tiny son.

When Emma drifted back to consciousness, Joseph was at her side. For the next two weeks, as Emma hovered near death, Joseph "never slept one hour in undisturbed quiet," said his mother.[58] He kept vigil at her bedside day and night, attending to her every need. Surely, his concern did much to excuse his faults in Elizabeth Hale's eyes.

With the passage of time, however, Joseph became anxious. He had heard nothing from Harris. The travel time, especially in the pleasant summer weather, should have taken no more than three or four days, then perhaps a week at home to check on the management of his farm, heal the breach with Dolly, and give Joseph's anxious family a detailed account of how he had spent the last two months with their son and daughter-in-law. With another three or four days to return, Martin should have been back within two weeks. But he was not.

By Independence Day, Joseph was probably drifting to the doorway several times a day, wondering if Martin would be driving up or at least sending a messenger to explain what was keeping him in Palmyra. He did not mention his uneasiness to Emma, "for fear of agitating her mind too much for the health of her body," as Lucy Smith recorded; but as Emma recovered, she could not have helped noting his anxiety. "I shall not be at ease until I know something about what Mr. Harris is doing," she finally said, urging him to go to Palmyra. At first, Joseph rejected the suggestion, begging his wife "not worry herself as he ... should not dare to be absent from her even one hour while her situation was so precarious." But Emma insisted that she would be

58. Unless otherwise noted, this section of my narrative is based on Anderson, *Lucy's Book,* 412-14.

fine. "Seeing her so cheerful and so willing to have him leave," the apprehensive Smith left for Manchester, traveling by stagecoach.

Back in Palmyra, trouble had indeed developed. Martin, true to his word, had read the manuscript pages in the evenings to five people: wife Lucy, his parents Nathan and Rhoda, both of them Quakers, his younger brother Preserved, and Dolly's widowed sister, Polly Cobb.[59] The reading had the desired effect. Dolly "seemed highly pleased with what she heard and entered into the spirit of it so much that she gave her husband the privilege of locking it up in a set of drawers" that she had not previously allowed him to touch and to which she alone had the key.[60] Evidently, this reconciliation was so heartwarming that Martin felt safe leaving the manuscript in her possession; but later, unable to resist the temptation to show it to an unnamed friend, Martin picked the lock with a penknife, damaging the bureau in the process.

When Dolly noticed the defaced piece of furniture, "her irracible temper knew no bounds," wrote Lucy Smith, "and an intolerable storm ensued throughout the house which descended with greatest force upon the head of the devoted husband." Martin was storing the manuscript in an unlocked drawer elsewhere in the house; and Dolly, according to the account Martin later gave Lucy Smith, appropriated it, giving it to a neighbor for safe keeping. When Harris discovered that the manuscript was missing, he immediately suspected Dolly, not only because of her hostility but because the Flanders Dyke episode showed that she would not hesitate to cross ethical boundaries to make a point. When he confronted her, according to John Clark, she retorted: "If this be a divine communication, the same being who revealed it to you can easily replace it."[61] Harris was "indignant at his wife beyond measure—he raved most violently, and it is said [he] actually beat Mrs. H[arris] with a rod—but she remained firm, and would not give up the manuscript."[62]

---

59. William Pilkington, "The Dying Testimony of Martin Harris …," Apr. 3, 1934, 2.

60. Anderson, *Lucy's Book,* 420.

61. John A. Clark to "Dear Brethren," Aug. 31, 1840, 98, in Vogel, *Early Mormon Documents,* 2:269. According to Lucy Smith's version, "she solemnly averred that she did not know anything about it whatever" (Anderson, *Lucy's Book,* 422).

62. Clark to "Dear Brethren," Aug. 31, 1840, 98. Harris talked to Clark at least twice, but another person may have been Clark's source on the matter of beating. "In one of his fits of rage," Dolly Harris testified, "he struck me with the but[t] end of a whip. … He beat me on the head four or five times, and the next day turned me out of doors twice, and beat me in a shameful manner" (Lucy Harris, Statement, Nov. 29, 1833, in Howe, *Mormonism Unvailed,* 254.) It is not clear if the beating occurred as a result of pilfering the manuscript or on an earlier occasion.

Meanwhile, Joseph rode north by stagecoach. Exhausted from caring for Emma and beside himself with worry, he could neither eat nor sleep. Disembarking, probably at Canandaigua, at 10:00 p.m., Joseph had twenty miles to walk before reaching the Smith farmstead. An unnamed fellow passenger in whom he confided, concerned at Smith's distraught condition, traveled the distance with him. It was almost dawn when they reached Manchester. By then, Smith was unable to walk without the stranger's assistance. The household was just stirring when they arrived, and Lucy promptly took over, feeding the stranger, who then returned to Canandaigua without even a few hours' rest.

After downing some pepper tea, Joseph sent a younger brother three miles down the road to Martin's place, asking that he breakfast with him. The family expected Harris by 8:00 a.m., but it was 12:30 p.m. before the old farmer appeared in view, his eyes cast downward. When he entered, Martin sank at the table. Normally an incessant talker, he said nothing. When Hyrum asked if he were sick, Martin pressed his hands to his temples and cried out, "Oh, I have lost my soul! I have lost my soul."

Joseph jumped up and blurted, "Martin, have you lost that manuscript? [H]ave you broken your oath and brought down condemnation upon my head as well as your own?"

"Yes," Martin sadly admitted, "it is gone and I know not where."

"Oh! My God!" Joseph groaned. He urged Martin to search for it again. But Martin said it would be no use: "I have even ripped open beds and pillows and I know it is not there."

This disclosure brought a new round of laments from Joseph: "Must I return to my wife with such a tale as this? I dare not do it, lest I should kill her at once. And how shall I appear before the Lord? Of what rebuke am I not worthy from the angel of the Most High?"

Joseph's family was also in tears. "Sobs and lamentations filled the house," recalled Lucy. Joseph paced the floor "grieving like a tender infant" until sunset. "I well remember that day of darkness," Lucy wrote, "both within and without. To us, at least, the heavens seemed clothed with blackness, and the earth shrouded with gloom. I have often said within myself, that if a continual punishment, as severe as that which we experienced on that occasion, were to be inflicted upon the most wicked characters who ever stood upon the footstool of the Almighty—if even their punishment were no greater than that, I should feel to pity their condition."[63]

63. Anderson, *Lucy's Book,* 423.

Joseph left the next morning for Harmony. "We parted with heavy hearts," wrote Mother Smith, "for it seemed as though all our fond anticipations which we had fed upon and which had been the source of so much secret gratification to us all was in a moment fled and fled forever."[64]

64. Ibid., 420.

14 | CONVERTING COUSIN COWDERY

These were days never to be forgotten—to sit under the sound of a voice dictated by the inspiration of heaven, awakened the utmost gratitude of this bosom!

—Oliver Cowdery, [Letter I] to W. W. Phelps, Sept. 7, 1834, 14

Despite his self-proclaimed powers in scrying the locations of lost objects, buried treasure, and envisioning the location of the golden plates and their interpretation, Joseph was either unable or decided not to reproduce the lost 116 pages of Book of Mormon manuscript.[1] It was a depressed young seer who returned to his wife shortly before Emma's twenty-fourth birthday on July 10, 1828. Joseph was anxious for her health, her recovery still overshadowed by their baby's recent death.

The bleak reality of the manuscript's disappearance effected a crisis of confidence in Joseph. Together he and Emma sought consolation by affiliating with local Methodists, including most of Emma's kin. The intent of the Wednesday evening class meetings was to foster an atmosphere of communal fellowship. "Here," wrote Methodist historian Thomas Morris, "where only pious friends are presumed to be present, where all would help and none would hinder us in the pursuit of spiritual life, we can freely talk over

1. Although a common assumption is that Dolly burned the pages in an attempt to end her husband's support of the Book of Mormon, evidence does not support this. Joseph proffered a revelation that said "wicked men" took the manuscript from Martin, not from his wife. Their purpose in doing so, the revelation states, was to "alter the words" of the original so that, if Joseph rewrote the manuscript, it would not agree with the altered version. This would prompt the "wicked men" to "say that [Smith] has lied in his words, and that he has no gift, and that he has no power" (D&C 10:8-18). As late as 1829, when he wrote the preface to the 1830 Book of Mormon, Smith believed that "some person or persons have stolen & kept [the manuscript] from me." One account alleges that Dolly gave the manuscript pages to a physician, Ezra Seymour, who kept them for years, reading them for entertainment to family members and his patients (William R. Hine, Affidavit, ca. Mar. 1885, 1). According to another version, J. R. Pratt, a Palmyra physician, told LDS Church Apostle Franklin D. Richards in 1880 that "he could put his hand on the manuscript which Martin Harris lost, in an hour, if it was needed" (Charles C. Richards, "An Address Delivered by Charles C. Richards ...," Apr. 20, 1947; Charles Richards was Franklin's son).

our hopes and fears, trials and deliverances, resolutions and prospects in the way to heaven. In a word, we may safely and prudently state our case as it is, whether encouraging or otherwise, and thereby secure the sympathizing prayers, counsels, exhortations, or admonitions of those in whom we have most confidence."[2]

Class meetings typically opened with a hymn. Attendees were urged to "sing lustily, and with a good courage."[3] No doubt Joseph and the others found joy in Emma's mellifluous voice. Next, the group knelt for the invocation, with a leader praying for the spiritual welfare of all present. Traditionally, the class leader then bore testimony of his spiritual condition, specifically how he had fared during the previous week. Attendees followed suit, asked "to reveal their troubles and triumphs," after which the leader offered "direction, counsel, or encouragement as might seem appropriate."[4] Participants were admonished to be frank—to reveal their spiritual struggles, hopes, fears, temptations, failures, and triumphs. John Wesley, co-founder of the Methodist Connection, observed that by sharing their testimonies, members "began to bear each other's burdens and naturally to care for each other."[5]

What peace Joseph and Emma received from Methodist worship services was soon shattered by a vocal faction within the close-knit congregation. Emma's cousin Joseph Lewis, son of Rev. Nathaniel Lewis, together with Joshua McKune accosted Joseph to tell him "plainly that such a character as he was a disgrace to the church, that he could not be a member of the church unless he broke off his sins by repentance, made public confession, renounced his fraudulent and hypocritical practices, and gave some evidence that he intended to reform and conduct himself somewhat nearer like a Christian than he had done." They warned that if he did not withdraw from the class, they would call for a disciplinary investigation. Lewis later said that Smith "immediately withdrew his name."[6] While Lewis thought Joseph had only been a member for three days, Michael Morse, Smith's brother-in-law, reported that "he was the 'leader' of the said 'class' and that to his certain knowledge Smith's name remained on the class book ... about *six months,* when it was simply 'dropped,' as Smith did *not* seek to become a full member."[7]

That October, two to three months after Joseph returned to Harmony

2. Thomas Morris, Introduction to John Miley, *Treatise on Class Meetings,* 10-11.
3. John H. Wigger, *Taking Heaven by Storm,* 84.
4. Ibid.
5. Qtd. in Kenneth Cain Kinghorn, *The Heritage of American Methodism,* 69.
6. Joseph and Hiel Lewis, "Mormon History, A New Chapter about to be Published," 1.
7. Michael Morse, Interviewed by William W. Blair, May 22, 1879, 191.

and notified Emma that his book was lost, his parents, "uneasy as to the consequences of his distress of mind," decided to visit their son and his wife.[8] En route they stopped in Fayette Township, New York, at the Peter Whitmer Sr. farmstead, "a point midway between the northern extremities of Lakes Cayuga and Seneca, two miles from Waterloo, seven miles from Geneva, and twenty-seven miles from Palmyra."[9] Evidently, the Smiths had earlier met David Whitmer, young Joseph's age, while he was in Palmyra on business and visiting a friend, Oliver Cowdery, a second cousin to Lucy Smith.[10] "A great many people in the neighborhood were talking about the finding of certain golden plates," Whitmer later stated. As they discussed the matter, Cowdery told Whitmer "he was acquainted with the Smith family, and he believed there must be some truth in the story of the plates, and that he intended to investigate the matter."[11]

The opportunity to do so came in the fall, at the beginning of the 1828 school term. A teaching position opened in the Manchester district schools.[12] Oliver's older brother Lyman, while living in nearby Arcadia, came to Manchester to interview for the position.[13] He may have heard of the vacancy from cousin Hyrum Smith, a trustee of the school board. Terms were agreed upon and Lyman was hired. The next day, however, he announced a change of plans, and requested the board hire Oliver instead. This was done, whereupon Cowdery requested that Joseph Sr. take him in as a boarder, that he might "become acquainted with his patrons in the school." Smith agreed. As soon as he settled into the family home, Oliver began asking the Smiths about the rumored golden plates. Initially, Father Smith hesitated, but the

8. Unless otherwise stated, my narrative in this section is based on Lavina Fielding Anderson, *Lucy's Book,* 423-30.

9. David Whitmer, "Interview," June 1, 1881, *Kansas City Journal,* 62. For evidence that Joseph and Lucy Smith met David Whitmer at this time, see Anderson, *Lucy's Book,* 449-50.

10. Cowdery's mother, Rebecca Fuller Cowdery, was the great-granddaughter of John Fuller and Mehitable Rowley, who were also the second great-grandparents of Lucy Mack Smith, Joseph Smith's mother. In addition, Mary Gates, a cousin of Joseph's maternal grandmother, Lydia Gates Mack, was married to Nathaniel Cowdery Jr., the brother of William Cowdery, Oliver's grandfather (Stanley R. Gunn, *Oliver Cowdery,* 33).

11. "Mormonism. Authentic Account of the Origin of This Sect," 1.

12. One may wonder why the destitute Joseph Smith Sr., soon to be cast into debtors' prison, did not assume the teaching position. But New Yorker Susan Fenimore Cooper explained: "An elderly person acting as master or mistress of a common school is an unheard of circumstance throughout the country; it may be doubted if such an individual could be found between the St. Croix and the Colorado" (Cooper, *Rural Hours,* 224).

13. Lyman Cowdery, who eventually became a lawyer and Ontario County, New York, probate judge, was born on March 12, 1802, in Wells, Vermont. He married Eliza Alexander on April 20, 1825, and died on April 22, 1881, in Elkhorn, Wisconsin.

young schoolmaster soon won his confidence. As the father related the details of his son's story, Cowdery's curiosity intensified.

Joseph and Lucy's trip to Pennsylvania whetted Oliver's desire to participate in his distant cousin's marvelous work. After leaving the Whitmer farm, the Smiths, walking since they could not afford a horse, were within three-quarters of a mile from Joseph and Emma's place when young Joseph ran to meet them. He had told Emma his parents were coming, "although he could not see us," wrote his mother. When Joseph saw his parents, his "countenance [was] blazing with delight," Lucy wrote. But the perceptive mother could also tell "a great and real trouble was seated at [his] heart." Later that night, Joseph told his parents that after he arrived home in Harmony in early July, "I commenced humbling myself in mighty prayer before the Lord." He pled for mercy, asked that he be "forgiven of all that I had done which was contrary to [his] will." In the midst of his entreaty, he said, an angel appeared. The messenger told Joseph he had sinned in delivering the manuscript "into the hands of a wicked man," and that he must pay the consequences by giving back the plates "into the hands of the angel from [whom] he had received them." The angel added that "it may be if you are sufficiently humble and penitent that you will receive them again on the 22 [of S]eptember [1828]."[14]

Soon afterwards, while gazing into his stone, Joseph voiced the first of dozens of messages he said were conveyed by God. This revelation, spoken in Joseph's own voice, was delivered in a quaint, third-person rhetoric, unlike the more authoritarian, first-person vernacular the prophet later utilized.

> 1 The works, and the designs, and the purposes of God, can not be [f]rustrated, neither can they come to nought, for God doth not walk in crooked paths; neither doth he turn to the right hand nor to the left; neither doth he vary from that which he hath said: Therefore his paths are strait and his course is one eternal round.
>
> 2 Remember, remember, that it is not the work of God that is frustrated, but the work of men: for although a man may have many revelations, and have power to do many mighty works, yet, if he boasts in his own strength, and sets at nought the counsel of God, and follows after the dictates of his own will, and carnal desires, he must fall and incur the vengeance of a just God upon him.
>
> 3 Behold, you have been intrusted with these things, but how strict

14. Anderson, *Lucy's Book,* 424-25.

were your commandments; and remember, also, the promises which were made to you, if you did not transgress them; and behold, how oft you have transgressed the commandments and the laws of God, and have gone on in the persuasions of men: for behold, you should not have feared man more than God, although men set at nought the counsel of God, and despise his words, yet you should have been faithful and he would have extended his arm, and supported you against all the fiery darts of the adversary; and he would have been with you in every time of trouble.

4 Behold thou art Joseph, and thou wast chosen to do the work of the Lord, but because of transgression, if thou art not aware thou wilt fall, but remember God is merciful: Therefore, repent of that which thou has done, and he will only cause thee to be afflicted for a season, and thou art still chosen, and wilt again be called to the work; and except thou do this, thou shalt be delivered up and become as other men, and have no more gift.

5 And when thou deliverdst up that which God had given thee sight and power to translate, thou deliverdst up that which was sacred, into the hands of a wicked man, who has set at nought the counsel of God, and has broken the most sacred promises, which were made before God, and has depended upon his own judgment, and boasted in his own wisdom, and this is the reason that thou hast lost thy privileges for a season, for thou hast suffered the counsel of thy director to be trampled upon from the beginning.

6 Nevertheless, my work shall go forth and accomplish my purposes, for as the knowledge of a Savior has come into the world, even so shall the knowledge of my people, the Nephites, and the Jacobites, and the Josephites, and the Zoramites, come to the knowledge of the Lamanites, and the Lemuelites and the Ishmaelites, which dwindled in unbelief, because of the iniquities of their fathers, who have been suffered to destroy their brethren, because of their iniquities, and their abominations: and for this very purpose are these plates preserved which contain these records, that the promises of the Lord might be fulfilled, which he made to his people; and that the Lamanites might come to the knowledge of their fathers, and that they might know the promises of the Lord, and that they may believe the gospel and rely upon the merits of Jesus Christ, and be glorified through faith in his name; and that through their repentance they might be saved: Amen.[15]

15. BC II: "A Revelation given to Joseph, in Harmony, Pennsylvania, July, 1828, after Martin had lost the Manuscript of the forepart of the book of Mormon, translated from the book of Lehi, which was abridged by the hand of Mormon."

During their visit, Joseph and Lucy Smith recounted not only the latest family and neighborhood news, but also Oliver Cowdery's interest in Joseph's book. They became acquainted with Isaac and Elizabeth Hale and other family members. "They [the Hales] were a lovely[,] intel[l]igent[,] and highly respectable Family ... pleasantly situated living in fine circumstances," remembered Lucy. During the Smiths' stay, there were apparently no difficulties over the animosity between Isaac and his son-in-law. Mother Smith wrote that the visit "passed very agreeably," and she and her husband returned to Manchester "relieved of a burden which was almost insupportable, and our present joy far overbalanced all our former grief."[16]

Upon their return home, Joseph and Lucy told Martin Harris of events in Harmony. Their recital prompted him to return to Pennsylvania. When he arrived in March 1829, Harris again tried to convince Joseph to show him the golden plates. Isaac Hale was also drawn into the drama.[17] Harris told him that it was imperative he "have a greater witness," and that he had talked with Joseph about it. But Smith told his former scribe that "he could not, or durst not show him the plates," said Hale. Joseph then agreed to walk into the woods, through the snow, where he said he had buried the plates. Upon his return, he informed Harris that he could follow his track back into the trees where he could "find the Book, and examine it for himself." But Martin was no more successful in finding the plates in the woods than his wife had been when she searched there previously.[18]

The next day, Isaac walked to Joseph and Emma's place. There he saw Joseph and Martin examining a paper. He later recalled reading such comments as *"my servent [sic] seeketh a greater witness, but no greater witness can be given him,"* and something about *"three that were to see the thing."* This may have been a reference to what eventually became Chapter IV in the *Book of Commandments,* a collection of Joseph's early revelations, which opens with: "Behold, I say unto you, that my servant Martin has desired a witness from my hand, that my servant Joseph has got the things of which he has testified, and borne record that he had received of me." Mention is made in verse 4

16. Anderson, *Lucy's Book,* 430-35.

17. My treatment of this incident, unless otherwise stated, is based on Isaac Hale's 1834 Statement.

18. In an 1859 interview, Martin seems to allude to this incident: "At one time, before the Lord showed them to me, Joseph said I should see them. I asked him, why he would break the commands of the Lord? He said, you have done so much I am afraid you will not believe unless you see them. I replied, 'Joseph, I know all about it. The Lord has showed to me ten times more about it than you know'" (qtd. in Joel Tiffany, "Mormonism—No. I," 166).

that "three shall know of a surety that these things are true, for I will give them power, that they may behold and view these things as they are." And Harris, after being criticized for a lack of humility, was promised a future "view of the things which he desireth to know" on the condition he "will go out and bow down before me, and humble himself in mighty prayer and faith."[19] Martin, perhaps once again feeling embarrassed, if not humiliated, returned to Palmyra, no doubt licking his wounds all the way home.

Joseph made no further efforts to involve Harris in producing his book until it came time to underwrite publication costs. In fact, Martin was scarcely back on his farmstead before another scribe was on his way. Sometime that same spring of 1829, Oliver Cowdery returned to the Smith home. Before supper, he told Father Smith that "it had been put into his heart" that he would visit young Joseph and become his scribe as soon as the school term finished in March. The next day, he again reportedly told his hosts that "the subject upon which we were yesterday conversing seems working in my very bones, and I cannot, for a moment, get it out of my mind." Samuel Harrison Smith was preparing to travel to Pennsylvania to help Joseph with spring farm work, and Cowdery resolved to accompany him. "I have made it a subject of prayer," Cowdery told the Smiths, "and I firmly believe that it is the will of the Lord that I should go. If there is a work for me to do in this thing, I am determined to attend to it." Father Smith advised the fervent young man first to "seek for a testimony for himself," which Cowdery did. Joseph later wrote that "[The] Lord appeared unto a young man by the name of Oliver Cowdery and shewed unto him the plates in a vision and also the truth of the work and what the Lord was about to do through me his unworthy servant therefore he was desirous to come and write for me to translate."[20] Lucy added that "from this time forth Oliver was so entirely absorbed in the subject of the record that it seemed impossible for him to think or converse about anything else."[21]

Meanwhile, Father Smith's three-year contract with seventy-year-old Lemuel Durfee was drawing to a close. The poverty-stricken Smiths were forced to vacate their frame house and move into the cramped log home occupied by Hyrum, his pregnant wife, Jerusha, and one-year-old daughter,

19. Similar phraseology appears in the Book of Mormon when King Benjamin, a major character, exhorts people to "humble yourselves before God; and ask in sincerity of heart that he would forgive you" (Mos. 4:10).

20. Joseph Smith History, 1832, in Dean C. Jesse, *The Papers of Joseph Smith,* 1:10.

21. Anderson, *Lucy's Book,* 433.

Lovina. "We now felt more keenly than ever," wrote Mother Smith, "the injustice of the measure which had placed a landlord over us on our own premises, and who was about to eject us from them." The small dwelling with two bedrooms plus a loft became home to twelve people: Hyrum's household, Joseph and Lucy, adult children Sophronia and Harrison, teenagers William and Katharine, youngsters Don Carlos and Lucy—and Oliver Cowdery. Lucy Smith, while not mentioning her family's failed attempts at money-digging, her husband's drinking, and sheer bad luck, attributed their reverses to having turned their backs "upon the world and set out in the service of God."

Lemuel Durfee, who would die on August 8, 1829, had come to the Smiths' aid in their darkest hour, purchasing their property and allowing them to live there for three years. He now wanted the farm and frame home for daughter Mary and her husband, Roswell Nichols. Lucy Smith complained to Cowdery that the Durfees were "wicked men who fear not God[,] neither do they regard man." Have the Durfees ever "lifted a finger to earn any part of that which they now claim?" she asked. "I tell you they have not." Obviously believing that religious differences, not economic necessity, had prompted Quaker Durfee's actions, Mother Smith wrote that she now "give[s] up all this for the sake of Christ and salvation, and I pray God to help me to do so, without a murmur or a tear." She also informed Oliver that the family could no longer house him comfortably. "Mother," Cowdery begged, according to Lucy, "let me stay with you, for I can live in any log hut where you and father live, but I cannot leave you."[22]

In April, when the weather was wet and miserable, Oliver and twenty-one-year-old Harrison set out on foot southward, a journey that would ultimately dictate both their fates. They stopped at the Whitmers en route. According to David Whitmer, Oliver assured him that "as soon as [he] found out anything either truth or untruth [about the golden plates] he would let me know."[23] Meanwhile, in Harmony, Joseph's progress on his book had slowed to a crawl. Emma's household labors consumed so much time that she could seldom scribe for him. Three days before Oliver and Harrison arrived, as Lucy later reported, Joseph became so concerned about the lack of progress that he knelt to implore God to send him a scribe. Mother Smith said that "he was informed that the same should be forthcoming in a few

22. Ibid., 437.

23. David Whitmer, qtd. in "Mormonism. Authentic Account of the Origin of This Sect," 1.

days." Accordingly, near sunset on Sunday evening April 5, 1829, when Cowdery extended his hand in greeting and explained why he came to Harmony, "Joseph was not at all surprised."[24]

That first night, the two cousins, who probably knew of each other but had never met, stayed up while Joseph told Oliver his "entire history as far as it was necessary for his information in those things which concerned him." No doubt Cowdery offered his own life story as well. Born in Vermont like Joseph, Cowdery, the eighth child of William Cowdery Jr. and Rebecca Fuller Cowdery, was ten months younger than his cousin. Since 1824, Oliver had been living in western New York near several of his siblings.[25] Most important, he, like Joseph, was also blessed with a special gift. "Behold thou hast a gift, and blessed art thou because of thy gift," Joseph would state in a soon-to-be-given revelation:

> Remember it is sacred and cometh from above; and if thou wilt inquire, thou shalt know mysteries which are great and marvelous: therefore thou shalt exercise thy gift, that thou mayest find out mysteries, that thou mayest bring many to the knowledge of the truth; yea, convince them of the error of their ways. Make not thy gift known unto any, save it be those which are of thy faith.—Trifle not with sacred things.[26]

In another revelation, Joseph identified Cowdery's gift as "the gift of working with the sprout."[27] This divining rod "hath told you things behold there is no other power save God that can cause this thing of Nature to work in your hands for it is the work of God & therefore whatsoever ye shall ask to tell you by that means that will he grant unto you that ye shall know."[28]

---

24. Anderson, *Lucy's Book,* 438.

25. Cowdery's oldest brother, Warren, was living in Freedom, New York, by 1816. The next year, siblings Dyer, Erastus, and Sally joined Warren in New York (Larry E. Morris, "Oliver Cowdery's Vermont Years and the Origins of Mormonism," 111). Oliver remained behind in Poultney, Vermont, with his father and stepmother until 1825.

26. BC V:5.

27. Sprout: "A shoot from the end of a branch" (Noah Webster, *American Dictionary of the English Language* [1828], s.v. "Sprout, 2").

28. "6th Commandment AD 1829," cited in Robin Scott Jensen et al., *The Joseph Smith Papers,* 15-16. The "sprout" reference, according to the editors of the Smith Papers, was at some point changed by Signey Rigdon to read "rod," the reading printed in BC VII:3. This was altered once again by Joseph Smith when he reprinted the text in the 1835 *Doctrine and Covenants:* "Now this is not all thy gift; for you have another gift, which is the gift of Aaron; behold, it has told you many things" (D&C 8:6). B. H. Roberts said in 1901 that "the gift which the Lord says [Cowdery] has in his hand meant a [divining] stick which was like Aaron's Rod. It is said Bro. Phineas Young got it from [Cowdery] and gave it to President [Brigham] Young who had it with him when he arrived in this valley and that it was with that stick that he pointed out where the [Salt Lake] temple should be built" (qtd. in John P. Hatch, *Danish Apostle,* 130-31).

Cowdery and Harrison must have brought Joseph some money, although the amount and the source are unknown. On Monday, April 6, Oliver helped Joseph secure written confirmation regarding the agreement with Isaac Hale to purchase for $200 the 13.5 acres he was farming. Joseph gave his father-in-in-law a down payment of $64. The agreement, witnessed by Oliver and Harrison, stipulated an additional $50 payment on May 1, less than a month away. The final payment of $86 would be made the following year, on May 1, 1830.[29] It was Tuesday, April 7, Cowdery later said, when the two men rolled up their sleeves and commenced to work on the English text of the Book of Mormon. Before long, however, provisions ran out. The two extra mouths had quickly depleted Joseph and Emma's stores. Isaac Hale would not help, so Joseph and Oliver walked upriver to Colesville in search of Joseph Knight Sr. who, with his wife, Polly, had visited Joseph and Emma in March.[30] But Knight was lumbering in the Catskills, and the cousins returned empty-handed to Harmony. Within a few days, however, Knight arrived with ten bushels of grain, six of potatoes, a barrel of mackerel, a pound of tea, and a ream of lined paper.

It is easy to envision Smith and Cowdery, two zealous young men, forestalling their bedtimes nightly with brains locked in heady conversation about the unfolding of Joseph's book. Cowdery was impressed that Joseph seemed to read his mind on occasion. He wrote to David Whitmer that, according to Whitmer's later statement, "Joseph had enquired of the Lord concerning him, and had told him secrets of his life that he knew could not be known to any person but himself, in any other way than by revelation from the Almighty."[31] Still, as Oliver labored with Joseph over the Book of Mormon narrative, he like others may have wondered about the absence of any golden plates.

Whitmer later explained—based upon discussions Joseph would also have had with Oliver—why the plates were not present during the transcription process. After Joseph was chastised for the loss of the 116 pages, he was told he "would not be permitted to see the 'plates' that the 'Characters' would appear before him & when he translated them correctly they would

29. Isaac Hale, Land Agreement with Joseph Smith, Apr. 6, 1829.

30. Knight wrote that near the end of March 1829, "I told my wife I must go Dow[n] and see Joseph again[. W]hy Do you go so soon for [,] said she[. S]ays I[,] Come go and see[;] and she went with me[. N]ext morning we went Down and found them well and were glad to see us[.] Joseph talked with us about his translating and some revelations he had Received and from that time my wife Began to Bel[i]eve" (Joseph Knight, Sr., "Reminiscence," 4).

31. David Whitmer, Interviewed by James H. Hart, Mar. 10, 1884; see also BC V:11.

disappear & new ones come in their place[;] if not translated correctly the first time they would remain until they were[.]"[32] Perhaps to demonstrate for Cowdery his ability to "translate" items that were not present, Joseph also scryed "from parchment, written and hid up by" John the Revelator of the New Testament. Gazing into his stone, the natural born seer envisioned:

> And the Lord said unto me, John my beloved, what desirest thou? And I said Lord, give unto me power that I may bring souls unto thee.— And the Lord said unto me: Verily, verily I say unto thee, because thou desiredst this, thou shalt tarry till I come in my glory:
>
> And for this cause, the Lord said unto Peter:—If I will that he tarry till I come, what is that to thee? For he desiredst of me that he might bring souls unto me: but thou desiredst that thou might speedily come unto me in my kingdom: I say unto thee, Peter, this was a good desire, but my beloved has undertaken a greater work.
>
> Verily I say unto you, ye shall both have according to your desires, for ye both joy in that which ye have desired.[33]

Cowdery, who years later became a lawyer, was drawn to Joseph's charisma. According to David Whitmer, the young seer told Oliver that "it was the will of heaven that he should be his scribe." Cowdery added that although he had not seen golden plates, he "knew of a certainty that he had a record of a people that inhabited this continent, and that the plates they were translating gave a complete history of these people."[34] The seer and his scribe did not attempt to reproduce the lost 116 pages. Smith later announced that he was "commanded of the Lord that I should not translate the same over again." In explanation, Joseph wrote a 284-word sentence which declared in part:

> I would inform you that I translated, by the gift and power of God, and caused to be written, one hundred and sixteen pages, the which I took from the Book of Lehi, which was an account abridged from the plates of Lehi, by the hand of Mormon; which said account, some person or persons have stolen and kept from me, notwithstanding my utmost exertions to recover it again—and being commanded of the Lord that I should not translate the same over again, for Satan had put it into their hearts to tempt the Lord their God, by altering the words, that they did

32. David Whitmer, Interviewed by M. J. Hubble, Nov. 13, 1886.
33. BC VI.
34. David Whitmer, qtd. in "Mormonism. Authentic Account of the Origin of This Sect," 1.

> read contrary from that which I translated and caused to be written; and if I should bring forth the same words again, or, in other words, if I should translate the same over again, they would publish that which they had stolen, and Satan would stir up the hearts of this generation, that they might not receive this work[.][35]

Thus, when Smith and Cowdery started their partnership, they began work, not on "The First Book of Nephi," which would come later but appear as the first book in the Book of Mormon, but on "The Book of Mosiah," which would appear later in the Book of Mormon.[36] It was apparently understood that Oliver, at least occasionally, would be allowed to scry as well. "[A]ssuredly as the Lord liveth," one heavenly promise to Cowdery began, you "shall receive a knowledge concerning the engravings of old records, which are ancient, which contain those parts of my scripture of which have been spoken, by the manifestation of my Spirit; yea, behold I will tell you in your mind and in your heart by the Holy Ghost, which shall come upon you and which shall dwell in your heart."[37] Elsewhere, Joseph delivered more reassurance: "Verily, verily I say unto you, that there are records which contain much of my gospel, which have been kept back because of the wickedness of the people; and now I command you, that if you have good desires, a desire to lay up treasures for yourself in heaven, then shall you assist in bringing to light, with your gift, those parts of my scriptures which have been hidden because of iniquity."[38]

But when Oliver attempted to scry, the stone—as Joseph once commented—was "as dark as Egypt."[39] Try as he might, Cowdery could not envision ancient characters. Frustrated, he could not understand why God's promise was not being fulfilled. When Joseph then gazed into the darkness, Cowdery was told:

> I would that you should continue [writing] until you have finished this record which I have intrusted unto you, and then behold, other records have I, that I will give unto you power that you may assist to translate:
>
> Be patient my son, for it is wisdom in me, and it is not expedient that you should translate at this present time. Behold the work which you are

35. Preface, 1830 Book of Mormon, iii.
36. For a treatment of this issue, see Brent Lee Metcalfe, "The Priority of Mosiah."
37. BC VII:1.
38. Ibid., V:12.
39. See Edward Stevenson, "The Three Witnesses to the Book of Mormon," 389.

called to do, is to write for my servant Joseph. … Do not murmur my son, for it is wisdom in me that I have dealt with you after this manner.

Behold you have not understood, you have supposed that I would give it unto you, when you took no thought, save it was to ask me; but behold I say unto you, that you must study it out in your mind; then you must ask me if it be right, and if it is right; I will cause that your bosom shall burn within you: therefore, you shall feel that it is right; but if it be not right, you shall have no such feelings, but you shall have a stupor of thought, that shall cause you to forget the thing which is wrong: therefore, you cannot write that which is sacred, save it be given you from me.

Now if you had known this, you could have translated: nevertheless, it is not expedient that you should translate now. Behold it was expedient when you commenced, but you feared and the time is past, that it is not expedient now.[40]

Joseph's own dictation process seems not to have shown any such sequence of study, hypothesis, and prayer. As G. St. John Stott notes: "Had Smith 'studied out' each line of his translation Cowdery would surely have noted and attempted to follow suit; and, for that matter, others who had watched Smith at work would have mentioned his habit of working line by line (or by any block that we can imagine) and testing his translation with prayer."[41] Although Smith frequently said that the Book of Mormon came through "the gift and power of God," no eyewitness account explicitly mentions prayer as an obvious part of the process. Later, Smith told Orson Pratt that he "translated" the plates by the "Spirit of Revelation and Prophecy."[42] Later still, while speaking publicly in Washington, D.C., in February 1840, Joseph said that the book "was communicated to him, direct from heaven. If there was such a thing on earth as the author of it, then he (Smith) was the author; but the idea that he wished to impress was, that he had penned it as dictated by God."[43]

During an 1839 sermon, Smith explained how he viewed the revelation process. "A person may profit by noticing the first intimations of the Spirit of Revelation," he said, "for instance when you feel pure Inteligence flowing unto you it may give you sudden strokes of ideas that by noticeing [sic] it you may find it, fulfilled the same day or Soon. (I.E.) Those things

40. BC VIII.

41. Stott, "The Seer Stone Controversy," 41.

42. Orson Pratt, quoting Joseph Smith, "Minutes of the School of Prophets, Salt Lake City, Jan. 14, 1871," in Robert J. Matthews, *"A Plainer Translation,"* 40.

43. Andrew F. Ehat and Lyndon W. Cook, *The Words of Joseph*, 34.

that were presented unto your minds by the Spirit of God will come to pass and thus by learning the Spirit of God. & understanding it you may grow into the principle of Revelation. Until you become perfect in Christ Jesus."[44] Joseph believed that everyone was entitled to personal revelation, asserting that "any man that does not receive revelation for himself is damned,"[45] but his own ability to scry was a relatively unique endowment. The gift of seeing was numbered among other New Testament gifts of the spirit as prophecy and tongues. The seer stone was merely one of the means whereby Joseph exercised his gift.

Once this episode established Joseph's superiority as seer, he and Cowdery returned to their task. Cowdery later said that after Smith dictated the account of Jesus' appearance to the Nephites in 3 Nephi, he and Joseph considered their own unbaptized state. "No men in their sober senses," Cowdery wrote, "could translate and write the directions given to the Nephites, from the mouth of the Savior ... without desiring a privilege of showing the willingness of the heart by being buried in the liquid grave, to answer a good conscience by the resurrection of Jesus Christ ... we only waited for the commandment to be given. Arise and be baptized."[46] Lucy Smith's version is different. She wrote that, shortly after Smith and Cowdery began working together, the seer received a commandment from God through his stone to "repair to the water, and attend to the ordinance of Baptism," since neither had yet been baptized. Accordingly, and in harmony with the instructions given in Mosiah, Joseph and Oliver found a quiet pool on the Susquehanna behind the house, immersed each other in the river, and came forth "greatly glorifying and praising God."[47] In his study of LDS priesthood authority, Gregory A. Prince notes, "Smith's and Cowdery's baptisms ... were thus divinely authorized, though not as a prerogative based on the duties of any [priesthood] office." Later accounts, as Prince observes, describe "additional elements such as authority from an angel conferred by the laying on of hands and tandem rather than simultaneous baptism, in contrast to the Book of Mormon model."[48]

---

44. Ibid., 5-6.

45. Ibid., 230.

46. Oliver Cowdery to W. W. Phelps, Sept. 7, 1834 [Letter I], *Latter Day Saints Messenger and Advocate* 1 (Oct. 1834): 15.

47. *History of the Church,* 1:44.

48. Gregory A. Prince, *Power from On High,* 5. Prince has developed a timetable of early Mormon and non-Mormon records which documents Smith and Cowdery's claim of a restoration of divine authority. The 1830 accounts support the appearance of angels. Beginning in late 1832, but not explicitly until late 1834, records note the receipt of priesthood from angels, and in

As Joseph and Oliver were returning to the house, according to Lucy, they stumbled upon Harrison Smith in a secluded spot engaged in vocal but secret prayer. Both Joseph and Oliver considered the prayer evidence of Harrison's "honesty of heart and zeal for religion," and the three returned to the river to baptize Harrison also. Harrison remained with Joseph and Emma, helping to maintain the farm and attending school until August 1829. In late summer, he returned to New York where he told family the good news about the progress of Joseph's work.[49]

When Martin Harris heard Harrison's report, he decided to see for himself. Wife Dolly, just as enthusiastically, decided to thwart her husband's intentions. According to Lucy Smith, Dolly rode through the neighborhood

---

1835 the angels were finally named (ibid., 7). Cowdery described the appearance of an angel—subsequently said to be John the Baptist—at the baptism:

> The Lord, who is rich in mercy and ever willing to answer the consistent prayer of the humble, after we had called upon him in a fervent manner, aside from the abodes of men, condescended to manifest to us his will. On a sudden, as from the midst of eternity, the voice of the Redeemer spake peace to us, while the veil was parted, and the angel of God came down clothed with glory, and delivered the anxiously looked for message, and the keys of the gospel of repentance. What joy! What wonder! What amazement!
>
> While the world were [w]racked and distracted—while millions were groping as the blind for the wall, and while all men were resting upon uncertainty as a general mass, our eyes beheld—our ears heard. As in the blaze of day; yes, more—above the glitter of the May sunbeam, which then shed its brilliancy over the face of nature. Then his voice, though mild, pierced to the centre, and his words, "I am thy fellow servant," dispelled every fear. We listened—we gazed—we admired. It was the voice of the angel from glory—it was a message from the Most High; and as we heard we rejoiced, while his love enkindled upon our souls, and we were wrapt in the vision of the Almighty. Where was room for doubt? Nowhere, uncertainty had fled, doubt had sunk, no more to rise, while fiction and deception had fled forever.
>
> But ... think further, think for a moment, what joy filled our hearts, and with what surprise we must have bowed, (for who would not have bowed the knee for such a blessing?) When we received under his hand the holy priesthood, as he said, in the name of Messiah, I confer this priesthood and this authority, which shall remain upon earth, that the sons of Levi may yet offer an offering unto the Lord in righteousness. (Cowdery to Phelps, [Letter I], 14-15.)

David Whitmer reported that, when he moved Smith and Cowdery to the Whitmer farm in June 1829, "I conversed freely with them upon this great work they were bringing about, and Oliver stated to me in Joseph[']s presence that they had baptized each other seeking by that to fulfill the command. ... I never heard that an Angel had ordained Joseph and Oliver to the Aaronic priesthood until the year 1834[,] 5. Or 6—in Ohio. My information from Joseph and Oliver upon this matter [is] they were commanded so to do by revealment through Joseph. I do not believe that John the Baptist ever ordained Joseph and Oliver as stated and believed by some, I regard that as an error, a misconception" (David Whitmer, Interviewed by Zenos H. Gurley, Jan. 14, 1885). See also Dan Vogel, "Evolution of Early Mormon Prieshtood Narratives," *Journal Whitmer Historical Association Journal* 34, no. 1 (Spring/Summer 2014): 58-80. For a different approach, see Mark Lyman Staker, "Where Was the Aaronic Priesthood Restored?: Identifying the Location of John the Baptist's Appearance, May 15, 1829," *Mormon Historical Studies* 12, no. 2 (Fall 2011): 142-59.

49. Harrison was actually baptized on May 25, 1829, according to Joseph Smith's history *(History of the Church,* 1:44), not on May 15, as Lucy has it.

"like a dark spirit, making diligent enquiry at every house" in hopes of gleaning solid evidence that Joseph did not have golden plates, and that his intention was to obtain "money from those who might be so credulous as to believe him." After she had assembled what she considered sufficient testimony, she entered a complaint before a magistrate at nearby Lyons, the Wayne County seat. She also asked lawyer Lyman Cowdery, Oliver's brother, to come to Lyons to "travel post haste" to Pennsylvania, should a decision be given against Joseph, with officers to assist them in "securing [Joseph Smith] and confining him in prison."[50]

Lucy Smith reported the court proceedings as she heard them from friends who were in attendance. The first witness, probably Peter Ingersoll, reported that the wooden box Joseph said housed the golden plates actually contained "nothing but sand; and he, Joseph Smith, said it was gold, to deceive the people." The second witness swore that Joseph told him that the box contained nothing but lead, and "he was determined to use it as he saw fit." The third witness declared that he once asked Joseph what was in his box and Joseph told him "there was nothing at all in the box," adding that "he had made fools of the whole of them, and all he wanted was, to get Martin Harris's money away from him."

Dolly Harris also submitted her own affidavit affirming that "she believed the chief object which Joseph Smith had in view, was to defraud her husband out of all his property, and that she did not believe that Joseph Smith had ever been in possession of the gold plates which he talked so much about." The magistrate then forbade the introduction of any more witnesses until he questioned Martin Harris. Harris "raised his hand to heaven," wrote Lucy Smith, and told the judge:

> I can swear, that Joseph Smith never has got one dollar from me by persuasion since God made me. I did once, of my own free will and accord, put fifty dollars into his hands, in the presence of many witnesses, for the purpose of doing the work of the Lord. This, I can pointedly prove; and I can tell you, furthermore, that I have never seen, in Joseph Smith, a disposition to take any man's money without giving him a reasonable compensation for the same in return. And as to the plates which he professes to have, gentlemen, if you do not believe it, but continue to resist the truth, it will one day be the means of damning your souls.

---

50. Unless otherwise stated, my narrative on this incident is derived from Anderson, *Lucy's Book*, 441-45.

After Harris, according to Lucy, the judge said no further witnesses were required, ordered his clerk to hand over the record of the proceedings, shredded it, and ordered the complainants to "go home about their business, and trouble him no more with such ridiculous folly." Meanwhile, back in Harmony, the ambience had darkened. "We had been threatened with being mobbed from time to time," Joseph later wrote, "and this, too, by professors of religion. And their intentions of mobbing us were only counteracted by the influence of my wife's father's family."[51] Even this support ebbed when Smith and Cowdery began to argue against the religious views of Isaac Hale's family, friends, and neighbors. "[F]eeling it to be our duty," Joseph later said, "we commenced to reason out of the Scriptures with our acquaintances and friends, as we happened to meet with them."[52] Although Joseph did not then suggest that he might organize his own church, he seems clearly to be moving in that direction. As he had earlier told Harrison: "We informed him of what the Lord was about to do for the children of men, and began to reason with him out of the Bible." Both Cowdery and Smith had labored extensively with the twenty-year-old Presbyterian, persuading "him concerning the gospel of Jesus Christ, which was now about to be revealed in its fulness."[53]

Joseph was convinced he knew what God had in mind for himself and for the rest of humanity. This confident assurance was likely what irked Isaac Hale and his Methodist friends and relatives, most of whom already viewed Joseph as a fraud. Emma's brother Alva, who had helped Joseph move to Harmony, testified in 1834 that "he knows Joseph Smith Jr. to be an imposter, and a liar."[54] Emma's Uncle Nathaniel Lewis added that he knew Joseph well and did not consider him "a man of truth and veracity; and that his general character in this part of the country, is that of an impostor, hypocrite and liar."[55] And sixty-nine-year-old Isaac, wrote Joseph, prior to Oliver Cowdery's arrival with means to avert the crisis, had been ready "to turn me out of doors."[56]

Joseph never commented publicly on the distress this breach caused Emma or if her loyalty wavered when he finally decided to relocate to a less hostile locale. Accordingly, while gazing into his stone, he was "commanded to write a letter to a man by the name of David Whitmer" to tell him that "he must come with his team immediately" to convey Joseph and Oliver to

51. *History of the Church,* 1:44.
52. Ibid.
53. Ibid.
54. Alva Hale, Affidavit, 1834 1.
55. Nathaniel Lewis, Statement, 1834, 1.
56. Joseph Smith, History, 1832, 6.

the Whitmer residence. The reason for haste, Smith wrote, was that "evil-designing people were seeking to take away [Joseph's] life, in order to prevent the work of God from going forth to the world."[57] Whitmer left his own account, in which he stated that Smith needed to leave the community quickly "on account of the persecutions and threats and the watchings that were going on in Harmony,—men trying to get possession of the plates."[58] Joseph was also looking for a new patron. He was broke and needed room and board from the well-to-do Peter Whitmer family. Father Whitmer, according to one account, was a "hard-working, God-fearing man, a strict Presbyterian [who] brought his children up with rigid sectarian discipline."[59]

When David Whitmer received Joseph's letter, he showed it to his parents and siblings, asking their advice. His father reminded him that he had sown a substantial amount of grain that needed to be harrowed. That, plus fertilizing, would take a minimum of two full working days. "You cannot go," his father said, "unless you get an evidence from God that it is very necessary."[60] This pleased David, said Lucy Smith, and he asked God what to do. Whitmer felt "the Spirit" urge him to go as soon as his wheat was harrowed. The next morning, as he surveyed his field, he concurred in his father's estimate that it would require two heavy days of work. He decided that if he could finish the work more quickly than it had ever been done before, he would consider the speed as "evidence that it was the will of God, that he should do all in his power to assist Joseph Smith in the work in which he was engaged." By noon, he had finished half the field; by suppertime, the remainder.

The next morning, he was astonished to discover the fertilizer already spread on his field. His sister reported that on the previous day, she had seen three men working in the field and assumed David had hired them. But David had not hired anyone, was never able to find out who the workers were, and concluded the event had been a miracle. He drove his two-horse rig the 135 miles to Harmony within two days; the speed must have been considerable. When he arrived, Whitmer said, Oliver told him they "knew just when I started, where I put up at night and even the name on the sign board of the hotel where I stayed each night." They knew this because Cowdery had requested Smith "to look in the Seer stone," after which he "told him

57. Anderson, *Lucy's Book,* 446.

58. David Whitmer, qtd. in Joseph F. Smith, Statement, Apr. 25, 1918.

59. "Special Correspondence," *Chicago Tribune,* Dec. 17, 1885.

60. Unless otherwise stated, my narrative in this section is based on Anderson, *Lucy's Book,* 447-49.

all these particulars of [Whitmer's] journey."[61] Whitmer, like Cowdery, fell under Smith's charisma. "Joseph Smith was a man of great magnetism," David would later say, "made friends easily, was liberal and noble in his impulses, tall, finely formed and full of animal life, but sprung from the most humble of circumstances."[62]

Earlier, Joseph had concluded that although he and Cowdery should go to the Whitmer farm in New York, Emma should stay temporarily behind with her parents. As he was packing, Joseph again gazed into his stone to ask "in what manner the plates should be conveyed to their point of destination." According to his mother, he was assured to "give himself no trouble about [that] but hasten to [W]aterloo and after he arrived a[t] Mr. Whitmore's house if he would repair immediately to the garden he would receive the plates from the hand of an angel to whose charge they must be committed for their safety."[63]

The three men arrived at the Whitmer farmstead in late May. On or near June 1, 1829, Joseph and Oliver resumed their work on the book. "It was a laborious work for the weather was very warm," said David Whitmer, "and the days were long and they worked from morning till night. But they were both young and strong and were soon able to complete the work." Many observers, including all members of the Whitmer family, were allowed to watch the scrying and dictation. Joseph and Oliver were not screened from view, and there were no golden plates present. David left many accounts, including:

> The way it was done was thus: Joseph would place the seerstone in a deep hat, and placing his face close to it, would see, not the stone, but what appeared like an oblong piece of parchment, on which the hieroglyphics would appear, and also the translation in the English language, all appearing in bright luminous letters. Joseph would then read it to Oliver, who

61. David Whitmer, Interviewed by James H. Hart, Mar. 10, 1884.

62. "David Whitmer Interviewed," *Saints' Herald,* Nov. 15, 1881, 347.

63. According to Edward Stevenson, Diary, Dec. 23, 1877. David Whitmer told him that en route to Waterloo, the three travelers passed

> an aged man about 5 feet 10, heavy set and on his back an old fashioned army knapsack strapped over his shoulders and something square in it, and he walked alongside of the wagon and wiped the sweat off his face, smiling very pleasant. David asked him to ride and he replied, "I am going across to the Hill Cumorah." Soon after they passed, they felt strangely and stopped but could see nothing of him ... and they asked the Lord about it. He said that the Prophet looked as white as a sheet and said that it was one of the Nephites, and that he had the plates.

Joseph F. Smith related essentially the same story, which he said David Whitmer told him personally (Joseph F. Smith, Statement, Apr. 25, 1918).

> would write it down as spoken. Sometimes Joseph could not pronounce the words correctly, having had but little education; and if by any means a mistake was made in the copy, the luminous writing would remain until it was corrected. It sometimes took Oliver several trials to get the right letters to spell correctly some of the more difficult words, but when he had written them correctly, the characters and the interpretation would disappear and the interpretation would disappear, and be replaced by other characters and their interpretation.
>
> When the seer-stone was not placed in the hat, no characters or writing could be seen therein, but when so placed then the hieroglyphics would appear as before described. Some represented but one word, or name, some represented several, and some from one to two lines.[64]

When Zenas H. Gurley, editor of the *Saints' Herald* (a publication of the Reorganized Church of Jesus Christ of Latter Day Saints, later Community of Christ), interviewed Whitmer in 1885, he specifically asked if Joseph used his stone "to finish up the translation." Whitmer replied, "[H]e used a stone called a 'Seers stone,' the 'Interpreters' having been taken away from him because of transgression. The 'Interpreters' were taken from Joseph after he allowed Martin Harris to carry away the 116 pages of Ms of the Book of Mormon as a punishment, but he was allowed to go on and translate by the use of a 'Seers stone' which he had, and which he placed in a hat into which he buried his face, stating to me and others that the original character appeared upon parchment and under it the translation in English."[65]

Shortly after Joseph and Oliver settled in at the Whitmer place, Emma arrived. She and Joseph occupied a second-story room to the right of the head of the stairs. Conditions in the crowded log home during the summer evidently caused Joseph to flare up in anger with his wife one morning. David recalled that as long as Joseph remained agitated, he could not scry. After a walk outside, a prayer in the orchard, and a request that Emma forgive him, Smith found that inspiration again flowed.[66]

---

64. Whitmer, Interviewed by Hart, Mar. 10, 1884.

65. "Questions Asked of David Whitmer at His Home in Richmond Ray County Mo. Jan. 14-1885 Relating to Book of Mormon, and the History of the Church of Jesus Christ of LDS by Elder Z. H. Gurley."

66. David Whitmer remembered that "Joseph quarrelled with his wife, and lost the spirit of revelation until he repented and made amends with his wife." David Whitmer, "Communication from Elder D. Whitmer," 765. The same year, he also told a lengthier version of the same experience:

> On one occasion the prophet had indulged in a stormy quarrel with his wife. Without pacifying her or making any reparation for his brutal treatment, he returned to the room in

Joseph did not hesitate to dispense revelations to the Whitmers. God's word functioned as a medium of exchange in the young prophet's visionary economy. He delivered revelations to David, John, and Peter Whitmer Jr. Each, in nearly identical words, was told of the marvelous work about to come forth. The field was white, ready to be harvested. It awaited only their sickles. While all the brothers were instructed to declare repentance to the people and bring souls to Jesus, David was also promised that, if he asked the Father in the name of the Son, having faith, he should receive the Holy Ghost and stand as a special witness to the truth of the Book of Mormon (D&C 14:8).

As the production of the manuscript drew to a close, Smith and Cowdery filled out copyright documents for the new book. The title page was submitted to R. R. Lansing, clerk of the Northern District of New York, on June 11, 1829. By the end of June, the Book of Mormon was finished. Joseph wrote to his parents, twenty-five miles away, asking them to tell Martin Harris the work was done. "That same evening," wrote Lucy Smith, "we conveyed this intelligence to Martin Harris, for we loved the man, although his weakness had cost us much trouble." Harris wanted to congratulate Joseph in person. At sunset the next day, he, Joseph Sr., and Lucy reached the Whitmer place. Cowdery and Smith entertained them by reading aloud from the completed manuscript. "It would be superfluous for me," wrote Lucy, to "say to any one who has read these pages that we were greatly rejoiced for it then appeared to us who did not realize the magnitude of the work which <could> hardly be said at that time to have begin[n]ing, as though the greatest difficulty was then surmounted."[67]

The next morning after breakfast, Joseph Sr., Lucy, Martin, Joseph Jr.,

---

the Whitmer residence to resume the work with the plates. The surface of the magic stone remained blank, and all his persistent efforts to bring out the coveted words proved abortive. He went into the woods again to pray, and this time was gone fully an hour. His friends became positively concerned, and were about to institute a search, when Joseph entered the room, pale and haggard, having suffered a vigorous chastisement at the hands of the Lord. He went straight in humiliation to his wife, entreated and received her forgiveness, returned to his work, and, much to the joy of himself and his anxious friends surrounding him, the stone again glared forth its letters of fire. (David Whitmer, Interviewed by *Omaha Herald,* Oct. 10, 1886.)

Joseph Smith III reported that, after his father died, some claimed "that [M]other was quarrelsome and was antagonistic to my father, and frequently made trouble for him." But young Joseph reported that "I never heard any quarreling or harsh language between them under any circumstances, and that even disagreements between them were not conducted in a noisy or angry manner, that mother's language was quiet and temperate, and so was father's" (Joseph Smith III, "What Do I Remember of Nauvoo," 337). Joseph III was eleven years old when his father was killed.

67. Anderson, *Lucy's Book,* 452.

and Oliver joined the Whitmers in reading, singing, and praying in the sitting room. Arising from his knees after the prayer, Joseph walked to Harris, looked into his eyes, and announced: "Martin Harris, you have got to humble yourself before your God this day, that you may obtain a forgiveness of your sins. If you do, it is the will of God that you should look upon the plates, in company with Oliver Cowdery and David Whitmer."[68] It was an electrifying moment. Two decades later, when Lucy Smith was recounting the episode, she averred that "a solemnity … thrills through my veins to this day, when it occurs to my recollection."

An ultimate moment of truth had arrived. Many had heard remarkable stories, anecdotes of golden plates, a gold breastplate, magical spectacles, a compass used in the Arabian wilderness, and a sword that once severed its owner's head in Jerusalem. But Joseph, who had done the telling, had yet to exhibit tangible proof.[69] Where Jesus gave evidence of himself by saying: "handle me and see," three adult men were now going to be shown the original Nephite record. Their collective witness would prove that true gold never feared the refiner's fire.

---

68. Ibid., 452.

69. Aside from his earlier promises to Martin and Dolly Harris, Joseph also told others they would see the golden plates. Alva Hale testified that Joseph told him "he should see the Plates from which he translated the book of Mormon," but when he arrived at the appointed time, "Smith did not show them, but appeared angry" (Alva Hale, Affidavit, Mar. 20, 1834). Nathaniel Lewis reported that Joseph told him "he was to exhibit the plates to the world, at a certain time, which was then about eighteen months distant. … After the time stipulated had passed away, Smith being at my house was asked why he did not fulfill his promise [to] show the golden Plates and prove himself an honest man? He replied that he, himself was deceived, but that [I] should see them if I were where they were" (Nathaniel Lewis, Statement, 1834). Levi Lewis declared: "With regard to the plates, Smith said God had deceived him—which was the reason he (Smith) did not show the plates" (Levi Lewis, Statement, 1834).

15 | ENVISIONING THE GOLDEN PLATES

> *[W]e, through the grace of God the Father, and our Lord Jesus Christ, have seen the plates which contain this record ... ; and we also know that they have been translated by the gift and power of God, for his voice hath declared it unto us; wherefore we know of a surety, that the work is true.*
>
> —Oliver Cowdery, David Whitmer, and Martin Harris, in 1830 Book of Mormon, 589

Residents of the area surrounding Fayette, New York, displayed more interest in Joseph's ministry than did skeptical neighbors and relatives in Harmony, Pennsylvania. "We found the people of Seneca county in general friendly, and disposed to enquire into the truth of these strange matters which now began to be noised abroad," Joseph later asserted. Doors opened, and gatherings, similar to Methodist class meetings, occurred. "We met with many from time to time," he recalled, "who were willing to hear us, and who desired to find out the truth as it is in Christ Jesus, and apparently willing to obey the gospel, when once fairly convinced and satisfied in their own minds."[1] The number of believers began to grow. Hyrum Smith, David Whitmer, Peter Whitmer Jr., and possibly John Whitmer were soon baptized in nearby Seneca Lake to cleanse them of sin and to manifest their newfound faith in Christ.

Although Smith and Cowdery baptized others, they were not yet inclined, or ready, to organize followers into a new church. But according to Joseph's 1838-39 history, he and Cowdery for some time "made this matter a subject of humble prayer."[2] The two knelt in "the chamber of Mr. Whitmer's house, in order more particularly to seek of the Lord what we now so earnestly desired." While they prayed, "the word of the Lord came ... commanding us that I should ordain Oliver Cowdery to be an Elder ... and that

1. *History of the Church,* 1:51.
2. Unless otherwise noted, my narrative of this incident is based on ibid., 1:60-61.

he also should ordain me to the same office." The men were to postpone the ordination, however, "until such times as it should be practicable to have our brethren, who had been and who should be baptized, assembled together, when we must have their sanction to our thus proceeding to ordain each other, and have them decide by vote whether they were willing to accept us as spiritual teachers or not." The two men were also authorized to "bless bread and break it ... and to take wine, bless it, and drink it."

Shortly afterwards, Joseph delivered a revelation to Cowdery and David Whitmer to trust the "things which are written [the Book of Mormon]; for in them are all things written, concerning my church, my gospel, and my rock." The two men were admonished to "cry repentance unto this people" and furthermore to "[a]sk the Father in my name in faith believing that you shall receive, and you shall have the Holy Ghost which manifesteth all things." In addition, they were instructed to "search out the twelve [disciples] which shall have the desires of which I have spoken; and by their desires and their works, you shall know them."[3]

By late June 1829, with the English text of the Book of Mormon nearing completion, Joseph was elated. The copyright had been secured on the 11th.[4] And now that he was nearly free from more than eighteen months of interrupted dictation, Joseph began planning a solemnization by witnesses to verify to the world that the golden plates actually existed. "We ascertained that three special witnesses were to be provided by the Lord," said Joseph, "to whom He would grant that they should see the plates from which [the Book of Mormon] should be translated."[5] Almost immediately thereafter, Joseph later said, it occurred to Oliver Cowdery, David Whitmer, and Martin Harris that they might be these three special witnesses. The trio wanted to believe and Smith wanted them to believe. So they asked him to look into his stone to find "if they might not obtain of him the privilege to be these three special witnesses."[6]

Some men and women are always more anxious than others to participate in a quest of transcendent spiritual significance. One wonders if Joseph's life would have been easier if the pool of potential witnesses had included

3. BC XV. The twelve disciples, also apostles, were not chosen until 1835, when the Church was headquartered in Kirtland, Ohio.

4. A common assumption is that Joseph Smith was listed as "Author and Proprietor" to satisfy copyright regulations. While authorship could have been attributed to divine inspiration, thereby foregoing the need for registered copyright, obtaining a copyright enabled Joseph to control the proceeds of book sales.

5. *History of the Church,* 1:52.

6. Ibid., 1:53.

people like Emma. Perhaps her involvement might have prevented her from subsequently contending against him "because of the things" which she had "not seen ..."[7] Allowing Dolly Harris a glimpse of the plates might have calmed the obstinate woman and saved her marriage. And Isaac Hale would have been an ideal witness to confirm his son-in-law's veracity. Instead, Hale went to the grave a decade later convinced that his daughter's husband was a fraud. But Emma, Dolly, and Isaac, God-fearing Christians all, were evidently not visionaries of the same inclination as Joseph, Oliver, David, and Martin—men whose spiritual orientation apparently predisposed them to a more mystical world view.

"Behold I say unto you, that you must rely upon my word," said Smith, transmitting God's word to Cowdery, Whitmer, and Harris, as the Book of Mormon neared completion, "which if you do, with full purpose of heart, you shall have a view of the plates, and also the breastplate, the sword of Laban, the Urim and Thummim, which were given to the brother of Jared upon the mount, when he talked with the Lord face to face, and the miraculous directors which were given to Lehi while in the wilderness, on the borders of the Red Sea."[8] "Seeing" the golden plates, and the array of artifacts said to accompany them, differed from "seeing" with one's physical eyes. Rather, it involved one's spiritual vision, where images appear in the mind's reality. In fact, one of the definitions of to "see" in Noah Webster's 1828 dictionary is: "To know by revelation."[9] Martin Harris left several

7. BC XXVI:3. Interestingly, Mary Whitmer, David's mother, claimed to have envisioned the golden plates around June 1, 1829. David attested that shortly after his arrival in Fayette,

> [M]y mother was going to milk the cows, when she was met by the same old man (judging by her description of him) who said to her "You have been very faithful and diligent in your labors, but you are tired because of the in crease of your toil, it is proper therefore that you should receive a witness that your faith may be strengthened?" There upon he showed her the plates. My father and mother had a large family of their own, the addition to it therefore of Joseph, his wife Emma and Oliver very greatly increased the toil and anxiety of my mother. And although she had never complained she had sometimes felt that her labor was too much, or at least she was perhaps beginning to feel so. This circumstance, however, completely removed all such feelings, and nerved her up for her increased responsibilities. (David Whitmer, Interviewed by Orson Pratt and Joseph F. Smith.)

8. 1835 *Doctrine and Covenants* XLII:1. This revelation, written for the three witnesses in 1829, was not included in the *Book of Commandments.* Ezra Booth, however, mentioned that he examined the manuscript in Missouri in 1831 (Booth, "Mormonism No. III," *Ohio Star,* Oct. 24, 1831). The use of Urim and Thummim in the text is an anachronism; the term was not publicly used in Mormonism until beginning about 1833. When this revelation was copied into the Kirtland Revelations Book in 1834-35, the text had already been altered to read as it does in the 1835 *Doctrine and Covenants* (H. Michael Marquardt, *The Joseph Smith Revelations,* 49).

9. Noah Webster, *American Dictionary of the English Language* (1828), s.v. "See," definition no. 14.

statements, to this effect. One second-hand source in 1838 reported that Harris said seeing the marvelous artifacts was like seeing "a city through a mountain."[10] In 1840, Palmyra minister John A. Clark asked Harris: "Did you *see* those plates?" Martin answered Yes. "Did you see the plates, and the engraving on them with your bodily eyes?" insisted Clark. "Yes," Harris replied, "I saw them with my eyes,—they were shown unto me by the power of God and not of man." "But did you see them with your natural,—your bodily eyes, just as you see this pencil-case in my hand?" Harris answered: "I did not see them as I do that pencil-case, yet I saw them with the eye of faith; I saw them just as distinctly as I see any thing around me,—though at the time they were covered over with a cloth."[11] John H. Gilbert, who typeset much of the Book of Mormon and sometimes conversed with Harris while doing so, recalled fifty years later that, in one of their conversations, he asked Harris if he had "really seen the plates with his naked eyes?—his reply was, No, but with spiritual eyes."[12]

The revelation on witnessing made it clear that the plates could not be seen with earthly eyes but only as Joseph had seen them—with faith and by God's heavenly power.[13] The witnesses were promised: "[I]t is by your faith that you shall obtain a view of [the artifacts] even by that faith which was had by the prophets of old."[14] Early Mormon convert-turned-critic Ezra Booth, after reading an early copy of this revelation, reflected:

> When in Missouri, I had an opportunity to examine a commandment given to these witnesses, previous to their seeing the plates. They were informed that they should see and hear those things by faith, and then they should testify to the world, as though they had seen and heard, as I see a man, and hear his voice: but after all, it amounts simply to this; that by faith or imagination, they saw the plates and the angel, and by faith or imagination, they heard the voice of the Lord.[15]

According to an 1830 newspaper account, Joseph claimed that "none could see [the golden plates] but he who was commanded;—that though they should lie in the middle of the street beneath the broad glare of a meridian

10. Stephen Burnett to Lyman E. Johnson, Apr. 15, 1838.

11. John A. Clark to Dear Brethren, Aug. 24, 1840, *The Episcopal Recorder,* 99.

12. John H. Gilbert to James T. Cobb, Mar. 16 1879, 5. Also see John H. Gilbert, "Memorandum, made by John H. Gilbert Esq, Sept. 8th, 1892."

13. 1835 *Doctrine and Covenants* XLII:2.

14. Ibid., 1.

15. Booth, "Mormonism No. III," Oct. 24, 1831.

sun, in the presence of hundreds, yet no eye but his could see them!"[16] Seeing with the "eye of faith," "spiritual eye," or "mind's eye" were relatively common expressions in early America. Nathan Cole, a Connecticut Congregationalist, received "the sealing evidence" of his salvation through a vision. "It seemed as if I really saw the gate of heaven by an Eye of faith," wrote Cole in 1740, "& the way for Sinners to Get to heaven by Jesus Christ; as plain as I ever saw anything with my bodily eyes in my life."[17] Jonathan Edwards's wife, Sarah, similarly stated: "I beheld [the children of God] by faith in their risen and glorified state, with spiritual bodies re-fashioned after the image of Christ's glorified body, and arrayed in the beauty of heaven. ... They appeared to my mind in all their reality and certainty, and as it were in actual and distinct vision; so plain and evident were they to the eye of my faith."[18]

An unnamed Presbyterian investigating a turn-of-the-century Kentucky revival observed: "I have heard men of respectability assert, that their manifestations of gospel truth were so clear, as to require some caution when they began to speak, lest they should use language which might induce their hearers to suppose they had seen those things with their bodily eyes."[19] A Scottish Methodist minister, James Robe, instructed his congregation how to interpret their experiences correctly "in the expressest, strongest, plainest manner [he] could, That Jesus Christ in the body cannot be seen by any with their bodily eyes in this life." If they thought they saw such sights, he let them know "that it was owing only to the strength of their imagination, to the disorder of their head, and of the humours of their bodies at that time; and that it was not real." When three women in his congregation "thought they saw a great and glorious light, for a very short time," he "examined into the circumstances" and learned "that their eyes had been shut at the time, and so easily convinced them, that it was not real, but imaginary, and that no weight was to be laid upon it by them."[20] Leigh Schmidt, a professor of religion at Princeton University, notes that having a visionary experience "with the eyes of [the] mind" or "by the eye of faith," as opposed to the "bodily eyes," might be accepted by ministers if such experiences were hedged about with proper restrictions.[21]

---

16. "Imposition and Blasphemy!!—Money Diggers, &c.," May 15, 1830.
17. Nathan Cole, qtd. in Ann Taves, *Fits, Trances, and Visions,* 69.
18. Qtd. in Serano E. Dwight, *The Life of President [Jonathan] Edwards,* 178.
19. Qtd. in Taves, *Fits, Trances, and Visions,* 109.
20. James Robe, qtd. in ibid., 62.
21. Leigh Eric Schmidt, *Holy Fairs,* 148.

In the September 2, 1832, issue of the *Liberal Advocate* of Rochester, New York, a "correspondent," who had attended a gospel meeting wrote that one of the converts exclaimed:

> My friends and Brethren, I have seen my Creator, he was like! [H]e was like! [H]e was like! A great lump of gold, and Jesus Christ was with him, and beckoned me to come to him, but the Devil touched my elbow and said don't go M_____, don't go. Then Jesus Christ separated from the father—came to me and shook hands, and said you must take up the cross and follow me, but the devil twitched my elbow again, and said don't go M_____ don't go.

When the meeting ended, the correspondent asked "how he could utter such blasphemy in public." The testifier replied, "Oh my friends, it was not with my carnal eye, but with my mind's eye that I saw these things."[22] Not only could some zealots see with a spiritual eye, but some could hear with a spiritual ear. "The things of the Spirit of God cannot be discovered but by spiritual, internal senses," wrote theologian John Fletcher in 1851. "They are the only medium by which an intercourse between Christ and our souls can be opened and maintained." Fletcher maintained that new ways of seeing and experiencing could regenerate souls, but these refined perceptions of the divine did not usually come from "our bodily external senses." He warned that we should be vigilant with those "who claim to have seen or heard too much with their 'bodily organs.'"[23]

In the Book of Mormon, Moroni writes, "There were many whose faith was so exceedingly strong, even before Christ came, who could not be kept from within the veil, but truly saw with their eyes the things which they had beheld with an eye of faith, and they were glad" (Eth. 12:19). Ezra Booth stated in 1831 that Joseph "does not pretend that he sees ... with his natural, but with his spiritual, eyes; and he says he can see ... as well with his eyes shut, as with them open. So also in translating.—The subject stands before his eyes in print, but it matters not whether his eyes are open or shut; he can see as well one way as the other."[24] According to Stephen Burnett, who heard Martin Harris speak to an Ohio congregation in 1838, Harris "never

22. Joseph W. Barnes, "Obediah Dogberry," 10-11.

23. John Fletcher, "On Evangelical Mysticism," in *The Works of the Reverend John Fletcher,* 4:284-88.

24. Ezra Booth, "Mormonism [I]," *Ohio Star,* Sept. 12, 1831.

saw the plates with his natural eyes only in vision or imagination" and that all the witnesses saw the plates "spiritually or in vision with their eyes shut."[25]

Both Brigham Young and Joseph Smith provided specific details on the Mormon perspective of envisioning with the "spiritual eyes." In an 1856 address, Young asked a group of Latter-day Saints:

> Where is the spirit world? Can you see it with your natural eyes? No. Can you see spirits in this room? No. Suppose the Lord should touch your eyes that you might see, could you then see the spirits? Yes, as plainly as you now see bodies, as did the servant of Elijah. If the Lord would permit it, and it was His will that it should be done, you could see the spirits that have departed from this world, as plainly as you now see bodies with your natural eyes; as plainly as brothers [Heber] Kimball and [Orson] Hyde saw those wicked disembodied spirit in Preston, England [in 1837]. They saw devils there, as we see one another; they could hear them speak, and knew what they said. Could they hear them with the natural ear? No. Did they see those wicked spirits with their natural eyes? No. They could not see them the next morning, when they were not in the spirit; neither could they see them the day before, nor at any other time; their spiritual eyes were touched by the power of the Almightly.[26]

Smith and a later associate, Sidney Rigdon, while "translating St. John's Gospel" in Hiram, Ohio, became rapt in heavenly ecstasy and jointly experienced in spirit what they called "The Vision," or "Vision of the Three Degrees of Glory," now published as Section 76 in LDS editions of the Doctrine and Covenants. Philo Dibble, an eye-witness, asserted fifty years later:

> The vision which is recorded in the Book of Doctrine and Covenants was given at the house of "Father Johnson," in Hyrum [Hiram], Ohio, and during the time that Joseph and Sidney were in the spirit and saw the heavens open, there were other men in the room, perhaps twelve, among whom I was one. During a part of the time—probably two-thirds of the time—I saw the glory and felt the power, but did not see the vision.
>
> The events and conversation, while they were seeing what is written (and many things were seen and related that are not written,) I will relate as minutely as is necessary.
>
> Joseph would, at intervals, say: "What do I see?" as one might say while looking out the window and beholding what all in the room could

25. Burnett to Johnson, Apr. 15, 1838.
26. Richard S. Van Wagoner, *The Complete Discourses of Brigham Young,* 2:1130.

> not see. Then he would relate what he had seen or what he was looking at. Then Sidney replied, "I see the same." Presently Sidney would say "what do I see?" and would repeat what he had seen or was seeing, and Joseph would reply, "I see the same."
>
> This manner of conversation was repeated at short intervals to the end of the vision, and during the whole time not a word was spoken by an other person. Not a sound nor motion made by anyone but Joseph and Sidney, and it seemed to me that they never moved a joint or limb during the time I was there, which I think was over an hour, and to the end of the vision.[27]

Smith, in an 1843 account of this same event, wrote: "I, Joseph, the prophet, in spirit beheld, And the eyes of the inner man truly did see Eternity sketch'd in a vision from God."[28] Smith and Rigdon's transcendent experience, which came through their spiritual eyes and ears during prayer, seems to have been similar to the witnessing experience of Joseph, Oliver, David, and Martin three years earlier. It was Sunday, probably June 28, 1829, when the moment arrived came for the Three Witnesses to envision the plates and other Nephite artifacts.[29] Smith accompanied the men into the nearby wood lot, a few hundred feet from the Whitmer home. "According to previous arrangement," they knelt and Joseph "commenced by vocal prayer to our Heavenly Father, and was followed by each of the others in succession."[30] Despite their desires and fervency of the men's appeal, the heavens remained closed. They prayed a second time, with the same result. "[We] failed at that time to see the plates or the angel who should have been on hand to exhibit them," Harris later said. The others, continued Harris, "believed it was because I was not good enough, or, in other words, not sufficiently sanctified."[31] So Martin moved away, deeper into the woods. In 1878, when he was seventy-three and the last surviving witness, David Whitmer said what happened next. The three of them were sitting on a log,

> when we were overshadowed by a light. It was not like the light of the sun, nor like that of fire, but more glorious and beautiful. It extended away round us, I cannot tell how far, but in the midst of this light, immediately

27. Philo Dibble, "Philo Dibble['s] Narrative," 303-4.

28. Joseph Smith to W. W. Phelps, "The Answer," 82.

29. My dating is based on Dan Vogel, *Early Mormon Documents,* 5:421.

30. *History of the Church,* 1:54.

31. Martin Harris, qtd. in Anthony Metcalf, *Ten Years before the Mast,* 71. Metcalf interviewed Harris in 1873 or 1874. Harris may have had in mind lingering fallout from the debacle of the loss of the 116 pages.

> before us … there appeared, as it were, a table, with many records on it, besides the plates of the Book of Mormon; also the sword of Laban, the Directors (i.e. the ball which Lehi had) and the Interpreters. I saw them just as plain as I see this bed … and I heard the voice of the Lord as distinctly as I ever heard anything in my life declaring that they (the plates) were translated by the gift and power of God.[32]

Whitmer recounted this same story, in greater or lesser detail, over the last decade of his life. (He died in 1888.) In 1881, he told a newspaper reporter that the celestial messenger said: "Blessed is the Lord and he that keeps his commandments." Then as the angel displayed the plates, and turned the pages, Whitmer said he heard another voice "that seemed to fill all space, musical as the sighing of a wind through the forest, … saying 'What you see is true; testify to the same.'"[33] After the vision, Smith then looked for Harris, whom he found kneeling on the loam of the forest floor. Anxiously, Harris confessed that he had "not yet prevailed with the Lord, and earnestly requested me to join him in prayer, that he also might realize the same blessings which we had just received." As soon as Joseph began to pray aloud, "the same vision was opened to our view, at least it was again opened to me." As Smith began telling Harris what he saw and heard, much as he would later do with Sidney Rigdon under similar circumstances, Martin cried out: "Tis enough; tis enough; mine eyes have beheld; mine eyes have beheld." The exuberant Harris sprang to his feet, shouting, "Hosanna," and praising God.[34]

Cowdery said little of the experience during the remainder of his life, which ended in 1850 at age forty-four. Harris did not say much either, although it was generally understood that the angel showed the golden plates to the trio.[35] In 1838, Martin reportedly stated in a public meeting that "he never saw the plates with his natural eyes only in vision or imagination."[36] In the late 1850s, when spiritualist Joel Tiffany asked him about

32. David Whitmer, Interviewed by Joseph F. Smith and Orson Pratt, Sept. 7-8, 1878. According to Whitmer, Joseph Smith said that this divine voice said, "These plates have been revealed by the power of God, and they have been translated by the power of God. The translation of them which you have seen is correct, and I command you to bear record of what you now see and hear" *(History of the Church,* 1:55).

33. David Whitmer, Interviewed by *Chicago Times,* Oct. 14, 1881. Elsewhere David said this was the "voice of God" speaking from heaven, "saying that the Book was true and the translation correct" (David Whitmer, Interviewed by William H. Kelley and G. A. Blakeslee, Jan. 15, 1882).

34. *History of the Church,* 1:55.

35. When asked in an interview what the angel's name was, David Whitmer said, "I do not know as no name was given" (David Whitmer, Interviewed by Zenos H. Gurley, Jan. 14, 1885).

36. Martin Harris, qtd. in Stephen Burnett to Lyman E. Johnson, Apr. 15, 1838.

the experience, Harris reportedly replied: "I am forbidden to say anything how the Lord showed them to me, except that by the power of God I have seen them."[37] He continued to affirm the spiritual or visionary nature of his experience throughout his life. Shortly before his death in 1875, he told Anthony Metcalf, who interviewed him in Utah in 1873 or 1874, what he had said to John A. Clark: "I never saw the golden plates, only in a visionary or entranced state." Elaborating, Martin related that during his prayer in the woods, "I passed into a state of entrancement; and in that state I saw the angel and the plates."[38]

David Whitmer, late in life, wrote:

> [W]e were in the spirit when we had the view, for no man can behold the face of an angel, except in a spiritual view, but we were in the body also, and everything was as natural to us, as it is at any time. Martin Harris, you say, called it "being in vision." We read in the Scriptures, Cornelius saw, in a vision, an angel of God, Daniel saw an angel in a vision, also in other places it states they saw an angel in the spirit. A bright light enveloped us where we were, that filled at noon day, and there in a *vision,* or in the *spirit,* we saw and heard just as it is stated in my testimony in the Book of Mormon.[39]

It was between 3:00 p.m. and 4:00 p.m. that afternoon, wrote Lucy Smith, when Joseph, accompanied by Cowdery, Whitmer, and Harris, returned to the Whitmer home. Mother Whitmer and Joseph and Lucy Smith were sitting in a bedroom when young Smith came into the room, threw himself on the bed, and exclaimed: "you do not know how happy I am the Lord has caused the plates to be shown to 3 more besides me who have also seen an angel and will have to testify to the truth of what I have said for they know for themselves that I do not go about to deceive the people."[40]

On June 26, 1829, a day or two before the witnesses envisioned the golden plates, the *Wayne Sentinel* published the first known public announcement of the Book of Mormon. Not mentioning that his print shop would be publishing the work, Egbert B. Grandin wrote:

> [I]n this particular region, for some time past, much speculation has existed, concerning a pretended discovery, through superhuman means, of

37. Martin Harris, qtd. by Joel Tiffany, "Mormonism—No. II," *Tiffany's Monthly,* Aug. 1859, 166.

38. Metcalf, *Ten Years before the Mast,* 70-71.

39. Whitmer to Metcalf, Apr. 2, 1887, in Metcalf, *Ten Years before the Mast,* 74.

40. Lavina Fielding Anderson, *Lucy's Book,* 453.

> an ancient record, of a religious and divine nature and origin, written in ancient characters impossible to be interpreted by any to whom the special gift has not been imparted by inspiration. It is generally known and spoken of as the *"Golden Bible."* Most people entertain an idea that the whole matter is the result of a gross imposition, and a grosser superstition. It is pretended that it will be published as soon as the translation is completed. Meanwhile we have been furnished with the following, which is represented to us as intended for the title page of the work—we give it as a curiosity.[41]

On Thursday, July 2, Joseph, Oliver, and several of the Whitmers visited the Smiths, who had returned to Manchester. While there, according to Lucy, "the male part of the company repaired to a little grove where it was customary for the family to offer up their secret prayers." Joseph had declared the previous March that three witnesses "and none else" would be allowed to "know of a surety" that he had "in his possession, the record of the Nephites."[42] But the witness experience with Cowdery, Whitmer, and Harris had been so successful that Joseph secured additional attestation from eight more witnesses. Lucy wrote that Joseph had been told the plates would be carried to the Smiths' grove "by one of the ancient Nephites." Accordingly, eight men—Christian Whitmer, Jacob Whitmer, Peter Whitmer Jr., John Whitmer, Hiram Page, Joseph Smith Sr., Hyrum Smith, and Harrison Smith—also envisioned the golden plates. "Joseph Smith, Jr. the Author and Proprietor of this work," they jointly attested,

> has shewn unto us the plates of which hath been spoken, which have the appearance of gold; and as many of the leaves as the said Smith has translated, we did handle with our hands; and we also saw the engravings thereon, all of which has the appearance of ancient work, and of curious workmanship. And this we bear record, with words of soberness, that the said Smith has shewn unto us, for we have seen and hefted, and know of a surety, that the said Smith has got the plates of which we have spoken. And we give our names unto the world, to witness unto the world that which we have seen: and we lie not, God bearing witness of it.[43]

No angel appeared as part of this final showing. Joseph was alone with the Eight Witnesses, who said little of their experience. A detailed, albeit

41. "Just about to ...," *Wayne Sentinel,* June 26, 1829, 3.
42. BC IV.
43. 1830 Book of Mormon, 590.

hearsay, description of the event was recorded by former Illinois Governor Thomas Ford, who obtained his information from an undisclosed second-hand source:

> It is related that the Prophet's early followers were anxious to see the plates; the Prophet had always given out that they could not be seen by the carnal eye, but must be spiritually discerned; that the power to see them depended upon faith, and was the gift of God, to be obtained by fasting, prayer, mortification of the flesh, and exercises of the spirit; that so soon as he could see the evidence of a strong and lively faith in any of his followers, they should be gratified in their holy curiosity. He set them to continual prayer, and other spiritual exercises, to acquire this lively faith by means of which the hidden things of God could be spiritually discerned; and at last, when he could delay them no longer, he assembled them in a room, and produced a box, which he said contained the precious treasure. The lid was opened; the witnesses peeped into it, but making no discovery, for the box was empty, they said, "Brother Joseph, we do not see the plates." The Prophet answered them, "O ye of little faith! How long will God bear with this wicked and perverse generation? Down on your knees, brethren, every one of you, and pray God for the forgiveness of your sins, and for a holy and living faith which cometh down from heaven." The disciples dropped to their knees, and began to pray in the fervency of their spirit, supplicating God for more than two hours with fanatical earnestness; at the end of which time, looking again into the box, they were now persuaded that they saw the plates.[44]

Harris reportedly said in 1838 that "the eight witnesses never saw [the plates] & hesitated to sign that instrument for that reason, but were persuaded to do it."[45] He clarified this statement in 1859 when he told Joel Tiffany that "no one, save Oliver Cowdery, myself, Joseph Smith,[J]r., and David Whitmer, ever saw [the plates]."[46] According to early Mormon convert Theodore Turley, Whitmer said in April 1839: "I handled those plates;

44. Thomas Ford, *History of Illinois,* 257-58.

45. Martin Harris, qtd. in Burnett to Johnson, Apr. 15, 1838. During a period of disillusionment with Joseph Smith, Harris reportedly said that "he never saw the plates, from which the book [of Mormon] purports to have been translated, except in vision, and ... any man who says he has seen them in any other way is a liar, Joseph [Smith] not excepted" (Harris, qtd. in "Mormonism," *Evangelist* [Carthage, Ohio] 6 [Oct. 1, 1838]: 226). In 1860, Brigham Young explained: "you who are spiritually minded, who have the visions of our mind opened ... the latter is inward. My inward eyes see, my inward hands handle, my inward taste tastes of the word of God" (Van Wagoner, *The Complete Discourses of Brigham Young,* 3:1567).

46. Martin Harris, qtd. in Tiffany, "Mormonism—No. II," 166.

there was fine engravings on both sides. I handled them. ... [t]hey were shown to me by a supernatural power."[47]

By whatever means or mechanism, the sheer force of Joseph's compelling, persuasive faith, together with their own consuming desire to believe and see, enabled eleven witnesses to come away from their spiritual ordeal in 1829 convinced they were participants in a transcendent occurrence. For the rest of their lives, none ever denied what he believed he had experienced under Joseph's guidance and instruction.

After the witnessing event in Manchester, Mother Smith reported that Joseph returned to the Smith log home where the "Angel again made his appearance to Joseph and received the plates from his hands."[48] David Whitmer added that after the plates were shown to him "by the power of God," they were "taken away by the angel to a cave, which we saw by the power of God while we were yet in the Spirit."[49] Brigham Young in 1877 said that Cowdery described the cave as being in Robinson Hill (Hill Cumorah). After the Book of Mormon English transcription was completed around July 1, 1829, "the angel instructed [Smith] to carry [the plates] back to the [H]ill Cumorah." Young continued: When Cowdery and Smith approached the hill, it opened before their eyes and "they walked into a cave, in which there was a large and spacious room" and laid the golden plates on

> a large table that stood in the room. Under this table there was a pile of plates as much as two feet high, and there were altogether in this room more plates than probably many wagon loads; they were piled up in the corners and along the walls, The first time they went there the sword of Laban hung upon the wall; but when they went again it had been taken down and laid upon the table across the gold plates; it was unsheathed, and on it was written these words: "This sword will never be sheathed again until the kingdoms of this world become the kingdom of our God and his Christ."[50]

Joseph's account was simpler: "When, according to arrangements, the messenger called for them, I delivered them up to him; and he has them in his

47. Theodore Turley, "Memoranda," 1845, LDS Church History Library. Appreciation to Dan Vogel for drawing my attention to this item.

48. Anderson, *Lucy's Book,* 457.

49. David Whitmer, Interviewed by E. C. Briggs and Rudolph Etzenhouser, Apr. 25, 1884.

50. Brigham Young, June 17, 1877, *Journal of Discourses,* 19:36. Dan Vogel believes that the cave story is basically folklore, likely based on a vision rather than on reality. See Vogel, *Early Mormon Documents,* 3:378-82.

charge until this day, being the second day of May, one thousand eight hundred and thirty-eight."[51]

Meanwhile, that summer, as negotiations for printing the dictation were underway, Smith family members began writing relatives about Joseph's marvelous work. On June 17, 1829, Hyrum Smith received a response to a letter he had written to Uncle Jesse Smith, who had taken young Joseph with him to Salem in 1813. Jesse, now in Stockholm, New York, flared up at Hyrum's attempt to spread the good news. Not only was Jesse skeptical of Joseph Jr.'s claims that "he has eyes to see things that are not," he accused his nephew of making "lead books, and declar[ing] to the world that they are of the most fine gold." Like Isaac Hale, Jesse labeled the "whole pretended discovery … a very clear and foolish deception, a very great wickedness, unpardonable, unless you are shielded by your ignorance."[52]

Despite Jesse's opposition, the Smith family maintained their course. In mid-June, Smith, Cowdery, and Harris began to seek ways and means to publish Joseph's book. Evidently, their first contact was nearby Macedon resident George Crane, a wealthy old Quaker "of intelligence, property, and high respectability."[53] The Smiths had first looked for his aid when they were about to lose their Manchester farm, encouraged by the fact that, as Mother Smith wrote, he "manifested a great friendship for us from our first acquaintance with him."[54] But this amity did not become support for the Book of Mormon despite Joseph's insistence that "he was moved by the spirit to call upon him for assistance."[55] Stephen S. Harding, a Smith family acquaintance, told a correspondent that Smith and Cowdery visited Crane, "who had manifested some interest in the pretended translation." They read several pages from Joseph's book to the elderly gentleman, who listened attentively. Then "in his straight forward, Quaker soberness," Harding wrote, Crane reportedly announced: "Joseph, thy book is blasphemous; and I counsel thee to mend thy ways, or thee will come to some bad end."[56] John W. Barber and Henry Howe, nineteenth-century New York historians, interviewed

51. *History of the Church,* 1:18-19.

52. Jesse Smith to Hiram [sic] Smith, June 17, 1829.

53. Pomeroy Tucker, *Origin, Rise, and Progress of Mormonism,* 37.

54. Anderson, *Lucy's Book,* 370.

55. Joseph Smith, qtd. in John W. Barber and Henry Howe, *Historical Collections of the State of New York,* 581.

56. Stephen S. Harding to Thomas Gregg, Feb. 1882, in Thomas Gregg, *The Prophet of Palmyra,* 40.

Palmyra area residents and wrote that Crane "bid [Smith] to go to work, or the state prison would end his career."[57]

Having failed to enlist Crane, Joseph and Martin turned to Palmyra publisher E. B. Grandin, a job printer, bookseller, and owner of the *Wayne Sentinel.* Grandin's shop, which he rented from his brother Philip Grandin, was a three-story building at the west end of "Thayer and Grandin's Row" on Main Street. The print shop was on the third floor, the bookbinding operation on the second, and the ground floor housed Grandin's bookstore. After pitching the book to Grandin, who was a few months younger than Smith, Harris, according to Pomeroy Tucker, "offered to give security by a mortgage upon his un[e]ncumbered farm for the cost of the printing and binding of the book." But Grandin balked, from both religious misgivings and concerns about the book's commercial viability, since he knew that many citizens opposed the publication. "[B]elieving the whole affair to be a wicked imposture and a scheme to defraud Mr. Harris, who was his friend,"[58] Grandin "advised against the supposed folly of the enterprise" and, with other Harris family friends and neighbors, sought to persuade Martin "to desist and withdraw his countenance from the imposture."[59] Their efforts, however, proved unsuccessful. After repeated consultations and careful consideration, Grandin refused to publish the work.

Undaunted, Smith and Harris traveled up the Erie Canal to Rochester, a boom town thirty miles westward, and talked to Thurlow Weed, publisher of the *Rochester Telegraph.* First, Joseph evidently went alone. In 1883, Weed remembered the budding seer as "[a] stout, round, smooth-faced young man, with the air and manners of a person without occupation." When he "said he wanted a book printed," Weed decided that Smith was a "shrewd, scheming fellow who … would impress one favorably in conversation." After telling Weed about the "golden Bible," Joseph pulled his seer stone from his pocket, put it in his stovepipe, and pronounced "a chapter of the 'Book

57. Barber and Howe, *Historical Collection of the State of New York,* 581. Pomeroy Tucker wrote that Crane "sternly rebuked Smith's pretensions, and denouncing them as in a high degree blasphemous and wicked. Mr. Crane kindly but earnestly admonished him, for his own good, to desist from his criminal pursuit, warning him that persistence therein would be certain to end in his death upon the gallows, or in some equally ignominious manner" (Tucker, *Origin, Rise, and Progress of Mormonism,* 37). W. H. McIntosh wrote that Crane "advised Smith to give up his scheme, or ruin would result to him, and it is well known, the Friend spoke prophetically" (McIntosh, *History of Ontario Co.,* 43).

58. Tucker, *Origin, Rise, and Progress of Mormonism,* 51.

59. "Mormonism and Joe Smith. The Book of Mormon or Golden Bible," *Wayne Democratic Press,* May 26, 1858.

of Mormon'" to Weed. The publisher, later to become a powerful New York politician, found the reading "so senseless, that I thought the man either crazed or a very shallow impostor, and therefore declined to become a publisher." Smith returned the next day with Harris and assured Weed that the book "was a divine revelation, and would be accepted, and that he would be accepted by the world as a prophet." Supposing that Weed had doubts about Smith's financial status, Harris "offered to become security for the expense of printing." Weed once again declined, advising Harris "not to mortgage his Farm and beggar his Family."[60]

After this second refusal, Smith and Harris crossed the street to the establishment of Elihu F. Marshall, a bookseller and publisher of the *Rochester Album.* Marshall, well-known for a popular spelling book, published in 1819, "gave his terms to Smith and his associates for the execution of their work, and his proffered acceptance of the proposed mode of security."[61] Martin gave an interview to the *Rochester Gem,* self-described as "a quaint little publication … dedicated to the literary and domestic interests of the community." The paper said Harris was in town "to make a contract for printing a large quantity of a work called the Golden Bible."[62]

Before the final papers were drawn up to complete the deal with Marshall, Smith and Harris returned to Palmyra and made another appeal to Grandin. They informed the young businessman that if he maintained his refusal, the book would be printed in Rochester and he would lose thousands of dollars. According to Henry Allen, Grandin's grandson, the printer "consult[ed] friends who felt that it was merely a business matter and that he would be in no way related to the religion." On that basis, "he consented."[63] Grandin went to work immediately. He took a few sample pages to John H. Gilbert, journeyman typesetter, who concluded that 5,000 copies could profitably be printed and bound for $3,000.[64]

---

60. Harriet A. Weed, *Autobiography of Thurlow Weed,* 1:358-59; Thurlow Weed, "Prospect of Peace with Utah," *Albany Evening Journal* 29 (May 19, 1858): 2; Thurlow Weed to Ellen E. Dickinson, Apr. 12, 1880, in Ellen E. Dickinson, *New Light on Mormonism … with [an] Introduction by Thurlow Weed,* 260-61.

61. Elihu F. Marshall, qtd. in "Mormonism and Joe Smith," May 26, 1858.

62. "Golden Bible," *Rochester Gem* 1 (Sept. 5, 1829): 70.

63. Henry M. Allen, "Letter to the Librarian of the Palmyra Library."

64. In 1830 America, publishers were not producing books in large print runs. And until 1820, 70 percent of all books circulating in America had been printed in Great Britain. At the time the Book of Mormon was printed, book runs usually ranged from 500 to 2,000 copies. Although the Bible, the most salable book in the country, was occasionally printed in a 10,000-copy edition, most printers felt that it was best "to be forced to reprint a successful book than to carry

One morning, as Joseph was preparing to walk to Palmyra to meet with Grandin, Alexander McIntyre, the Smith family physician, stopped by to warn the Smiths that forty men had gathered up the road with "the view of waylaying Joseph." Presumably, the men had asked McIntyre to take charge of their group because he was a ranking peer in Palmyra's Mount Moriah Masonic Lodge. In addition, the Book of Mormon reflects, in portions, an anti-Masonic posture. When McIntyre refused, they appointed William T. Huzzy, also a Freemason.[65] When Lucy Smith heard the scheme, she urged Joseph to stay home. But he "smiled at my fears," she remembered, and said, "[N]ever mind, mother, just put your trust in God, and nothing will hurt me to day." He then walked out the door.

As soon as he approached the nearby David Jackway farm, Joseph saw a pack of men sitting atop a fence rail. He removed his hat as he came abreast of the first man. In his good-natured way, Joseph smiled and said: "Good morning, Mr. Huzzy." He then passed through the throng, greeting each man in turn. "While they were pondering in amazement," Lucy wrote, "he passed on, leaving them perched upon the fence, like so many roosting chickens, and arrived at Palmyra without being molested." That night, Joseph returned a happy man. "Well, mother, the Lord has been on my side to-day," he announced, "the devil has not overpowered me in any of my proceedings. Did I not tell you that I should be delivered from the hands of all my enemies! They thought they were going to perform great feats; they have done wonders to prevent me from getting the book printed; they mustered themselves together, and got upon the fence, made me a low bow, and went home, and I'll warrant you they wish they had stayed there in the first place. Mother, there is a God in heaven, and I know it."[66]

On August 17, 1829, Joseph, Martin, and Grandin signed the contract. Grandin agreed "to execute five thousand copies of the said Book in the manner and form following—The volume to consist of six hundred octavo pages (more or less.)—edited and closely printed on new type and fine paper.—The full edition to be bound in calf, completed and delivered on or

---

on ... [their] shelves a large remainder of a volume that had failed to make its way" (Helmut Lehmann-Haupt, Lawrence C. Roth, and Rollo G. Silver, *The Book in America,* 40.)

65. Pomeroy Tucker, also a member of the Mount Moriah Lodge, wrote that Huzzy, "a notorious wag," was intimately acquainted with Joseph Smith. It was Huzzy (and a friend, Azel Vandruver) who, when denied a look at the golden plates, exclaimed, "Egad! I'll see the critter, live or die!" and jerked the covering off to reveal "a large tile-brick" (Tucker, *Origin, Rise, and Progress of Mormonism,* 32).

66. Anderson, *Lucy's Book,* 458.

before the first day of July in the year of our Lord one thousand eight hundred and thirty." In return, Smith and Harris promised to pay him $3,000 in three equal installments, the first at the time of signing, the second in November 1829, and the final upon delivery of the books.[67] Lucy Smith wrote that Harris committed to paying half of the costs, Joseph and Hyrum the other 50 percent. Unlike Harris, however, they had no money for collateral.[68]

Grandin purchased a new set of small pica type. In March 1829, he had bought a single-pull Washington press, constructed of iron, which he now readied for the job. Grandin's shop worked on the project eleven hours a day, six days a week, for more than seven months.[69] When the print team drew the first proof-sheet of the title page from the press in mid-August, Joseph Sr., Joseph Jr., Oliver Cowdery, Martin Harris, and Stephen S. Harding, a twenty-one-year-old lawyer, were there to observe. Fifty-three years later, Harding recalled:

> Mr. Grandin and two or three typos [typesetters] were present, as if curious in seeing the first impression of the title page. [Pomeroy] Tucker took up the ink-balls and made the form ready; then laying the blank sheet upon it, with one pull at the lever the work was done; then taking the impression, looked at it a moment, passed it to Cowdery, who scanned it carefully, and passed it to the prophet himself, who seemed to be examining every letter, and without speaking gave it into the hands of his father and Harris. It was then returned to Tucker. Of course we all looked at it with more or less curiosity, and the work was pronounced excellent.

67. Harris mortgaged 151 acres of his farm to Grandin on August 25, 1829. The mortgage stipulated that Harris was to pay "the sum of three thousand dollars at or before the expiration of eighteen months from the date thereof," which was February 25, 1831 (Martin Harris, Mortgage to Egbert B. Grandin, Aug. 25, 1829). Today, $3,000 would have a value approaching $60,000. See also Michael Hubbard MacKay and Gerrit J. Dirkmaat, *From Darkness unto Light: Joseph Smith's Translation and Publication of the Book of Mormon* (Provo, Utah: Brigham Young University Religious Studies Center/Salt Lake City: Deseret Book Co., 2015), 187.

68. According to Lorenzo Saunders, Interview, Nov. 12, 1884, 4, the Smiths, while Joseph's book was being printed, first thought they would become rich from its sale. Hyrum had told Lorenzo and Orlando Saunders, while working in the grain fields with them in the fall of 1828, that "this is the last year I am going to Swing the Cradle." When asked why, he explained, "I am going to take up this Mormonism ... Joseph Smith my brother will be the richest man in the United states."

69. In addition to John H. Gilbert, John H. Bortles, Thomas McAuley, and William Van Camp also worked on the production of the Book of Mormon. Pomeroy Tucker was foreman of the print shop. Luther Howard did the binding. Case, Abbey, & Co., of nearby Shortsville, New York, reportedly manufactured the paper used in the first edition (Charles F. Milliken, *A History of Ontario County, New York and Its People,* 1:415). For the technical background of the printing process, see Gayle Goble Ord, "The Book of Mormon Goes to Press."

Tucker, who was my cousin, then handed it to me, saying: "Here, Steve, I'll give this to you. You may keep it as a curiosity."[70]

John H. Gilbert, journeyman printer, who subsequently set most of the type, recalled years later when he was a master printer:

> Hyrum Smith brought the first installment of manuscript, of 24 pages, closely written on common foolscap paper;—he had it under his vest, and vest and coat closely buttoned over it. At night Smith came and got the manuscript, and with the same precaution carried it away. The next morning with the same watchfulness, he brought it again, and at night took it away. This was kept up for several days. The title page was first set up, and after proof was read and corrected, several copies were printed for Harris and his friends. On the second day—Harris and Smith being in the office—I called their attention to a grammatical error, and asked whether I should correct it? Harris consulted with Smith a short time, and turned to me and said; "The Old Testament is ungrammatical, set it as it is written."[71]

There was not a single punctuation mark in the entire manuscript, Gilbert said. "The sentences were all run in without capitals, or other marks to designate where one left off and another began, and it was no easy task to straighten out the stuff."[72] After he had worked with the manuscript for several days, Gilbert said to Hyrum one morning, "Mr. Smith, if you would leave this manuscript with me, I would take it home with me at night and read and punctuate it, and I could get along faster in the day time, for now I have frequently to stop and read half a page to find how to punctuate it." Hyrum, remembering the lost 116 pages, replied, "This is pretty important business, young man, and I don't know as we can trust this manuscript in

---

70. Harding to Gregg, Feb. 1882, 46. Harding was invited to the Smith home after the day's events. In 1875, while living in Cincinnati, Harding, then sixty-five, provided a colorful account to the *Cincinnati Times* of that walk to the Smith home in Manchester. "The party left Grandin's office and started down the lane leading to the log cabin where the Prophet resided. 'Joe' was about twenty-two; lean, lank, limber, fair complexion, light hair, his face rather cadaverous, and pitted like a pig skin. He was dressed indifferently—poor hat, tow pants, and unpresentable shirt." Harding wrote that Father Smith, while walking, carried a "huge jug of vinegar [cider]." Although Harding stated he had no taste for vinegar, he "kept close to the old man only to enjoy the 'gurgle' of the vinegar, which produced a music in his emotions that was altogether indescribable." Harding declared, "This was a party for a painter and one of the most excruciating of all the ludicrous affairs of my life" ("A Profane Revelation").

71. John H. Gilbert, "Memorandum, made by John H. Gilbert Esq, Sept. 8th, 1892."

72. John H. Gilbert, qtd. in "Joe Smith: Something about the Early Life of the Mormon Prophet." A study of photographs of the original surviving manuscript pages proves this to be essentially true.

your possession." But after consideration, Gilbert was allowed to work with about "a quire of paper, or 48 [numbered] pages, at a time,"[73] with the understanding that the manuscript pages would be returned as soon as he was finished with them.

To prevent another disaster like Harris's loss of the 116 manuscript pages, Joseph directed Cowdery to make a copy (now called the Printer's Copy) which was used in the production work. The original transcription was kept secure in the Smith home. Peter Whitmer Jr., a former constable, remained at the Smith home to guard the writings and act as a bodyguard while the courier, either Hyrum or Oliver, walked the manuscript pages daily back and forth between Manchester and Palmyra. Martin, who was nearly always present while the book was being printed, told Stephen Harding that the "angel of the Lord" appeared to Joseph and informed him that because "the devil had appeared in the form of a man or woman, and had possessed himself of the sacred MS.," it was necessary that "at least three witnesses" watch over the manuscript when it was in the printers hands.[74]

Once the financial arrangements and security were established, and the book was at press, Joseph returned to Emma, who was once again in Harmony. On October 22, he wrote to Cowdery:

> Respected Sir I would in form you that I arrived at home on Sunday morning the 4th after having a prosperous Journey, and found all well, the people are all friendly to <us> except a few who are in opposition to evry thing unless it is some thing that is exactly like themselves and two of our most formadable persacutors are now under censure and are cited to a tryal in the church for crimes which if true are worse than all the Gold Book business. We do not rejoice in the affliction of our enimies but we shall be glad to have truth prevail there begins to be a great call for our books in this country the minds of the people are very much excited when they find there is a copy right obtained and that there is really [a] book, about to be printed I have bought a horse of [Josiah] Stowell and want some one to come after it as soon as convenient Mr. Stowell has a prospect of getting five or six hundred dollars he does not know certain that he can get it but he is a going to try and if he can get the money he wants to pay it in immediately for books we want to hear from you and know how you prosper in the good work, give our best respects to Father & Mother and all our brothers and Sisters, To Mr. Harris and all the

73. Ibid.
74. Gregg, *The Prophet of Palmyra,* 37.

> company concerned tell them that our prayers are put up daily for them that they may be prospered in every, good word and work and that they may be preserved from sin here and from the consequence of sin hereafter and now dear brother be faithful in the discharge of evry duty looking for the reward of the righteous and now may God of his infinite mercy keep and pre=serve us spotless untill his coming and receive us all to rest with him in eternal repose through the attonement of Christ our Lord Amen.[75]

While Smith was back in Harmony, devotees in Fayette township began to preach the gospel as they had been commanded the previous June. "The Book of Mormon was still in the hands of the printer," said David Whitmer, "but my brother, Christian Whitmer, had copied from the manuscript the teachings and doctrine of Christ, being the things which we were commanded to preach."[76] Elsewhere, in the *Wayne Sentinel* offices where the Book of Mormon was being printed, the newly inked proofs were being stored, but not securely. On Sundays and evenings, when Grandin's press was not being used, Abner Cole, a free-thinking local lawyer, whom Lucy Smith said had become "destitute of Money [and] property," had access to the place, and took some loose pages from Joseph's book.[77] On September 2, Cole published the first issue of *The Reflector,* a satirical newspaper, which he distributed in areas outside the reach of the *Wayne Sentinel,* which the Smith family read. Using the pseudonym, Obediah Dogberry, Cole enlivened his weekly paper with jabs at Joseph's book-to-be. In the inaugural dispatch, Cole announced: "The Golden Bible, by Joseph Smith Junior, author and proprietor, is now in press and will shortly appear, Priestcraft is short lived!" In the December 9 issue, he announced that "at the solicitation of many of our readers we have concluded to commence publishing *extracts* from it." True to his word, the sometime solicitor printed an extract corresponding to 1 Nephi 1:1 through 1 Nephi 2:33.

On Sunday, December 27, 1829, Hyrum began to feel that something was amiss in the printing office. He expressed his concerns to Oliver, who

75. This letter appeared in Dean C. Jessee, comp. and ed., *The Personal Writings of Joseph Smith,* 227-28. Cowdery received the letter on November 5, and responded on November 6, 1829. "[M]y only motive in this writing," Cowdery said, in part, "is to inform you of my prospects and hopes and my desires and my longings to be freed from sin and to rest in the King=dom of my Savior and my redeemer when I begin to write of the mercys of God I know not when to stop but time and paper fail" (Cowdery to Smith, Nov. 6, 1829).

76. David Whitmer, *An Address to All Believers in Christ,* 32.

77. Anderson, *Lucy's Book,* 470. Cole, who was born about 1782, had served locally as a justice of the peace (1814-15), a constable (1818), and a road overseer.

was still living in the Smith home. After some debate about whether walking to town would violate the Sabbath, they decided it was necessary to quell their apprehension. Arriving at Grandin's office, they saw Cole at work. When Hyrum asked why he was working on Sunday, Cole explained that he was issuing a weekly newspaper and had access to the facility only when Grandin was not using it. Smith and Cowdery picked up a back issue of *The Reflector* and read that Cole had promised readers "one form of Joe Smith's Gold Bible each week." It was evident to Hyrum that Cole intended to publish the principal portion of the book "in such a way that [he] would not be obliged to pay the Smiths for it."[78] Shocked and angry, Hyrum challenged him. "[W]hat right have you to print the Book of Mormon in this manner?" he asked, "Do you not know that we have secured the copyright?" "It is none of your business," Cole replied, "I have hired the press, and will print what I please, so help yourself." "Mr. Cole," rejoined Hyrum, "that manuscript is sacred, and I forbid your printing any more of it." "Smith," exclaimed Cole, "I don't care a d[am]n for you: that d[amne]d gold bible is going into my paper, in spite of all you can do."

Hyrum and Cowdery returned home and told Joseph Sr. what they had found. The elder Smith determined to go to Harmony as soon as weather permitted to appraise young Joseph of the copyright infringement. Cowdery wrote to Joseph on December 28, explaining that Father Smith "is going directly to your country."[79] Father and son returned to Manchester in mid-January, fighting a blizzard. "The weather was so extremely cold," Lucy wrote, that her husband and son "came near perishing before they arrived at home." As soon as Joseph Jr. thawed out, he hiked into Palmyra to the Grandin office where he encountered Cole. "How do you do Mr[.] Coles," Joseph hailed, "you seem hard at work." "How do you do, Mr. Smith," answered Cole.[80] Examining one of Cole's freshly printed pages, Joseph said, "Mr. Cole, that book, [the Book of Mormon] and the right of publishing it, belongs to me, and I forbid you meddling with it any further." The words had scarcely left Joseph's mouth when Cole, a pugilist,[81] threw off his coat, rolled

78. Unless otherwise noted, my narrative on this incident is based on Anderson, *Lucy's Book,* 470-75.

79. Oliver Cowdery to Joseph Smith, Dec. 28, 1829.

80. Cole and Joseph had likely known each other since the Smith family first moved to Palmyra in 1816-17. Both families were living on west Main Street. Joseph was ten, and Cole, an overseer of highways from April 1816 to April 1817, was in his early to mid-thirties.

81. In a brief character sketch, Cole characterized himself as one who "Flogs fop or fool where're they'r [sic] found, / And single-handed stands his ground" (qtd. in Egbert Bratt Grandin,

up his sleeves, and bellowed as he pumped his fists, "[D]o you want to fight, sir? Do you want to fight?—I will publish just as what I'm a mind to and now if you want to fight just come on." "Well now," replied Joseph who was less than half Cole's forty-seven years, "you had better keep on your c<oa>t for it's cold and I am not going to fight you nor anything of that sort but you have got to stop printing my book sir[,] I assure you for I know my rights and shall maintain them."

Cole persisted. "Sir[,] ... if you think you are the best man just take off your coat and try it." Not willing to be provoked, Joseph replied: "Mr. Cole ... there is Law—and you will find that out if you did not know it before but I shall not fight you for that would do no good and there is another way of disposing <of> the affair that will answer my purpose better than fighting." Joseph suggested arbitration, to which Cole agreed. Armed with this copyright documentation, Joseph prevailed, and Cole "made us no further trouble," wrote Lucy.[82]

While Joseph was in Palmyra settling the Cole affair, his father signed an agreement on January 16, 1830, with Harris. "I hereby agree," attested Joseph Sr., "that Martin Harris shall have an equal privilege with me & my friends of selling the Book of Mormon of the Edition now printing by Egbert B. Grandin until enough of them shall be sold to pay for the printing of the same or until such times as the said Grandin shall be paid for the printing the aforesaid Books or copies."[83]

Joseph had scarcely made the 150-mile return trip to Harmony, however, when additional trouble broke out in Palmyra in the late winter or early

---

Diary, Jan. 1, 1831). In the March 16, 1830, issue of his newspaper, Cole, who had received a letter from Luther Howard, bookbinder of the Book of Mormon, demanding that he be removed as a subscriber, derided Howard, calling him a "'*little* lump of anguish,' who measures something more than four feet in his shoes ... who professes, *obstentatiously* [sic], to belong to a Calvinist church ... while he *privately* advocates the 'Gold Bible'" ("We have only to regret ...," *[Palmyra] Reflector,* Mar. 16, 1830, 89).

82. Cole, after moving to Rochester, published an eight-page weekly, the *Liberal Advocate,* from February 23, 1832, until November 22, 1834. He declared that "EQUAL RIGHTS and FREE DISCUSSION will be fearlessly advocated and maintained. Sectarian *dogmas* or tenets will be investigated and compared." A freethinker, Cole was labeled by one writer as an "opponent of intolerance, hypocrisy, and fanaticism (as he perceived these things)" (Barnes, "Obediah Dogberry," 1). Cole died in Rochester on July 13, 1835.

83. Simon Gratz Autograph Collection. An old debt incurred by Father Smith resulted in legal action three days after he signed the agreement with Harris. When Lemuel Durfee's estate was being inventoried, it included a $36.50 promissory note signed by Smith and Abraham Fish. Durfee's son, on January 19, entered a plea before Justice Nathan Pierce against the two men. The account was turned over to Constable S. Southworth for collection and resolved in September (H. Michael Marquardt and Wesley P. Walters, *Inventing Mormonism,* 131).

spring of 1830. While Cowdery and an unnamed son of Dr. Gain Robinson were working on a printing project, "a party of restless religionists," Lucy later asserted, "began to counsel together, as to the most efficient means of putting a stop to our proceedings."[84] Robinson overheard the men. One of the ringleaders said, "Now gentlemen this golden bible … is destined to bring down every thing before it if there is not a stop put to it." Implying that ministers would become unemployed, the speaker asked, "Shall we endure this gentlemen?" To which cries of "No! No!" erupted. The group decided to send a delegation to visit Lucy Smith during the day to ask her to read from the manuscript. A distraction would draw Lucy away from the manuscript momentarily, during which one of the men would toss it into the fireplace. The backup plan, if the book was published, was to encourage everyone in the community to boycott Joseph's book.

Cowdery related the plans he and Robinson had overheard. Lucy reminded him that the place was guarded around the clock, and she would not retrieve the manuscript if men came for that purpose. Moreover, she kept the manuscript in a chest under her bed with the headboard physically resting on the box so that it could not be extracted without moving the bed. Four days later, three men appeared at the Smith home. "Mrs. Smith," one of them began, "we hear you have a gold bible and we came to see you [if] you [would be] so kind as to show it to us." She answered:

> No gentlemen, we have got <no> gold bible and neither have we ever had anything of the kind, but we have a translation of some gold plates which was sent to the world to bring the plain[n]ess of the Gospel to the children of men and also to give a history of the people that used to inhabit this country and I then proceeded to give them the substance of what is contained in the book of Mormon particularly the principles of religion which it contains. But added I the Universalists come here wonderful[l]y affraid that their religion will suffer loss—The Presbyterians are frightened least their sallery will come down[.] The Methodists come and they rage for they worship a God without body or parts and the doctrine we advocate comes in contact with their views.

One of the men then asked if they could see the manuscript. Lucy again refused: "No sir you cannot see it we have done exhibiting the manuscript altogether I have told you what was in it and that must <suffice>."

---

84. Unless otherwise noted, my narrative at this point is based on Anderson, *Lucy's Book,* 460-68.

Thus thwarted, the men next convened a mass meeting at which citizens voted to shun the Book of Mormon. The group sent a committee to Grandin and, according to Lucy, "inform[ed] him of the resolutions which they had passed, and also to explain to him the evil consequences which would result to him therefrom."[85] They encouraged him to stop the press, telling him that the Smiths had lost all their property and could only pay their share of the printing costs through sale of the books—which no one would buy. But Smith and Harris jointly "succeeded in removing [Grandin's] fears, so that he went on with the work, until the books were printed, which was in the spring of eighteen hundred and thirty."[86]

With scarcely a shilling in his pocket, however, and needing additional support, Joseph had little recourse but to keep up the pressure on Harris to continue funding his needs.[87] About this time or earlier, Joseph had directed a compelling revelation at Harris: "A commandment of God and not of man to you, Martin," it declared.[88] After calling upon Harris to "repent, lest I smite you by the rod of my mouth, and by my wrath, and by my anger," the

85. Anderson, *Lucy's Book,* 476.

86. Mother Smith added that "These trips back, and forth, exhausted nearly all our means, yet they seemed unavoidable" (ibid.)

87. Evidently about this same time, it was suggested that Joseph try to sell the copyright in Canada. Hiram Page, one of the eight Book of Mormon witnesses, wrote:

> Joseph thought this would be a good oprtunity to get a handsom Sum of money which was to be (after the expencis were taken out) for the exclusive benefit of the Smith famly and was to be at the disposal of Joseph according to Oliver Cowdery Joseph Knights, Hiram Page and [Josiah Stowell] were chosen (as I understand by revlation) to do the busianess. ... the necessary prepration was made (by them) in a Sly manor So as to keep martin Haris from drawing a Share of the money. ... when we got [to Kingston]; there was no purcheser neither were they authorized at kingston to buy rights for the provence; but little york was the place where Such busianess had to be done; we were to get 8,000 dollars. (Hiram Page to William E. McLellin, Feb. 2, 1848.)

The men returned "nearly starved, completely wearied, with no money nor copyright sold either" (John L. Traughber to James T. Cobb, ca. 1881, 311).

David Whitmer remembered that Joseph inquired of the Lord by gazing "into the hat in which he placed the stone." When the men returned empty-handed, Whitmer said, "we were all in great trouble; and we asked Joseph how it was that he had received a revelation from the Lord ... and the brethren had utterly failed in their undertaking. Joseph did not know how it was, so he enquired of the Lord about it, and behold the following revelation came through the stone: '*Some revelations are of God: some revelations are of man: and some revelations are of the devil.*'" "This was a lesson for our benefit," Whitmer added, "and we should have profited by it in [the] future more than we did" (David Whitmer, *An Address to All Believers in Christ,* 30; emphasis his). For a copy of this revelation, see "23 Commandment AD 1830," cited in Robin Scott Jensen et al., *The Joseph Smith Papers,* 30-33. For more, see Stephen Kent Ehat, "'Securing' the Prophet's Copyright in the Book of Mormon: Historical and Legal Context of the So-called Canadian Copyright Revelation," *BYU Studies* 50, no. 2 (2011): 4-70.

88. BC XVI. See also MacKay and Dirkmaat, *From Darkness unto Light,* 190-93.

revelation commanded: "Impart a portion of thy property; Yea, even a part of thy lands and all save the support of thy family. Pay the printer's debt. …" In the face of such admonition, Martin needed little additional incentive to keep up his support.

Grandin's shop continued to turn out page after page, day after day, until finally, with evidently little fanfare, the Book of Mormon was advertized for sale in his bookstore on March 26, 1830. Harris gave one of the first books to his older brother, Emer, who after reading it, like millions since, followed in Martin's footsteps to become a believer in the dreams and visions of Joseph Smith.

16 | JOSEPH'S BOOK

> *[T]here can be no doubt as to the possession of a vividly strong, creative imagination by Joseph Smith, the Prophet, an imagination, it could with reason be urged, which, given the suggestions that are to be found in the "common knowledge" of accepted American Antiquities of the times ... would make it possible for him to create a book such as the Book of Mormon is.*
>
> —B. H. Roberts, *Studies of the Book of Mormon,* edited by Brigham D. Madsen, 250

One easily imagines the adolescent Joseph exploring the slopes of the glacial drumlin he would later identify as the Hill Cumorah. The mount, the highest elevation in the area, from a distance looks much like an immense Indian mound or tumulus, rising apart and mysterious in the gently rolling landscape. From the summit of the hill is an awe-inspiring view, the type of attraction a curious, creative youth like young Joseph would naturally have been drawn to. His keen imagination would no doubt been further fired by local folklore, abundant with romantic yarns. In them, stories emerged of ancient fortifications, epic battles, and human massacre. Such tales, common to the day, would have captured young Joseph's fantasy.

Indian mounds, nearly a dozen of which dotted the western New York landscape within a fifty-mile radius of young Smith's home,[1] are generally divided into three types: temple or altar mounds,[2] fortification mounds,[3] and

1. There was a burial mound in Clifton Springs, a little more than five miles south of the Smith farm. About ten miles away, near Victor, was a mound containing graves topped with an ancient fortification which showed evidence of once having been picketed. Three additional mounds stood ten miles south in Canandaigua, where the Smiths occasionally conducted business. East of Canandaigua, on the road to Geneva, was the circular wall of one of New York's most famous ancient fortifications ("New World Antiquities," 5).

2. "A Gentleman in Pompey, N.Y.," *Palmyra Herald,* Feb. 19, 1823, 2, suggested that "many of these fortifications were not forts, but religious temples, or places of public worship."

3. En route to western New York when he was ten or eleven, young Joseph passed by several prominent palisaded fortification mounds and abandoned village sites along the Mohawk River. Similar bastions are described in the Book of Mormon. See Alma 50:1-4; and also Alma 48:8, 49:18.

burial mounds[4] in which excavations often unearthed skeletons and ancient artifacts. The Rev. Thaddeus Mason Harris, who toured regions northwest of the Allegheny Mountains in 1803, wrote: "The vast mounds and walls of earth, discovered in various parts of this western region have excited the astonishment of all who have seen or heard of them. ... These works are scattered over the whole face of the country."[5] DeWitt Clinton, New York's governor, in 1817 described a mound near Ridgeway, Genesee County, New York, containing piles of skeletons. "They were deposited there by their conquerors," he hypothesized.[6]

The editor of the January 21, 1818, *Palmyra Register* speculated that the remains of one such mound were "doubtless killed in battle and hastily buried."[7] The following year, on May 26, the *Register* added that "this country was once inhabited by a race of people, at least, partially civilized, & that this race has been exterminated by the forefathers of the present and the late tribes of Indians in this country." A popular history of New York, published in 1824 when Joseph was nineteen, related a tradition of the Seneca, an Iroquois tribe, that "before and after that remote period, when the ancestors of the Senecas sprung into existence, the country, especially about the lakes, was thickly inhabited by a race of civil, enterprising, and industrious people, who were totally destroyed, and whose improvements were taken possession of by the Senecas."[8] The book's authors added that the Seneca had exterminated a highly civilized white race who had built numerous fortifications near the Great Lakes and eastern woodlands as a defense against the savage

4. In 1820, Caleb Atwater, postmaster of Circleville, Ohio, published in *Archaeologia Americana* his "Description of the Antiquities Discovered in the State of Ohio and Other Western States." In one mound, he reported, was "a great quantity of human bones." He speculated that these remains were undoubtedly "of those who had been slain in some great and destructive battle. First, because they belonged to persons who had attained their full size; ... and secondly, they were here in the utmost confusion, as if buried in a hurry" (qtd. in "New World Antiquities," 3). The Book of Mormon mentions burial mounds in Alma 2:38, 16:11, and 28:11.

5. Thaddeus Mason Harris, qtd. in "New World Antiquities," 1.

6. DeWitt Clinton, qtd. in "New World Antiquities," 3.

7. Orson Pratt, in his 1840 treatment of the discovery of the golden plates, wrote that in the great battles of the Book of Mormon "tens of thousands were frequently slain, after which they were piled together in great heaps upon the face of the ground, and covered with a shallow covering of earth, which will satisfactorily account for those ancient mounds, filled with human bones, so numerous at the present day, both in North and South America" (Orson Pratt, *An Interesting Account of Several Remarkable Visions and of the Late Discovery of Ancient American Records,* 9). An 1834 publication reported that early Mormon missionaries preached that "the mounds throughout the western states, which have heretofore excited so much curiosity, are the remains of the cities of the Nephites and Lamanites" ("The Book of Mormon," *The Unitarian,* 43).

8. John V. N. Yates and Joseph W. Moulton, *History of the State of New-York Including Its Aboriginal and Colonial Annals,* 40.

red natives. The authors reported a number of popular conjectures about the origin of this alleged white race, including the hypothesis that they were descendants of ancient Israelites.

While not speculating on the origins of the American aborigines, Joseph Smith Sr. reportedly told neighbor Roswell Nichols sometime before he left the area in 1830 that "the ancients, half of them melted the ore and made the gold and silver, while the other half buried it deeper in the earth, which accounted for these hills."[9] Another neighbor, William Stafford, recalled in 1833 that Joseph Sr. told him earlier that "[n]early all the hills in this part of New York were thrown up by human hands, and in them were large caves" brimming with treasure.[10]

While Joseph Jr. was in some ways a singular visionary, he was by no means the first to speculate on the origins of the earliest Americans. As soon as Europeans began to explore the interior of the continent, conjectures multiplied about who the native inhabitants were and from which branch of the human tree they derived. The subject became one of the world's great mysteries. Some early theorists viewed them as Egyptian. Others supposed them to be Phoenicians, Welsh, Irish, Japanese, Chinese, Tartars, or Norse.[11] The most widely cited theory, however, was that American Indians were Israelites—descendants of biblical patriarchs Abraham, Isaac, and Jacob. This scenario was perhaps first expounded in print by Joannes Fredericus Lumnius in 1567. Portuguese Jew Antonio de Montezinos (1644), Jewish Rabbi Manasseh ben Israel (1650), and English clergyman Thomas Thorowgood expanded on the theory. Thorowgood co-authored a 1660 work with John Eliot of Massachusetts, known as the "Apostle to the Indians," *Jews in America, or Probabilities That Those Indians Are Judaical, Made More Probable by Some Additionals to the Former Conjectures.* Other book-length treatments of the topic included James Adair's *History of the American Indians* (1775), Elias

9. Roswell Nichols, Statement, Dec. 1, 1833, in Eber D. Howe, *Mormonism Unvailed,* 257-58. Traveling through Missouri in 1838, Joseph Jr. visited some Indian mounds which he believed "were probably erected by the aborigines of the land, to secrete treasures" *(History of the Church,* 3:37).

10. William Stafford, Statement, in Howe, *Mormonism Unvailed,* 237. In an 1835 letter to Oliver Cowdery, W. W. Phelps called Cumorah "the artificial hill of North America" and further explained: "Around that mound died millions of the Jaredites. ... [T]here too, fell the Nephites" (W. W. Phelps to Oliver Cowdery, *Messenger and Advocate* 2, no. 2 [Nov. 1835]: 221).

11. For discussions of the various theories of origin of Native Americans, see J. M. Adovasio and Jake Page, *The First Americans;* Michael H. Crawford, *The Origins of Native Americans;* Thomas D. Dillehay, *The Settlement of the Americas;* Brian M. Fagan, *Ancient North America;* Daniel Lavallee, *The First South Americans;* Reader's Digest, *Mysteries of the Ancient Americas;* B. H. Roberts, *Studies of the Book of Mormon;* and Dan Vogel, *Indian Origins and the Book of Mormon.*

Boudinot's *A Star in the West; or, a Humble Attempt to Discover the Long Lost Ten Tribes of Israel* (1816), Caleb Atwater's "Description of the Antiquities Discovered in the State of Ohio and Other Western States," in *Archaeologia Americana* (1820), Ethan Smith's *View of the Hebrews* (1823, 1825), and Josiah Priest's *The Wonders of Nature and Providence, Displayed* (1825).[12]

Other New Englanders, including Samuel Sewall (commissioner of the Society for the Propagation of the Gospel in New England), Jonathan Edwards, Roger Williams, and William Penn, shared the view that the American Indians were Israelites. Moreover, just two years before Joseph Smith began working in earnest on the Book of Mormon, New Yorker Mordecai M. Noah was quoted in the October 11, 1825, *Wayne Sentinel,* Smith's hometown newspaper, as saying: "Those who are conversant with the public and private economy of the Indians, are strongly of [the] opinion that they are the lineal descendants of the Israelites, and my own researches go far to confirm me in the same belief."[13]

In 1840, in one of the earliest published treatments of Joseph's life, Orson Pratt wrote that the angel who appeared to young Joseph in 1823 "manifest[ed] to him, that the 'American Indians' were a remnant of Israel."[14] While Joseph found himself in the mainstream of New England divines on this issue, like most nineteenth-century Americans, he did not distinguish among the cultures and lifestyles of the hundreds of different Native American tribes and clans. Instead, he believed that these groups belonged to a single race, called *Lamanites.* During the early 1820s, the young seer must have sensed that a history of the American Indians could fill that perplexing gap in the history of the world and satisfy the curiosity of those who had long wondered about that culture. Simultaneously, the publication of such a history could provide both money and respect. In 1835, his cousin and confidant, Oliver Cowdery, described Smith's 1823 thinking:

> A history of the inhabitants who peopled this continent, previous to its being discovered to Europians [sic] by Columbus, must be interesting to every man; and as it would develop the important fact, that the present race were descendants of Abraham, and were to be remembered in the immutable covenant of the Most High to that man, and be restored to a knowledge of the gospel, that they, with all nations might rejoice, seemed to inspire further thoughts of gain and income from such a valuable

12. Priest's work sold 22,000 copies (Adovasio, *The First Americans,* 18).
13. Mordecai M. Noah, "M. M. Noah's Speech," *Wayne Sentinel,* Oct. 11, 1825, 1.
14. Pratt, *An Interesting Account,* 3.

history. Surely, thought [Smith], every man will seize with eagerness, this knowledge, and this incalculable income will be mine.[15]

Joseph was a syncretist who freely borrowed ideas from his environment. Thus, as I read and interpret the earliest historical sources, including eye-witness testimony, Joseph did not "translate"—at least not in any commonly accepted definition of the term—the text of the Book of Mormon. Rather, he "scryed" or "envisioned" it through a process of "seeing" that drew, at a minimum, upon both his innate creative intelligence and his own experience with his intellectual, religious, political, economic, and familial worlds.[16] For example, the inspiration for Joseph's story of golden artifacts was no doubt informed, in significant part, by reports of the discovery of metal plates at several eastern American sites. In 1775, trader James Adair described two brass plates and five copper plates that were possessed by a band of Tuccabatches Indians. One member of the tribe said that "he was told by his forefathers that those plates were given to them by the man we call God; that there had been many more of other shapes. ... [S]ome had writing upon them which were buried with particular men."[17] Palmyra newspaperman Orsamus Turner reported in 1850 that a New York plowman in 1809 unearthed an "Ancient Record, or Tablet." According to Turner, this plate "had engraved upon one side of it ... what would appear to have been some record, or as we may well imagine some brief code of laws."[18] In 1821, the *Western Farmer*, another Palmyra newspaper, reported that Erie Canal diggers found "several brass plates," skeletons, and fragments of pottery.[19]

Accounts of buried metal plates and the persistent myth of a lost Indian book may have also inspired Congregational minister Ethan Smith of

---

15. Oliver Cowdery, [Letter VII] to W. W. Phelps, July 1835, 156.

16. This approach obviously departs from that which sees the Book of Mormon as a "translation" of a genuinely ancient history of the various peoples of the Americas. I do not argue for the superiority of my interpretation, merely that it makes the most sense to me. Nor do I suggest that Joseph was a fraud—conscious or otherwise—according to the generally accepted definition of the term. Joseph was a religious visionary who constructed a belief system composed, syncretically, from a wide variety of elements. Of the authorship of Isaiah, J. Reuben Clark, at the time a member of the First Presidency of the LDS Church, admonished in words that he also applied to the Bible as a whole: "Who wrote Isaiah ... are matters that do not in any way affect either the supreme literary value of the great prophecies and poems that the book contains, or that these are the word of God to his children. What prophet, what poet wrote them is of no consequence, since whoever he was or they were, they were inspired of God. So with all the books of the whole Bible" (J. Reuben Clark Jr., "The World Crisis Today," *LDS Church News*, June 16, 1945, 11).

17. Adair, *The History of the American Indians*, 178.

18. O[rsamus] Turner. *Pioneer History of the Holland Purchase of Western New York*, 668-69.

19. "Discoveries on the Canal," 1.

Poultney, Vermont, to write about the legend. Dartmouth-educated Smith (no known relation to Joseph), who ministered to the congregation of which Oliver Cowdery's family were members, wrote in 1823 that the Indians once had "a book which they had for a long time preserved, but having lost the knowledge of reading it, they concluded it would be of no further use to them; and they buried it with an Indian chief." Although he did not cite a source for this legend, he added that the Indians "once, away in another country, had the old divine speech, the book of God; they shall at some time have it again, and shall then be happy."[20]

Ethan Smith was influenced about the origins of the American Indians by ideas current at Dartmouth College in Hanover, New Hampshire. Its founder, Rev. Eleazar Wheelock, and successors believed that Christians were under an obligation to spread the gospel among the Indians because they were "the descendants of Abram."[21] When Smith wrote *View of the Hebrews,* he, like the Book of Mormon text, speculated that there were two classes of people in ancient America, one barbarous and the other civilized:

> It is highly probable that the more civilized part of the tribes of Israel after they settled in America became wholly separated from the hunting and savage tribes of their brethren; that the latter lost the knowledge of their having descended from the same family with themselves; that the more civilized part continued for many centuries, that tremendous wars were frequent between them and their savage brethren until the former became extinct.

"This hypothesis," added Smith, "accounts for the ancient works, forts, mounds, and vast enclosures as well as tokens of a good degree of civil government which are manifestly very ancient and for centuries before Columbus discovered America."[22]

A popular theory among some writers is that Smith's *View of the Hebrews* was an important source of inspiration—perhaps on par with, or second only to, the King James Version of the Bible (KJV)—for the basic story line of the Book of Mormon. For some, the structural similarities between the two books seem too substantial to be mere coincidence. After years of studying the

20. Ethan Smith, *View of the Hebrews,* 130, 223. According to Poultney church records, at the time of the writing and publication of *View of the Hebrews,* Cowdery's stepmother and three of his sisters were members of the congregation (David Persuitte, *Joseph Smith and the Origins of the Book of Mormon,* 7-8).

21. David M'Clure and Elijah Parish, *Memoirs of the Rev. Eleazar Wheelock, D.D.,* 106.

22. Roberts, *Studies of the Book of Mormon,* 332.

Book of Mormon, B. H. Roberts, one of seven presidents of the First Council of Seventy (the third-ranked body in the hierarchy of the LDS Church) and one of Mormonism's best-known theologians, opined in the 1920s:

> [O]n subjects widely discussed, and that deal in matters of widespread public interest, there is built up in the course of years, a community knowledge of such subjects, usually referred to as "matters of common knowledge" to which non-readers of books or of periodicals, and to which even the ignorant have more or less of access, through hearing such subjects discussed at the gathering places of the common people; the village store, the wheelwright's shop, the town meeting, and post office, the social meetings of the community, the gathering and dispersing throngs in attendance upon church services—in all such places the people hear and absorb knowledge of such subjects as are of general interest, until there is formed what I have referred to as "common knowledge" of things. ... Such "common knowledge" existed throughout New England and New York in relation to American Indian origins and cultures; the prevailing ideas respecting the American Indians throughout the regions named were favorable to the notion that they were of Hebrew origin. ... And with the existence of such a body of knowledge, or that which was accepted as "knowledge," and a person of vivid and constructive imaginative power in contact with it, there is little room for doubt but that it might be possible for Joseph Smith to construct a theory of origin for his Book of Mormon in harmony with these prevailing notions; and more especially since this "common knowledge" is set forth in almost handbook form in the little work of Ethan Smith *View of the Hebrews.*[23]

Both Ethan Smith and Joseph Smith identify American Indians—drawing on Ezekiel 37:15-17 in the King James Bible—as the "stick of Joseph or Ephraim" (the northern Ten Tribes of Israel) which is expected to be reunited with the "stick of Judah" (the Jews of the southern kingdom of Judah). Moreover, each work reflects the lifelong admonition of Dartmouth's Rev. Eleazar Wheelock, who asserted during his inauguration that it was the obligation of the American (gentile) nation of Christians, in the last days, to gather the remnant and to "make the Redeemer known" among them, *"that the manifestation of Jesus Christ, among the heathen,* will powerfully and effectually draw them unto him."[24] Chapter 4 of *View of the Hebrews* appeals to the "Christian Nation" of the United States "to become the instrument for

23. Ibid., 153-54.

24. M'Clure and Parish, *Memoirs of the Rev. Eleazar Wheelock,* 17-19; emphasis Wheelock's.

teaching the gospel to the American Indians and restore them to the favor and blessing of God."[25] The title page of the Book of Mormon, which Joseph said was found on one of the golden plates, attests that the work was written "to the Lamanites, which are a remnant of the House of Israel. … that they may know the covenants of the Lord, that they are not cast off forever: and also to the convincing of the Jew and Gentile that JESUS is the CHRIST, the ETERNAL God."

The Book of Mormon tells of the transoceanic migrations of two ancient groups of Middle Eastern families to the Americas. The first group, called Jaredites, came to the apparently previously unpopulated New World ca. 2247 B.C.E., at the time of the confusing of tongues at the Tower of Babel, as described in Genesis 11.[26] This group then evolved into a great civilization, ostensibly covering all of North America "from sea to sea, with towns and cities,"[27] before battling itself to extinction about 600-300 B.C.E., on and near the Hill Ramah (Cumorah) in Joseph's New York neighborhood. According to the Book of Mormon, millions were slain. Oliver Cowdery wrote that "the entire power and national strength of both the Jaredites and Nephites were destroyed" in the region of Cumorah.[28]

The Nephites were part of the second migration to the pre-Columbian Americas, said to have taken place in the late sixth century B.C.E. (1 Ne. 18:23-25). This migration consisted of two small groups—Lehites and Mulekites—both Hebrew immigrants from the Middle East. They merged sometime after their separate arrivals in the New World. The Book of Mormon explains that these people "did multiply and spread, and did go forth from the land southward to the land northward, and did spread insomuch that they began to cover the face of the whole earth, from the sea south, to the sea north, from the sea west, to the sea east."[29] Nephite and Lamanite cultures, whose histories are chronicled in the Book of Mormon, are described on the title page as "a remnant of the House of Israel." Elsewhere, Joseph explained that these peoples "are the Indians that now inhabit this country."[30]

25. Roberts, *Studies of the Book of Mormon,* 336.

26. Joseph described the arrival of the Jaredites as the "first settlement" in ancient America (Joseph Smith, "Church History," 707).

27. Joseph Smith Jr., "Facts Are Stubborn Things," 922.

28. Cowdery, [Letter VII] to W. W. Phelps, July 1835, 157.

29. 1830 Book of Mormon, 412 (Hel. 3:8 in 1981 LDS edition). In the Book of Mormon (LDS) editions between 1879 to 1920, footnotes identified the land southward as South America, the land northward as North America, the sea south as the Atlantic, south of Cape Horn, the sea north as the Arctic, north of North America, the sea west as the Pacific, and the sea east as the Atlantic.

30. Joseph Smith, "Church History," 707.

Joseph's book chronicles wars, migrations, kings, and religious activities of these enlightened New World Christians. The civilization's climax is a visit by the resurrected Jesus Christ to these Israelites, who possessed "a correct knowledge of the gospel, and the plan of restoration and redemption."[31] Christian churches were organized among them, baptisms by immersion administered, and all the blessings and privileges of the New Testament dispensation enjoyed, with the peculiar gifts of speaking with tongues, prophesying, performing miracles, and similar practices hundreds of years before the appearance of the Jesus in the flesh in the Middle East.

Interestingly, these Christian American Hebrews, who were said to have populated the Americas from about 600 B.C.E. to about 400 C.E., were annihilated in internecine warfare on the same Hill Cumorah where the Jaredites had met their ultimate fate. Despite living centuries before Joseph Smith, these Book of Mormon peoples encountered religious and political difficulties that were similar to those the eastern United States underwent in Joseph's youth. And although the book presents itself as a literal history of Hebrew peoples, it mentions none of the prominent Jewish holidays, is replete with references to Jacksonian American politics, alludes to the anti-Masonic furor of the late 1820s, and engages in such early nineteenth-century theological controversies as infant baptism, free will, Original Sin, and the efficacy of works. The book also tends to partake of the general millennial anticipation of Joseph's day.

Joseph's Book of Mormon has impacted the lives of millions of people since 1830. With more than 150 million copies published in more than 100 languages, the book is unquestionably a work of global significance, undergirding a world-wide religious movement reportedly approaching 16 million adherents. Yet I wonder if the work is sometimes revered more for its heritage than for its contents. Mormons have been taught from the earliest days of Joseph's ministry that the Book of Mormon, the faith's keystone text, is a literal record of God's dealings with the ancient inhabitants of the Americas. But probably only a small percentage of followers are familiar with the difficulties such claims have created since the book's 1830 publication. Many are unaware of a secondary literature of some 6,000-plus titles scrutinizing the book's and its interpreters' empirical claims.[32] The main conclusion of this particular growing body of work is that there is no element in the Book of

31. Oliver Cowdery, [Letter IV], to W. W. Phelps, Feb. 1835, 79.
32. Scott McLemee, "Latter-day Studies."

Mormon that cannot be explained naturalistically.[33] An overview of critical issues regarding the ancient historicity of the Book of Mormon follows.

Language

Joseph Smith said: "There was no Greek or Latin upon the plates from which I, through the grace of God, translated the Book of Mormon."[34] Evidently unknown to him, however, *Christ* is a Greek word, as are *Lachoneus, Timothy, Jonas, Alpha,* and *Omega*—all of which appear in the book. Joseph's ear was naturally attuned to seventeenth-century English, the language of the regularly used King James Bible which he heard preached from the pulpit as well as read in his home by both parents. As he began to dictate the English text of the Book of Mormon, Joseph tried to emulate much of the cadence and flow of the Bible. B. H. Roberts pointed out that the language in the 1830 Book of Mormon reflected the English of New England in the early 1800s and that it "is evidently but little influenced by any attempt to follow the idiom of an ancient language." Roberts also observed that the type of grammatical errors found in the Book of Mormon are those expected from someone who was "unlearned in the English language."[35]

The vernacular of the Book of Mormon's first edition is often rural western New York. Questions about the grammar of the 1830 text later led Joseph, with Oliver Cowdery's help, to make more than a thousand changes for the book's second edition, published in 1837 in Kirtland, Ohio.[36] As linguist and Book of Mormon scholar Royal Skousen notes: "The language of our current text of the Book of Mormon differs in a number of important ways from the original text."[37]

---

33. The opposing point of view may be best documented in the publications of a variety of organizations and on-line web sties, notably FAIR (Foundation for Apologetic Information and Research), *Interpreter: A Journal of Mormon Scripture,* and the Neal A. Maxwell Institute for Religious Scholarship.

34. Joseph Smith Jr., "Meaning of the Word Mormon," 194.

35. B. H. Roberts, *Defense of the Faith and the Saints,* 1:278.

36. The 1837 Book of Mormon may have been hurried into print because of Joseph's financial difficulties. On June 25, 1833, he wrote to printer W. W. Phelps, "As soon as we can get time, we will review the manuscripts of the Book of Mormon, after which they will be forwarded to you" *(History of the Church,* 1:363). Smith also revised the 1840 edition. By that point, however, Cowdery had left the Church, taking the printer's manuscript with him. Orson Pratt prepared a new LDS edition in 1879, and James E. Talmage prepared a 1920 LDS edition. The 1981 LDS edition was prepared under the supervision of the Scriptures Publication Committee.

37. Royal Skousen, "The Original Language of the Book of Mormon," 29. Some examples of Smith's imperfect grammar, which were changed in the second edition, are:

"The armies of the Lamanites are a marching towards the city of Cumeni" (Alma 57:31).

"They was yet wroth" (1 Ne. 4:4).

After skimming an early edition of the Book of Mormon, Mark Twain wrote, admittedly derisively but perhaps cogently of Joseph's attempt to impart a Bible-like authority to the text: "the result is a mongrel—half modern glibness, and half ancient simplicity and gravity. ... Whenever he found his speech growing too modern—which was about every sentence or two—he ladled in a few such Scriptural phrases as 'exceeding sore,' 'and it came to pass,' etc and made things satisfactory again."[38] In fact, the 1830 edition used the phrase "and it came to pass" more than 1,200 times—almost 200 times in 1 Nephi alone. In 1 Nephi 3:21-29, the phrase begins eight of nine verses. In the sixty-nine verses of Ether 14 and 15, it appears thirty-nine times. In the 1837 edition, Joseph removed at least forty-seven "and it came to pass" expressions.

In addition to incorrect grammar, the text is sometimes long-winded. One speech, assigned to Nephi, reads:

> Wherefore hearken, O my people, which are of the House of Israel, and give ear unto my words: for because that the words of Isaiah are not plain unto you, nevertheless they are plain unto all they that are filled with the spirit of prophecy. But I give unto you a prophecy, according to the spirit which is in me; wherefore I shall prophesy according to the plainness which hath been with me from the time that I came out from Jerusalem with my father: for behold, my soul delighteth in plainness unto my people, that they may learn; yea, and my soul delighteth in the words of Isaiah, for I came out from Jerusalem, and mine eyes hath beheld the things of the Jews, and I know that the Jews do understand the things of the Prophets, and there is none other people that understand the things which were spoken unto the Jews, like unto them, save it be that they are taught after the manner of the things of the Jews.[39]

Another repetitive passage reads: "And thus did the thirty and eighth year pass away, and also the thirty and ninth, and forty and first, and the forty and second; yea, even until forty and nine years had passed away, and also the fifty and first, and the fifty and second; yea, and even until fifty and nine years had passed away."[40] Such wordiness is puzzling since Nephite

---

"This shall be your language in them days" (Hel. 13:37).
"I have wrote to them" (3 Ne. 26:11).
"Adam and Eve, which was our first parents" (1 Ne. 5:11).
"That all might see the writing which he had wrote" (Alma 46:19).

38. Mark Twain, *Roughing It,* 107.
39. 1830 Book of Mormon, 103 (2 Ne. 25:4-5).
40. 1830 Book of Mormon, 514 (4 Ne. 1:6).

writers comment how they economized their narrative to save space (Jarom 1:2, 14; Mormon 9:33).

Yet the Book of Mormon also contains such memorable expressions as Lehi's "Adam fell that men might be; and men are, that they might have joy" (2 Ne. 2:25); as well as Nephi's stirring lament: "Behold, my soul is rent with anguish because of you, and my heart is pained" (1 Ne. 17:47). And King Benjamin captures the Christian's duty in a single sentence: "[W]hen ye are in the service of your fellow beings ye are only in the service of your God" (Mosiah 2:17).

After the 1830 witnessing experience, Oliver Cowdery, David Whitmer, and Martin Harris testified: "[W]e also know that [the golden plates] have been translated by the gift and power of God, for his voice hath declared it unto us."[41] Joseph added in his history further words from God: "These plates have been ... translated by the power of God. The translation of them which you have seen is correct."[42] This claim, if interpreted literally, seems to contradict the fact that more than 12,000 changes "of all varieties" have been made to the book's text in the ensuing years since 1830.[43] Poor communication with copiers and typesetting errors have been put forth as plausible reasons, but they are not fully satisfying. True, the most common changes were tidying the book's problematic English grammar: 891 changes of *which* to *who,* 177 changes of *exceeding* to *exceedingly,* 162 changes of *was* to *were,* 74 of *is* to *are,* and 10 of *done* to *did.*[44]

More significant, however, are the theological modifications, including changes of meaning. For example, in 2 Nephi 30:6, *white* appeared in the 1830 and 1837 editions. Joseph changed this word—though not every occurrence—to the less racist *pure* in the 1840 edition. In Mosiah 21:28 and Ether 4:1, the first edition had *Benjamin* (who was long dead at this point) where *Mosiah* now appears. "Such is the nature of the errors in question," stated B. H. Roberts, a noted Book of Mormon student, "and so interwoven are they throughout the diction of the book, that they may not be disposed of by saying they result from inefficient proof-reading or referring them to the mischievous disposition of the 'typos,' or the unfriendliness of the publishing house. The errors are constitutional in their character, they are of the web and woof of the style and not such errors as may be classed as

41. "The Testimony of Three Witnesses," 1830 Book of Mormon, 589.
42. *History of the Church,* 1:54-55.
43. Hal Houghey, *A Review of the Reprint of the Original Book of Mormon,* 550.
44. George A. Horton Jr., "Understanding Textual Changes in the Book of Mormon," 28.

typographical. Indeed, the first edition of the Book of Mormon is singularly free from typographical errors."[45]

In light of what early witnesses said about how Joseph envisioned the Book of Mormon, one may wonder why corrections were necessary since God not only reportedly waited until a word had been spelled before continuing, but also declared the entire completed book "correct." David Whitmer, in nearly a dozen interviews, described his understanding in these terms. On one occasion, he said that "God gave to Brother Joseph the gift to see the sentences in English, when he looked into the hat in which was placed the stone."[46] He added that Smith stated "to me and others that the original character appeared upon parchment and under it the translation in [E]nglish, which enabled him to read it readily."[47] He told another interviewer that "a spiritual light would shine forth, and parchment would appear before Joseph, upon which was a line of characters from the plates, and under it, the translation in English; at least, so Joseph said."[48] And on another occasion, he described how Smith "would hold the interpreters to his eyes and cover his face with a hat, excluding all light, and before his eyes would appear what seemed to be parchment, on which would appear the characters of the plates in a line at the top, and immediately below would appear the translation in English, which Smith would read to his scribe, who wrote it down exactly as it fell from his lips. The scribe would then read the sentence written, and if any mistake had been made, the characters would remain visible to Smith until corrected, when they faded from sight, to be replaced by another line."[49] "The tablets or plates were translated by Smith, who used a small oval, kidney-shaped stone," Whitmer said in 1881, "that seemed endowed with the marvelous power of converting the characters on the plates, when used by Smith, into English, who would then dictate to

45. B. H. Roberts, cited in Francis W. Kirkham, *A New Witness for Christ in America,* 1:200-201. See Robert J. Matthews, "Answer to a Gospel Question": "Changes and corrections have been necessary to correct copying and printing errors and to clarify the message of this book of scripture. Corrections of this sort are normal whenever new editions of a book are printed. Mistakes such as typographical errors, misspellings, misplaced or dropped words, and ambiguities noted in one edition are usually corrected in the text." Matthews asserts, incorrectly in my opinion, that "none of these changes, individually or collectively, alters the message of the Book of Mormon" (qtd. in *A Sure Foundation: Answers to Difficult Gospel Questions,* 33, 34).

46. David Whitmer, *An Address to All Believers in Christ,* 37.

47. David Whitmer, Interviewed by Zenos H. Gurley, Jan. 14, 1885.

48. J. L. Traughber Jr., Interview, Oct. 1879.

49. David Whitmer, Interviewed by the *Kansas City Journal,* June 1, 1881.

Cowdery what to write. Frequently, one character would make two lines of manuscript, while others made but a word or two words."[50]

Martin Harris corroborated the essence of Whitmer's accounts in an 1870 interview: "By aid of the seer stone, sentences would appear and were read by the Prophet and written by Martin, and when finished he would say, 'Written,' and if correctly written, that sentence would disappear and another appear in its place, but if not written correctly it remained until corrected."[51] Another eyewitness, Joseph Knight Sr., agreed: Smith "put the urim and thummim into his hat and Darkned his Eyes then he would take a sentence and it would apper in Brite Roman Letters then he would tell the writer and he would write it then <that would go away> the next sentance would Come and so on. But if it was not Spelt rite it would not go away till it was rite[.]"[52]

These first-hand descriptions of the process, echoing what Smith told Whitmer, Harris, and Knight, seem to suggest that the textual accuracy of the English version of the Book of Mormon should be absolute. The book was, according to friendly sources, dictated virtually word for word through God's gift and power. The need to make a thousand changes for the second edition (1837) would seem to be unnecessary considering such a claim of word-for-word perfection.[53] If Joseph produced the Book of Mormon in the manner indicated by Harris, Whitmer, Knight, and others, one might assume the process was a simple recitation of words scryed through the seer stone.

B. H. Roberts wrote extensively on this subject. He objected to the claim that God revealed the text word-for-word, noting that the resulting grammatical errors meant "assigning such errors to God." If it could be concluded, he continued, "that the language of the Book of Mormon, word-for-word, and letter-for-letter, was given to the prophet by direct inspiration of God, acting upon his mind, then again God is made responsible for the language errors in the Book of Mormon—a thing unthinkable."[54]

---

50. David Whitmer, Interviewed by the *Chicago Times,* Oct. 14, 1881.

51. Edward Stevenson, "One of the Three Witnesses: Incidents in the Life of Martin Harris," Nov. 30, 1881.

52. Joseph Knight Sr., "Reminiscence," 3.

53. Royal Skousen writes: "The evidence does not support theories that Joseph Smith composed the text himself or that he took the text from some other source. Instead, it indicates that the Lord exercised what I refer to as 'tight control' over the word-by-word translation of the Book of Mormon. In particular, the evidence suggests that Joseph Smith saw specific words written out in English and read them off to the scribe, and that the accuracy of the resulting text depended on the carefulness of Joseph and his scribe" (Royal Skousen, "Evidence from the Original Manuscript," 23).

54. Roberts, *Defense of the Faith and the Saints,* 2:278. Edward H. Ashment observes:

If Joseph mechanically read a divinely inspired English text in his stone, any resulting grammatical and textual errors would seem to have originated with God. Furthermore, if every word of the original text were divinely revealed, one wonders how Joseph could have presumed—unless God so directed—to attempt any revision of the text. Clearly, it is the book's message and teachings, and not its exact words, that Joseph believed were inspired of God.

Hebrew Holidays

Since Lehi and his family are reported to have came from Jerusalem, one may reasonably expect to find traces of Israelite manners and customs surviving among Book of Mormon peoples. We are told that these early American colonists spoke and read both Hebrew and Egyptian and observed the Law of Moses (1 Ne. 1:2; 4:15, 5:9; Mosiah 1:1-4; Alma 26:15; 3 Ne. 1:24; Eth. 1:33). Yet Lehi and his clan had scarcely left the boat before the Book of Mormon discourses on the church of the Lamb of God, speaks of Protestant-style evangelism, and delivers exhortations suffused with doctrines of nineteenth-century Christianity. Although Nephi did build a temple (2 Ne. 5:16) after the manner of Solomon's temple in Jerusalem, there are no subsequent references to the animal sacrifices and national festivals so common to Solomon's era. The Book of Mormon does not once unequivocally name or describe the celebration of one of the numerous Israelite feasts or festivals.[55]

The most important holiday in ancient Hebrew culture was the Passover, a spring festival commemorating the exodus from Egypt. The Hebrew names for the festival are *hag ha-Pesah* ("the feast of the Passover"), because God's angel of death "passed over" the children of Israel, while slaying the firstborn among the Egyptians, and *hag ha-Massot* ("the feast of Unleavened Bread").[56] Exodus 12:14 enjoins: "This day shall be a memorial; and ye shall keep it a feast to the Lord throughout your generations; ye shall keep it a feast by an ordinance forever." Should readers not expect to find Lehi and his descendants in some fashion observing *Pesah*—perhaps as many as 630 times—in the New World before the reported visit of the resurrected Jesus?

"Those who claim every word of the text of the Book of Mormon is of divine origin thus obligate themselves to the assertion that the original manuscript is the only text which is acknowledged by God, because it would be the most 'accurate,'—every grammatical error or unintelligible idea must remain so, because that is how God intended it to be" (Edward H. Ashment, "The Book of Mormon—A Literal Translation?," 11).

55. Terrence L. Zink and John W. Welch hypothesize that King Benjamin's sermon, delivered at the temple in the city of Zarahemla around 124 B.C.E., was a celebration of an "Israelite festival" (Zink and Welch, "King Benjamin's Speech in the Context of Ancient Israelite Festivals," 127-66).

56. *Encyclopaedia Judaica,* 13:165.

In fact, this important festival, referenced seventy-seven times in the Bible, is not once named or identifiably described in the Book of Mormon text.[57]

As part of Passover, the Israelites were also under solemn commandment to "observe the feast of unleavened bread ... in your generations by an ordinance for ever" (Exod. 12:17). God instructed: "Seven days shall ye eat unleavened bread; even the first day ye shall put away leaven out of your houses; for whosoever eateth unleavened bread; even the first day ye shall put away leaven out of your houses: for whosoever eateth leavened bread from the first day until the seventh day, that soul shall be cut off from Israel" (Exod. 12:15). While unleavened bread is mentioned forty-three times in the Bible, it is not mentioned once in the Book of Mormon.[58]

In addition, other festivals such as the feast of weeks *(Shavuot),* the feast of tabernacles *(Sukkot),* the feast of harvest, the feast of the ingathering, the feast of the seventh month, the feast of dedication, the feast of the Lord, and the feast of the Jews, mentioned forty-four times in the Bible, do not appear in the Book of Mormon.[59] Even the Jewish Sabbath, so crucial to Israelite culture, is mentioned only five times in the Book of Mormon. Circumcision, sacrifices, burnt offerings, and ceremonial uncleanness are seldom discussed. Yet Alma 30:3 stresses: "the people did observe to keep the commandments of the Lord; and they were strict in observing the ordinances of God, according to the law of Moses; for they were taught to keep the law of Moses until it should be fulfilled." (In the Old World, Mosaic law did not become canonical until about 400 B.C.E.)

It seems apparent that Nephite history and theology are influenced more by a modern Christian world view than by an ancient Hebrew one. The idiom and piety of the righteous Israelite colonists of the Book of Mormon more closely resembles nineteenth-century evangelical Christians of Joseph Smith's own day than that of ancient law-abiding Hebrews. No evidence has emerged in the historical record of a Christ-centered religious culture in the Old World until at least the first century C.E. Moreover, even a casual reading of Old Testament books of Ezra and Nehemiah supplies evidence that while the descendants of Lehi in America were enjoying the redemptive faith in Christ, the Jews of the diaspora, who had returned from Babylon to rebuild Jerusalem, were being continually enjoined by God to obey the law of Moses, not to pursue a Christianity which did not yet exist. To maintain

57. Jerald and Sandra Tanner, "Joseph Smith's Attempt to Save the Book of Mormon," 10.
58. Ibid.
59. Ibid.

the traditions so central to their survival as a people, diaspora Jews reinterpreted the law, replacing the physical temple of Jerusalem with a spiritual one, and weaving complex patterns of duties, prayers, and observances that orthodox Jews were bound to follow. Not a thread of this pattern developed in the Book of Mormon culture of ancient America.

Anthropology and Genetics

It has long been thought that, respecting the origin of the American Indians, the Book of Mormon echoes popular nineteenth-century speculation. Although the book does not unequivocally state that Native Americans are descended from Israelites, Joseph Smith and nearly every other early Mormon leader affirmed that they did. (See Appendix 2.) W. W. Phelps and Parley P. Pratt, two prominent early converts to Mormonism, aptly captured that concept for many nineteenth-century Mormons: "That wonderful conjecture, which left blank ... the origin ... of the American Indians, was done away by the Book of Mormon," Phelps exclaimed in 1833.[60] Pratt, writing four years later, declared that the Book of Mormon "reveals the origin of the American Indians, which was before a mystery."[61]

The ethnological findings of generations of researchers since the 1830s reveal a different picture of the culture and peoples of ancient America. Beginning in the eighteenth century, most scientists were convinced that the first Americans originated in northeastern Asia. George Louis Leclerc, Conte de Buffon, a famed French naturalist, recognized the resemblance between Amerindians and various Asian factions. He concluded in 1749 that these two groups shared a common origin and that the New World was originally peopled by Asians.[62] That determination is now viewed by nearly all scholars as scientific fact. Virtually all Native Americans are Asiatic who "separated from their Asian neighbors about 40,000-50,000 years ago and from each other in what may have been three or more separate waves of migration across Beringia 7,000-15,000 years ago."[63] Although molecular anthropologists are now able to identify descendants of ancient Israelites, no connection to Semitic bloodlines has appeared in Central America, Polynesia, or elsewhere among Native Americans.[64] Mitochondrial DNA testing has correlated Native American

60. W. W. Phelps, "The Book of Mormon," 58.

61. P[arley] P. Pratt, *A Voice of Warning,* 135.

62. C. D. G. Buffon, *Historic Naturelle* (1749), qtd. in Michael H. Crawford, *The Origins of Native Americans,* 3.

63. Thomas W. Murphy, "Lamanite Genesis, Genealogy, and Genetics," 48.

64. Anthropologist Thomas W. Murphy attests that "to date no intimate genetic link has

genetic heritage almost exclusively to East Asia and post-Columbian colonists. Even the remains of dogs from pre-Columbian American sites show that they "originated from multiple Old World lineages of dogs that accompanied late Pleistocene humans across the Bering Strait."[65]

When asked about DNA evidence and the Book of Mormon, Michael Crawford, a biological anthropologist at the University of Kansas, states: "I don't think there is one iota of evidence that suggests a lost tribe from Israel made it all the way to the New World."[66] Oxford geneticist Bryan Sykes and Russian geneticist Micoslava Derenko both concur that "the Indian gene pool is Siberian, not Middle Eastern."[67] Mesoamerican groups, including those occupying hypothetical Book of Mormon lands, are members of the same Asian families. These groups have been in America for tens of thousands of years longer than any purported Book of Mormon peoples.

In short, from the Bering Strait to the Straits of Magellan, the western hemisphere was populated long before the arrival of the Jaredites in—according to the Book of Mormon—approximately 2200 B.C.E. While there were certainly uninhabited areas on the American continent at the time, most of the land mass was clearly, though perhaps scarcely, populated.

The Book of Mormon seems not to accommodate easily this scientific reality. Instead, it declares that America, the land where the Middle-Eastern Jaredites first settled, was "the land of promise, which was choice above all other lands, which the Lord God had preserved for a righteous people" (Eth. 2:7). Nephi, also writing of the American continent, says: "[W]e have obtained a land of promise, a land which is choice above all other lands; a land which the Lord God hath covenanted with me should be a land for the inheritance of my seed; Yea, the Lord have covenanted this land unto me, and to my children forever, and also those who should be led out of other countries by the hand of the Lord." He then adds that "it is wisdom that this land should be kept as yet from the knowledge of other nations; for behold, many nations would overrun the land, that there would be no place for an inheritance" (2 Ne. 1:5, 8).

Some Mormon writers suggest that the Nephites and Lamanites were, in fact, one of many ancestral sources for present-day Native Americans. They

---

been found between ancient Israelites and indigenous Americans, much less within the time frame suggested by the Book of Mormon" (ibid., 48).

65. Rich Deem, "DNA Evidence and Molecular Genetics Disprove the Book of Mormon," 4.

66. Michael Crawford, qtd. in Murphy, "Lamanite Genesis, Genealogy, and Genetics," 53.

67. Bryan Sykes and Micoslava Derenko, qtd. in Suzan Mazur, "Mormons in the Olympic Spotlight."

suggest that Lamanites were a small isolated group, and that the bulk of the American Indians came from Asia or elsewhere. This assertion, however, requires one to ignore dozens of statements to the contrary from LDS Church leaders, including those made by virtually every president of the Church since 1830. To most readers, the Book of Mormon is not about a small number of Middle Eastern colonists tucked away in a corner of Mesoamerica. Rather, the story the Book of Mormon recounts is of voyaging Israelites who arrive in a likely unpeopled hemisphere where they "began to cover the face of the whole earth, from the sea south to the sea north, from the sea west to the sea east" (Hel. 3:8). Their numbers swell until they become "as numerous almost, as if were the sand of the sea" (Morm. 1:7).[68] Then, driven by pride and unrighteousness, they launch into extensive civil wars that terminate in the annihilation of two of the three peoples (the Lamanites, or ancestors of the American Indians, were victors) in approximately 421 C.E. As Joseph Smith explained in his 1842 letter to John Wentworth, editor of the *Chicago Democrat,* in words that Joseph said were divinely inspired: "the history of ancient America is unfolded" in the Book of Mormon "from its first settlement by a colony that came from the tower of Babel." He added that the "Jaredites were destroyed about the time that the Israelites came from Jerusalem, who succeeded them in the inheritance of the country."[69] His language seems not to leave any room in early America for cultures other than the Jaredite and Nephite/Lamanite civilizations. As molecular biologist Simon Southerton, a former LDS Church bishop, writes: "Decades of serious and honest scholarship have failed to uncover credible evidence that these Book of Mormon civilizations ever existed. No Semitic languages, no Israelites speaking these languages, no wheeled chariots or horses to pull them, no swords or steel to make them. They remain a great civilization vanished without a trace, the people along with their genes."[70]

---

68. John C. Kunich, a Harvard Law School graduate and judge advocate in the U.S. Air Force, concludes: "It is apparent that the large numbers of Book of Mormon peoples could not have been produced from the tiny Lehi-Mulek colonizing groups. No growth rate even close to the rate of increase prevalent from 590 B.C. to A.D. 390 would have produced the population sizes described in the scriptures, even if there had been no wars" (Kunich, "Multiply Exceedingly: Book of Mormon Population Sizes," 36-37.

69. Joseph Smith to John Wentworth, *History of the Church,* 4:537; emphasis mine. Smith added that the Angel Moroni told him "there was a book deposited, written upon gold plates, giving an account of the former inhabitants of this continent, and the source from whence they sprang" (ibid., 706-7). Smith borrowed a large portion of his letter to Wentworth from Orson Pratt's 1840 work, *An Interesting Account.*

70. Southerton, *Losing a Lost Tribe,* 199.

Archaeology

> [N]]othing, absolutely nothing, has ever shown up in any New World excavation which would suggest to a dispassionate observer that the Book of Mormon, as claimed by Joseph Smith, is a historical document relating to the history of early migrants to our hemisphere.
>
> —Michael Coe, "Mormons and Archaeology," 41

The Book of Mormon narrative is abundant with details of the history and culture of three vast ancient civilizations, the Jaredites, Nephites, and Lamanites. It names thirty-eight cities, gives the names and relative locations of rivers and seas, describes agricultural items, domestic animals, and metallurgy, and chronicles massive wars and epic migrations of peoples. If the book were history, like the Bible, one would expect archaeologists to find physical evidence confirming the presence of these cities, as Old World archaeologists have found for Jerusalem, Jericho, Capernaum, Bethsaida, and Beersheba. Yet not one of the hundreds of places in the Book of Mormon has been definitely located anywhere in the Americas, despite more than a century of searching. This quest may be the most ambitious hunt for a vanished civilization since Heinrich Schliemann's (1822-90) successful search for Troy. As Michael Coe, a Mesoamerican archaeologist at Yale University and author of *Breaking the Maya Code,* concludes: "As far as I know there is not one professionally trained archaeologist, who is not a Mormon, who sees any scientific justification for believing the foregoing [that Hebrew immigrants built a civilization in ancient America as described in the Book of Mormon] to be true, and I would like to state that there are quite a few Mormon archaeologists who join this group."[71]

One of those Mormons, lawyer-turned-amateur-archaeologist Thomas Stuart Ferguson, conceded: "With all these great efforts it cannot be established factually that anyone, from Joseph Smith to the present day, has put his finger on a single point of terrain that was a Book-of-Mormon geographical place. And the hemisphere has been pretty well checked out by competent people. Thousands of sites have been excavated."[72] In short, it seems

71. Coe, "Mormons and Archaeology," 41.

72. Thomas Stuart Ferguson, *Written Symposium on Book-of-Mormon Geography,* 1. Ferguson (1915-83) later renounced his belief in a genuinely ancient Book of Mormon, according to Stan R. Larson, *Quest for the Gold Plates: Thomas Stuart Ferguson's Archaeological Search for the Book of Mormon.* Larry S. Ferguson, Thomas's son, in a posthumous edition of one of his father's books, included a testimonial from his father: "The greatest witness to the truthfulness of the Book of Mormon is the book itself. But many are the external evidences that support it" (Bruce W. Warren and Thomas Stuart Ferguson, *The Messiah in Ancient America,* 283).

improbable that archaeologists will ever discover the immense Nephite cities of Zarahemla and Bountiful. John Carlson, adjunct assistant professor of anthropology at the University of Maryland, said in 1984: "I think the chances of evidence for the Book of Mormon civilizations' being found as very, very small. Very vanishingly small."[73] Coe minces no words: "Forget the so-far fruitless quest for Jaredites, Nephites, Mulekites, and the lands of Zarahemla and Bountiful; there is no more chance of finding them than of discovering the ruins of the bottomless pit described in the book of Revelation."[74]

While a central assertion of the Book of Mormon is that large Christian civilizations existed in ancient America prior to the birth of Jesus, civilizations that derived from migrations of people from the Old to the New World, the Smithsonian Institution and the National Geographical Society, two of America's premier scientific centers, have stated for the record that no archaeological evidence supports this belief. The Department of Anthropology at the Smithsonian's National Museum of Natural History, in a 1997 "Statement Regarding the Book of Mormon," announced: "Smithsonian archaeologists see no direct connection between archeology of the New World and the subject matter of the book."[75] A 1998 spokesperson for the Society wrote: "The Book of Mormon is clearly a work of great spiritual power[;] millions have read and revered its words, first published by Joseph Smith in 1830. Yet Smith's narration is not generally taken as a scientific source for the history of the Americas. Archaeologists and other scholars have long probed the hemisphere's past, and the [National Geographic] Society does not know of anything found so far that has substantiated the Book of Mormon."[76]

None of the 303 proper names found in the Book of Mormon has been discovered on the thousands of deciphered inscriptions in the New World. And despite the fact that Book of Mormon peoples are portrayed as Hebrew-speaking, Reformed Egyptian-writing Christians, no unequivocally ancient inscriptions have been found in Hebrew or anything remotely Egyptian.[77] Furthermore, none of the pre-Columbian religious discoveries from ancient America reflect evidence of a Christian culture.

The first proposed model of the Book of Mormon's geography

73. John Carlson, "Book of Mormon Archaeology," 43.

74. Coe, "Mormons and Archaeology," 48.

75. "Information from the National Museum of Natural History."

76. Julie Crain, Research Correspondent for the National Geographic Society, to Luke Wilson, Aug. 12, 1998.

77. Moroni recorded that his people still spoke Hebrew but that the plates were written in a script called "reformed Egyptian" (Morm. 9:32-34).

encompassed the entire Western Hemisphere. As Dan Vogel, a historian of early Mormonism, summarizes: "It is absolutely clear that Joseph Smith and the early Mormons associated the Book of Mormon with the Mound Builder myth and that they consistently held the belief that the Book of Mormon contained the history of a people who landed in South America and were destroyed in the Great Lakes region."[78]

Oliver Cowdery, in an 1835 letter to W. W. Phelps, described the Hill Cumorah in Manchester, New York, as the location where "the entire power and national strength of both the Jaredites and Nephites were destroyed."[79] Later that year, Phelps added, "Around that mound [i.e., Cumorah] died millions of the Jaredites. ... In that day, her inhabitants spread from sea to sea. ... There too, fell the Nephites."[80] In a second letter, Phelps referred to other North American areas as Book of Mormon lands. Respecting the Great Plains, which he termed "the centre of America," Phelps wrote: "The world will never value the land of Desolation, as it is called in the Book of Mormon, for anything more than hunting ground."[81]

Joseph Smith not only allowed these statements of his associates to stand without modification, his own declarations reveal his belief that much of the Book of Mormon unfolded in North America. For example, on June 4, 1834, when Joseph's traveling company on its way to Missouri arrived at the Mississippi River, he wrote a letter to his wife, identifying the surrounding country as Nephite territory. "The whole of our journey," he wrote, was spent "wandering over the plains of the Nephites, recounting occasionally the history of the Book of Mormon, roving over the mounds of that once beloved people of the Lord, picking up their skulls & their bones, as proof of its divine authenticity."[82] A month earlier, members of Joseph's company had climbed atop a

78. Dan Vogel, "The New Theory of Book of Mormon Geography," 12.

79. Oliver Cowdery, [Letter VII] to W. W. Phelps, July 1835, 157. To any who attempt to relocate the Hill Cumorah away from New York, Joseph Fielding Smith wrote in 1956: "It is difficult for a reasonable person to believe that such men as Oliver Cowdery, Brigham Young, Parley P. Pratt, Orson Pratt, David Whitmer, and many others could speak frequently of the spot [in New York] where the Prophet Joseph Smith obtained the plates as the Hill Cumorah, and not be corrected by the Prophet, if that were not the fact. That they did speak of this hill in the days of the Prophet in this definite manner is an established record of history" (Joseph Fielding Smith, *Doctrines of Salvation,* 3:232). In 1990, the secretary to the First Presidency wrote: "The Church has long maintained, as attested to by references in the writings of General Authorities, that the Hill Cumorah in western New York state is the same as referenced in the Book of Mormon" (F. Michael Watson, letter dated Oct. 16, 1990).

80. W. W. Phelps to Oliver Cowdery, *Messenger and Advocate,* Nov. 1835, 220.

81. Phelps, "The Far West," 33.

82. Joseph Smith to Emma Smith, June 4, 1834, in Dean C. Jessee, *The Personal Writings of Joseph Smith,* 324.

burial mound near the Illinois River, dug into the soil, and uncovered a skeleton.[83] Wilford Woodruff, one of Smith's traveling companions, wrote:

> While on our travels we visited many of the mounds which were flung up by the ancient inhabitants of this continent, probably by the Nephites & Lamanites. We visited one of those Mounds and several of the brethren dug into it and took from it the bones of a man. Brother Joseph had a vission [sic] respecting the person he said he was a white Lamanite ... his name was Zelph. ... Zelph was a large thick set man and a man of God, he was a warrior under the great prophet / Onandagus/ that was known from the hill Camorah / or east sea / to the Rocky mountains. The above knowledge Joseph received in a vision.[84]

And on September 25, 1838, when Joseph and others were traveling through Huntsville, Randolph County, Missouri, he "told the brethren that that place ... was the ancient site of the [Book of Mormon] city of Manti."[85] Two years later, in 1838, he named a place north of Far West, Missouri, Tower Hill, "a name I gave the place in consequence of the remains of an old Nephite altar or tower that stood there."[86] Several revelations received between 1828 and 1831 named the American Indians as Lamanites, and Missouri as the land of the Lamanites (D&C 3, 10, 19, 28, 30, 32, 49, 54). As archaeological discoveries in South America and Mesoamerica began to unfold in the late 1830s and early 1840s, however, the efforts of Joseph and his associates to identify Book of Mormon lands shifted to focusing on the southern hemisphere. According to Frederick G. Williams, a counselor in the governing First Presidency, Joseph reportedly explained that Lehi and his family landed at 30 degrees south latitude, in Chile.[87]

Descriptions of Nephite fortifications during the final years of their

83. This mound—Naples-Russell Mound Number 8 (Pike County)—is a "typical prehistoric Middle Woodland mortuary complex of the Hopewell culture" (Stanley B. Kimball, *Heber C. Kimball,* 31).

84. Wilford Woodruff, *Wilford Woodruff's Journal,* 1:10. For additional information, see Kenneth W. Godfrey, "The Zelph Story"; Kenneth W. Godfrey, *What Is the Significance of Zelph in the Study of Book of Mormon Geography?;* Sandra Tanner, "Zelph—The White Warrior." See also two Internet documents without identified authors: "The Zelph Incident" and "The Zelph Story."

85. George Reynolds and Janne M. Sjodahl, *Commentary on the Book of Mormon,* 2:324.

86. *History of the Church,* 3:35.

87. Joseph's statement was recorded by Frederick G. Williams and later referred to by Franklin D. Richards and James A. Little, *A Compendium of the Doctrines of the Gospel,* 289. Much earlier, however, an 1830 Ohio newspaper (Warren Ishom, editor) referred to the Lehi party's landing in Chile: "This new Revelation, they say is especially designed for the benefit, or rather for the christianizing of the Aborigines of America; who, as they affirm, are a part of the tribe of Manasseh, and whose ancestors landed on the coast of Chili [sic] 600 years before the coming of

dynasty, when they were besieged by Lamanite raiders, depict structures like those created by the Iroquois of western New York: villages encircled by wooden palisades and further protected by moats and trenches: "And upon the top of these ridges of earth [Moroni] caused that there should be timbers, yea, works of timbers built up to the height of a man, round about the cities. And he caused that upon those works of timbers there should be a frame of pickets built upon the timbers round about; and they were strong and high" (Alma 50:2-3). Hundreds of these ancient strongholds have been discovered in western New York and elsewhere in the eastern United States. They, and not the huge stone cities of the southern hemisphere, correspond more closely to the descriptions in the Book of Mormon.

"[I]f a sincere student of the Book of Mormon will conscientiously read and study the Book itself and will plot out all the locations mentioned," Joseph E. Vincent, editor of *California Archaeologist,* explained at a 1963 archaeological symposium at LDS Church-owned Brigham Young University, "he will find that all Book of Mormon lands lie within a five or six hundred mile radius, and that this area could not possibly extend from Chile to New York."[88] This caused many Mormon scholars to look elsewhere for the Hill Cumorah's location. For the past quarter of a century, some anthropologists and Book of Mormon students have attempted to work out a "new paradigm for the Book of Mormon—one that shifts Book of Mormon events from a full-hemispheric to a limited geography model."[89] But this interpretation revises traditional Church teachings that Book of Mormon events took place across the western hemisphere. The book itself prophesied America as the promised land, a nation fulfilling a sort of millennium, a divinely ordained new order. While the book may have benefitted from Joseph Smith's fertile imagination, it is short on verifiable ancient history.

Nineteenth-Century Revival Scenes

The Book of Mormon "is the product of Joseph's early thought, shaped by the evangelical and revivalist influences in early nineteenth century New England," wrote LDS scholar J. Frederic Voros Jr.[90] Young Smith's exposure to this religious ambience, as already discussed, actually began during a period of religious enthusiasm in Palmyra, New York, in 1817, when he was

Christ, and from them descended all the Indians of America" (Warren Isham, "The Golden Bible, or, Campbellism Improved").

88. Joseph E. Vincent, Untitled Comments, 68.

89. Dan Wotherspoon, "Reframing the Book of Mormon," 19.

90. J. Frederic Voros Jr., "Was the Book of Mormon Buried with King Follett?," 15.

twelve. B. H. Roberts has written: "It is clearly established now that these scenes of religious frenzy were common in the vicinage where Joseph Smith resided in his youth and early manhood … and Joseph Smith himself came in contact with these emotional phenomena in his own experience."[91] One of the more dramatic manifestations of religious enthusiasm in the meetings young Joseph attended was the "falling exercise" or "lying slain in the spirit." Men and women, overcome emotionally by preaching, would collapse, then remain motionless for hours, even days, before reviving. Typically, when once again animated, they would jump to their feet, then break forth into extravagant expressions of joy and praise to the Lord Jesus who they claimed had redeemed them from their sins during their stupor.

As noted previously, to many early American observers and participants, like the boy Joseph, such strange happenings became models of authentic Christian conversion experiences. Hence, when Smith dictated a conversion scene in the Book of Mormon, he drew upon his own observations and experiences. Nearly every instance of spiritual transformation related in the Book of Mormon reflects typical eighteenth- and nineteenth-century New Light Methodist and Presbyterian rebirth experiences. Benjamin Abbott, a Methodist itinerant minister, while preaching in the early 1780s, noted that a "young man was struck to the floor, and many said that he was dead." Abbott, who had seen this phenomenon many times before, assured the audience that the man was merely "lying Slain in the spirit." After three hours, however, even he became concerned. The man's skin had grown cold, his fingers were stiff, and could not be straightened. Fortunately, he soon revived, "prais[ing] God for what he had done for his soul."[92] Methodism historian Jesse Lee, a participant in revivalistic enthusiasm, reported in 1810:

> It was quite common for sinners to be seized with a trembling and shaking, and from that to fall down on the floor as if they were dead; and many of them have been convulsed from head to foot, while others have retained the use of their tongues so as to pray for mercy, while they were lying helpless on the ground or floor. … It was truly affecting to see [Christians] collecting round the penitent sinners, and praying for them … until some of the mourners would get converted; and then to see the young converts leaping up with streaming eyes and calling upon all present to praise God for what he had done for their souls.[93]

91. Roberts, *Studies of the Book of Mormon,* 308.
92. Benjamin Abbott, qtd. in John H. Wigger, *Taking Heaven by Storm,* 108.
93. Kenneth Cain Kinghorn, *The Heritage of American Methodism,* 34.

Jacob Young (1776-1859) while attending a Methodist meeting in Kentucky, observed: "[T]he congregation was melted into tears; I could compare it to nothing but a storm of wind. ... [T]he congregation nearly all rose from their seats, and began to fall upon the floor like trees thrown down by a whirlwind." Young looked on with amazement: "[M]y tears flowed freely, my knees became feeble, and I trembled like Belshazzar; my strength failed and I fell upon the floor." During another meeting the following day while listening to a woman singing, Young again fell to the floor, lying there for "many hours, having no recollection of any thing that passed, only that my mind was dark, and my soul greatly distressed." Then near midnight, a "light appeared to shine from the south part of heaven, and God, in mercy, lifted up the light of his countenance upon me, and I was translated from the power of darkness into the kingdom of God's dear son." Recovering, Young jumped up and began to shout and cry aloud. A few days later, he gained assurance of his conversion through a prophetic dream in which Christ showed him his name written in the Book of Life.[94]

An unnamed Presbyterian investigating a Kentucky revival in 1800 "conversed with many who fell under the influence of comfortable feelings" and was surprised by the orthodox account "they [gave] of their exercises as they lay entranced." Their minds, he said, "appeared wholly swallowed up in contemplating the perfections of God, as illustrated in the plan of salvation; and while they lay apparently senseless, and almost lifeless, their minds were more vigorous and their memories more retentive and accurate than they had ever been before."[95] Richard Garrettson, a Methodist preacher living in Petersburg, Virginia, in 1787, reported that "hundreds of saints were so overcome with the power of God, that they fell down as in a swoon. ... During this time, they were happy beyond description; and when they came to themselves, it was with loud praises to God, and with tears, and speeches enough to break a cork, or melt the hardest heart."[96]

Philip Bruce, a presiding Methodist elder near Norfolk, Virginia, stated in 1788 that "as soon as the preacher begins to speak, the power of GOD appears to be present; which is attended with trembling among the people, and falling down; some lie void of motion or breath, others are in strong convulsions; and thus they continue, till the Lord raises them up, which is

94. Jacob Young, *Autobiography of a Pioneer,* 23.

95. Qtd. in Ann Taves, *Fits, Trances, and Visions,* 108.

96. R[ichard] Garrettson, "An Account of the Revival of the Work of God," 302.

attended with emotions of joy and rapture."[97] LaRoy Sunderland, prominent Methodist reformer and later luminary in the Methodist Wesleyan Church, described preaching in 1823 with the result that people "wept, fell upon the floor, become cold and rigid in their muscular systems; their eyes were closed, or elevated and set; some of them fell into a state of trance, and all the singing, praying, rejoicing and other manifestations which took place during that sermon, we supposed to have been produced by the 'power of the Holy Ghost,' operating on the minds of the people."[98]

Several of these kinds of falling exercises appear in the Book of Mormon. For example, Alma, one of the principal characters in the book, after being reproved by an angel for his wickedness:

> became dumb that he could not open his mouth; yea, and he became weak, even that he could not move his hands; therefore he was taken by those that were with him, and carried helpless, even until he was laid before his father ... and his father rejoiced, for he knew that it was the power of God.
>
> And it came to pass after they [the people assembled] had fasted and prayed for the space of two days and two nights, the limbs of Alma received their strength and he stood up and began to speak unto them, bidding them to be of good comfort; for, said he, I have repented of my sins and have been redeemed of the Lord, behold, I am born of the Spirit. (Mosiah 27:19-20, 23-24.)

The reborn Alma then preached a sermon that revealed as much maturity of thought and knowledge of the scriptures as the oldest and wisest preacher described in the Book of Mormon. The same thing later happened to Lamoni, a Lamanite king:

> And it came to pass that after he [a prophet by the name of Ammon] had said all these things, and expounded them to the king, that the king believed all his words. And he began to cry unto the Lord, saying: O Lord, have mercy: according to thy abundant mercy which thou hast had upon the people of Nephi, have upon me and my people. And now, when he had said this, he fell unto the earth, as if he were dead. And it came to pass that his servants took him and carried him in unto his wife and laid him upon a bed, and he lay as if he were dead for the space of two days and two nights. (Alma 18:40-43.)

97. "An Extract of a Letter from Philip Bruce," 563.
98. LaRoy Sunderland, *The Trance, and Correlative Phenomena,* 11-12.

Preparations were made for the king's burial, but Ammon interfered, promising that the next day the stricken king would rise from his near-death slumber. Sure enough, on the third day, "It came to pass that he arose," just as Ammon had predicted. And not only did he arise, "he stretched forth his hand unto the woman [his wife], and said: blessed be name of the Lord, and blessed art thou; for as sure as thou livest, behold, I have seen my Redeemer." But after he uttered these words, "his heart was swollen within him, and he sunk again with joy." The queen followed suit, "being overpowered by the Spirit." Ammon, looking on, began to pray, but "was also overpowered with joy; and thus they all three had sunk to the earth." The servants of the king, seized with fear, began to pray. "And it came to pass that they did call on the name of the Lord, in their might, even until they had all fallen to the earth." After, everyone remained slain in the spirit for several hours. The queen was the first to stir, assisted by "a certain woman" who had been converted years before and fully understood the queen's predicament:

> And it came to pass that she went and took the queen by the hand, that perhaps she might raise her from the ground; and as soon as she touched her hand she arose and stood upon her feet, and cried with a loud voice saying, O blessed Jesus, who has saved me from an awful hell! O blessed God have mercy on this people. And when she had said this, she clasped her hands, being filled with joy, speaking many words which were not understood. (Alma 19.)

Soon after this falling exercise, the father of Lamoni, king of all Lamanites, was converted. After a long sermon by the prophet Aaron,

> [T]he king did bow down before the Lord upon his knees; yea, even he did prostrate himself upon the earth, and cried mightily, saying: O God, Aaron hath told me that there is a God; and if there is a God, and if thou art God, wilt, thou make thyself known unto me, and I will give away all my sins to know thee, and that I may be raised from the dead, and be saved at the last day. And now when the king had said these words, he was struck as if he were dead. (Alma 22:17-18.)

The king remained in this condition for a time, when Aaron took him by the hand and pulled him to his feet. The unnamed king immediately began to preach and extol the Lord Jesus so "that his whole household were converted unto the Lord." Before being "struck as if he were dead," he was an agnostic. When he came out of his swoon, he was able to present the Christian plan of salvation so persuasively that his household was converted.

Book of Mormon characters also deliver such traditional gospel phrases as these: "encircled about eternally in the arms of his love" (2 Ne. 1:15); "the Spirit of the Lord ... has wrought a mighty change ... in our hearts" (Mosiah 5:2); "the grave shall have no victory ... the sting of death should be swallowed up in the hopes of glory" (Alma 22:14); "O that ye would awake ... awake from a deep sleep ... and shake off the awful chains by which ye are bound" (2 Ne. 1:13); "put on the armour of righteousness" (2 Ne. 1:23); "And they arose and came forth out of the water rejoicing, being filled with the spirit" (Mosiah 18:14); "his heart was swollen with sorrow within his breast" (Hel. 7:6); "And see that ye have faith, hope, and charity, and then ye will always abound in good work" (Alma 7:24); "Repent all ye ends of the earth, and come unto me, and be baptized in my name, and have faith in me, that ye may be saved" (Moro. 7:34); and "if ye have not charity, ye are nothing, for charity never faileth" (Moro. 7:46).

Other Book of Mormon phrases, popular among nineteenth-century revivalists, according to Book of Mormon researcher Mark Thomas,[99] include: "infinite atonement" (Alma 34:9-16); "day of grace" (Mormon 2:15); "He should not come to redeem them in their sins, but to redeem them from their sins" (Alma 11:36-37); and "the God of nature suffers" (1 Ne. 19:12).

Anachronistic Domestic Animals

> Ship-building and sailing, use of magnetic compass, overseas navigation, wheeled vehicles drawn by horses, tent manufacture, linen manufacture, many agricultural products from the Old World, wheat and barley, vineyards and wine presses, domestic animals from the Old World, glass manufacture, and so forth. All these paint a scene that seems to be quite foreign to what I am familiar with in the archeological record of the New World.
>
> —Raymond T. Matheny, "Book of Mormon Archaeology," 20

Horses

Horses are explicitly referenced fourteen times in the Book of Mormon text. The 1830 edition announces that the Nephites "did till the land, and raise all manner of grain, and of fruit, and flocks of herds, and flocks of all

99. Mark D. Thomas, "The Meaning of Revival Language in the Book of Mormon."

manner of cattle, of every kind, and goats, and wild goats, and also much horses" (p. 145). Archaeologist Michael Coe questions this picture:

> [T]here is an inherent improbability in specific items that are mentioned in the Book of Mormon as having been brought to the New World by the Jaredites and/or Nephites. Among these are the horse (extinct in the New World since about 7,000 B.C.), the chariot, wheat, barley, and metallurgy (true metalworking based upon smelting and casting being no earlier in Mesoamerica than about 800 A.D.). The picture of this hemisphere between 2,000 B.C. and A.D. 421 presented in the [Book of Mormon] has little to do with the early Indian cultures as we know them, in spite of much wishful thinking.[100]

In Joseph Smith's Book of Mormon, the Jaredite, Nephite, and Lamanite cultures built their empires on the backs of draft animals conventional in the Mediterranean, European, and modern American world: cattle, cows, oxen, and asses (Eth. 9:18-19; 1 Ne. 18:25; Enos 1:21; 3 Ne. 3:22, 4:46, 6:1). The Nephites and Lamanites went to war with horse-drawn conveyances (Alma 18:9, 20:6; 3 Ne. 3:22, 21:14). Yet it was established long ago that indigenous peoples did not use beasts of burden, nor even the wheel itself. Proof of domestic animals has not appeared in any form, neither in physical evidence such as skeletal remains nor in surviving representations in sculpture, mural art, ceramic pieces, sculpture art, or any other artistic medium. Moreover, as Charles C. Mann, a correspondent for *Science* and the *Atlantic Monthly,* noted in his 2005 book *1491: New Revelations of the Americas before Columbus,* "Because the Western Hemisphere had no cows, horses, or camels, smallpox had no chance to evolve there. Indians had never been exposed to it—they were 'virgin soil,' in epidemiological jargon."[101] Conversely, substantial evidence has been discovered of pre-Columbian deer, jaguars, coati-mundis, tapir, monkeys, sloths, and a host of domesticated dogs, turkeys, llamas, alpacas, and guinea pigs, the true animals of Central and South America.

Two of major anachronisms of the Book of Mormon are its mentions of horses and elephants. Horses originated in North America tens of thousands of years ago as small three-toed creatures of the woodlands, and by late Pleistocene times (which ended 10,000 years ago), they looked much like today's Grevey's zebra. They disappeared entirely, however, at the end of the last great Ice Age when a massive extinction of North American megafauna

---

100. Coe, "Mormons and Archeology," 42.
101. Charles C. Mann, *1491: New Revelations of the Americas before Columbus,* 87.

also swept away the mastodon, mammoth, rhinoceros, sabertooth cat, camel, and short-faced bear.

Remains of early horses have been found in numerous ancient sites such as La Brea in California, Tierra del Fuego at the southern tip of South America, and Lagoa Santa in Brazil. Though these remains have been found in direct association with the vestige of humans, thus demonstrating the contemporaneity of the two, these early peoples had a simple, nomadic hunting culture. They did not ride horses nor use them as beasts of burden; they simply hunted and ate them. The animal has been extinct in the Americas for approximately 10,440 years.[102]

The horse was unknown in pre-Columbian history at the coming of Europeans. Columbus brought horses to Hispaniola on his second voyage, but the animal's impact upon the New World was not felt until 1519, when Hernando Cortez set out from the port of Trinidad, Cuba, on an expedition which within two years would bring Mexico under Spanish domination. He brought with him sixteen Spanish horses.[103] The Coronado expedition in 1540 brought a thousand horses and mules from Mexico into the American Southwest. This group traveled from as far west as the South Rim of the Grand Canyon to as far east as Kansas. Historians have surmised that many of the animals escaped and produced mustangs (i.e., wild horses). John C. Ewers, a historian of the horse in America, notes: "There is no mention of encounters with stray horses or mounted Indians in any account of Spanish expeditions to the Great Plains in the later years of the 16th and early years of the 17th century."[104] For example, Cabeza de Vaca's sixteenth-century expedition into the interior of America (Florida, Texas, New Mexico, Arizona) saw many Indians, representing a host of tribes, but none had horses.[105] Cortez and Pizarro evoked terror and amazement in indigenous Americans who first thought that manlike figures grew from the four-legged beasts' backs.

The period between 1540 and 1880 in the history of the Indian tribes of the Great Plains is known as "the Horse Culture Period."[106] Early seventeenth-century Spanish settlements, particularly near Santa Fe, furnished "just

102. J. M. Adovasio and Jake Page, *The First Americans,* 119.

103. William H. Prescott, *History of the Conquest of Mexico and History of the Conquest of Peru,* 144. When the Indians first killed one of the horses in battle, it "was borne off in triumph." The remains were sent to the different towns in the area. "The circumstance troubled the Spanish commander, as it divested the animal of the supernatural terrors with which the superstition of the natives had usually surrounded it."

104. John C. Ewers, *The Horse in Blackfoot Indian Culture,* 2.

105. Cabeza de Vaca, *Adventures in the Unknown Interior of America.*

106. Ibid., 1.

the items necessary to encourage the adoption of horses by the Indians to the east—friendly contact through trade, [an] ample supply of horses, and examples of the advantages of the new servants."[107] By 1750, wild horses, descendants of abandoned and escaped animals, had spread as far north as the Canadian border, and all Plains Indian tribes had herds of the versatile creatures.

Elephants

> The two genera, Mammuthus and Mammut, disappeared from North America about 10,000 years ago, and in South America at that time three genera of gomphotheres (Cuvieronius, Haplomastodon, and Stegomastodon, also considered mastodonts) died out. ... The genus Elephas (the Asian elephant) was present in Africa and Asia, but never in the New World. Loxodanta (the African elephant) was always restricted to Africa.
>
> —Gary Haynes, *Mammoths, Mastondonts, and Elephants,* 3

In even more distant times—four million years ago—mammoths and mastodons, both originating in Africa, had expanded their range into Europe and Asia, then into North America via the Siberian land bridge. During the late Pleistocene Period, mastodons were common in the eastern forests of North America. The first mammoths in the New World were a breed of southern mammoth that had slowly adapted to the cold of northeastern Asia, then readapted to slightly warmer climes in the southwestern parts of the United States, then continued to move southward, eventually populating South America as well.

When all mammoths finally ran up against the withering forces unleashed at the end of the Pleistocene, approximately 10,000 years ago, they vanished except for a population of woolly mammoths that survived in the frigid steppes of Wrangel Island off Alaska until Roman times, approximately 4,000 years ago.[108] The modern elephant is related to but did not descend from mastodons and mammoths. Thus, the Book of Mormon's reference to elephants in America during the Jaredite period of the Book of Mormon is an impossibility. Although there is ample evidence of ancient mammoths and mastodons in America, the first elephant did not arrive until 1796, and came by boat. Captain Jacob Crowninshield purchased the beast in India and shipped it to the New World. For more than a dozen years, the pachyderm

107. Ibid., 3. See "Indian Horse Distribution Map," 5.

108. Adovasio and Page, *The First Americans,* 66. These mammoths were a dwarf species.

toured New England, Pennsylvania, and the Carolinas. The second elephant in America, "Old Bet," arrived in the country in 1815 and toured New England alive, and later stuffed, until 1821. The third elephant, "Columbus," was on constant display in the eastern United States from 1818 until 1847.[109]

The Book of Mormon's reference to elephants may have been inspired by the greatest curiosity on display in America at the time of Joseph Smith's birth: the eleven-foot-tall skeleton of the American *incognitum*, or mastodon, on display at the Philadelphia Museum owned by portrait artist and polymath Charles Willson Peale. The curiosity had been excavated by Peale from a farm in the Hudson River Valley four years before Joseph's birth. Paul Semonin, in his study of national identity, observed that "this mythical creature helped them imagine themselves as new rulers of the Natural World."[110]

Anachronistic Agricultural Products

In the Book of Mormon, Mosiah 9:9 recounts the agricultural success of the Nephites during their first century: "And we began to till the ground, yea, even with all manner of seeds, with seeds of corn, and of wheat, and of barley, and with neas, and with sheum, and with seeds of all manner of fruits." However, according to a statement issued by the Smithsonian Institution in 1996: "None of the principal Old World domesticated food, plants or animals (except the dog) occurred in the New World in pre-Columbian times. American Indians had no wheat, barley, oats, millet, rice, cattle, pigs, chickens, horses, donkeys, camels, before 1492."[111]

The lack of archaeological evidence, summarized by the Smithsonian's statement, cannot reasonably accommodate the Book of Mormon's picture of the Nephites growing wheat, figs, and grapes, as well as barley, the cereal on which their national economy was based (Mosiah 7:22, 9:9; Alma 11:7, 15; Mosiah 9:9; Hel. 11:17; 3 Ne. 14:16; Mosiah 9:9, 3 Ne. 18:18). No botanical remains of these Old World staples have ever been discovered in the Americas. Although evidence of historic barley has been found in Native American sites in Arizona, it was a species native only to North America and found in a limited region. Brigham Young University archaeologist Raymond T. Matheny commented that a 1983 *Science* magazine article describing this find in a pre-Columbian setting is "wrongly claimed as support for the Book of Mormon because the barley described was not a domesticated old world

109. R. J. Brown, "The Elephant Comes to America," 1-2.

110. Paul Semonin, "Peale's Mastodon."

111. "The Smithsonian Institution's 1996 'Statement Regarding the Book of Mormon.'"

barley," introduced to the New World by the Nephites.[112] Instead of wheat and barley being staples of the true early Native American and Mesoamerican diet, the most frequently consumed agricultural products were maize, beans, squash, potatoes, tomatoes, chocolate, and manioc.

Borrowings from the King James Bible

Joseph Smith was probably more familiar with the King James Version of the Bible than with any other book. He most likely had never heard of earlier translations of the scriptures such as the Septuagint (130 B.C.E.), William Tyndale's Bible (1526), Thomas Cromwell's Great Bible (1539), the New Testament produced in Calvinist Geneva (1557), the Geneva Bible (1560), and the Bishops' Bible (1568). The King James Version, first published in 1611, and the occasional almanac, were likely among the few books the pious but impoverished Smith family owned. The Bible was used daily in the family's devotionals. Its phrases adorned their language. In fact, young Joseph probably learned to read from the KJV. By his own testimony, he began an intensive study of the sacred work at age twelve.

When Joseph began dictating the Book of Mormon, he not only did so in the language of King James's England, but also borrowed wholesale from His Majesty's translation of the Bible. The ancient literary patterns in the Book of Mormon actually reflect the rhetorical shadows of the KJV in Joseph's language. Hundreds of verses in the Book of Mormon appear either in part or exactly as they were translated in King James English. For example, compare the following:

1830 1 Ne. 52-56 (1981 1 Ne. 20-21) // Isa. 48-49
1830 2 Ne. 75-78 (1981 2 Ne. 7-8) // Isa. 50-51
1830 3 Ne. 479-85 (1981 3 Ne. 12-14) // Matt. 5-7
1830 3 Ne. 503-505 (1981 3 Ne. 24-25) // Mal. 3-4

Such an approach made a powerful appeal to and impact upon religionists of the day. The Book of Mormon cites twenty complete chapters from the KJV, including Exodus 20:2-17; Isaiah 2-12; 48-54; and Malachi 3-4. Quotations from Isaiah 49-54 in 1 Nephi are especially problematic since most scholars maintain that Isaiah 40-66 were written after the Babylonian exile, about 587 B.C., by an unknown author called "deutero-Isaiah."[113]

The text of Isaiah in the Book of Mormon is not always the same as the

112. Matheney, "Book of Mormon Archaeology," 28.
113. See George D. Smith, "Isaiah Updated."

KJV. Of 433 Isaiah verses in the Nephite record, Joseph modified about 233 during his dictation. Yet 199 verses are word for word the same as the 1611 English rendition. The Sermon on the Mount from the book of Matthew is included nearly verbatim in the Book of Mormon. Many of the sayings in this sermon may have been genuine sayings of Jesus. And while it is conceivable that Jesus could have paraphrased these couplets during a sermon in the New World, the likelihood that he could pronounce them in precisely the same language which would later be chosen by Matthew seems unlikely.

Elsewhere in the Book of Mormon, in sections ostensibly written during the Old Testament time frame, are hundreds of phrases and quotations from the KJV New Testament. As one researcher has noted, "Even the 'prophecies' appearing in the Old Testament portion of the book are often given in the New Testament wording that accompanies their fulfillment. John the Baptist, for example, is predicted to come and prepare the way for One 'mightier than I,' 'whose shoe's latchet I am not worth to unloose' (1 Ne. 10:8//Luke 3:16; 1 Ne. 10:8//John 1:27). Similarly, there shall be 'one fold, and one shepherd,' and 'one faith and one baptism' (1 Ne. 22:25//John 10:16; Mosiah 18:21//Eph. 4:5)."[114]

Another problem is that when the Book of Mormon quotes the KJV, it includes the text's italicized words, which are not present in the original Greek and Hebrew versions. The King's translators placed these words in italics in the text to clarify sentence structure. Mosiah 14, for example, contains the thirteen italicized words from Isaiah 53, yet the King's translators would not be born for another ten centuries. Furthermore, known translation errors in the KJV also appear verbatim in the Book of Mormon. For example the KJV translates the Hebrew *chuppah* as meaning *defense* ("for upon all the glory of Zion shall be a defence"), when the more correct English translation is *canopy.* 2 Nephi 14:5 follows the KJV in this translation error. The same is true of Isaiah 5:25 and 2 Nephi 15:25. Here the Hebrew *suchah* is translated as *refuse,* not *torn,* as it appears in both Isaiah and 2 Nephi.

Even given the Book of Mormon's errors and inconsistencies, one must still deal with the question of how Joseph was able to dictate the extensive passages from the KJV. The most obvious explanation is that Joseph had a KJV in front of him. B. H. Roberts surmised that "[w]hen Joseph Smith saw that the Nephite record was quoting the prophecies of Isaiah, of Malachi and the words of the Savior, he took the English Bible and compared these

114. Wesley P. Walters, *The Book of Mormon Today,* 5.

passages as far as they paralleled each other, and finding that in substance, in thought, they were alike, he adopted our English translation."[115] Roberts's supposition seems to be incorrect. In an 1881 interview, "[David] Whitmer emphatically asserts as did [Martin] Harris and [Oliver] Cowdery, that while Smith was dictating the translation he had no manuscript notes or other means of knowledge save the seer stone and the characters as shown on the plates."[116] Joseph's eldest son, Joseph Smith III, asked his mother about her experience as the prophet's scribe and particularly "whether he had not some manuscript or book, or paper copy, from which he read to the scribe." According to her son, Emma explained: "This could not have been done; for he could not have had any such manuscript or book without her finding it out." Joseph then asked if Emma thought his father might "have had some work from which he would commit to memory and so dictate from memory." Emma explained that this was not a possibility, either, because "when not engaged in translating he was busy at work about the premises, or with other parties."[117]

A possible answer to the question about how Smith could dictate those extensive KJV passages without a Bible or notes—in addition to the possibility that Whitmer and Joseph III were mistaken—may be the Smith family's remarkable memory retention, a trait called eidetic imagery.[118] "Young people in particular," according to J. Arthur Thomson, "are often able to make almost photographically precise pictures of what they see, especially when it strikes the chord of interest. ... All eye-minded people have something of the gift, but some have it extraordinarily, and have cultivated it still more."[119] For example, in 1823 thirteen-year-old Jane Wilson, winner of an annual public competition sponsored by the New York Sunday School Union, "recited 1,650 Bible verses from memory."[120] In 1835, Thomas Carlyle loaned Volume 1 of his massive, just-completed *The French Revolution* to his friend,

---

115. B. H. Roberts, in Kirkham, *A New Witness for Christ in America,* 1:203.

116. David Whitmer, Interviewed by the *Chicago Times,* Oct. 14, 1881.

117. Joseph Smith III, "Letter to R[obert] Patterson," 177.

118. This ability is also known as photographic memory or the ability to remember not only content but its visual arrangement. See "Causes of Savantism."

119. J. Arthur Thomson, *Riddles of Sciences,* n.p. For additional sources on the development of memory strategies and photographic memory, see R. V. Kail, *The Development of Memory in Children;* Mary J. Carruthers, *The Book of Memory: A Study of Memory in Medieval Culture;* Frances A. Yates, *The Art of Memory;* D. F. Bjorkland and B. R. Zeman, "Children's Organization and Metamemory Awareness in Their Recall of Familiar Information"; and L. Hasher and R. T. Zacks, "Automatic and Effortful Processes in Memory."

120. Joseph W. Barnes, "Obediah Dogberry," 5.

John Stuart Mill. Mill, in turn, showed it to a friend who read it but left the pages in a jumble when it was returned. Carlyle's charwoman mistook it for trash and threw it in the fire. Legend has it that Carlyle "rewrote Volume One (which would be published, to great acclaim, four years later) from memory."[121] Martin Harris also may have possessed an excellent memory. He could "quote more scripture than any man in the neighborhood," remembered one acquaintance.[122] Reportedly, he memorized entire books from the Bible and would later "defy any man to show me any passage of scripture that I am not posted on or familiar with."[123] Karma Thinley Rinpoche, master of the Kagyu and Sakya traditions in the Himilayan region, was born into the noble family of Bongsar in 1931 in the Nangchen area of Kham, Eastern Tibet. He possessed a memory so phenomenal he could memorize entire texts within one day.[124] Some Christians in China memorized large sections of the Bible when Communists took control of the country in 1949.[125] Shawn Nelson, of the Mission Valley Christian Fellowship, overheard that a teacher had "memorized roughly 20 books of the New Testament." This information stimulated Nelson to begin memorizing himself, using a technique called Suntereo,[126] and at his peak was able to recall nineteen books from memory.[127]

According to George A. Smith, his (and Joseph Smith's) grandfather, Asael Smith, was a "man of extraordinary retentive memory," who "possessed a great knowledge of the Bible, so much so that he could read it as well without the book as with it."[128] According to William Hyde, a close friend of Joseph Smith Sr., Father Smith's "memory was something extraordinary. He could repeat several chapters of a book verbatim after it had been read rapidly."[129] An unnamed reporter writing for the *Philadelphia Sun* in 1831 stated that Joseph Jr. "possessed a remarkably retentive memory" and impressed Martin Harris by committing "several chapters of the New Testament to memory." While scrying with his stone, Joseph "refers Harris to a chapter in the Bible which he had learned by rote; and which he reads from the plates, with surprising

121. "The Writer's Almanac."

122. Thomas Gregg, *The Prophet of Palmyra,* 37.

123. Martin Harris to Mr. Emerson, 5.

124. "Karma Thinley Rinpoche."

125. "Memorize the Bible in One Year."

126. A Greek New Testament word meaning to "carefully keep in mind, preserve in memory" ("Memorize the Bible. Literally").

127. Ibid.

128. George A. Smith, Aug. 2, 1857, JD, 5:101.

129. William Hyde, "Birth of Mormonism."

accuracy."[130] Thurlow Weed reported that Smith placed his seer stone "in his hat, from which he read a chapter of the 'Book of Mormon.'"[131]

In 1888, one of Joseph's biographers, J. H. Kennedy, stated that Joseph's "mind was retentive," although he provided no evidence for this assertion.[132] William Law, Joseph's counselor in the First Presidency in Nauvoo, said that "Joseph had a wonderful memory."[133] Joseph's son, Joseph III, had, according to Israel A. Smith (Joseph III's son), a "most remarkable memory—most notable for a man then in his eighties." As Joseph III sank into delirium on his deathbed,

> we heard him reciting at great lengths [sic] passages from some work unknown to those at his bedside. However, when we called in my sister, Mrs. Audentia Anderson, she recognized them as long quotations from [J. G.] Holland's *Bitter Sweet.*
>
> Back of that some months I will remember him, sitting in the dark night of his blindness (for he was totally blind during the last four years of his life) and reciting in its entirety a long poem [sic] called *The Tale of the Dismal Swamp* [by Harriet Beecher Stowe].
>
> He was specially fond of poetry and often had surcease from pain and physical misery by repeating the poems he learned when but a boy.[134]

That Joseph Jr.'s memory was abundant enough to recall lengthy biblical passages during his dictation of the Book of Mormon seems proven in his own history. When reporting the 1823 appearance of an angel, Joseph inventoried the messenger's remarkable scriptural citations: part of the third chapter of Malachi, all of the fourth chapter of Malachi, the eleventh chapter of Isaiah, Acts 22-23, Joel 2:28-32, and "many other passages of Scripture."[135] Not only was eighteen-year-old Joseph apparently able to recognize the source of each of these scriptures, but fifteen years later, when he first put the messenger's words to paper, he was able not only to recall all scriptures cited, but their exact wording, which varies on occasion from their biblical reference.

Len Oakes, in his study of prophetic charisma, comments on the astute memory often found in charismatic leaders:

---

130. "The Mormonites," in *[Philadelphia] Sun,* Aug. 18, 1831.
131. Harriet A. Weed, *Autobiography of Thurlow Weed,* 1:359.
132. J. H. Kennedy, *Early Days of Mormonism,* 15.
133. William Law, "The Mormons in Nauvoo," July 3, 1887.
134. Israel A. Smith, "My Father's Last Years," 475.
135. *History of the Church,* 1:12-13.

> A lasting impression one retains of any charismatic leader one gets close to is of his singular memory. … Memory is not a trait that impresses a researcher in the field doing a short-term investigation, so it tends to be overlooked in studies of charisma. Few scholars mention it, and then just to note in passing that charismatic leaders have excellent memories. But because memory is central to most cognitive functioning, this study sought comments from followers regarding the "central gift" or any "semimagical quality" or "extraordinary gift … that seemed utterly striking" possessed by the leaders. All the followers agreed that the leaders had good memories.[136]

Non-Uniqueness

> Behold thou [Joseph Smith] wast called and chosen to write the book of Mormon.
>
> —BC XXV:1

Joseph's mental state during the dictation of the Book of Mormon differs from shamanistic possession, classical mysticism, and reports of automatic writing. He neither lost consciousness of his surroundings nor became disassociated from his personal identity. Unlike cases of spirit writing or channeled texts, he did not claim to hear a voice or take dictation from another personality. In 1831, when Hyrum Smith asked him for details about the coming forth of the Book of Mormon, Joseph replied, "[I]t was not intended to tell the world all the particulars."[137] Three years later during an 1834 speech at Henrietta, New York, Joseph stated with equal reticence, "[M]any would disbelieve that a recent revelation had been made to him … but that a revelation from heaven was given to him, and by him had been faithfully transcribed, for the benefit of all who should receive his testimony."[138] On at least two other occasions, he identified his translation ability with what he called the "Spirit of revelation."[139] First, in April 1829 he promised Oliver Cowdery that he too would be able to translate "engravings of old records" by the "manifestation of my Spirit; yea, behold I will tell you in your mind and in your heart by the Holy Ghost, which shall come upon you and which shall dwell in your heart."[140] Prior to 1833, he told Orson

136. Len Oakes, *Prophetic Charisma,* 62-63.
137. Donald Q. Cannon and Lyndon W. Cook, *Far West Record,* 23.
138. Joseph Smith, qtd. in "Interview with the Mormon Prophet," 1.
139. BC VII:2.
140. Ibid. VII:1.

Pratt that he had translated the plates by "the spirit of revelation."[141] Even if there were no golden plates to translate, as G. St. John Stott has written, "to say that Smith could not translate is not to say that he did not think that he could. ... [H]e would instead have trusted that his words *were* a translation because they came to him by what he thought was the inspiration of God."[142]

In 1839, Joseph explained, "[W]hen you feel pure Inteligence flowing unto you it may give you sudden strokes of ideas."[143] Perhaps when Joseph looked into his seer stone, he felt such surges of "pure intelligence" flowing into his mind that he believed his dictation was a revelation from God. Thus, as he explained, when the word of God came by the spirit of revelation, it came not as a vision but as "sudden strokes of ideas"—concepts which entered his thinking process. This information agrees with such Book of Mormon accounts as "the word of the Lord came into my mind," "I had heard the voice of the Lord speaking unto me in very word," or "the words of the Lord which he doth put into my heart" (Enos 1:10, Jac., 7:5, Hel. 13:5). Stott therefore argues: "Given that Smith had no awareness of the subtleties of the subconscious mind, and given also his willingness to challenge the conventional wisdom that God no longer spoke to man—there was nothing unreasonable in his thinking that his intuitions were the word of God."[144]

Dr. Herbert Benson and William Proctor, the former a Harvard Medical School researcher, propose in their 2003 book, *The Breakout Principle,* a theory that may explain how Joseph and others engender creative projects that seem beyond their natural abilities. A "break-out," they explain, "may be triggered by traditional relaxation-response techniques, such as silently repeating a word, prayer, or phrase—or engaging in a repetitive physical activity—while assuming a passive attitude. Or the Breakout may be evoked by other means, such as immersion in one's personal belief system, in acts of altruism, in a significant personal encounter, or in a mental state that we call *total abandon.*"[145] Concentrating on the seer stone in his hat, Joseph may have been experiencing the requisite "total abandon" during his scrying. Benson and Proctor continue: "A Breakout typically leads to additional experiences or states of mind, which can result in improved personal performance and the generation of life-changing insights. In all cases, the essential element for a Breakout involves the decisive

141. "Minutes of the School of Prophets, Salt Lake City, Jan. 14, 1871."

142. G. St. John Stott, "The Seer Stone Controversy," 38.

143. Andrew F. Ehat and Lyndon W. Cook, *The Words of Joseph Smith,* 5.

144. Stott, "The Seer Stone Controversy," 48.

145. Herbert Benson and William Proctor, *The Break-Out Principle,* xi-xii; emphasis theirs.

breaking of prior thought and emotional patterns"—precisely what Smith was doing when scrying the Book of Mormon.[146]

When responding to claims that Joseph wrote the Book of Mormon, Hugh Nibley, a professor of religion at Brigham Young University, commented that such assertions are "based on the simple proposition that since people have written books, somebody, namely Smith or a contemporary, wrote this one. But to make this thesis stick is to show not only that people have written big books, but that somebody has been able to produce a big book like this one. But no other such book exists. Where will you find another work remotely approaching the Book of Mormon in scope and daring?"[147]

Mohammed

In fact, there are many books that devotees would certainly consider equal, if not superior, to the Book of Mormon "in scope and daring."[148] One such work is the Quran (Arabic for "recitation"), brought forth through the instrumentality of Mohammed. Born in the Arabian desert in the sixth century, Mohammed, like Joseph Smith, seemed poor material for a prophet. Uneducated and semi-illiterate, he made a living as a caravan driver until he married a rich widow. Yet he brought forth a message that ignited the flame known today as Islam, a religion that is a way of life for nearly a billion people.

Like Mormonism, Islam is based in a revealed book, the Quran, the tangible of the divine. Its readers are often impressed with the power and beauty of the language. It is difficult to imagine how a work of such literary quality

146. Ibid., xii.

147. Hugh Nibley, *Since Cumorah,* 138.

148. In his survey "Spirit Writing: Another Look at the Book of Mormon," Scott C. Dunn, in addition to the works I have already cited, mentions other spirit writers. Jane Roberts, a housewife from Elmira, New York, susceptible to trances, channeled "Seth," a "discarnate intelligence," and produced fourteen texts dealing with complex philosophical and metaphysical subjects beyond her own educational experience. Levi H. Dowling, born in 1844, was commissioned by "Visel the Goddess of Wisdom" to record *The Aquarian Gospel of Jesus the Christ,* a "transcription from the Akashic Records," recounting a previously unknown ministry of Jesus. The *Urantia Book,* 2,097 pages long, has sold more than 100,000 copies since its appearance in 1955. Also a channeled text, its subject is "the organization and administration of the universes, of the genesis and destiny of man and his relation to God, and of the teachings of Jesus Christ" (John Koffend, "The Gospel According to Helen," 77). Visionary William Blake said his epic *Jerusalem* (1804) was "dictated to him." Robert Graves was working on a historical novel in 1943 when "a sudden overwhelming obsession interrupted me. It took the form of an unsolicited enlightenment on a subject I knew almost nothing of. ... My mind worked at such a furious rate all night, as well as all the next day, that my pen found it difficult to keep pace with the flow of thought. ... Within three weeks, I had written a 70,000-word book about [an] ancient Mediterranean Moon-Goddess," published as *The White Goddess* in 1948.

could have emanated from an illiterate desert-dweller. Roger du Pasquier, a Swiss journalist and Islam specialist, has written:

> The central miracle of Islam was, and remains the Quranic revelation. To this day no one has put forward a defensible explanation of how an unlettered caravan merchant of the early seventh century might have been able, by his own devices, to produce a text of such inimitable beauty, of such capacity to stir emotion, and which contained knowledge and wisdom which stood so far above ideas current at that time. The studies carried out in the West which try to determine the "sources used by Muhammad," or to bring to light the psychological phenomenon which enabled him to draw inspiration from his "subconscious," have demonstrated only one thing; the anti-Muslim prejudice of their authors.[149]

According to Mohammed, the angel Gabriel spoke the words of the Quran to him over a twenty-three-year period (610-632 C.E.). Although the Quran, like the Book of Mormon, has been shown to contain errors, its readers, like Book of Mormon readers, are instructed to verify its truthfulness through prayer. "And if you are in doubt," states the Quran, "as to that which We have revealed to Our slave (Muhammad), then produce a sûrah (chapter) of the like thereof, and call your witnesses beside Allah if ye are truthful" (Sûrah 2:23). Another verse challenges: "Or say they: He hath invented it? Say: Then bring a sûrah (chapter) like unto it, and call (for help) on all ye can besides Allah, if ye are truthful" (Sûrah 10:38).[150]

Jakob Lorber

Another individual who produced a work in many ways equal to the Book of Mormon is the Austrian mystic Jakob Lorber (1800-64), a contemporary of Joseph Smith. On March 15, 1840, Lorber, a musician living in Graz, Austria, had a spiritual experience that shook him deeply. Early one morning, he heard a voice coming from the region of his heart calling him to be "God's Scribe." The voice, later identified as Jesus Christ, told him, "Take up your pen and write!" According to Lorber's biographer, "When he had written down all he had heard with his Inner Ear in the course of that day, it had become clear to him that he had been given a most extraordinary mission from the world beyond."[151]

149. Roger du Pasquier, *Unveiling Islam,* 3.

150. Muhammed Marmaduke Pickthall, trans., *The Glorious Koran.*

151. Kurt Eggenstein, *The Prophet Jakob Lorber Predicts Coming Catastrophes and the True Christianity,* 5.

For the rest of his life, Jakob spent several hours each day recording the dictations of the Inner Voice. His first complete work was "The Household of God," an account of the Old Testament. His magnus opus was "The Great Gospel of John," consisting of eleven volumes—10,000 hand-written pages. It is a day-by-day account of the final three years of Christ's life on earth.

Lorber's manuscripts grew daily over his twenty-four-year ministry. "The extensive manuscripts left by Lorber," wrote his biographer, "show no corrections or revisions. There was no need for these, for what he wrote was not the product of his own mind."[152] In 1858, in a letter to a friend, Lorber described the process: "I always perceive the most holy Word of the Lord in the region of my heart, like a thought of utmost clarity, pure and light, as spoken words. No one else, however close to me, can hear anything of a voice, yet for me this voice of Grace sounds forth more clearly than the loudest material sound."[153]

Unlike Joseph Smith, Lorber neither engaged in preaching nor received any income from his work. His writings, collectively referred to as the *Neuoffenbarung,* or New Revelation, are held by the Lorber Verlag in Germany. The writings, according to Lorber's biographer and friend Karl Ritter von Leitner, speak of "the nature of God, the universe and man and their reciprocal relations, providing a really comprehensive answer to mankind's age-old questions as to whence, whither and why of life."[154] A sample of his work from the "Explanation of the Biblical Gospel of John Revealed by the Lord Jesus to His prophet Jakob Lorber" reads:

> About the baptism with water
> and with the spirit (John 3:22)
>
> 22. After this, Jesus went into Judea with his disciples, stayed there with them, and baptised.
>
> 1. When day had fully dawned, we got on our way and went into Judaea which actually belong[s] to Jerusalem, surrounded this city in the same way as today a district lies around its principal town. One could easily walk through the whole land in a few days.
>
> 2. And what did I actually do in this land? The verse says that I was staying there with them and then baptised. Here arise the questions who, in fact "they" were and what it means that I stayed with them. "They" are above

152. Ibid., 5-6.
153. Karl Ritter Von Leitner, *Jakob Lorber,* 15.
154. "Jakob Lorber."

all the disciples, whose number had again increased by a few in Jerusalem, but then also all those who believed in and sympathized with My teaching.

3. And all those who adopted My teaching in full faith were openly baptised by Me with water, but secretly with the spirit of My eternal love and wisdom and thereby obtained the power to be called "God's children." That is what I was doing as I was staying there. The teaching and what I did was partly recorded by the other three evangelists and need not be stated here. This actually consisted mainly in illustrating all the serious defects from which the Jews and Pharisees were suffering and in preaching the love for God and one's neighbour.

First I described all the weakness, admonished the sinners to repent, warned all who adopted My teaching against reverting to the old leaven of the Pharisees and, in corroboration of My most gentle teaching, performed miraculous acts needed for these so very materialistic times. I also healed many sick, freed the possessed from the unclean spirits and took on more and more disciples.[155]

Pearl Curran/Patience Worth

Living in St. Louis, Missouri, Pearl Curran in May 1913, while using the Ouija board, received the first of many messages from a mysterious entity, who first called herself "Pat C." Later Pat returned and spelled out, "Oh, why let sorrow steel thy heart?" Two months later, on July 8, the entity finally revealed herself as "Patience Worth," born in Dorset, England, in the seventeenth century. While still a young girl, she and her family immigrated to America, where young Patience was killed by Indians.

From 1913 until Curran's death in 1938, Patience Worth transmitted an incredible amount of material through Curran. Some of the material was in her quaint seventeenth-century dialect, and some in more modern English. One night, Worth dictated twenty-two poems. In one five-year stretch, she wrote 1.6 million words, more than six times the length of the Book of Mormon. One of her full-length novels, *Hope Trueblood* (1918), was acclaimed in the literary world though none of the reviewers was aware of the circumstances which prompted the work. *Telka* (1928), a poem of 60,000 words, made accurate use of Middle English terminology. *The Sorry Tale* (1917), a 325,000-word book, substantially longer than the Book of Mormon, is a treatment of the life of a "parallel Christ." Like the Book of Mormon,

155. "Explanation of the Biblical Gospel of John Revealed by the Lord Jesus to His Prophet Jakob Lorber," 35.

the plot unfolds against the social, domestic, and political background of an ancient culture—Palestine and Rome, using the language and customs of Greeks, Arabians, Romans, and several Jewish sects of which Curran was completely unfamiliar. This opus was written in 108 days, a rate of 3,000 words per evening, as revealed directly to Curran.

Curran's knowledge of Bible lands was limited to what she had learned in Sunday school. She quit school at age fifteen, was not an avid reader, rarely traveled, and, like Joseph Smith, possessed no books in her home that could have been used as reference materials. A sample from her novel *The Sorry Tale* reads:

> And upon the cross still suffered He, for the transgressor of the Jews beside Him lived. And they that watched laughed, and behold, they saw that they stirred and they brought forth vinegar, the wine of the people, and offered it that He might live long to suffer.
>
> And it was true that the Jews had fallen fearful, and one and another departed unto the temples to pray and hide. And Rome remained to glut upon the feast. And they had called out against the Son of God, and fallen weary of His words, for He forgave them, and spake in tones to the heavens, crying out that the Father forgive, for the Jews knew that Rome had lain their backs open.
>
> And the transgressor cried out long in his agony, and he turned unto Jesus Christus, speaking out: "Mercy!" And the Rome's men spake unto Him: "If thou art the Son of God, save thyself and him."
>
> And the transgressor spake: "Why do this unto Him? He hath done naught unto thee, and I have perverted the laws and undone them." And Jesus Christus turned His head slow unto the transgressor and spake: "Behold, thou shalt enter the new land this day and be with the Father even as I." And lo, they looked upon Him at this, for He was uttering prophecy even in death. And he hung, His beauteous head wet of blood and crowned of thorns, even as man had made His days thorned, and His precious flesh was illumined with the flames of the lightning.
>
> And behold, the earth quaked. And it was true that the tombs gave up [sic] dead. Their bodies were shaken free. And when the mighty peal had fallen like a trumpet, like a bird that flees singing, sounded out: "It is finished!" And His head sunk, and He turned unto the withered form of Hatte, hanging limp and broken, and the smile of God broke upon His countenance, and it was o'er.[156]

156. Patience Worth (communicated through Mrs. John H. Curran), *The Sorry Tale,* 635-36.

Helen Schucman

Since 1976, when it was first published, more than 2.5 million copies of *A Course in Miracles* have been sold in nineteen-plus different languages, spawning thousands of independent study groups worldwide. The *Course* was channeled through an "inner voice" manifested to Helen Schucman, a Jewish atheist research psychologist and professor of medical psychology at Columbia University's College of Physicians and Surgeons in New York City. In 1965, after several months of symbolic dreams and psychic experiences, her colleague, William Thetford, also a professor at Columbia, encouraged her to record her impressions. Her first flash was to write: "This is a course in miracles." In the book's preface, Schucman wrote: "That was my introduction to the Voice. It made no sound, but seemed to be giving me a kind of inner dictation which I took down in a shorthand notebook. The writing was never automatic. It could be interrupted at any time and later picked up again. It made me very uncomfortable, but it never seriously occurred to me to stop."[157]

The result, after ten years of dictation, was a 1,500-page manuscript, published in 1976 as a three-volume work ("Text," "Workbook for Students," and "Manual for Teachers"), usually bound in one, which promised to bring the miracles of love and inner harmony into readers' lives. The implied author of the massive work is Jesus Christ, speaking in the first person. As author John Koffend wrote, *A Course in Miracles* is an "epiphenomenon, a quasi-religious fad that sells books, somewhat like Norman Vincent Peale's *The Power of Positive Thinking,* that in an earlier generation enjoyed immense but transient popularity, particularly among distressed Americans looking for effortless shortcuts to peace of mind."[158]

A sample from Schucman's work respecting the concept of salvation tells us: "Never forget that the Sonship is your salvation, for the Sonship is your Self. As God's creation It is yours, and belonging to you It is His. Your Self does not need salvation, but your mind needs to learn what salvation is."[159] Respecting the historicity of Jesus Christ, she wrote, "God would not have us be alone because He does not will to be alone. That is why He created His Son, and gave him the power to create with Him."[160]

Judy Skutch, founder of the nonprofit Foundation for Inner Peace, which publishes the *Course* and promotes it as a teaching tool, explained

157. Qtd. in Debi Miller, "A Course in Miracles," 3.
158. Koffend, "The Gospel According to Helen," 77.
159. *A Course in Miracles,* 200.
160. Ibid., 150

in 2000: "The Course is Christian in statement. Its purpose is to help us achieve a universal spiritual experience. Whatever path we choose, the purpose is always to help us reach a state where we recognize our oneness with the All."[161] One devotee has written, "The Course is designed to draw out minds into a completely different way of thinking, a thought system based on God, love, forgiveness, caring and sharing. It also puts heavy emphasis on human relationships. It could be called a course in the healing of relationships, for it is how we see and relate to others that puts us in touch with our own true nature and state of being."[162] Another advocate said in 2002, "I personally believe that the influence of the Course has barely begun, and that people will be studying and discussing it hundreds of years from now."[163]

Although many adherents consider the Quran, "The Great Gospel of John," *The Sorry Tale,* and *A Course in Miracles* equal to or perhaps even surpassing the Book of Mormon, as noted American literary critic Harold Bloom has written, "There are enigmatic splendors in the Book of Mormon, whether it was revealed to Joseph Smith or whether it emerged from his indubitable religious genius."[164] And the Book of Mormon, like the Quran and *A Course in Miracles,* has impacted the lives of millions of readers worldwide since its release more than 185 years ago.

The Changing Place of Joseph's Book

Although there has been renewed academic and popular interest in the Book of Mormon since the mid-1980s, for nearly a century and a half it was mostly left to draw dust on library back shelves. Not until 1961 did LDS Church-owned Brigham Young University require undergraduates to study the book; the LDS Sunday School curriculum did not include the Book of Mormon as a separate course of study until 1972.[165] LDS historian Grant Underwood comments:

> As we step back to take a larger look at Book of Mormon usage in early years, we can make a number of general observations. First, compared to the Bible, the Book of Mormon was hardly cited at all. ... To a people who have come to prize the Book of Mormon as "the keystone" of

161. Judy Skutch, qtd. in Koffend, "The Gospel According to Helen," 86.
162. Miller, "A Course in Miracles," 4-5.
163. Allen Watson, "The Story of the Course."
164. Harold Bloom, Review of Terryl L. Givens, *By the Hand of Mormon: The American Scripture that Launched a New World Religion.*
165. Terryl L. Givens, *By the Hand of Mormon,* 236, 238.

> their religion, it may come as a surprise to learn that in the early literature the Bible was cited nearly twenty times more frequently than the Book of Mormon. Such a ratio is corroborated in the unpublished sources as well. During his proselyting peregrinations at this period of time, [LDS Apostle] Orson Pratt kept a fairly detailed record of the scriptures used in his sermons. Bible passages were listed ten times more frequently than Book of Mormon ones. Moreover, in the 173 Nauvoo [Illinois] discourses of the prophet Joseph Smith for which contemporary records exist, only two Book of Mormon passages have been cited while dozens of biblical passages were.[166]

As Robert A. Gunderson, artifacts manager for the Community of Christ (formerly Reorganized Church of Jesus Christ of Latter Day Saints) in Independence, Missouri, notes: "five years after the Book of Mormon was first published it was virtually ignored by [Joseph] Smith and [Sidney] Rigdon in defining the doctrinal beliefs of the church."[167] As Joseph's theology developed, he paid less attention to—or at least emphasized less—the Book of Mormon and more attention to the ongoing revelations that were eventually incorporated into the Doctrine and Covenants.

166. Grant Underwood, "Book of Mormon Usage in Early LDS Theology," 52-53.

167. Robert A. Gunderson, "From the Dust to the Dusty," 81. For example, the "Lectures on Faith," first published in the 1835 Doctrine and Covenants as the "Doctrine of the Church of the Latter Day Saints," contains 123 biblical references but only seven Book of Mormon references. Joseph Smith's dedicatory prayer at the Kirtland, Ohio, temple in 1836 made nine biblical references, thirty-four references to his own revelations, but only four to the Book of Mormon. In his widely publicized King Follett discourse, delivered in Nauvoo, Illinois, in 1844, Joseph explicitly stated that he would base his doctrinal proofs on the Bible. In addition to many biblical references, he cited the Book of Moses, the Book of Abraham, and Doctrine and Covenants, but not the Book of Mormon. Ibid., 82.

17 | THE CHURCH OF CHRIST

The disinherited classes, especially the unlettered, have been more moved by emotional religion; and emotional religion is at times animated by a revolt against the religious style, the liturgy, and the clergy of the upper-class church, which is at the same time a revolt against aristocratic manners and morals.

—Richard Hofstadter, *Anti-Intellectualism in American History,* 56

The precise moment when Joseph felt inspired to form a new church, one animated by both his spiritual quest and yearnings as well as imbued by the Christianity of the King James Bible, is unknown. David Whitmer, however, recalled that generalized preaching occurred "during the time the book [of Mormon] was being translated."[1] The publication of Joseph's book signaled to the world his coming of age. It manifested that the twenty-four-year-old was more than a natural born money-digging village seer. If a "tough as hickory" brawler like Andrew Jackson could win the U.S. presidency, and a semiliterate frontiersman like Tennessean Davy Crockett could be elected to Congress mainly on the basis of his reported bear-hunting prowess, then a country farm lad like Joseph, who claimed heavenly revelations, could become a prophet of God.

The release of Joseph's Book of Mormon was the first tangible step in what early Mormonites, as members of Joseph's Church of Christ were sometimes called, termed "the restoration of all things." That phrase, as historian D. Michael Quinn writes, "eventually encompassed a remarkable theology, a radical world view, and an ethnic sense of 'peopleness' among those who have always preferred to be known as Latter-day Saints."[2] As non-Mormon historian Jan Shipps argues, Mormonism became "a new religious movement," in essence a new world religion.[3]

1. David Whitmer, Interviewed by *Kansas City Journal,* June 1, 1881.
2. D. Michael Quinn, *The Mormon Hierarchy,* 4.
3. Jan Shipps, *Mormonism,* esp. Chap. 7, "The Millennial Vision Transformed."

In 1828, a small throng of loosely organized, anti-creedal disciples began converging around the standard of Joseph's prophetic proclamations and events surrounding the coming forth of his book. At that early point, the young prophet was distinguished by his angelic charge to translate and publish the Book of Mormon. "He has a gift to translate the book," a 1829 revelation reported, "and I have commanded him that he shall pretend to no other gift, for I will grant him no other gift" (BC IV:2). David Whitmer believed that during the eight months preceding the formal organization of the Church, the faith was as organized as it needed to be and, was closer to primitive Christianity than at any other time in its subsequent history.[4]

From 1828 to May 1829, as Quinn notes, "'my church' was an unorganized body of 'my people' who had no priestly 'authority' and which required no religious ordinances." Joseph and Oliver Cowdery, after baptizing each other in mid-1829, also immersed dozens of other believers in Joseph's mission. These baptisms, however, were to remit sin, signal a commitment to Christ, but not to enter an organization. The gathering of adherents until April 6, 1830, lacked an institutional form and required only a profession of faith and repentance.

However, although a formal ecclesiastical organization did not yet exist, it was anticipated. Joseph delivered a revelation to his father in February 1829 which promised that "a marvelous work is about to come forth among the children of men" (BC III:1).[5] A month later, another revelation, delivered to Martin Harris, announced: "I will establish my church, like unto the church which was taught by my disciples in the days of old" (IV:5). And in May 1829, the divine voice added: "if this generation harden not their hearts, I will establish my church among them" (ibid.). Later, when Joseph was riding from Harmony to Manchester with Joseph Knight, he told his benefactor that "there must be a Church formed But Did not tell when."[6]

Joseph probably first told his family in the fall of 1828 that he believed all churches were wrong.[7] Until that point, Mother Smith, Hyrum, Harrison,

4. David Whitmer, *An Address to All Believers in Christ,* 28-33, 45-48.

5. This same message was communicated to Oliver Cowdery (V:1), Hyrum Smith (X:1), Joseph Knight (XI:1), and David Whitmer (XII:1).

6. Joseph Knight, "Reminiscence," 2.

7. Lucy Smith wrote to her brother in January 1831. Interestingly, she made no mention of a "first vision," but instead promoted Joseph's book as the family's source of inspiration:

> [B]y reading [the Book of Mormon] our eyes are opened that we can see the situation in which the world now stands; that the eyes of the whole world are blinded; that the churches have all become corrupted, yea every church upon the face of the earth; that the

and Sophronia were congregants at Palmyra's Western Presbyterian Church. Sometime in September 1828, they stopped attending meetings. On March 3, 1830, a committee of the Rev. Alfred E. Campbell and Elders Henry Jessup, and George Beckwith was appointed to visit the Smiths to measure their spirituality.[8] Lucy gave the men no testimony of young Joseph's "first vision." Instead, she offered a history of the Book of Mormon, "dwelling particularly upon the principles of religion therein contained." She later explained that she "endeavoured to show them the similarity between these principles, and the simplicity of the gospel taught by Jesus Christ in the New Testament." The fervent Lucy complained that, despite these Book of Mormon principles, "the different denominations are very much opposed to us. The Universalists are alarmed lest their religion should suffer loss, the Presbyterians tremble for their salaries, the Methodists also come, and they rage."

After listening, Beckwith, the group's spokesman, reportedly replied, "Mrs. Smith, you and the most of your children have belonged to our church for some length of time, and we respect you very highly. You say a great deal about the Book of Mormon, which your son has found, and you believe much of what he tells you, yet we cannot bear the thoughts of losing you." He then urged: "I wish that if you do believe those things, you would not say anything more upon the subject—I do wish you would not." Lucy answered: "[I]f you should stick my flesh full of faggots, and even burn me at the stake, I would declare, as long as God should give me breath, that Joseph has got that Record, and that I know it to be true."

The visitors saw the futility of continuing the discussion and left, encountering Hyrum outside. "Mr. Smith, do you not think that you may be deceived about that Record, which your brother pretends to have found?" asked Beckwith. Hyrum answered no, and asked Beckwith to read the book when it was in print and then ask God to witness if it was true. After a brief discussion, the Presbyterians turned to Harrison who, like his brother Joseph, was proficient in the scriptures. In response to their arguments, he

---

gospel of Christ is nowhere preached. This is the situation which the world is now in, and you can judge for yourselves if we did not need something more than the wisdom of man to show us the right way.

God, seeing our situation, had compassion upon us, and has sent us this revelation [the Book of Mormon] that the stumbling block might be removed, that whomsoever would might enter. He now established His Church upon the earth as it was in the days of the Apostles. (Lucy Mack Smith to Solomon Mack and wife, Jan. 6, 1831.)

8. Unless otherwise noted, my treatment of this incident is based on the narrative in Lavina Fielding Anderson, *Lucy's Book,* 467-70.

referenced Isaiah 56:9-11: "All ye beasts of the field come to devour, yea, all ye beasts in the forest. His watchmen are blind: they are all ignorant, they are all dumb dogs, they cannot bark; sleeping, lying down, loving to slumber. Yea, they are greedy dogs which can never have enough, and they are shepherds that cannot understand: they all look to their own way, every one for his gain, from his quarter." After so pointed a reception, the three gentlemen, asserted Mother Smith, "left without ceremony."

A week later, just sixteen days before the first printed edition of the Book of Mormon became available, the Presbyterian committeemen reported that they had again visited the Smiths and had "received no satisfaction." The Smiths "acknowledged that they had entirely neglected the ordinances of the church for the last eighteen months and that they did not wish to unite with us any more." They were summoned to appear before the session on March 24, 1830, to answer charges of "[n]eglect of public worship and the Sacrament of the Lord's Supper for the last eighteen months."[9] When the session met on March 29, just three days after the Book of Mormon was offered publicly for sale, the above charges were sustained on the testimony of Henry Jessup, Harvey Shel, Robert W. Smith, and Frederick U. Sheffield. The church then suspended Lucy, Hyrum, and Harrison Smith from membership.[10]

Eight days later, on April 6, the entire Smith family aligned itself with Joseph's new church. His father and Martin Harris were both baptized this day in Crooked Brook, which bisects the Smiths' farm. When Joseph Sr. exited the water, Joseph Jr. grabbed his hand and shouted, "Oh! My God I have lived to see my father baptized into the true church of Jesus Christ."[11] Lucy wrote that her son "covered his face <and sobbed upon his father's bosom like an infant>." Joseph Knight Sr. added his recollection:

> old Brother Smith and Martin Harris was Babtised[,] Joseph was fild with the Spirrit to a grate Degree to see his Father and Mr. Harris that he had Bin with so much [and] he Bust out with greaf and Joy and Seamed as tho the world Could not hold him[.] he went out into the Lot and appeared to want to git out of site of every body and would sob and Crie and Seamed to Be so full that he could not live[.] oliver and I went after him

9. "Records of the Sessions of the Presbyterian Church in Palmyra," 2:11-12.

10. Ibid.

11. Unless otherwise stated my treatment of this incident is taken from Anderson, *Lucy's Book,* 477.

and Came to him and after awhile he Came in But he wasd the most wrot upon that I ever saw any man. But his joy seemed to Be full[.].[12]

Although no contemporary records were kept of this meeting, tradition asserts that it convened at the Peter Whitmer Sr. home in Fayette, New York. The evidence seems compelling, however, that the founding caucus more probably met in the cramped Smith log home in Manchester, where Joseph and Lucy Smith still lived with Hyrum and his family.[13] The 1833 *Book of Commandments* (an early version of the Doctrine and Covenants) contains six revelations dated April 6, 1830. Each of the beneficiaries of these revelations—Oliver Cowdery, Hyrum Smith, Harrison Smith, Joseph Smith Sr., Joseph Knight Sr., and Joseph Smith Jr.—attended the Church's organization on this same date. Yet the headnote for each revelation states that it was given in Manchester (BC XVII, XVIII, XIX, XX, XXI, and XXII). Fayette is twenty-five miles distant, which would have required a round trip of fifty miles in a single day—an unlikely occurrence.

In addition, the first newspaper to mention the event, the Mormon-produced *Evening and the Morning Star* published in Independence, Missouri, beginning in 1832, stated clearly: "Soon after the book of Mormon came forth, containing the fulness of the gospel of Jesus Christ, the church was organized on the sixth of April, in Manchester; soon after, a branch was established in Fayette, and the June following, another in Colesville, New York."[14] Joseph's younger brother William also identified Manchester as the site of organization.[15] In addition, the revelation received by the prophet

12. Joseph Knight Sr., "Reminiscence," 6.

13. For an overview of this point, see H. Michael Marquardt, "An Appraisal of Manchester as Location for the Organization of the Church." See also H. Michael Marquardt, "Manchester as the Site of the Organization of the Church on April 6, 1830," *John Whitmer Historical Association Journal* 33, no. 1 (Spring/Summer 2013): 141-53; and Marquardt, "Historical Setting of Mormonism in Manchester, Ontario County, New York," *John Whitmer Historical Association Journal* 35, no. 2 (Fall/Winter 2015): 62-108. For a contrary interpretation, see Karen Lynn Davidson, David J. Whittaker, Mark Ashurst-McGee, and Richard L. Jensen, eds., *The Joseph Smith Papers: Histories, Volume 1: Joseph Smith Histories, 1832-1844* (Salt Lake City: The Church Historian's Press, 2012), 496n21; Davidson, Jensen, and Whittaker, eds., *The Joseph Smith Papers: Histories, Volume 2: Assigned Histories, 1831-1847* (Salt Lake City: The Church Historian's Press, 2012), 115n12; and especially Michael Hubbard MacKay, *Sacred Space: Exploring the Birthplace of Mormonism* (Provo, Utah: Religious Studies Center, Brigham Young University, 2016).

14. W. W. Phelps, "Rise and Progress of the Church of Christ," 84. Phelps was not among the original members, so his account must be considered, at best, second-hand.

15. William Smith, *William Smith on Mormonism,* 14. Smith mentions that his family "went to my brother Hyrum's house" in 1829, and that "[i]t was in this house that the first conference of the Church of Jesus Christ of Latter Day Saints was held, on the 6th day of April, 1830, at which I was present."

during the charter meeting is identified in the *Book of Commandments* XXII:1 as "given in Manchester, New-York, April 6, 1830."

Near noon on that Tuesday,[16] close to sixty people assembled to witness the organization of the Church of Christ, the same name given to the Christian Nephite church in the Book of Mormon (Mosiah 18:17; 3 Ne. 26:21, 27:8, 28:23; Moro. 6:4). The meeting was simple. Twenty-four-year-old Joseph called the gathering to order after prayer and then asked "our brethren to know whether they accepted us [Joseph and Oliver] as their teachers in the things of the Kingdom of God, and whether they were satisfied that we should proceed and be organized as a Church according to said commandment which we had received."[17]

After the group consented, Oliver Cowdery, Hyrum Smith, Peter Whitmer Jr., Harrison Smith, and David Whitmer joined with Joseph Smith as a quorum of six to meet New York's legal requirements for incorporating a religious society.[18] Joseph then pronounced a revelation. Apostle Cowdery was designated to ordain Brother Joseph "a seer, a translator, a prophet, an apostle of Jesus Christ, [and] an elder of the church through the will of God the Father, and the grace of our Lord Jesus Christ." The flock of disciples was then admonished to "give heed unto all [Smith's] words and commandments … for his word ye shall receive, as if from mine own mouth, in all patience and faith." In addition, members were told that God inspired Joseph "to move the cause of Zion in mighty power for good." The revelation closed: "Yea, and thus saith the Lord God, lo, lo, to the Jews" (BC XXII).

The sacrament of the Lord's supper followed. "We then took bread, blessed it, and brake it with them," said Joseph, "also wine, blessed it, and drank it with them." Smith and Cowdery next laid their hands on individuals who had previously been baptized "that they might receive the gift of the Holy Ghost, and be confirmed members of the Church of Christ." In

16. Edward Stevenson to President John Taylor, Jan. 7, 1878.

17. *History of the Church,* 1:77.

18. "An Act to Provide for the Incorporation of Religious Societies" was passed by the New York State Legislature on April 5, 1813. Although the organizers of the Church met the legal requirements, according to historian Larry C. Porter, who spent considerable time searching for the "elusive incorporation record," a formal written statement of organization has never been found (Larry C. Porter, "Organizational Origins of the Church of Jesus Christ, 6 April 1830," 157). David Stott, a New York attorney, asserts, however, that the Church was complying with a different set of legal rules. "When seeking out what legally took place on April 6, 1830, historians have assumed the church members tried to form a 'religious corporation,'" Stott says. But instead of being organized as a "religious corporation," Stott suggests, the Church was organized as a "common-law religious society," the model for an organizational meeting not found in the statutes (Michael De Groote, "BYU Symposium," 2).

Joseph's retrospective 1839 recital, he said that "the Holy Ghost was poured out upon us to a very great degree." Under the Spirit's influence, "some prophesied" and the entire group "praised the Lord, and rejoiced exceedingly." The ensemble then dismissed, Smith concluded, "with the pleasing knowledge that we were now individually members of and acknowledged of God," as members of the Church of Christ, which was now "organized in accordance with commandments and revelations given by Him to ourselves in these last days."[19]

A few days later on Sunday, April 11, a gathering was held in the Peter Whitmer Sr. home in Fayette, where Oliver delivered the Church's first formal discourse, then baptized six new members, including Hiram Page; his wife, Katharine Whitmer Page; Katherine's brothers Christian and Jacob Whitmer, and their wives, sisters Anne Schott and Elizabeth Ann Schott. Five days later, Joseph proclaimed another revelation "in consequence of some desiring to unite with the church without re-baptism, who had previously been baptized." Because "in these last days" all of the previous "covenants have I caused to be done away in this thing," rebaptism was required as "a new and an everlasting covenant" (BC XXIII).[20] One week later, Oliver baptized Peter Whitmer Sr., Mary Whitmer, William and Elizabeth Jolly and their son Vincent, Richard [Ziba] Peterson, and Elizabeth Anne Whitmer (who would later marry Cowdery) in nearby Seneca Lake.[21]

In late April, the impoverished Smith and Cowdery, possibly having worn out their welcome in the crowded Whitmer home in Fayette, left to visit the more prosperous Joseph Knight family in Colesville, New York. The Knights were Universalists but, according to Smith, "were willing to reason with me upon my religious views, and were, as usual, friendly and hospitable." Several meetings were held in the neighborhood where "we had

19. *History of the Church,* 1:78.

20. Of interest in this revelation is the lack of reference to priesthood authority and its restoration through angelic ordination, ideas that retrospectively became a part of this earlier period. As Dan Vogel notes: "Smith and Cowdery, as is true for many religious founders, emphasized the charismatic aspects of their authority at first and only later sought to bureaucratize it by stressing the more legalistic elements of priesthood" (Vogel, *Joseph Smith,* 495).

21. *History of the Church,* 1:81. Rev. Diedrich Willers, a minister of the German Reform Church in the Fayette area, wrote his superiors on June 18, 1830, that the Mormons were rebaptizing members of various denominations and forming a new Christian church. "With their baptism by immersion," he reported, "they are winning over many members of the Baptist Church—the general as well as the particular Baptists." He added that he knew the Whitmers and that over the previous nine years they had been "adherents of the Methodists, the Reformers, the Presbyterians, Mennonites, and Baptists" (Diedrich Willers Jr. to Reverend Brethren, June 18, 1830).

many friends, and some enemies."[22] During this period, Newel Knight, a close friend of Smith, while suffering religious anxiety, slumped into convulsions. His alarmed wife sent for Smith. When Joseph arrived, Knight was "suffering very much in his mind, and his body acted upon in a very strange manner; his visage and limbs distorted and twisted in every shape and appearance possible to imagine; and finally he was caught up off the floor of the apartment and tossed about most fearfully."[23]

Knight's family and neighbors, witnessing the disturbing scene, saw Joseph catch hold of Knight's hand, whereupon the overwrought man said he was possessed of the devil and knew that the prophet had the power to cast him out. Acting on Knight's faith, as well as his own, Joseph commanded the devil to depart. Newel declared that he saw the devil leave and vanish. The sufferer's grotesque facial expressions relaxed, and his body's distortions ceased. Knight said that the visions of eternity were then opened to him. In his weakened condition, reminiscent of the "falling down exercise," he was placed on his bed, but he said he felt himself "attracted upward, and remained for some time enwrapt in contemplation, insomuch that I knew not what was going on in the room." In this state, his body seemed to elevate until he felt the ceiling beams press against his shoulder and head. Many present were convinced of God's power and later joined the Church. Ultimately, the incident became viewed as the first miracle of the fledgling church. Joseph affirmed that "it was done not by man, nor by the power of man, but it was done by God, and by the power of godliness."[24]

Soon afterwards, Joseph returned to Fayette. He later recalled that the Book of Mormon was then

> accounted as a strange thing. No small stir was created by its appearance. Great opposition and much persecution followed the believers of its authenticity. But it had now come to pass that truth had sprung out of the earth, and righteousness had looked down from heaven, so we feared not our opponents, knowing that we had both the Father and the

---

22. *History of the Church,* 1:81.

23. Unless otherwise noted, my narrative is taken from *History of the Church,* 1:82-84.

24. *History of the Church,* 1:83. Knight's sister-in-law, Emily Austin, who attended many of the Mormon meetings at Colesville during this time, wrote that "the excitement was great, insomuch that many were overcome by the spirit, and were, seemingly, unconscious of all around them. On awakening from this trance, they would say they were happy, and had seen angels and talked with them. However, I did not feel interested in this direction. It had hitherto appeared most simple of all things, and I was decidedly against such proceedings" (Emily M. Austin, *Mormonism,* 37).

> Son, because we had the doctrines of Christ, and abided in them; and therefore we continued to preach and to give information to all who were willing to hear.[25]

From the beginning, Joseph's book, priced at $1.75, failed to capture much of a market in western New York. During the last week of March 1830, as Joseph was returning to Manchester with Joseph Knight Sr., they encountered a discouraged Martin Harris in the roadway, his satchel filled with newly printed copies of the Book of Mormon. "The Books will not sell for no body wants them," Harris said. "I think they will sell well," countered Smith. Worried about the loss of his farm if the books did not sell, Harris replied: "I want a commandment." "Why?" Joseph answered, "Fulfill what you have got." But the anxious Harris would not be put off. "I must have a commandment," Harris insisted. "A commandment of God and not of man to you, Martin, given ... by him who is eternal," was bestowed shortly thereafter: "I command you, that thou shalt not covet thine own property, but impart it freely to the printing of the book of Mormon" (BC XVI:27). But Joseph's book still did not sell even when the asking price was lowered to $1.25. Palmyra resident Pomeroy Tucker recalled: "The book ... fell dead before the public. ... It found no buyers, or but very few."[26] The Rev. John Sherer of the American Home Missionary Society, while ministering in Colesville, New York, told a correspondent six months after publication: "Their books remain unsold; <except> here and there. ... It is thought the great speculation, which they probably anticipated, will prove a losing busi=nesss."[27]

Both Joseph and Martin made strenuous exertions to promote the book's sale, as did Harrison and Joseph Smith Sr.[28] Albert Chandler worked in Luther Howard's book bindery where the Book of Mormon was bound in 1830. He recorded in 1898, "Martin Harris ... gave up his entire time to advertising the Bible to his neighbors and the public generally in the vicinity of Palmyra. He would call public meetings and address them himself."[29] One observer wrote in the local paper that Martin "was daily seen on the streets inviting his friends and neighbors to buy. His form was conspicuous with a

25. *History of the Church,* 1:84.

26. Pomeroy Tucker, *Origin, Rise, and Progress of Mormonism,* 60-61.

27. John Sherer to Absalom Peters, Nov. 18, 1830.

28. In October 1845, Lucy Smith told a conference of Saints that Harrison "had to sell them [copies of the Book of Mormon] to buy us victuals I want to speak of this that you may not complain of hard times" (Anderson, *Lucy's Book,* 478).

29. Qtd. in William Alexander Linn, *The Story of the Mormons,* 48.

grey suit of homespun, his head surmounted by a large stiff hat, while under his arm he carried several copies of the book."[30] Despite early efforts, most of the 5,000 copies of the Book of Mormon remained in storage until the church became established in Ohio.[31]

"Embryonic Mormonism was strikingly primitivistic during its earliest months," notes Peter Crawley, an expert on early Mormon imprints.[32] This characteristic had its origins in the Church's original deployment as much like a Methodist class, the form of worship Joseph had grown up with. "Methodism's style and tone," write historians Nathan O. Hatch and John H. Wigger, "worked their way deep into the fabric of American life, influencing nearly all other mass religious movements that would follow it."[33] At his core, Joseph exhibited a Methodist, or Methodist-enlightened, temperament. Peter Cartwright, a Methodist minister who spent a day with the prophet in Springfield, Illinois, in the 1840s, recalled in his 1856 autobiography Joseph telling him: "[A]mong all the Churches in the world the Methodist was the nearest right, and that, as far as they went, they were right. But they had stopped short by not claiming the gift of tongues, of prophecy, and of miracles." Joseph further added that "[w]e Latter-day Saints are Methodists, as far as they have gone, only we have advanced further."[34]

Early Mormonism, in many ways, may be considered old-fashioned Methodism. An 1841 feature in Horace Greeley's paper noted: "Setting aside the near approach of the Millennium and the Book of Mormon, [the Mormons] resemble in faith and discipline the Methodists, and their meetings are marked by the fervid simplicity that characterizes that body of Christians."[35] Although there were certainly differences between the two religions, the principal agenda of each was "to usher in the kingdom of God on earth."[36] Joseph Smith, like John Wesley, "developed a theology of the royal road of salvation which is best characterized as a *working* theology, designed

30. "Old Newspapers—No. 25," *Palmyra Courier,* May 31, 1872.

31. The preface to the 1837 edition of the Book of Mormon notes a "pressing call" for the book, the 1830 edition having "some time since been distributed."

32. Peter Crawley, "The Passage of Mormon Primitivism," 26.

33. Nathan O. Hatch and John H. Wigger, *Methodism and the Shaping of American Culture,* 16.

34. Cartwright, *Peter Cartwright's Autobiography,* 343. See also Christopher C. Jones, "'We Latter-day Saints Are Methodists': The Influence of Methodism on Early Mormon Religiosity," M.A. thesis, Brigham Young University, August 2009; and Jones, "The Power and Form of Godliness: Methodist Conversion Narratives and Joseph Smith's First Vision," *Journal of Mormon History* 37, no. 2 (Spring 2011): 88-114.

35. "The Book of Mormon," *New-Yorker,* Jan. 1841.

36. John H. Wigger, *Taking Heaven by Storm,* 181. For Mormon parallels, see D&C 6:3, 11:3, 12:3, 14:3, and 65:5-6.

to help persons on their way to heaven. The grace of God was interpreted in various stages as enabling the fundamental transformation of the individual through a conversion experience in which God was the prime mover, Christ the mediator, and the individual a full participant as responder."[37]

Mormons adopted a view similar to Wesley's maxim that "[All] ought above all else to be people going on to perfection."[38] And both the Methodist Episcopal Church and Joseph's Church of Christ harnessed powerful undercurrents of popular belief that had previously found little institutional recognition. Mormonism and Methodism were primarily driven and constrained by "the needs, hopes, and fears of ordinary people," and almost entirely governed by those from the middle and lower classes.[39] Both groups imbued common people—farmers, mechanics, merchants, and artisans—with the belief that they as individuals and as communities could overcome folly, eradicate vice, and improve their lot in life. It is also evident that Mormons and Methodists resembled each other in practicing a pragmatic trial-and-error approach to religion, willing to drop or modify unsuccessful methods. And finally, as each movement grew, its organizational complexity increased.

From the beginnings of the two societies, each demonstrated a strong dislike for aristocratic, European-style clericalism. A variety of lay leadership positions were open to ordinary men of both traditions. "Everyday folk," claims Nathan O. Hatch, professor of history and provost at the University of Notre Dame, "rather than college-educated gentlemen" assumed ministerial duties.[40] And preachers of both movements rejected written-out sermons, which Hatch described as "a read discourse with a stiff theological spine."[41] Instead, informally trained Methodist preachers and Mormon missionaries opted for spontaneous, led-by-the-Spirit-type jeremiads that were audience-centered, colloquial, improvised, and often emotional.

Both religions asserted that God could speak to anyone, even those traditionally excluded from authority. Both groups put great stock in signs, wonders, and ecstatic experiences. Many early Methodists and Mormons believed in the efficacy of dreams, visions, and supernatural direction, and

37. Frederick A. Norwood, *The Story of American Methodism,* 17. For Mormon parallels, see D&C 4, 11, 14, 16.

38. Norwood, *The Story of American Methodism,* 50. D&C 68:13 reads: "[W]herefore, continue in patience until ye are perfected"; and members of the School of Prophets are commanded to "be perfected in their ministry" (D&C 90:8).

39. Wigger, *Taking Heaven by Storm,* 5.

40. Hatch and Wigger, *Methodism and the Shaping of American Culture,* 37.

41. Ibid.

were not afraid to base day-to-day decisions on such phenomena. Each religion rejected predestination: the idea that God ordained some souls for eternal life and others for eternal damnation. While both organizations believed that God's grace was offered to all through Christ's atonement, they also believed that baptism was the means by which individuals entered the church. American Methodists and Mormons followed the Arminian line of thinking, writes Hatch, that "God's grace is resistible." While he may reach out to us, the theory proposes, we are free either to accept or reject his offer of eternal salvation.[42]

The term *liberty* was also a theological keystone in both religions. "The strikingly eclectic use of the word *liberty* in early Methodist discourse," writes David Hempton, professor of church history at Boston University, "is not merely incidental, but is suggestive of much deeper resonance for both men and women."[43] Joseph's Book of Mormon contains ten anecdotes related to "liberty," including the oft-cited account of an angry Moroni, chief commander of the Nephite armies, who "rent his coat; and ... took a piece thereof, and wrote upon it, In memory of our god, our religion, and freedom, and our peace, our wives, and our children; and he fastened it upon the end of a pole thereof ... and he called it the title of liberty."[44] In addition, Joseph spoke of the American concept of liberty in his public addresses.[45] Elsewhere in the Book of Mormon, America is called "a land of liberty" (2 Ne. 1:7).

At its outset in nineteenth-century America, Methodism was utterly an evangelistic movement. Likewise, the very being of the fledgling Church of Christ lay in missionary work. Mormon missionaries and Methodist itinerants, common men who burned with the Spirit and who hungered for respect and opportunity, viewed the whole country as a "vast field ripe for the harvest of souls."[46] Intriguingly, the first official mission of both traditions was to the indigenous American Indian. During its 1820 General Conference in Baltimore, the Missionary Society of the Methodist Episcopal Church was founded. In his episcopal address, William McKendree,

42. John H. Wigger, "'Fighting Bees': Methoidist Itinerants and the Dynamics of Methodist Growth, 1770-1820," in Hatch and Wigger, *Methodism and the Shaping of American Culture,* 129.

43. David Hempton, "Methodist Growth in Transatlantic Perspective, ca. 1770-1850," in Hatch and Wigger, *Methodism and the Shaping of American Culture,* 58.

44. 1830 Book of Mormon, 350-51.

45. See, for example, "Joseph Smith to Mr. Editor," Jan. 22, 1840, in Dean C. Jessee, *The Personal Writings of Joseph Smith,* 455-58; and Joseph's July 9, 1843, diary entry in Andrew F. Ehat and Lyndon W. Cook, *The Words of Joseph Smith,* 229.

46. Norwood, *The Story of American Methodism,* 15; BC X, XI, XII. See Joseph's early statements that "the field is white already to harvest" in D&C 6:3, 11:3, 12:3, 14:3.

bishop of Virginia, stated: "Perhaps we have not paid sufficient attention to the voice of Providence, calling to … [a] spread of the Gospel among the Indians. … [A]t this moment your attention is emphatically called to this subject by an address from the Wyandotte Indians, requesting us to send missionaries among them." McKendree, like Joseph Smith, believed that Christianized Indians could and should play a significant part in the development of the new American Republic.[47]

Both Methodist itinerants and Mormon missionaries were ordained elders, were issued licenses authorizing them to represent their respective churches, and were called and "set apart" for their assignments at annual general conferences. They served in their fields of labor under the supervision of "presiding elders," traveled "without purse or scrip," and, as both leaders and lay persons, supported themselves by whatever resources they could muster to extend the movement and to evangelize those within their reach. A basic rule for Methodist preachers, later adopted by their Mormon counterparts, was "let your motto be, 'Holiness to the Lord.' Avoid all lightness, jesting, and foolish talking."[48] Elements of both preaching traditions drew on startling verbal images of an apocalyptic vision, impending divine judgment, and the necessity of "fleeing the wrath to come," as the final scene was called in both cultures.

Both groups held weekly prayer/testimony meetings, usually on a weekday evening, where devotees could bear testimony to the group, bringing "the interior life of each person out into a communal sharing of the drama of salvation and commitment," as described by historian of religions Donald Mathews in his study of the "psychodynamics of orality" in early Methodist revivals.[49] There was also a similarity in their worship or communion services, which consisted of prayer, singing, partaking of a token piece of bread, and a sip or two of water or wine, followed by one or more sermons, then closed by a benediction. In nearly all public meetings in both cultures, congregants knelt together in prayer. The Mormon baptismal prayer, as outlined first in 3 Nephi 11:25 of the Book of Mormon, like the benediction in Methodist

47. Kenneth Cain Kinghorn, *The Heritage of American Methodism,* 169.

48. Adam Clarke, "A Letter to a Preacher (1800)," 103. For Mormon parallels, see D&C 20:69, 46:33. Joseph Smith, in describing the millennial city of the New Jerusalem, said (slightly paraphrasing Zechariah 14:20) that therein "even upon the bells of the horses shall be written *Holiness to the Lord" (History of the Church,* 2:358). Elsewhere, he said that on each temple in Zion must be written: "Holiness to the Lord" (ibid., 1:359).

49. Donald G. Mathews, "Evangelical America: The Methodist Ideology," qtd. in David Hempton, "Methodist Growth in Transatlantic Perspective," in Hatch and Wigger, *Methodism and the Shaping of American Culture,* 57.

services, closes with a trinitarian supplication: "In the name of the Father, and of the Son, and of the Holy Ghost."

Mormonism, like Methodism, was a social process as much as an ecclesiastical movement. The church became not only a vessel of salvation but also a way of life. Both sets of believers were singing folks. Former Methodist Emma Smith selected favorite Methodist songs from the Methodist hymnal of her youth for inclusion in the first Mormon hymn book, *A Collection of Sacred Hymns,* published in 1835.[50] Beloved women like Emma were called "elect ladies" in both traditions.[51] Strong older women like Lucy Mack Smith were lovingly revered as "mothers in Israel."[52]

Another value among both early Methodists and Mormons was an emphasis on writing letters, keeping journals, and compiling statistics, even among barely literate missionaries and preachers. Writings by members of both groups "abound with intimations of divine communications, prophetic whispers, and special guidances."[53] The most profound Mormon adoption of a Methodist tenet, however, was dependence on the inner witness of the Holy Ghost. John Wesley stressed "the witness of the spirit," which he interpreted as "an inward impression on the soul whereby the spirit of God immediately and directly witnesses to my spirit that I am a child of God ... that all my sins are blotted out and I am reconciled to God."[54] In Mormon theology, the "witness of the Spirit," roughly akin to the "gift of the Holy Ghost," has impacted the faith from the beginning. The essence of Mormon understanding on this issue is captured in the Methodist-style exhortation of the last surviving Nephite, Moroni:

> Behold, I would exhort you that when ye shall read these things, if it be wisdom in God that ye should read them, that ye would remember how merciful the Lord hath been unto the children of men, from the creation of Adam even down unto the time that ye shall receive these things, and ponder it in your hearts.
>
> And when ye shall receive these things, I would exhort you that ye would ask God, the Eternal Father, in the name of Christ, if these things are not true; and if ye shall ask with a sincere heart, with real intent,

50. John Wesley's 1780 hymnal was titled *A Collection of Hymns, For the Use of the People Called Methodists.*

51. BC XXVI:2; Wigger, *Taking Heaven by Storm,* 163.

52. Wigger, *Taking Heaven by Storm,* 151-72; for a Mormon parallel, see Lavina Fielding Anderson, *Lucy's Book,* 59n21.

53. John Smith to John Wesley, Aug. 21, 1747, 259.

54. John Wesley, qtd. in Leo Rosten, *Religions in America,* 129.

> having faith in Christ, he will manifest the truth of it unto you, by the power of the Holy Ghost.
>
> And by the power of the Holy Ghost ye may know the truth of all things. (Moro. 10:3-5.)

On February 16, 1832, Joseph Smith announced that the mysteries of God's kingdom "are only to be seen and understood by the power of the Holy Spirit, which God bestows on those who love him, and purify themselves before him" (D&C 76:114-16). No doubt, Wesley would have said "amen" to that sentiment.

Most of the thirty-some baptized members of the newly organized Church of Christ were located in three villages in upstate New York: Manchester, Fayette, and Colesville. At Joseph's call, they assembled at the Whitmer farmstead, where the Church's first general conference was held June 9, 1830. The prophet offered the invocation, then read Ezekiel 14 aloud. Verse 21 describes the Lord's "four sore judgments upon Jerusalem, the sword, and the famine, and the noisome beast, and the pestilence, to cut off from it man and beast." The next verse, however, was probably interpreted as a reference to Book of Mormon peoples: "Yet, behold, therein shall be left a remnant that shall be brought forth, both sons and daughters: behold, they shall come forth unto you, and ye shall see their way and their doings: and ye shall be comforted concerning the evil that I have brought upon Jerusalem."

As part of the conference business, Harrison Smith was ordained an elder, Hyrum and Joseph Sr. priests. Ten brethren received licenses—Methodist-like documents certifying that they were authorized to represent the Church of Christ. The prophet then read aloud the "Articles and Covenants of the Church of Christ," a revelatory document containing instructions about the Church's structure and order (BC XXIV).[55] Afterward, according to Oliver Cowdery's 1830 record, an "Exhortation [was delivered] by Joseph Smith jr."[56] Joseph's history, recorded in 1838-39 added: "Much exhortation and instruction was given, the Holy Ghost was poured out upon us in a miraculous manner—many of our number prophesied, whilst others had the heavens opened to their view, and were so overcome that we had to lay them on beds or other convenient places."[57]

55. A composite document which included Oliver Cowdery's 1829 "Articles and Covenants" was presented to the Church at its first conference in Fayette, New York, on June 9, 1830.

56. Joseph Smith, "Remarks delivered on June 9, 1830 at Fayette, Seneca County, New York," in Donald Q. Cannon and Lyndon W. Cook, *Far West Record,* 2.

57. Joseph Smith, "Manuscript History of the Church," rpt. in Dan Vogel, *Early Mormon Documents,* 1:106.

Newel Knight was one of those who experienced a somewhat dramatic variation on this "falling exercise." The catalepsy trance is as old as religion itself. Persons of spiritually sensitive or easily enkindled temperaments when overcome by intense religious feeling sometimes swoon. Knight later claimed he could not understand why he was on a bed "as he felt no sense of weakness." Like other eighteenth- and nineteenth-century enthusiasts, Knight reported that he "felt his heart filled with love, with glory, and pleasure unspeakable." While entranced, he saw "a vision of the future burst upon him." With his spiritual eyes, he "beheld the Lord Jesus Christ, seated at the right hand of the majesty on high." When Knight and the others recovered, "they shouted hosannas to God and the Lamb, and rehearsed the glorious things which they had seen and felt, whilst they were yet in the spirit." Smith's history interprets these events, not as manifestations common in Methodist gatherings for more than a century, but as God's personal approbation:

> Such scenes as these were calculated to inspire our hearts with joy unspeakable, and fill us with awe and reverence for that Almighty being, by whose grace we had been called to be instrumental in bringing about, for the children of men, the enjoyment of such glorious blessings as were now at this time poured out upon us. To find ourselves engaged in the very same order of things as observed by the holy Apostles of old; to realize the importance and solemnity of such proceedings; and to witness and feel with our own natural senses, the like glorious manifestations of the powers of the Priesthood, the gifts and blessings of the Holy Ghost, and the goodness and condescension of a merciful God unto such as obey the everlasting gospel of our Lord Jesus Christ, combined to create within us sensations of rapturous gratitude, and inspire us with fresh zeal and energy in the cause of truth.[58]

The conference then adjourned to reconvene on September 26. Shortly afterwards, David Whitmer baptized twelve in Seneca Lake, including Joseph Smith's siblings: Katharine, William, and Don Carlos. Joseph then returned to his home and wife in Harmony, Pennsylvania. While there, he began contemplating the "conjecture and conversation" he heard respecting the "lost books" of the Bible. He was particularly intrigued that "Jude ... quotes the Prophecy of Enoch, the seventh from Adam."[59] Accordingly, while in nearby Colesville, Smith reported that the Lord "reveal[ed] the

58. *History of the Church,* 1:85-86.
59. Ibid., 1:132.

following doings of olden times, from the prophecy of Enoch" which was contained in the "Writings of Moses." This disclosure, identified as "revealed to Joseph Smith the Prophet, in June 1830," was eventually included as the Book of Moses, an item in the *Pearl of Great Price,* later adopted as one of the LDS Church's books of canonized scripture.[60]

In the second half of June 1830, Joseph, accompanied by Emma, Oliver Cowdery, and Whitmer brothers John and David, visited the Knight family twenty miles away in Colesville where they found that Joseph Knight Sr., who had finished reading the Book of Mormon and was satisfied it was true, wished to be baptized. So did other members of the Knight family, along with Emma Smith. On Saturday, June 26, a stream on the Knight property was dammed to make a pond. Shortly afterwards, however, some local men and boys wrecked the dam before the baptisms could be performed. The next day, Sunday, Cowdery preached at a meeting in the large Knight barn. Several attendees bore witness of the truthfulness of the Book of Mormon and the doctrines of repentance, baptism for the remission of sins, and the laying on of hands for the gift of the Holy Ghost. A few ruffians attended the services and harassed the congregants: "Cald them fools and said they ware Decived."[61]

Early on Monday morning, June 28, the dam was repaired and thirteen new converts were baptized. Local men and boys jeered the participants, asking if they "had been washing sheep."[62] Ultimately, about fifty men clamored around Knight's house where the Mormonites had retreated. Smith later described the mob as "raging with anger" and wanting to "commit violence upon us." But the small group of Mormons instead moved to Newel Knight's nearby home where the gang continued to mock them.

A meeting had been appointed for that evening to confirm the newly baptized as members of the Church. But as the disciples gathered, Constable Ebenezer Hatch stepped forward and arrested Smith. Joseph said he was arrested for "setting the country in an uproar by preaching the Book of

---

60. Between June and September, Joseph, according to Dan Vogel, "dictated Moses 2:1-5:43a; on October 21, Moses 5:43b-51 in Fayette, New York; on November 30, Moses 5:52-6:18; on December 1, Moses 6:19-52a, probably in Fayette; and later in December, Moses 6:52a-8:12, including the 'Prophecy of Enoch'" (Vogel, *Early Mormon Documents,* 1:138-39). The Book of Moses, published in the *Pearl of Great Price,* was canonized by the LDS Church in 1880.

61. Knight, "Reminiscence," 7. Abram W. Benton, also of Colesville, commenting in April 1831 on Mormon converts, called them "a few weak and silly women, and still more silly men, whose minds are shrouded in a mist of ignorance, which no ray can penetrate, and whose credulity the utmost absurdity cannot equal" (Abram W. Benton, "Mormonites," 1).

62. Joseph Knight Jr., "Joseph Knight's Incidents of History ...," 2.

Mormon."[63] In reality, he was rearrested on the same charge he had narrowly escaped in March 1826 when he was accused of being "a disorderly person and an Impostor." While awaiting her husband's hearing before Joseph P. Chamberlain, a South Bainbridge justice of the peace,[64] Emma arranged to stay with her sister, Elizabeth Hale Wasson, who lived between Colesville and Harmony.

Joseph Knight Sr. later explained the prophet's arrest as the work of locals who "made a Catspaw [a dupe] of a young fellow By the name of Docter Benton in Chenengo County to sware out a warrent against Joseph for as they said pertending to see under ground."[65] Knight loyally followed the arrested Smith to the village, but it was too late to start proceedings that night. Knight asked the penurious prophet if he wanted a lawyer. Smith said he did, and Knight hired James Davidson, a local farmer who practiced law part-time and was, like most attorneys, self-trained.

The next morning, July 1, Davidson remarked that "it looked like a squaley [stormy, windy] Day" and recommended also hiring John S. Reed (1784-1878), another local farmer/lawyer. Knight complied. The circulation of sensational charges against Smith attracted many spectators to the trial; but according to Reed's 1861 reminiscence, the young prophet "sat thare aparently as unconcarned as if he was in his [own] farthers house. When a hard witness would com[e] upon the stand [and I] would say to him that our case Looked bad he said with a smile apon his countanance [I] shall be cleared[;] doe your duty and fear not."[66]

After a day-long trial, a multitude of witnesses failed to provide incriminating testimony against Joseph. When Josiah Stowell and two of his daughters furnished unqualified commendations of Joseph's character, the case was dismissed. Frustrated, Smith's antagonists sought to pursue their case in neighboring Broome County, serving the warrant, as Joseph later recalled, "at the very moment that I was acquitted by this [Chenango County] court."[67] The charge was that "he, the said Joseph Smith, Jr., had been guilty

63. *History of the Church,* 1:88. New York State law defined a "disorderly person" as "all jugglers [deceiver, trickster, cheat, conjuror], and all persons pretending to have skill in physiognomy, palmistry, or like crafty science, or pretending to tell fortunes, or to discover where lost goods may be found" *(Laws of the State of New York, Revised, 1813,* 1:114, sec. I). Smith's lawyer, John S. Reed, wrote to Brigham Young in 1861 that Joseph was arrested "for the crime of Glass Looking and Juglin forten [fortune]" (John S. Reed to Brigham Young, Dec. 6, 1861).

64. For Judge Chamberlin's "Bill of Costs," see Vogel, *Early Mormon Documents,* 4:267-70.

65. Joseph Knight Sr., "Reminiscence," 7.

66. Reed to Young, Dec. 6, 1861, 1.

67. Joseph Smith, "Manuscript History of the Church," 45, in Vogel, *Early Mormon Documents,* 1:119.

of a breach of the peace, against the good people of the State of New York, by looking through a certain stone to find hid treasures, &c, within the Statute of Limitation."[68] A constable escorted Smith to a nearby tavern where he was held for the night, starved, and mistreated. Newel Knight said that Joseph's mockers, in a parody of Jesus's passion, "Spit upon him, pointed their fingers at him, say=ing prophecy, p<ro>phesy."[69]

Between the two court hearings, Reed and Joseph Knight Sr. rode to Hezekiah Peck's house in Colesville where a group of Mormon women, including Emma Smith, had gathered "for the purpose of praying for the deliverance of the Prophet of the Lord." When the women came out to the wagon, Reed was greatly affected by the sight of Emma's "crimson cheeks … wet with tears that came streaming from her eyes. … [I]t seemed that her very heart strings [were] broken with grief."[70] Reinvigorated, Reed went with Knight to Colesville, the seat of Broome County, again to defend Smith, with Davidson's assistance, before Justice Joel K. Noble. "These men," Joseph later reported, "although not regular lawyers, were upon this occasion able to put to silence their opponents, and convince the court that I was innocent. They spoke like men inspired of God."[71] According to Reed, Smith's opponents had spared "[n]either talents nor money … to ensure them success. They employed the ablest lawyer in that county, introduced twenty witnesses before dark, but proved nothing."[72]

After the judge deliberated for thirty minutes, Joseph was brought back into the chambers. "Mr. Smith," a spokesman said, "we have had your case under consideration, examined the testimony, and find nothing to condemn you; and therefore you are discharged." But the judge proceeded nonetheless to "reprimand him severely," said Reed, "not because anything derogatory to his character in any shape had been proven against him … but merely to please those fiends in human shape who were engaged in the unhallowed persecution of an innocent man, sheerly on account of his religious opinions."[73]

Justice of the Peace Noble, however, recalled the trial, almost twelve years later, differently. "Proof [was] manifested by I think 43 witnesses," he remembered, "Proof [that] Jo. [was] a vagrant idler, lazy ([but] not [a]

68. "Mormonism," in *New England Christian Herald,* Nov. 7, 1832, 23.
69. Newel Knight, Autobiography, 7.
70. Qtd. in *History of the Church,* 6:395.
71. Ibid., 1:91-94.
72. Ibid., 6:395.
73. Ibid., 6:396.

drunkard) but now and then drunk. [Also a] liar [and] deceiver. Jo [was] a nuisance to good society … [and] any thing but a good man."[74]

After Joseph left the courtroom, a mob swarmed about him, threatening to "railride me, and tar, and feather me."[75] He found sanctuary at the nearby home of Emma's brother-in-law, Benjamin Wasson. "We got him away that night," said Reed, "from the midst of three hundred people without his receiving any injury; but I am well aware that we were assisted by some higher power than man; for to look back on the scene, I cannot tell how we succeeded in getting him away. I take no glory to myself: it was the Lord's work and marvelous in our eyes."[76] The next day, July 4, Joseph and Emma arrived home in Harmony.

A few days later, Joseph returned to the Knight home with Cowdery to confirm those who had recently been baptized. The duo had scarcely arrived when someone spotted them, and a gang of miscreants began to gather. The two Mormons left town with the gang in pursuit. They traveled throughout the night, arriving safely in Harmony the next morning.[77] "Thus were we persecuted on account of our religious faith," Joseph recorded, "in a country the Constitution of which guarantees to everyman the indefeasible right to worship God according to the dictates of his own conscience—and by men, too, who were professors of religion, and who were not backward to maintain the right of religious liberty for themselves, though they could thus wantonly deny it to us."[78]

---

74. Joel King Noble to Jonathan B. Turner, Mar. 8, 1842, 2.

75. *History of the Church,* 1:96.

76. Ibid., 6:396.

77. Richard Bushman suggests that on this long, anxious night, Smith and Cowdery received the Melchizedek Priesthood from the trio of ancient apostles Peter, James, and John (Bushman, *Joseph Smith and the Beginnings of Mormonism,* 163, 240-41). Joseph, while never specifically dating this significant event, several years later said that it took place "in the wilderness between Harmony, Susquehanna county, and Colesville, Broome county, on the Susquehanna River" (Joseph Smith to the Church of Jesus Christ of Latter Day Saints, Sept. 6, 1842). But David and John Whitmer later told Edward Stevenson that "they do not have any knowledge of, neither do the records show, concerning Peter, James, and John's coming to the prophet Joseph" (qtd. in Joseph Grant Stevenson, *The Stevenson Family History,* 1:177-78). William E. McLellin, who joined the Church in August 1831, wrote: "I never heard of John the Baptist ordaining Joseph and Oliver. I heard not of James, Peter, and John doing so" (McLellin to J. L. Traughber, Aug. 25, 1877). And though McLellin reported he heard Smith tell the story of the Church's founding, "I never heard of … John, or Peter, James and John" (McLellin to Elder D. H. Bays, May 24, 1870). The first public announcement of these angelic ordinations occurred in Kirtland, Ohio, on February 12, 1834 *(History of the Church,* 2:25).

78. *History of the Church,* 1:97. On August 28, 1830, Smith and John Whitmer wrote to the Colesville Saints:

> Were it not for the prayers of you few, the Almighty would have thundered down his wrath upon the inhabitants of that place, but be not faint, the day of your deliverance is not

Throughout the month of July 1830, the prophet continued to issue revelations and pronouncements intended to enhance his position within the fold of the faithful and to articulate his financial needs. Commanded to "Magnify thine office," he was told to sow his fields and then "go speedily unto the church, which is in Colesville, Fayette and Manchester, and they shall support thee; and I will bless them both spiritually and temporally." In the event "the church" did not provide assistance, the revelation warned: "I will send upon them a cursing instead of a blessing." The revelation then defined for the Church what Joseph's role would be:

> [T]hou shalt continue in calling upon God in my name, and writing the things which shall be given thee by the Comforter; And expounding all scriptures unto the church, and it shall be given thee in the very moment, what thou shalt speak and write; and they shall hear it, or I will send unto them a cursing instead of a blessing: For thou shalt devote all thy service in Zion. And in this thou shalt have strength. Be patient in afflictions, for thou shall have many: But endure them, for lo, I am with you, even unto the end of thy days. And in temporal labors thou shalt not have strength, for this is not thy calling. (BC XXV:4-14.)[79]

At the same time, the prophet also delivered a revelatory communiqué to Emma, who had voiced concerns about not being included in the circle of those who had seen the golden plates and about how they would survive after Joseph abandoned farming. The message began soothingly:

> Emma, my daughter in Zion, a revelation I give unto you, concerning my will: Behold thy sins are forgiven thee, and thou art an elect lady,

---

> far distant for the judgements of the Lord are already abroad in the earth and the cold hand of death will soon pass through your neighborhood, and sweep away some of your most bitter enemies, for you need not suppose that God will be mocked at, and his commandments be trampled under their feet. … But brethren be not discouraged when we tell you of perilous times, for they must shortly come, for the sword, famine, and pestilence are approaching, for there shall be great destructions upon the face of this land. (Smith to Colesville Saints, Aug. 28, 1830.)

79. Joseph's brother William, also wanting others to labor on his behalf, importuned an RLDS priesthood quorum in 1883 when he was seventy-two:

> I respectfully submit to this conference that I am at liberty, should they be so impressed by the spirit of the Master, to go into the field of labor, wherever this conference may deem it wisdom that I should go; and it is further my desire and wish to be relieved from the monotony of a life confined on a farm where necessity of hard labor like a canker worm is constantly destroying my ministerial and spiritual food and spiritual life, and that my temporal days and temporal life may be prolonged, I ask this conference to make such action in my case as will give me a life and place that will enable me to add my testimony with the rest of my brethren that are here in conference for the coming year, as the Lord by his good spirit shall direct. (William Smith, qtd. in "Ministry Reports.")

> whom I have called. Murmur not because of the things which thou hast not seen, for they are withheld from thee, and from the world, which is wisdom in me in a time to come. And the office of thy calling shall be for a comfort unto my servant Joseph, thy husband, in his afflictions, with consoling words, in the spirit of meekness. And thou shalt go with him at the time of his going, and be unto him for a scribe, that I may send Oliver whithersoever I will. And thou shalt be ordained under his hand to expound scriptures, and to exhort the church, according as it shall be given thee by my Spirit: For he shall lay his hands upon thee, and thou shalt receive the Holy Ghost, and thy time shall be given to writing, and to learning much. And thou needest not fear, for thy husband shall support thee from the church: For unto them is his calling. (BC XXVI:1-9.)[80]

Emma was satisfied; but within days another challenge to the prophet's authority arose. Second Elder Oliver Cowdery, having returned to Fayette, wrote to Smith alleging that the "Articles and covenants of the Church of Christ" contained an erroneous phrase—part of what is now verse 37: "and truly manifest by their works that they have received of the Spirit of Christ unto a remission of their sins." Cowdery then commanded Smith "in the name of God to erase those words, that no priestcraft be amongst us."[81] The previous year, Cowdery had issued a revelation which appears to have been an early version of "The Articles and Covenants." This document is titled "A commandment from God unto Oliver how he should build up his church & the manner thereof." It includes most of the Articles and Covenants, but not the phrase Cowdery considered erroneous. Possibly, as Peter Crawley reasons, "[S]ome of his anxiety resulted from what he [Cowdery] perceived to be an unauthorized addition to a revelation directed to him."[82]

Joseph traveled to Fayette to diffuse the situation. Cowdery had convinced the Whitmers of his position, but the prophet persuaded them that the offending phrase was indeed correct. Meanwhile, Isaac Hale had become increasingly irritated with his son-in-law. The hard-working hunter/farmer was angry that his daughter and son-in-law were essentially living off the sweat of others' brows. To make matters worse, two years earlier Joseph

80. The phrase "support thee from the church" was later changed to: "support thee in the church." Compare 1835 *Doctrine and Covenants* 48:2.

81. Priestcraft: "The stratagems and frauds of priests; fraud or imposition in religious concerns; management of selfish and ambitious priests to gain wealth and power, or to impose on the credulity of others" (Noah Webster, *American Dictionary of the English Language* [1828], s.v. "Priestcraft").

82. Crawley, "The Passage of Mormon Primitivism," 28.

had contracted with Hale to buy the thirteen-acre farm on which he and Emma were living, but he had not yet completed the purchase. Pressed by his father-in-law, Joseph paid the mortgage in full on August 25, 1830, with money he borrowed from a lending company.[83]

In early September, Newel and Sally Knight had visited the Smiths in Harmony. Neither Sally nor Emma had been formally confirmed as new members of the Church of Christ after their baptisms, so Joseph planned a small service to complete this stage of admission. The prophet evidently set out to purchase a bottle of wine for the sacrament but had only gone a short distance before realizing he had no money. "I was met by a heavenly messenger," he later reported, "and received the following revelation: 'Listen to the voice of Jesus Christ ... for behold, I say unto you, that it mattereth not what ye shall eat, or what ye shall drink, when ye partake of the sacrament, if it so be that ye do it with an eye single to my glory; remembering unto the Father my body which was laid down for you, and my blood which was shed for the remission of your sins: Wherefore, a commandment I give unto you, that you shall not purchase wine, neither strong drink of your enemies: Wherefore, you shall partake of none except it is made new among you'" (BC XXVIII:1-5). Returning to his home where grapes were ripening, he and his friends pressed out some juice and "partook together of the Sacrament, after which we confirmed these two sisters into the Church, and spent the evening in a glorious manner. The Spirit of the Lord was poured out upon us, we praised the Lord God, and rejoiced exceedingly."[84]

Despite promises of spiritual abundance, what Joseph called "a spirit of persecution" began to brew in the neighborhood, spurred by Emma's maternal uncle, Nathaniel Lewis. His strategy was to persuade Isaac Hale no longer to provide Joseph and Emma a sanctuary. Joseph's version is that Lewis "told him [Hale] falsehoods concerning me of the most shameful nature, which turned the old gentleman and his family so much against us that they would no longer promise us protection."[85] Although Joseph is not specific about the "shameful" falsehoods, Lewis later made an affidavit declaring, also in non-specific terms, that "Joseph Smith Jr. is not a man of truth and veracity; and that his general character in this part of the country,

83. Hale signed over the Harmony property to Smith on this date with John Whitmer and Jesse Lane as witnesses. Smith gave George H. Noble & Co. his promissory note for $190.95. For these documents, see Vogel, *Early Mormon Documents,* 4:424-35.

84. *History of the Church,* 1:108.

85. Ibid.

is that of an impostor, hypocrite and liar."[86] Whatever the details, the Harmony folk began to turn against Joseph.

Benefactor Newell Knight was summoned from Colesville to transport the needy Smiths to Fayette, where Peter Whitmer Sr., "having heard of the persecutions against us … invited us to go and live with him." Emma's adieu to her parents, relinquishing all hope for a reconciliation between her husband and father, was painful. The day she and Joseph climbed aboard Knight's wagon marked the last time she would ever see her girlhood home, her mother, or her father. In early September, the displaced couple arrived at Fayette, "amidst the congratulations of our brethren and friends."[87] Emma by now was pregnant with twins who would be born April 30, 1831, and like baby Alvin die in infancy. Lucy Smith wrote:

> Emma's health at this time was quite delicate, yet she did not favor herself on this account, but whatever hands found to do, she did with her might, until she went so far beyond her strength, that she brought upon herself a heavy fit of sickness, which lasted four weeks. And, although her strength was exhausted, still her spirits were the same, which, in fact, was always the case with her, even under the most trying circumstances. I have never seen a woman in my life, who would endure every species of fatigue and hardship, from month to month, and from year to year, with that unflinching courage, zeal, and patience, which she has ever done.[88]

After the Smiths squeezed themselves into their Fayette lodgings, Joseph discovered that Hiram Page, one of the Book of Mormon eight witnesses, supported by Cowdery and the Whitmers, was claiming to receive his own inspiration through a small black seer stone. Page was conveying revelations about the building of the new Zion and the true order of the Church.[89] According to Newel Knight, Page had "quite a roll of papers full of these revelations," which were "in contradiction to the New Testament and the revelations of these last days."[90] Pages's scrying activities should not be surprising, considering that, in an embryonic congregation like the Church of Christ, everyone was expected to enjoy divine intuition. But the

86. Nathaniel Lewis, Statement, Mar. 20, 1834, in Vogel, *Early Mormon Documents,* 4:488-89.

87. *History of the Church,* 1:109.

88. Anderson, *Lucy's Book,* 503.

89. Hiram Page, five years older than Joseph Smith, had married Catherine Whitmer in 1825.

90. Newel Knight, Journal, 64.

prophet, apparently still nettled by Cowdery's presumption, declared that Page's claims "were entirely at variance with the order of God's house, as laid down in the New Testament, as well as in our late revelations."[91] Accordingly, he pronounced a revelation putting both Cowdery and Page in their place: "[N]o one shall be appointed to receive commandments and revelations in this church excepting my servant Joseph." Furthermore, "thou shalt not command him who is at thy head, and at the head of the church." The revelation instructed Cowdery to "take thy brother Hiram between him and thee alone, and tell him that those things which he hath written from that stone are not of me, and that satan deceiveth him" (BC XXX:2, 6, 11).[92]

At the scheduled three-day September general conference, Page was on the agenda. The prophet convinced those present, including Page, to renounce the stone and any revelations received through it. The conference then voted that Joseph alone was to "receive and write Revelations & Commandments for this Church."[93] The prophet later testified that "much of the power of God manifested amongst us; the Holy Ghost came upon us, and filled us with joy unspeakable; and peace, and faith, and hope, and charity abounded in our midst."[94] To prove his sincerity, Page gave up the stone, which was pulverized into dust.[95]

In another move, intended to deflect any further challenges from Cowdery, Joseph in September, just prior to the fall conference, assigned his second-in-command to undertake a distant mission, far removed from the seat of authority in the Church of Christ. "Behold I say unto you, that you

91. *History of the Church,* 1:110.

92. The same issue of primacy arose in 1831 when a woman named Hubble began receiving revelations in Kirtland, Ohio, on behalf of others. The prophet responded: "And this ye shall know assuredly, that there is none other appointed unto you to receive commandments and revelations until he [Smith] be taken, if he abide in me. But verily, verily I say unto you, that none else shall be appointed unto this gift except it be through him, for if it be taken from him he shall not have power, except to appoint another in his stead" (BC XLV:3-4). In 1833, Joseph wrote to a Church member in Missouri: "[I]t is contrary to the economy of God for any member of the Church, or any one, to receive instructions for those in authority, higher than themselves. ... [I]f any person have a vision ... it must be for his own benefit and instruction" *(History of the Church,* 1:338).

93. Cannon and Cook, *Far West Record,* 3.

94. *History of the Church,* 1:115.

95. Martin Harris's brother, Emer, made the following statement in Provo, Utah, on April 6, 1856: "Br Hiram Page Dug out of the earth a black stone put it in his pocket[.] When he got home he looked at it it Contained a Sentence on paper to be [illegible] it as soon as he wrote one sentence another sentence came on the stone until he wrote 16 pages. Br Joseph was told of the fact one person asked Joseph if it was right he said he did not know but he prayed and got revelation that the stone was of the devil then it was Broke to powder and the writings burnt it was a work of the power of darkness" (Emer Harris, Statement, Apr. 6, 1856).

shall go unto the Lamanites and preach my gospel unto them," declared this revelation, "and cause my church to be established among them." Joseph's revelation then linked this mission with the future site of the anticipated city of New Jerusalem: "[I]t is not revealed, and no man knoweth where the city shall be built ... [but] it shall be on the borders by the Lamanites" (BC XXX:8-9).

The Church of Christ, numbering about sixty, had learned by revelation that God wanted them to be "gathered in unto one place, upon the face of this land, to prepare their hearts, and be prepared in all things, against the day when tribulation and desolation are sent forth upon the wicked: For the hour is nigh, and the day soon at hand" (BC XXIX:9). By "the day," the revelation meant the Millennium and second coming of Jesus, but the righteous first had to assemble in Zion, the city of refuge. Mormon eyes turned westward, where this New Jerusalem would rise on borders shared with the Lamanites.

Since the War of 1812, the federal government had encouraged Indians to move west. On May 26, 1830, Congress passed the Indian Removal Act, after four months of debate. U.S. President Andrew Jackson signed the bill into law authorizing him to transfer and resettle Native American tribes to lands west of the Mississippi River. Many of them were already living in the region of present-day Kansas and Oklahoma.[96] Their displacement was a political reality of the burgeoning nation; but from the time the Puritans landed in New England, the Christian conversion of the Indians had been a project dear to the Anglo-American heart. Joseph Smith had declared as early as July 1828 that the golden plates had been preserved for nearly two millennia so that the "Lamanites might come to the knowledge of their fathers, and that they might know the promises of the Lord, and that they may believe the gospel and rely upon the merits of Jesus Christ, and be glorified through faith in his name; and that through their repentance they might be saved" (BC II:6).

The Book of Mormon underscored this doctrine. Enos 1:15-16 explained that the records were sacred, preserved from marauders so that God could eventually "bring them forth unto the Lamanites in his own due

96. Jackson believed that there could be no peace for the Indians east of the Mississippi: "By persuasion and force they [i.e., our ancestors] have been made to retire from river to river and from mountain to mountain, until some of the tribes have become extinct and others have left but remnants to preserve for a while their once terrible names. Surrounded by the whites with their arts of civilization, which by destroying the resources of the savage doom him to weakness and decay, the fate of the Mohegan, the Narragansett, and the Delaware is fast overtaking the Choctaw, the Cherokee, and the Creek. That this fate surely awaits them if they remain within the limits of the States does not admit of a doubt." (Qtd. in H. W. Brands, *Andrew Jackson, His Life and Times,* 435-36.)

time." Jarom 1:2 indicates that the plates "are written for the intent of the benefit of our brethren the Lamanites." Mormon, one of the last Nephite survivors, addressed the victorious Lamanites in these terms: "I would speak somewhat unto the remnant of this people who are spared … that they may know of the things of their fathers; yea, I speak unto you, ye remnant of the house of Israel" (Morm. 7:1). His son, Moroni, Joseph's future angelic messenger, lamented as the curtains fell upon Nephite culture: "I write a few more things, that perhaps they may be of worth unto my brethren, the Lamanites, in some future day" (Moro. 1:4).

The Mormons viewed the government's relocation of the American Indians as God's work. W. W. Phelps, editor of an official Mormon newspaper, in 1832 wrote: "[T]hanks to him who rules all things after the counsel of his own will, and whose words never fail, the people of the United States, are already witnesses of the fulfilling of this prophecy, for they daily behold the children of God, gathering into his kingdom, ready to meet the Lord when he comes in his glory. … When we see Indians gathered home by the government, we must exclaim the hand of the Lord is too plain in all this."[97]

In October 1830, Joseph, speaking for God, extended Cowdery's missionary call to Peter Whitmer Jr., Parley P. Pratt, and Ziba Peterson. They were to journey to the western borders of the nation and deliver the Book of Mormon message to these dark-skinned Israelites. Their assignment underscored the Mormon understanding of the origin and history of these frontier Indians but went further in offering a prophecy of their conversion to Christianity. Joseph's revelations foresaw their becoming a "white and delightsome people" (2 Ne. 30:6) who "will marshal themselves, and shall become exceedingly angry, and shall vex the Gentiles with a sore vexation" (D&C 87:5). The missionaries expected that their Indian brothers and sisters, not differentiated as tribes, would embrace the Book of Mormon, recognize that they were a remnant of the House of Israel, and accept Jesus as Messiah.

On October 17, as the four missionaries were making their preparations in Manchester, New York, they bound themselves by a covenant that Cowdery recorded in these terms:

> I, Oliver, being commanded of the Lord God, to go forth unto the Lamanites, to proclaim glad tidings of great joy unto them, by presenting

97. W. W. Phelps, "The Book of Mormon," 59. Phelps later wrote that the arrival of some 360 Kickapoos and Pottowattamies at eastern Independence, Missouri, fulfilled one of Isaiah's promises (see Phelps, "Israel Will Be Gathered," 101).

> unto them the fullness of the gospel of the only begotten son of God, and also, to rear up a pillar, as a witness where the Temple of God shall be built, in the glorious New Jerusalem; and having certain brothers with me, who are called of God to assist me, whose names are Parley, Peter, and Ziba, do therefore most solemnly covenant before God, that I will walk humbly before him, and do this business, and this glorious work according as he shall direct me by the Holy Ghost; ever praying for mine and their prosperity, and deliverance from bonds, and from imprisonments, and whatsoever may befall us, with all patience and faith.—Amen.[98]

Joseph, David, Parley, Ziba, and Peter also signed this testament. Then the four elders departed. Their route led west for more than 1,500 miles through the heartland of a sparsely settled country. They would travel nearly the entire distance carrying bedrolls and packs loaded with foodstuffs, clothing, and as many copies of the Book of Mormon as they could heft, courtesy of Martin Harris. They were young and strong, unintimidated by great distances, quickened by a new faith. They started their mission at the height of a glorious Indian summer, armored in the conviction that they were embarked upon God's holy errand.

98. Rpt. in Ezra Booth, "Letter VIII."

18 | TO THE OHIO

> *Wherefore I the Lord, knowing the calamity which should come upon the inhabitants of the earth, called upon my servant Joseph, and spake unto him from heaven, and gave him commandments ... and all this that it might be fulfilled, which was written by the prophets: The weak things of the world should come forth and break down the mighty and strong ones ....*
>
> —BC I:4

The Mormonite missionaries to the Lamanites did not immediately make a beeline toward their destination—the "borders by the Lamanites" near present-day Kansas City. Instead they preached their way west, toward Buffalo, New York. There, wrote Parley P. Pratt, they taught "the gospel in its fulness, and distributed the record of their forefathers among ... the Catteraugus Indians."[1] As there was no Catteraugus tribe, Pratt meant the Cattaraugus Reservation of the Seneca Nation, forty miles south of Buffalo on the shores of Lake Erie, near present-day Irving. This preserve was created in 1797 from 2.6 million acres of lands ceded to the Holland Land Company by the Six Iroquois Nations.[2] Five Iroquois reservations were created in this acreage on the Niagara frontier: the Tonawanda, Allegany, Cattaraugus, and Tuscarora Reservations, and the Buffalo Creek Reservation, site of present-day West Seneca, New York.

This latter location, nearer to Buffalo, is the second possible site for the Lamanite missionaries' 1830 visit. Little was accomplished there, however, because language difficulties made it next to impossible to communicate with the Seneca tribesmen.[3] The missionaries left behind two copies of the

1. Parley P. Pratt, *Autobiography of Parley Parker Pratt*, 57.

2. This Seneca compromise was made at the Treaty of Big Tree nearly Buffalo, New York ("Seneca Indians—Useful Resources on and off the Web"; "Information about the Seneca Indians from THIS Seneca's perspective"; "Early Cattaraugus County History").

3. The Seneca were ultimately ordered from their lands in the Treaty of Buffalo Creek (1838), by the terms of which the remaining four Seneca reservations in New York (Buffalo

Book of Mormon, then set off southwesterly towards Pennsylvania and the Western Reserve area of the Buckeye State. There, near Cleveland, lived Sidney Rigdon, a Reformed Baptist minister whom Pratt had known for several years. The four missionaries arrived near the Rigdon place in Mentor, Ohio, on Thursday, October 28. Dividing into pairs, they began to proselytize. Oliver Cowdery and Pratt first knocked on Rigdon's door. After listening to their reports of the coming forth of the Book of Mormon, and praise of the prophet, Rigdon rebuffed them. "He had one Bible," the clergyman said, "which he believed was a revelation from God and with which he pretended to have some acquaintance; but with respect to the book they had presented him, he must say that he had considerable doubt."[4] Sidney did agree to read this new Bible, however, and spent the entire night doing so by candlelight. The next evening, Cowdery and Pratt preached to a large crowd in Rigdon's assembly hall. At the conclusion of his remarks, Pratt invited Rev. Rigdon's comments. "The information they had that evening received," he later observed, was of an extraordinary character, and "certainly demanded their most serious consideration."[5] After the services ended, Pratt and Cowdery walked Rigdon home where they stayed, talking deep into the night. Promising to finish the Book of Mormon, Rigdon agreed to "frankly tell them his mind and feelings on the subject."[6]

When Cowdery and Pratt returned a day or two later, Rigdon had almost fulfilled the promise. His son Wycliffe remembered that his father "got so engaged in [the book] that it was hard for him to quit long enough to eat his meals. He read it both day and night."[7] Rigdon was anxious to find out what he could about Joseph Smith. When Cowdery related that his twenty-four-year-old cousin had "hardly a common school education," Rigdon responded: "[I]f that was all the education he had, he never wrote the book."[8] In his own later account of this conversation, Sidney "expressed the utmost amazement

---

Creek, Tonawanda, Cattaraugus, and Allegany) were sold after which provisions were made for the Senecas to relocate in Kansas. The corrupt treaty was protested, however, and a new one endorsed in 1842. This treaty allowed the sale of Buffalo Creek and Tonawanda, but preserved the Allegany and Cattaraugus Reservations. As a result of the Buffalo Creek treaties, some Senecas moved near "the borders of the Lamanite" in Kansas. Most did not, and of those who did, all but two returned (Anthony F. C. Wallace, *Death and Rebirth of the Seneca,* 2; "Seneca," *Encyclopedia of North American Indians,* 2).

4. *History of the Church,* 1:123-24; Karl Keller, "'I Never Knew a Time When I Did Not Know Joseph Smith,'" 23.

5. *History of the Church,* 1:124.

6. Ibid.

7. Wycliffe Rigdon, qtd. in Keller, "'I Never Knew a Time,'" 24.

8. Ibid.

that such a man should write a book which seemed to shed a flood of light on all the old scriptures, open all their profoundest mysteries, and give them perfect consistency." If God ever gave a revelation to man, Rigdon concluded, "surely this must be divine."[9] Despite his enthusiasm, Sidney craved a divine sign of assurance. According to Disciples of Christ historian Amos Sutton Hayden, "the sign appeared, and he was convinced that Mormonism was of God!"[10] Rigdon in 1834 described this sign as a vision:

> [T]o my astonishment I saw the different orders of professing Christians passing before my eyes, with their hearts exposed to view, and they were as corrupt as corruption itself. That society to which I belonged [the Reformed Baptists] also passed before my eyes, and to my astonishment it was as corrupt as the others. Last of all that little man who bro't me the Book of Mormon [Cowdery], passed before my eyes with his heart open, and it was as pure as an angel; and this was a testimony from God; that the Book of Mormon, was a Divine Revelation.[11]

Meanwhile, the success of Mormon missionary work in the area was astonishing. Word spread like a wildfire that preachers from the East had brought an apocalyptic message. And many listeners were prepared to welcome it. "There were many at the time who believed the millennium was at hand," wrote Hayden,

> and in 1830 there were those who were convinced it had dawned. ... The long-expected day of gospel glory would very soon be ushered in. ... These glowing expectations formed the staple of many sermons. They were the continued and exhaustless topic of conversation. They animated the hope and inspired the zeal to a high degree of the converts and many of the advocates of the gospel. Millennial hymns were learned and sung with a joyful fervor and hope surpassing the conception of worldly and carnal professors. It was amid a people full of these expectations, and with hearts fired with these things, that Mormonism was brought, and there is small wonder that it found a welcome.[12]

9. Sidney Rigdon, Interviewed by Austin W. Cowles, in Cowles, "The Mormons," 61.

10. Amos Sutton Hayden, *Early History of the Disciples in the Western Reserve,* 186.

11. Sidney Rigdon, qtd. in Eber D. Howe, *Mormonism Unvailed,* 217.

12. Hayden, *Early History of the Disciples in the Western Reserve,* 183. "From about 1810 to 1845," wrote Curtis Dahl, an observer of the American scene in 1959,

> an influential though now half-forgotten group of American poets, novelists and painters had celebrated, though only artistically, terrific, blood-curdling destruction ... preferably by cataclysmic supernatural forces, of whole cities, nations, races or indeed of the world itself.

After a few weeks of fervid activity and intense exhortation, in October and November, 127 souls, including Rigdon ultimately, gathered at the river, were baptized, and became enveloped in the folds of the new church. The number of new converts far exceeded the entire membership in the East. Cowdery wrote to Joseph on November 12, 1830, informing him that fifty-five people had recently been baptized in northern Ohio. Cowdery introduced Rigdon in the letter, advising Smith that "sooner or later" the dynamic new disciple would travel east to meet the prophet. "Receive him [as] if from my own bosom, for he is as I am," Cowdery wrote, unaware that Rigdon's influence in the young church would quickly eclipse his own.[13]

Despite their success, Cowdery and the other missionaries felt they could postpone their journey no longer as autumn advanced into winter. After ordaining Rigdon, Isaac Morley, Lyman Wight, John Murdock, and others to the ministry, they sent a second letter to the prophet asking him to appoint a presiding elder to superintend the rapidly growing work. On January 4, 1831, the prophet dispatched twenty-eight-year-old John Whitmer to fill this assignment.

On November 16, 1830, Eber D. Howe, editor of the *Painesville* [Ohio] *Telegraph,* announced the missionaries' departure "for the regions beyond the Mississippi, where [Smith] contemplated founding a 'City of Refuge' for his followers, and converting the Indians under his prophetic authority."[14] Other newspapers along the way picked up the story of the epic trek. The missionaries to the Lamanites "are now on their way to the Western Indians, for whose benefit the new Revelation [the Book of Mormon] was especially designed," wrote Warren Isham, editor of the *Observer and Reflector,* only two days later. Isham also reported Cowdery's claim that these "Aborigines of America" were "part of the tribe of Manasseh ... and from them descended all the Indians of America," but as fast as they converted, they would "become white men."[15] The *Republican Advocate* of Wooster, Ohio, reported two weeks later that the wayfarers "have now gone west of the Mississippi, where

These connoisseurs of holocausts, dilettantes of disaster, form an American "School of Catastrophe" that bridges the gap between literature and painting and offers an amusing yet valuable insight into the taste of early nineteenth-century America. (Dahl, "The American School of Catastrophe," 380.)

13. Newel Knight, Journal, qtd. in Dan Vogel, *Joseph Smith,* 542.

14. Eber D. Howe, "The Book of Mormon," *Painesville* [Ohio] *Telegraph,* Nov. 16, 1830, 3. It documents this quotation: announced the missionaries' departure "for the regions beyond the Mississippi, where [Smith] contemplated founding a 'City of Refuge' for his followers, and converting the Indians under his prophetic authority."

15. Warren Isham, "The Golden Bible, or Campbellism Improved."

they say is a holy spot, and there they are to establish a New Jerusalem, into which will be gathered all the Natives who they say are descendants of Manasseh. They say they are led by the spirit and will know the ground when they place their feet on it."[16]

Meanwhile, in distant Manchester, New York, financial disaster once again menaced the Smith family. Joseph Sr. was sentenced to thirty days in debtors' prison, and Hyrum fled the county to avoid creditors. Years later, reflecting on this phase of his life, Joseph Jr. would say: "I brought salvation to my father's house, as an instrument in the hand of God, when they were in a miserable situation."[17] But he would not procure sufficient Church monies to sustain his extended family until after he settled in Ohio, where there were more affluent Saints. There he would establish, at least temporarily, a fragile utopian dream of communitarianism, where men "had all things common and sold their possessions and goods, and parted them to all men, as every man had need" (Acts 2:44-45). Joseph's principle, which he called "the more perfect law of the Lord,"[18] was especially suited to benefit the chronically indigent like the Smiths.

Early America distinguished between the "impotent poor," who were incapable of work (for example, the elderly and the severely disabled), and the "able poor," who could labor to help support themselves. This latter class was generally viewed as irresponsible and undeserving of charity, their own bad habits (intemperance) and character defects (laziness) assumed to be the cause of their poverty.[19] Care of the poor, however, had become part of a rising tide of general social reform, and change was in the air. On November 27, 1824, New York State passed legislation mandating that the supervisors of each county "direct the purchase of one or more tracts of land, not exceedingly the quantity of two hundred acres, and thereon build and erect, for the accommodation, employment and use of the said county, one or more suitable buildings, to be denominated the poor house of that county."[20]

16. "The Golden Bible," *Republican Advocate* [Wooster, Ohio], Dec. 4, 1830.

17. Joseph Smith Jr. to William Smith, Dec. 18, 1835, in Dean C. Jessee, *The Personal Writings of Joseph Smith,* 116.

18. The earliest revelation in Kirtland pertaining to Smith's personal financial matters commanded the Saints to "provide for him food and raiment and whatsoever thing he needeth to accomplish the work, wherewith I have commanded him" (BC XLV:12).

19. The "Report of the Secretary of [New York] State in 1824 on the Relief and Settlement of the Poor" noted that "at least 1585 male persons were reduced to the state [of poverty] by the excessive use of ardent spirits" (2).

20. "1824 Law Establishing County Poorhouses in New York," www.poorhousestory.com/1824 law.htm (accessed Apr. 26, 2004).

Joel Weed, the father of Joseph Smith's fellow New Yorker, Thurlow Weed, was a man seemingly cut from the same pattern as Joseph Smith Sr. According to his son, Weed had "an earnest desire to do the best he could for his children" but "was doomed to earn his bread by the sweat of his brow" as "a farmer." Like the Smiths, calamity seemed to follow the Weeds with the result "that we were always poor, sometimes very poor." He explains it as "misfortune rather than the fault of my parents, for they were always struggling to promote the welfare of their children."[21] His father "worked hard, but never prospered. The debtor's prison, therefore, was ever staring us in the face," and Weed Sr. was not alone in dreading imprisonment.[22]

Joseph Sr. was condemned to debtors' prison at nearby Canandaigua in early October 1830, while Hyrum barely escaped that fate shortly thereafter as his own finances began to unravel. On April 7, 1830, the day after the new church was inaugurated, Hyrum signed a promissory note to a local farrier who shod his horse. By September, the debt remained unpaid, and Justice Nathan Pierce issued an execution to collect the balance on the threat of incarceration. On October 26, Constable Nathan Harrington attempted to serve the warrant but returned empty handed: "No property to be found Nor [Body]," reported the official. Hyrum had already left town for Colesville, New York.[23]

Joseph Sr., like Hyrum, could have escaped his creditors, since in late September the prophet had commanded him to "go forthwith to Waterloo, and prepare a place for our family, as our enemies also sought his destruction in the neighborhood in which we then resided."[24] But the fifty-nine-year-old Smith hesitated. Shortly after Hyrum fled with his family, several of his note holders called on Lucy Smith, seeking information about Hyrum's whereabouts. Typically in that period, when creditors heard that their debtor might be leaving the area, having liquidated most of his belongings to fund travel, they sought to obtain a settlement of their promissory note while the debtor was still available.[25]

---

21. Harriet A. Weed, *Autobiography of Thurlow Weed,* 1-2.

22. Ibid., 6.

23. Lucy Smith told this story as an example of Hyrum's religious devotion, omitting his legal difficulties: "Hyrum had settled up his business, for the purpose of being at liberty to do whatever the Lord required of him: and he requested Joseph to ask the Lord for a revelation concerning the matter. The answer given was, that he should take a bed, his family, and what clothing he needed for them, and go straightway to Colesville, for his enemies were combining in secret chambers to take away his life" (Lavina Fielding Anderson, *Lucy's Book,* 487).

24. Ibid.

25. For a discussion of this procedure, see Richard L. Bushman, *Joseph Smith and the Beginnings of Mormonism,* 41, and Tom Kelleher, "The Debit Economy of 1830s New England."

Once again, Lucy found herself caught in the middle, a victim of others' actions. She became anxious, understandably fearful of where this new round of unpleasantness would lead. The morning after the note holders called on Lucy, an elderly Quaker, probably thinking that Father Smith would also flee, called on him. "Friend Smith," the man announced, "I have a note against thee of fourteen dollars, which I have lately bought, and I have come to see if thou hast the money for me."[26] Smith did not. He could, however, pay six dollars. The collector refused partial payment, saying he would "not wait one hour," and warning Father Smith that if he did not pay in full immediately, he would go forthwith to jail. Reportedly, the only condition upon which he would grant forgiveness of the debt was that Smith would burn all copies of the Book of Mormon he had been trying to sell in the area. Father Smith refused. "No sir, I shall not do that," he responded. "Very well," said the Quaker, "thee shall go to jail then."

Lucy quickly intervened, offering her gold beads that she said would more than cover the debt. The Quaker insisted on cash and called in the constable who was waiting in the yard. "You are my prisoner," intoned the officer as he grabbed Smith's shoulder. Mother Smith pled for extra time, but the men departed (after eating Father Smith's dinner), escorting Smith to Canandaigua to serve a thirty-day sentence and leaving Mother Smith alone with eight-year-old daughter Lucy. Jailing the poor was often an attempt not only to prevent the debtor from fleeing, but to coerce payment if the creditor suspected hidden assets or to force the incarcerated or family members to pay the debt.[27]

The next day "a pert young gentleman" called on Mother Smith, again looking for Hyrum and saying he was collecting a debt Hyrum owed to Alexander McIntyre, the family's physician.[28] The next morning, Lucy paid the debt in corn and beans. That night, sitting at the fireside, feeling sorry

26. Unless otherwise stated, my text here is based on Anderson, *Lucy's Book,* 489-96. Joseph Sr. had earlier gotten into financial difficulties after the death of his benefactor Lemuel Durfee Sr. An execution order had been issued on May 7, 1830, for constable Sylvester Southworth to collect $37.50 plus interest and legal fees from Father Smith and Abraham Fish. The two men struggled for nearly four months to liquidate that debt (Nathan Pierce, Docket Book [1827-30], 25).

27. Tom Kelleher, "Welfare and Workfare in 1830s New England"; and Kelleher, "The Debit Economy of 1830s New England."

28. On December 2, 1830, Joseph wrote a note warning Hyrum to "beware of the freemasons, [Dr. Alexander] McIntyre heard that you were in Manchester and he got out a warrant and went to your father's to distress the family but Harrison overheard their talk and they said that they cared not for the debt, if they only could obtain your body. ... Therefore beware of the Freemasons" (Joseph Smith to Colesville Saints, Dec. 2, 1830, copied into Newel Knight, Journal, 196-207).

for herself and her jailed husband, Mother Smith heard a loud knock. When she opened the door, a stranger entered asking for Hyrum. While she was explaining his absence, several other men also came into the room, claiming that they too were collecting McIntyre's debts. Lucy tried to explain that the debt was paid, but the men said they did not believe her and insisted on taking corn stored in her loft. Lucy glanced out the window and "almost turned … giddy" at the roadway crowded with men holding candles and lamps. Fearing that her house was going to be "pillaged by a banditti of blacklegs, religious bigots, and cut-throats," Lucy rushed into her bedroom, knelt in prayer, and "begged that [the Lord] would not let my children fall into their hands … that they might be satisfied with plunder without taking life." At this moment, her powerful nineteen-year-old son William bounded in, crying, "In the name of God, what is this host of men doing here? Are they robbing or murdering? What are they about?" Mother Smith told him that they had taken his father to jail, were hunting Hyrum in vain, and were now insisting on plundering the house. William, who as an adult achieved a height of six feet three inches—the tallest of the Smith males—was known to favor a good brawl.[29] He grabbed a large handspike and sprang up the stairs, clearing out the miscreants who were in the process of removing the corn, then dashed out into the dooryard into the midst of the crowd, swinging his makeshift weapon and yelling, "Away from here, you cut-throats, instantly, or I will be the death of every one of you." They evidently believed what he said and soon dispersed in the darkness down Stafford Road.

Shortly afterwards, Harrison, ill and exhausted from a Book of Mormon sales trip, arrived, apparently with money in his pocket. Mother Smith told him about Father Smith's arrest, spent the night nursing him, and sent him off to Canandaigua at sunrise to effect Joseph Sr.'s release. Although Harrison had money to pay his father's debt, the jailer would not release Father Smith because it was Sunday, the Lord's day.

Mother Smith later wrote that her husband was "confined in the same dungeon with a man committed for murder." His cellmate, Eli Bruce, was

29. William's son, Edson Don Carlos Smith, remembered his father as "well built and of powerful physique, standing six foot three in his stocking feet" ("Episodes in Genealogical Research," 8). In 1883, at age seventy-two, William wrote that because of the many insults that came his way as a boy, "I got into a great many quarrels and contentions with the young men of the neighborhood on the same account, but invariably came off victorious" *(William Smith on Mormonism,* 13). Later in a Kirtland bout of fisticuffs with his prophet-brother, William whipped him so soundly he was "not able to sit down, or rise up, without help" (Joseph Smith Jr. to William Smith, Dec. 18, 1835, in Jessee, *The Personal Writings of Joseph Smith,* 114).

not a murderer, but a Niagara County sheriff convicted on charges related to the abduction and disappearance of the famous anti-Mason William Morgan. "Had a long talk with the father of *the Smith,"* wrote Bruce in his diary, "who according to the old man's account, is the particular favorite of Heaven! To him Heaven has vouchsafed to reveal its mysteries; he is the herald of the latter-day glory. The old man avers that he is commissioned by God to baptize and preach this new doctrine. He says that our Bible is much abridged and deficient; that soon the Divine will is to be known to all, as written in the *new Bible,* or *Book of Mormon."*[30]

Within a day or two, Harrison made arrangements to move his poverty-stricken parents and siblings to The Kingdom, a hamlet on the Seneca River a mile west of Seneca Falls, New York.[31] He succeeded only "after much fatigue and perplexities of various kinds," wrote Lucy. "The family moved into a house belonging to an individual by the name of [Fuller] Kellog and were welcomed into the neighborhood by a throng of generous, warm-hearted folks."[32]

In their new quarters, the Smiths carried on their custom of family devotionals, singing, and offering prayers. "The neighbours soon became aware of this," Mother Smith remembered, "and it caused our house to become a place of evening resort, for some dozen or twenty persons."[33]

Meanwhile, back in the Western Reserve, while awaiting his new presiding elder, Sidney Rigdon had immersed himself in a multitude of evangelist activities in the area. Though he now had, in the new Church of Christ, a religion to match his manner, Sidney had not met the man behind it all, the prophet Joseph. Possibly to satisfy some lingering doubts about the new direction his life had taken, Rigdon traveled to Manchester with Edward Partridge, a Painesville hatter and one of Rigdon's Reformed Baptist parishioners.[34]

30. Diary of Eli Bruce, Nov. 5, 1830, qtd. in Robert Morris, *The Masonic Martyr,* 266-67, emphasis his.

31. Four months later, Father Smith was still being sought by additional creditors. The prophet warned Hyrum from far-off Kirtland that David Jackaways "has threatened to take father with a supreme writ in the spring[. Y]ou had <bet[t]er> Come to Fayette and take father along with you[.] Come in a one horse wagon if you Can[.] Do not Come threw Buf[f]alo for th[e]y will lie in wait for you" (Joseph Smith Jr. to Hyrum Smith, Mar. 3-4, 1831, in Jessee, *The Personal Writings of Joseph Smith,* 230-31).

32. Anderson, *Lucy's Book,* 105. Larry Porter has documented that although the Smith rental home no longer stands, it was "on the north side of State Highway 5, north of the Seneca River, in the Kingdom" (Porter, "A Study of the Origins of the Church of Jesus Christ of Latter-day Saints," 105).

33. Anderson, *Lucy's Book,* 105.

34. John Whitmer asserted that although Edward Partridge was "desirous to know the

By mid-December when the two men arrived at Stafford Road, the log home was empty, the frame house occupied and the farmstead managed by Roswell Nichols. Rigdon and Partridge traversed the neighborhood seeking "further information respecting the doctrine which [the prophet] preached." Neighbors, said Lucy Smith, reportedly testified to the integrity of the Smith family on all matters except religion, explaining young Joseph as having deceived his family about the golden Bible. Rigdon and Partridge, however, waved the criticisms aside as mere prejudice.[35]

On the evening that Rigdon and Partridge reached the Kingdom, they found a meeting in progress with the prophet, preaching to a small congregation. After he finished, Joseph asked for comments. Partridge, soon to become the young church's first bishop, arose. He introduced himself and explained that he and his traveling companion had just arrived from Kirtland, via Manchester. Mother Smith, with evident gratification, recorded that his comments focused on their personal knowledge of "what [the Smiths] had sacrificed for [their] faith," and having heard that their "veracity was not questioned upon any other point than that of our religion," he requested baptism.

Rigdon and Partridge were welcomed into the fold. Smith was particularly pleased that men of important social stature, motivated by pure faith,[36] would be heaven sent all the way from Ohio to further God's work. Smith pronounced an impressive message as Rigdon's reward:

> Behold, verily, verily I say unto my servant Sidney, I have looked upon thee and thy works. I have heard thy prayers and prepared thee for a greater work. Thou art blessed for thou shalt do great things. Behold thou wast sent forth, even as John [the Baptist], to prepare the way before me, and before Elijah, which should come, and thou knew it not. …
>
> [T]he time of my coming … is nigh at hand … and I have sent forth the fulness of my gospel by the hand of my servant Joseph: and in weakness have I blessed him. … Wherefore watch over him, that his faith fail not … and a commandment I give unto thee, that thou shalt write for him: and the scriptures shall be given, even as they are in mine own bosom, to the salvation of mine own elect. …

---

truth of these things," he did not have "confidence enough to inquire at the hand of God, Therefore he sought testimony of man, and he obtained it, and received the truth and obeyed the divine requirements" (Bruce N. Westergren, *From Historian to Dissident,* 4).

35. Anderson, *Lucy's Book,* 504. Partridge and Rigdon evidently did not interview Smith's creditors nor were they seemingly aware that Joseph Sr. was then in jail.

36. BC XXXVII and XXXVIII.

> Tarry with him, and he shall journey with you; forsake him not, and surely these things shall be fulfilled. And inasmuch as ye do not write, behold it shall be given unto him to prophesy. And thou shalt preach my gospel, and call on the holy prophets to prove his words, as they shall be given him. … Fear not, little flock, the kingdom is yours, until I come. Behold I come quickly.[37]

For his part, the thirty-seven-year-old Rigdon also became immediately enamored of the charismatic young prophet, then a few days shy of his twenty-fifth birthday. Together, Smith felt assured, they could save the elect from the "wrath to come." They promptly settled down in The Kingdom to focus their fused energy on the Bible revision the prophet had been working on intermittently since finishing the Book of Mormon. Although the LDS Church today designates this reworking of the Bible as the "Joseph Smith Translation (JST)" while the Community of Christ (formerly RLDS Church) calls it the "Inspired Version," no ancient manuscripts were used, and neither Joseph nor Sidney was fluent in any foreign language. From Smith's description, the procedure, like that used in regard to the Book of Mormon, was an "inspired" revision, not a translation in the usual definition of the term. Joseph, armed with a prophet's understanding, modified existing biblical excerpts rather than restored actual passages which had been lost or altered from the original manuscripts.

While participating enthusiastically in this ambitious project, Rigdon also labored to convince the prophet to relocate to Ohio among Sidney's followers. There, Rigdon presumably assured Smith, he would be free from harassment and persecution. Proselytizing would be more fruitful in the Western Reserve, and Smith would be closer to the Indian nations on the frontier where he, speaking for the Lord, had already proclaimed the New Jerusalem would soon rise. Not least among the enticements for immigrating to Kirtland Mills, as the place was then called, were the financial considerations: a larger market for Book of Mormon sales and a general acceptance among Rigdon's supporters of communitarianism, or sharing all things in common. As the biographies of both men confirm, they were visionaries, usually with no visible means of support, who generally relied upon others for financial support. Amos Sutton Hayden observed in his history of the Disciples of Christ in the Western Reserve that Smith's and Rigdon's "long cherished hopes and anticipations of living without work were to be realized. Thus, from almost a state of beggary

37. Ibid. XXXVII.

... they were immediately well furnished with the 'fat of the land' by their fanatical followers, many of whom were wealthy."[38]

Before relocating with his new convert "to the Ohio," as the prophet designated the region,[39] Smith and Rigdon traversed Joseph's New York haunts, preaching and prophesying "great judgments that should come in the last days, and destruction upon the wicked."[40]

The decision to make the trip was finalized in late December 1830 when, at Canandaigua, a revelation advised the two men: "[I]t is not expedient in me that ye should translate any more until ye shall go to the Ohio, and this because of the enemy and for your sakes. And again, I say unto you that ye shall not go until ye have preached my gospel in those parts, and have strengthened up the church whithersoever it is found, and more especially in Colesville: for behold they pray unto me in much faith."[41]

After preaching for ninety minutes at the Canandaigua courthouse on December 24, Rigdon and Smith met with William Wine Phelps, editor of Canandaigua's anti-Masonic newspaper, the *Ontario Phoenix.* Phelps later asserted that his conversation with Rigdon lasted ten hours, during which the new Mormon spokesman told him that the Book of Mormon was true and that "he knew it by the power of the Holy Ghost, which was again given to man in preparation for the millennium."[42] A day or two later, Rigdon sermonized in Palmyra in the meeting hall—which Martin Harris had secured—of the Young Men's Library Society on the third floor of Exchange Row on Main, where the Book of Mormon had been printed and bound. A small audience, which included Lorenzo Saunders and Pomeroy Tucker, gathered to hear the famous preacher. "I saw Rigdon in 1830 preach with the Bible in one hand and the Book of Mormon in the other," remembered Saunders more than fifty years later. "He said the Bible was now fulfilled and done away and the book of Mormon was to take its place."[43] For his

38. Hayden, *Early History of the Disciples in the Western Reserve,* 214.

39. The prophet's designation, "to the Ohio," was geographically incorrect. The Ohio River begins in Pittsburgh, Pennsylvania, where the Allegheny and Monongahela Rivers meet. For the most part, the Ohio flows southwestward, forming the southern boundaries of the states of Ohio, Indiana, and Illinois, and the northern boundaries of West Virginia and Kentucky. The Ohio empties into the Mississippi River at Cairo, Illinois, and courses nowhere near the Kirtland/Mentor area.

40. John Corrill, *A Brief History of the Church of Christ,* 8. John Whitmer wrote that Joseph was prophesying: "God is about to destroy this generation, and Christ will descend from heaven in power and great glory, with all the holy angels with him to take vengeance upon the wicked and they that know not God" (Westergren, *From Historian to Dissident,* 8).

41. BC XXXIX.

42. William W. Phelps to E. D. Howe, Jan. 15, 1831, in Howe, *Mormonism Unvailed,* 274.

43. Lorenzo Saunders, Interview, Sept. 17, 1884, 9.

part, Tucker recalled more than three decades later that Rigdon cited several Book of Mormon passages to emphasize that the Bible and Book of Mormon "were both equally the Word of God; that neither was perfect without the other; and that they were inseparably necessary to complete the everlasting gospel of the Savior Jesus Christ."[44]

Before Smith and Rigdon visited Colesville, they attended the Church's third conference, held in Peter Whitmer's log home in Fayette on Sunday, January 2, 1831. In response to questions about the rumored relocation to Ohio, "the Prophet enquired of the Lord in the presence of the whole congregation," wrote Church Historian John Whitmer. He then sat at a table dictating while Rigdon transcribed. In part, the message said:

> But behold, verily, verily I say unto you, that mine eyes are upon you; I am in your midst and ye cannot see me, but the day soon cometh that ye shall see me and know that I am: for the vail of darkness shall soon be rent, and he that is not purified shall not abide the day: wherefore gird up your loins and be prepared. Behold the kingdom is yours and the enemy shall not overcome. ... And now I show unto you a mystery, a thing which is had in secret chambers. ... And I hold forth and deign to give unto you greater riches, even a land of promise; a land flowing with milk and honey, upon which there shall be no curse when the Lord cometh: and I will give it unto you for the land of your inheritance, if you seek it with all your hearts: and this shall be my covenant with you, ye shall have it for the land of your inheritance, and for the inheritance of your children forever, while the earth shall stand, and ye shall possess it again in eternity, no more to pass away.
>
> But verily I say unto you, that in time ye shall have no king nor ruler, for I will be your king and watch over you. Wherefore, hear my voice and follow me, and you shall be a free people, and ye shall have no laws but my laws, when I come, for I am your Lawgiver.
>
> And again I say unto you, that the enemy in the secret chambers, seeketh your lives: Ye hear of wars in far countries, and you say that there will soon be great wars in far countries, but ye know not the hearts of them in your own land. ... And that ye might escape the power of the enemy, and be gathered unto me a righteous people, without spot and blameless: Wherefore, for this cause I gave unto you the commandment, that ye should go to the Ohio: and there I will give unto you my law; and there you shall be endowed with power from on high. ... And if ye seek

44. Tucker, *Origin, Rise, and Progress of Mormonism,* 76-79.

> the riches which it is the will of the Father to give unto you, ye shall be the richest of all people; for ye shall have the riches of eternity: And it must needs be that the riches of the earth is mine to give.[45]

The doomsday rhetoric that characterized the prophet's teachings during this period was necessary. Obviously, much of his success would depend on the extent to which he could reconfigure the existing web of familial, social, economic, and political interactions into a spiritual vision compelling enough to draw adherents away from their daily routines and into a life that assumed heroic dimensions. They must become a peculiar people seeking to achieve the new Millennium.[46]

Many Mormons in New York were well-to-do-farmers, hesitant to uproot themselves from their prosperous farmsteads. But the prophet, according to John Whitmer, announced that "God is about to destroy this generation, and Christ will descend from Heaven in power and great glory, with all the holy angels with him, to take vengeance upon the wicked, and they that know not God."[47] Whitmer wrote in 1831 that when the revelation was first read ordering the move to Ohio, "the solemnities of eternity rested on the congregation." But then another reaction set in. Some men resisted, believing "that Joseph had invented it himself to deceive the people that in the end he might get gain."[48] For a time, Smith and Rigdon maintained intense pressure in preaching that, on the one hand, warned the people of "the wrath to come," while, on the other, promised a new land of inheritance. Most of the Mormon converts fell into line and began to dispose of their properties and goods in any way they could. The Whitmers were among the first to liquidate their assets, selling their valuable 100-acre farm to Charles Stuart for $2,200, shortly after the prophet voiced his revelation.[49]

John Whitmer was dispatched to Ohio in early January 1831 to carry the new commandments and revelations voiced by the prophet and recorded by Rigdon. Sidney also sent a letter of introduction with Whitmer urging the Kirtland/Mentor Saints to "receive him, for he is a brother greatly

45. BC IX:6-33.

46. See Richard S. Van Wagoner, *Sidney Rigdon,* 75.

47. Qtd. in F. Mark McKiernan and Roger D. Launius, *An Early Latter Day Saint History,* 32.

48. Westergren, *From Historian to Dissident,* 12.

49. Newel Knight wrote: "It was at this conference that we were instructed as a people, to begin the gathering of Israel, and a revelation was given to the prophet on this subject. Having returned home from conference, in obedience to the commandment which had been given, I together with the Colesville Branch, began to make preparations to go to Ohio. ... As might be expected, we were obliged to make great sacrifices of our property" (Knight, Autobiography and Journal, 47).

beloved, and an Apostle of this church." In that letter, Rigdon instructed his friends in Ohio that they were "living on the land of promise and that there at Kirtland is the place of gathering."[50]

Following the conference, Smith witnessed the marriage of his eighteen-year-old sister Katharine to Wilkins Jenkins Salisbury on January 8, 1831. David Whitmer married Julia Ann Jolly the next day. Then Smith and Rigdon traveled to Colesville where they stayed with Joseph Knight for several days while Rigdon preached to small gatherings. During one of these engagements, some local bullies evidently threatened the prophet and his spokesman. "The Spirit of the Lord fell upon Sidney," wrote John Whitmer, basing his account on information from Rigdon or Smith, "and he spoke with boldness, and he preached the gospel in its purity; but they laughed him to scorn, he being filled, with the Holy Spirit, he cried aloud O, ye heavens give ear and ye angels attend. I bear witness in the name of Jesus Christ that this people is sealed up to everlasting destruction."[51]

After a quick business trip to Harmony in mid-January, during which Smith rented his home to Joseph McKune Jr., who purchased it in 1833,[52] the prophet and Rigdon returned to Seneca County where Rigdon preached at the courthouse in Waterloo, scolding his audience for the "want of 'charity and brotherly love' among the prevailing sects and denominations of professing christians." After pronouncing "dreadful vengeance on the whole state of New York, and [Waterloo] in particular," he advised listeners to "flee from the wrath to come" and follow him "beyond the western waters" to safety.[53] Rigdon then caught a stage for Kirtland, arriving there on February 1. The Palmyra *Reflector,* edited by Joseph Smith's antagonist Abner Cole, reported with unfettered cynicism on February 1 that "the Prophet, Spouse, and whole 'holy family' (as they style themselves,) will follow Rigdon, so soon as their deluded or hypocritical followers, shall be able to dispose of what little real property they possess in this region."[54]

Joseph and Emma, five months pregnant with twins, had already started for Ohio, probably on January 27, riding in Joseph Knight Jr.'s fifty-dollar

50. Rigdon commented on Whitmer's arrival, noting that the more important part of his mission was "to inform the brethren that the boundaries of the promised land, or the New Jerusalem, ... the township of Kirtland, a few miles west of this, is the eastern line and the Pacific Ocean the western line" (Sidney Rigdon to Ohio Saints, Jan. 4, 1831, rpt. in Howe, *Mormonism Unvailed,* 111).

51. Westergren, *From Historian to Dissident,* 13.

52. Dan Vogel, *Early Mormon Documents,* 5:452.

53. "Mr. Editor," 95.

54. Ibid.

sleigh, driven by reliable Father Knight.[55] En route, they preached at Joseph and Lucy Smith's home in The Kingdom, and at the Macedon homes of Calvin and Sophronia Stoddard, and Martin Harris's brother Preserved. Mother Smith wrote that "they baptized some in both places after which [the prophet] proceeded on his journey."[56] The small company then burst forth out of New York on a long, cold sleigh ride that would take them to the promised land and a new life.

At any time, along those hundreds of miles of frozen roadway to Ohio, had Joseph consulted his peep stone, would he have foreseen the loss only two years later of Jackson County, Missouri, site of his New Jerusalem, and failure to redeem the land of Zion through force? Have watched the collapse of the bank-like Kirtland Safety Society, and his own flight from disillusioned followers into Missouri, to launch new policies of gathering that five years later would result in the exodus of his people to nearby Illinois? Have realized that Christ's second advent was not "at the doors"? Most sobering, would he have seen his own murder at age thirty-eight in company with brother Hyrum, deaths that would permanently scar the collective psyche of his followers? Or have realized that at the moment bullets pierced his body and he fell from the second-story window of a small jail in western Illinois on June 27, 1844, he would transform from hero into icon?

55. Joseph Knight Jr., "Joseph Knight's Incidents of history," 2.
56. Anderson, *Lucy's Book,* 506.

EPILOGUE

Towering genius ... thirsts and burns for distinction; and, if possible, it will have it. ... Is it unreasonable then to expect, that some man possessed of the loftiest genius, coupled with ambition sufficient to push it to its utmost stretch, will at some time, spring up among us?

—Abraham Lincoln, "Address Before the Young Men's Lyceum," 1:113-14

The brigades of Mormon elders launched around the world during Joseph's lifetime and throughout much of the career of his Utah-based successor Brigham Young did not speak of a wondrous visitation from God and the Lord Jesus to the boy Joseph. Instead, they testified that an uneducated farm boy, one of the weak things of the earth, directed by an angel and empowered by Heaven, "translated" an ancient record of God's dealings on the American continent. The narrative disclosing the coming forth of this record and its message resonated for many of Smith's contemporaries. "When darkness covered the earth, and gross darkness the people," wrote William W. Phelps, only three years after the Church's organization,

> when no man did walk in the old paths, nor did search out the everlasting gospel; when men built up churches in the glory of the world; and when all flesh had become so corrupt, that a few more years might have left the cities of the world, like Sodom and Gomorrah, the Lord our Savior, saw fit in his great goodness, endless mercy, and infinite wisdom, to send an angel and signify unto man, that there was a sacred record to be unfolded in the eyes of all nations, containing the fulness of the gospel. It was the book of Mormon. ... This was welcome news to them that looked for the gathering of the righteous, in the last days.[1]

Early Mormonites announced that divine revelation existed not only in biblical epochs, but continued in their own age. Mormons asserted that Smith was a prophet like Ezekiel, Isaiah, and Elijah, possessing a special connection to a transcendent force. As psychologist Len Oakes cautions, however, "the most consistent thing about prophets has been their failure."[2] Many of

1. W. W. Phelps, "The Book of Mormon," 57.
2. Len Oakes, *Prophetic Charisma,* 178.

Joseph's ambitious projects failed. He and his successors either retooled or discarded the unworkable, impractical ideas. He was mistaken in embracing the popular belief of the day that the second advent and millennial reign of Christ was "nigh at hand." But other early Americans were also proven wrong that the end time was imminent, and that humankind was in the latter days. Moreover, the themes of millennialism, modern revelation, and the restoration of Christianity to its ancient purity—the bases upon which Joseph and his followers built early Mormonism—were compelling to many during the 1830s and 1840s, a period when the religious ferment of antebellum America spawned a multitude of religious and social movements. Seekers yearned "for some moral absolute."[3] They followed the charismatic Smith not "out of fear or monetary inducement, but out of love, passionate devotion, [and] enthusiasm."[4] Most importantly, they believed in him and his message.

The Book of Mormon gave—and continues to offer—a promissory vision that included solidarity of purpose. A contemporary Mormon scholar notes: "The religious genius of the book was its ability to speak to Joseph Smith's world and answer the theological dilemmas facing those looking for further light and knowledge." The Book of Mormon's essential mission—"to bring people to the new-yet-old gospel revealed to Joseph Smith"—could not have been achieved "had the book not effectively communicated the fully developed Christian message expected by the early converts to Mormonism."[5] As Oakes points out, charismatics like Smith learn "to speak the inner language of one's followers better than they can articulate it themselves, and to use it to influence them. What the leader seeks is some handle on people's emotions that allows him to appear extraordinary and to project a prophetic image, to speak in language clearer than the truth."[6]

The Book of Mormon tells us that God chose America's earliest inhabitants to be his people, as he chose the Israelites of the Old World. Americans, like the Jews, are to redeem themselves and ultimately humanity. American historian Kenneth Winn points out that "Americans in fact had gladly shouldered this burden up through the time of the Founding Fathers. Unfortunately, by Smith's day, they had turned away from building the just and holy society, and were embracing all manner of vice and wickedness. The entire

3. A. J. Jones, and R. M. Anservits, "Saint-Simon and Saint-Simonism," 1,104.

4. R. C. Tucker, "The Theory of Charismatic Leadership," 735.

5. Blake T. Ostler, "The Book of Mormon as a Modern Expansion of an Ancient Source," 113.

6. Oakes, *Prophetic Charisma,* 90.

society seemed to teeter on the brink of irredeemable corruption. If Americans would not return to godly ways, they were doomed."[7] Thus, the Book of Mormon urged Americans to renew their sense of mission, to repent and return to their former holy walk, that they might again be a people the world could emulate. If they ignored this message or failed in their mission, the Lord's judgment will thunder at the door. Joseph, like many of his day, looked back to a "golden age" of virtue and equality that he hoped to renew.

The Book of Mormon reads in many places like an indictment of Jacksonian America. Nathan Hatch finds it to be "a document of profound social protest, an impassioned manifesto by a hostile outsider against the smug complacency of those in power and the reality of social distinctions based on wealth, class and education."[8] This strong cultural critique was a principal source of the Church's "populist" appeal:

> By revealing an up-to-date Bible, and insisting upon God's active supernatural presence, Smith gave authoritative answers to many seeking secure moorings. More strikingly ... [the Book of Mormon] conveyed the unmistakable claim that common people had the right to shape their own faith and to take charge of their own religious destiny. These populist themes resonated powerfully with Smith's earliest disciples, young men who were characteristically poor, uprooted, unschooled, and unsophisticated like himself.[9]

Like all of God's prophets, Joseph perceived the divine word largely through the prism of his own experience. It was not necessary for him to convert followers to a new world view. He needed only to tap into powerful undercurrents of popular belief that enabled ordinary people to reach beyond themselves. For their part, devotees found a source of spiritual meaning, fellowship, community, and destiny while achieving the coherence and comfort of belonging. What makes the movement so unique is the synergistic vitality of both its leadership and membership, energy which guarantees the survival of the faith when many of its counterparts failed. As John Greenleaf Whittier wrote of Joseph and other nineteenth-century prophets:

> In listening to these modern prophets, I discovered, as I think, the great secret of their success in making converts. They speak to a common feeling; they minister to a universal want. They contrast strongly the

7. Kenneth Winn, *Exiles in a Land of Liberty,* 18.
8. Nathan O. Hatch, *The Democratization of American Christianity,* 116.
9. Ibid., 121.

> miraculous power of the Gospel to the apostolic time with the present state of our nominal Christianity. They ask for the signs of divine power; the faith, overcoming all things, which opened the prison doors of the apostles, gave them power over the elements, which rebuked disease and death itself, and made visible to all the presence of the Living God. They ask for any declaration in the Scriptures that this miraculous power of faith was to be continued to the first confessors of Christianity. They speak a language of hope and promise to weak, weary hearts, tossed and troubled, who have wandered from sect to sect, seeking in vain for the primal manifestations of the divine power.[10]

Few men knew or loved Joseph better than Brigham Young. And perhaps no one has ever captured more precisely why the prophet won and kept the hearts of his people. "Joseph Smith, the Prophet of the last days," said Young in 1862, "had a happy faculty of reducing the things of heaven to the capacity of persons of common understanding, often in a single sentence throwing a flood of light into the gloom of ages. He had power to draw the spirits of the people who listened to him to his standard, where they communed with heavenly objects and heavenly principles, connecting the heavenly and the earthly together—in one blending flood of heavenly intelligence."[11]

Joseph's legacy flourishes even as the Mormon prophet continues to engender controversy. Oakes contends, somewhat pessimistically: "We realize that ... at the core of our noblest ideals lies a terrible delusion: that much of what we call 'truth' is just a defense against the unknown."[12] While some do become disenchanted when they come to know Brother Joseph more fully "unfiltered" by superstition and sentiment, to borrow Oakes's phrase, many men and women continue to look for ways to sustain themselves through the challenges of each new day. To millions worldwide, Joseph's revelation continues to fulfill that need.

10. John Greenleaf Whittier, "A Mormon Conventicle," 302-3.
11. Brigham Young, July 13, 1862, JD 9:310.
12. Oakes, *Prophetic Charisma,* 195.

APPENDIX 1 | ACCOUNTS OF CLAIMED SUPERNATURAL VISIONS

Many men and women have reported encountering a heavenly being or beings, in visions or apparitions. To believers, these incidents are glimpses of transcendental illumination beamed into history. To skeptics, such experiences are an irrational window into humanity's subjective experience of itself. "Perhaps the biggest mistake we can make about the mystical experience is to take it too seriously," argues Len Oakes, a psychologist specializing in religious charisma:

> Typically the mystic believes that he alone has the truth, or that the "God" who spoke with him is the only true God, or that his is the only path to salvation. But this cannot be so. Mystics invariably contradict each other, and clearly not all can be right. One seer meets Jesus, another meets Krishna, another meets the Great White Brotherhood or the Void or whatever, each of which is "God" or "the Highest." These beliefs are mere self-serving fancies, and the degree to which the prophet uncritically accepts his vision is a measure of his limitations. ... Yet it is tempting to think that mystical utterances reveal some great truth if only we could interpret them correctly. Perhaps they do, but only about the mystic who has them.[1]

We have yet to understand fully the complexities of human beings' spiritual lives. That such experiences shape perceptions of life and inspire hopes for transcendence and immortality cannot be disputed. An estimated 50 million, or more, living Americans today report some kind of Christian-oriented "born again" experience.[2] Below is a brief chronological sampling of a variety of religionists from many cultures who have claimed a profound encounter which they interpreted as sacred and of which a record exists. As evidence that such phenomena are common to human experience, I include examples from 2000 B.C.E. to 1988 C.E. The year cited is the approximate year of the apparition.

1. Len Oakes, *Prophetic Charisma,* 106-7.
2. T. Robbins, "Cults, Converts, and Charisma," 4.

Abraham (ca. 2000 B.C.E.)

Now the Lord had said unto Abram, Get thee out of thy country, and from thy kindred, and from thy father's house, unto a land that I will shew thee:

And I will make of thee a great nation, and I will bless thee, and make thy name great; and thou shalt be a blessing:

And I will bless them that bless thee, and curse him that curseth thee: and in thee shall all families of the earth be blessed. (Gen. 12:1-3.)

Isaac (ca. 1900 B.C.E.)

And the Lord appeared unto him, and said, Go not down into Egypt; dwell in the land which I shall tell thee of:

Sojourn in this land, and I will be with thee, and will bless thee; for unto thee, and unto thy seed, I will give all these countries, and I will perform the oath which I sware unto Abraham thy father;

And I will make thy seed to multiply as the stars of heaven, and I will give unto thy seed all these countries; and in thy seed shall all the nations of the earth be blessed;

Because that Abraham obeyed my voice, and kept my charge, my commandments, my statutes, and my laws. (Gen. 26:2-5; also v. 24.)

Jacob (ca. 1800 B.C.E.)

And God appeared unto Jacob again, when he came out of Padanaram, and blessed him.

And God said unto him, Thy name is Jacob: thy name shall not be called any more Jacob, but Israel shall be thy name: and he called his name Israel.

And God said unto him, I am God Almighty: be fruitful and multiply; a nation and a company of nations shall be of thee and kings shall come out of thy loins;

And the land which I gave Abraham and Isaac, to thee I will give it, and to thy seed after thee will I give the land. (Gen. 35:9-12.)

Moses (late 1300s B.C.E.)

Then went up Moses, and Aaron, Nabab, and Abihu, and seventy of the elders of Israel:

And they saw the God of Israel: and there was under his feet as it were a paved work of a sapphire stone, and as it were the body of heaven in his clearness.

And upon the nobles of the children of Israel he laid not his hand: also they saw God, and did eat and drink. (Exod. 24:9-11.)

Zoroaster (660 B.C.E.)

As the holy one I recognized thee, Mazda Ahura, when Good Thought (Vohu Manah) came to me and asked me, "Who art thou? To whom dost thou belong? By what sign wilt thou appoint the days for questioning about thy possessions and thyself?"

Then said I to him: "To the first (question), Zarathustra am I, a true foe to the Liar, to the utmost of my power, but a powerful support would I be to the Righteous, that I may attain the future things of the infinite Dominion, according as I praise and see thee, Mazda."

As the holy one I recognized thee, Mazda Ahura, when Good Thought came to me. To his question, "For which wilt thou decide?" (I made reply), "At every offering of reverence to thy Fire, I will bethink me of Right so long as I have power, Then show me Right, upon whom I call."

And when thou saidst to me, "To Right shalt thou go for teaching," then thou didst not command what I did not obey: "Speed thee, ere my Obedience come, followed by treasure-laden Destiny, who shall render to men severally the destinies of the two-fold award."[3]

Saul of Tarsus (40 C.E.)

And as he journeyed, he came near Damascus: and suddenly there shined round about him a light from heaven:

And he fell to the earth, and heard a voice saying unto him, Saul, Saul, why persecutest thou me?

And he said, Who art thou, Lord? And the Lord said, I am Jesus whom thou persecutest: it is hard for thee to kick against the pricks.

And he trembling and astonished said, Lord, what wilt thou have me to do? And the Lord said unto him, Arise, and go into the city, and it shall be told thee what thou must do.

And the men which journeyed with him stood speechless, hearing a voice, but seeing no man. (Acts 9:3-7.)

Muhammad (620 C.E.)

According to Muslim tradition, Muhammad often visited a cave a few

3. James Hope Moulton, *Early Zoroastrianism,* 365-66.

miles north of Mecca. One night ("The Night Of Power and Excellence," Muslims call it) there rose in vision before him the archangel Gabriel, the Messenger of God, who cried "Recite!"

> "RECITE thou in the name of thy Lord who created;—
> Created man from CLOTS OF BLOOD:—
> Recite thou! For thy Lord is the most Beneficent,
> Who hath taught the use of the pen:—
> Hath taught Man that which he knoweth not."[4]

St. Rosa of Viterbo (1235-52)

Saw Jesus suspended on the cross, nailed by his hands and feet, crowned with thorns, with many marks of torture on his body. She fainted at the sight of the wounds. When she recovered consciousness she is said to have seen Jesus, gazed at him and conversed with him, he telling her of his love for the human race.[5]

Sister Maria Jesus Agreda (1620)

Maria Fernandez Coronel was born on April 2, 1602, in Agreda, Spain. She donned the blue habit and took her vows as a nun in the Franciscan order. In 1620, the teenage Sister Maria Jesus Agreda began experiencing visions, or raptures. While cloistered in her convent, she would meditate for hours, oftentimes the entire day. From 1620 to 1631, she related to her fellow sisters more than 500 wondrous stories of spiritual travels to a faraway land where she met savages and told them of the "word of Christ." Firmly convinced of the reality of her spiritual travels or bi-location, she wrote a book in which she described, in great detail, her missionary work in the New World. Ultimately the Church brought her to trial, accusing her of heresy. During the height of the hearing, however, an expedition of returning conquistadors and friars arrived in Spain with a wondrous tale of their own. Spanish explorers, adventuring in an unexplored region north of Mexico had encountered numerous Native American tribes who already knew of Jesus Christ, having been taught of the Savior by a white-skinned "Blue Lady," who "appeared to many, drifting in a blue haze while she preached the word of the Lord in their native languages."

The rapid Spanish conquest and control of New Mexico in the fifteenth

4. *The Koran,* trans. J. M. Rodwell, *Everyman's Library,* XCVI:19.
5. Wiebe, *Visions of Jesus,* 17.

and Sixteenth Centuries may have been partially due to Sister Agreda's missionary efforts on behalf of the Catholic Church. Ultimately the Franciscans baptized more than 50,000 people and established twenty-five missions.[6]

George Fox (1642)

Born in 1624 in Leicestershire, England, Fox was the son of a weaver in an English village. At age eighteen he left home in search of religious experience and later reported in his journal various personal religious experiences or direct revelations which he called "openings," that corrected, he believed, the traditional concepts of faith and practice in English religious life. He placed the God-given inward light above creeds and scripture and regarded personal experience as the true source of authority. During 1649-60 the Society of Friends came into being though group members were usually simply called Quakers.[7]

Emanuel Swedenborg (1744)

On a certain night, a man appeared to him in the midst of a strong shining light, and said, "I am God the Lord, the Creator, and Redeemer; I have chosen thee to explain to men the interiour and spiritual sense of the sacred writings. I will dictate to thee what thou oughtest to write." After this period, "his spiritual sight was so opened, that he could see in the most clear and distinct manner, what passed in the spiritual world, and converse with angels and spirits in the same manner as with men."[8]

Thomas Rankin (1770s)

One day, in the midst of anxiety over his soul, he fell into a deep trance. "Sleeping I was not, and waking I was not," he later wrote. "Some may think or suppose, what I am going to say was only a dream; but of the contrary of this, I am as much assured of, as I know I am at this moment a living man." Having not yet been converted, Rankin was convinced he was a sinner destined to hell. In his vision he "clearly saw, my soul doomed to everlasting flames. ... Around my bed, stood with eager looks, a company of damned spirits, ready to conduct my soul to endless torments." The vision did end with his demise into hell, however, but with a revelation of Christ. "In the twinkling of an eye, I beheld the heavens open and part asunder and the

6. "The Blue Nun."
7. "Fox, George," inWendy Doniger, *Merriam-Webster's Encyclopedia of World Religions,* 356.
8. Hannah Adams, *Dictionary of All Religions and Religious Denominations,* 202.

appearance of the glorified humanity of the Son of God. I thought I cried aloud, 'There is the Lord Jesus Christ! There is the Redeemer of lost and undone mankind!'"[9]

Ann Lee (1736-84)

I saw in vision the Lord Jesus in his Kingdom and glory. He revealed to me the depth of man's loss, what it was, and the way of redemption therefrom. Then I was able to bear an open testimony against the sin that is the root of all evil; and I felt the power of God flow into my soul like a fountain of living water. From that day I have been able to take up a full cross against all the doleful works of the flesh.[10]

Zilpha Elaw (b. 1790)

Zilpha Elaw's search for spiritual meaning began with a dream at age fourteen. "It was a prevailing notion in that part of the world with many," she later wrote, "that whatever a person dreamed between the times of twilight and sunrise, was prophetically ominous, and would shortly come to pass." Later, she believed her prayers were answered when one night she "distinctly saw" Jesus approach her "with open arms, and a most divine and heavenly smile upon his countenance. As He advanced towards me, I felt that his very looks spoke, and said, 'Thy prayer is accepted, I own thy name.'" She was sure this apparition was not merely an illusion because the cow she was then milking also "bowed her knees and cowered down upon the ground" when Christ appeared.[11]

James Finley (early 1800s)

A Kentuckian at the turn of the nineteenth century, Finley had spent most of the day in a hollow log reading, praying, and weeping. The next morning, he arose and went to his barn to pray:

> "Just as I passed the corner of the house on my way, suddenly God poured upon me the Holy Spirit in such a manner, in such a measure, that I fell, my whole length, in the snow, and shouted, and praised God so loud, that I was heard over the neighborhood. As soon [as] I was able to rise, I returned to the house, and my wife having risen, I caught her in my arms,

9. Thomas Rankin, qtd. in Wigger, *Taking Heaven by Storm,* 113-42.
10. "Lee, Ann," in Doniger, *Merriam-Webster's Encyclopedia of World Religions,* 657.
11. Wigger, *Taking Heaven by Storm,* 122.

and ran around the house, shouting, 'Salvation! Salvation![']... While thus exercised, I felt as though some one had spoken to me, 'Go preach my Gospel.' I instantly replied, 'Yes, Lord, if thou will go with me.'"[12]

Solomon Mack, Joseph Smith's Grandfather (1810)

"My mind was imagining, but agitated. I imagined many things; it seemed to me that I saw a bright light in a dark night. When contemplating on my bed which I could not account for, but I thought I heard a voice calling to me again. I thought I saw another light of the same kind, all which I considered as ominous of my own dissolution. I was in distress that sleep departed from my eyes and I literally watered my pillow with tears that I prayed eagerly that God would have mercy on me, that he would relieve me and open the eyes of my understanding and enable me to call him as I ought. ... I could not sleep and took to reading, I was distressed to think how I had abused the sabbath and had not taken warning from my wife. About midnight I saw a light about a foot from my face as bright as fire, the doors were all shut and no one stirring in the house, I thought by this that I had but a few moments to live, and O! What distress I was in; I prayed that the Lord would have mercy on my soul and deliver me from this horrible pit of sin. I thought my self that I had been such a vile wretch that the Lord would not have mercy on me, and I thought as I had slighted so many warnings from my companion, and so abused the sabbath; but I perceived my body and soul was in danger.

"Another night soon after I saw another light as bright as the first, at a small distance from my face, and I thought I had but a few moments to live, and not sleeping nights, and reading, all day I was in misery. ... Another time, in the dead of the night I was called by my christian name, I arise up to answer to my name. The doors all being shut, and the house full, I thought the Lord called, and I had but a moment to live. ... The calls, I believe were for me to return to the Lord who would have mercy on me."[13]

Solomon Chamberlain (1816)

"[T]he Lord shewed me in a vision, that there was no people on the earth that was right, and that faith was gone from the earth, excepting a few and that all Churches were corrupt. I further saw in the vision, that he would soon raise up a Church, that would be after the Apostolic Order, that there

12. W. P. Strickland, *Autobiography of Rev. James B. Finley,* 177.
13. Solomon Mack, *A Narraitve [sic] of the Life of Solomon Mack,* 19-20.

would be in it the same powers, and gifts that were in the days of Christ, and that I should live to see the day, and that there would a book come forth, like unto the Bible and the people would be guided by it, as well as the Bible."[14]

John Samuel Thompson (1822)

"[I]n a glare of brightness exceeding tenfold the brilliancy of the meridian Sun. The Lord said 'I commission you to go and tell mankind that I am come; and bid every man to shout victory!'"[15]

Asa Wild (1823)

"[T]he Lord ... told me that the Millennial state of the world is about to take place; that in seven years literally [1830], there would scarce a sinner be found on earth; that the earth itself, as well as the souls and bodies of its inhabitants, should be redeemed, as before the fall, and become as the garden of Eden. He told me that all of the most dreadful and terrible judgments spoken in the blessed scriptures were to be executed within that time, that more than two thirds of the inhabitants of the world would be destroyed by these judgments ... He also told me that every denomination of professing christians had become extremely corrupt; many of which had never had any true faith at all; but are guided only by depraved reason, refusing the teaching of the spirit ... which alone can teach us the true meaning of the [scriptures]. ... He told me further, that he had raised up, and was now raising up, that class of persons signified by the angel mentioned by the Revelator XIV. 6,7, which flew in the midst of heaven; having the everlasting gospel to preach, that these persons are of an inferior [social] class, and small learning; that they were rejected by every denomination as a body; but soon, God will open their way, by miracles, judgments, &c. That they will have higher authority, greater power, superior inspection, and a greater degree of holiness than was ever experienced before. ... Furthermore he said that all the different denominations of professing christians constituted the New Testament Babylon ... that he is about to call out all his sincere children who are mourning in Zion, from oppression and tyranny of the mother of harlots; and that the severest judgments will be inflicted on the false and fallen professors of religion."[16]

---

14. Solomon Chamberlain, *A Sketch of the Experience of Solomon Chamberlain,* qtd. in Larry C. Porter, "Solomon Chamberlain's Missing Pamphlet," 131-32.

15. John Samuel Thompson, *Christian Guide,* 71.

16. "Remarkable VISION and REVELATION, as Seen and Received by Asa Wild of Amsterdam (N.Y.)," 4.

Billy Hibbard (1825)

"I saw Jesus Christ at the right hand of God, looking down upon me, and God the Father looking upon him. ... [A]s I looked up I saw heaven open, and Jesus at the right hand of God, and the Heavenly hosts surrounding the throne, adoring the Father and Son in the most sublime strains."[17]

James G. Marsh (1838)

When he was about nine years old, James Marsh, son of Thomas B. Marsh, experienced "a remarkable vision, in which he talked with the Father and many of the ancient prophets face to face, and beheld the Son of God coming in his glory." He related that the Lord showed him his own name written in the Book of Life, and also his celestial mansion awaiting him in heaven.

During his four-day illness, he continually manifested a desire to his parents to depart and be with the Lord. "If it is the will of God to take me, I do not wish to stay," he told his parents. His father prayed that the Lord would take him. "My son," father Marsh asked, "are you confident that if you die now your spirit will rest in the celestial paradise?" The boy answered, "Yes, sir." Then "my son, go in peace and expect to come forth at the resurrection of the just where you and I will again strike hands." He again answered, "Yes, sir, I will," and immediately he fell asleep without a struggle or a groan.[18]

Bernadette of Lourdes (1858)

Marie-Bernarde Soubirous was born to a poor family in Lourdes, France, in 1844. Between February 11 and July 16, 1858, at the age of fourteen, she is said to have had a series of visions of the Virgin Mary, who revealed her identity with the words "I am the IMMACULATE CONCEPTION." Young Bernadette steadfastly defended the genuineness of these visions, despite strong opposition from her family members, local church authorities, and others. To escape public attention she boarded in the local school run by the Sisters of Charity of Nevers. In 1866 she was granted admission into the novitiate in the mother house at Nevers. She remained there until her 1879 death. She was canonized in 1933.[19]

---

17. B[illy] Hibbard, *Memoirs of the Life and Travels of B. Hibbard,* 1, 17, 23, 72, 118.

18. "Obituary of James G. Marsh," 48.

19. "Bernadette of Lourdes, Saint," in Doniger, *Merriam-Webster's Encyclopedia of World Religions,* 124.

Ellen G. White (1844-1915)

"I have had no claims to make, only that I am instructed that I am the Lord's messenger. … Early in my work I was asked several times, Are you a prophet? I have ever responded, 'I am the Lord's messenger.' I know that many have called me a prophet, but I have made no claim to this title. My Saviour declared me to be His messenger. 'Your work,' He instructed me, 'is to bear My word. Strange things will arise; and in our youth I set you apart to bear the message to the erring ones, to carry the world before unbelievers, and with pen and voice to reprove from the Word actions that are not right. Exhort from the Word. I will make My Word open to you. … My spirit and My power shall be with you.'"[20]

Granville Oral Roberts (1920s)

"[God] called me to take His healing power to my generation. His words rang clear to me: 'Son, I am going to heal you and you are to take the message of my healing power to your generation.'"[21]

Andrée and Gilberte Degeimbre, Fernande Golberte, and Albert Voisin (1932)

The first few times the Blessed Virgin Mary appeared in Beauraing, Belgium, to five children, ranging in age from nine to fifteen years old, she was some distance away from the group, and said nothing. Ultimately she appeared in Beauraing more than thirty times between November 19, 1932, and January 3, 1933, and announced who she was on December 23. "I would like a church built here," she announced, "so that people can come here on pilgrimage." One of the children was promised by The Blessed Virgin, "I shall convert the sinners." To another she announced, "I am the queen of heaven and the Mother of God; pray always." These apparitions in Beauraing were fully approved by the Holy See on July 2, 1949.[22]

John Occhipinti (1958)

John Occhipinti grew up in a very devout Catholic home in Connecticut and New Jersey. He became serious about his faith at age eighteen (1958) while attending Bible college in Texas. As he was praying for an ill roommate he saw a person whom he identified as Jesus standing near his roommate's

20. Qtd. in Denis Fortin, "Ellen G. White and the Gift of Prophecy," 9.
21. Oral Roberts, *The Call,* 22.
22. "Our Lady of Beauraing," 1-4.

bed. He laid his hand on the roommate's brow, then disappeared. At that instant his roommate jumped from bed and ran down the halls of the dorm shouting, "I've been healed, I've been healed." Occhipinti described Jesus as traditional [in appearance], with a long white robe, shoulder length hair, a short beard, and eyes that seemed to be on fire. He seemed to be about six feet tall, exhibited no radiance, and seemed as solid as any ordinary person.[23]

Zeitun, Egypt, Appearances of the Virgin Mary (1968)

On April 2, 1968 the Virgin Mary appeared at night over the domes of the church of St. Mary at Zeitun, Egypt. According to one account, "she appeared in luminary and spiritual figure and for the first time in history, she continued her manifestation in an uninterrupted way on consecutive nights. Each time the appearance would last for several hours each night and was seen by thousands of people of different faiths and nationalities." Multitudes came to see her each night for thirty months. She was dressed "like a queen with a laminating [sic] scarf covering her head." Some nights she would wear a crown on her head, with "sparkling jewels and a small cross on it." On other occasions she would appear "carrying Jesus Christ as a baby over her left arm."[24]

Our Lady of Akita (1973)

In Akita, Japan, on June 12, 1873, Sister Agnes Sasagawa, a Christian nun, while in prayer, witnessed rays of light emanating from the tabernacle. In the coming days after her experience, Sister Agnes noticed the wounds of the stigmata on the inside of her left hand. The cross-shaped wounds profusely bled, causing considerable pain. In the chapel stood a three-foot statue of the Virgin Mary carved from Katsura wood. While praying on July 6, 1973, Sister Agnes heard a voice coming from the statue which was glowing in light. "My daughter, my novice," spake the statue, "you have obeyed me well in abandoning all to follow me. Is the infirmity of your ears painful? Your deafness will be healed, be sure. Does the wound of your hand cause you to suffer? Pray in reparation for the sins of men. Each person in this community is my irreplaceable daughter. Do you say well the prayer of the Handmaids of the Eucharist? Then, let us pray it together: 'Most Sacred Heart of Jesus, truly present in Holy Eucharist, I consecrate my body and soul to be entirely one with Your Heart, being sacrificed at every instant

23. Ibid., 76-77.
24. "The Appearance of The Virgin Mary in Zeitun, Egypt."

on all the altars of the world and giving praise to the Father pleading for the coming of His Kingdom. Please receive this humble offering of myself. Use me as You will for the glory of the Father and the salvation of souls. Most holy Mother of God, never let me be separated from Your Divine Son. Please defend and protect me as Your Special Child. Amen.'"

When the prayer was finished, the Heavenly Voice said: "Pray very much for the Pope, Bishops, and Priests. Since your Baptism you have always prayed faithfully for them. Continue to pray very much ... very much. Tell your superior all that passed today and obey him in everything that he will tell you. He has asked that you pray with fervor."

Later that day several other nuns noticed drops of blood flowing from the right hand of the carving. The bleeding continued until September 29, at which time the statue began to sweat an essence of perfume. On January 4, 1975, the statue started to cry and continued to do so at intervals for seven years, crying a total of one hundred and one times.

Ultimately Our Lady of Akita gave Sister Agnes three messages. On April 22, 1984, after an eleven-year investigation, Bishop John Shojiro, with Holy See approval, declared the events to be of supernatural origin.[25]

Maureen Hason (1982)

Jesus appeared before her open eyes, extending his hands toward her in a gesture of compassion. He was wearing a white robe, had brown hair and beard, and a tanned complexion. His face was sad, and although he did not say anything to her, he communicated with his eyes. She could tell by the look on his face that he knew her through and through, and that he loved her. She saw that she had been living her own life without his help. What his face said was, "I've been here all along. If you would have just come to me I would have been able to help you." At that moment she came to an understanding of the Christian doctrine of forgiveness, and the meaning of the belief that "Jesus is the Lord of everything." This event was the turning point in her religious life.[26]

Rose Fairs (1988)

While Fairs was lying in her bed early one morning on October 29, 1988, Jesus appeared about six to eight feet away, standing in her doorway. "He wore a robe, off-white in color, loosely tied up by a cord." She was attracted to

25. "Our Lady of Akita."
26. Wiebe, *Visions of Jesus,* 70-71.

his face, "especially his eyes." He had brown curly hair with a beard to match, and blue eyes. This point puzzled her because she didn't think that a Jew would have blue eyes. His facial expression was pleasant, but he did not smile. He said nothing, and did not convey a message of any type. Rose believes the purpose of his visit "was simply to let her know that he exists."[27]

27. Ibid., 60-61.

APPENDIX 2 | MEANINGS OF *LAMANITE* IN MORMON CULTURE

The [Book of Mormon] was written by many ancient prophets by the spirit of prophecy and revelation. Their words, written on gold plates, were quoted and abridged by a prophet-historian named Mormon. The record gives an account of two great civilizations. One came from Jerusalem in 600 B.C., and afterward separated into two nations, known as the Nephites and the Lamanites. The other came much earlier when the Lord confounded the tongues at the tower of Babel. This group is known as the Jaredites. After thousands of years, all were destroyed except the Lamanites, and they are the principal ancestors of the American Indians.

—Introduction, Book of Mormon (1981)[1]

Since 1830, the vast majority of Joseph Smith's disciples have believed precisely what this introduction to the Book of Mormon asserts: the native aborigines of the Americas are lineal descendants of the Lamanites, the surviving remnant of all Book of Mormon cultures. As such, these peoples are deemed modern-day Israelites. The idea that the Hebrew ancestors of today's Native Americans lived everywhere in the Western hemisphere from Alaska to the southern tip of South America, including the Pacific Islands, is one of the better-known concepts in Mormon history. Virtually every prominent Mormon Church leader from Joseph Smith to the present has shared this interpretation.

Beginning in the last half of the twentieth century, however, a small but articulate group of researchers has attempted to revise this long-held tradition. Their motive is to defend the integrity of the Book of Mormon as an ancient historical record in the face of increasing archaeological, cultural, and social challenges—most recently an abundance of DNA studies—that

1. In 2007, the wording "the principal ancestors of the American Indians" was officially changed to "among the ancestors of the American Indians."

have established an Asian, rather than Semitic or Middle Eastern, ancestry for virtually all Amerindians.[2]

As one Book of Mormon researcher has stated, "Apologetic scholars now recognize (1) that Book of Mormon events could not have spanned North, Central, and South America, and (2) that modern Amerindians are predominantly of East Asian ancestry."[3] Seemingly, in an attempt to circumvent the conclusion that the Book of Mormon is Joseph Smith's solution for the controversies of his age, born of early American myths that American Indians were of Semitic origin, some writers continue to promote the concept that the Book of Mormon's founding Hebrew colonists were a small cluster of settlers who peopled a very limited tract of Mesoamerica. These Israelites supposedly interacted with the much larger indigenous populations of North and South America who were Asiatic. In time, this theory postulates, interbreeding with this Asian stock effectively extinguished the founding colonies' unique Middle Eastern genetic code and the Lamanites as a distinguishable people were no more.[4]

The major problem with this attempted solution is that LDS Church leaders, from Joseph Smith to members of the Church's current leadership, have consistently made explicit statements identifying *all* North and South American Indians, as well as Polynesian islanders, as literal Lamanites—Semitic descendants of the original colonists in the Book of Mormon.[5] A half-century ago, Joseph Fielding Smith, then president of the LDS Church's Quorum of the Twelve Apostles and eventually tenth Church president, unequivocally rejected the so-called "limited geography" theory of Book of Mormon lands:

---

2. Jeffrey Meldrum and Trent D. Stephens have observed: "99.6% of Native American genetic markers studies so far exhibit Siberian connections. ... There has been little if any evidence seriously considered by the mainstream scientific community that would indicate a Middle East origin, or any other source of origin, for the majority of contemporary Native Americans" (Meldrum and Stephens, "Who Are the Children of Lehi?" 41-42). A 2009 article in *Science Daily* announced that Kari Britt Schroeder of the University of California, Davis, and other researchers found that all Native Americans are descended from a single migration across the Bering Strait. Their study appeared in the journal *Molecular Biology and Evolution* ("A Quantum Leap in DNA Studies"). Brent Lee Metcalfe, "Reinventing Lamanite Identity," 20-25, lists some ten articles treating the DNA evidence.

3. Metcalfe, "Reinventing Lamanite Identity," 20.

4. See John L. Sorenson, *An Ancient American Setting for the Book of Mormon;* Meldrum and Stephens, "Who Are the Children of Lehi?"; John L. Sorenson and Matthew Roper, "Before DNA"; Michael F. Whiting, "DNA and the Book of Mormon"; and Blake T. Ostler, "Assessing the Logical Structure of DNA Arguments against the Book of Mormon," 70-72.

5. For a scholarly overview of DNA, Native American, and Book of Mormon geography issues, see Simon G. Southerton, *Losing a Lost Tribe.*

> Within recent years there has arisen among certain students of the Book of Mormon a theory to the effect that within the period covered by the Book of Mormon, the Nephites and Lamanites were confined almost within the borders of the territory comprising Central America and the southern portion of Mexico; the Isthmus of Tehuantepec probably being the "narrow neck" of land spoken of in the Book of Mormon rather than the Isthmus of Panama. ... This modernistic theory of necessity, in order to be consistent, must place the waters of Ripliancum and the Hill Cumorah some place within the restricted territory of Central America, notwithstanding the teaching of the Church to the contrary for upwards of 100 years. ... In the light of revelation it is absurd for anyone to maintain that the Nephites and Lamanites did not possess this northern land. ... In the face of this evidence coming from the Prophet Joseph Smith, Oliver Cowdery and David Whitmer, we cannot say that the Nephites and Lamanites did not possess the territory of the United States and that the Hill Cumorah is in Central America.[6]

A brief but representative selection of the teachings of prominent LDS authorities equating *Lamanite* with "American Indian" and thus effectively challenging the "limited geography" theory of Book of Mormon lands appears chronologically below.

Joseph Smith

[1828:] And for this very purpose are these [gold] plates preserved, which contain these records—that the promises of the Lord might be fulfilled, which he made to his people;

And that the Lamanites might come to the knowledge of their fathers, and that they might know the promises of the Lord. (D&C 3:19-20.)

[1830:] [The Book of Mormon] is my word to the Gentile, that soon it may go to the Jew, of whom the Lamanites are a remnant. (D&C 19:27.)

At this time [October 1830] a great desire was manifested by several of the elders respecting the remnants of the house of Joseph, the Lamanites, residing in the west—knowing that the purposes of God were great respecting that people, and hoping that the time had come when the promises of the Almighty in regard to them were about to

6. Joseph Fielding Smith, "Where Is the Hill Cumorah? Book of Mormon Establishes Location of Historic Region," 2-3.

be accomplished, and that they would receive the gospel, and enjoy its blessings.[7]

And that which I have appointed [Parley P. Pratt] is that he shall go with my servants, Oliver Cowdery and Peter Whitmer, Jun., into the wilderness among the Lamanites. (D&C 32:2.)

[1831:] And thus you shall take your journey into the regions westward, unto the land of Missouri, unto the borders of the Lamanites. (D&C 54:8).

In contemplating the degraded state of the Lamanites and the lack of civilization, refinement and religion among the people generally, the Prophet exclaimed in yearning prayer: When will the wilderness blossom as the rose? When will Zion be built up in her glory, and where will thy Temple stand, unto which all nations shall come in the last days? (D&C 57: headnote.)

[1833:] The Book of Mormon is a record of the forefathers of our western tribes of Indians; having been found through the ministration of an holy angel, and translated into our own language by the gift and power of God, after having been hid up in the earth for the last fourteen hundred years, containing the word of God which was delivered unto them. By it we learn that our western tribes of Indians are descendants from that Joseph which was sold into Egypt, and that the land of America is a promised land unto them.[8]

[1835:] It has been said by many of the learned and wise men, or historians, that the Indians or aborigines of this continent, are of the scattered tribes of Israel. It has been conjectured by many others, that the aborigines of this continent are not of the tribes of Israel, but the ten tribes have been led away into some unknown regions of the north. Let this be as it may, the prophecy I have just quoted (Deut. 30:1-4) "will fetch them," in the last days, and place them in the land which their fathers possessed.[9]

[1836:] One of the most important points in the faith of the Church of the Latter-day Saints, through the fullness of the everlasting Gospel, is the gathering of Israel (of whom the Lamanites constitute a part)—that happy time when Jacob shall go up to the house of the Lord, to worship Him in spirit and in truth, to live in holiness. … The Book

7. *History of the Church,* 1:118.
8. Ibid., 315.
9. Ibid., 2:261.

of Mormon has made known who Israel is, upon this continent. And while we behold the government of the United States gathering the Indians, and locating them upon lands to be their own, how sweet it is to think that they may one day be gathered by the Gospel![10]

[1842:] In this important and interesting book the history of ancient America is unfolded, from its first settlement by a colony that came from the tower of Babel, at the confusion of languages to the beginning of the fifth century of the Christian Era. We are informed by these records that America in ancient times has been inhabited by two distinct races of people. The first were called Jaredites, and came directly from the Tower of Babel. The second race came directly from the city of Jerusalem, about six hundred years before Christ. The Jaredites were destroyed about the time that the Israelites came from Jerusalem, who succeeded them in the inheritance of the country. The principal nation of the second race fell in battle towards the close of the fourth century. The remnant are the Indians that now inhabit this country.[11]

The Church's First Missionaries, 1830

[The Lamanite missionaries] are now on their way to the Western Indians, for whose benefit the new Revelation was especially designed. The Indians, as fast as they are converted are to become white men. …

This new Revelation, they say is especially designed for the benefit, or rather for the christianizing of the Aborigines of America; who, as they affirm, are a part of the tribe of Manasseh, and whose ancestors landed on the coast of Chili [sic] 600 years before the coming of Christ, and from them descended all the Indians of America.[12]

Parley P. Pratt (1807-57)

It was now October, 1830. A revelation had been given through the mouth of this Prophet, Seer, and Translator, in which Elders Oliver Cowdery, Peter Whitmer, Ziba Peterson and myself were appointed to go into the wilderness through the western States, and to the Indian territory. … After traveling for some days we called on an Indian nation at or near Buffalo; and spent part of a day with them, instructing them in the knowledge of the record of their forefathers.[13]

10. Ibid., 358.
11. Ibid., 4:537-38.
12. Qtd. in Warren Isham, "The Golden Bible, or Campbellism Improved."
13. Parley P. Pratt, *Autobiography of Parley Parker Pratt,* 47.

Thus ended our first Indian Mission, in which we had preached the gospel in its fullness, and distributed the record of their forefathers among three tribes, viz: the Catteraugus Indians, near Buffalo, N.Y., the Wyandots of Ohio, and the Delawares west of Missouri.[14]

Oliver Cowdery

[1831:] I am informed of another tribe of Lamanites lately who have an abundance of flocks of the best kinds of sheep and cattle, and they manufacture blankets of a superior quality. The tribe is very numerous; they live three hundred miles west of Santa Fe, and are called Navajos.[15]

[1835:] The Nephites who were once enlightened, had fallen from a more elevated standing as to favor and privilege before the Lord, in consequence of the righteousness of their fathers, and now falling below, for such was actually the case, were suffered to be overcome, and the land was left to the possession of the red men, who were without intelligence, only in the affairs of their wars; and having no records, only preserving their history by tradition from father to son, lost the account of their true origin, and wandered from river to river, from hill to hill, from mountain to mountain, and from sea to sea, till the land was again peopled, in a measure, by a rude, wild, revengeful, warlike and barbarous race. Such are our Indians.[16]

Brigham Young

[1853:] These Indians are the seed of Israel, through the loins of Joseph who was sold into Egypt; they are the children of Abraham, and belong to the chosen seed; were it not so, you would never have seen them with dark, red skins. This is in consequence of the curse that has been placed upon them, which never would have come upon them in the world, had their fathers not violated the order of God, which was formerly among them; for in proportion to the light they sinned against, so were they reduced by the curse of God, which has been visited upon their children for many generations. They are of the House of Israel, and the time has come for the Lord to favor Zion, and redeem Israel. We are here in the mountains, with these Lamanites for our neighbors, and I hesitate not to say, if this people possessed the faith

14. Ibid., 57.
15. Oliver Cowdery to General William Clark, 432-33.
16. Oliver Cowdery to W. W. Phelps, "Letter VII," July 1835, 158.

they ought to have, the Lord Almighty would never suffer any of the sons of Jacob to injure them in the least.[17]

[1855:] Before the Book of Mormon was printed, and immediately after Joseph Smith obtained the plates, and the revelations he received concerning this record being the record of the Nephites, and of the Lamanites, who are the fathers of the present aborigines of our country, and in which the Lord told him that He was about to set His hand the second time to gather Israel, the war commenced against him; this was long before the book was printed.[18]

[1866:] I am sorry to say that we see the descendants of this very people now in a very low and degraded state. I refer to the aborigines or native Indians of this continent. But this is in consequence of their apostasy and turning from God. The aborigines of this country are the descendants of this very people whom Jesus visited, to whom He delivered his gospel, and among whom he organized his Church. They were obedient for over three hundred years, and served God with an undivided heart, after which they began to apostatize. For three hundred years the people on the continent of North and South America were benefitted by the work of the Savior in organizing his Church and revealing every principle and ordinance calculated to assist them back into the presence of God.[19]

[1870:] We have Israel in our midst; we live upon their land; we have communion with them and we are under the necessity of feeding and clothing them to a certain extent; and to preserve peace with them at present, until they come to a knowledge of the truth. I mean the Lamanites, the aborigines of our country. They are of the House of Israel.[20]

Wilford Woodruff

[1857:] The American Indians, whose origin has long been a subject of dispute, and which the learned have sought in vain to come to a knowledge of, are here set forth in their true character, through the instrumentality of their records which have been revealed [the Book of Mormon], and that they are about to have restored to them the blessings of the gospel and the holy priesthood, with all its attendant

17. Brigham Young, May 8, 1853, JD 1:106.
18. Brigham Young, Feb. 18, 1855, JD 2:179.
19. Brigham Young, May 29, 1870, JD 13:174-75.
20. Brigham Young, Oct. 6, 1870, JD 13:262.

privileges, which were enjoyed by their progenitors, and thereby become a civilized and righteous nation in their own land.[21]

[1893:] Remember in like pity the dwindling remnants of the House of Israel, descendants of thy servant Lehi. Restore them, we pray thee, to thine ancient favor, fulfill in their completeness the promises given to their fathers, and make of them a white and delightsome race, a loved and holy people as in former days.[22]

Orson Pratt

[1842:] It was also made manifest to him [Joseph Smith], that the "American Indians" were a remnant of Israel; that when they first emigrated to America, they were an enlightened people, possessing a knowledge of the true God, enjoying his favour.

The principal nation of the second race [Nephites], fell in battle towards the close of the fourth century. The remaining remnant, having dwindled into an uncivilized state, still continue to inhabit the land, although divided into a "multitude of nations," and are called by Europeans the "American Indians."

We have also stated when, and by whom they [the gold plates] were written; that they contain the history of nearly one-half of the globe, from the earliest ages after the flood, until the beginning of the fifth century of the Christian era.[23]

[1859:] [The Book of Mormon] professes to contain the history of part of the tribe of Joseph, who came out of the land of Jerusalem 600 years before Christ, and colonized the American continent. These Indian tribes are their descendants.[24]

Those who survived the overwhelming judgments of war and famine were left only to sink into the lowest depths of degradation and misery. Their descendants are called by us American Indians.[25]

[1868:] He [Jesus] appeared on this great Western Hemisphere, peopled by numerous nations—the remnants of the House of Israel, of whom our American Indians are the descendants. They saw Jesus as well as the Jews at Jerusalem. They beheld the wounds in His hands, His

21. "Important Notice to the Saints," 1,066.

22. Dedicatory Prayer for the Salt Lake Temple, in G. Homer Durham, *The Discourses of Wilford Woodruff,* 346.

23. Orson Pratt, *An Interesting Account of Several Remarkable Visions,* 10.

24. Orson Pratt, Jan. 2, 1859, JD 7:33.

25. Orson Pratt, Aug. 14, 1859, JD 7:213.

feet, and in His side. They saw Him descend clothed in a white robe; they saw Him come down into the midst of their assemblies, in the northern portion of what we call South America.[26]

[1872:] The Lord led one of the Prophets, whose name was Lehi and his sons, and one or two other families from the land of Jerusalem to this American continent. This was about six hundred years before Christ; of these families the American Indians are the descendants.[27]

The Twelve Apostles

[1845:] To all the Kings of the World;
To the President of the United States of America;
To the Governors of the several States;
And to the Rulers and People of all Nations: …

We also bear testimony that the "Indians" (so called) of North and South America are a remnant of the tribes of Israel; as is now made manifest by the discovery and revelation of their ancient oracles and records.

And that they are about to be gathered, civilized, and made one nation in this glorious land.

[God] will assemble the Natives[,] the remnants of Joseph in America; and make of them a great, and strong, and powerful nation: and he will civilize and enlighten them and will establish a holy city, and temple, and seat of government among them, which shall be called Zion.

The despised and degraded son of the forest, who has wandered in dejection and sorrow, and suffered reproach, shall then drop his disguise, and stand forth in manly dignity, and exclaim to the Gentiles who have envied and sole him: "I am Joseph: does my father yet live?" Or, in other words: I am a descendant of that Joseph who was sold into Egypt. You have hated me, and sold me, and thought I was dead. But lo! I live, and am heir to the inheritance, titles, honors, priesthood, sceptre, crown, throne, and eternal life and dignity of my fathers who live for evermore.

Let the Government of the United States also continue to gather together, and to colonize the tribes and remnants of Israel (the Indians), and also to feed, clothe, succor, and protect them, and endeavor to civilize and unite; and also to bring them to the knowledge of their

26. Orson Pratt, June 14, 1868, JD 12:252.
27. Orson Pratt, Feb. 4, 1872, JD 15:69-70.

Israelitish origin, and of the fulness of the gospel which was revealed to, and written by, their forefathers on this land; the record of which has now come to light.

[God] has revealed the origin and the Records of the aboriginal tribes of America, and their future destiny.—And we know it.[28]

John Taylor

[1853:] Where will you find a more corrupt set than the descendants of Ephraim, so far fallen and so debased a set as the Indians that dwell in these mountains, and that roam wildly over the broad prairies of this country? Their fathers have got to do something for them to bring them forth to inherit the promises. It is for Abraham to feel after his seed, and be interested in their welfare.[29]

George Q. Cannon

[1868:] When America was discovered by white men from Europe the Indian race covered the continent from the Atlantic to the Pacific. … All the people then were red. … The Book of Mormon teaches us that these people were the children of Laman and Lemuel, and other men who were white, but who, because of their wickedness, brought this curse of a red skin upon their children. … When the Nephites were destroyed, the red men spread all over the land and split up into nations and tribes. … There are many promises made by the Lord in the book of Mormon to the Indians. The gospel of Jesus Christ is to be declared unto them. They are to come to the knowledge of the truth, and many generations shall not pass away among them, before they will become a white and delightsome people. … They are the descendants of Abraham, the friend of God. God covenanted with their fathers that, in the last days, he would remember and save them. They have a great work to do yet among the Gentiles. They are the Lord's battle-axe, and He will use them to do His work. Many of them may perish, but a remnant must be saved.[30]

[1877:] The Lord has revealed many things about the Indians. But the people

28. Although Apostle Parley P. Pratt authored the "Proclamation," Wilford Woodruff claimed that the document fulfilled "an express commandment of God" ("Important Notice to the Saints"). Brigham Young wrote to Pratt affirming the Twelve's approval: "We have to say in relation to your proclamation that we approve of it and are pleased with it" (Brigham Young to Parley P. Pratt, May 26, 1845, 14).

29. John Taylor, June 12, 1853, JD 1:157.

30. George Q. Cannon, "Editorial Thoughts," *Juvenile Instructor,* June 1, 1868, 84.

of the world do not believe them. The Lord has said they will not all be destroyed; but a remnant shall be spared, and they will yet be mighty and shall become a white and pleasant people. … It is hard for many of those who call themselves Saints to believe the words of the Lord concerning the Lamanites, or, as we call them, Indians. The Lamanites are so few and the Gentiles are so many, and the Lamanites have so little power and are so low and degraded, that doubting Saints cannot see how they can escape destruction. But the Lord has said they shall escape, and his word must be fulfilled.[31]

Erastus Snow

[1882:] If the Spirit gives me liberty I will pursue the train of thought that has passed through my mind while Brother Richards has been speaking upon the spirit that has gone abroad upon the remnants of the house of Israel who occupy this land, the American Indians whom we understand to be the descendants of the Nephites, the Lamanites, the Lemuelites and the Ishmaelites who formerly possessed this land, whose fathers we have an account of in the Book of Mormon. Those who are most familiar with their history, and with the history of our settlements in these mountains for the last thirty years—the manner in which we have sent out our colonies to locate upon the land of the Lamanites. … [T]hose, I say, who are best acquainted with our labors in this direction will best appreciate the results.[32]

James E. Talmage

[1890:] The Lamanites, while increasing in numbers, fell under the curse of divine displeasure; they became dark in skin and benighted in spirit, forgot the God of their fathers, lived a wild nomadic life, and degenerated into the fallen state in which the American Indians—their lineal descendants—were found by those who rediscovered the western continent in later times.[33]

[T]he existing Indian tribes are descendants of the immigrants whose history is contained in the Book of Mormon, and that therefore they have sprung from progenitors who were of the house of Israel.[34]

[1915:] The Nephites suffered extinction about 400 A.D., but the Lamanites

31. George Q. Cannon, "Editorial Thoughts," *Juvenile Instructor,* Aug. 1, 1877, 174.
32. Erastus Snow, Feb. 5, 1882, JD 23:8-9.
33. James E. Talmage, *A Study of the Articles of Faith,* 260.
34. Ibid., 284.

lived on in their degraded course, and are today extant upon the land as the American Indians.[35]

About 400 A.D. the last great battle was fought near the hill Cumorah; and the Nephite nation became extinct. The degenerate remnant of Lehi's posterity, the Lamanites or American Indians, have continued until this day.[36]

B. H. Roberts

[1906:] It was for this purpose that the record which had been intrusted to Joseph [Smith] had been preserved, that the promises of God might be fulfilled that he had made to the ancient inhabitants of America, that their descendants—the American Indians—might know the promises of the Lord made to their father, and believe the gospel and rely upon the merits of Jesus Christ, and be glorified and saved through faith in his name, by their faith and repentance.[37]

Spencer W. Kimball

[1946:] You Polynesians of the Pacific are called Samoan or Maori, Tahitian or Hawaiian, according to your islands. There are probably sixty million of you on the two continents and on the Pacific Islands, all related by blood ties. The Lord calls you Lamanites, a name which has a pleasant ring, for many of the grandest people ever to live upon the earth were so called. In a limited sense, the name signifies the descendants of Laman and Lemuel, sons of your first American parent, Lehi, but you undoubtedly possess also the blood of the other sons, Sam, Nephi, and Jacob. And you likely have some Jewish blood from Mulek, son of Zedekiah, King of Judah. The name Lamanite distinguishes you from other peoples. It is not a name of derision or embarrassment, but one of which to be very proud.[38]

[1949:] We still find race prejudice and intolerance on the part of many non-Indians concerning the Lamanites. Often they are excluded from cafes, hotels, schools, and are made to feel unwelcome in church gatherings.

You have read of their weaknesses and sins and crimes. You have seen them languishing under their curse. They have suffered much

35. James E. Talmage, *Jesus the Christ,* 49.
36. Ibid., 742.
37. B. H. Roberts, *A Comprehensive History of the Church,* 1:113.
38. Edward L. Kimball, *The Teachings of Spencer W. Kimball,* 596-97.

and endlessly. But have you recalled their virtues, their strengths, and the promises and covenants made to them?

Have they not eaten husks long enough? Has not their day of restoration come? Can we not forgive their trespasses, that we might in turn be forgiven?[39]

[1960:] The day of the Lamanites is nigh. For years they have been growing delightsome, and they are now becoming white and delightsome, as they were promised. In this picture of the twenty Lamanite missionaries, fifteen of the twenty were as white as Anglos; five were darker but equally delightsome. The children in the home placement program in Utah are often lighter than their brothers and sisters in the hogans on the reservation.

At one meeting a father and mother and their sixteen-year-old daughter were present, the little member girl—sixteen—sitting between the darker father and mother, and it was evident she was several shades lighter than her parents—on the same reservation, in the same hogan, subject to the same sun and wind and weather. There was the doctor in a Utah city who for two years had had an Indian boy in his home who stated that he was some shades lighter than the younger brother just coming into the program from the reservation. These young members of the Church are changing to whiteness and to delightsomeness.[40]

[1971:] *Who are the Lamanites?* The term *Lamanite* includes all Indians and Indian mixtures, such as the Polynesians, the Guatemalans, the Peruvians, as well as the Sioux, the Apache, the Mohawk, the Navajo, and others. It is a large group of great people. … *Lamanites share a royal heritage.* I should like to address my remarks to you, our kinsmen of the isles of the sea and the Americas. Millions of you have blood relatively unmixed with gentile nations. … Columbus called you "Indians," thinking he had reached the East Indies. … The Lord calls you *Lamanites.*[41]

George P. Lee (First Native American LDS General Authority)

[1976:] I have a testimony of the Book of Mormon, the history of my forefathers. America was founded so that the gospel could be restored and

39. Ibid., 610.
40. Spencer W. Kimball, "The Day of the Lamanite," 922-23.
41. Qtd. in Edward L. Kimball, *The Teachings of Spencer W. Kimball,* 596.

so that this sacred record could be brought back to my people and to anyone who will listen.[42]

Bruce R. McConkie

[1979:] When Columbus discovered America, the native inhabitants, the American Indians as they were soon to be designated, were a people of mixed blood and origin. Chiefly they were Lamanites, but such remnants of the Nephite nation as had not been destroyed had, of course, mingled with the Lamanites. ... Thus the Indians were Jews by nationality (D&C 57:4), their forefathers having come out from Jerusalem, from the kingdom of Judah. (2 Ne. 33:8-10). ... But with it all, for the great majority of the descendants of the original inhabitants of the Western Hemisphere, the dominant blood lineage is that of Israel. The Indians are repeatedly called Lamanites in the revelations to the Prophet, and the promise is that in due course they "shall blossom as the rose" (D&C 49:24), that is, become again a white and delightsome people as were their ancestors a great many generations ago.[43]

Official LDS Church Missionary Pamphlet

[1982:] Lehi's people and Mulek's people eventually merged and became one nation, the ancestors of the American Indians. The Book of Mormon is the ancient history of this people, telling of their wars, movements, kings, and their religion—which was the religion of Israel, for these people were Israelites and practiced the law of Moses.[44]

Ted E. Brewerton

[1995:] Many migratory groups came to the Americas, but none was as important as the three mentioned in the Book of Mormon. The blood of these people flows in the veins of the Blackfoot and the Blood Indians of Alberta, Canada; in the Navajo and the Apache of the American Southwest the Inca of western South America; the Aztec of Mexico; the Maya of Guatemala; and in other native American groups in the Western Hemisphere and the Pacific islands.[45]

---

42. George P. Lee, "But They Were in One," 99. At this time, Lee was the only Native American LDS general authority.

43. Bruce R. McConkie, *Mormon Doctrine,* 32-33.

44. "What Is the Book of Mormon?" 1982, 3.

45. Ted E. Brewerton, "The Book of Mormon," 30-31.

Gordon B. Hinckley

[1984:] Thou Kind and Gracious Father, our hearts swell with gratitude for thy remembrance of the sons and daughters of Lehi. … We thank Thee O God, for lifting the scales of darkness which for generations clouded the vision of the descendants of Lehi.[46]

[1999:] "I sense a great spirit of gratitude for this new [Ecuadoran] temple," remarked President Hinckley. "The Saints have waited a very, very long time." He continued: "It has been a very interesting thing to see the descendants of Father Lehi in the congregations that have gathered in the temple. So very many of these people have the blood of Lehi in their veins, and it is just an intriguing thing to see their tremendous response and their tremendous interest."[47]

James E. Faust

[2000:] We invoke Thy blessings upon this nation of Mexico where so many of the sons and daughters of Father Lehi dwell. Bless these Thy children.[48]

Thomas S. Monson

[2000:] May Thy eternal purposes concerning the sons and daughters of Lehi be realized in this sacred house. May every blessing of the eternal gospel be poured out upon them, and may the suffering of the centuries be softened through the beneficence of Thy loving care.[49]

Clate W. Mask Jr.

[2004:] I love meeting the children of Lehi in spotless white in the numerous temples in the Mexico South Area, where I am currently serving. … I have seen humble descendants of Lehi come down from the mountains to that temple [in Guatemala] and openly weep as they stood there in awe."[50]

Jeffrey R. Holland

[2006:] While we talk about the children of Lehi blossoming as a rose,

---

46. Gordon B. Hinckley, "Dedicatory Prayer of the Guatemala City, Guatemala Temple."
47. Gordon B. Hinckley, qtd. in "Remarks at the Dedication of the Guayaquil, Ecuador Temple," 74.
48. James E. Faust, "Bring New Light and Understanding," 4.
49. Thomas S. Monson, "Prayer at Dedication of Villahermosa, Mexico Temple, May 21, 2000."
50. Clate W. Mask Jr., "Standing Spotless before the Lord," April 2004, LDS General Conference Address, at https://www.lds.org/general-conference/2004/04/standing-spotless-before-the-lord?lang=eng.

you [Navajos, Hopis, Zunis, Apaches, and Utes] are blossoming individually.[51]

Dieter F. Uchtdorf

[2011:] You [Guatemalans] are truly children of our wonderful Father Lehi.[52]

Juan A. Uceda

[2015:] We are working here [in Peru] among the children of Lehi, they have the blood of Israel and they respond to the message of the gospel of Jesus Christ.[53]

Neil L. Andersen

[2016:] They [the Navajo Nation] are the children of Lehi ...[54]

51. Qtd. in "Children of Lehi: Gospel Is First Loyalty," *LDS Church News,* March 25, 2006; at http://www.ldschurchnewsarchive.com/articles/48683/Children-of-Lehi-Gospel-is-first-loyalty.html.

52. Qtd. in "Quetzaltenango Guatemala Temple: 2,400 Youth Participate in Cultural Celebration," *LDS Church News,* December 10, 2011, at http://www.ldschurchnewsarchive.com/articles/61817/Quetzaltenango-Guatemala-Temple-2400-youth-participate-in-cultural-celebration.html.

53. Qtd. in "Temple Dedication Highlights Unforgettable Father's Day in Peru," *LDS Church News,* June 25, 2015, at http://www.deseretnews.com/article/865631427/Temple-dedication-highlights-unforgettable-Fathers-Day-in-Peru.html?pg=all.

54. Qtd. in "Church Strengthens Ties to Navajo Nation," *LDS Church News,* January 21, 2016, at http://www.deseretnews.com/article/865645895/Church-strengthens-ties-to-Navajo-Nation.html?pg=all.

BIBLIOGRAPHY

Abbreviations

BC	*A Book of Commandments: For the Government of the Church of Christ, Organized According to Law, on the 6th of April 1830.*
Conference Report	*Report of the Semi-Annual Conference of the Church of Jesus Christ of Latter-day Saints.* Salt Lake City: Church of Jesus Christ of Latter-day Saints, semi-annual.
D&C	[Joseph Smith Jr. et al.]. *Doctrine and Covenants of the Church of Jesus Christ of Latter-day Saints: Containing Revelations Given to Joseph Smith the Prophet, with some Additions by His Successors in the Presidency of the Church.* Salt Lake City: Deseret Book, for the Church, 1981.
History of the Church	Joseph Smith Jr. et al., *History of the Church of Jesus Christ of Latter-day Saints,* edited by B. H. Roberts, 2d ed. rev. (6 vols. 1902–12, Vol. 7 1932. Rpt., Salt Lake City: Deseret Book, 1977 printing).
JD	*Journal of Discourses.* 26 vols. Liverpool and London: Latter-day Saints Booksellers Depot, 1855–86.
Journal History	Journal History of the Church of Jesus Christ of Latter-day Saints. Chronological scrapbook of typed entries and newspaper clippings, 1830-present. LDS Church History Library.
LDS Church History Library	Archives and Library of the Church History Department, Church of Jesus Christ of Latter-day Saints, Salt Lake City.
Lee Library	L. Tom Perry Special Collections, Harold B. Lee Library, Brigham Young University, Provo, Utah.
RLDS History	*The History of the Church of Jesus Christ of Reorganized Latter Day Saints.*
TS	*Times and Seasons.* Commerce/Nauvoo, Illinois. 1839-45.

Frequently Cited Works

Aberbach, Alan David. *In Search of An American Identity: Samuel Latham Mitchill, Jeffersonian Nationalist.* New York: Peter Lang, 1988.

"Abracadabra, a Magical Formula Used by the Gnostics." www.avsands.com/abracadabra-av.htm (Dec 3, 2001).

An Account of a Trance or Vision of Sarah Alley. Poughkeepsie, New York: Power, 1798.
"Account of monies received in tuition in Moor's I.C. School from Aug. 1814 to Aug. 1815." "Moor's Indian Charity School Records, 1760-1915." DA 403, Box 1, fd. 1. Rauner Special Collections Library, Dartmouth College, Hanover, New Hampshire.
"An Act for Supporting Ministers of the Gospel." *1787 Vermont Laws,* Oct. 1, 1787.
Adair, James. *The History of the American Indians.* London: N.p., 1775.
Adams, Donald R., Jr. "Wage Rates in the Early National Period: Philadelphia, 1785-1830." *Journal of Economic History,* Sept. 1968, 402-12.
Adams, Hannah. *Dictionary of All Religions and Religious Denominations.* 4th ed. New York: James Eastburn & Co., 1817.
Adams, Vivian McConkie. "All Prophets Knew, Testified of Him." www.needessays.com/essay/009596.html (Aug. 31, 2004).
Adovasio, J. M., and Jake Page. *The First Americans: In Pursuit of Archaeology's Greatest Mystery.* New York: Random House, 2002.
Agricola, Georgius. *De Re Metallica, translated from the First Latin Edition of 1556.* Ed. Herbert Clark Hoover and Lou Henry Hoover. New York: Dover Publications, 1950.
Agrippa, Henry Cornelius. *Three Books of Occult Philosophy.* London: Gregory Moule, 1651. Reprint, St. Paul, MN: Llewellyn Publications, 2004.
_____. *His Fourth Book of Occult Philosophy.* Robert Turner, trans. London: Thomas Books, 1665.
à Kempis, Thomas. *An Extract of the Christian's Pattern; or, A Treatise of the Imitation of Christ,* edited by John Wesley. Philadelphia: Dickins, 1794.
Alderman, R. W., Letter to Arthur B. Deming, Dec. 25, 1884. *Naked Truths about Mormonism* 1 (Jan. 1888): 3.
Alexander, Archibald, ed. *Sermons of the Log College.* Ligonier, Pennsylvania: Solio Deo Gloria Publications, 1993.
Alexander, Thomas G. "The Place of Joseph Smith in the Development of American Religion: A Historiographical Inquiry." In Bryan Waterman, ed., *The Prophet Puzzle,* 1-24.
_____. "The Reconstruction of Mormon Doctrine." In Gary James Bergera, ed. *Line upon Line,* 53-66.
Alirangues, Loretta M. "Funerary Practices in Early and Modern America." www.morbidoutlook.com/nonfiction/articles/2003 06 america.html (Jan. 25, 2005).
Allen, Henry M. "Letter to the Librarian of the Palmyra Library," Mar. 1964. E. B. Grandin File. King's Daughters Library, Palmyra, New York.
Allen, James B. "Emergence of a Fundamental: The Expanding Role of Joseph Smith's First Vision in Mormon Religious Thought." *Journal of Mormon History* 7 (1980): 43-61.
_____. "Second Only to Christ: Joseph Smith in Modern Mormon Piety." In Stephen D. Ricks, Donald W. Parry, and Andrew H. Hedges, eds., *The Disciple as Witness: Essays on Latter-day Saint History and Doctrine in Honor of Richard Lloyd Anderson.* Provo, Utah: FARMS, 2000. 1-35.
_____. "The Significance of Joseph Smith's 'First Vision' in Mormon Thought." *Dialogue: A Journal of Mormon Thought* 1 (Autumn 1966): 29-45.
_____., and Glen M. Leonard. *The Story of the Latter-day Saints.* 2d ed. rev. and enl. Salt Lake City: Deseret Book, 1992.

"American Ballads and Songs." http://sniff.numachi.com/~rickheit/dtrad/pages/tiCALOMELL:TTredflag.html (Jan. 19, 2005).

"Amniomancy." www.oldwivestales.net/QandAarticle1013.html (Aug. 5, 2004).

"The Ancient Trade of Coopering." www.beaverbuckets.com/beaver_den_news_spr_o1.htm (Oct. 27, 2004).

Anderick, Mrs. S. F. Affidavit, June 24, 1887. *Naked Truths about Mormonism* 1 (Jan. 1888): 2.

Anderson, Galusha. *When Neighbors Were Neighbors* (Boston, 1911), 106. Cited in Gregory Van Dussen, "The Bergen Camp Meeting in the American Holiness Movement." *Methodist History* 21, no. 2 (Jan. 1983): 77-90.

Anderson, Lavina Fielding. *Lucy's Book: A Critical Edition of Lucy Mack Smith's Family Memoir.* Salt Lake City: Signature Books, 2001.

Anderson, Mary Audentia. *Ancestry and Posterity of Joseph Smith and Emma Hale.* Independence, Missouri: Herald Publishing House, 1929.

Anderson, Richard Lloyd. *Investigating the Book of Mormon Witnesses.* Salt Lake City: Deseret Book, 1981.

_____. *Joseph Smith's New England Heritage: Influences of Grandfather Solomon Mack and Asael Smith.* Salt Lake City: Deseret Book, 1971.

_____. "Joseph Smith's New York Reputation Reappraised." *BYU Studies* 10 (Spring 1970): 283-314.

_____. "The Mature Joseph Smith and Treasure Searching." *BYU Studies* 24 (Fall 1984): 489-560.

_____. "Personal Writings of the Book of Mormon Witnesses." In Noel B. Reynolds, ed., *Book of Mormon Authorship Revisited,* 39-60.

Anderson, Robert D. *Inside the Mind of Joseph Smith: Psychobiography and the Book of Mormon.* Salt Lake City: Signature Books, 1999.

Anderson, Rodger I. *Joseph Smith's New York Reputation Reexamined.* Salt Lake City: Signature Books, 1990.

Andover, Vermont. Vital Records, Book A, p. 191. Marriage of Luman Walters and Harriet Howard, Nov. 3, 1819. LDS Church History Library.

"Another Testimony: Statement of William Smith, Concerning Joseph, the Prophet." *Deseret Evening News,* Jan. 20, 1894, 12.

Anthon, Charles. "A Fact in the Mormon Imposture." Letter, Aug. 12, 1844. Rpt. *New-York Observer,* May 3, 1845.

_____. Letter to Eber D. Howe, Feb. 17, 1834, in Eber D. Howe, *Mormonism Unvailed,* 270-72.

_____. Letter to Thomas Winthrop Coit, Apr. 3, 1841. *Church Record* (Flushing, New York) 1 (Apr. 7, 1841): 231-32. Rpt. in John A. Clark, *Gleanings by the Way,* 233-38. For convenience, see Dan Vogel, ed., *Early Mormon Documents,* 4:382-86.

"The Appearance of The Virgin Mary in Zeitun, Egypt." www.st-peter-st-paul-coptic-orthodox-church.org/story.htm (Apr. 19, 2005).

"Appendicitis." www.medimall.co.uk/appendicitis.htm (Sept. 2, 2003).

"Appendicitis Symptoms." http://ks.essortment.com/appendicitissym rexu.htm (Dec. 27, 2004).

Arrington, Leonard J., and Davis Bitton. *The Mormon Experience.* New York: Alfred A. Knopf, 1979.

"The Articles and Covenants of the Church of Christ." *Evening and Morning Star* 1, no. 1 (June 1832): 1-2.

Ashment, Edward H. "The Book of Mormon—A Literal Translation?" *Sunstone* 5, no. 2 (Mar.-Apr. 1980): 10-14.

Ashurst-McGee, Mark. "The Josiah Stowell Jr.-John S. Fullmer Correspondence." *BYU Studies* 38 (1999): 108-17.

_____. "Moroni: Angel or Treasure Guardian?" *Mormon Historical Studies* 2, no. 2 (2001): 39-76.

_____. "A Pathway to Prophethood: Joseph Smith Junior as Rodsman, Village Seer, and Judeo-Christian Prophet." M.A. thesis, Utah State University, 2000.

Aslan, Reza. *No god but God: The Origins, Evolution, and Future of Islam.* New York: Random House Trade Paperbacks, 2006.

"Aussie Minister's Amazing Feats of Memory Make Him Champion of the Universe." www.redhotchilli.com/news/article40725030953.htm (Dec. 2, 2004).

Austin, Emily M. *Mormonism; or, Life among the Mormons.* Madison, Wisconsin: M. J. Cantwell, 1882.

Backman, Milton V., Jr. "Awakening in the Burned-over District: New Light on the Historical Setting of the First Vision." *BYU Studies* 6 (Spring 1969): 301-20.

_____. *Joseph Smith's First Vision: Confirming Evidence and Contemporary Accounts.* Salt Lake City: Bookcraft, 1980.

_____. *Joseph Smith's First Vision: The First Vision in Historical Context.* Salt Lake City: Bookcraft, 1971.

_____., and James B. Allen. "Membership of Certain of Joseph Smith's Family in the Western Presbyterian Church of Palmyra." *BYU Studies* 10 (Summer 1970): 482-84.

Bailey, Raymond T. "Emma Hale: Wife of the Prophet Joseph Smith." M.A. thesis, Brigham Young University, 1952.

Baker, Frank, ed. *The Works of John Wesley: Letters II, 1740-1755.* Oxford, England: Claredon, 1982.

Barben, Arnold H. *Notes on "The Kingdom."* Seneca Falls, New York: Seneca Falls Historical Society, n.d.

Barber, John W., and Henry Howe. *Historical Collections of the State of New York.* New York: S. Tuttle, 1842, 406-7. Rpt. in Dan Vogel, ed., *Early Mormon Documents,* 3:312-14.

Barnes, Joseph W. "Obediah Dogberry: Rochester Freethinker." *Rochester History* 36, no. 3 (July 1974): 1-24.

Barton, N. E. "Joe Smith's Youthful Days. Deacon Stowell's Long Hunt for God—His Belief that Smith Could See Fifty Feet into the Earth." *Bainbridge [New York] Republican,* Aug. 23, 1877, 2.

Bateman, Samuel (1832-1911). Diary, 1886-88, 1899-1909. Typescript, MS 1899. Lee Library.

Bauder, Peter. *The Kingdom and Gospel of Jesus Christ: Contrasted with That of Anti-Christ. A Brief Review of Some of the Most Interesting Circumstances, Which Have Transpired since the Institution of the Gospel of Christ, from the Days of the Apostles.* Canajoharie, New York: Printed by A. H. Calhoun, 1834.

Bean, Willard. *A. B. C. History of Palmyra and the Beginning of "Mormonism."* Palmyra, New York: Palmyra Courier Co., 1938.

_____. "How We Got the Hill Cumorah." *Deseret News,* Jan. 29, 1943. Willard Bean Scrapbook, Lee Library.

_____. "Report of 2 May 1917 interview of Dr. Pratt conducted by Willard Bean." Qtd. in Rand Hugh Packer, "History of Four Mormon Landmarks in Western New York," 47.

_____. "Scrapbook." Lee Library.

Beardsley, Levi. *Reminiscences: Personal and Other Incidents; Early Settlement of Otsego County.* New York: Charles Vinten, 1852. In Louis C. Jones, ed., *Growing Up in the Cooper Country—Boyhood Recollections of the New York Frontier.* Syracuse, New York: Syracuse University Press, 1965.

Becker, Carl L. "Everyman His Own Historian." In *The Vital Past: Writings on the Uses of History.* Edited by Stephen Vaughn. Athens: University of Georgia Press, 1985, 1-22.

Bedell, George C., Leo Sandon Jr., and Charles T. Wellborn. *Religion in America,* 2d ed. New York: Macmillan Publishing, 1982.

Beer, Andrew. *Farmers' Calendar, or Utica Almanack, for the Year of Our Lord, 1816.* Utica, New York: Seward and Williams, 1815.

Behrens, Richard K. "Hyrum Smith: The Dartmouth Years Revisited on His 200th Birthday." Unpublished paper, 2000. Photocopy in my possession, used by permission.

Bell, Whitfield J., Jr. *The Colonial Physician and Other Essays.* New York: Science History, 1975.

Benes, Peter, ed. *Wonders of the Invisible World, 1600-1900: The Dublin Seminar for New England Folklife Annual Proceedings, 1992.* Boston: Boston University Press, 1995.

Bennett, James Gordon. "Mormonism—Religious Fanaticism—Church and State Party," Pt. 1, *Morning Courier and Enquirer,* Aug. 31, 1831. Rpt. in *Christian Register* (Boston), Sept. 24, 1831, and Dan Vogel, ed., *Early Mormon Documents,* 3:283. See also www.gbennett.f9.co.uk/gb-timeline.htm (July 23, 2004).

_____. "Mormon Religion—Clerical Ambition—Western New York—The Mormonites Gone to Ohio," Pt. 2, *New York Morning Courier and New-York Enquirer,* Sept. 1, 1831. Rpt. in *Christian Register* (Boston), Sept. 24, 183, and Dan Vogel, ed., *Early Mormon Documents,* 3:281.

Bennett, John Cook. *The History of the Saints, or, An Exposé of Joe Smith and Mormonism.* Boston: Leland & Whiting, 1842.

Bennett, Richard E. "'Read This I Pray Thee': Martin Harris and the Three Wise Men of the East." *Journal of Mormon History* 36, no. 1 (Winter 2010): 178-216.

Benson, Herbert, and William Proctor. *The Breakout Principle.* New York: Scribner, 2003.

[Benton, Abram W.] "Mormonites." *Evangelical Magazine and Gospel Advocate* (Utica, New York) 2 (Apr. 9, 1831): 120.

Benton, Josiah Henry. *Warning Out in New England, 1656-1817.* Boston: W. B. Clarke, 1911.

Berge, Dale L. "Archaeological Work at the Smith Log House." *Ensign,* Aug. 1985, 24-26.

_____. *Archaeology at the Boyhood Home of Joseph Smith, Jr., Palmyra, New York.* Provo, Utah: Brigham Young University Museum of Peoples and Cultures, 2003.

Bergen, F. D. "Current Superstitions." *Memoirs of the American Folk-Lore Society.* Boston: N.pub., 1896.

Bergera, Gary James. "Joseph Smith and the Hazards of Charismatic Leadership." In Bryan Waterman, ed., *Prophet Puzzle,* 239-58.

_____, ed. *Line upon Line: Essays on Mormon Doctrine.* Salt Lake City: Signature Books, 1989.

_____. "The Orson Pratt-Brigham Young Controversies: Conflict within the Quorums, 1853-1868." *Dialogue: A Journal of Mormon Thought* 13 (Summer 1980): 7-49.

Berrett, LaMar C., ed. *Sacred Places: New England and Eastern Canada, a Comprehensive Guide to Early LDS Historical Sites.* Salt Lake City: Bookcraft, 1999.

_____. *Sacred Places: New York and Pennsylvania, A Comprehensive Guide to Early LDS Historical Sites.* Salt Lake City: Deseret Book, 2000.

Besterman, Theodore. *Crystal Gazing: A Study in the History, Distribution, Theory and Practice of Scrying.* 1920. Rpt., Kila, Montana: Kessinger Publishing, n.d.

"Bible Dictionary." In *The Holy Bible Containing the Old and New Testaments Translated Out of the Original Tongues: And With the Former Translations Diligently Compared and Revised, by His Majesty's Special Command, Appointed to be Read in Churches.* Salt Lake City: Church of Jesus Christ of Latter-day Saints, 1981.

Bidamon, Emma Smith. Interviewed by Nels Madson and Parley P. Pratt, 1877.

_____. Letter to Emma S. Pilgrim, Mar. 27, 1876. Community of Christ, Library-Archives, Independence, Missouri.

Bissell, Josiah. Letter to Charles G. Finney, Sept. 15, 1829. Charles Finney Papers, Oberlin College Archives.

Bjorkland, D. F., and B. R. Zemand. "Children's Organization and Metamemory Awareness in Their Recall of Familiar Information." *Child Development* 53 (1982): 799-810.

Blackman, Emily C. *History of Susquehanna County, Pennsylvania.* Philadelphia: Claxton, Remsen & Haffelfinger, 1873.

Blackstone, William. *Commentaries on the Laws of England.* Oxford: Claredon Press, 1765.

Blair, William W. Letter to Editors, May 22, 1879, *Saints' Herald* 26 (June 15, 1879), 190-91.

_____. Journal. Community of Christ, Library-Archives, Independence, Missouri. Also qtd. in Dan Vogel, ed., *Early Mormon Documents,* 4:340-42.

Bland, John M. "Men Who Would Be 'Kings.'" www.friktech.com/rel/kings1.htm (Aug. 28, 2003).

Bloch, Ruth R. "American Feminine Ideals in Transition: The Rise of the Moral Mother, 1785-1815." *Feminist Studies* 4 (June 1978): 101-20.

Bloom, Harold. *The American Religion: The Emergence of the Post-Christian Nation.* New York: Simon & Schuster, 1992.

_____. *Genius: A Mosaic of One Hundred Exemplary Creative Minds.* New York: Warner Books, 2002.

_____. Review of *By the Hand of Mormon: The American Scripture that Launched a New World Religion,* by Terryl L. Givens. www.oup-usa.org/search97cgi/s97_cgi?action+View&VdkVgwKey+%2E%2E%2F%2E% (Mar. 15, 2002).

"The Blue Nun." http://shell.amigo.net/~tmv/Special Inv4.html (Apr. 19, 2005).

"Boatmen's Friend Society to the Forwarders, Merchants, and Others." *Rochester Daily Advertiser* (1826-56), Aug. 20, 1830.

Bok, Sissela. *Lying: Moral Choice in Public and Private Life.* New York: Vintage Books, 1989.

_____. *Secrets: On the Ethics of Concealment and Revelation.* New York: Vintage Books 1984.

A Book of Commandments for the Government of the Church of Christ, Organized According to Law, on the 6th of April 1830. Zion. Independence, Missouri: W. W. Phelps, 1833.

The Book of Fate: A New and Complete System of Fortune Telling ... Carefully Rendered into English, and Arranged from the Manuscripts of an Adept. New York: Nafis & Cornish, 1817.

Book of Mormon. Palmyra, New York: Printed by E. B. Grandin for the Author, 1830. Current editions cited in this work include: (1) *Book of Mormon: Another Witness for Christ.* Salt Lake City: Church of Jesus Christ of Latter-day Saints, 1981; (2) *Book of Mormon.* Authorized Edition. Independence, Missouri: Community of Christ, 1908, 1966; and (3) *Book of Mormon.* Revised Authorized Edition. Independence, Missouri: Church of Christ [Temple Lot], 1990.

"The Book of Mormon." *Evening and Morning Star* 1, no. 8 (Jan. 1833): 57-59.

"The Book of Mormon." *Evening and Morning Star* 1, no. 12 (May 1833): 98.

"The Book of Mormon." *The New-Yorker,* Jan. 1841. www.lavazone2.com/dbroadhu/New York/miscNew YorkC2.htm (Oct. 11, 2004).

Book of Moses ["Revealed in 1830"]. *Pearl of Great Price,* 1851; Salt Lake City: Church of Jesus Christ of Latter-day Saints, 1982.

Booth, Ezra. "Letter Number VIII." *[Ravenna] Ohio Star,* Dec. 8, 1831.

_____. "Mormonism [I]." *Ohio Star,* Sept. 12, 1831. Rpt. in *[Painesville] Telegraph,* Oct. 25, 1831. www.lavazone2.com/dbroadhu/Ohio/paintel2.htm (Apr. 23, 2003).

_____. "Mormonism No. II." *Ohio Star,* Oct. 9, 1831. Rpt. in *[Painesville] Telegraph,* Nov. 1, 1831. www.lavazone2.com/dbroadhu/Ohio/paintel2.htm (Apr. 23, 2003).

_____. "Mormonism No. III." *Ohio Star,* Oct. 24, 1831. Rpt. in *[Painesville] Telegraph,* Nov. 8, 1831. www.lavazone2.com/dbroadhu/Ohio/paintel2.htm (Apr. 23, 2003).

_____. "Mormonism No. IV." *Ohio Star,* Oct. 31, 1831. Rpt. in *[Painesville] Telegraph,* Nov. 15, 1831. www.lavazone2.com/dbroadhu/Ohio/paintel2.htm (Apr. 23, 2003).

_____. "Mormonism No. V." *Ohio Star,* Nov. 7, 1831. Rpt. in *[Painesville] Telegraph,* Nov. 22, 1831. www.lavazone2.com/dbroadhu/Ohio/paintel2.htm (Apr. 23, 2003).

_____. "Mormonism No. VI." *Ohio Star,* Nov. 14, 1831. Rpt. in *[Painesville] Telegraph,* Nov. 29, 1831. www.lavazone2.com/dbroadhu/Ohio/paintel2.htm (Apr. 23, 2003).

Boudinot, Elias. *A Star in the West: or a Humble Attempt to Discover the Long Lost Tribes of Israel.* Trenton, New Jersey: D. Fenton, S. Hutchinson and J. Dunham, 1816.

Bowen, Norman R., ed. *Elizabeth W. Kane, A Gentile Account of Life in Utah's Dixie, 1872-73: Elizabeth Kane's St. George Journal.* www.signaturebooks.com/dixie.htm (Aug. 10, 2004).

BoxArt. "A Glossary of Divination." www.angelfire.com/tx/afaceinacrowd/glossdiv.html (Sept. 2, 2004).

Boyd, Alexander. Letter to William Boyd, Nov. 26, 1810. Rauner Special Collections, Library, Dartmouth College, Hanover, New Hampshire.

Braden, Clark, and E. L. Kelley. *Public Discussion of the Issues between the Reorganized Church of Jesus Christ of Latter Day Saints and the Church of Christ (Disciples) Held in Kirtland, Ohio, Beginning February 12, and Closing March 8, 1884 between E. L.*

Kelley, of the Reorganized Church of Jesus Christ of Latter Day Saints and Clark Braden, of the Church of Christ. St. Louis: Clark Braden, 1884.

Bradford, M. Gerald, and Alison V. P. Coutts. *Uncovering the Original Text of the Book of Mormon: History and Findings of the Critical Text Project.* Provo, Utah: FARMS, 2002.

Bradley, Joshua. *Accounts of Religious Revivals in Many Parts of the United States from 1815 to 1818.* Albany, New York: G. J. Loomis & Co., 1819.

Brand, John. *Observations on the Popular Antiquities of Great Britain.* 3rd ed., 3 vols. 1777. Reprint, London: Henry G. Bohn, 1849.

Brands, H. W. *Andrew Jackson: His Life and Times.* New York: Doubleday, 2005.

Brewerton, Ted E. "The Book of Mormon: A Sacred Ancient Record." *Ensign,* Nov. 1995, 30-31.

Brewster, James Colin. *Very Important! To the Mormon Money Diggers.* Springfield, Illinois: Author, 1843.

"A Brief History of Palmyra." *Palmyra, New York History and Genealogy.* www.palmyrany.com/history.htm (May 21, 2003).

"A Brief History of Patronage." http://es.rice.edu/ES/humsoc/Galileo/Student_Work/Florence96/jessdave/patronage.html (Oct. 10, 2002).

"A Brief History of Steel." www.tf.uni-kiel.de/matwis/amat/def en/kap 5/advanced/tf 1 4.html (Apr. 2, 2003).

Brieger, G. H. "Therapeutic Conflicts and the American Medical Profession in the 1860s." *Bulletin of Historical Medicine* 41 (1967): 215-22.

Briggs, Edmund C. "A Visit to Nauvoo in 1856." *Journal of History* 9 (Jan. 1916): 454.

Brill, Steve ("Wildman"). *Identifying and Harvesting Edible and Medicinal Plants in Wild (and Not So Wild) Places.* New York: HarperCollins Publishers, 2002.

Broadhurst, Dale. "Uncle Dale's Readings in Early Mormon History: Newspapers of New York." www.lavazone2.com/dbroadhu/New York/miscNew YorkSg.htm (Sept. 15, 2003).

Brodie, Fawn M. *No Man Knows My History: The Life of Joseph Smith the Mormon Prophet.* New York: Alfred A. Knopf, 1945.

Brooke, John L. *The Refiner's Fire: The Making of Mormon Cosmology, 1644-1844.* Cambridge, Massachusetts: Cambridge University Press, 1994.

Brooks, Juanita, ed. *On the Mormon Frontier: The Diary of Hosea Stout.* 2 vols. Salt Lake City: University of Utah Press/Utah Historical Society, 1964.

Brothers, Richard A. *A Revealed Knowledge of the Prophecies and Times.* 2 vols. West Springfield, Massachusetts: Edward Gray, 1797.

Brown, C. W. "Manchester in the Early Days." *Shortsville Enterprise,* Mar. 11, 1904. In *Shortsville Free Press* file. Lee Library.

Brown, R. J. "The Elephant Comes to America." www.historybuff.com/library/refelephant.html (Nov. 3, 2003).

Burn, Richard. *The Justice of the Peace, and Parish Officer.* 12th ed. 3 vols. London: Strahan and Woodfall, 1772.

Burnet, David Staats. "Something New—The Golden Bible." *Evangelical Inquirer* (Dayton, Ohio) No. 10, 1 (Mar. 7, 1831): 217-20. www.solomonspalding.com/docs/1831i05a.htm (Feb. 4, 2005).

Burnett, Stephen, Letter to Lyman E. Johnson, Apr. 15, 1838, Joseph Smith Letterbook (1837-43), 2:64-66. Joseph Smith Papers, LDS Church History Library. For convenience, see Dan Vogel, ed., *Early Mormon Documents,* 2:288-93.

Bush, George, ed. *The Memorabilia of Swedenborg; or, The Spiritual World Laid Open.* New York: John Allen, 1846.

_____. *Statement of Reasons for Embracing the Doctrines and Disclosures of Emanuel Swedenborg.* New York: Allen, 1846.

Bushman, Richard L. *Believing History: Latter-day Saint Essays,* ed. Reid L. Neilson and Jed Woodworth. New York: Columbia University Press, 2004.

_____. "The Character of Joseph Smith." *BYU Studies* 42, no. 2 (2003): 23-34.

_____. "The First Vision Story Revived." *Dialogue: A Journal of Mormon Thought* 4 (Spring 1969): 82-93.

_____, ed. *The Great Awakening: Documents on the Revival of Religion, 1740-1745.* Chapel Hill: University of North Carolina Press, 1969.

_____. *Joseph Smith and the Beginnings of Mormonism.* Urbana: University of Illinois Press, 1984.

_____. "A Joseph Smith for the Twenty-First Century." *BYU Studies* 40, no. 3 (2001): 155-71.

_____, with the assistance of Jed Woodworth. *Joseph Smith: Rough Stone Rolling.* New York: Alfred A. Knopf, 2005.

Butler, Jon. *Awash in a Sea of Faith: Christianizing the American People.* Cambridge, Massachusetts: Harvard University Press, 1990.

_____. "Magic, Astrology and the Early American Religious Heritage." *American Historical Review* 84 (Apr. 1979): 317-46.

Butts, Isaac. Statement, ca. 1885. *Naked Truths about Mormonism* 1 (Jan. 1888): 2.

Campbell, Alexander. "The Book of Mormon Reviewed, and Its Divine Pretensions Exposed." *[Painesville] Telegraph.* Mar. 15, 1831. www.lavazone2.com/dbroadhu/Ohio/paintel2.htm (Apr. 23, 2003).

_____. *Christian Baptism, with Its Antecedents and Consequences* (1851). www.mun.ca/rels/restmov/texts/acampbell/Cbac/CBAC212.HTM.

Cannon, Donald Q. "Joseph Smith in Salem (D&C 111)." In Robert L. Millet and Kent P. Jackson, eds., *Studies in Scripture, Volume 1: The Doctrine and Covenants.* Sandy, Utah: Randall Book Co., 1984. 432-437.

_____. "Palmyra, New York: 1820-1830." In Larry C. Porter, Milton V. Backman, and Susan Easton Black, eds., *Regional Studies ... New York,* 1-13.

_____, ed. *Regional Studies in Latter-day Saint Church History: New England.* Provo, Utah: Department of Church History and Doctrine, 1988.

_____. "Topsfield, Massachusetts: Ancestral Home of the Prophet Joseph Smith." *BYU Studies* 14, no. 1 (Autumn 1973): 56-76.

_____., and Lyndon W. Cook, eds. *Far West Record: Minutes of the Church of Jesus Christ of Latter-day Saints, 1830-1844.* Salt Lake City: Deseret Book, 1983.

_____., Arnold K. Garr, and Bruce A. Van Orden, eds. *Regional Studies in Latter-day Saint Church History: The New England States.* Provo, Utah: Religious Studies Center, Brigham Young University, 2004.

Cannon, George Q. "Editorial Thoughts." *Juvenile Instructor* 3 (June 1, 1868): 84.

_____. "Editorial Thoughts." *Juvenile Instructor* 12 (Jan. 1, 1877): 174.

_____. *Life of Joseph Smith.* Salt Lake City: Juvenile Instructor Office, 1888.

Capron, Joseph. Nov. 8, 1833 statement in Eber D. Howe, *Mormonism Unvailed,* 258-60.

"Captain John Smith Describes the Susquehanna." www.dnr.state.md.us/publiclands/susquehannahistory.html (May 10, 2005).

"Captain Kidd—Pirate's Treasure Buried in the Connecticut River." www.bio.umass.edu/biology/conn.river/kidd.html (Feb. 18, 2004).

Card, Zina Young Williams. Letter to Franklin D. Richards, July 31, 1896. F. D. Richards Letter Collection, LDS Church History Library.

Carey, George G. "Folklore from the Printed Sources of Essex County, Massachusetts." *Southern Folklore Quarterly* 32 (Mar. 1968), 30.

Carey, Jacqueline. *Angels: Celestial Spirits in Legend and Art.* New York: MetroBooks, 1997.

Carlson, John. "Book of Mormon Archaeology: What Does the Evidence Really Show?" Seminar presentation during Aug. 25, 1984, panel discussion at Sunstone Theological Symposium, Salt Lake City. Typescript, 43-44. Lee Library.

Carroll, Robert Todd. "Automatic Writing." *The Skeptic's Dictionary.* http://skepdic.com/autowrite.html (Dec. 3, 2001).

_____. "Divination (Fortune Telling)." *The Skeptic's Dictionary.* http://skepdic.com/divinati.html (Sept. 25, 2003).

_____. "Dowsing (a.k.a. Water Witching)." *The Skeptic's Dictionary.* http://skepdic.com/dowsing.html (Dec. 3, 2001).

_____. "Scrying." *The Skeptic's Dictionary.* http://skepdic.com/scrying/html (Dec. 3, 2001).

_____. "The Unconscious Mind." http://skepdic.com/unconscious.html (Dec. 3, 2001).

Carroll, Roger. *Lebanon, 1761-1994: The Evolution of a Resilient New Hampshire City.* West Kennebunk, Maine: Phoenix Publishing, 1994.

Carruthers, Mary J. *The Book of Memory: A Study of Memory in Medieval Culture.* Cambridge, England: Cambridge University Press, 1992.

Carter, George F. "Maize in Asia and Elephants in America." www.equinox-project.com/v20091.htm (Mar. 17, 2003).

Cartwright, Peter. *Peter Cartwright's Autobiography.* Cincinnati: Cranston & Curts, 1856, http://olivercowdery.com/smithhome/1850s/1856Cart.htm (Sept. 9, 2004).

"Caul." http://healthlink.mcw.edu/article/901311432.html (Aug. 5, 2004).

"Caul." www.fact-index.com/c/ca/caul.html (Aug. 5, 2004).

"Caul, or Face Veil, Occasionally Present at Birth." http://healthlink.mcw.edu/article/901311432.html (Aug. 5, 2004).

"Cauls." http://theshadowlands.net/cauls.htm (Aug. 9, 2004).

"Causes of Savantism." http://dubiniserver.colorado.edu/prj/jsl/causes.html (Apr. 1, 2003).

Chandler, Clay L. "Scrying for the Lord: Magic, Mysticism, and the Origins of the Book of Mormon." *Dialogue: A Journal of Mormon Thought* 36 (Winter 2003): 43-78.

"Changing Medical Practices in Early America." http://dpisinfo.com/wb/medhistory.html (Mar. 9, 2004).

Chapman, Glen. "The Elephant and the Book of Mormon." www.2s2.com/chapmanresearch/elephant.html (July 27, 2001).

_____. "Horses and the Book of Mormon." www.2s2.com/chapmanresearch/user/documents/horses.html (July 27, 2001).

Chase, Abel D. Affidavit, May 2, 1879. Wyl, *Mormon Portraits,* 230-31.

_____. Interviewed by William H. Kelley and Edmund L. Kelley, Manchester, New York, Mar. 6, 1881. William Kelley, Notebook No. 5, p. 9. William H. Kelley Papers, Community of Christ, Library-Archives, Independence, Missouri.

Chase, Abner. *Recollections of the Past.* New York: n.p., 1846.
Chase, Willard. Affidavit. Sworn before Frederick Smith, Justice of the Peace of Wayne County, Dec. 11, 1833. In Eber D. Howe, *Mormonism Unvailed,* 240-48.
_____. Obituary, *Palmyra Courier,* Mar. 17, 1871.
_____. Obituary. *The American Wesleyan,* Apr. 10, 1871. Courtesy Bill Clark.
Chatters, James C. *Ancient Encounters: Kennewick Man and the First Americans.* New York: Simon & Schuster, 2001.
Chauncy, Charles. *Enthusiasm Described and Caution'd Against* [1742] in *The Great Awakening: Documents Illustrating the Crisis and Its Consequences,* ed. Alan Heimert and Perry Miller. New York: Bobbs-Merrill, 1967.
_____. "A Letter from a Gentleman in Boston to Mr. George Wishart ... of Edinburgh." In *The Great Awakening: Documents on the Revival of Religion, 1740-1745,* ed. Richard L. Bushman. Chapel Hill: University of North Carolina Press, 1989, 118-19.
_____. *Seasonable Thoughts on the State of Religion in New England.* Boston, 1743; Reprint, Hicksville New York: Regina Press, 1975.
Child, Hamilton. *Gazetteer and Business Directory of Broome and Tioga Counties, N.Y. for 1872-3.* Syracuse, New York: Journal Office, 1873.
_____. *Gazetteer and Business Directory of Chenango County, N.Y., for 1869-70.* Syracuse, New York: Journal Office, 1869.
_____. *Gazetteer and Business Directory of Wayne County, N.Y. for 1867-8.* Syracuse, New York: Journal Office, 1867.
"Chronological List of Students: Moor's Charity School and Dartmouth College." www.avcnet.org/ne-do-ba/odn edo2.html (Oct. 3, 2002).
Clark Chase Family Group Record. www.familysearch.org/Eng/Search/AF/family group record.asp?familyid+2279466 (July 29, 2003).
Clark, J. Reuben, Jr. "The World Crisis Today." *LDS Church News,* June 16, 1945, 11.
Clark, John A. *Gleanings by the Way.* Philadelphia: W. J. & J. K. Simon, 1842.
_____. Letter to Dear Brethren, Aug. 24, 1840. *The Episcopal Recorder* (Philadelphia) 18 (Sept. 5, 1840): 94-99. Rpt. in John A. Clark, *Gleanings by the Way,* 217, 222-31. Rpt. in Dan Vogel, ed., *Early Mormon Documents,* 2:260-69.
_____. Letter to Dear Brethren, Aug. 31, 1840, *The Episcopal Reader* (Philadelphia) 18 (Sept.12, 1840): 98-99. Rpt. in Dan Vogel, ed., *Early Mormon Documents,* 2: 269-71.
Clarke, Adam. "A Letter to a Preacher (1800)." In Adam Clarke and Thomas Coke, *The Preacher's Manual.* Nashville: Stevenson, 1857.
Clayton, William. Conference Minutes, Nauvoo, Illinois, Oct. 8, 1845. In Dan Vogel, ed., *Early Mormon Documents,* 1:223.
Cleland, Robert Glass, and Juanita Brooks. *A Mormon Chronicle: The Diaries of John D. Lee, 1848-1876.* San Marino, California: Huntington Library, 1955.
Clifford, Alan C. "Charles Wesley (1707-88)." www.igracemusic.com/igracemusic/hymnbook/authors/charles wesley.html (Feb. 4, 2005).
Clinton, William Jefferson. *My Life.* New York: Alfred A. Knopf, 2004.
Cocherell, B. L. "The Ephod, Breastplate, Urim, Thummin, and Theraphim." www.bibleresearch.org/leadersbook8/b8w17.html (June 2, 2003).
Coe, Michael. "Mormons and Archaeology: An Outside View." *Dialogue: A Journal of Mormon Thought* 8, no. 2 (Summer 1973): 20-48.

Cohn, Norman. Review of Ginzburg's *The Night Battles: Witchcraft and Agrarian Cults in the Sixteenth and Seventeenth Centuries.* www.holysmoke.org/wb/wb0208.htm (Aug. 12, 2004).
Cole, Nathan. "The Spiritual Travels of Nathan Cole." Unpublished manuscript. Connecticut Historical Society. Extract rpt. in Richard L. Bushman, ed., *The Great Awakening: Documents on the Revival of Religion, 1740-1745,* 68-70.
"Communication." *Wayne Sentinel* 1 (Sept. 15, 1824): 3.
"Communication from Elder D. Whitmer." *Saints' Herald* 33 (Dec. 4, 1886): 764-65.
Compton, Todd. *In Sacred Loneliness: The Plural Wives of Joseph Smith.* Salt Lake City: Signature Books, 1997.
Conkling, J. Christopher. *A Joseph Smith Chronology.* Reprint, Salt Lake City: Deseret Book, 1979.
Conover, George S., ed. *History of Ontario County, New York.* Syracuse, New York: D. Mason and Co., 1888.
"Contract with E. B. Grandin." *Ensign,* Dec. 1983, 41.
"Converted Lamanites." *Liahona: The Elders' Journal* (Independence, Missouri) 6 (June 20, 1908): 48-49.
Conway, Alan, ed. *The Welch in America: Letters from the Immigrants.* Minneapolis: University of Minnesota Press, 1961.
Cook, Lyndon W. *David Whitmer Interviews: A Restoration Witness.* Orem, Utah: Grandin Book Co., 1991
_____. *The Revelations of the Prophet Joseph Smith: A Historical and Biographical Commentary of the Doctrine and Covenants.* Provo, Utah: Seventy's Mission Bookstore, 1981.
_____. *William Law: Biographical Essay, Nauvoo Diary, Correspondence, Interview.* Orem, Utah: Grandin Book Co., 1994.
Cook, Thomas L. *Palmyra and Vicinity.* Palmyra, New York: Palmyra Courier Journal, 1930.
Cooley, Arnold James. *A Cyclopaedia of Six Thousand Practical Receipts, and Collateral Information in the Arts, Manufactures, and Trades, Including Medicine, Pharmacy, and Domestic Economy.* New York: B. Appleton & Co, 1848.
Cooper, James Fenimore. *The Pioneers: Or the Sources of the Susquehanna, a Descriptive Tale.* New York: Charles Wiley, 1823.
Cooper, Susan Fenimore. *Rural Hours,* 1850. Rpt., edited by Rochelle Johnson and Daniel Patterson, Athens: University of Georgia Press, 1998.
Cooper, William. *A Guide in the Wilderness; or, the History of the First Settlements in the Western Counties of New York, with Useful Instructions to Future Settlers.* Dublin, Ireland: Gilbert and Hodges, 1810.
"A Copy of the Several Lists of the Mens [sic] Names Liable to Work on the Highways in the town of Palmyra in the Year 1804 …" In Dan Vogel, *Early Mormon Documents,* 3:411-14.
Corbett, Pearson H. *Hyrum Smith, Patriarch.* Salt Lake City: Deseret Book, 1963.
"Correspondence." TS 4 (Feb. 15, 1843): 97-98.
Corrill, John. *A Brief History of the Church of Christ of Latter Day Saints (Commonly Called Mormons) Including an Account of Their Doctrine and Discipline, with the Reasons of the Author for Leaving the Church.* St Louis: Printed for the Author, 1839.
A Course in Miracles. Glen Ellen, California: Foundation for Inner Peace, 1992.

Cowdery, Elizabeth Ann Whitmer. Affidavit, Feb. 15, 1870. Qtd. in William E. McLellin to "My Dear Friends," Feb. 1870, Community of Christ, Library-Archives, Independence, Missouri.

Cowdery, Oliver. "The Articles of the Church of Christ." 1829. LDS Church History Library. Published in Robert J. Woodford, "The Historical Development of the Doctrine and Covenants," 288.

_____. *Cowdery's Letters on the Bringing in of the New Dispensation.* Burlington, Wisconsin: Free Press Print, 1899.

_____. Letter to General William Clark, May 7, 1831, TS 5 (Feb. 15, 1844): 432-33.

_____. Letter to Joseph Smith, Nov. 6, 1829, Joseph Smith Letterbook, 1:6-8, Joseph Smith Papers, LDS Church History Library. For convenience, see Dan Vogel, ed., *Early Mormon Documents,* 2:404-406.

_____. Letter to Joseph Smith, Dec. 28, 1829, Joseph Smith Letterbook, 1:4-5, Joseph Smith Papers. LDS Church History Library. For convenience, see Dan Vogel, ed., *Early Mormon Documents,* 2:407-408.

_____. [Letter I] to W. W. Phelps, Sept. 7, 1834, *Latter Day Saints' Messenger and Advocate* 1 (Oct. 1834): 13-16.

_____. [Letter III]. Dec. 1834, *Latter Day Saints' Messenger and Advocate* 1 (Dec. 1834): 41-43.

_____. [Letter IV:] "Rise of the Church." Feb. 1835, *Latter Day Saints' Messenger and Advocate* 1 (Feb. 1835): 77-80.

_____. [Letter V]. Mar. 1835, *Latter Day Saints' Messenger and Advocate* 1 (Mar. 1835): 95-96.

_____. [Letter VI]. Apr. 1835, *Latter Day Saints' Messenger and Advocate* 1 (Apr. 1835): 108-12.

_____. [Letter VII]. July 1835, *Latter Day Saints' Messenger and Advocate* 1 (July 1835): 155-59.

_____. [Letter VIII]. Oct. 1835. *Latter Day Saints' Messenger and Advocate* 2 (Oct. 1835): 195-202. Four of these letters were reprinted five years later in Nauvoo and may be found in the following issues of TS: Letter III, TS 2 no. 3 (Dec. 1, 1840): 225-26; Letter IV, TS 2, no. 4 (Dec. 15, 1840): 241-43; Letter IV, TS 2, no. 10 (Mar. 15, 1841): 343-45; Letter IV, TS 2, no. 11 (Apr. 1, 1841): 360-64, 377-80.

Cowles, Austin W. "The Mormons: Pen and Pencil Sketches Illustrating their Early History, I." *Moore's Rural New-Yorker* (Rochester, New York), Jan. 2, 1869. www.lavazone2.com/dbroadhu/New York/misNew YorkS3.htm (Oct. 19, 2004).

Cowles, George W. *Landmarks of Wayne County.* Syracuse, New York: D. Mason & Co., 1895.

Coxe, Trench. *A View of the United States of America.* Dublin: P. Wogan, 1795.

"The Craft of the Seer." www.tartans.com/seer2.html (June 4, 2002).

Crain, Julie, Research Correspondent for the National Geographic Society. Letter to Luke Wilson, Aug. 12, 1998. Photocopy.

Crawford, Michael H. *The Origins of Native Americans: Evidence from Anthropological Genetics.* Cambridge, England: Cambridge University Press, 1998.

Crawley, Peter. "The Passage of Mormon Primitivism." *Dialogue: A Journal of Mormon Thought* 13, no. 4 (Winter 1980): 26-37.

Cross, Whitney R. *The Burned-Over District: The Social and Intellectual History of Enthusiastic Religion in Western New York, 1800-1850.* Ithaca, New York: Cornell University Press, 1950.

Cuming, F. H. *An Address, Delivered at the Laying of the Cap-Stone, of the Ten Combined Locks at Lockport, on the Anniversary of St. John the Baptist, June 24, 1825.* Lockport, New York: Orsamus Turner, 1825.

Curtis, Susan. "Early Nineteenth-Century America and the Book of Mormon." In Dan Vogel, ed., *The Word of God,* 81-96.

Dahl, Curtis. "The American School of Catastrophe." *American Quarterly* 11 (1959): 375-82.

Davenport, Frederick Morgan. *Primitive Traits in Religious Revivals.* 1905. Rpt., Honolulu: University Press of the Pacific, 2000.

"David Whitmer Interviewed." *Saints' Herald,* Nov. 15, 1881, 347.

Davies, Rupert E., ed. *The Works of John Wesley.* 26 vols. Nashville: Abingdon, 1989.

Dee, Genet Bingham, ed. and comp. *A Voice from the Dust: A Sacred History of Ancient Americans.* Salt Lake City: Deseret News Press, 1939.

Deem, Rich. "DNA Evidence and Molecular Genetics Disprove the Book of Mormon." www.godandscience.org/cults/dna.html (Sept. 30, 2003).

De Givry, Grillot. *Witchcraft, Magic, and Alchemy.* Trans. by J. Courtenay Locke, Boston: Houghton Mifflin Co., 1931.

De Groote, Michael. "DNA Shows Joseph Smith Was Irish." www.mormontimes.com/DB_Index.php?linkTrack=mtEmail&id=1722 (Oct. 25, 2004).

_____. "BYU Symposium: LDS Church's First Legal Status." www.mormontimes.com/print/?id=13814 (Mar. 18, 2010).

De Quincey, Thomas. *The Confessions of an English Opium-eater.*London: Folio Society, 1822.

Deming, Arthur B. Collected Papers. Chicago Historical Society, Chicago.

Deno, Andrea. "Sigmund Freud, 1856-1939: The Family Story." www.acigarisjustacigar.com/family (Aug. 9, 2004).

Deuel, Nancy R. "A Historical Time Line of North American Horses." www.cavalry.org/Horse_History.htm (Apr. 22, 2002).

De Vaca, Cabeza. *Adventures in the Unknown Interior of America.* www.eldritchpress.org/cdv/rel.htm (Feb. 19, 2004).

Devendorf, John C. "Battles of New York." www.fortklock .com/Battles.htm (May 4, 2004).

Dibble, Philo. "Philo Dibble['s] Narrative." *Early Scenes in Church History.* Salt Lake City: Juvenile Instructor Office, 1882, 74-96.

_____. *Juvenile Instructor,* May 15, 1892, 303-304.

"Dictionary of American Fighting Ships." www.hazegray.org/danfs/frigates/essex1.htm (Feb. 12, 2003).

Dillehay, Thomas D. *The Settlement of the Americas: A New Prehistory.* New York: Basic Books, 2000.

"Discoveries on the Canal." *Western Farmer* (Palmyra, New York), Sept. 19, 1821, 1.

"Divination." www.paralumun.com/divination.htm (Nov. 1, 2001).

"The Divining Rod." *American Journal of Science and Arts* 11 (Oct. 1826): 201-12.

"The Divining Rod." *Worcester Magazine and Historical Record* 1 (Oct. 1825): 27-29.

Dogberry, Obediah (pseud. Abner Cole). "Book of Pukei." *[Palmyra] Reflector,* June 12, 1830, 36-37; July 7, 1830, 60. www.lavazone2.com/dbroadhu/New York/wayn1830.htm (Sept. 15, 2003).

Dow, George Francis, and John Henry Edmonds. *The Pirates of the New England Coast, 1630-1730.* Salem, Maine: Marine Research Society, 1923.

Dow, Lorenzo. *History of Cosmopolite.* Wheeling, Virginia: Martin, 1848.

Dubler, Alice M. *Manchester through the Years.* Houghton, New York: Houghton College Press, 1954.

Dunn, Scott. "Automaticity and the Dictation of the Book of Mormon." In Dan Vogel and Brent Lee Metcalfe, eds., *American Apocrypha: Essays on the Book of Mormon,* 17-46.

_____. "Spirit Writing: Another Look at the Book of Mormon." *Sunstone,* June 1985, 17-26.

du Pasquier, Roger. *Unveiling Islam.* www.crescentlife.com/heal%20the%20world/orientalism,_misinformation_&_islam.htm.

Durfee, Isaac, and Lumon Harrison. "Minutes of the Survey of a Public Highway," June 13, 1820. Rpt. in Dan Vogel, ed., *Early Mormon Documents,* 3:420-21.

Durfee, Lemuel. Account Book. 1820s, Microfilm of holograph. LDS Church History Library.

Durham, G. Homer, ed. *The Discourses of Wilford Woodruff.* Salt Lake City: Bookcraft, 1990.

Dwight, Serano E. *The Life of President [Jonathan] Edwards.* New York: Carvill, 1830.

"Early Cattaraugus County History." www.hopefarm.com/cattarny.htm (Oct. 25, 2005).

Eaton, Anna Ruth. *The Origin of Mormonism.* New York: Woman's Executive Committee of Home Missions, 1881.

Eaton, Horace. *The Early History of Palmyra: A Thanksgiving Sermon, Delivered at Palmyra, N.Y., November 26, 1857, By Horace Eaton, Pastor of the Presbyterian Church, Palmyra, New York.* Rochester, New York: Press of A. Strong and Co., 1858.

_____. *The Great Physician: A Sermon on Occasion of the Death of Alexander McIntyre, M.D., Delivered in the Presbyterian Church, Palmyra, N.Y., July 24, 1859.* New York: Printed by John F. Trow, 1860.

_____. *A Memorial of the Celebration at Palmyra, N.Y., of the Centennial Fourth of July, 1876.* Rochester, New York: E. R. Andrews, 1876.

"Effects of Drunkenness." *Palmyra Register,* June 23, 1820, 2.

Eggenstein, Kurt. "Lorber's Method of Recording the Inner Voice." www.disk-plus-buch.de/kee/1/c-invoic.htm (Sept. 8, 2003).

_____. *The Prophet Jakob Lorber Predicts Coming Catastrophies and the True Christianity.* Beitigheim, Germany.: Valkyrie Publishing House, 1975.

Ehat, Andrew F., and Lyndon W. Cook, eds. *The Words of Joseph Smith: The Contemporary Accounts of the Nauvoo Discourses of the Prophet Joseph.* Religious Studies Monograph Series, No. 6. Provo, Utah: Brigham Young University Religious Studies Center, 1980.

"1824 Law Establishing County Poorhouses in New York." www.poorhousestory.com/1824 law.htm. (Apr. 26, 2004).

Ekman, Paul. *Telling Lies: Clues to Deceit in the Marketplace, Politics, and Marriage.* New York: W. W. Norton & Co., 2001.

Ellis, Arthur J. *The Divining Rod: A History of Water Witching.* The Department of the Interior, United States Geological Survey, Washington, D.C.: Government Printing Office, 1938.

Ellis, Elisabeth Gaynor, and Anthony Esler. *World History: Connections to Today.* Englewood Cliffs, New Jersey: Prentice-Hall, 1999.

Emerson, Charles Phillips, Jr., and Jane Sherburn Bragdon. *Essentials of Medicine: The Art and Science of Medical Nursing.* Philadelphia: J. B. Lippinscott, 1955.

Enders, Donald L. "The Joseph Smith, Sr., Family: Farmers of the Genesee." In Susan Easton Black and Charles D. Tate Jr., eds., *Joseph Smith: The Prophet, the Man,* 213-25.

_____. "'A Snug Log House': A Historical Look at the Joseph Smith, Sr., Family Home in Palmyra, New York." *Ensign,* Aug. 1985, 14-23.

"Episodes in Genealogical Research: New Light on William Smith." *Deseret News,* July 27, 1935, 8.

"Esquire: Dictionary Entry and Meaning." Hyperdictionary entry in www.hyperdictionary.com/search.aspx.

The Essential Joseph Smith. Foreword by Marvin S. Hill. Salt Lake City: Signature Books, 1995.

"Explanation of the Biblical Gospel of John Revealed by the Lord Jesus to His prophet Jakob Lorber." www.j-lorber.com/English/Text/GEJ1.html (Apr. 19, 2005).

"Extract from Stephens's 'Incidents of Travel in Central America.'" TS 3 (Sept. 15, 1842): 911-15.

"An Extract of a Letter from Philip Bruce, Elder of the Methodist Episcopal Church, to Bishop Coke, dated Portsmouth, Virginia, March 25, 1788." *Arminian Magazine* [Philadelphia] 2 (Nov. 1790): 563-64.

Evans, John Henry. *Joseph Smith: An American Prophet.* New York: Macmillan, 1943.

Ewers, John C. *The Horse in Blackfoot Indian Culture: With Comparative Material from Other Western Tribes.* Washington, D.C.: U.S. Government Printing Office, 1955.

Fagan, Brian M. *Ancient North America.* London: Thames and Hudson, 2005.

Farmer, John, and Jacob B. Moore. *Gazetteer of the State of New-Hampshire.* Concord, New Hampshire: Jacob B. Moore, 1823.

Farnsworth, Samuel. "Account of the Typhous Fever Which Prevailed in This Place, Beginning the First of the Month [July 1812]." Rauner Special Collections Library, Dartmouth College, Hanover, New Hampshire.

_____. "Nathan Smith's Class Notes, Lecture 2." Oct. 20, 1812. Rauner Special Collections Library, Dartmouth College, Hanover, New Hampshire.

Faulring, Scott H., ed. *An American Prophet's Record: The Diaries and Journals of Joseph Smith.* Salt Lake City: Signature Books/Smith Research Associates, 1987.

Faust, James E. "Bring New Light and Understanding." Excerpt from prayer at dedication of Tuxla Guitierrez Mexico Temple, *LDS Church News,* Mar. 18, 2000, 4.

_____. "'A Wondrous Day' at Temple Dedication." *LDS Church News,* Aug. 7, 1999, 10.

Ferguson, Thomas Stuart. *Written Symposium on Book-of-Mormon Geography: Response of Thomas S. Ferguson to the Norman & Sorenson Papers.* http://trialsofascension.net/mormon/archaeology.html (Sept. 27, 2004).

"Fifty Years of Farming in Vermont." www.moravek.net/ovisnosti/addiction-history.htm (Oct. 10, 2002).

Finberg, Laurence, M.D., and Ronald E. Kleinman, M.D. *Saunders Manual of Pediatric Practice.* Philadelphia: W. B. Sanders Co., 2002.

Finney, Charles G. *What a Revival of Religion Is.* New York: N.p., 1835. In *Religion in America,* edited by George C. Bedell, Leo Sandon Jr., and Charles T. Wellborn, 167-71.

Firmage, Mary Brown. Interviewed by Richard S. Van Wagoner, Aug. 11, 1986. Richard S. Van Wagoner Collection, Manuscripts Division, J. Willard Marriott Library, University of Utah, Salt Lake City.

Fleming, Stanford. *Children and Puritanism: The Place of Children in the Life and Thought of the New England Churches, 1620-1847.* New Haven, Connecticut: Yale University Press, 1933.

Fletcher, John. "On Evangelical Mysticism." In *The Works of the Reverend John Fletcher, Late Vicar of Madely.* 4 vols. New York: Lane and Scott, 1851.

Flibbert, Joseph, K. Davis Goss, Jim McAllister, Bryant F. Tolles, Jr., Richard B. Trask. *Salem: Cornerstones of a Historic City.* Beverly, Massachusetts: Commonwealth Editions, 1999.

Forbes, Thomas Rogers. *The Midwife and the Witch.* New Haven, Connecticut: Yale University Press, 1966.

Ford, Charles V. *Lies! Lies! Lies!: The Psychology of Deceit.* Washington, D.C.: American Psychiatric Press, 1996.

Ford, Thomas. *History of Illinois.* Chicago: n.p., 1854.

Fortin, Denis. "Ellen G. White and the Gift of Prophecy: The Test of a Prophet." www.andrews.edu/~fortind/EGWTest.htm (May 29, 2002).

Fowler, John. *Journal of a Tour through the State of New York in the Year 1830 with Remarks on Agriculture in Those Parts Most Eligible for Settlers.* London: Whittaker, Treacher, and Arnot, 1831.

Fowler, William W. "The Story of Mrs. Martin J. (Nancy) Van Alstine." *Woman of the American Frontier.* www.fortklock.com/Van%20Alstine.htm (May 10, 2003).

Fraiberg, Selma. "Tales of the Discovery of the Secret Treasure." *Psychoanalytic Study of the Child* 9 (1954): 218-41.

Friedman, David M. *A Mind of Its Own: A Cultural History of the Penis.* New York: Penguin Books, 2003.

"Gain C. and Caius C. Robinson Invoice Book, 1819-1831." Original at Palmyra King's Daughters Free Library, Palmyra, New York. Also in LDS Church History Library. For convenience, see Dan Vogel, ed., *Early Mormon Documents,* 3:433-34.

Garber, Marjorie. "Our Genius Problem." *Atlantic Monthly,* Dec. 2002, 65-72.

Garrett, Susan R. "Messengers of God." www.pcusa.org/today/archive/believe/wpb0004.htm (Oct. 25, 2004).

Gilbert, F. C. *Divine Predictions of Mrs. Ellen G. White Fulfilled.* South Lancaster, Massachusetts: Good Tidings Press, 1922.

Gilbert, John H. Letter to James T. Cobb, Feb. 10, 1879, LDS Church History Library.

_____. Letter to James T. Cobb, Mar. 16, 1879, LDS Church History Library.

_____. "Memorandum of John H. Gilbert, Esq., Sept. 8, 1892, Palmyra, New York," 3. Palmyra King's Daughters Free Library, Palmyra, New York. For convenience, see Dan Vogel, ed., *Early Mormon Documents,* 2:542-48.

Giles, Charles. *Pioneer: A Narrative of the Nativity, Experience, Travels, and Ministerial Labours of Rev. Charles Giles.* New York: G. Lane & P. P Sandford, 1844.

Giles, John D. "Survey Made of Flora of Sacred Grove: Elder Giles Makes Report of Results to Presiding Bishopric." *LDS Church News*, Feb. 24, 1945, 6, 12.

Givens, Terryl L. *By the Hand of Mormon: The American Scripture that Launched a New World Religion.* New York: Oxford University Press, 2002.

Goddard, M. E., and Henry V. Partridge. *A History of Norwich, Vermont.* Hanover, New Hampshire: Dartmouth Press, 1905.

Goddard Space Flight Center. "Science Question of the Week." www.gsfc.nasa.gov/scienceques2001/20020315.htm. (Apr. 28, 2004).

Godfrey, Kenneth W. *What Is the Significance of Zelph in the Study of Book of Mormon Geography.* Provo, Utah: FARMS, 1999. http://farms.byu.edu/display.php?table=jbms&passthru=T.

_____. "The Zelph Story." *BYU Studies* 29, no. 2 (Spring 1989): 31-56.

Goen, C. C., ed. *The Works of Jonathan Edwards.* 4 vols. New Haven, Connecticut: Yale University Press, 1972.

"GOLD BIBLE." *The Reflector* (Palmyra, New York), Dec. 9, 1829. www.lavazone2.com/dbroadhu/New York/wayn1830.htm (Sept. 15, 2003).

"GOLD BIBLE." *The Reflector* (Palmyra, New York), Jan. 6, 1831. www.lavazone2.com/dbroadhu/New York/wayn1830.htm (Sept. 15, 2003.

"GOLD BIBLE, NO. 2." *The Reflector* (Palmyra, New York), Jan. 18, 1831. www.lavazone2.com/dbroadhu/New York/wayn1830.htm (Sept. 15, 2003).

"GOLD BIBLE, NO. 3." *The Reflector* (Palmyra, New York), Feb. 14, 1831. www.lavazone2.com/dbroadhu/New York/wayn1830.htm (Sept. 15, 2003).

"GOLD BIBLE, NO. 4." *The Reflector* (Palmyra, New York), Feb. 1, 1831. www.lavazone2.com/dbroadhu/New York/wayn1830.htm (Sept. 15, 2003).

"GOLD BIBLE, NO. 5." *The Reflector* (Palmyra, New York), Feb. 28, 1831. www.lavazone2.com/dbroadhu/New York/wayn1830.htm (Sept. 15, 2003).

"GOLD BIBLE NO. 6." *The Reflector* (Palmyra, New York), Mar. 19, 1831. www.lavazone2.com/dbroadhu/New York/wayn1830.htm (Sept. 15, 2003).

"Golden Bible." *The Gem* (Rochester, New York), Sept. 5, 1829, reprinted from *The Palmyra Freeman,* Aug. [no day], 1829. www.lavazone2.com/dbroadhu/New York/wayn1830.htm (Sept. 15, 2003). Also reprinted in *Rochester Advertiser and Telegraph,* Aug. 31, 1829, and *The Gem* (Rochester, New York), Sept. 5, 1829, and *Painesville Telegraph and Geauga Free Press,* Sept. 22, 1829.

"The Golden Bible." *Republican Advocate* (Wooster, Ohio), Dec. 4, 1830. www.lavazone2.com/dbroadhu/Ohio/miscohio.htm (Mar. 17, 2005).

Goss, K. David. "The Maritime History of Salem." In Joseph Flibbert, K. David Goss, Jim McAllister, Bryant F. Tolles Jr., and Richard B. Trask, *Salem Cornerstones of a Historic City.* Beverly, Massachusetts: Memoirs Unlimited, 1999.

Grace, William to Maj. Roberdeau, Apr. 10, 1823. Rpt. in Richard B. Stout, "A Singular Discovery."

Grandin, Egbert Bratt, Diary, 1831-41. Microfilm of holograph. LDS Church History Library.

Granstrom, Chris. "Sweet Taste of Spring." *Smithsonian,* Apr. 2002, 20-22.

"The Great Age of Sail." *Destination Salem.* www.salemorg/maritime.asp (July 12, 2003).

Greeley, Horace. *Recollections of a Busy Life.* New York: J.B. Ford, 1868.

"Green Mountain Boys to Thomas C. Sharp," Feb. 15, 1844. Thomas C. Sharp and Allied Anti-Mormon Papers, Beinecke Rare Book and Manuscript Library, Yale

University, New Haven, Connecticut. For convenience, see Dan Vogel, ed., *Early Mormon Documents,* 1:597.

Gregg, Thomas. *The Prophet of Palmyra.* New York: John B. Alden, 1890.

Grimm, Jacob, and Wilhelm Grimm. *Household Tales,* trans. Margaret Hunt. London: George Bell, 1884.

Grunder, Rick. "Martin Harris/Charles Anthon/Dr. Mitchell Story." www.xmission.com/nplporter//lds/inprogress/anthon.htm (Mar. 9, 2006).

Gunderson, Robert A. "From the Dust to the Dusty: The Rise and Fall of the Book of Mormon in the Life and Ministry of Joseph Smith, Jr." *John Whitmer Historical Association Journal* 22 (2002): 75-88.

Gunn, Stanley R. *Oliver Cowdery: Second Elder and Scribe.* Salt Lake City: Bookcraft, 1962.

Gutch, E., and Mabel Peacock. *Examples of Printed Folk-Lore Concerning Lincolnshire.* London, Folk-Lore Society, 1908.

Hale, Alva. Affidavit. Affirmed to and subscribed before Charles Dimon, J.P., Mar. 20, 1834. In Eber D. Howe, *Mormonism Unvailed,* 262-66.

Hale, Isaac. Land Agreement with Joseph Smith, Apr. 6, 1829. LDS Church History Library.

_____. Statement. Affirmed to and subscribed before Charles Dimon, J.P., Mar. 20, 1834. In *Susquehanna Register* and *Northern Pennsylvanian* 9 (1 May 1834): 1. Rpt. in Dan Vogel, ed., *Early Mormon Documents,* 4:281-89.

Hall, Courtney Robert. *A Scientist in the Early Republic: Samuel Latham Mitchill.* New York: N.pub., 1934.

Hancock, Mary Salisbury. "The Three Sisters of the Prophet Joseph Smith." *Saints' Herald* pt. 1, 101 (Jan. 11, 1954): 34-36; pt. 2, 101 (Jan. 18, 1954): 58-59; and pt. 3, 101 (Jan. 25, 1954): 82-83, 95.

Harding, Stephen S. Letter to Thomas Gregg, Feb. 1882. In Thomas Gregg, *The Prophet of Palmyra,* 34-56.

Hardy, B. Carmon. *Solemn Covenant: The Mormon Polygamous Passage.* Urbana: University of Illinois Press, 1992.

Harris, Abigail. Statement, Nov. 28, 1833. In Eber D. Howe, *Mormonism Unvailed,* 253.

Harris, Emer. Statement, Apr. 6, 1856. Utah Stake General Minutes, 1855-60. LR 9629, Series 11, Vol. 10, p. 273. LDS Church History Library.

Harris, Lucy ("Dolly"). Statement Nov. 29, 1833. In Eber D. Howe, *Mormonism Unvailed,* 254.

Harris, Martin. Letter to Mr. Emerson, Nov. 23, 1870. *Millennial Star,* Jan. 1, 1877. Qtd. in Ronald W. Walker, "Martin Harris: Mormonism's Early Convert," 33.

_____. Mortgage to Egbert B. Grandin, Aug. 25, 1829, Mortgages, Liber 3, 325, Wayne County Clerk's Office, Lyons, New York. For convenience, see Dan Vogel, ed., *Early Mormon Documents,* 3:473-77.

Hasher, L., and R. T. Zacks. "Automatic and Effortful Processes in Memory." *Journal of Experimental Psychology* 108 (1979): 356-88.

Hatch, Ephraim. *Joseph Smith Portraits: A Search for the Prophet's Likeness.* Provo, Utah: Religious Studies Center, Brigham Young University, 1998.

Hatch, John P., ed. *Danish Apostle: The Diaries of Anthon H. Lund, 1890-1921.* Salt Lake City: Signature Books/Smith-Pettit Foundation, 2006.

Hatch, Nathan O. *The Democratization of American Christianity.* New Haven, Connecticut: Yale University Press, 1989.

_____. "Mormon and Methodist: Popular Religion in the Crucible of the Free Market." *Journal of Mormon History* 20, no. 1 (Spring 1994): 24-44.

_____., and John H. Wigger, eds. *Methodism and the Shaping of American Culture.* Nashville: Kingswood Books, 2001.

Hawthorne, Nathaniel. "The Haunted Mind." Qtd. in F. O. Matthiessen, *American Renaissance: Art and Experience in the Age of Emerson and Whitman.* London, n.p.; 1941.

Hayden, Amos Sutton. *Early History of the Disciples in the Western Reserve.* Cincinnati: Chase and Hall, 1875.

Haynes, Gary. *Mammoths, Mastodonts, and Elephants: Biology, Behavior, and the Fossil Record.* Cambridge, Massachusetts: Cambridge University Press, 1991.

Hays, Bonnie. "Palmyra, Believe It or Not." http://wxxi.org/canaltowns/transcripts/bhays.htm (Nov. 9, 2004).

Hayter, Early W. *The Troubled Farmer, 1850-1900: Rural Adjustment to Industrialism.* Dekalb: Northern Illinois University Press, 6-7.

Hayward, Oliver S., M.D., and Constance E. Putnam. *Improve, Perfect, and Perpetuate: Dr. Nathan Smith and Early American Medical Education.* Hanover, New Hampshire: University Press of New England, 1998.

Herbermann, Charles, et al. *The Catholic Encyclopedia.* 15 vols. New York: Robert Appleton, 1912.

Herndon, Ruth Wallis. *Unwelcome Americans: Living on the Margin in Early New England.* Philadelphia: University of Pennsylvania Press, 2001.

Hibbard, B[illy]. *Memoirs of the Life and Travels of B. Hibbard, Minister of the Gospel.* New York: J. C. Totten, 1825.

Hiland, Paul, and Robert Parks. *History of Wells, Vermont.* Rutland, Vermont: Charles E. Claremont Manufacturing Co., 1877.

Hill, Donna. *Joseph Smith: The First Mormon.* Garden City, New York: Doubleday, 1977.

Hill, Marvin S. "Brodie Revisited: A Reappraisal." *Dialogue: A Journal of Mormon Thought* 7 (Winter 1972): 72-85.

_____. "The First Vision Controversy: A Critique and Reconciliation." *Dialogue: A Journal of Mormon Thought* 15, no. 2 (Summer 1982): 31-46.

_____. "Joseph Smith and the 1826 Trial: New Evidence and New Difficulties." *BYU Studies* 12 (Winter 1972): 223-33.

_____. "Money Digging Folklore and the Beginnings of Mormonism: An Interpretive Suggestion." *BYU Studies* 24 (Fall 1984): 473-88.

_____. "On the First Vision and Its Import in the Shaping of Early Mormonism." *Dialogue: A Journal of Mormon Thought* 12, no. 1 (Spring 1979): 90-99.

_____. *Quest for Refuge: The Mormon Flight from American Pluralism.* Salt Lake City: Signature Books, 1989.

Hill, Nan. "Joe Smith Lived and Married Here." *Afton Enterprise,* July 20, 1939. Newspaper clipping. U. Grant Baker Collection, LDS Church History Library. For convenience, see Dan Vogel, ed., *Early Mormon Documents,* 4:205-207.

Hill, Ralph Nading, ed. *The College on the Hill: A Dartmouth Chronicle.* Hanover, New Hampshire: Dartmouth Publications, 1964.

Hinckley, Gordon B. "Colonia Juarez Temple Dedication." Prayer at dedication of Colonia Juarez Chihuahua Temple. *LDS Church News,* Mar. 13, 1999, 9.
_____. "The Cornerstones of Our Faith." *Ensign,* Nov. 1984, 52.
_____. "Dedicatory Prayer of the Guatemala City, Guatemala Temple." www.ldschurchtemples.com/cgi- bin/prayers.cgi?guatemala_city&chronological (Sept. 1, 2004).
_____. "Dedicatory Prayer of the Mexico City Temple." www.mrm.org/multimedia/text/dna-bom.html (Sept. 1, 2004.)
_____. "Praise to the Man." *Ensign,* Aug. 1983, 2-6.
_____. "Rise to the Glories of the Past." Excerpts from the dedicatory prayer at the Cochabamba Bolivia Temple, *LDS Church News,* May 13, 2000, 4.
Hine, William R. Affidavit, ca. Mar. 1885. Arthur B. Deming, ed. *Naked Truths about Mormonism* 1 (Jan. 1888): 2.
Hirsch, J. M. "Tapping into a Sweet Success Story." *Salt Lake Tribune,* Mar. 17, 2004, B2.
"Historic Lebanon, New Hampshire." www.lebanonnhhistory.org/exhibits/timeline/1700-69.html (May 10, 2003).
"A Historical Sketch of Windsor, Broome County, New York." *Binghamton Daily Republican,* Aug. 18, 1880, 3.
"Historicity of the First Vision." www.lightplanet.com/response/vision.htm (Aug. 25, 2003).
"The History and Mystery of Old Cape Cod." www.barnstablepatriot.com/cccompanion/chapter 2.html (Mar. 6, 2003).
"History of Brigham Young." *Millennial Star* 26 (Feb. 20, 1864): 118-19.
"History of Joseph Smith." TS 3 (Mar.-Oct. 1841): 726-28, 748-49, 753-54, 771-73, 785-86, 801-4, 817-18, 832-33, 853-54, 865-67, 884-85, 897-98, 915-17, 926, 943-44; 4 (Nov.-Dec. 1842): 12-13, 22-23, 40, 41, 61-62, 71-72, 92-93, 108, 117-19, 130-31, 146-47, 172, 304-5, 320-21, 336-38, 352-54.
"History of the Mohawk Palatines." www.geocities.com/christman 19/mvfkswjearly.html.
"The History of a Nephite Coin: A Personal Experience of Elder Richard M. Robinson of Grantsville, Utah, Recorded Dec. 30, 1934." Typescript, LDS Church History Library.
"A History of the Vermont Apple Industry." www.vermontapples.org/seasons.html (Apr. 1, 2004).
Hofstadter, Richard. *Anti-intellectualism in American Life.* New York: Vintage Books, 1963.
Holland, David. "Priest, Pastor, and Power: Joseph Smith and the Question of Priesthood." In *Archive of Restoration Culture: Summer Fellows' Papers, 1997-1999.* Provo, Utah: Joseph Fielding Smith Institute, 2000, 9-16.
Holland, Jeffrey R. "An Analysis of Selected Changes in Major Editions of the Book of Mormon—1830-1920." M.A. thesis, Brigham Young University, 1966.
Holley, Vernal. *Book of Mormon Authorship,* 2d ed. Salt Lake City: Vernal Holley, 1989.
Holt, Brian. *Jesus: God or the Son of God?: A Comparison of the Arguments.* Mt. Juliet, Tennessee: Tellway Publishing, 2002.
Holzapfel, Richard Neitzel, and T. Jeffrey Cottle. *Old Mormon Palmyra and New England: Historic Photographs and Guide.* Santa Ana, California: Fieldbrook Productions, 1991.

Horton, George A., Jr. "Understanding Textual Changes in the Book of Mormon." *Ensign,* Dec. 1983, 24-28.

Horton, James P. *A Narrative of the Early Life, Remarkable Conversion, and Spiritual Labours of James P. Horton.* N.p.: n.p., 1846. Qtd. in Leigh Eric Schmidt, *Hearing Things,* 56-57.

Hotchkin, James H. *A History of the Purchase and Settlement of Western New York, and the Rise, Progress, and Present State of the Presbyterian Church in that Section.* New York: W. M. Dodd, 1848.

Houghey, Hal. *A Review of the Reprint of the Original Book of Mormon,* No. 5, *Firm Foundation,* Sept. 1, 1959, 550.

"The Household Cyclopedia." www.msong.org/cyclopedia/medicine.html (Dec. 27, 2004).

Howard, Richard P. "Adjusting Theological Perspectives to Historical Reality." *Saints' Herald* 129 (Sept. 1, 1982): 28.

_____. "Joseph Smith's First Vision: The RLDS Tradition." *Journal of Mormon History* 7 (1980): 23-30.

Howe, Eber D. "The Book of Mormon." *Painesville [Ohio] Telegraph,* Nov. 16, 1830, 3.

_____. *Mormonism Unvailed: or, A Faithful Account of that Singular Imposition and Delusion, from Its Rise to the Present Time.* Painesville, Ohio: E. D. Howe, 1834.

Howe, James. Clipping from undated and unidentified newspaper, Jonathan B. Turner Papers. Illinois Historical Society Library, Springfield.

Howell, Nathaniel W., Walter Hubbell, Ansel D. Eddy, Henry Chapin, Jared Willson, and Lewis Jenkins. Letter to Ancil Beach, Jan. 1832, 1-2. Walter Hubbell Collection, 1831-33 Correspondence, Princeton University Library, Princeton, New Jersey. For convenience, see Dan Vogel, ed., *Early Mormon Documents,* 3:15.

Huggins, Ronald V. "From Captain Kidd's Treasure Ghost to the Angel Moroni: Changing *Dramatis Personae* in Early Mormonism." *Dialogue: A Journal of Mormon Thought* 36 (Winter 2003): 17-42.

Hulbert, Charles F. Undated newspaper clipping in Scrapbook. Qtd. in Larry C. Porter, "A Study of the Origins of the Church of the Church," 104.

Hullinger, Robert N. *Joseph Smith's Response to Skepticism.* Salt Lake City: Signature Books, 1992.

Hume, David. *Essays: Moral, Political, and Literary,* edited by Eugene F. Miller. Indianapolis: Liberty Classics, 1987.

Huntington, Ray L., and David M. Whitchurch. "'Eighteen Hundred and Froze to Death': Mount Tambora, New England Weather, and the Joseph Smith Family in 1816." In Donald Q. Cannon, Arnold K. Garr, and Bruce A. Van Orden, eds., *Regional Studies … New England States,* 87-98.

Hyde, Orson. *Ein Ruf aus der Wuste, einke Stimme aus dem Schoose der Erde.* Frankfurt, Germany: N. pub., 1842. English translator not identified. For convenience, see Dan Vogel, ed., *Early Mormon Documents,* 1:161-68.

Hyde, William. "Birth of Mormonism. The Story of an Old Man Who Was There When the Tables of Stone Were Found." *Chicago Times,* Oct. 14, 1888. For convenience, see Dan Vogel, ed., *Early Mormon Documents,* 3:188.

"Important Notice to the Saints." TS 6 (Oct. 9, 1845): 1,066.

"Imposition and Blasphemy!! Money-Diggers, &c." *The Gem, of Literature and Science* (Rochester, New York), May 15, 1830. www.lavazone2.com/dbroadhu/New York/miscNew YorkSf.htm (May 1, 2003).

"In the Summer of the Year." *Syracuse Journal,* Feb. 16, 1867. www.lavazone2.com/dbroadhu/New York/miscNew YorkSg.htm (Oct. 19, 2004).

"Information about the Seneca Indians from THIS Seneca's Perspective." http://home.alltel.net/cjimerson/seneca.htm (Oct. 25, 2005).

"Information from the National Museum of Natural History—Smithsonian Institution." www.godandscience.org/cults/Smithsonian.html (Aug. 21, 2001).

Ingersoll, Peter. Affidavit, Dec. 2, 1833. Sworn before Wayne County Judge Thomas P. Baldwin. In Eber D. Howe, *Mormonism Unvailed,* 232-33.

"Inhabitancy and Warning Out." Subsection in *History of Chelmsford.* www.usigs.org/library/books/ma/Chelmsford1917/chel570ch11.htm (Mar. 6, 2003).

"An Interesting Document: Articles of Agreement between Joe Smith, the Father of Mormonism, and Other Persons in 1825." *Salt Lake Tribune,* 23 Apr. 1880, 4. For convenience, see Dan Vogel, ed. *Early Mormon Documents,* 4:411-13.

"Interview with the Mormon Prophet." *Evangelical Magazine and Gospel Advocate* (Utica, New York), Apr. 5, 1834.

Investigator. "The Mormons in Nauvoo: Three Letters from William Law on Mormonism—An Honest Man's Views and Remorse." *Salt Lake City Tribune,* 3 July 1887, 6.

"Iroquois Landscape." New York State Department of Economic Development. www.iloveny.com/travel ideas/culture il.asp (May 5, 2004).

Isham, Warren. "The Golden Bible." *Observer and Telegraph,* Nov. 18, 1830. www.lavazone2.com/dbroadhu/Ohio/miscohio.htm (Mar. 17, 2005).

Isselbacher, Kurt J., M.D., Raymond D. Adams, M.D., Eugene Braunwald, M.D., Robert G. Petersdorf, M.D., and Jean D. Wilson, M.D. *Harrison's Principles of Internal Medicine,* 9th ed. New York: McGraw-Hill, 1980.

"Jakob Lorber." www.jakoblorber.co.nz/JakobLorber.html (Nov. 3, 2003).

"Jakob Lorber the New Revelation." www.amaluxherbal.com/jakob lorber and the new revelation.htm (Nov. 3, 2003).

James, Jane Manning. "Autobiography." 1902, LDS Church History Library.

James, William. *No. 64 (#4476). Manuscript Essays and Notes.* Cambridge, Massuchestts: Harvard University Press, 1988.

_____. *The Varieties of Religious Experience: A Study in Human Nature; Being the Gifford Lectures on Natural Religion Delivered at Edinburgh in 1901-1902.* New York: New American Library, 2003.

Jarratt, Devereaux. *The Life of the Reverend Devereaux Jarratt, Rector of Bath Parish, Dinwiddie County, Virginia. Written by Himself, in a Series of Letters Addressed to the Rev. John Coleman, One of the Ministers of the Protestant Episcopal Church, in Maryland.* 1806; reprint, New York: Arno Press, 1969.

Jennings, Warren A. "The First Mormon Mission to the Indians." *Kansas Historical Quarterly* 38 (Autumn 1971): 288-99.

Jenson, Robin Scott, Robert J. Woodford, Steven C. Harper, eds. *The Joseph Smith Papers—Revelations and Translations, Manuscript Revelation Books.* Salt Lake City: Church Historian's Press, 2009.

Jeremiah Hurlburt v. Joseph Smith Sr. and Alvin Smith, June 26, 1819, Ontario County Records Center and Archives, Canandaigua, New York. For convenience, see Dan Vogel, ed., *Early Mormon Documents,* 3:385-88.

Jessee, Dean C. "The Early Accounts of Joseph Smith's First Vision." *BYU Studies* 9 (Spring 1969): 275-94.

_____. "Joseph Knight's Recollection of Early Mormon History." *BYU Studies* 17 (Autumn 1976): 29-39.

_____. "New Documents and Mormon Beginnings." *BYU Studies* 24 (Fall 1984): 397-428.

_____. "The Original Book of Mormon Manuscript." *BYU Studies* 10 (Spring 1970): 259-78.

_____, ed. *The Papers of Joseph Smith, Vol. 1: Autobiographical and Historical Writings.* Salt Lake City: Deseret Book, 1989.

_____, ed. *The Papers of Joseph Smith, Vol. 2: Journal, 1832-1842.* Salt Lake City: Deseret Book, 1992.

_____, comp. and ed. *The Personal Writings of Joseph Smith.* Salt Lake City: Deseret Book, 1984.

_____. "The Writing of Joseph Smith's History." *BYU Studies* 11 (Spring 1971): 439-73.

"Joe Smith, the Mormon Prophet." *Rochester Daily Union and Advertiser,* Oct. 1, 1867. www.lavazone2.com/dbroadhu/New York/miscNew YorkS3.htm (Oct. 19, 2004).

"Joe Smith: Something about the Early Life of the Mormon Prophet." *Detroit Post and Tribune,* Dec. 3, 1877, 3.

"John Dee, Astrologer to the Queen." www.mystae.com/restricted/streams/gnosis/dee.html (Aug. 9, 2004).

Johnson, John, and Elizabeth Jones. *An Interesting Discussion of the Fundamental Doctrine of the Christian Religion,* 4th ed. London: Hodson, 1818.

Johnson, Ludwell H., III. "Men and Elephants in America." *Scientific Monthly,* Oct. 1952, 215-21.

Johnson, Rochelle, and Daniel Patterson, eds. Susan Fenimore Cooper, *Rural Hours.* Athens: University of Georgia Press, 1998.

Jones, A. J., and R. M. Anservits. "Saint-Simon and Saint-Simonism: A Weberian View." *American Journal of Sociology* 80, no. 5 (1975): 1,095-1,123.

Jones, Louis C., ed. *Growing Up in the Cooper Country: Boyhood Recollections of the New York Frontier.* Syracuse, New York: Syracuse University Press, 1965.

Jones, W. R. "'Hill-Diggers' and 'Hell-Raisers': Treasure Hunting and the Supernatural in Old and New England." In Peter Benes, ed., *Wonders of the Invisible World,* 97-126.

"Joseph Smith—His Early Attempts at Imposture." *Syracuse Journal,* Dec. 2, 1875. www.lavazone2.com/dbroadhu/New York/miscNew YorkS3.htm (Oct. 19, 2004).

Joseph Smith Sr. v. Jeremiah Hurlburt, Feb. 17, 1819, Ontario County Records Center and Archives, Canandaigua, New York. For convenience, see Dan Vogel, ed., *Early Mormon Documents,* 3:385-88.

Kail, R. V. *The Development of Memory in Children.* San Francisco: Freeman, 1979.

Kane, Elizabeth W. *A Gentile Account of Life in Utah's Dixie, 1872-73: Elizabeth Kane's St. George Journal,* edited by Norman R. Bowen. Salt Lake City: Tanner Trust Fund, 1995. Also www.signaturebooks.com/dixie.htm (Aug. 10, 2004).

"Karma Thinley Rinpoche." www.inthelight.co.nz/spirit/gurus/karma007.htm (Apr. 1, 2003).

Karp, Mary. "Anesthesia." *World Book Encyclopedia,* 1992, 1:436.

Katz, Edward, and Peter Paulson. "A Brief History of the Divining Rod in the United States." *Journal of the American Society for Psychical Research* 42 (Oct. 1948): 119-31; 43 (Jan. 1949): 3-18.

Kaufman, Martin. *American Medical Education: The Formative Years, 1795-1910.* Westport, Connecticut: Greenwood, 1976.

Kelleher, Tom. "The Debit Economy of 1830s New England." 2001. Old Sturbridge Village—Online Resource Library. www.osv.org/learning/Document Viewer.php?Action=View & DocID=1947 (June 22, 2005).

_____. "Welfare and Workfare in 1830s New England: Jails, Prisons, Work Houses, and Poor Farms." 1997. Old Sturbridge Village—Online Resource Library. www.osv.org/learning/Document Viewer.php?Action=View & DocID=1824.

Keller, Karl, ed. "'I Never Knew a Time When I Did Not Know Joseph Smith': A Son's Record of the Life and Testimony of Sidney Rigdon." *Dialogue: A Journal of Mormon Thought* 1 (Winter 1966): 15-42.

Keller, Roger R. "Presbyterianism in New York State to 1838." In Alexander L. Baugh and Andrew H. Hedges, eds., *Regional Studies in Latter-day Saint Church History: New York-Pennsylvania.* Provo, Utah: Brigham Young University Department of Church History and Doctrine, 2002. 1-28.

_____. "Unitarianism: Part of the Background of the Restoration." In Donald Q. Cannon, Arnold K. Garr, and Bruce A. Van Orden, eds., *Regional Studies ... New England States.* 99-122.

Kelley, E. L. Papers, "Miscellany." Community of Christ, Library-Archives, Independence, Missouri. For convenience, see Dan Vogel, ed., *Early Mormon Documents,* 2:146-64.

Kelley, William H. "The Hill Cumorah, and the Book of Mormon: The Smith Family ... from Late Interviews." *True Latter Day Saints' Herald* 28 (June 1, 1881): 166-67.

_____. Notebook, No. 5, 1-16. William H. Kelley Papers. Community of Christ, Library-Archives, Independence, Missouri. For convenience, see Dan Vogel, ed., *Early Mormon Documents,* 2:83-87.

Kendall, Edward Augustus. *Travels through the Northern Parts of the United States in the Years 1807 and 1808.* 3 vols. New York: I. Riley, 1809.

Kendig, Daniel S. Statement. *The History of Seneca Co., New York.* Philadelphia: Everts, Ensign & Everts, 1876.

Kennedy, David M., Thomas A. Bailey, and Mel Piehl. *The Brief American Pageant: A History of the Republic,* 3d. ed. Lexington, Massachusetts: D.C. Heath and Co., 1993.

Kennedy, James Harrison. *Early Days of Mormonism: Palmyra, Kirtland, and Nauvoo.* New York: Charles Scribner's Sons, 1888.

Kett, Joseph F. "Growing Up in Rural New England, 1800-1840." In *Anonymous Americans,* edited by Tamara K. Hareven. Englewood Cliffs, New Jersey: Prentice-Hall, 1971.

"Kidd's Island: A Story of the Dorrillite Imposture." *Chicago Magazine: The West As It Is.* Chicago: J. Gager and Co. for Chicago Mechanics' Institute, 1857.

Kimball, Edward L., ed. *The Teachings of Spencer W. Kimball.* Salt Lake City: Deseret Book, 1982.

Kimball, Spencer W. "The Day of the Lamanite." *Improvement Era,* Dec. 1960, 922-23.

_____. *The Lamanite and the Gospel.* Provo, Utah: Brigham Young University Press, 1969.

_____. Letter to ___________. Feb. 2, 1963. UA 617, Box 1, fd. 5. Lee Library.

_____. "Our Paths Have Met Again?" *Ensign,* Dec. 1975, 2-7.

Kimball, Stanley B. "The Anthon Transcript: People, Primary Sources, and Problems." *BYU Studies* 10 (Spring 1970): 325-64.

_____. *Heber C. Kimball: Mormon Patriarch and Pioneer.* Urbana: University of Illinois Press, 1981.

King, Janet. "Vermont Civil War Medicine." http://vermontcivilwar.org/medic/medicine2.shtml (Dec. 27, 2004).

Kinghorn, Kenneth Cain. *The Heritage of American Methodism.* New York: Abingdon Press, 1999.

Kirkham, Francis W. *A New Witness for Christ in America: The Book of Mormon.* 2 vols. Independence, Missouri: Zion's Printing and Publishing, 1951.

"Kirtland Council Minute Book." Microfilm. LDS Church History Library.

Kittridge, George Lyman. *Witchcraft in Old and New England.* Cambridge, Massachusetts: Harvard University Press, 1929.

Knight, Joseph, Jr. "Joseph Knight's Incidents of History from 1827 to 1844/Aug. 16, 1862/compiled from loose sheets/in J[oseph]. K[night]'s possession/T[homas] B[ullock].," Joseph Knight, Jr., File, LDS Church History Library. Rpt. in Dan Vogel, ed., *Early Mormon Documents,* 4:71-73.

Knight, Joseph, Sr. "Reminiscence." Ca. 1835-47. Holograph. LDS Church History Library. In Dan Vogel, ed., *Early Mormon Documents,* 4:11-24.

Knight, Newel (1800-47). Autobiography and Journal, ca. 1846-47. Holograph. LDS Church History Library.

Koffend, John. "The Gospel According to Helen." *Psychology Today,* Sept. 1980, 74-90.

The Koran. Trans. J. M. Rodwell. Everyman's Library, No. 380. London: J. M. Dent and Sons, 1909.

Kraut, Ogden. *Seer Stones.* Dugway, Utah: Ogden Kraut, ca. 1967.

Kunich, John C. "Multiply Exceedingly: Book of Mormon Population Sizes." *Sunstone* 14, no. 3 (June 1990): 27-44.

Lane, George. "Revival of Religion on Ontario District." *Methodist Magazine* 8 (1825): 160.

Lapham, Fayette. "Interview with the Father of Joseph Smith, the Mormon Prophet, Forty Years Ago. His Account of the Finding of the Sacred Plates." *Historical Magazine* 7 (May 1870): 305-90.

Larabee, Leonard W., ed. *The Papers of Benjamin Franklin.* 24 vols. New Haven, Connecticut: Yale University Press, 1959-84.

Larson, Stanley R. *Quest for the Gold Plates: Thomas Stuart Ferguson's Archaeological Search for the Book of Mormon.* Salt Lake City: Freethinker Press/Smith Research Associates, 1996.

_____. "A Study of Some Textual Variations in the Book of Mormon Comparing the Original and the Printer's Manuscripts, and the 1830, the 1837, and the 1840 Editions." M.A. thesis, Brigham Young University, 1974.

_____. "Textual Variants in Book of Mormon Manuscripts." *Dialogue: A Journal of Mormon Thought* 10, no. 4 (Autumn 1977): 8-30.

Lavallee, Daniel. *The First South Americans: The Peopling of a Continent from the Earliest Evidence to High Culture.* Salt Lake City: University of Utah Press, 1995.

Law, William. "Dr. Wyl and Dr. Wm. Law. A Deeply Interesting Talk on Old Nauvoo Days. Astounding Revelations of Darkness." *Salt Lake Tribune,* July 31, 1887. www.geocities.com/Heartland/Meadows/1247/lawint.htm (Oct. 29, 2003).

_____. "The Mormons in Nauvoo. Three Letters from William Law on Mormonism. An Honest Man's Views and Remorse." *Salt Lake Tribune,* July 3, 1887, 6.

Laws of the State of New-York, Revised and Passed at Thirty-Sixth Session of the Legislature. 2 vols. Independence, Missouri: Zion's Printing and Publishing, 1951.

Lee, George P. "But They Were in One." *Ensign,* May 1976, 26-27.

Lee, Jesse. *A Short History of the Methodists in the United States of America.* Baltimore: Magill & Clime, 1810.

"Legends of the Lakes." Qtd. in *Ontario County in the Finger Lakes.* Canandaigua, New York: Ontario County, 1999.

Lehmann-Haupt, Hellmut, Lawrence C. Roth, and Rollo G. Silver. *The Book in America.* 2nd ed. New York: n.p., 1951.

"Lemuel Durfee Jr. Obituary." *Palmyra Courier,* Apr. 21, 1871.

"Lemuel Durfee [Sr.] Probate Papers," filed Jan. 22, 1830. Wayne County Clerk's Office, Lyons, New York. For convenience, see Dan Vogel, ed., *Early Mormon Documents,* 3:486.

Lewis, Joseph, and Hiel Lewis. "Mormon History: A New Chapter about to Be Published." *Amboy Journal,* Apr. 30, 1879, 1. Also W. Wyl [pseud]., *Mormon Portraits,* 79-81. For convenience, see Dan Vogel, ed., *Early Mormon Documents,* 4:301.

Lewis, Levi, Statement. 1834. Qtd. in "Mormonism." *Susquehanna Register, and Northern Pennsylvanian* 9 (May 1, 1834): 1.

Lewis, Nathaniel. Qtd. in "Mormonism and the Mormons." *Methodist Quarterly Review* 3, no. 1 (1843): 111-22.

_____. Statement. Affirmed and subscribed before Charles Dimon, J.P., Mar. 20, 1834. "Mormonism." *Susquehanna Register and Northern Pennsylvanian,* May 1, 1834. For convenience, see Dan Vogel, ed., *Early Mormon Documents,* 4:288-89.

Lewis, Sophia. Statement in *Susquehanna Register, and Northern Pennsylvanian,* May 1, 1834. For convenience, see Dan Vogel, ed., *Early Mormon Documents,* 4:298.

Libby, Jean, ed. *From Slavery to Salvation: The Autobiography of Rev. Thomas W. Henry of the A.M.E. Church.* Jackson: University Press of Mississippi, 1994.

Lincoln, Abraham. "Address before the Young Men's Lyceum of Springfield, Illinois, Jan. 27, 1838." In Roy P. Basler, *The Collected Works of Abraham Lincoln.* New Brunswick, New Jersey: Rutgers University Press, 1953, 1:113-14.

Linn, William Alexander. *The Story of the Mormons from the Date of their Origin to the Year 1901.* 1902. Rpt., New York: Macmillan, 1923.

"List of the Polls and Rateable Estate of the Town of Lebanon in the County of Grafton, and the Invoice and Assessments—Thereon Made by the Select Men of Said Town for the Year 1813 ... 1814." Lebanon Town Clerk's Office, Lebanon, New Hampshire. For convenience, see Dan Vogel, ed., *Early Mormon Documents,* 1:663-65.

Litvag, Irving. *Singer in the Shadows: The Strange Story of Patience Worth.* New York: Popular Library, 1972.

"Log Cabin." *Columbia Encyclopedia,* 6th ed., 2001. www.bartleby.com/65/lo/logcabin.html (Mar, 8, 2004).

Long, Clement. *Serving God with the Mind: A Discourse Commemorative of Rev. Roswell Shurtleff.* Concord, New Hampshire: McFarland & Jenks, 1861.

Loomis, Chauncey. "Experience on Beaver Island with James J. Strang." In Vickie Cleverley Speek, *God Has Made Us a Kingdom: James Strang and the Midwest Mormons.* Salt Lake City: Signature Books, 2006.

Lovejoy, Evelyn M. Wood. *History of Royalton, Vermont, with Family Genealogies, 1769-1911.* Burlington, Vermont: Free Press Printing, 1911.

Lyell, Charles. *Principles of Geology or the Modern Changes of the Earth and Its Inhabitants.* London: John Murray, 1872.

Mack, Solomon. *A Narraitve [sic] of the Life of Solomon Mack.* Windsor, Vermont: Solomon Mack, ca. 1811. LDS Church History Library.

Madsen, Gordon A. "Joseph Smith's 1826 Trial: The Legal Setting." *BYU Studies* 30 (Spring 1990): 91-108.

Madsen, Nels. "A Visit to Mrs. Emma Smith Bidamon." 1877. Signed statement. LDS Church History Library.

Magnus, Albertus. *Egyptian Secrets; or, White and Black Art for Man and Beast.* N.p., 1880.

Mais, Charles. *The Surprising Case of Rachel Baker, Who Prays and Preaches in Her Sleep.* New York: Whiting and Watson, 1814.

"Making 1,000 Pounds of Maple Sugar." LDS Church Museum exhibit, Mar. 11, 2005.

Mann, Charles C. *1491: New Revelations of the Americas before Columbus.* New York: Alfred A. Knopf, 2005.

"The Manuscript." *Detroit Gazette,* May 16, 1823. www.lavazone2.com/dbroadhu/MI/miscmich.htm (Mar. 23, 2005).

"Manuscript History of the Church." Book A-1. Microfilm, Lee Library. For convenience, see Dean C. Jessee, ed., *The Papers of Joseph Smith,* 1:265-386. Also Manuscript History of the Church, Vol. A-1. LDS Church History Library. In Dean C. Jessee, ed., *The Personal Writings of Joseph Smith.* Salt Lake City: Deseret Book, 1984, 665-66.

Marquardt, H. Michael. "An Appraisal of Manchester as Location for the Organization of the Church." *Sunstone* 16 (Feb. 1992): 49-57.

_____. "Early Texts of Joseph Smith's Revelations, 1828-1833." *Restoration* 1 (July 1982): 8-11.

_____. *The Joseph Smith Revelations: Text and Commentary.* Salt Lake City: Signature Books, 1999.

_____. *The Rise of Mormonism: 1816-1844.* Longwood, Florida: Xulon Press, 2006.

_____, and Wesley P. Walters. *Inventing Mormonism: Tradition and the Historical Record.* San Francisco: Smith Research Associates, 1994.

Massey, John Stewart. "Ginseng, Folklore Cure-All, Is Being Regarded Seriously." *Smithsonian* 6 (Feb. 1976): 105.

Matheny, Deanne G. "Does the Shoe Fit? A Critique of the Limited Tehauntepec Geography." In Brent Lee Metcalfe, ed., *New Approaches to the Book of Mormon,* 269-328.

Matheny, Raymond T. "Book of Mormon Archaeology: What Does the Evidence Really Show?" Seminar presentation during Aug. 25, 1984, panel discussion at Sunstone Theological Symposium, Salt Lake City. Typescript in Lee Library, 19-26.

Mather, Frederick G. "The Early Days of Mormonism." *Lippincott's Magazine* 26 (Aug. 1880): 198-221.

_____. "The Early Mormons: Joe Smith Operates at Susquehanna." *Binghamton Republican,* July 29, 1880. For convenience, see Dan Vogel, ed., *Early Mormon Documents,* 4:345-60.

Matthews, Robert J. *"A Plainer Translation": Joseph Smith's Translation of the Bible.* Provo, Utah: Brigham Young University Press, 1975.

Mazur, Suzan. "Mormons in the Olympic Spotlight: Polygamy and Scripture Threaten to Steal Some of the Thunder from the Winter Games in Utah." *Financial Times,* Feb. 9, 2002. http://globalarchive.ft.com (Mar. 1, 2002).

McCallum, James D. "Eleazar Wheelock: Founder of Dartmouth College." Mss. Series #4, 79. Rauner Special Collections Library, Dartmouth College, Hanover, New Hampshire.

McCaughey, Robert A. "Columbia and Higher Learning in America," 1-12. http://c250.columbia.edu/c250_events/symposia/history_century_timeline.html (May 26, 2006).

M'Clure, David, and Elijah Parish, eds. *Memoirs of the Rev. Eleazar Wheelock, D.D.: Founder and President of Dartmouth College and Moor's Charity School, with a Summary History of the College and School.* Newburyport, New Hampshire: Edward Little & Co., 1811.

McConkie, Bruce R. *Mormon Doctrine.* Salt Lake City: Bookcraft, 1958.

McConkie, Mark L. *The Father of the Prophet: Stories and Insights from the Life of Joseph Smith, Sr.* Salt Lake City: Bookcraft, 1993.

McCrae, Thomas. "Typhoid Fever." *Modern Medicine: Its Theory and Practice,* edited by William Osler, 4 vols. Philadelphia: Lea Bros. and Co., 1907.

McGuire, Ross, and Nancy Grey Osterud. *Working Lives: Broome County, New York, 1800-1930.* Binghamton, New York: Roberson Center for the Arts and Sciences, n.d.

[McIntosh, W. H.] *History of Ontario Co., New York.* Philadelphia: Everts, Ensign and Everts, 1876.

_____. *History of Seneca Co., New York, 1786-1876.* Philadelphia: Everts, Ensign and Everts, 1876.

_____. *History of Wayne County, New York: With Illustrations Descriptive of Its Scenery, Palatial Residences, Public Buildings, Fine Blocks, and Important Manufactories.* Philadelphia: Everts, Ensign & Everts, 1877.

McKelvey, Blake. "Rochester and the Erie Canal." *Rochester History* 11, nos. 3-4 (July 1949): 1-24.

McKiernan, F. Mark, and Roger D. Launius, eds. *An Early Latter Day Saint History: The Book of John Whitmer—Kept by Commandment.* Independence, Missouri: Herald Publishing House, 1980.

McKune, Joshua. "Statement." *Susquehanna Register and Northern Pennsylvanian* 9 (May 1, 1834): 1. For convenience, see Dan Vogel, ed., *Early Mormon Documents,* 4:325.

McLeister, Ira F., and Roy S. Nicholson. *Conscience and Commitment: A History of the Wesleyan Methodist Church of America.* Marion, Indiana: Wesley Press, 1976.

McLellin, William E. Letter to Elder D. H. Bayt, May 24, 1870. *True Latter Day Saints' Herald* 17 (Sept. 15, 1870): 556.

_____. Letter to "My Dear Friends," Independence, Missouri, Feb. 1870. Community of Christ, Library-Archives, Independence, Missouri.

_____. Letter to J. L. Traughber, Aug. 25, 1877, in *Salt Lake Tribune,* Dec. 4, 1985.

McLemee, Scott. "Latter-day Studies: Scholars of Mormonism Confront the History of What Some Call 'the Next World Religion.'" *Research: The Chronicle of Higher Education* 48, no. 28 (Mar. 22, 2002): A14-A16.

Meldrum, Jeffrey, and Trent D. Stephens. "Who Are the Children of Lehi?" *Journal of Book of Mormon Studies* 12, no. 1 (2003): 38-51.

Melish, John. *Travels in the United States of America in the Years 1806 and 1807 and 1809, 1810 and 1811.* Philadelphia: N. pub., 1812.

"Memorize the Bible. Literally." www.mvcf.com/church/ministries/suntereo/ (Apr. 1, 2003).

"Memorize the Bible in One Year." www.retta.org/study/1year.htm (Apr. 1, 2003).

Merriam-Webster's Encyclopedia of World Religions. Ed. Wendy Doniger. Springfield, Massachusetts: Merriam-Webster, 1999.

Merrill, Byron R. "Joseph Smith and the Lamanites." In Susan Easton Black and Charles D. Tate, Jr., eds., *Joseph Smith: The Prophet, The Man,* 187-202.

Metcalf, Anthony. *Ten Years before the Mast.* Malad City, Idaho: Author, 1888.

Metcalfe, Brent Lee., ed. *New Approaches to the Book of Mormon: Explorations in Critical Methodology.* Salt Lake City: Signature Books, 1993.

_____. "The Priority of Mosiah: A Prelude to Book of Mormon Exegesis." In Brent Lee Metcalfe, ed., *New Approaches to the Book of Mormon,* 395-444.

_____. "Reinventing Lamanite Identity." *Sunstone,* Issue 131, Mar. 2004, 20-25.

"Michael Morse. Interviewed by William W. Blair, May 8, 1879." In William W. Blair. Journal. Community of Christ, Library-Archives, Independence, Missouri.

Miley, John. *Treatise on Class Meetings.* Cincinnati: Poe & Hitchcock, 1866.

"Millennium." www.wordtrade.com/religion/milleniu.htm (May 8, 2003).

Miller, Debi. "A Course in Miracles." www/bliss2000.com/Blisseng/courseng.htm (Nov. 25, 2002).

Miller, Russell E. *The Larger Hope: The First Century of the Universalist Church in America, 1770-1870.* Boston: Unitarian Universalist, 1979.

Milliken, Charles F. *A History of Ontario County, New York and Its People.* 2 vols. Canandaigua, New York: Lewis Historical Publishing Co., 1911.

Minutes of the Annual Conferences of the Methodist Episcopal Church. Report 446: 1824. Qtd. in H. Michael Marquardt and Wesley Walters, *Inventing Mormonism,* 17.

Minutes of the Ontario Baptist Association. Rochester, New York: Printed by Everand Peck, 1825.

"Minutes of the Quorum of the Twelve." Jan. 20, 1843. Brigham Young Collection. LDS Church History Library.

"Minutes of a Special Conference of the Church of Jesus Christ of Latter Day Saints, held in the city of Nauvoo, Illinois., Commencing on the 6th of October, 1843." TS 4 (Sept. 15, 1843): 331.

"Mitchill, Samuel Latham, 1764-1831." William L. Clements Library, University of Michigan, Samuel Latham Mitchill Papers. www.clements.umich.edu/webguides/M/Mitchill.html (May 26, 2006).

"Money Digging." *Palmyra Herald Canal Advertiser,* July 24, 1822. Rpt. in www.lavazone2.com/dbroadhu/New York/miscNew YorkSg.htm (Sept. 11, 2003).

"Money Digging." *Windsor [Vermont] Journal,* Jan. 17, 1825. Rpt. in "Money Digging," *Wayne Sentinel,* Feb. 16, 1825, 1.

"Money Digging." *Wayne Sentinel,* Feb. 16, 1825.

"Money Digging." *Lyons Advertiser,* Aug. 29, 1827. www.lavazone2.com/dbroadhu/New York/miscNew YorkS0.htm (May 1, 2003).

Monson, Thomas S. "Prayer at Dedication of Villahermosa, Mexico Temple, May 21, 2000." *LDS Church News,* May 27, 2000, 6.

Moore, Margaret B. "Salem and Hawthorne." www.hawthorneinsalem.org/ScholarsForum/SalemAnd Hawthorne.html (Feb. 15, 2003).

Moore, William. "The 1823 Detroit Manuscript: A Book of Mormon Prequel." www.solomonspalding.com/SRP/saga/sagao2b.htm (Apr. 15, 2003).

Morain, William D. *The Sword of Laban: Joseph Smith, Jr., and the Dissociated Mind.* Washington, D.C.: American Psychiatric Press, 1998.

Moreno, Fred. "Audubon's Friendship with Samuel Latham Mitchill." http://nyasdev.enforme.com/sne/update.asp?updatedD=9 (Mar. 28, 2005).

"The Mormon Delusion." *New-York Observer,* Nov. 12, 1831. www.lavazone2.com/dbroadhu/New York/miscNew YorkC1.htm (Sept. 28, 2004).

"Mormon Leaders at Their Mecca. ... Joe Smith's Life at Palmyra." *New York Herald,* June 25, 1893, 12. For convenience, see Dan Vogel, ed., *Early Mormon Documents,* 3:200-202.

"Mormonsim." *New England Christian Herald,* Nov. 7, 1832, 22-23. Boston Wesleyan Association. S. W. Wilson and S. O. Wright, editors. Signature Books Keepsake, No. 5.

"Mormonism." *Evangelist* (Carthage, Ohio) 6 (Oct. 1, 1838): 226.

"Mormonism. Authentic Account of the Origin of This Sect from One of the Patriarchs. Discovery of the Plates, and the Translation of the Book of Mormon—Polygamy an Excrescence." *Kansas City Daily Journal,* June 5, 1881, 1.

"Mormonism and Joe Smith: The Book of Mormon or Golden Bible." *Wayne Democratic Press,* May 26, 1858. www.lavazone2.com/dbroadhu/New York/miscNew YorkS3.htm (Oct. 19, 2004).

"Mormonism in Its Infancy." *Newark [New Jersey] Daily Advertiser,* Aug., 1856. www.lavazone2.com/dbroadhu/MA/midatlan.htm (Sept. 10, 2003).

Morris, Larry E. "Oliver Cowdery's Vermont Years and the Origins of Mormonism." *BYU Studies* 39, no. 1 (2000): 106-29.

Morris, Robert. *The Masonic Martyr: The Biography of Eli Bruce, Sheriff of Niagara County, New York.* Louisville, Kemtucky: Morris and Monsarrat, 1861.

Morse, Michael. Interviewed by William W. Blair, May 22, 1879. *Saints' Herald* 26 (June 15, 1879): 190-91.

Moseley, Hardwick, ed. *The Romance of North America.* Boston: Houghton Mifflin Co., 1952.

"A Most Extraordinary ..." *Western Farmer* (Palmyra, New York), Jan. 30, 1822. www.lavazone2.com/dbroadhu/New York/miscNew YorkSg.htl (Sept. 11, 2003).

Moulton, James Hope. *Early Zorastrianism.* London: Constable and Co., 1913.

"Mrs. Joe Smith. An Interviewed by the Widow of the Noted Mormon Leader." *Wellsville [New York] Daily Reporter,* Oct. 27, 1844. www.lavazone2.com/dbroadhu/New York/misc.New YorkS3.htm (Sept. 19, 2004).

"Mrs. John A. Curran Tells Story of Patience Worth Experience." *St. Louis Globe-Democrat,* Nov. 3, 1915, 110-11.

Muhl, Anita M. "Automatic Writing Combined with Crystal Gazing as a Means of Recalling Forgotten Incidents." *Journal of Abnormal Psychology and Social Psychology* 19, no. 3 (Oct.-Dec. 1924): 264-73.

Muir, Sir William. *Life of Mohamet.* London: Smith, Elder and Co., 1878.

Murphy, Thomas. "Lamanite Genesis, Genealogy, and Genetics." In Dan Vogel and Brent Lee Metcalfe, eds., *American Apocrypha: Essays on the Book of Mormon,* 47-78.

_____. "Simply Implausible: DNA and a Mesoamerican Setting for the Book of Mormon." *Dialogue: A Journal of Mormon Thought* 36 (Winter 2003): 109-32.

Nash, Eugene Beauharnais, M.D. "Leaders in Typhoid Fever." www.homeoint.org/books5/nashtyphoid/typhoid4.htm (Mar. 17, 2004).

"Nathaniel Hawthorne." In *Virtual American Biographies.* From *Appleton's Cyclopedia of American Biography.* Eds. James Grant Wilson and John Fiske. 6 vols. New York: D. Appleton and Co., 1887-89. www.famousamericans.net/nathanielhawthorne (Feb. 13, 2003).

"Necromancy." *New Advent Catholic Encyclopedia.* www.newadvent.org/cathen/050486.htm (May 16, 2005).

"Necromancy." *Occultopedia.* www.occultopedia.com/n/necromancy.htm (May 5, 2002).

"Necromancy: Or Divination by Means of the Spirits of the Dead." www.sacred-texts.com/bos/bos195.htm (May 16, 2005).

Neibaur, Alexander. Journal, Feb. 5, 1841-Jan. 1861. LDS Church History Library.

"Newel Knight's Journal." *Scraps of Biography—Tenth Book of the Faith Promoting Series,* Juvenile Instructor Office. Salt Lake City, 1883.

Newell, Fanny. *Memoirs of Fanny Newell Written by Herself.* Kennebec, Minnesota: Hallowell, 1824.

_____. *Diary of Fanny Newell.* Boston: Peirce, 1848.

Newell, Linda King, and Valeen Tippets Avery. *Mormon Enigma: Emma Hale Smith, Prophet's Wife, "Elect Lady," Polygamy's Foe.* Garden City, New York: Doubleday and Co., 1984.

The New-England Primer, Improved, Being an Easy Method to Teach Young Children the English Language. New York: Daniel D. Smith, 1807.

"New Light on Joseph Smith's First Vision." www.irr.org/mit/fvision.html (Oct. 15, 2002).

"New World Antiquities." www.xmission.com/~research/central/vogel3.htm (June 10, 2003).

New York Manuscript Census (Federal) and Indexes for 1800, 1810, 1820, 1830, 1840, 1850, 1860, 1870.

"New York State Newspaper Project." Wayne County (New York) Newspapers. http://unix.2nysed.gov/nysnp/359.htm. (July 30, 2003).

Nibley, Hugh W. *An Approach to the Book of Mormon.* Salt Lake City: Council of the Twelve Apostles of the Church of Jesus Christ of Latter-day Saints, 1957. Reprint, Salt Lake City: Deseret Book, 1978.

_____. *The Myth Makers.* Salt Lake City: Bookcraft, 1961.

_____. *Since Cumorah: The Book of Mormon in the Modern World.* Salt Lake City: Deseret Book, 1967.

Nichols, Roswell. Statement, Dec. 1, 1833. In Eber D. Howe, *Mormonism Unvailed,* 257-58.

"Nineteenth Century Revivals." In Geoff Waugh, *Fire Fell: Revival Visitations.* www.christiankword.org/revival/2-1800.html (Apr. 3, 2002).

"No author, untitled and undated statement." George A. Smith Papers, Manuscripts Division, J. Willard Marriott Library, University of Utah, Salt Lake City.

Noah, Mordecai M. Qtd. in "M. M. Noah's Speech," *Wayne Sentinel,* Oct. 11, 1825, 1.

Noble, Joel King. Letter to Jonathan B. Turner, Mar. 8, 1842, Turner Collection, Illinois State Historical Library, Springfield. For convenience, see Dan Vogel, ed., *Early Mormon Documents,* 4:106-11.

Norris, John V. "Many Medical Advances in Last Half-Century." www.phxsg.org/johnnorris/norris71.htm (Jan. 19, 2005).

North, Gary. *Crossed Fingers.* Tyler, Texas: Institute for Christian Economics, 1996.

Norwood, Frederick A. *The Story of American Methodism: A History of the United Methodists and Their Relations.* Nashville, Tennessee: Abingdon Press, 1974.

Noss, John B. *Man's Religions.* New York: Macmillan Co., 1967.

Nyberg, D. *The Varnished Truth: Truth Telling and Deceiving in Ordinary Life.* Chicago: University of Chicago Press, 1993.

Nyman, Monte S., and Robert L. Millet, eds. *The Joseph Translation: The Restoration of Plain and Precious Things.* Provo, Utah: Brigham Young University Religious Studies Center, 1985.

Oakes, Len. *Prophetic Charisma: The Psychology of Revolutionary Religious Personalities.* Syracuse, New York: Syracuse University Press, 1997.

Oaks, Dallin H. "The Witness: Martin Harris." *Ensign,* May 1999, 35-37.

"Obituary of James G. Marsh." *Elders' Journal* 1, no. 3 (July 1838): 48.

"Observations on the Pathology and Treatment of Necrosis." *Philadelphia Monthly Journal of Medicine and Surgery* 1, no. 1 (June 1827): 11-19; vol. 1, no. 2 (July 1827): 66-75. Rpt. in Nathan R. Smith, ed., *Medical and Surgical Memoirs,* 97-121, in *Medical Classics* 1, no. 8 (Apr. 1937): 820-38.

"Of Mastodons, Mammoths and Other Giants of the Pleistocene." http://unmuseum.mus.pa.us/mastodon.htm (Apr. 3, 2002).

"The Old Mohawk-Turnpike Book." www.rootsweb.com/~nyherkim/journey1.html (Mar 25, 2004).

"Old Newspapers—No. 25." *Palmyra Courier,* May 31, 1872.

"Old Wives Tales." www.oldwivestales.net/QandAarticle1013.html (Aug. 5, 2004).

Omer, George E., Jr. "An Army Hospital: From Dragoons to Rough Riders—Fort Riley, 1853-1903." www.kancoll.org/khq/1957/57 4 omer.htm (Jan. 20, 2005).

Ontario County. Deeds, Book G, p. 345, Ontario County Records Center and Archives, Canandaigua, New York.

Ontario County Clerk's Office. Miscellaneous Records, Book C, pp. 385-88. Canandaigua, Ontario County, New York.

"Origin of Mormonism. Joe Smith and His Early Habits. How He Found the Golden Plates. A Contemporary of the Prophet Relates Some Interesting Facts." *San Francisco Chronicle,* May 14, 1893, 12. For convenience, see Dan Vogel, ed., *Early Mormon Documents,* 3:211.

Ostler, Blake T. "Assessing the Logical Structure of DNA Arguments against the Book of Mormon." *Sunstone,* Dec. 2004, 70-72.

_____. "The Book of Mormon as a Modern Expansion of an Ancient Source." *Dialogue: A Journal of Mormon Thought* 20 (Spring 1987): 66-123.

"Our Lady of Akita." www.medjugorjeusa.org/akita.htm (Apr. 19, 2005).

"Our Lady of Beauraing." www.marypages.com/beauraingEnglandhtm (Apr. 19, 2005).

Owens, Lance S. "Joseph Smith: America's Hermetic Prophet." In Bryan Waterman, ed., *The Prophet Puzzle,* 155-72.

Packer, Rand Hugh. "History of Four Mormon Landmarks in Western New York: The Joseph Smith Farm, Hill Cumorah, the Martin Harris Farm, and the Peter Whitmer, Sr., Farm." M.A. thesis, Brigham Young University, 1975.

Page, Hiram. Letter to William [E. McLellin], Feb. 2, 1848. Community of Christ, Library-Archives, Independence, Missouri.

Paine, Thomas. *The Age of Reason.* 1796. Edited by Moncure D. Conway. www.infidels.org/library/historical/thomas paine/age of reason/part1.html (Aug. 10, 2003).

Palmer, Grant H. *An Insider's View of Mormon Origins.* Salt Lake City: Signature Books, 2002.

_____. Interviewed by Richard S. Van Wagoner, Sept. 12, 2004.

_____. Letter to Richard S. Van Wagoner, Oct. 4, 2004.

_____. "My Recollection of Viewing Three 'Seer Stones' in the First Presidencies [sic] Vault in June 1966." Statement written for Richard S. Van Wagoner on Dec. 15, 2003.

"Palmyra." Undated clipping from *Wayne County Journal.* Willard Bean Scrapbook, Lee Library.

Palmyra, New York, 1789-1964, 175th Year. Palmyra, New York: N. pub., 1964.

Palmyra, New York. Cemetery File. Courtesy Beth Hoad, Palmyra, New York.

"Palmyra, New York. Highway Survey, June 13, 1820." Old Town Record, 1793-1870, 221. Township Office, Palmyra, New York. For convenience, see Dan Vogel, ed., *Early Mormon Documents,* 3:420-21.

"Palmyra Village." *Palmyra Herald,* June 19, 1822, 2.

Partridge, Eric. *A Dictionary of Slang and Unconventional English.* New York: Macmillan, 1967.

Payne, Samantha. Affidavit, June 29, 1881. Published in *Ontario County Times,* July 27, 1881. For convenience, see Dan Vogel, ed., *Early Mormon Documents,* 2:172-73.

Pearce, Stewart. *Annals of Luzern County.* Philadelphia: N. pub., 1866.

Pearl of Great Price: Being a Choice Selection from the Revelations, Translations, and Narrations of Joseph Smith, First Prophet, Seer, and Revelator to the Church of Jesus Christ of Latter-day Saints. Liverpool, England: F. D. Richards, 1851.

Peck, George. *Early Methodism within the Bounds of the Old Genesee Conference, from 1788 to 1828.* New York: Carlton and Porter, 1860.

_____. *The Life and Times of Rev. George Peck, D.D., Written by Himself.* New York: Nelson and Phillips, 1874.

_____. "Mormonism and the Mormons." *Methodist Quarterly Review* 2 (Jan. 1843): 112-15.

Pendered, Norman C. *Blackbeard: The Fiercest Pirate of All.* Manteo, North Carolina: Times Printing Co., n.d. www.ocracoke-nc.com/blackbeard/tales/blcknc0a.htm (Sept. 15, 2004).

Perkins, Mrs. George [Julia Anna Shepard]. *Early Times on the Susquehanna.* Binghamton, New York: Herald Co. of Binghamton, 1906.

Persuitte, David. *Joseph Smith and the Origins of the Book of Mormon.* 2d. ed. Jefferson, North Carolina: McFarland & Co., 2000.

Peterson, J. W. "Another Testimony: Statement of William Smith, Concerning Joseph, the Prophet." *Deseret Evening News,* Jan. 20, 1894, 11.

Phelps, W. W. "The Book of Mormon." *Evening and the Morning Star* 1, no. 8 (Jan. 1833): 57-59.

_____. "The Far West." *Evening and the Morning Star* 1, no. 5 (Oct. 1832): 33.

_____. "Israel Will Be Gathered." *Evening and the Morning Star* 2, no. 13 (June 1833): 101.

_____. "Letter No. 11." *Messenger and Advocate* 2 (Oct. 2, 1835): 193-95.

_____. Letter to Eber D. Howe, Jan. 15, 1831. In Eber D. Howe, *Mormonism Unvailed,* 274.

_____. Letter to Oliver Cowdery, *Messenger and Advocate* 1, no. 1 (Sept. 1835): 177-79.

_____. Letter to Oliver Cowdery, *Messenger and Advocate* 2, no. 2 (Nov. 1835): 220.

_____. "Rise and Progress of the Church of Christ." *Evening and the Morning Star* 1, no. 11 (Apr. 1833): 84.

Pickthall, Muhammed Marmaduke, trans. *The Glorious Koran: A Bi-Lingual Edition with English Translation, Introduction and Notes.* London: George Allen & Unwin, 1976.

Pierce, Nathan, Docket Book (1827-30). Manchester township Office, Clifton Springs, New York. For convenience, see Dan Vogel, ed., *Early Mormon Documents,* 3:491-92.

Pilkington, William. "Address Delivered in the Lewisville Ward." Rigby Stake, Apr. 23, 1939. Typescript. LDS Church History Library.

_____. "A Biography [Autobiography] of William Pilkington, Jr. Written by Himself." 1938. LDS Church History Library. For convenience, see Dan Vogel, ed., *Early Mormon Documents,* 2:361.

_____. "The Dying Testimony of Martin Harris, As Given to William Pilkington by Martin Harris Himself in Clarkston, Cache County, Utah." Affidavit (holograph), Apr. 3, 1934. LDS Church History Library.

"Plain Truth." *Palmyra Register,* July 5, 1820, 2.

Poe, Edgar Allen. "A Chapter on Autography (Part I)." *Graham's Magazine,* Nov. 1841, 224-34. www.eapoe.org/works/misc/autogc1.htm.

"Poor Laws." *The Dictionary of English History,* rev. ed. London: Cassell and Co., 1928.

"Poor Masters." *Western Farmer* (Palmyra, New York) Apr. 3, 1822, 3.

"Poorhouse History of Wayne County." www.poorhousestory.com/WAYNE.htm (Apr. 26, 2004).

Porter, Larry C. "The Church in New York and Pennsylvania, 1816-1831." In F. Mark McKiernan, Alma R. Blair, and Paul M. Edwards, eds., *The Restoration Movement: Essays in Mormon History.* Lawrence, Kansas: Coronado Press, 1973. 27-61.

_____. "The Colesville Branch and the Coming Forth of the Book of Mormon." *BYU Studies* 10 (Spring 1970): 365-85.

_____. "The Joseph Knight Family." *Ensign,* Oct. 1978, 39-45.

_____. "Organizational Origins of the Church of Jesus Christ, 6 April 1830." In Larry C. Porter, Milton V. Backman Jr., and Susan Easton Black, eds., *Regional Studies in*

Latter-day Saint Church History: New York. Provo, Utah: Brigham Young University Department of Church History and Doctrine, 1992. 149-64.

_____. "The Restoration of the Priesthood." *Religious Studies Center Newsletter* 9 (3 May 1995): 1-12.

_____. "Reverend George Lane: Good 'Gifts,' Much 'Grace,' and Marked 'Usefulness.'" *BYU Studies* 9 (Spring 1969): 321-40.

_____. "Solomon Chamberlain: Early Missionary." *BYU Studies* 12 (Spring 1972): 314-318.

_____. "A Study of the Origins of the Church of Jesus Christ of Latter-day Saints in the States of New York and Pennsylvania, 1816-1831." Ph.D. diss., Brigham Young University, 1971. Rpt., "Dissertations in Latter-day Saint History Series," Provo, Utah: Joseph Fielding Smith Institute for Latter-day Saint History/BYU Studies, 1971.

_____. "Was the Church Legally Incorporated at the Time It Was Organized in the State of New York?" *Ensign,* Dec. 1978, 26-27.

Pratt, Henry. Letter to [son] Addison Pratt, May 26, 1838. Holograph. LDS Church History Library.

Pratt, Orson. "Cumorah." *The Contributor* 3 (1882): 357-59.

_____. *Divine Authenticity of the Book of Mormon—A Series of 6 Pamphlets.* Liverpool, England: Franklin D. Richards, 1850-51. *New Mormon Studies.* CD-ROM, Smith Research Associates, 1998.

_____. *An Interesting Account of Several Remarkable Visions and of the Late Discovery of Ancient American Records.* Edinburgh, Scotland: Ballantyne and Hughes, 1840.

_____. "Number 1: Divine Authenticity of the Book of Mormon," 1-18.

_____. "Number 2: More Revelation Is Indispensably Necessary," 18-34.

_____. "Number 3: The Bible and Tradition, without Further Revelation, an Insufficient Guide," 35-51.

_____. "Number 4: Evidences of the Book of Mormon and Bible Compared," 51-68.

_____. "Number 5: The Book of Mormon Confirmed by Miracles," 68-85.

_____. "Number 6: Prophetic Evidence in Favor of the Book of Mormon," 85-102.

Pratt, Parley P. *Autobiography of Parley Parker Pratt,* edited by Parley P. Pratt Jr. New York: Russell Brothers, 1874.

Prescott, William H. *History of the Conquest of Mexico and History of the Conquest of Peru.* New York: Modern Library, 1952.

Price, Ebenezer. *A Chronological Register of Boscawen, in the County of Merrimack, and State of New-Hampshire, from the First Settlement of the Town to 1820.* Concord, New Hampshire: Jacob B. Moore, 1823.

Price, Robert M. "Joseph Smith: Inspired Author of the Book of Mormon." In Dan Vogel and Brent Lee Metcalfe, *American Apocrypha: Essays on the Book of Mormon,* 321-66.

_____. "Joseph Smith in the Book of Mormon." *Dialogue: A Journal of Mormon Thought* 36 (Winter 2003): 89-96.

Priest, Josiah. *The Wonders of Nature and Providence, Displayed.* Albany, New York: E. & E. Hosford, 1825.

Prince, Gregory A. *Power from On High: The Development of Mormon Priesthood.* Salt Lake City: Signature Books, 1995.

Prince, Walter Franklin. "Automatic Writing Combined With 'Crystal Gazing.'" *Journal of Abnormal and Social Psychology* 20 (1925-26): 34-42.

_____. "Psychological Tests for the Authorship of the Book of Mormon." *American Journal of Psychology* 28 (July 1917): 373-89.

"A Profane Revelation." *Salt Lake Daily Tribune,* Jan. 6, 1875. www.lavazone2.com/dbroadhu/Utah/tribune/.htm (Nov. 10, 2004).

"The Prophet J. Lorber Predicts Coming Catastrophes and the True Christianity." www.disk-plus-buch.de/kee/0-eggen.htm (Nov. 3, 2003).

Purple, W[illiam] D. "Joseph Smith, the Originator of Mormonism. Historical Reminiscences of the Town of Afton." *Chenango Union* (Norwich, New York) 30 (May 3, 1877): 3. For convenience, see Dan Vogel, ed., *Early Mormon Documents,* 4:127-37.

"Questions Asked of David Whitmer at His Home in Richmond Ray County Mo. Jan. 14-1885 Relating to Book of Mormon, and the History of the Church of Jesus Christ of LDS by Elder Z. H. Gurley." Holograph. LDS Church History Library.

Quinn, D. Michael. *Early Mormonism and the Magic World View.* Rev. and enl. ed. Salt Lake City: Signature Books, 1998.

_____. "The First Months of Mormonism: A Contemporary View by Rev. Diedrich Willers." *New York History* 54 (July 1973): 317-33.

_____. "From Sacred Grove to Sacral Power Structure." *Dialogue: A Journal of Mormon Thought* 17 (Summer 1984): 9-34.

_____. "Joseph Smith's *Experience* of a Methodist 'Camp Meeting' in 1820." *Dialogue: A Journal of Mormon Thought. Dialogue* Paperless: E-paper #3. Expanded version (Definitive). Dec. 20, 2006.

_____. "Latter-day Saint Prayer Circles." *BYU Studies* 19, no. 2 (Fall 1978): 79-105.

_____. *The Mormon Hierarchy: Origins of Power.* Salt Lake City: Signature Books/Smith Research Assocites, 1994.

_____. "Socioreligious Radicalism of the Mormon Church: A Parallel to the Anabaptists." In Davis Bitton and Maureen Ursenbach Beecher, eds., *New Views of Mormon History,* 363-86.

Quitman, Frederick H. *A Treatise on Magic: or, On the Intercourse between Spirits and Men; with Annotations.* Albany, New York: n.p., 1810.

Randi, James. *Conjuring: Being a Definitive Account of the Venerable Arts of Sorcery, Prestidigitation, Wizardry, Deception, and Chicanery and of the Mountebanks and Scoundrels Who Have Perpetrated These Subterfuges on a Bewildered Public.* New York: St. Martin's Press, 1992.

_____. *An Encyclopedia of Claims, Frauds, and Hoaxes of the Occult and Supernatural.* New York: St. Martin's Press, 1997.

Raymond, Rossiter W. "The Divining Rod." *Transactions of the American Institute of Mining Engineers* 11 (Feb. 1883): 411-46.

Reader's Digest. *Mysteries of the Ancient Americas: The New World before Columbus.* Pleasantville, New York: The Reader's Digest Association, 1992.

"Record of Births, Deaths, Marriages and Miscellaneous Items." Book A, p. 129. Tunbridge Town Clerk's Office, Tunbridge, Vermont. For convenience, see Dan Vogel, ed., *Early Mormon Documents,* 1:631.

"A Record of Strangers Who Are Warned Out of Town, 1813-1818," p. 53. Norwich Town Clerk's Office, Norwich, Vermont. For convenience, see Dan Vogel, ed., *Early Mormon Documents,* 1:668.

Records of "The First Baptized [sic] Church in Palmyra." American Baptist Historical Society, Rochester, New York.

"Records of Junius F. Wells." Qtd. in "Joseph Smith Memorial History Book." For convenience, see Porter, "A Study of the Origins of the Church," 5.

"Records of the Sessions of the Presbyterian Church in Palmyra," Vol. 2. Western Presbyterian Church, Palmyra, New York. For convenience, see Dan Vogel, ed., *Early Mormon Documents,* 3:496-501.

Reed, John S. Letter to Brigham Young, Dec. 6, 1861, Brigham Young Collection. LDS Church History Library. For convenience, see Dan Vogel, ed., *Early Mormon Documents,* 4:121-25.

Reid, Daniel G., ed. *Dictionary of Christianity in America.* Downers Grove, Illinois: InterVarsity Press, 1990.

Reid, Max. *The Mohawk Valley: Its Legends and Its History.* New York: Knickerbocker Press, 1901. www.fortklock.com/RFeidch11.htm (Mar. 25, 2004).

Reimherr, Otto. "The Susquehanna: Mormonism's Jordan." *Susquehanna University Studies* 11, no. 2 (1980): 71-89.

"Remarkable VISION and REVELATION, as Seen and Received by Asa Wild, of Amsterdam, (N.Y.)." *Wayne Sentinel,* Oct. 22, 1823, 4.

"Remarks at the Dedication of the Guayaquil, Ecuador Temple." In "News of the Church," *Ensign,* Oct. 1999, 74.

Remsburg, John E. "Six Historic Americans." www.infidels.org/library/historical/john_remsburg/six_historic-americans/chapter_2.1 (Oct. 24, 2002).

"Report of the Secretary of [New York] State in 1824 on the Relief and Settlement of the Poor." www.poorhousestory.com/YATES REPORT ENTIRE.htm (Apr. 26, 2004).

Report of the Vermont Board of Agriculture, 1920-22. Qtd. in "A History of the Vermont Apple Industry." www.Vermontapples.org/seasons.html (Apr. 2, 2004).

"Rev. Willard Chase Departed This Life in Palmyra, N.Y., March 10, 1871, in the 74th Year of His Age." *The American Wesleyan,* Apr. 10, 1871. Photocopy courtesy of Bill Clark, Indianapolis, Indiana.

Reynolds, George, and Janne M. Sjodahl. *Commentary on the Book of Mormon.* 7 vols. Ed. and arranged by Phillip C. Reynolds. Salt Lake City: Deseret News Press, 1956-62.

Richards, Charles C. "An Address Delivered by Charles C. Richards at the Sacrament Meeting, held in … Salt Lake City, Utah, Sunday Evening, April 20, 1947." Signed typescript, LDS Church History Library.

Richards, Franklin D., and James A. Little. *A Compendium of the Doctrines of the Gospel.* Salt Lake City: Deseret News, 1882.

"The Riddel and Orn Family Tree Pages." www.riddel.com/tree/fam/famoo293.htm (Nov. 12, 2002).

Rigdon, Sidney. Interviewed by Austin W. Cowles, "The Mormons: Pen and Pencil Sketches, Illustrating their Early History." *Moore's Rural New Yorker,* Jan 23, 1869. Lee Library.

_____. Letter (revelation) to Stephen Post, Dec. 1, 1866. Listed as section 26 in Copying Book A. Stephen Post Collection, LDS Church History Library. For convenience, see Richard S. Van Wagoner, *Sidney Rigdon,* 413.

____. Revelation. Section 70 in Copying Book A. Stephen Post Collection, LDS Church History Library. For convenience, see Richard S. Van Wagoner, *Sidney Rigdon,* 371-72.

Riley, I. Woodbridge. *The Founder of Mormonism: A Psychological Study of Joseph Smith Jr.* New York: Dodd, Mead & Co., 1903.

Ring, Wilson. "Mystery Treasure Still Tempting N.H. Searchers." *Salt Lake Tribune,* June 20, 2004, A14.

Rittner, Don. "Crossing That Bridge When You Come to It!" www.themesh.com/his28.html (May 4, 2004).

"Roads." www.townofrussia.com/ROADS.html (May 4, 2004).

Robbins, T. "Cults, Converts, and Charisma: The Sociology of New Religious Movements." *Contemporary Sociology* 36, no. 1 (Spring): entire issue.

Roberts, B. H. *A Comprehensive History of the Church of Jesus Christ of Latter-day Saints,* 6 vols. 1930; Salt Lake City: Church of Jesus Christ of Latter-day Saints, 1965 printing.

_____. *Defense of the Faith and the Saints.* 2 vols. Salt Lake City: Deseret News, 1907, 1912.

_____. "Joseph Smith: The Prophet-Teacher." www.helpingmormons.org/josephsmith.htm (Sept. 9, 2003).

_____. *Mormonism: Its Origin and History.* Independence, Missouri: Press of Zion's Printing and Publishing Co., 1923.

_____. *New Witnesses for God.* 2 vols. Salt Lake City: Deseret News, 1909.

_____. "The Probability of Joseph Smith's Story." www2.ida.net/graphics/shirtail/probabil.htm (Oct. 29, 2003).

_____. *Studies of the Book of Mormon,* edited by Brigham D. Madsen. 2d. ed. Salt Lake City: Signature Books, 1992.

_____. "Translation of the Book of Mormon." *Improvement Era,* Apr. 1906, 425-36.

Roberts, George. *The Substance of a Sermon (But Now More Enlarged) Preached to, and at the Request of the Conference of the Methodist Episcopal Church, Held in Baltimore, March, 1807.* Baltimore: Henry Foxall, 1807.

Roberts, Oral. *The Call.* Garden City, New York: Doubleday, 1971.

Robinson, (Dr.) Gain. Store Day Books and Account Books, 1825-29, 1826-28, 1827-29. King's Daughters' Library, Palmyra, New York. LDS Church History Library. The first lampblack entry of Sept., 18, 1827, "Joseph Smith for Son," is in the 1826-29 book, p. 301, and in the 1827-29 book, n.p.

Robinson, Richard N. "The History of a Nephite Coin." Dec. 30, 1934. Signed by Robinson and his wife. LDS Church History Library.

Rogers, Joseph. Statement, May 16, 1887. *Naked Truths about Mormonism* (Apr. 1888): 1.

Romig, Ronald E. "The Lamanite Mission." *Journal of the John Whitmer Historical Association* 14 (1994). www.jwha.info/jclm14.htm (Jan. 30, 2003).

Rorabaugh, W. J. *The Alcoholic Republic: An American Tradition.* New York: n.p., 1979.

Ross, Kenneth J., Reference Librarian, Presbyterian Historical Society. Email to Richard S. Van Wagoner, Nov. 18, 2004.

Rosten, Leo. *Religions in America: A Completely Revised and Up-to-Date Guide to the Faiths, Churches, and Denominations in the United States.* New York: Simon and Schuster, 1963.

Russell, Bertrand. "How I Write." *Portraits from Memory and Other Essays.* London: n.p. 1965.

Russell Stoddard v. Joseph Smith. Feb. 18, 1825. Common Pleas Transcripts, Ontario County Record Center and Archives, Canandaigua, New York.

Russell, William D. "A Further Inquiry into the Historicity of the Book of Mormon." *Sunstone* 7, no. 5 (Sept./Oct. 1982): 20-27.

"Salem Heads of Household, 1790 United States Census." www.geocities.com/Heartland/Meadows/2770/sale1790.txt (Feb. 3, 2004).

Salisbury, Katharine Smith. Affidavit, Apr. 15, 1881. Community of Christ, Library-Archives, Independence, Missouri.

_____. "An Angel Told Him: Joseph Smith's Aged Sister Tells about Moroni's Talk." *Kansas City Times,* Apr. 11, 1895. www.lavazone2.com/dbroadhu/Missouri/Miss1881.htm (Oct. 13, 2004.) For convenience, see Kyle R. Walker, "Katharine Smith Salisbury's Recollections," 5-19.

_____. "Dear Sisters." *Saints' Herald* 33 (May 1, 1886): 60.

_____. "Reminiscences of Joseph Smith, As Told by His Sister, Catherine Smith-Salisbury, to Her Grandson, Herbert S. Salisbury." *Saints' Herald* 60 (Oct. 8, 1913): 982-84.

Saunders, Benjamin. Interviewed by William H. Kelley, ca. Sept. 1884: Box 2, fd. 44, p. 19. "Miscellany." Community of Christ, Library-Archives, Independence, Missouri. For convenience, see Dan Vogel, ed., *Early Mormon Documents,* 2:136-140.

Saunders, Lorenzo. Affidavit, July 21, 1887. *Naked Truths about Mormonism* 1 (Jan. 1888): 2.

_____. Interviews, Sept. 17, 1884; Sept. 20, 1884; and Nov. 12, 1884. "Miscellany 1795-1948." E. L. Kelley Papers, and Box 2, fd. 44, p. 19. Community of Christ, Library-Archives, Independence, Missouri. For convenience, see Dan Vogel, ed., *Early Mormon Documents,* 2:154.

_____. Letter to Thomas Gregg, Jan. 28, 1885. Charles A. Shook, *The True Origin of the Book of Mormon,* 315.

Schenck, Lewis Bevens. *The Presbyterian Doctrine of Children in the Covenant.* New Haven, Connecticut: Yale University Press, 1940.

Schmidt, Leigh Eric. *Hearing Things: Religion, Illusion, and the American Enlightenment.* Cambridge, Massachusetts: Harvard University Press, 2000.

_____. *Holy Fairs: Scottish Communions and American Revivals in the Early Modern Period.* Princeton, New Jersey: Princeton University Press, 1989.

Schultz, Suzanne M. *Body Snatching: The Robbing of Graves for the Education of Physicians in Early Nineteenth Century America.* Jefferson, North Carolina: McFarland & Co., 1992.

Scot, Reginald. *Discovery of Witchcraft … Whereunto Is Added an Excellent Discourse on the Nature and Substance of Devils and Spirits, in Two Books: The First by the Aforesaid Author: The Second Now Added in This Third Edition, as Succedaneous to the Former … With Nine Chapters at the Beginning of the Fifteenth Book of the Discovery.* London: Andrew Clark, 1665.

Scott, Sir Walter. *Letters on Demonology and Witchcraft.* New York: J. and J. Harper, 1831.

"Scrying." www.fortunecity.com/roswell/price/112/scry.html (Oct. 18, 2001).

Searles, Asa B. Reminiscence. *History of Lee County.* Chicago: H. H. Hill and Co., 1882.

Semonin, Paul. "Peale's Mastodon: The Skeleton in Our Closet." www.common-place.org/vol-04/no-02/semonin/.

"Seneca Indians—Useful Resources on and off the Web." www.senecaindians.com/seneca resources.htm (Oct. 25, 2005).

"The Shaker Song Tradition at Union Village, Ohio: The Golden Plates Manuscript." www.shakerwssg.org/shaker song tradition at union v.htm (Dec. 18, 2003).

Shaller, M. *Reckoning with Reagan: America and Its President in the 1980s.* New York: Oxford University Press, 1992.

"Shaping the Age of Expansion." http://xroads.virginia.edu/~MA02/volpe/canal/impact body.html (July 15, 2004).

Shaw, Ralph R., and Richard H. Shoemaker. *American Bibliography: A Preliminary Checklist, 1801-1819: Corrections, Author Index.* New York: Scarecrow Press, 1966.

Sherer, John. Letter to Absalom Peters, Nov. 18, 1830. American Home Missionary Society Archives, Amistad Research Center, Tulane University, New Orleans. For convenience see Dan Vogel, ed., *Early Mormon Documents,* 4:91-93.

Sheriff, Carol. *The Artificial River: The Erie Canal and the Paradox of Progress, 1817-1862.* New York: Hill and Wang, 1996.

Shipps, Jan. "Joseph Smith and Mormonism." www.lds-mormon.com/shipps joseph smith.shtml (Dec. 23, 2003).

_____. *Mormonism: The Story of a New Religious Tradition.* Urbana: University of Illinois Press, 1985.

_____. "The Prophet Puzzle: Suggestions Leading Toward a More Comprehensive Interpretation of Joseph Smith." *Journal of Mormon History* 1 (1974): 3-20. In Bryan Waterman, ed., *The Prophet Puzzle,* 25-48.

_____, and John W. Welch, eds. *The Journals of William E. McLellin, 1831-1836.* Urbana: University of Illinois Press/Provo, Utah: BYU Studies, 1994.

Shook, Charles A. *Cumorah Revisited; or, "The Book of Mormon" and the Claims of the Mormons Reexamined from the Viewpoint of American Archaeology and Ethnology.* Cincinnati: Standard Publishing, 1910.

_____. *The True Origin of the Book of Mormon.* Cincinnati: Standard Publishing Co., 1914.

Shultz, Suzanne M. *Body Snatching: The Robbing of Graves for the Education of Physicians in Early Nineteenth Century America.* Jefferson, North Carolina: McFarland & Co., 1992.

Sibly, Ebenezer. *A New and Complete Illustration of the Occult Sciences.* London: Champante & Whitrow, 1784.

Simms, Jeptha R. *The Frontiersmen of New York.* Albany: N.p., 1883. www.fortklock.com/simmsturnpike.htm (May 4, 2004).

"A Singular Discovery." *Detroit Gazette,* Apr. 16, 1823. www.lavazone2.com/dbroadhu/NE/miscne01.htm (Aug. 30, 2004).

Skinner, Charles M. *Myths and Legends of Our Own Land.* Detroit: Singing Tree Press, Book Tower, 1969.

Skousen, Royal. "Evidence from the Original Manuscript." *Journal of Book of Mormon Studies* 7, no. 1 (1998): 23-31.

_____. "John Gilbert's 1892 Account of the 1830 Printing of the Book of Mormon." In Stephen D. Ricks, Donald W. Parry, and Andrew H. Hedges, eds., *The Disciple as Witness: Essays on Latter-day Saint History and Doctrine in Honor of Richard Lloyd Anderson.* Provo, Utah: FARMS, 2000.

_____. "New Evidence about Book of Mormon Scribes." *Insights* (Jan. 1993): 1.

_____. "The Original Language of the Book of Mormon: Upstate New York Dialect, King James English, or Hebrew?" *Journal of Book of Mormon Studies* 3, no. 1 (Spring 1994): 28-38.

_____. "Piecing Together the Original Manuscript." *BYU Today,* May 1992, 18-24.

_____. *The Printer's Manuscript of the Book of Mormon: Typographical Facsimile of the Entire Text in Two Parts.* Provo, Utah: FARMS, 2001.

_____. "Towards a Critical Edition of the Book of Mormon." *BYU Studies* 30, no. 1 (Winter 1990): 41-69.

_____. "Translating the Book of Mormon: Evidence from the Original Manuscript." In Noel B. Reynolds, ed., *Book of Mormon Authorship Revisited,* 61-94.

Sloan, Douglas. *The Scottish Enlightenment and the American College Ideal.* New York: Columbia University Teachers College Press, 1971.

Smith, Caroline Rockwell. Statement, Mar. 25, 1885. *Naked Truths about Mormonism* 1 (Apr. 1888): 1.

Smith, Don Carlos. "Smith Family Genealogy Record [ca. 1840]." LDS Church History Library.

Smith, Elias. *The Life, Conversion, Preaching, Travels, and Sufferings of Elias Smith.* Portsmouth, New Hampshire: Beck & Foster, 1816.

Smith, Emily A. *The Life and Letters of Nathan Smith, M.B., M.D.* New Haven, Connecticut: Yale University Press, 1914.

Smith, Emma [Hale] (see also Emma Smith Bidamon), comp. *A Collection of Sacred Hymns, for the Church of the Latter Day Saints.* Kirtland, Ohio: F. G. Williams & Co., 1835.

Smith, Ethan. *View of the Hebrews.* 2d ed. Poultney, Vermont: Smith & Shute, 1825.

Smith Family of New England. http://freepages.genealogy.rootsweb.com/walkersj/Smith.htm (Mar. 15, 2003).

Smith, Francis. "Americana in Drumlin Square." www.rootsweb.com/~nywayne/history/drumlins1.html (Oct. 14, 2003).

Smith, George A. Letter to editor. *Wayne County Journal,* May 6, 1875. Willard Bean Scrapbook, Lee Library.

Smith, George Albert. "Journal." 1870-1951. Microfilm of holograph. George Albert Smith Papers. Ms 36, Box 73, book 4, Manuscripts Division, J. Willard Marriott Library, University of Utah, Salt Lake City.

Smith, George D. "Defending the Keystone: Book of Mormon Difficulties." *Sunstone* 6, no. 3 (May-June 1981): 45-50.

_____. "Isaiah Updated." In Dan Vogel, ed., *The Word of God,* 113-30.

_____. *Nauvoo Polygamy: "But We Called It Celestial Marriage ..."* Salt Lake City: Signature Books, 2008.

_____, ed. *An Intimate Chronicle: The Journals of William Clayton.* Salt Lake City: Signature Books/Smith Research Associates, 1991.

Smith, Israel A. "My Father's Last Years (A Memory of President Joseph Smith)." *Saints' Herald,* Nov. 6, 1834, 474-75.

Smith, Jesse. Letter to Hiram [sic] Smith, June 17, 1829. Joseph Smith Jr., Letterbook 2, 59-60. Joseph Smith Jr. Collection, Lee Library.

Smith, Joseph [Jr.]. "Answers to Questions ..." *Elders' Journal* 1 (July 1838): 42-44. Revised version in *History of the Church,* 3:38-30.

_____. "The Book of the Law of the Lord," entry of Aug. 23, 1842, 179. Original in First Presidency's Vault, Church of Jesus Christ of Latter-day Saints, Salt Lake City, Utah. For convenience, see Dan Vogel, ed., *Early Mormon Documents,* 1:173.

_____. Book of Mormon. Palmyra [New York]: E. B. Grandin, 1830. Current editions being used include: Church of Jesus Christ of Latter-day Saints [Salt Lake City], 1981. Community of Christ [Independence, Missouri], 1908—authorized Edition; and 1966—Revised Authorized Edition. Church of Christ [Temple Lot], 1990.

_____. "Church History." TS 3 (Mar. 1, 1842): 707.

_____. "Facts Are Stubborn Things." TS 3 (Sept. 15, 1842): 922.

_____. "History, 1832." Joseph Smith Letterbook, 1:1-6, Joseph Smith Papers, LDS Church History Library. For convenience, see Dean C. Jessee, ed., *The Personal Writings of Joseph Smith,* 4-14, and Dan Vogel, ed., *Early Mormon Documents,* 1:27.

_____. "History Draft, 1839." In Dan Vogel, ed., *Early Mormon Documents,* 1:68.

_____. *Inspired Version—The Holy Scriptures: Containing the Old and New Testaments; An Inspired Revision of the Authorized Version.* Independence, Missouri: Herald Publishing House, 1971.

_____. "[Letter] to the Church of Jesus Christ of Latter Day Saints," Sept. 6, 1842. TS 3 (Oct. 1, 1842): 934-36.

_____. "Letter to Colesville Saints," Aug. 28, 1830. Newel Knight Journal, 128-36, ca. 1846, in private possession. For convenience, see Dan Vogel, ed., *Early Mormon Documents,* 11-15.

_____. Letter to John Wentworth. TS 3 (Mar. 1, 1842): 708.

_____. "[Letter] to the *Times and Seasons.*" TS 4, no. 23 (Oct. 15, 1843): 375.

_____. Letter to W. W. Phelps. Printed as "The Answer." TS 4, no. 6 (Feb. 1, 1843): 82.

_____. Manuscript *History of the Church,* vol. A-1. LDS Church History Library. In Dean C. Jessee, ed., *The Personal Writings of Joseph Smith,* 665-66.

_____. "Meaning of the Word Mormon." TS 4 (May 15, 1843): 194.

_____, et al. *History of the Church of Jesus Christ of Latter-day Saints,* edited by B.H. Roberts, 2nd ed. rev. Salt Lake City: Deseret News Press, 6 vols. Published 1902-12, vol. 7 published 1932; 1978 printing by Deseret Book.

Smith, Joseph, Sr. "Blessing on Emma Smith." In Dan Vogel, ed., *Early Mormon Documents,* 1:472.

_____. "Blessing on Hyrum Smith, Dec. 18, 1833." Patriarchal Blessing Book 1:2-3. LDS Church History Library. For convenience, see Dan Vogel, ed., *Early Mormon Documents,* 1:469.

_____. "Blessing on Joseph Smith Jr., Dec. 9, 1834." In Patriarchal Blessing Book 1:3-4. LDS Church History Library. For convenience, see Dan Vogel, ed., *Early Mormon Documents,* 1:471, or www.xmission.com/~research/about/pathb2.htm.

_____. Introductory Comments: Patriarchal Blessing Book 1:1-2. LDS Church History Library. For convenience, see Dan Vogel, ed., *Early Mormon Documents,* 1:467.

_____. "Patriarchal Blessing Given to Wilford Woodruff," Apr. 15, 1837. http://idafab.tripod.com/blessings/hpb01.html (Apr. 8, 2003).

_____, and Alvin Smith, Promissory Note, Mar. 27, 1818, Ontario County Records Center and Archives, Canandaigua, New York. For convenience, see Dan Vogel, ed., *Early Mormon Documents,* 3:385.

_____, vs. Jeremiah Hurlburt, 17 Feb. 1819; Jeremiah Hurlburt vs. Joseph Smith Sr. and Alvin Smith, June 26, 1819, Ontario County Records Center and Archives, Canandaigua, New York. For convenience, see Dan Vogel, ed., *Early Mormon Documents,* 3:385-88.

Smith, Joseph, III. "Last Testimony of Sister Emma." *Saints' Herald* 26 (Oct. 1, 1879): 289-90. Also published in *Saints' Advocate* 2 (Oct. 1879): 49-52.

_____. Letter to Mrs. E. Horton, Mar. 7, 1900. Community of Christ, Library-Archives, Independence, Missouri. For convenience, see Dan Vogel, ed., *Early Mormon Documents,* 1:546-47.

_____. Letter to R[obert] Patterson. *Saints' Herald,* Mar. 24, 1883, 177-79.

_____. "Notes of Interview with Emma Smith Bidamon." Feb. 1879. Miscellany, Community of Christ, Library-Archives, Independence, Missouri. For convenience, see Dan Vogel, ed., *Early Mormon Documents,* 1:536-40.

_____. "What Do I Remember of Nauvoo." In *Journal of History,* 3, no. 1 (Jan. 1910): 337-38.

_____, and Heman C. Smith. *History of the [Reorganized] Church of Jesus Christ of Latter Day Saints, 1805-1890,* 4 vols.; continued by F. Henry Edwards as *The History of the [Reorganized] Church of Jesus Christ of Latter Day Saints,* Vols. 5-8. Independence, Missouri: Herald House, 1897-1903, 1967 printing.

Smith, Joseph F. "Joseph Smith as a Boy." *Millennial Star* 67 (1905): 802-805.

_____. "Remarks Made by President Joseph [F.] Smith Following the Reading of the Preceding Paper." *Journal of History* [published by RLDS Church], 1 (Jan. 1908): 41.

_____. Statement, Apr. 25, 1918. Joseph F. Smith Collection, LDS Church History Library. Rpt. in Lyndon W. Cook, *David Whitmer Interviews,* 48-51.

Smith, Joseph Fielding. *Doctrines of Salvation.* Comp. and ed. by Bruce R. McConkie. 3 vols. Salt Lake City: Deseret Book, 1954-56.

_____. "Where Is the Hill Cumorah?: Book of Mormon Establishes Location of Historic Region." *LDS Church News,* Feb. 27, 1954, 2-3.

_____, ed. and comp. *Teachings of the Prophet Joseph Smith.* Salt Lake City: Deseret News Press, 1954.

Smith, Lucy Mack. Letter to Solomon and Ester Mack, Jan. 6, 1831, Waterloo, New York. MS 3468. LDS Church History Library. Granddaughter Candace Barker sent the original to Joseph Fielding Smith, received Sept. 5, 1906; published in *Elders' Journal,* Nov. 1, 1906, 59-62.

_____. Letter to William Smith, Jan. 23, 1845, Nauvoo. Holograph. Ms 15550. LDS Church History Library.

_____. Letter to William Smith, Jan. 4, 1849. *Melchisedic and Aaronic Herald* 1 no. 2 (Mar. 1849): 1.

_____. Minutes of Address, uncatalogued, General Conference, Oct. 8, 1845. Copy by Curtis E. Bolton. Access no. 211325-ARCH-94, LDS Church History Library. Qtd. in Lavina Fielding Anderson, *Lucy's Book,* 54.

Smith, Nathan, M.D. "Observations on the Pathology and Treatment of Necrosis." *Philadelphia Monthly Journal of Medicine and Surgery* 1, no. 1 (June 1827): 11-19;

vol. 1, no. 2 (July 1827): 66-75. Rpt. in *Medical and Surgical Memoirs,* 97-121. In *Medical Classics* 1, no. 8 (Apr. 1937): 820-38.

_____. *A Practical Essay on Typhous Fever.* New York: E. Bliss, and E. White, 1824.

Smith, William B. Interviewed by J. W. Peterson and W. S. Pender, July 4, 1891. *The Rod of Iron* 3 (Feb. 1924): 67.

_____. "Notes Written on 'Chambers' Life of Joseph Smith,'" ca. 1875. LDS Church History Library.

_____. "The Old Soldier's Testimony. Sermon preached by Bro. William B. Smith, in the Saints' Chapel, Detroit, Iowa, June 8th, 1884. Reported by C. E. Butterworth." *Saints' Herald* 31 (Oct. 4, 1884): 642-43.

_____. "Sermon by Elder Wm. B. Smith." *Zion's Ensign* (Independence, Missouri), Aug. 27, 1892. www.lavazone2.com/dbroadhu/Missouri/Miss1881.htm (Oct. 14, 2004).

_____. Statement in *Saints' Herald* 31 (4 Oct. 1884): 644.

_____. *William Smith on Mormonism.* Lamoni, Iowa: Herald Steam Book and Job Office, 1883.

_____. "W[illia]m B. Smith's Last Statement." *Zion's Ensign* (Independence, Missouri) 5 (Jan. 13, 1894): 6. Rpt. as "Statement of William Smith, Concerning Joseph, the Prophet," *Deseret Evening News,* Jan. 20, 1894, 11. For convenience, see Dan Vogel, ed., *Early Mormon Documents,* 1:510-13.

"The Smithsonian Institution's 1996 'Statement Regarding the Book of Mormon.'" www.jefflindsay.com/LDSFAQ/smithsonian.shtml (July 27, 2001).

"Some Account of Joseph Smith and the Mormon Imposture Chiefly Compiled from *Chamber's Miscellany* and the Rev. H. Caswell." Warnminister, England: W. H. Tayler, 1845(?). LDS Church History Library.

Sorenson, John L. "Ancient America and the Book of Mormon Revisited." *Dialogue: A Journal of Mormon Thought* 4 (Summer 1969): 81-95.

_____. *An Ancient American Setting for the Book of Mormon.* Salt Lake City: Deseret Book, 1985.

_____. "When Lehi's Party Arrived in the Land, Did They Find Others There?" *Journal of Book of Mormon Studies* 1, no. 1 (Fall 1992): 1-34.

_____, and Matthew Roper. "Before DNA." *Journal of Book of Mormon Studies* 12, no. 1 (2003): 5-23.

Southerton, Simon G. *Losing a Lost Tribe: Native Americans, DNA, and the Mormon Church.* Salt Lake City: Signature Books, 2004.

"Special Correspondence." *Chicago Tribune,* Dec. 17, 1885. Rpt. in Lyndon W. Cook, *David Whitmer Interviews,* 171-80.

Spofford, Horatio Gates. *A Gazetteer of New York.* Albany, New York: N.p., 1813.

Squier, E[phraim] G. *Antiquities of the State of New York.* Buffalo, New York: N.p., 1851.

Stafford, Christopher M. Affidavit, Mar. 23, 1885. *Naked Truths about Mormonism* 1 (Apr. 1888): 1.

Stafford, Cornelius R. Statement, Mar. 23, 1885. *Naked Truths about Mormonism* 1 (Jan. 1888): 3.

Stafford, William. Affidavit, Dec. 9, 1833. Sworn before Wayne County Judge Thomas P. Baldwin. In Eber D. Howe, *Mormonism Unvailed,* 237.

Staker, Susan. "Secret Things, Hidden Things: The Seer Story in the Imaginative Economy of Joseph Smith." In Dan Vogel and Brent Lee Metcalfe, eds., *American Apocrypha,* 235-74.

Stenhouse, T. B. H. *The Rocky Mountain Saints …* New York: D. Appleton and Company, 1873.

Stevenson, Edward. Diary. LDS Church History Library. Qtd. in Lyndon W. Cook, *David Whitmer Interviews,* 10-13.

_____. Letter to President John Taylor, Jan. 7, 1878, reporting Dec. 22-23, 1877, interview with David Whitmer, LDS Church History Library. For convenience, see Lyndon W. Cook, *David Whitmer Interviews,* 16.

_____. "One of the Three Witnesses: Incidents in the Life of Martin Harris." *Deseret News,* Nov. 30, 1881. Rpt. *Millennial Star* 44 (6 Feb. 1882): 86-87. For convenience, see Dan Vogel, ed., *Early Mormon Documents,* 2:320-21.

_____. *Reminiscences of Joseph, the Prophet, and the Coming Forth of the Book of Mormon.* Salt Lake City: Edward Stevenson, 1893.

_____. "The Thirteenth Witness to the Plates of the Book of Mormon." *Millennial Star* 55 (Mar. 27, 1893): 214-16.

_____. "The Three Witnesses to the Book of Mormon," No. III. *Millennial Star* 48 (June 21 1886): 389-91.

Stevenson, Joseph Grant. *The Stevenson Family History: Consisting of Biographical Sketches of the Joseph Stevenson Family Which Came to America in 1828, Including Sketches of the Lives of Their Wives and Husbands.* 2 vols. Provo, Utah: Joseph Grant Stevenson, 1955.

Stilwell, Lewis D. *Migration from Vermont.* Montpelier: Vermont Historical Society, 1948.

Stocker, Rhamanthus M. *Centennial History of Susquehanna County, Pennsylvania.* Philadelphia: R.T. Peck and Co., 1887.

Stommel, Henry, and Elizabeth Stommel. *Volcano Weather: The Story of 1816, the Year without a Summer.* Newport, Rhode Island: Seven Seas, 1983.

Stothers, Richard B. "The Great Tambora Eruption in 1815 and Its Aftermath." *Science* 224, no. 4654 (June 15, 1984): 1191-98.

Stott, G. St. John. "Joseph Smith's 1823 Vision: Uncovering the Angel Message." *Religion* 18, no. 4 (1988): 347-62.

_____. "New Jerusalem Abandoned: The Failure to Carry Mormonism to the Delaware." *Journal of American Studies* 21, no. 1 (1987): 71-85.

_____. "The Seer Stone Controversy: Writing the *Book of Mormon.*" *Mosaic: A Journal for the Interdisciplinary Study of Literature* 19, no. 3 (Summer 1986): 35-53.

Stout, Hosea. *On the Mormon Frontier: The Diaries of Hosea Stout, 1844-1861.* Edited by Juanita Brooks. 2 vols. Salt Lake City: University of Utah, 1964.

Stout, Richard B. "A Singular Discovery: The Curious Manuscript, Mitchill, and Mormonism." www.olivercowdery.com/smithhome/2000s/2001RBSt.htm (Sept. 23, 2003).

Stowell, Josiah, Jr. Letter to John S. Fullmer, Feb. 17, 1843. Holograph, LDS Church History Library.

Stowell, William Henry Harrison. *Stowell Genealogy.* Rutland, Vermont: Tuttle Co., 1922.

Strickland, W. P. *Autobiography of Rev. James B. Finley; or, Pioneer Life in the West.* Cincinnati: Methodist Book Concern, 1855.

Strickland, William. *Journal of a Tour in the United States of America, 1794-95.* New York: New-York Historical Society, 1971.

Sunderland, LaRoy. *The Trance, and Correlative Phenomena.* Chicago: James Walker, 1868.
A Sure Foundation: Answers to Difficult Gospel Questions. Salt Lake City: Deseret Book, 1988.
"Swedenborg, Emanuel." Wendy Doniger, ed., *Merriam-Webster's Encyclopedia of World Religions,* 1,041.
Swedenborg, Emanuel. *Swedenborg's Journal of Dreams, 1743-1744,* commentary by Wilson Van Dusen. New York: Swedenborg Foundation, 1986.
Talmage, James E. *Jesus the Christ: A Study of the Messiah and His Mission according to Holy Scriptures both Ancient and Modern.* Salt Lake City: Deseret Book Co., 1915.
_____. *A Study of the Articles of Faith: Being a Consideration of the Principal Doctrines of the Church of Jesus Christ of Latter-day Saints.* Salt Lake City: Church of Jesus Christ of Latter-day Saints, 1890.
Tanner, Jerald, and Sandra Tanner. *Joseph Smith's 1826 Trial.* Salt Lake City: Modern Microfilm, 1971.
_____. "Joseph Smith's Attempt to Save the Book of Mormon." www.xmission.com/~country/reason/blkhol1.htm (July 27, 2001). Tanner, Sandra. "Evolution of the First Vision and Teaching on God in Early Mormonism." www.geocities.com/Athens/Delphi/3750/first.vision.html (Oct. 29, 2003).
_____. "Zelph—The White Lamanite Warrior." www.utlm.org/onlineresources/zelph.htm (Aug. 21, 2001).
Tate, Charles D., Jr. "John H. Gilbert's Work on the Book of Mormon." In Larry C. Porter, Milton V. Backman Jr., and Susan Easton Black, *Regional Studies in Latter-day Saint Church History: New York.* Provo, Utah: Brigham Young University Department of Church History and Doctrine, 1992. 113-19.
Taves, Ann. *Fits, Trances, and Visions: Experiencing Religion and Explaining Experience from Wesley to James.* Princeton, New Jersey: Princeton University Press, 1999.
Taylor, Alan. "The Early Republic's Supernatural Economy: Treasure Seeking in the American Northeast, 1780-1830." *American Quarterly* 38 (Spring 1986): 6-34.
_____. "The Great Change Begins: Settling the Forest of Central New York." *New York History* 75 (July 1995): 265-90.
_____. "Rediscovering the Context of Joseph Smith Jr.'s Treasure-Seeking." *Dialogue: A Journal of Mormon Thought* 19 (Winter 1986): 18-28.
Terr, Lenore. *Unchained Memories: True Stories of Traumatic Memories, Lost and Found.* New York, Basic Books, 1994.
"Testimony of Brother E. Thayer Concerning the Latter Day Work." *True Latter Day Saints' Herald* 3 (Oct. 1862): 79-80, 82-84. Also www.lavazone2.com/dbroadhu/Ohio/sain1860.htm.
Thatcher, Virginia S., and Alexander McQueen, eds. *The New Webster Encyclopedic Dictionary of the English Language.* Chicago: Consolidated Book Publishers, 1980.
"Theodore Roosevelt." www.bartleby.com/people/RsvltT.html (Mar. 9, 2006).
Thomas, Keith. "An Anthropology of Religion and Magic." *Journal of Interdisciplinary History* 6 (Summer 1975): 91-109.
_____. *Religion and the Decline of Magic.* New York: Charles Scribner's Sons, 1971.
Thomas, Mark D. *Digging in Cumorah: Reclaiming Book of Mormon Narratives.* Salt Lake City: Signature Books, 1999.
_____. "Scholarship and the Book of Mormon." In Dan Vogel, ed., *The Word of God,* 63-80.

_____. "The Meaning of Revival Language in the Book of Mormon." *Sunstone* 8, no. 3 (May-June 1983): 19-38.

Thomas, Northcote W. *Crystal Gazing: Its History and Practice, with a Discussion of the Evidence for Telepathic Scrying.* London: Alexander Moring, Ltd. 1905.

Thompson, D[aniel] P[ierce]. *May Martin; or, The Money Diggers. A Green Mountain Tale.* Montpelier, Vermont: E. P. Walton, 1835.

Thompson, John E. "'The Facultie of Abrac': Masonic Claims and Mormon Beginnings." *Philalethes,* Dec. 1982, 9, 15.

Thompson, John H., ed. *Geography of New York State.* Syracuse, New York: Syracuse University Press, 1966.

Thompson, John Samuel. *Christian Guide.* Utica, New York: A. G. Dauby, 1826.

Thompson, R[obert]. B. "An Address Delivered at the Funeral of Joseph Smith Sen. Late Patriarch of the Church of Jesus Christ of Latter Day Saints, September 15th, 1840." TS 1, no. 11 (Sept. 1840): 170-73.

Thompson, William. "Mormonism." *Susquehanna Register and Northern Pennsylvanian* 9 (May 1, 1834): 1.

Thompson, Zadock. *Natural History of Vermont.* Rutland, Vermont: Charles E. Tuttle, 1972.

Thomson, J. Arthur. *Riddles of Sciences.* Aberdeen: Liveright,1932. Qtd. in www.survivalafterdeath.org/articles/thomson/crystalgazing.htm.

Thorndike, Lynn. *A History of Magic and Experimental Science during the First Thirteen Centuries of Our Era.* 2 vols. London: N.p., 1923.

Tiffany, Joel. "Mormonism—No. I." *Tiffany's Monthly* 5 (June 1859): 165-66.

_____. "Mormonism—No. II." *Tiffany's Monthly* 5 (Aug. 1859): 163-70.

"To the Honorable General Assembly of the State of Vermont, Next to Be Convened at Woodstock," Oct. 15, 1807, 1. Tunbridge Town Clerk's Office, Tunbridge, Vermont. For convenience, see Dan Vogel, ed., *Early Mormon Documents,* 1:656.

"To the Public." Joseph Smith Sr., Letter to the editor, Sept. 25, 1824. *Wayne Sentinel* 2 (Sept. 29, 1824), 3. Also in the issues of Oct. 6, 13, 20, 27, and Nov. 3.

Toyton, Evelyn. *Growing Up in America: 1830-1860.* Brookfield, Connecticut: Millbrook Press, 1995.

Traughber, John L., Jr. Interviewed, October 1879, Richmond, Missouri. *Saints Herald* 26 (Nov. 15, 1879): 341-42. In Lyndon W. Cook, *David Whitmer Interviews,* 52-56.

_____. Letter to James T. Cobb, ca. 1881. Rpt. in William Wyl, *Joseph Smith, the Prophet,* 311.

"Treasure Seeking." www.belinus.co.uk/folklore/Files4/ThomasTreasure Seeking.htm (Nov. 11, 2002).

Troll, Rich. "Samuel Tyler Lawrence: A Significant Figure in Joseph Smith's Palmyra Past." *Journal of Mormon History* 32, no. 2 (Summer 2006): 38-86.

Troskansky, Betty, comp. *Writings of James Reeves, Palmyra's First Historian.* Palmyra, New York: Betty Troskansky, 1989.

Tucker, Pomeroy. "The Mormon Imposture—The Mormon Aborigines." *Wayne Democratic Press* (Lyons, New York) 3 (June 2, 1858): 2. For convenience, see Dan Vogel, ed., *Early Mormon Documents,* 3:68.

_____. "Mormonism and Joe Smith: The Book of Mormon or Golden Bible." *[Lyons, New York.] Wayne Democratic Press,* May 26, 1858. For convenience, see Dan Vogel, ed., *Early Mormon Documents,* 3:66.

_____. *Origin, Rise, and Progress of Mormonism: Biography of Its Founders and History of Its Church.* New York: D. Appleton & Co., 1867.

Tucker, R. C. "The Theory of Charismatic Leadership." *Daedalus* 97, no. 3 (1968): 731-56.

"Tunbridge Anabaptist Society Petition," Nov. 12, 1799. Tunbridge Town Records, p. 443. Tunbridge Town Clerk's Office, Tunbridge, Vermont. For convenience, see Dan Vogel, ed., *Early Mormon Documents,* 1:636-37.

Turner, O[rsamus]. *History of the Pioneer Settlement of Phelps and Gorham's Purchase, and Morris's Reserve. To Which Is Added, a Supplement or Continuation of the Pioneer History of Ontario, Wayne, Livingston, Yates and Allegheny.* Rochester, New York: Erastus Darrow, 1851. Also http://home1.gte.net/dbroadhu/Restor/Lib/Tur18511a.htm (accessed July 16, 2002).

_____. *Pioneer History of the Holland Purchase of Western New York.* Buffalo, New York: George H. Derby and Co., 1850.

Tuttle, Daniel S. "A Document Discovered." *Utah Christian Advocate* 23 (Salt Lake City) 3 (Jan. 1886): 1. For convenience, see Dan Vogel, ed., *Early Mormon Documents,* 4: 239-56.

_____. "Mormons." In Philip Schaff, ed., *A Religious Encyclopaedia.* 2 vols. New York: Funk and Wagnalls, 1883. 2:1,576.

_____. *Reminiscences of a Missionary Bishop.* New York: Thomas Whittaker, 1906.

Twain, Mark. *Roughing It.* 1872. Rpt., Berkeley: University of California Press, 1997.

Tyler, Alice Felt. *Freedom's Ferment.* Minneapolis: University of Minnesota Press, 1944.

"Types of Divination." http://athena523.tripod.com/divination/typesdiv.htm (Aug. 9, 2004).

"Typhoid Fever." www.emedicine.com/med/topic2331.htm (Mar. 17, 2004).

"Typhus." http://en.wikipedia.org/wiki/Typhus (Mar. 17, 2004).

Underwood, Grant. "Book of Mormon Usage in Early LDS Theology." *Dialogue: A Journal of Mormon Thought* 17 (Autumn 1984): 35-74.

U.S. Bureau of the Census. 1820 census. Farmington, Ontario County, New York, 1820, 318, Family No. 524. Original in National Archives, Washington, D.C. For convenience, see Dan Vogel, ed., *Early Mormon Documents,* 3:422-23.

_____. *Manuscript Census (Federal) and Indexes, New York,* 1800, 1810, 1820, 1830, 1840, 1850, 1860, 1870.

_____. *Vermont.* 1790, 1800, 1810, 1820.

Van Dam, Cornelis. *The Urim and Thummim: A Means of Revelation in Ancient Israel.* Winona Lake, Indiana: Eisenbrauns, 1997.

Vanderdocs, Cornelius (from W. H. Homer Jr.). Martin Harris Farm, Palmyra, New York, Dec. 18, 1959, 1-7. Lee Library.

Vanderhoof, E. W. *Historical Sketches of Western New York.* Buffalo, New York: Matthews-Northrup Works, 1907.

Van Dine, Warren L. "Some Descriptive Material about List of Nine Prominent People of Salisbury Descent (from the Wilkins J. Salisbury—Catherine Smith marriage of 1831)." LDS Church History Library.

Van Wagoner, Richard S. "Joseph Smith: The Gift of Seeing." *Dialogue: A Journal of Mormon Thought* 15 (Summer 1982): 48-68.

_____. *Mormon Polygamy: A History.* 2d ed. Salt Lake City: Signature Books, 1989.

_____. "Sarah M. Pratt: The Shaping of an Apostate." *Dialogue: A Journal of Mormon Thought* 19 (Summer 1986): 69-99.

_____. *Sidney Rigdon: Portrait of Religious Excess.* Salt Lake City: Signature Books, 1994.

_____, ed. *The Complete Discourses of Brigham Young.* 5 vols. Salt Lake City: Smith-Pettit Foundation, 2009.

_____, and Steven C. Walker. *A Book of Mormons.* Salt Lake City: Signature Books, 1982.

Vermont General Index to Vital Records. Entries for birth of Alvin Smith on Feb. 11, 1798, for birth of "Hiram Smith" on Feb. 9, 1800, for marriage of Luman Walters on Nov. 3, 1819, and for the birth of Luman Walters's child on May 15, 1821. Family History Library, Church of Jesus Christ of Latter-day Saints, Salt Lake City, Utah.

"Vermont Timeline." www.dhca.state.vt.us/HistoricSites/html/timeline.html (July 26, 2004).

Vincent, Joseph E. Untitled comments. In *Papers of the Fourteenth Annual Symposium on the Archaeology of the Scriptures.* Ed. Forrest R. Hauck. Provo, Utah: BYU Dept. of Extension Publications, 1963.

"Visitor Tells of His Boyhood Days at Palmyra, N.Y." *Deseret Evening News,* Nov. 10, 1915, B-2.

Vogel, Dan. "Anti-Universalist Rhetoric in the Book of Mormon." In Brent Lee Metcalfe, ed., *New Approaches to the Book of Mormon,* 21-52.

_____. "The Earliest Mormon Concept of God." In Gary James Bergera, ed., *Line upon Line,* 17-33.

_____, ed. *Early Mormon Documents,* 5 vols. Salt Lake City: Signature Books, 1996-2003.

_____. "Echoes of Anti-Masonry: A Rejoinder to Critics of the Anti-Masonic Thesis." In Dan Vogel and Brent Lee Metcalfe, eds., *American Apocrypha,* 275-320.

_____. "The New Theory of Book of Mormon Geography: A Preliminary Examination." Privately circulated, 1985.

_____. *Indian Origins and the Book of Mormon: Religious Solutions from Columbus to Joseph Smith.* Salt Lake City: Signature Books, 1986.

_____. "James Colin Brewster: The Boy Prophet Who Challenged Mormon Authority." In Roger D. Launius and Linda Thatcher, eds., *Differing Visions,* 120-39.

_____. *Joseph Smith: The Making of a Prophet.* Salt Lake City: Signature Books, 2004.

_____. "Joseph Smith's Family Dynamics." *John Whitmer Historical Association Journal* 22 (2002): 51-74.

_____. "The Locations of Joseph Smith's Early Treasure Quests." *Dialogue: A Journal of Mormon Thought* 27 (Fall 1994): 197-231.

_____. "More on Treasure Seeking." Letter to John H. Wittorf. *Dialogue: A Journal of Mormon Thought* 28 (Winter 1995): viii-x.

_____. "Mormonism's 'Anti-Masonick Bible.'" *John Whitmer Historical Association Journal* 9 (1989): 17-30.

_____. "The Prophet Puzzle Revisited." In Bryan Waterman, ed., *The Prophet Puzzle,* 49-68.

_____. *Religious Seekers and the Advent of Mormonism.* Salt Lake City: Signature Books, 1988.

_____. "The Validity of the Witnesses' Testimonies." In Dan Vogel and Brent Lee Metcalfe, eds., *American Apocrypha,* 79-122.

_____, ed. *The Word of God: Essays on Mormon Scripture.* Salt Lake City: Signature Books, 1990.

_____, and Brent Lee Metcalfe, eds. *American Apocrypha: Essays on the Book of Mormon.* Salt Lake City: Signature Books, 2002.

Vogt, Evon Z., and Ray Hyman. *Water Witching USA.* 2nd ed. Chicago: University of Chicago Press, 1979.

"The Voice of the Spirit." *Evangelical Inquirer* (Dayton, Ohio), Oct. 4, 1830, 102-104.

Von Goores, J. *Die Christliche Mystik,* 4 vols. Regensbureg: N.p., 1836-42.

Von Leitner, Karl Ritter. *Jakob Lorber: A Short Biography.* Bietigheim, Germany: N.p., 1930.

Voros, J. Frederic, Jr. "Was the Book of Mormon Buried With King Follett?" *Sunstone,* Mar. 1987, 15-18.

Waite, Arthur E. *Book of Ceremonial Magic.* 1911; rpt. New Hyde Park, New York: University Books, 1961.

Waldron, Stuart. "Scrying." www.mystic-mouse.co.uk/WisdomTexts/Scrying.htm (Oct. 9, 2002).

Walker, Helen. "We Remember … the Erie Canal." www.cgazette.com/towns/Newark/history/918323473078.htm (Nov. 9, 2004).

Walker, John Phillip, ed. *Dale Morgan on Early Mormonism: Correspondence and A New History.* Salt Lake City: Signature Books, 1986.

Walker, Kyle R. "The Joseph S. and Lucy Mack Smith Family." In *United by Faith: The Joseph Sr. and Lucy Mack Smith Family.* Edited by Kyle R. Walker. American Fork, Utah: Covenant Communications, 2005, 156-74.

_____. "Katharine Smith Salisbury: Sister to the Prophet." *Mormon Historical Studies* 3, no. 1 (2002): 5-34.

_____. "Katharine Smith Salisbury and Lucy Smith Millikin's Attitudes toward Succession, the Reorganized Church, and Their Smith Relatives in Utah." *Mormon Historical Studies* 3, no. 2 (2002): 165-71.

_____. "Katharine Smith Salisbury's Recollections of Joseph's Meetings with Moroni." *BYU Studies* 41, no. 3 (2002): 5-19.

Walker, Ronald W. "Joseph Smith: The Palmyra Seer." *BYU Studies* 24 (Fall 1984): 461-72.

_____. "Martin Harris: Mormonism's Early Convert." *Dialogue: A Journal of Mormon Thought* 19 (Winter 1986): 29-43.

_____. "The Persisting Idea of American Treasure Hunting." *BYU Studies* 24 (Fall 1984): 429-59.

_____. "Seeking the 'Remnant': The Native American during the Joseph Smith Period." *Journal of Mormon History* 19, no. 1 (Spring 1993): 1-32.

Walker, Sylvia. Statement, Mar. 20, 1885. *Naked Truths about Mormonism* 1 (Apr. 1888): 1.

Wallace, Anthony F. C. *Death and Rebirth of the Seneca.* New York: Random House, 1972. Qtd. in Mary Durke Becker, "Seneca." www.college.hmco.com/historyreaderscomp/naind/html/na 035300 seneca.htm.

Wallcut, Thomas. Letter to James Freeman, Oct. 31, 1789. Thomas Wallcut Papers. American Antiquarian Society, Worcester, Massachusetts.

Walters, Wesley P. "The Abduction of Emily (Coburn) Austin." *Gospel Anchor* 10 (May 1984): 22-31.

_____. *The Book of Mormon Today.* Grand Rapids, Michigan: Gospel Truths Ministries, 1992.

_____. "The Book of Mormon Today: Challenges to Its Relevance and Authenticity." www.irr.org/mit/Book-of-Mormon-Today.html (May 13, 2003).

_____. "Joseph Smith's Bainbridge, N.Y., Court Trials." *Westminster Theological Journal* 36 (Winter 1974): 123-55.

_____. "Joseph Smith's Move to Palmyra and Manchester, N.Y." Unpublished paper, 1987. Photocopy courtesy of H. Michael Marquardt.

_____. "The Mormon Prophet Attempts to Join the Methodists." www.utlm.org/onlineresources/josephsmithmethodist.htm (May 12, 2004).

_____. "New Light on Mormon Origins from Palmyra (N.Y.) Revival." *Bulletin of the Evangelical Theological Society* 10 (Fall 1967): 227-44. Rpt. in *Dialogue: A Journal of Mormon Thought* 4 (Spring 1969): 59-81.

Warren, Bruce W., and Thomas Stuart Ferguson. *The Messiah in Ancient America.* Provo, Utah: Book of Mormon Research Foundation, 1987.

Waterman, Bryan, ed. *The Prophet Puzzle: Interpretive Essays on Joseph Smith.* Salt Lake City: Signature Books, 1999.

Waters, John L. "Using Scrying to See How a Genius Works." www.humboldt.edu/~jlw47/usingscrying.html (Oct. 10, 2002).

Watson, Allen. "The Story of the Course." www.circleofa.com/acimstry.html (Nov. 25, 2002).

Watson, David Lewis. *The Early Methodist Class Meeting: Its Origins and Significance.* Nashville: Disciples Resources, 1987.

Watson, F. Michael (secretary to the First Presidency of the LDS Church). Letter to Darrel L. Brooks, Oklahoma City, Oct. 16, 1990. Photocopy in my possession.

[Watson, James Fanning]. *Methodist Error; or, Friendly Christian Advice to Those Methodists Who Indulge in Extravagant Emotions and Bodily Exercises.* Trenton, New Jersey: D. & E. Fenton, 1819.

"We have only to regret ..." *[Palmyra] Reflector,* Mar. 16, 1830, 89.

Webster, Noah. *An American Dictionary of the English Language.* In 2 vols. New York: S. Converse, 1828; facsimile reprint, 1967, 1995.

Webster, Richard. *Dowsing for Beginners: How to Find Water, Wealth, and Lost Objects.* St. Paul: Llewellyn Publications, 2001.

"Webster's 1828 Dictionary, Electronic Version by Christian Technologies, Inc." http://65.66.134.201/cgi-bin/webster/webster.exe?search for texts web1828=colic (Oct. 26, 2004).

"The Wedding of Aurelia Weeks Smith, 1829." Old Sturbridge Village—Online Resources Library, www.osv.org/learning/DocumentViewer.php?Action+View&DocID+1134 (June 22, 2005).

"The Wedding of William Sumner Barton and Elizabeth Ann Jennison, 1849." Old Sturbridge Village—Online Resources Library, www.osv.org/learning/DocumentViewer.php?Action+View&DocID+1134 (June 22, 2005).

Weed, Harriet A., ed. *Autobiography of Thurlow Weed.* 2 vols. Boston: Houghton, Mifflin and Co., 1883.

Weed, Thurlow. "The Beginning of Mormonism." *Albany Evening Journal* (July 31, 1854). For convenience, see Dan Vogel, ed., *Early Mormon Documents,* 3:328.

_____. Letter to Ellen E. Dickinson, Apr. 12, 1880. In Ellen E. Dickinson, *New Light on Mormonism … with [an] Introduction by Thurlow Weed.* New York: Funk and Wagnals, 1885, 260-61.

_____. "Prospect of Peace with Utah." *Albany Evening Journal* 29 (May 19, 1858): 2.

Weibye, Jens C. A. "6th Daybook. From January 1st 1880 to December 31st 1881." LDS Church History Library.

Weider, Ben. "The Assassination of Napoleon." www.napoleon-series.org/ins/weider/c assassination w.html (Jan. 19, 2005).

[Welch, Ernest L.], comp. *"Grip's" Historical Souvenir of Seneca Falls, N.Y.* Syracuse, New York: Ernest L. Welch, 1904. No. 17, p. 20.

Welch, John W. "A Book You Can Respect." *Ensign,* Sept. 1977, 45-48.

_____. "Chiasmus in the Book of Mormon." *BYU Studies* 10 (Autumn 1969): 69-84.

_____. "Jesse Smith's 1814 Protest." *BYU Studies* 33 (1993): 131-44.

_____. "What Does Chiasmus in the Book of Mormon Prove?" In Noel B. Reynolds, ed., *Book of Mormon Authorship Revisited,* 199-224.

Wells, Junius F. "The Birthplace of the Prophet Joseph Smith." *Millennial Star* 67 (Liverpool, England: Heber J. Grant, 1905): 461.

_____. "The Smith Family in Vermont." In Evelyn M. Wood Lovejoy, *History of Royalton, Vermont, with Family Genealogies, 1769-1911.* Burlington, Vermont: Free Press Printing, 1911.

Westergren, Bruce N., ed. *From Historian to Dissident: The Book of John Whitmer.* Salt Lake City: Signature Books, 1995.

"The Westminster Confession of Faith." In *The Book of Confessions.* New York: Office of the General Assembly, 1983.

What Is the Book of Mormon? Missionary brochure. Salt Lake City: Church of Jesus Christ of Latter-day Saints, 1982.

"What Is So Special about the Caul?" www.caulbearer.org/Special%20about%20the%20 Caul.htm (Aug. 9, 2004).

Whiting, Michael F. "DNA and the Book of Mormon: A Phylogenetic Perspective." *Journal of Book of Mormon Studies* 12, no. 1 (2003): 24-37.

Whitmer, David. *An Address to All Believers in Christ, by a Witness to the Authenticity of the Book of Mormon.* Richmond, Missouri: David Whitmer, 1887.

_____. "Communication from Elder D. Whitmer." *Saints' Herald,* Dec. 4, 1886, 764-65.

_____. Interview by the *Saints' Herald,* June 1888. Printed in *Saints' Herald* 28 (July 1, 1881): 198.

_____. Interviewed by *Chicago Times,* Oct. 14, 1881, Richmond, Missouri. Printed Oct. 17, 1881.

_____. Interviewed by E. C. Briggs and Rudolph Etzenhouser, Apr. 25, 1884, Richmond, Missouri. Printed in *Saints' Herald,* June 21, 1884. For convenience, see Lyndon W. Cook, *David Whitmer Interviews,* 125-29.

_____. Interviewed by James H. Hart, Mar. 10, 1884, Richmond, Missouri. Printed in *Deseret News,* Mar. 25 1884. For convenience, see Lyndon W. Cook, *David Whitmer Interviews,* 110-16.

_____. Interviewed by Joseph F. Smith and Orson Pratt, Sept. 7-8, 1878, Richmond, Missouri, Joseph F. Smith Diary, LDS Church History Library. For convenience, see Lyndon W. Cook, *David Whitmer Interviews,* 25-26.

_____. Interviewed by *Kansas City Journal,* June 1, 1881, printed June 5, 1881. For convenience, see Lyndon W. Cook, *David Whitmer Interviews,* 59-71.
_____. Interviewed by M. J. Hubble, *Chicago Inter–Ocean.* Rpt., *Saints' Herald* 33 (Nov. 13, 1886): 707. M. J. Hubble Family Papers, Missouri Historical Society. Rpt. in *BYU Studies* 14, no. 4 (Summer 1974): 484-86.
_____. Interviewed by *Omaha Herald,* Oct. 10, 1886. For convenience, see Lyndon W. Cook, *David Whitmer Interviews,* 193-207.
_____. Interviewed by William H. Kelley and G. A. Blakeslee, Jan. 15, 1882. Printed *Saints' Herald,* Mar. 1, 1882. For convenience, see Lyndon W. Cook, *David Whitmer Interviews,* 86.
_____. Interviewed by Zenos H. Gurley, Jan. 14, 1885. LDS Church History Library.
_____. Letter, Dec. 9, 1886. *Saints' Herald* 34 (Feb. 5, 1887): 92.
_____. Letter. Feb. 5, 1887. *Saints' Herald.* www.xmission.com/~country/reason/dw let1.htm (Oct. 13, 2004).
Whitney, Terry. "Nathaniel Hawthorne's Early Life: Introduction." www.hatrhorneinsalem.com/Life&Times/BiographicalInfo/Earlylife/Introduction.html (Feb. 15, 2003).
Whittier, John Greenleaf. *Legends of New-England.* Hartford, Connecticut: Hanmer and Phelps, 1831. www.hti.umich.edu/cgi/t/text/-fb21cf&view=main&idno=WhittLegen (May 24, 2002).
_____. "A Mormon Conventicle." *Millennial* Star 10 (Oct. 1, 1848): 302-303.
_____. *The Supernaturalism of New England.* Norman: University of Oklahoma Press, 1969.
Wiebe, Phillip H. *Visions of Jesus: Direct Encounters from the New Testament to Today.* Oxford, England: Oxford University Press, 1997.
Wigger, John H. "'Fighting Bees': Methodist Itinerants and the Dynamics of Methodist Growth, 1770-1820." In Nathan O. Hatch and John H. Wigger, eds., *Methodist and the Shaping of American Culture,* 87-133.
_____. *Taking Heaven by Storm: Methodism and the Rise of Popular Christianity in America.* Urbana: University of Illinois Press, 1998.
Willers, Diedrich, Jr. "Ambition and Superstition." Miscellaneous Undated Items. Diedrich Willers Papers, Cornell University, Ithaca, New York. Qtd. in Dan Vogel, *The Making of a Prophet,* 582n11.
_____. Letter to Reverend Brethren, June 18, 1830. Willers Collection, Carl A. Kroch Library, Cornell University, Ithaca, New York. For convenience, see Dan Vogel, *Early Mormon Documents,* 5:277-78.
Willey, Aaron C. "Observations on Magical Practices." *Medical Repository* 2 (1816): 378-80.
"William Wood Gerhard (1809-1872)." http://chronicles.dickson.edu/encyclo/g/ed gerhardWW.htm (Mar. 18, 2004).
"William Wood Gerhard." www.famousamericans.net/williamwoodgerhard/ (Mar. 18, 2004).
Williston, Rev. Seth. Letter to C. Davis, Ontario County, Apr. 29, 1799. *New York Missionary Magazine* 1 (Jan. 1800): 35-38.
Wills, Book 47, pp. 7-11. Surrogate's Court, Manhattan Borough, New York County, New York. Ontario County Miscellaneous Records, Book C, pp. 342-44, Ontario

County Records Center and Archives, Canandaigua, New York. For convenience, see Dan Vogel, *Early Mormon Documents,* 1:277, 3:424.

Wineapple, Brenda. *Hawthorne: A Life.* New York: Alfred A. Knopf, 2003.

Winn, Kenneth. *Exiles in a Land of Liberty: Mormons in America, 1830-1846.* Chapel Hill: University of North Carolina Press, 1989.

"Winter Wheat." http://collections.ic.gc.ca/agrican/pubweb/hs270105.asp (Feb. 3, 2004).

Wirthlin, LeRoy S. "Joseph Smith's Boyhood Operation: An 1813 Surgical Success." *BYU Studies* 21 (Spring 1981): 131-54.

_____. "Joseph Smith's Surgeon." *Ensign,* Mar. 1978, 59-60.

_____. "Nathan Smith (1762-1828) Surgical Consultant to Joseph Smith." *BYU Studies* 17 (Spring 1977): 319-38.

Woman's Society of the Western Presbyterian Church, comp. "Palmyra, New York." 1907. www.rootsweb.com/~nywayne/history/palpresb.html (Apr. 21, 2003).

"The Wonderful World of Scrying." www.dcsi.net/~bluesky/scrying.htm (Oct. 9, 2002).

Wood, George B., and Franklin Bache, M.D. *The Dispensatory of the United States of America.* 6th ed. Philadelphia: Grigg & Elliot, 1845.

Wood, Gordon S. "Evangelical America and Early Mormonism." *New York History* 61, no. 4 (Oct. 1980): 359-86.

Wood, Wilford C. *Joseph Smith Begins His Work.* Vol. 1: *Book of Mormon, 1830.* Salt Lake City: Wilford Wood, 1959.

_____. *Joseph Smith Begins His Work.* Vol. 2: *The Book of Commandments, the Doctrine and Covenants, the Lectures on Faith, Fourteen Articles of Faith.* Salt Lake City: Wilford Wood, 1962.

Woodruff, Wilford. *Wilford Woodruff's Journal, 1833-1898.* Typescript. Edited by Scott Kenney. 9 vols. Midvale, Utah: Signature Books, 1983-85.

Woodward, Cal. "Documents Show Nixon Misled Public on Cambodian Actions." *[Provo, Utah] Daily Herald,* Nov. 17, 2005, A5.

Woodward, Daniel. "Birthplace and Early Residence of Joseph Smith, Jr." *Historical Magazine* 7 (Nov. 1870): 315-16. For convenience, see Dan Vogel, *Early Mormon Documents,* 1:624.

Worms, Abraham ben Simeon of. *The Book of the Sacred Magic of Abra-Melin the Mage.* Trans. S. L. McGregory Mathers. London: J. M. Watkins, 1898.

Worth, Patience (communicated through Mrs. John H. Curran). *The Sorry Tale.* New York: Henry Holt and Co., 1917.

Wright, Carroll D. *History and Growth of the United States Census.* Washington, D.C.: Government Printing Office, 1900.

Wright, Dennis A., and Geoffrey A. Wright. "The New England Common School Experience of Joseph Smith Jr., 1810-16." In *Regional Studies in Latter-day Saint Church History: The New England States.* Edited by Donald Q. Cannon, Arnold K. Garr, Bruce A. Van Orden. Provo, Utah: Religious Studies Center, Brigham Young University, 1988, 237-59.

Wright, Henry Clarke. *Human Life.* Boston: Bela Marsh, 1849. Excerpt reprinted in Louis C. Jones, *Growing Up in the Cooper Country,* 93-187.

"The Writer's Almanac." www.writersalmanac.org/docs/99 10 11.htm (Sept. 2, 2003).

"Written Charms." www.folkmagic.co.uk/magic/writtencharms.htm (Aug. 10, 2004).

Wyl, W. (pseud. Wilhelm Ritter Von Wymetal). *Joseph Smith, His Family, and His Friends [Mormon Portraits].* Salt Lake City: Tribune Printing and Publishing, 1886.

Yates, Frances A. *The Art of Memory.* Chicago: University of Chicago Press, 2001.

Yates, John V. N., and Joseph W. Moulton. *History of the State of New-York Including Its Aboriginal and Colonial Annals.* New York: A. T. Goodrich, 1824. www.olivercowdery.com/texts/1824Yate.htm (Oct. 2, 2003).

"Year without a Summer." www.fact-index.com/m/mo/mount_tambora.html (Feb. 14, 2004).

"Year without a Summer." www.worldhistory.com/wiki/Y/Year-Without-A-Summer.htm (Feb. 14, 2004).

Young, Brigham. Letter to Parley P. Pratt, May 26, 1845, Brigham Young Letterpress Copybook, Aug. 27, 1844-May 25, 1845, 14. LDS Church History Library.

_____. "Preaching in Tooele County by Brigham Young, Heber C. Kimball, George A. Smith, and George Q. Cannon, July 13-15, 1866." Miscellaneous Minutes. Edyth Romney Typescripts, LDS Church History Library.

_____. Unpublished Address, Oct. 7, 1866. Recorded by George D. Watt. Brigham Young Collection. LDS Church History Library. In Van Wagoner, *Complete Discourses of Brigham Young,* 4:2378.

_____. Unpublished Discourse. LDS General Conference, Oct. 8, 1854. In Van Wagoner, *Complete Discourses of Brigham Young,* 2:853.

Young, Jacob. *Autobiography of a Pioneer; or the Nativity, Experience, Travels, and Ministerial Labors of Rev. Jacob Young with Incidents, Observations, and Reflections.* Cincinnati: Cranston and Curts, n.d. [ca. 1857].

Zaroski, Dan. "Research on Coopering: A Brief History of the Trade of Coopering and Reference List." www.interlog.com/~zaroski/info.html (Sept. 11, 2003).

Zink, Terrence L., and John W. Welch. "King Benjamin's Speech in the Context of Ancient Israelite Festivals." In *King Benjamin's Speech Made Simple.* Eds. John W. Welch and Stephen D. Ricks. Provo, Utah: FARMS, 1999, 127-66.

INDEX

Note: JS = Joseph Smith Jr.

ABOUT THE AUTHOR AND HIS WORK

Richard S. Van Wagoner was the author of *Mormon Polygamy: A History* (1985, 2nd ed. 1989), *Lehi: Portraits of a Utah Town* (1990), *Sidney Rigdon: A Portrait of Religious Excess* (1994), *Pioneering Lehi City: A 150-Year Pictorial History* (2002), editor of *The Complete Discourses of Brigham Young,* five volumes (2010), and coauthor of *A Book of Mormons* (1982). He published articles in *BYU Studies*, *Dialogue: A Journal of Mormon Thought*, *Sunstone*, *Utah Historical Quarterly*, and *Utah Holiday*. He received writing awards from the Dialogue Foundation, the John Whitmer Historical Association, the Mormon History Association, and the Utah State Historical Society. He earned an M.S. degree from Brigham Young University (Provo, Utah) in 1970. Trained as a clinical audiologist, he owned and operated Mountain West Hearing Center in Salt Lake City. He was a lifelong resident of Lehi, Utah; a founding member of the Lehi Historical Preservation Commission; and served as Lehi City's Historical Archivist. He was a co-founder, a member of the Board of Directors, and a member of Editorial Advisory Committee of Signature Books (Salt Lake City).

When he passed away in his sleep at age sixty-four on Sunday morning, October 10, 2010, Van Wagoner had completed work on his biography of the early years of Joseph Smith. He had twice revised the finished manuscript, reviewed and approved two rounds of copy editing, and assembled, ordered, and captioned a preliminary selection of illustrations. Thus, in preparing this biography for publication five years later, minimal work was needed to bring the manuscript up to date. A final round of proofing silently corrected some remaining minor errors. Mention of relevant publications that appeared during the interim was also silently introduced into some of the footnotes. In no instance, however, did the publication of subsequent research by other scholars necessitate the revision of any of Van Wagoner's narrative. While we are saddened that Van Wagoner is not alive to witness the publication of his masterwork, we are grateful for his example and his scholarship.

A B C D E F G H I J K L M
N O P Q R S T U V W X Y Z

a b c d e f g h i j k l m
n o p q r s t u v w x y z

a b c d e f g h i j k l m
n o p q r s t u v w x y z

This book was set in Adobe Caslon Pro, a revival of oldstyle fonts designed by William Calson in 1725. As one of the earliest British typefaces, it was popular among English and American printers, and was used in printing the United States Declaration of Independence. *Natural Born Seer: Joseph Smith, American Prophet, 1805-1830* was printed on fifty-pound natural offset stock and case bound by Sheridan Books in Ann Arbor, Michigan.